'OFT IN DANGER'

The Life and Campaigns of General Sir Anthony Farrar-Hockley

Jonathon Riley

Helion & Company

Helion & Company Limited
26 Willow Road
Solihull
West Midlands
B91 1UE
Tel. 0121 705 3393
Fax 0121 711 4075
Email: info@helion.co.uk
Website: www.helion.co.uk
Twitter: @helionbooks
Visit our blog http://blog.helion.co.uk/

Published by Helion & Company 2015
Designed and typeset by Bookcraft Ltd, Stroud, Gloucestershire
Cover designed by Paul Hewitt, Battlefield Design (www.battlefield-design.co.uk)
Printed by Gutenberg Press Limited, Tarxien, Malta

Text © Jonathon Riley 2015
Photographs © as individually credited
Maps © Steve Waites 2014, unless otherwise credited

Front cover: TFH as CO 3 Para, 1964. (Airborne Forces Museum)
Rear cover: From a collection of official photographs held by Sergeant Alfred Stanley
Morgan, A Company 6 (RW) Para.

ISBN 978-1-910777-25-1

British Library Cataloguing-in-Publication Data.
A catalogue record for this book is available from the British Library.

For details of other military history titles published by Helion & Company Limited contact
the above address, or visit our website: http://www.helion.co.uk.

We always welcome receiving book proposals from prospective authors.

Contents

List of Illustrations

List of Maps

Foreword

by Field Marshal Lord Bramall KG GCB OBE MC

I did not get to know Tony Farrar-Hockley at all well until the early 1970s when, although infantrymen, we both came to command armoured divisions in Germany on the central front of NATO. I was, of course, well aware – as was the whole army – of his outstanding record as a fighting soldier, going back 30 years, but it was not until we had the opportunity to work together as neighbouring comrades-in-arms that I came fully to appreciate his many talents both as a soldier and as a highly intelligent human being.

It was all too obvious that he possessed in full measure all the qualities needed to be a good, vigorous and effective commander whose troops, because of his leadership, would be bound to give the best possible account of themselves if we had ever been called upon to fight in those tense days when the Cold War was still at its height. Some of his qualities were even more obvious on the far more peaceful sports field. Tony enjoyed his cricket, but was not a particularly skilful performer; yet when our two divisional sides played against each other, he insisted on captaining his side (as I did mine) and in the field he would stand at the closest of close short legs, almost in touching distance of the batsman, wearing none of the protective clothing often used by modern cricketers. When called upon to bat he would resolutely get on to the front foot and attack the bowling whatever hostile short-pitched deliveries were being sent down at him. We both enjoyed the needle matches played between our two sides.

It was also obvious that he was a man of keen intellect with a very strong literary bent, which was borne out by the formidable and much-respected body of his published works. These were not only about the Korean War, in which he had been so involved (including writing the official British history of that war), but also about battlefields and commanders of other wars elsewhere. In all of these, his own critical analyses directly benefitted from his professional knowledge as an experienced practitioner himself. Unlike many academic historians he really knew about war and the pressures and stresses on commanders it involved; and all this showed in his vivid and austere style of writing.

Above all, he was a most delightful colleague and companion for whom I formed an enormous liking – as well as a very high regard. He was warm-hearted with a great capacity for kindness, compassion and concern for others – and a stimulating conversationalist who had a very good sense of humour and enjoyed a good argument. So it never surprised me that he was widely popular not only in the army, but also in academic circles at Oxford where he found the time to read for a Defence Fellowship.

Altogether, Tony Farrar-Hockley was a man of many parts, and this immaculately researched book, written by a battlefield-experienced commander himself and so aptly titled *Oft in Danger*, is a very good read. It provides a most interesting insight into the life and the times of a very significant military figure who has contributed so much not only often heroically on the field of battle, but also in the wider field of modern history; to its development and the analysing of the lessons that we should, although more often than not do not, learn from them.

I therefore strongly commend this book to those who are intrigued by military history generally, as so many are, and who like to be made aware of the realities and heroics of the actual battlefield.

Dwin Bramall
Field Marshal
March 2015

Author's Preface

There is a tendency in the modern world for great men and women to be sneered at; their achievements belittled; their greatness mocked; and their failing magnified. If, dear reader, this is what you seek from this book then I fear you have wasted your money, for you will not find it. I took this project on because I admired and respected Tony Farrar-Hockley greatly; indeed I count him among the most significant influences of my own military life and career. This is not to say that I have set out to write a hagiography. None of us is perfect and great people are often flawed – sometimes deeply so. Where TFH was wrong, or where his faults were obvious, I have done my best to show this and explain them, and not apologise. He, I am certain, would not have done so.

TFH, or 'Farrar the Para' as we all knew him when I was a youngster, belonged to that generation of senior officers who had started their military service in the Second World War and continued through the various campaigns of the 1940s, 1950s and 1960s. They had seen the world change from being dominated by the great dictators and the struggle against them, to being dominated by the threat of Russian and Chinese Communism. They had taken part in hot wars like Korea, and the Cold War at its deepest and darkest. They had confronted the challenges of post-colonial insurgencies and seen these develop into recognisably modern terrorism in Northern Ireland. They had seen a huge army, based on compulsory service, shrink as its commitments reduced; as economic pressures mounted; and as it returned to the voluntary, professional principle after a quarter of a century of National Service. These were momentous times and, before the fall of the Berlin Wall, with only Northern Ireland and a few chances of action elsewhere, we thought that we would not see the like again; we saw TFH and his contemporaries – like Dwin Bramall, Nigel Bagnall, 'Roly' Gibbs and the rest – as giants, in whose footsteps we would never be likely to tread.

Well, in 1989 the world changed and the chaos that followed it has meant that the current generation of military commanders has had at least some experience comparable with theirs, but the army has continued its decline in size and it seems unlikely that future generations will be able to say the same. For this reason, among others, I have thought it important to give a series of snapshots of what the British Army was like during the years from 1939 to the mid-1980s – as well as telling the story of Tony Farrar-Hockley as a great soldier, a great commander and a great scholar. The title of the book says much about TFH himself, for if ever there was a man who was oft in danger, it was him; but it also explains that this is a survey of the military scene in which he was so much a figure during the second half of the 20th century.

Acknowledgements

I would like to thank many people and institutions for their help, without which this biography could not have been written. First, to the Farrar-Hockley family: Linda, Dair, Hilary, Victoria, Briony Smith and Rosemary Howell for their encouragement, many suggestions and their knowledge of TFH and his life – little of which was recorded.

Next I would like to acknowledge and thank all those whom I interviewed or helped me with interviews for their time, their trouble and their memories: Pat Beaumont, Larry Bohana, Desmond Bowen, Lord Bramall – who has also written the foreword – Clive Brennan, Pat Butler, Peter Cavendish, David Charles, Peter Chiswell, Francesco di Cinito, Peter Crocker, Peter Cronk, Paddy Deacon, John Edwards, Jack Ellis, Graham Farrell, Roy Giles, Teddy Gueritz, Jeremy Hickman and Mrs Hickman, Glyn Hughes, David Keenan, Sir Frank Kitson, Robert McAfee, Cliff Meredith, Charles Messenger, Malcolm Ross-Thomas, Mike Motum, Ted Olive, Jacko Page, Sir Thomas Prickett, Toby Sewell, John Stevens, Mike Tillotson, Leighton Thomas, Andrew Watson, Martin Vine, Anthony Vivian, Mike Walsh, Peter Walter, Bryan Webster.

Next, Jonathan Baker and the staff at the Parachute Regiment Museum and Archive, Duxford; Kevin Mason, Shirley Williams, Allan Poole and Kelly Davies at the Royal Welch Fusiliers Archives, Wrexham and Bodelwyddan Castle; the trustees of the Royal Welch Fusiliers Museum for permission to use material from *The Red Dragon, The Royal Welch Fusiliers 1919-1945* (6th (RW) Para in Italy, France and Greece) and *Regimental Records, Volume VI* (6th (RW) Para in Palestine) – as well as other material from the archives as noted in the bibliography and source notes; George Streatfeild, the trustees and staff of the Regiments of Gloucester Museum for material related to the regiment between 1939 and 1954; Major Dominic Spencer and his family for the use of the diary of Major Fleming-Jones, 6th (RW) Para); the staff at the Liddell-Hart Centre for Military History, King's College London; the staff at the Imperial War Museum Photographic Archive; Max Arthur for material from *Men of the Red Beret*; Francesco di Cinito for material on 2 Parachute Brigade in Italy; Carol Oxwell, the archivist at *Sixth Sense* in Germany; Brigadier Ahmed Aideed Al Masareh, Director of Moral Guidance, JHQ Jordanian Army; Mr Amjad Adaileh, Director of the Arabic Press Department, Communications and Information Division at the Royal Hashemite Court, Amman, Jordan; and Ms Alia Al-Kadi, Press Officer at the same department, for their assistance in research in the Jordanian archives; the Archives of Exeter School; Alasdair Goulden, John Stevens and Nick Keyes, who reviewed the work as it was in progress and corrected my many lapses; my daughter Victoria, who acted as my researcher at several key points.

Last, but by no means least, Steve Waites, who has drawn the maps for this book to such a high standard – as he has done for my last nine books.

1

'The Spirit of Adventure' TFH's Early Life and Schooling, 1924-1939

Mr David Griffin and his wife Emily were not happy in the spring of 1920 – not happy at all. Their daughter Beatrice – Bea – had announced that she intended to marry; not that, at the age of 32, they were against the idea of her marrying. However she intended to marry Arthur Hockley – and to the Griffins, this Hockley simply would not do. The Griffins were a solidly respectable, middle-class professional family who lived in what was still the village of Ealing. Here, David owned and ran the first estate agency in the area and served as a councillor and Mayor. They were moreover staunch members of the Anglican Church, given to the high, Anglo-Catholic tendency. They had a firm view of right and wrong and of their place in society: Emily was, after all, descended from Sir Cloudesley Shovell – an Admiral of the Fleet and a Knight, even if he had been lost in one of the greatest ship-wreck disasters in British history.* They maintained a considerable house, which later became part of Ealing Studios; a motor car; and a full staff of domestic servants, gardeners and a chauffeur. Bea – Agnes Beatrice to give her her full name – was their second child; she was not physically robust, indeed rather thin, but of strong character and in spite of her parents' objections, she was determined to have her way. However the Griffins' eldest daughter, Bea's elder sister Maud, had already married someone of whom the Griffins could not approve – and now her sister appeared to be going the same way. What, they wondered between themselves, had they done, that God and his angels should punish them so?

As well as the girls, there were also five boys; the eldest, their third child after Maud and Bea, was Frank, who had gone into business in South America. Next came Cyril, who fell out with his father and ran away to sea, sailing round the world on a clipper ship; later he became senior partner of the family business. After Cyril came Arthur; then Bernard, who was ordained in the Anglican Church; and finally Stanley, who had been wounded while serving in the Middlesex Regiment during the Great War and who eventually joined the family business – becoming senior partner on Cyril's retirement.

---

* Admiral of the Fleet Sir Cloudesley Shovell (c.1650-October 1707) fought in many of the important battles of the Anglo-Dutch Wars of 1665-1667 and 1672-1674, the Nine Year's War (1689-1698) and the War of the Spanish Succession (1702-1713). He became a popular hero and Commander-in-Chief of the fleet, but his life was brought to an end in the disastrous shipwreck in the Isles of Scilly in October 1707. He also served as MP for Rochester from 1695 until his death.

David Griffin, TFH's maternal grandfather.
(Farrar-Hockley family)

TFH's brother, Ted, in the uniform of the
Merchant Marine. (Farrar-Hockley family)

TFH's father in the uniform of the Royal
Flying Corps. (Farrar-Hockley family)

By contrast, Arthur Hockley had been born into a working class family on 6 August 1891 at Tottenham in North London[1] and he was therefore a few years younger than Beatrice. His father, George Hockley, was a customs house officer from Woodford Green in Essex,[2] who later moved to Tottenham. Arthur had served in the Great War as a private in the glamorous Royal Flying Corps in 1918, to which he may have been transferred from the Royal Field Artillery or the Army Service Corps – the records are ambiguous.[3] Early in life, Arthur had fallen out badly with his family and had made the breach formal by later taking his middle name, Farrar, and hyphenating it with his surname. He was a widower, with three children from his first marriage: Margaret, born in 1912; Sheila, born in 1913; and the youngest, Edward (Ted), born in 1916. Arthur was in the newspaper business as a journalist and editor. He edited two magazines devoted to the motor trade but was thought to be more interested in the commercial aspects of advertising revenue than in journalism. He was, by all accounts, evil-tempered, violent at times and impossible. Ted was clearly terrified of him, but he was also irresistibly charming, good-looking and of great presence. Beatrice fell for him. Her parents feared the worst – and they were proved right.[4]

After their marriage in 1921,[5] Arthur and Beatrice went to live first in Brentford and then in Coventry.[6] They had two children: the first being Pamela (Pam), born in 1922 and the second being Anthony (Tony), born on 8 April 1924,[7] the subject of this book. Anthony will from here on be referred to as 'TFH', which is how he became known in the army in later life and how most readers, therefore, will know him. His second Christian name – Heritage – was given in thanks to the doctor who delivered him after a difficult labour, but interestingly his entry in the Coventry Register of Births, Marriages and Deaths gives the surname as Griffin Hockley; his father therefore changed his surname to Farrar-Hockley soon afterwards and Griffin was

TFH with his mother and sister, Pam. (Farrar-Hockley family)

dropped from both children's names. When he was five years old, TFH remembered all the children being called in to their father in turn – he of course was last. Arthur and Beatrice were separating and the children were all given the choice of whether they stayed with their mother or their father. Unsurprisingly, perhaps, all the children – including Beatrice's three step-children – chose to stay with their mother. This, perhaps, explains the close relationship TFH enjoyed with his siblings – especially his sister Margaret.

Beatrice took the children and went back to Ealing. Thereafter, Arthur would occasionally see his children, usually one at a time, but he became a far less important figure in their lives than their mother and her family. From the age of five, therefore, TFH came under the influence of a devoutly Christian family, an influence which was to stay with him all his life. Here he learned some important lessons – not least the value of mutual respect between superiors and subordinates. His formidable grandmother, whom TFH greatly admired, caught him one day giving what can only be described as cheek to the chauffeur – who of course could not answer back. He was left in no doubt whatsoever that this was not how one carried on. TFH remembered. He remembered too, in later life, an episode when he was only four years old:

> Armistice Day, 1928. In the crowded street of an English city there is a slowing of people and vehicles. A maroon sounds. Traffic and talk, all movement and noise cease. A small boy looks up at his mother's face in silence. He wonders why she looks so grave.
> The child was [me] … When I asked my mother why we had to stand so still and quietly, she explained in simple words. I understood what she said but I did not comprehend it.[8]

In Ealing, he was at once sent to Miss Gundry's school, where he learned his letters and developed an early love of reading. Miss Gundry's has long vanished – she herself appears in the records of Sheet School near Petersfield in 1946, so it is possible that the school was evacuated there during the war and never returned. At the age of seven, in 1931, he went on to Ealing Preparatory School – then located in Langtry Road. By 1935, the three older children had left home – Ted had joined the Merchant Navy – and at this point, Beatrice moved with Pam and TFH to Exmouth. Here she joined her mother's cousin, Molly Tatham, at Nutwell Lodge. Molly was the widow of Jack Tatham, a doctor and army officer,[9] and she needed a companion. She therefore offered Beatrice a home, which Bea was glad to accept. There, in October 1937, TFH's childhood ended. He entered Exeter School as a day-boy at the age of 13.[10]

The school traced its origins to the opening of the Exeter Free Grammar School on 1 August 1633, which was founded mainly to educate the sons of the City freemen. Exeter's wealthy merchants provided the funding, with enough bequests to pay the headmaster £50 a year and to install the school in the medieval buildings of St John's Hospital, which had stood on the south side of the High Street since the 12th century. The buildings had lain unused since the Henrician confiscations which attended the destruction of the medieval church in England – and with it, all the social services (including education and healthcare) that the church had provided for the ordinary people.

The upper floor of the nave of the chapel became the large grammar schoolroom until 1868 when it was concluded that the buildings and site were too confined. Following the Endowed Schools' Act of 1872, the City's education was reorganised and under a Scheme of 1876,

TFH with his sister
Pam and lifelong
friend Nan Bazin.
(Farrar-Hockley family)

some new schools were formed (including The Maynard School) and a new governing body was constituted for the grammar school. This consisted of representation from the County, the City and Oxford and Cambridge Universities. In 1876 the headmaster, Henry Newport, resigned. His successor, Edward Harris, re-opened the school in 1877 and moved it to Victoria Park Road, in new buildings designed by noted architect William Butterfield. The school occupies this 25-acre (100,000 m²) site to this day.[11]

In 1920, the governors decided that it was no longer possible for them to continue to run the school without considerable financial assistance. The Exeter Education Authority agreed to assist but only if the school came under its direct control. In April 1921, therefore, admin-istration of the school was handed over to the City. It then became a 'maintained' school until 1929 when it became an 'aided' school – thus regaining charge of its own finances under a newly-appointed governing body. Its alumni included John Graves Simcoe, the first Lieutenant-Governor of Upper Canada; David Collins, the first Governor of Tasmania; Harry Pennell, who had captained Scott's ship, the *Terra Nova,* and later captained the *Queen Mary*; Sir Harry Veitch, the horticulturalist and founder of the Chelsea Flower Show; and a wealth of artists, scientists and sportsmen.

This was the school's status when TFH arrived in October 1937. It had around 200 boys, including a small contingent of boarders, and was run by the headmaster, J.L. Andrews, very much as any minor public school of the time would have been: a strict insistence on uniform and behaviour; a solid core of teaching to address the curriculum laid down for the school certificate; plenty of sport; and membership of the Junior Division of the Officers' Training Corps (OTC) mandatory for all those over the age of 13.[12] The school was divided into four houses – three of which were named after prominent Devonians: School, Buller, Drake and Raleigh. Given that there were few boarders, and these all in School House, the house system

Raleigh House, Exeter School, in July 1938. The headmaster, J.L. Andrews, is seated fifth from the left and on his left is the housemaster, Bernard Foster. TFH is sitting cross-legged in the front row, third from the right. (*The Exonian*, 1938)

was chiefly geared towards sports and games. TFH joined Raleigh House, under Mr Bernard Foster, and entered the Lower V form

There is little in the young TFH that presaged the soldier and scholar of later life. He was average in his school work; he loved English, History and French, but hated Mathematics and never really mastered it. He later said that but for the war, he felt he would have made a career either in the Anglican Church or the law.[13] In later life he developed a photographic memory, with the ability to read anything and retain it entirely for long periods of time. Perhaps he was born with this skill, but did not choose to exercise it until his interest was truly fixed on a subject. Once he had engaged this ability, it could – like any other ability – be trained. He had no eye for a ball and as the school did not offer an alternative to the standard diet of rugby, soccer and cricket he did not feature in any of the school sides. However, he had suffered from infantile asthma and this may have inhibited his ability to play games. He was never a house prefect. He joined the school's Amateur Dramatic Society, which he loved, and which certainly helped him to train his memory. In March 1939 he took part in the school play, '*The Importance of Being Earnest*', as Cecily Cardew. A review in *The Exonian* recorded that A.H. Farrar-Hockley and W.A. Bond had taken to heart the remark that 'style, not sincerity, is the vital thing. Sincerity in this play is an unimportant attribute. Both had some very charming poses; both helped to give Wilde's amazing stuff its true value and put across the wit of this farce …'[1]

TFH also joined the Lympstone Sea Scouts. For a boy who was not good at ball games, this gave him the opportunity to learn to sail a dinghy, another love that stayed with him all his life, and to sail and row a whaler. He also learned to swim and achieved the Royal Life-Saving Society's Bronze Medallion in 1938.[15] Cyril Tuckfield, Assistant Scoutmaster from 1929 to

1933 and the Scoutmaster until 1948, left an account of one summer's expedition in the troop's 25-foot whaler *Silver Arrow* up the River Dart to a campsite just below Galmpton:[16]

ORCHARD : SMITH : COOMBES : R . URWIN : D . RHYS-JAMES ;
FARRAR-HOCKLEY : PETERS : CECIL   HUGHES : BOND : FULFORD .
THEO

The cast of *The Importance of being Earnest*, as named. (*The Exonian*, 1939)

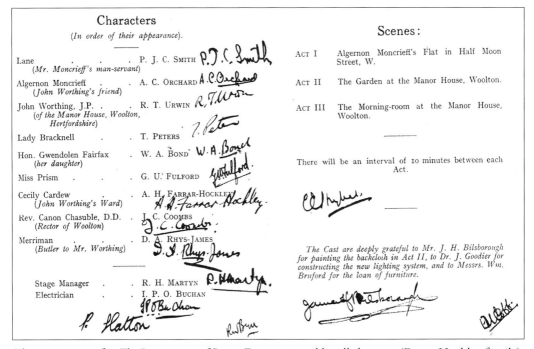

The programme for *The Importance of Being Earnest*, signed by all the cast. (Farrar-Hockley family)

There were seven of us, my first mate, Robert Bursey, Charlie Venus, Leslie Hodge, Tim Tapscott, A. Smith and Anthony Hockley, as usual, providing a little comic relief by arriving with a suitcase and his golf clubs over his shoulder! …

TFH was clearly well established as an amateur dramatist:

Our campsite was … just below Galmpton. Our approach had not been unobserved and we were greeted by five children whose parents lived in the lodge behind the boat house. They … helped us to carry our gear as we meandered in 'Line Ahead' through the undergrowth that lined the shore, all carrying some package or other. One could not but notice the resemblance to the many popular films of explorers trekking through the African jungle and Hockley was not slow to take advantage of the opportunity for a bit of acting, much to our enjoyment… .

At 9:30 p.m. just as it was dusk, we prepared to turn in, when we heard shrieks of laughter from Hockley's tent. I looked inside to discover the cause of the outburst and found that our eccentric friend had packed a typewriter into his suitcase, but had forgotten his blankets![17]

Mr Cyril Tuckfield, Tim Tapscott and TFH sailing with the Exmouth Sea Scouts. (Farrar-Hockley family)

TFH also entered the OTC and, within it, the Fife and Drum Corps. The OTC had begun life in 1859 as an offshoot of the Volunteer Movement and, like many other school corps, had then become a cadet company of a volunteer battalion – in this case, the 1st Volunteer Battalion of the Devon Rifles. In 1908 it had joined the Junior Division of the OTC, but was renamed again in 1937 as the Junior Training Corps (JTC), reflecting a new role in which it trained as a militia force to be mobilised at need in addition to its traditional tasks. When TFH joined it in 1937 it was commanded by Captain E.M. Cobb who in 1940 handed over to Captain R.W. Bell.[18] Bell's view of matters is summed up in his notes in the school journal: 'In spite of militia training, an OTC should still be an officer-producing unit, and it should be remembered that no-one is fit to give orders until he has first learnt to obey orders himself'.[19]

In his years in the OTC, TFH learned many basic skills that were to help him later on: drill, weapon training, map reading, minor tactics – and discipline. One Old Exonian recalled that:

> When I first joined [the JTC] in 1943 the junior company had to wear 1914-18 War-type uniform with brass buttons, peak caps and puttees. Wasn't the material itchy! Our rifles (no firing pins) were 1896 or so models, but there were some SMLEs* and Canadian weapons… Field days were a great event. Often these were on Woodbury Common, but I recall others on Pearce's Hill, Matford and others on East Hill, Ottery.[20]

Each year at the start of the summer vacation, the corps marched off for a two-week annual camp at Budleigh Salterton, Oakhampton, or some other local training establishment. Given that TFH seems not to have paid great attention to his prep outside school hours, and that he was not playing in any school side, joining organisations like the Sea Scouts and the JTC that provided interesting outdoor activities was a thoroughly good way, as he saw it, of filling his leisure hous.

After corps camp, the school holidays – especially the long summer vacation – were often spent with Bernard and his family at St Lladoc's Rectory in Ladock, Cornwall about six miles (nine kilometres) north-east of Truro. Here TFH and his siblings became great friends with their cousin Rosemary, who was five years younger than TFH. Rosemary remembered that by his early teens, TFH had lovely manners – no doubt at the insistence of his Griffin grandparents; and that he had a close and devoted relationship with all his brothers and sisters – especially Margaret, or 'Peg' – who later developed into something of an eccentric and who was married and divorced three times during her life. Although he was the youngest, he did not act like the youngest. Indeed, he was a leader from a very early age, always initiating games and taking the lead, but he was also full of fun, laughter and good-humour. A favourite game was 'highwaymen', using an upturned table as the coach to be robbed. TFH, of course, was always the highwayman!

The strong sense of right and wrong that the Griffins imparted to him was obvious in one episode that Rosemary recalled when TFH was perhaps 14. The garden at Ladock was full of large, fine trees in which the children loved to climb and play. One day, TFH got hold of a saw and cut out several branches from a particularly fine cypresses tree in order to make a sort

---

*   Short Magazine *Lee-Enfield*; the .303-inch, No. 4 rifle on general issue to the army.

The Corps of Drums of Exeter School JTC, 1938. The Officer Commanding, Captain R.W. Bell,
is seated centre; TFH is the drummer standing on the extreme left. (Exeter School Archives)

of den, with seats, inside the tree. Luncheon was then announced and the children took their
places in the dining room – the Rector at the head of the table – and the food was brought
up from the kitchen and formally served. While they were there, the head gardener entered
the room and asked to speak to the Rector – a thing almost unheard of, that the outdoor staff
should come in (and during luncheon to boot), but the gardener was in a great rage and would
not be put off.

'Sir,' he said, 'someone has taken a saw and cut off parts of one of my finest trees!' The
Rector also grew angry and immediately guessed who was responsible. Before anyone could
say another word, however, TFH jumped to his feet.

'Yes,' he said, 'I did it – and I am very sorry for it.'

This was risking a severe beating and the other children were very grateful and impressed
that he should without hesitation accept the whole blame. So too was the Rector, who valued
moral courage, and so TFH escaped his thrashing.[21]

As the 1930s went on, TFH and his friends could not but be aware of the worsening situation in Europe. The emergence of the Nazi Party in power in Germany in 1933 and the
outbreak of the Spanish Civil War made an impact, but according to TFH himself, it was
events after 1936 that impressed them more. This was because by that time, at the age of 14
or 15, TFH was able to go to the cinema – especially on a Saturday. Here, he saw the newsreels – particularly those of Pathé – in which the doings of the Germans and Italians featured

large. Mussolini, 'a familiar figure of fun', and the annexation of Austria particularly stuck in his memory.[22]

By 1939, TFH knew what was coming and knew what he wanted to do; and the memory of the war was there in the school, as in many others. Seventy old Exonians had died in the Great War – a remarkable figure for so small a place.[23]

Looking back in later life, TFH recalled that:

> My adolescent judgement of the [Great] War, formed from the novels and historical accounts, the movies and plays which reflected it, was that it had been on the whole an exciting event. It did not affect my ideas or spirit any more than the stories of the battles … in the old Wild West except that I could hear about the war from participants. I envied their experience.
>
> Looking back upon those years in which I grew up between the wars, I see now that that experience accounted for so much of what was happening around me.[24]

By the end of the first winter of the war, therefore, TFH felt that he had done all he could at school and now was the time to 'melt away' even though he was only 16.[25] His literary bent now, perhaps surprisingly, came to the fore and in March 1940, the school journal published a poem by him entitled: 'Written on Hearing of the Outbreak of War, September, 1939'. Writing poetry at that age, at that time, in an English public school was a brave thing to do. The poem reflects the feelings of many of that generation on hearing the news that all the sacrifices of 20 years before had been for nothing:

> So it has come.
> All that we fought and strove against – in vain,
> And Peace has fled on wild wings.
> The Tyrant stands astride his neighbour's land,
> And with mailed fist destroys his prey,
> As rebel hordes in Rome's last days
> Demolished house and temple wall.
> Must we, again, through folly of one Power
> Lose all the flower of Britain's youth?
> Once more must minds be snapped by strain,
> And others warped by fear and pain?
> O, would that God might guide our minds
> And we his instruments become,
> Than this, the horror of another war,
> But we are free to work our wills.
>
> So we will fight, and once again
> The glories of another field,
> The courage of yet other men,
> Will give us hope, though they
> Become but twisted bodies on a broken field.

There is less horror in a wounded man,
Or even in flying bullets overhead,
Than in the sorrow on a woman's face
When she has heard of dear ones dead,
Or children crying 'midst a ruined home,
Or old men, white hair stained with blood,
Who, straightening, shake gnarled fists
And curses to the blackened sky,
So this is War. May God forgive
All those that break the Peace.[26]

The poem speaks of many things of which TFH, as yet, knew nothing, but it does reflect the experience of a generation who had grown up with the legacy of the Great War; passed the wounded men begging in the streets, or seen the lingering effects of shell-shock and gas poisoning. It is, too, overtly Christian in its tone, reflecting TFH's strong beliefs and sense of outrage.

The war immediately changed the tempo of life:

There were air raid warnings and dispersal points... there was the study of aircraft silhouettes to be able to qualify for air spotting; bugles were sounded to mark the end of lessons as the chapel bell was reserved for announcing an invasion ... the appearance of Old Boys in uniform making visits, particularly heroes such as Commander Harwood who took part in the hunt of the *Graf Spee* which was one of the few events at that time which the British could take with pride.

The staff of course were decimated ... there was a succession of masters who never seemed to stay for very long, and it is a matter of regret that we were particularly vicious to them, as obviously their shortcomings were the very reason they were not in uniform.

I can recall seeing a ME 110 flying overhead, and there is the memory of meals being cooked over open fires for school lunches after the blitz, before power could be restored.[27]

All this excitement was too much to bear. In addition to the feeling of being left out of the war, TFH knew that although he was good at some subjects – English and History in particular, as the poem demonstrates – his grasp of Mathematics and Science was poor; he felt sure that he would not matriculate and so gain a school certificate.[28] Why stay on, therefore? On 1 September 1939, just before the Advent term was due to begin, TFH packed a bag, left a note for his mother and, with his friend Tom Trow, he reported to the depot of the Gloucestershire Regiment at Horfield Barracks, Bristol to enlist as a private soldier in the British Army at the age of 15.

2

'Half-way to Being a Soldier' Joining Up, 1941-1942

The Glosters, a famous regiment of the British Army, had been raised in 1694 by Colonel John Gibson. In 1751 it became the 28th Regiment of Foot and was re-named the 28th (North Gloucestershire) Regiment of Foot in 1782. After the Childers Reforms, the regiment amalgamated with the 61st (South Gloucestershire) Regiment of Foot to form the two-battalion Gloucestershire Regiment on 1 July 1881. It had raised 25 battalions during the Great War and its members had won six VCs. Its most prized distinction was the Back-Badge, gained as a result of its conduct at the Battle of Alexandria in 1801 when, attacked from front and rear by the French, the Commanding Officer had ordered the rear rank to turn about. Then, facing both ways, the regiment had delivered the devastating volleys of musketry for which the British Army was famous – so seeing off the French. In memory of that day the regiment's badge was the Sphinx, with a wreath of immortelles: a small version of the badge was ever after worn on the back of the regiment's head-dress.

The regiment's depot was not, surprisingly, in Gloucester, but in Bristol – probably because there were more recruits to be had in a major city than in a small cathedral town. Horfield Barracks had been built in 1845 and were therefore older than was usual for regimental depots, most of which had been built in the late 1870s or early 1880s to house Childers' new regiments; by 1939 it was nearing the end of its life.* Of course, there were other regiments closer to home, not least the Devons in Exeter itself. TFH felt however that if he were to enlist in the Devons then he would be spotted in no time – it was full of officers who knew his family socially – and he would be found out. *The Exonian* in July 1940, for example, listed 11 officers in the Devons who had attended Exeter School along with three times that number of NCOs and men. The Glosters were close enough, but also far away enough to provide a degree of camouflage.[1] Here at Horfield Barracks, having lied about his age in time-honoured fashion, TFH was enlisted, attested and put into the military system. For the next day or two it was the standard fare for a new recruit: medical examination, hair mown like a convict, kit issue and then learning how to swab, scrub and shine; to bull and blanco, under the watchful eye of a senior trained soldier or corporal – but only for a day or two. His mother was having none

---

* As early as 1938, correspondence between the regiment and Southern Command had led to an agreement in principle that a new depot would be built in 'a more central position' in Gloucestershire, but that this would have to wait while funds were found (112/Southern/4367 (QMG1) dated 9 July 1938). However, it was not until 1958 that the depot was eventually closed and sold off and training transferred to the new depot of the Wessex Brigade (*Bristol Evening World,* Thursday 24 September 1957).

The Glosters' Depot, Horfield Barracks, Bristol, where the young TFH joined the army. (GLRRM 05283.2)

A recruit's kit layout, such as TFH would have had to master on enlistment. (GLRRM 04858)

of it and she turned up at the barracks, demanded to see the officer commanding the depot and told him TFH's real age. In no time at all, as TFH recalled, 'I was hauled back to school.'[2]

There he stayed until April 1941. It was back to lessons where, being in his own words 'a lazy boy,' he was placed in the Remove.[3] It was also back to the OTC, in which he completed Certificate 'A',* became the solo drummer of the band and was promoted to Lance-Corporal[4] – and it was back to amateur dramatics. In March 1940, the school play was Shaw's '*Man and Superman*' in which TFH was once again cast in a female part, that of Ann Whitefield. *The Exonian* recorded, probably with deep irony, that:

The cast of *Man and Superman*; from left: A.C. Orchard, TFH, Roger Urwin,
Gandy Bradford. (*The Exonian*, 1940)

The first appearance of Ann Whitefield (A.H. Farrar-Hockley) suggested that, in this story of a Don Juan who is the quarry instead of the huntsman, the trail might be a long one but there could be only one result. She moved with grace, had all sorts of coquetry and cajolery at her finger tips and in her eyes; and surely the voices of the Sirens could have been no more alluring than her deep dulcet tones.[5]

TFH also made another poetic venture – this time paraphrasing Rudyard Kipling and making reference to his short period of military service in a poem entitled 'Half-way to Being a Soldier':

---

* There were two levels of examinations in military skills for the OTC, which were held twice a year in March and November. These awarded Certificates 'A' and 'B'. Certificate 'A' was designed primarily for members of the Junior Division of the OTC in schools and 'B' for the Senior Division at the universities; both examinations contained written and practical elements. Although the examinations were voluntary, successful candidates gained some advantages. For example, the holder of Certificate 'B' was entitled to a commission in the Special Reserve of Officers or the Territorial Force.

If you've slept with your boots unlaced on your feet,
With only your cap 'neath your head,
And naught but a greatcoat underneath,
Without anything overhead;
If you've slept with your pack half across your back,
And your hand lying on your gun,
You are half-way to being a soldier, my son,
To being a soldier, my son.

If you've been in a trench that is nearest the foe,
And listened to shrapnel's shrieks overhead,
'Till you've caught your breath from sheerest funk
At the thought of lying dead;
If you've longed to turn back at the rifles' crack
But kept right on at a run,
You are half-way to being a soldier, my son,
To being a soldier, my son.[6]

There are another two stanzas in this vein, which might have made experienced soldiers – who *had* experienced shrapnel or the crack-and-thump of a passing bullet – comment that schoolboys should keep quiet about things of which they knew nothing. One wonders what an older, wiser, TFH thought about these poetic fancies in later life.

In early January 1941, still three months short of his 17th birthday, TFH sat down with his mother and persuaded her that he could not wait any longer. Bea saw that he was not to be denied and reluctantly, she gave in and promised not to bring him home again, but made him wait until his birthday. He was attested before a magistrate on 15 January at Glastonbury,[7] giving his date of birth a year earlier than it had actually been, and enlisted into the army on 9 April 1941.[8] So it was back once more to the army – this time to the Exeter Recruiting Office. By now, there was a steady stream of conscripts entering the army and the recruiting officer looked somewhat quizzically at young TFH; what was the hurry? He would be called up soon enough, in his turn. So TFH had to tell the officer that he wanted to enlist as a regular soldier rather than be conscripted. In that case, he could have the choice of four infantry regiments: the Devons, the Somerset Light Infantry, the Duke of Cornwall's Light Infantry or the Glosters. Having gone first to the Glosters, TFH decided to stay with his original choice. He expected to be sent straight back to Horfield Barracks. However, the recruiting officer was no fool and had a very good idea that TFH was under age. He was, therefore, to his surprise, posted to the 70th (Young Soldiers) Battalion of the regiment, which was then at Glastonbury, as No. 5192664 Pte Farrar-Hockley, A.H.

Young Soldiers battalions had been first formed during the Great War, from what had originally been the Training Reserve, and were designed to provide a reserve of trained manpower for battalions in the theatres of war. As the army still enlisted boys at this time, and Parliament would not allow soldiers under the age of 19 to be sent overseas, these battalions carried out home service duties and training. At the close of the Great War, the army discharged the great mass of its war-enlisted men, but still had commitments to meet. Much of the force sent to occupy the Rhineland from 1918 under Sir Herbert Plumer, for example, was therefore provided by these battalions.[9] Young Soldiers battalions were again formed from the summer of 1940 onwards, often around a cadre of older men fit only for home service, supplemented by soldiers who had enlisted voluntarily, but were too young to serve overseas. As *The Red Dragon* recorded: 'In the summer of 1940, so many boys under 18 were volunteering for the Army [TFH was not alone] that the War Office decided to form Young Soldier battalions, and each regiment was ordered to supply the necessary officers and NCOs for its new battalion'.[10] They were usually numbered 70th and 71st in a regiment's order of battle and were often very large – sometimes up to 1,000-strong. The 70th Queen's, for example, reported its strength at the same date as TFH enlisted, as 43 officers and 922 NCOs and men.[11] A Young Soldiers company had been formed in the 8th (Home Service) Battalion of the Glosters in May 1940 at Stroud Road Drill Hall in Gloucester; this company was later expanded into the 70th (Young Soldiers) Battalion in October of that year.[2]

As well as undertaking training and providing a reserve of manpower – for many were fearful of the same casualty rates as in the Great War – Young Soldiers battalions were also given operational tasks in order to release regular troops. These included static guards on aerodromes until the Aerodrome Defence Corps relieved them; or anti-parachute operations, for which they were organised as counter-attack battalions; or internal security to prevent looting in the aftermath of bombing; or assistance to the ARP. Young Soldiers battalions were affiliated to a field force brigade and when fully trained were assigned an aerodrome or given a role within a sub-area or sub-district. Usually, companies rotated through a cycle of training, operations, exercises and recreation. All companies also changed their locations regularly so that everyone would know the whole area and all the tasks allocated to the unit. As many soldiers as could be spared would also be sent on specialist courses.[13] TFH's experience with the 70th Glosters followed this pattern:

A group of the 70th (Young Soldiers) Battalion of the Glosters in 1942, showing the uniforms and vehicles then in use. (GLRRM 05378)

We went into a training cycle while also doing military duties; I remember doing anti-parachute duties around Weston-Super-Mare (we were stationed at Brent Knoll at the time)… I also remember that there was bombing in Bristol and Bath and the lower echelons of human life started looting so that troops were called in. In my platoon we lost three chaps killed from bombing, one in my section. He had been posted in a place that seemed as safe as possible but when the bombs came down, he was killed. Of course there was nothing I could have done about it but still, I felt it was my responsibility. I felt it.[14]

The companies of the 70th Glosters spent time at various locations including the mud flats at Slimbridge – later the home of Peter Scott's Wildfowl Trust – Whitchurch Airport in Bristol, Abbots Leigh on the Clifton Suspension Bridge, Bristol City Docks, Avonmouth Docks and Brockley Airfield (later Bristol Airport).[15]

The battalion was commanded by Lieutenant-Colonel Gavin Young of the Welsh Guards,* whom TFH remembered as 'a wonderful CO at reaching out to us soldiers and NCOs and setting very high standards.'[16]

Very early on in his service, Young spotted TFH as a potential officer – having achieved Certificate 'A' at school. He was a lance-corporal by July 1941, a corporal on 8 December and a full-blown regular soldier, rather than a junior, in January 1942;[17] TFH's Platoon Sergeant, Jim Homer, warned him that he was being considered for a commission. TFH immediately felt that the gaffe would be blown when he had to produce his birth certificate, showing that he had enlisted under age and what was more, lied about it. This would hardly be the sort of conduct required of an officer and a gentleman, even in wartime: 'So I said to Jim Homer, "*No, I want to stay here longer and get more experience and be better trained before I go to an OCTU.*" Homer thoroughly approved of this, so I stayed put.'[18] As a result, TFH became a Sergeant: 'A wonderful experience; when I put those chevrons up, I felt a great weight of authority; a Sergeant was a hell of a fellow!'[19] In later life, even as a General, TFH always attended the annual past and present dinner of the Glosters Sergeants' Mess – sitting in the front row of the preceding AGM and voting as a full member and afterwards, paying as a member for his own dinner.[20]

However, there was no escaping his fate. His medical records describe him as fit, 5 feet 9 inches tall, 142 lbs in weight with a 40-inch chest, fresh complexion, blue eyes; and he had the good opinion of all his seniors. In the early summer of 1942, Young said he would have no more excuses from Farrar-Hockley:

I was still worried about the birth certificate but in the end I only had to produce my Army Form B217 – my record of attestation and service.† With that, the system

---

*   He was the father of Gavin David Young (1928-2001), the celebrated travel writer and *Guardian* journalist.
†   Army Form B217 consisted of the following sections:
     a. Questions put to the Recruit before Enlistment.
     b. Oath taken by the Recruit on Attestation.
     c. Certificate of Magistrate or Attesting Officer.
     d. Description on Enlistment.
     e. Certificate of Medical Examination.

TFH as a Cadet at 161 OCTU.
(Col J.W. Sewell)

simply accepted me. Then of course I didn't have a school certificate. I wrote down the subjects I had passed on the application form, went to an interview in Taunton which I sailed through and, as I was keen to become a regular officer, I was delighted to find that I was to attend 161 OCTU at Sandurst.[21]

Before the war, there had been considerable discussion about the future of officer training and of the two fee-paying colleges at Sandhurst and Woolwich. Suggestions from Leslie Hore-Belisha[22] and committees under Lord Willingdon in 1937[23] and Lord Strathcona in 1938[24] had all looked at ways to bring in more officers – as well as to widen the social base from which most officers were drawn. On the eve of the Second World War, around 90 percent of the army's officers were from the public schools and 30 percent from 10 major schools with army classes.[*] Before any decisions could be made, both Sandhurst and Woolwich were closed on mobilisation in September 1939, as, in the light of experience during the First World War, no regular commissions were to be granted in time of major war. The senior cadets of both establishments were commissioned at once. The juniors were called up into the Territorial Army as private soldiers – for Gentlemen Cadets were not actually in the army – and they were then

---

f. Certificate of Primary Military Examination.
g. Certificate of Approving Field Officer.
h. Military History Sheet.
i. Statement of Services.
* Eton, Harrow, Marlborough, Wellington, Rugby, Winchester, Hurstpierrepoint, Tonbridge and Felsted.

dispersed to various Officer Cadet Training Units, according to the arm or branch for which they were intended.[25]

Initially, the selection of more officers needed for the expanding army was carried out on the basis of recommendation by the Commanding Officer, followed by an interview with a senior regular officer. This method not only produced insufficient numbers, it also failed to produce the right quality: 25 percent of candidates selected by this means were failing the officer training courses that followed selection.[26] From the summer of 1942, personnel selection officers were put in place to assist commanding officers in identifying suitable candidates and the senior officer's interview was replaced by a command interview board – administered by the Local Command Headquarters and headed by a permanent president (usually a full colonel from the Reserve, assisted by commanding officers from nearby units). These boards, however, did little to improve matters: '... a candidate still stood or fell by the first impression he created. 'An awesome business', related Henry Longhurst, 'not improved by the thought that one's entire future may be dependant upon the state of another man's liver'.[27]

It was to one of these boards that TFH was sent, run by Western Command, and from which he passed successfully into officer training. He could equally well have gone before the newly-created War Office selection boards, which were now also up and running and replacing the command boards. It was these, more rigorous, boards that reduced failure rates to a mere eight percent in the OCTUs.[28]

Sandhurst was now the home of 161 Infantry Officer Cadet Training Unit (RMC), under the command of Lieutenant-Colonel C.A.M. Scott, whose task was to train officers for emergency commissions in the infantry. TFH joined the OCTU on 10 July 1942 and was posted to A Company (red),[29] in the Old Building which had been completed in 1812. Here, his

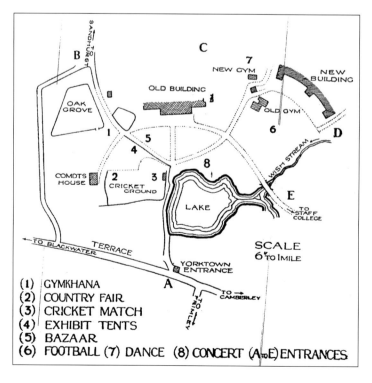

Sandhurst, as it would have appeared in 1942 (from the *RMC Magazine and Record,* 1921)

friend J.W. 'Toby' Sewell remembered that the pre-war regime of the college still endured, with even the college servants in residence to clean the cadets' rooms and polish their kit.[30] After a month, the OCTU was moved into the Edwardian red-brick New Buildings, to make more room for 101 (Royal Armoured Corps) OCTU, which trained officers for the cavalry, Reconnaissance Corps and Royal Tank Regiment; the function of the cavalry in war being to add tone to what would otherwise be a vulgar brawl, its officers could scarcely be expected to put up with any accommodation less stylish than that provided in the iconic Old Building. Another move was made before the last month of their training, this time further afield, to Mons Barracks at Aldershot – the move was made in column of route, with each company mounted on the infamous Sandhurst bicycles – which had later to be returned, as college property, at the insistence of 101 OCTU![31] Here in Aldershot the unit later became known as the 'Mons Officer Cadet Training Unit (Aldershot)'. After the war, it merged with Eaton Hall OCTU and became Mons Officer Cadet School. As such, it continued to train officers for short-service commissions in the Regular Army until it was wound up and merged back into Sandhurst in 1972.

In wartime, the tough, intensive course lasted for four months and was based on the infantry training syllabus which was used as a vehicle to teach and assess the cadets' leadership abilities. The main subjects were drill, weapon training, physical training, tactics, trekking and battle camp, sports and games, and competitions. The Standing Orders of the OCTU made it clear that officer cadets must demonstrate to the staff by their behaviour at all times, that they possessed the essential qualities of self-discipline, self-confidence and responsibility for others.[32] The directing staff of the OCTU were all selected for their combat experience: A Company was under the command of Major R.E.T. (Roger) St John of the Royal Northumberland Fusiliers;* his three captain instructors, who acted as platoon commanders, were all officers who had won Military Crosses in action: Edward Lisle Kirby of the Green Howards, and later the Royal Welch Fusiliers; H. Woods of the Royal Ulster Rifles; and L.H. Williams of the West Yorkshires. They and the tough senior NCOs of the company were charged with making sure that the future officers who passed through their hands would be capable of commanding troops in combat against some of the best soldiers in the world: the German and Japanese armies. The cadets were put through an unrelenting series of exercises during which they would, in turn, fill command appointments. Many of these exercises took place on local training areas, but there was a long exercise at the OCTU's battle camp in Snowdonia which included an 18-mile march and an inter-platoon competition. The final exercise took place around Guildford and included an assault crossing of the River Wey, a move to Frensham Ponds and an assault on the ridge above the lakes supported by *Churchill* tanks.[33]

During the last month of the course, TFH's thoughts began to turn towards the unit in which he would serve as a commissioned officer. He had achieved, in his own words:

> … a reasonable report and I began to think about the Airborne. I had been on a gas course while with 70th Glosters and there I had seen men with the Airborne badges.

---

*   Later Major-General Roger Ellis Tudor St John CB MC (1911-1998). He commanded 1st Battalion the Royal Fusiliers (City of London Regiment). After the war he served in the Mau Mau Rebellion in Kenya and was later, appropriately enough, President of the Regular Commissions Board.

These were admirable men and one wanted to be part of the front edge of the army, which they represented. Little did I know that there was a dearth of officers volunteering for the Airborne.[34]

I was on a [gas] course at Tregantle Fort* and whilst I was there I saw a bunch of bright and lively NCOs. I asked them who they were with and they said the Airborne Forces. Then, in early 1942, when they were looking for more people I thought: *"Gosh! Well, I'll volunteer!"* And that was that.[35]

TFH's choice-of-arm form in his record of service shows his first choice to have been the Royal Fusiliers on the ground that he had lived in London for eight years. He was, however, at first commissioned into the Wiltshire Regiment[36] and very nearly posted to the 7th Battalion of that regiment.[37] It was well known, though, among the other cadets and the staff that TFH had enlisted under age and he was regarded as very competent – even possessing, already, something of a presence[38] – and the Airborne needed officers. The commandant's report on him concluded that 'This officer cadet has done well and will make an excellent officer'.[39] Having applied for the Airborne, therefore, his wish was duly granted and, when he passed out of the OCTU on 5 November – his Emergency Commission and seniority back-dated to 8 August 1942[40] – he was transferred with effect from 11 November to the Parachute Battalion of the Royal Welch Fusiliers as No. 251309 2nd Lieutenant Farrar-Hockley.[41]

A pre-war Gentleman Cadet with one of the infamous bicycles, on one of which TFH and his fellow cadets made the move from Sandhurst to Aldershot in 1942 (from the *RMC Magazine and Record*, 1922)

---

*   9-21 March 1942 (AF B166a in TFH's record of service).

3

'Jumping thro' the hole'
The 6th (Royal Welch) Parachute
Battalion in Britain and North
Africa, 1942-1943[1]

TFH, not yet 19 years old and therefore still too young for active service abroad, joined the 6th (Royal Welch) Parachute Battalion at Larkhill on Salisbury Plain on 11 November 1942.[2] He had no connections with Wales whatsoever and it is possible that his posting to this battalion was simply the choice of the system; it was the 6th Battalion's turn to receive a new officer, and so to the 6th Battalion he went. However, the commandant at Sandhurst had been Brigadier Jimmy Bruxner-Randall[*] of the Royal Welch Fusiliers and it is also perfectly possible that, being well aware of TFH's latent potential, he pulled a few strings – thus TFH made the second of his three regimental affiliations. The battalion had seen no active service thus far during the war and so although TFH had the usual daunting prospect for a new, and very young, officer – that of meeting his first platoon – he did not have the even more daunting prospect of commanding a platoon of men who had faced the enemy's fire. Some of the older officers had seen active service between the wars or in the early period of the war. Captain Thomas Jones, for example, had been awarded the Distinguished Conduct Medal and had been commissioned from the ranks; Nigel Stockwell,[†] the Second-in-Command, had seen service on the North-West Frontier and in the Sudan. This was, therefore, an untried battalion, in a new role, in which a newly commissioned officer could make his way on his merits.

The 6th Battalion had been born as the child of a new policy in the formation of specialist units. In 1940, several units had been formed by gathering individual volunteers and raising a unit from them – a method which had been successful in some cases and near-disastrous in others. The 5th Battalion Scots Guards, for example, had been formed from skiing enthusiasts, winter sportsmen and polar explorers in all three services for operations in Finland. It had got as far as collective training at Chamonix in France before the Finns sued for peace and the battalion was broken up. It was probably just as well, since being almost entirely made up of officers who had voluntarily suspended their commissions, its fighting cohesion was questionable.[3] Several parachute battalions had also been started in this way. Some – like the first four battalions of the Parachute Regiment – had survived; others – like the 60th Queen's – had not.

---

[*]   Brigadier James Gerald Bruxner-Randall (1890-1982) served throughout both World Wars.

[†]   Nigel Clifton Stockwell RWF (1909-1976) served in Burma with the RWAFF and later in the Nigeria Regiment.

TFH soon after he was commissioned, wearing the uniform and badges of the Royal Welch Fusiliers. (Farrar-Hockley family)

On the credit side, the Independent Companies – the forerunners of the Army Commandos – had been formed by taking volunteers from the territorial infantry divisions of the army. Some of these fought with courage and determination in Norway under Colonel, later Major-General, Colin Gubbins, the wartime head of SOE.[4]

The results of calling for volunteers had to date, therefore, been variable. It was also realised that calling for volunteers tended to deplete the quality of standard infantry battalions by drawing off their best men. The Germans had discovered this in 1917 and 1918 when they formed their *Sturmbatallionen* – units which not only contained the best motivated men, but which also took the highest percentages of casualties. It was therefore decided to take entire, formed units and call for volunteers from within the unit – thus making use of the loyalties, traditions, cohesion and administrative systems already there.

To represent all the nations of the United Kingdom in the Airborne Forces, battalions were chosen from England, Scotland, Northern Ireland and Wales. The 10th Battalion The Royal Welch Fusiliers was selected to represent Wales. It had been formed in March 1939 when the government had decided to double the size of the Territorial Army. The method chosen was for each existing TA battalion to provide a nucleus of officers, NCOs and specialists, with up to two full companies of men and their equipment, to form a mirror-image second-line unit. Both units would then be brought up to strength by recruiting, conscription and new kit issues – thus the 7th Battalion of the Royal Welch Fusiliers, which recruited in Merionethshire and Montgomery, provided the basis for the 10th. Recruiting was brisk and the battalion formed without much fuss, although at the cost of operational effectiveness as a small number of experienced officers and NCOs struggled to manage a large influx of new men.

Of all the parachute battalions raised in this way during the war, 6th (RW) Para was the only one that received permission from the King to preserve in its new title the name of its parent regiment – perhaps because the King was Colonel-in-Chief of the regiment. Royal Welch traditions that were held dear were fiercely maintained: the Goat, the Flash – that bunch of black ribbons, the last relic of the pigtail, which adorns the back of every Royal Welch Fusilier[5] – and the celebration of St David's Day were all retained; the private soldiers were, until the very end of the battalion's existence, always called 'Fusilier' and not 'Private'. Most of the fusiliers were, of course, Welshmen from mid-Wales and not a few were Welsh-speaking; they stuck together strongly. In July 1942, all those on leave or detachment were summoned by telegram to return at once by their Commanding Officer, Lieutenant-Colonel Charles 'Lepro' Pritchard.[*] On 9 July, only three days after he took command, Pritchard paraded the battalion and told them that 'from 0001 hours tomorrow we will cease to be 10 RWF and we will instead become the 6th Parachute Battalion Royal Welch Fusiliers'[6] – they were to be re-roled, he said, with the option for every man of either volunteering for parachute training or being transferred elsewhere. The vast majority, 25 officers and 527 NCOs and men, decided to give it a try.[7] Not all were totally enthusiastic, as Sergeant Cliff Meredith later recalled, but the ties of comradeship persuaded most to have a go.[8] The result was therefore very close to the required jumping strength of a parachute battalion (the norm was around 50 percent volunteering[9]) – although not all of the men made it through training. Possibly the incentive of an extra two bob a day in parachute pay helped; more likely, the incentive was getting into action after three years of waiting for their war to start. One officer said as much in a letter to a friend: '... vanity, bravado, browned-off-ness with the infantry, a feeling of the utter absurdity of spending three years of one's life in khaki without even getting an interesting psychological experience ...'[10]

Those who did not were posted to other battalions of the Royal Welch Fusiliers and replaced by individual volunteers. Indeed, as early as 2 August – the day after the official formation of 6th (RW) Para – the Second-in-Command of the new battalion went off to visit other Welsh battalions to call for, and vet, volunteers. Only two weeks later, 69 more volunteers arrived from the 70th (Young Soldiers) Battalion of the Royal Welch and the War Diary shows a steady trickle of officers and men both leaving and joining from then on.[11] The scale of this turn-over can be judged by the fact that by April the following year, the battalion was still just over 100 men short of its mobilised strength.[12]

The battalion joined 2 Parachute Brigade, under Brigadier Ernest Down,[†] part of Lieutenant-General Frederick ('Boy') Browning's 1st Airborne Division. It consisted of the already-formed and trained 4th Parachute Battalion and two new battalions, still to be trained: the 5th (Scottish) Parachute Battalion, formed from the 8th Queen's Own Cameron Highlanders; and the 6th (Royal Welch) Parachute Battalion, later renamed 6th Battalion (Royal Welch) the Parachute Regiment. 'There was,' recalled TFH, 'a good deal of rivalry with the Jocks in 5 Para and one night they painted our Goat pink, which did *not* go down well.'[1] The brigade also had an attached parachute engineer company, signal company and a field ambulance – but no organic artillery. There was also very little in the way of motorised transport and much emphasis was therefore placed on the men's physical fitness, as they would be expected to cover long distances on foot under heavy load.

The battalion assembled at Hardwick Hall Camp, near Chesterfield – the parachute selection centre – on 1 August and on 6 August they put on the patches of the Airborne Forces. Before embarking on preliminary training, officers and men had to pass a two-week selection course at Hardwick Hall, an intense programme of physical tests, assault courses, cross-country and road marches in small squads under Army PT Corps instructors.

*   Pritchard, Charles Hilary Vaughan ('Lepro') DSO DL JP RWF, (1905-1976). He was commissioned in 1927; see his obituaries in *The Times* 31 March and 1 April 1976.

†   Later Lieutenant-General Sir Earnest Edward ('Eric') Down KBE CB (late Dorsets) (1902-1980).

The Flash as worn by 6th (RW) Para, an order signed off by Neill Boys as Adjutant of the battalion. (6th (RW) Para War Diary, RWF Museum/Archives)

Subject :- Dress.   10/08.

Os. C. Coys., Q.M., R.S.M.

Further to this H.Q. 10/51 of 1 Jun 44.

1.   The wearing of the Regimental Flash will be confined to S.D., B.D. and K.D. Jackets. It may be worn on Bush shirts when these are worn OUTSIDE the shorts or slacks.

2.   Flashes will be made to conform with the dimensions given below. Existing Flashes will be altered as far as possible to conform with these dimensions.

    (a) Length Officers - 9 inches.
                W.Os.   - 7 inches.
                O.Rs.   - 6 inches.
    (b) Width of ribbon   - 2¼ inches.
    (c) Width of "fan"   - 6 inches.
    (d) Length of hem   - ½ inch (showing)

3.   Half the hem will be worn inside the collar and buttoned to the collar.

Field.   Captain.
9 Jul 44.   Adjutant 6th Bn. (Royal Welch) Para. Regt.
(NMB/EMH)

Lieutenant-Colonel 'Lepro' Pritchard, the first CO of 6th (RW) Para and later Commander 2 Independent Para Brigade. (RWF Museum/Archives)

The fitness regime prior to undertaking parachute training weeded out many volunteers.
(Airborne Forces Museum)

'It was double-marching everywhere,' recalled Jack Ellis, 'training was intensive, all day and every day without a break.'[14] Those who did not show the required levels of stamina and self-discipline went no further.

For those who cleared this first hurdle, the next stage was parachute training at No. 1 Parachute Training School at Ringway, near Manchester. The CO was determined that the battalion would master the role and he led the way, qualifying with Nigel Stockwell on 16 August.

Pritchard's nickname, 'Lepro' – short for 'Leprechaun', derived from his almost wild fervour for all things Welsh. He was later Commander Airborne Establishments from 1946 to 1948 having made a major contribution during the Second World War to the development of Airborne Forces. Before the war, however, he had been one of the idlest officers of the Royal Welch Fusiliers – and this in a regiment whose officers thought and talked of nothing but hunting, racing and polo! While serving with the 2nd Battalion at Bingen on the Rhine in 1927, he had actually gone off to Paris for the weekend while on duty as Battalion Orderly Officer, leaving a telephone number with the Orderly Sergeant – an offence which, if discovered and taken seriously, might well have led to a trial by court-martial. However, the war had, in TFH's words, 'transformed him into a human dynamo. He was out and about training with us all day, working on papers until midnight, and determined that we should be at least good at our work, if not actually the very best.'[15]

Nigel Stockwell ended the war as a temporary brigadier commanding a brigade in 82nd (West African) Division under his cousin, Major-General Hughie Stockwell. Like everyone else, Pritchard started the two weeks at Ringway with ground training, which taught the trainee how to exit correctly from an aircraft, how to control his parachute and how to land without injury. Fuselages of *Whitley* aircraft were used for this, along with what was known as 'Kilkenny's Circus'* in the Ringway hangars: trapezes, wooden chutes and the fan – a revolving drum from which a cable with a parachute harness attached simulated the speed of a descent and the rate of impact on landing. There was also the roundabout – invented by the Poles – which was a 100-foot tower with a long steel arm protruding from the top, from which a parachute with a man suspended beneath it could be first hoisted up and then, once properly in position, released. Most people found the swings and slides pretty friendly, the roundabout alarming and the fan terrifying – but they learned that the terrors lay chiefly in the imagination, and the training received on this special equipment was of real value when the actual business of jumping from aircraft began.[1]

Parachute training at Ringway: fitting parachutes. (Airborne Forces Museum)

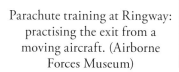

Parachute training at Ringway: practising the exit from a moving aircraft. (Airborne Forces Museum)

---

*   Named after the officer who devised and supervised parachute training – Wing Commander J.C. Kilkenny OBE RAF.

Parachute training at Ringway: that awful
balloon! (Airborne Forces Museum)

Parachute training at Ringway: the tower.
(Airborne Forces Museum)

The next stage in the training came in the second week with chill mornings and standing
around in Tatton Park, waiting for balloons to go up with their cargoes of four apprehensive
men in the small cages below the balloon. Once the tethered balloon reached 700 feet, the
instructor would open a trap door in the floor and one by one the trainees – sitting around
the hole with their legs dangling and their chutes attached to a static line – would assume
the correct position and on the word of command 'go', would exit. Jumping from a balloon
was generally felt to be far more frightening than jumping from an aircraft – an aircraft's
slipstream tended to pull the parachutist through the air as he fell; however, the jump from a
balloon was a dead weight, straight-down drop with around 120 feet of fall before the canopy
deployed. As one poet put it:

One morning very early,
Damp and cold and dark,
They took me in a so-called bus
Out to Tatton Park.
In keeping with the weather,
Said I to one and all,
'I take a dim and misty view
Of jumping thro' the hole.
Jumping thro' the hole, jumping thro' the hole,
I'll always keep my trousers clean,
When jumping thro' the hole'.[17]

The subsequent enjoyment of floating down was, however, rudely interrupted by an instructor on the ground – shouting instructions on keeping position ready for landing through a megaphone.

The two balloon drops were followed by anxious waiting in the corners of hangars for the weather men to decide whether or not conditions were fit for flying, in order to complete the five required aircraft jumps from a *Whitley*. These were done first in 'slow pairs', then in 'quick pairs', then in sticks of five men and finally in sticks of 10. The men learned to adopt the right position in the aircraft door so as to avoid somersaults when dropping or twisting the parachute's rigging lines together, or having the canopy invert. One after another the men passed through, received their wings, and went on 14 days' leave; or they were found to be 'unsuitable for employment in a parachute battalion' (i.e. they refused to jump) and were posted. In some cases they died, for parachuting was dangerous. On 17 November, around the time that TFH joined the battalion, Corporal James Lewis

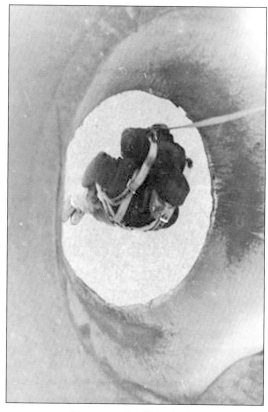

'Jumping thro' the hole'.
(Airborne Forces Museum)

and four fusiliers* were killed in a training accident. On the other hand, while at Ringway, the food was better than the usual rations, the accommodation was comfortable and there were the girls of the WRAF![18]

On 31 August, the battalion moved to No. 6 Camp at Bulford for a few weeks under canvas and from there – on 7 October – to Newcombe Lines, Larkhill on Salisbury Plain, just below Stonehenge. It was here that TFH joined the battalion. Almost immediately, however, he went off to do the two phases of parachute training[19] and having successfully completed these he was posted to C Company. His Company Commander, always a strong and abiding influence on a young officer, was Major Leonard Holden. Among the other battalion characters were Lieutenant Neill Boys,[†] the mortar officer; John Neill,[‡] one of his fellow subalterns; and Humphrey ('Huff') Lloyd-Jones, who commanded B Company. A fluent Welsh speaker, he always carried a walking stick, which during a drop was tied to his wrist with a length of string, while his rimless glasses were taped to his ears.[20] Then there was the regimental signals

---

*   Stan Reader, Ray Towler, Albert Williams and Ivor Williams.
†   Neill McPherson Boys (1918-2005). See his obituary in *Y Ddraig Goch*, February 2007.
‡   John Morris Neill MC (1919-1961) had been commissioned in 1941. He later returned to the RWF and was killed in a traffic accident in Berlin. See his obituary in *Y Ddraig Goch*, March 1962.

Lieutenant Tony Crosland, Signals
Officer and later Intelligence Officer
of 6th (RW) Para.
(RWF Museum/Archives)

officer, Anthony Crosland* – later a Labour Cabinet Minister and writer on socialist ideas. Crosland could have been a very difficult proposition – full of extreme left-wing ardour as he was; however, the challenge of parachuting and the increased chance of action seem to have engaged his interest. Later, as adjutant and intelligence officer of the battalion, he proved a skilled operator. TFH related one anecdote about a route-march on 1 May, probably in North Africa. The battalion was about to be dismissed at the end of the march when Crosland's platoon broke into a spirited rendition of the socialist anthem, 'The Red Flag'. 'Lepro', who had a rather high-pitched voice, became almost apoplectic in trying to make himself heard above the singing and the suppressed amusement – or horror – of the rest of the battalion, eventually telling Crosland's Company Commander to 'get rid of that bloody shower!'

TFH was very fortunate to have as his first Platoon Sergeant, in No. 12 Platoon, Cliff Meredith – a consummate professional but also a kindly man who guided the young TFH through the various pitfalls that awaited a young officer. They remained friends for the rest of TFH's life.† Meredith later recalled that 'As a new boy, he was keen to show his mettle. He stood out from the other officers and men who had joined us from other units, displaying a rugged personality. He soon became known as a no-nonsense officer, who kept his men sharp and well informed.'[21] TFH, for his part, recalled later that 'the men we had were of very high quality and one had the help one needed to be an effective officer.' For their part, one of his fusiliers recalled later when talking to TFH's son Dair, that in an effort to give himself more gravitas than his 18 years might provide, TFH first grew a moustache and then took up smoking a pipe. 'Neither worked,' said the old soldier, 'but it didn't matter – we all loved him anyway.'[22] Another soldier, Jack Ellis, remembered that TFH was from the first day 'a very good leader, everyone respected him and it was obvious that all he wanted was action.'[23]

---

*   Anthony Crosland (1919-1977) was commissioned into The Royal Welch Fusiliers in April 1941. He was later MP for Grimsby and was Foreign Secretary under James Callaghan before his early death from a stroke at the age of 58.

†   John Clifford (Cliff) Meredith MBE (b. 1920) – commissioned from the ranks as RSM of 2 RWF in Malaya in 1956 and served as QM with several RWF battalions until his retirement as a captain in 1961. He now lives in North Wales.

Before any encounter with the enemy, however, there was the terror of terrors: the regimental sergeant major. As it happened, this was RSM F.T. (Frederick) Langford, a strict disciplinarian and veteran of the last year of the Great War – but no terror. He habitually went around with a happy smile on his face – perhaps the outward expression of what he was: a deeply religious man and a contented, courageous spirit with an infectious keenness which lifted everyone who met him.

If the battalion's training had been hard before, it was doubly hard now. Many individual officers and NCOs went off on specialist training courses, while the regime of physical training (route marches of up to 25 miles), lectures, weapon training and parachute training was relentless. Tactical training exercises for platoons and companies also began, both by day and by night. Just after a bitterly cold Christmas the battalion was visited by Lieutenant-Colonel Simon Hill, who until recently had commanded 21st Parachute Battalion. He had returned badly wounded from North Africa, and he told the men of the doings of his old unit there. TFH was clearly injured at this time; the War Diary shows him as being discharged from Shaftesbury Military Hospital on New Year's Day 1943 – but gives no reason why he was there.[24]

While the battalion was on Salisbury Plain, the fusiliers were allowed local liberty for walking-out on some evenings in Salisbury or Winchester. Lorries were always laid on to make sure that the men got back to camp at the appointed time and the battalion orderly officer had to accompany the transport to ensure that all the men were accounted for. One evening, TFH found himself on this detail and as the fusiliers were noisily clambering aboard the lorries, a pretty, red-haired young ATS girl came up to him. 'I'm sorry to cause you trouble, Sir,' she said, 'but please can you help? You see, I've missed my own transport and I'll be in awful trouble if I don't get back to camp. Please could I hitch a ride with you?' TFH at first felt inclined to refuse, but soon gave in. By the time he had dropped her off, he had learned her name: Margaret Wells,* but she was always, always known as 'Pat' – no-one quite knew why. He had also got her to agree to see him again.

This was the start of TFH's first big love affair, one that was to last for the next 40 years. Pat was five years his senior – the difference in their ages was practically a State secret. She was an orphan from King's Lynn in Norfolk, who had been adopted and brought up by a family on the Royal Estate at Sandringham. She had left her adoptive home to enlist early in the war and was, by this time, a corporal driver. She was pretty, lively, not shy about coming forward and TFH soon fell head-over-heels. She in turn was equally smitten. In peacetime a relationship between a male officer and a female NCO would never have been tolerated – especially in a regiment with such traditional views on these things as The Royal Welch Fusiliers – but this was wartime and much licence was allowed (not least because there were many of both sexes from good families who had enlisted in the ranks). Within a year they had become engaged.

So matters went on until orders for a move were received at the end of March 1943. Before the battalion left for active service – to return God only knew when – TFH and Pat decided that they would marry. TFH was still under 21 and legally, therefore, he had to have his father's permission. He had seen little of his father and when he went to ask permission – using a day of his short pre-embarkation leave – his father refused. Shocked, TFH hastily engaged a

---

*   Margaret Bernadette Wells (b. 11 January 1919).

solicitor and went to court to ask a judge to rule that the circumstances were exceptional. The judge, however, supported his father and the two had therefore to wait. Given that within 12 months TFH could do as he wished, but in the intervening time he might easily be killed in action, this spiteful, petty refusal is very hard to understand. It provoked a final rift between TFH and his father which was never healed.[25] There was time for no more than a day or so with his mother. Molly Tatham had died at the beginning of the war and Beatrice had gone to live, briefly, at Ladock. However, she soon bought a house in Exeter – 'Siddowes', in Courtenay Road – on the southern edge of the city just off the main A377 Alphington Road. This house she kept for a short time until she moved again to 'Arnecliffe' in Phillips Avenue, Exmouth. She was soon joined by the young Briony Smith – later to be TFH's PA/researcher – who lived with her until 1944 when Bea was taken ill and, as a result, moved back to Ealing to be nearer the rest of her family, where she bought 18 Byron Road.

As a result of the various turmoils, the Griffin family took Pat under their wing – although she remained in the ATS. It was soon apparent that TFH and his career were what mattered first and last to her. She was, however, not at all trained in either housekeeping or mother-hood and was more than a little overawed, at first, by the Griffins, whose lifestyle was several degrees smarter than that in which she had grown up. However, as each got to know the other, the atmosphere relaxed. Stanley in particular, who was running the family estate agency in Ealing, took great pains with her and soon discovered that she loved music – as he did – and had a wonderful soprano voice.

*　　*　　*

On 2 April, with embarkation leave over, the whole of the 1st Airborne Division – to which 2 Para Brigade was assigned – paraded in front of King George VI. The King, unsurprisingly, inspected 6th (RW) Para.

Mobilisation was completed on 6 April and on 13 April the battalion moved by train to Gourock on the Firth of Clyde. For security reasons on the journey, their red berets were kept out of sight and khaki forage caps were worn. At Gourock they embarked in the troop-ship *Nieuw Holland* and steamed out into the North Atlantic at 1:30 a.m. on the morning of 16 April. Any prospect of a monotonous sea voyage was immediately dispelled by constant physical training, weapon-training exercises and TEWTs* for the officers and NCOs under 'Lepro' Pritchard's eagle eye. In the rare intervals of a stand-easy, the men could watch the other ships of the convoy and its escorts, constantly on watch against the threat of German submarines. Troopships were not known for comfort – especially on the troop decks, where the men were crowded into bunks or hammocks, messing in shifts and with limited washing facilities, canteen or recreation. For TFH as a Platoon Commander, therefore, there was a real need to keep the men so busy that they had no time to notice any of the shortcomings and so tired that they would sleep as soon as they fell into their beds.

On the night of 21 April, the distinctive, dark shape of Gibraltar could be seen to port and the lights of Tangier to starboard. By morning, the convoy was sailing through the blue waters of the Mediterranean. On the seventh day out, the battalion learned that it was to land

---

*   Tactical Exercise Without Troops.

King George VI and Queen Elizabeth inspecting 6th (RW) Para prior to embarkation for North Africa. (RWF Museum/Archives)

at Oran, in French North Africa, to concentrate inland and then to link up with the rest of 1st Airborne Division. Oran had been captured from the Vichy French on 9 November 1942 – a day after the initial Allied landings in French North Africa* – after a heavy battle. The assault had included parachute landings and in subsequent operations, the First Army had pushed eastwards to catch the German *Panzer Armee Afrika* between them and the British Eighth Army advancing from Egypt. In spite of the setback of the Kasserine Pass, the Allies had made rapid progress. On 9 March 1943, Erwin Rommel handed over his command and returned to Germany. By the time that 6th (RW) Para arrived, the final stages of Operation *Vulcan* were in progress in Tunisia. On 13 May, the German and Italian forces in Africa surrendered.

For most of the men on the convoy, the red cliffs of North Africa appearing above the horizon must have been an exciting sight; they had, in all likelihood, never been outside Britain before. That evening – 22 April 1943 – part of the convoy stood in to port, where 2 Para Brigade disembarked. After a march over rough stone in pelting rain, which seemed endless but was in fact only about a mile, the men reached an embussing area where they climbed aboard American three-ton trucks, driven by an African-American unit – perhaps the first time that many of the soldiers had ever seen a black man. From there they were driven

---

*   The Anglo-American operation, *Torch*, led by General Dwight Eisenhower.

to the Oran railway sidings, where at around 4:00 a.m. the men piled into hard, third-class carriages, were locked in as a protection against the nocturnal activities of thieving Arabs, and slept as well as they could.[26]

TFH awoke next morning to find himself passing through a country of green cornfields dotted with red poppies; of vineyards; and of occasional ancient olive groves. After frequent halts, the train – travelling first east, then south – reached the small town of Perregaux, about 60 miles inland from Oran. After a wash, a shave, weapon-cleaning and breakfast the men marched round the town to stretch their legs, glad to be wearing their red berets again. Three-ton trucks then took them up the foothills, over the mountains and half-way down the other side to the larger town of Mascara. To TFH it seemed impossibly, brilliantly white in the morning sun. Heading south again for three miles over a rough, pot-holed track the convoy passed through the village of Tizi, then joined a straight highway towards a distant range of hills. About five miles beyond Tizi they turned off under the shadow of a great bare hill, followed a track past two farms standing amid lemon and olive trees, rounded a final corner

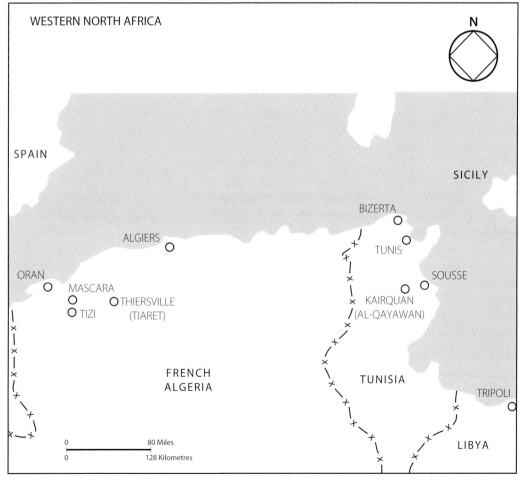

Western North Africa.

– and TFH came face-to-face with No. 2 Stockade: the prisoner of war camp that was to be his – and his battalion's – temporary home.

The days that followed were full of yet more new experiences: the climate, the American food, the anti-malarial Mepacrine tablets, the nesting Maribou storks and the tank bathing at Tizi. Above all, there was the rain, which arrived every evening in torrents. In a matter of minutes tiny rivulets became swollen streams; within an hour of the first drops falling, rivers rushed beneath some of the tents, washing the men's equipment away in a flood of muddy water.

After the rains, a period of fine weather followed and the battalion moved to a new tented camp beyond Thiersville, closer to Mascara. Section and platoon training began in earnest in the hills, along with route marches over the rough hills, covered with scrub and thorn bushes, shooting on improvised ranges and the imposition of strict food and water discipline.[27] Company exercises among the olive groves followed, up and down the valleys, in and out of the white-washed plaster of the Arab villages. Everywhere the thick red dust clung to skin and clothing – making it an uncomfortable time for all as the battalion mastered tactical march discipline, picqueting high ground, and the attack by day and night.[28]

The training day, which began at 0600 hrs with reveille, breakfast and PT, ended with supper at 1800 hrs unless there was a night exercise. On two afternoons a week, TFH had also to plan sports for his platoon and on Sundays after church parade, to supervise make-and-mend. He had little time for recreation, therefore. However, sometimes in the evening he could visit the nearby USAAF Airfield, sit out in the warm, still night and watch the latest American movies. Sometimes Captain Emrys Jones and his concert party entertained him and his fellows from the back of a three-ton truck. Corporal Boland and Fusilier Haughton would sing, or Fusilier Masters would give his version of Arthur Tracey's favourite music-hall song 'It's My Mother's Birthday Today' – and when the laughter had died, when those renowned funnymen Sergeant Corfield and Colour-Sergeant Rowland had taken their final bow, the whole audience would fall silent and listen to the beautiful singing of Emrys Jones himself. Then he would stop and say, 'Come on now, let's have the chorus,' and the night would echo with 500 Welsh voices.

On 4 May, TFH was promoted to the war-substantive rank of Lieutenant: no longer a one-pip wonder. For the rest of the month, the battalion was busy with tactical training and their first parachute training since arriving in Africa – also their first experience of dropping from American aircraft by day and by night. The reason for this became clear when Pritchard called the battalion together at the edge of the cornfield beside their camp and told them an operation was impending, though for security reasons he could not say when or where. In fact, the 1st Airborne Division was to become part of General Bernard Montgomery's Eighth Army, which with Mark Clark's US Fifth Army was preparing to invade Sicily, in Operation *Husky*. Each day the battalion trained in an area chosen for its resemblance to the country where they were to operate. Where necessary, the ground had been altered, and along the roads, false taped signs had been erected — 'Piccadilly', 'Regent Street', 'Oxford Street', 'Strand' — code-words for the roads and tracks in the operational area. Time after time the battalion moved into the exercise area, took up positions, deployed, concentrated and moved back to start all over again until they knew the position of every other man in their companies; every rock and stone; every patch of scrub – but Pritchard himself, having formed, trained and led the battalion thus far, was denied the chance to lead it into combat. On 19 May he was promoted to Colonel and became Deputy Commander of 2 Para Brigade. His successor was

Lieutenant-Colonel John Goodwin of the Welch Regiment, who had until now been Second-in-Command of the 4th Parachute Battalion.[29]

Brigade-level rehearsal exercises continued into early June in the area of Oued Taria, 12 miles south of Mascara. At last, on 13 June, the news came that the battalion was to move 650 miles north-east to Sousse, on the curve of the North African coastline below Tunis. The advance parties left by air on 24 June – the remainder following by road. When TFH and his platoon arrived, they found tents already pitched in the shade of the olive groves close to the road from Sousse to the Holy City of Kairouan. Lest they should think they were being pampered, they were immediately told to get their picks and shovels out and dig slit trenches. All around, the other units of 1st Airborne Division were doing the same. Here, at Kairouan, began the final stage of training to bring the men to the peak of physical fitness required for operations, but TFH was again taken into hospital along with two other officers and 12 men. The War Diary noted that – presumably given the imminence of operations – these officers and men were particularly required to return to the battalion.[30] However there would be no immediate return, as TFH and the others had contracted typhoid fever.[31]

With the end of the final training on 7 July the officers were briefed and then the whole battalion was marched into the briefing hut to be shown models of the operation area, maps of the enemy dispositions in Sicily, and the plans for the assault from the sea. Sicily was to be invaded by Allied forces from the American, British and Canadian armies, structured as two task forces. The Eastern Task Force (also known as Task Force 545) was led by General Sir Bernard Montgomery and consisted of the British Eighth Army. It was to land on a front of two corps: XIII Corps would land between Syracuse and Avola on 10 July and XXX Corps to the south of them, around Pachino. The Western Task Force (Task Force 343) was commanded by the redoubtable Lieutenant-General George S. Patton and consisted of the Seventh United States Army. The two task force commanders reported to Field Marshal Sir Harold Alexander, Commander of the 15th Army Group.

Two British and two American landings by Airborne Forces preceded the amphibious assaults just after midnight on 10 July. The British force was led by the 21st Independent Parachute Company (Pathfinders) who were to mark landing zones for the leading elements of the 1st Airborne Division, which was to seize the Ponte Grande – a major bridge over the River Anape, just south of Syracuse – and hold it until the British 5th Infantry Division arrived from the beaches at Cassibile, seven miles away. Glider-borne troops from 1 Airlanding Brigade were meanwhile to seize landing zones inland.[32] In the final version of the plan for the division, Operation *Fustian*, C Company Group, under Leonard Holden – including TFH's platoon – was to secure a bridge vital to the advance of XIII Corps and then to destroy the light flak gun positions on the far side. The remainder of the battalion was to seize the rising ground to the north of the bridge and to form a bridgehead.[33]

On 8 July, Montgomery himself came and spoke to the men once again, raising the levels of excitement and anticipation to new heights. Containers were issued and packed; parachutes issued and checked; ammunition broken out and distributed; kit checked, and checked, and checked again – but it was not to be, for the plan went badly awry. Strong winds of up to 45 knots blew the troop-carrying aircraft off course. The US force was badly scattered over south-eastern Sicily between Gela and Syracuse and worse still, the aircraft had been engaged by anti-aircraft fire from the Allied fleet, which brought down 23 aircraft. Half the US paratroopers failed to reach their rallying points. The British air-landing troops fared little better;

only 12 of the 147 gliders landed on target and 69 crashed at sea. A platoon of the South Staffordshire Regiment, which had landed on target, captured Ponte Grande and fought off German and Italian counter-attacks. The British force held out until about 1530 hrs when they were forced to surrender – only 45 minutes before the leading elements of 5th Infantry Division arrived from the south.

On 10 July, shortly before the battalion was to move and while the initial airborne action was in progress in Sicily, all but C Company's tasks were put on hold due to the changing situation. C Company, with the Mortar and *Vickers* Medium Machine-gun Platoons, packed their containers and moved out to airfields 20 miles away near El Djem. When they had emplaned, a liaison officer brought the news that the operation was postponed for 24 hours. Another hot day was passed beneath the olive trees and once again C Company group set off for the airfield early on 11 July. Then, out of the heat haze, there suddenly emerged a fast-moving jeep that made straight for the leading aircraft. One by one the men heard the news, shouted above the roar of the engines: the operation was cancelled.

For TFH, although it was galling for the battalion to have missed its chance of action, it meant that he himself had not been doubly disappointed – for he was still in hospital recovering from typhoid and had the battalion dropped, he would have missed it. Even before the spell in hospital he had been frustrated at not seeing action;[34] now he fumed and fidgeted all the more, anxious to rejoin his platoon before the drop, but forbidden from doing so; now he could relax, for there would be another chance.[35] The troops too could relax, for there was, perhaps, some slight consolation in a glorious two days' rest along the beaches and in the shining waters of the Mediterranean near Salines de Ras Dinas, with only one hour's physical training daily under the bronzed figure of Sergeant Instructor Jenkins. This was the first relaxation of more than a few hours since 6th (RW) Para had landed in North Africa. During this period both Brigadier Down and Major-General George Hopkinson,[*] the general officer commanding the division, came and spoke to the battalion to explain what had happened and why, and how the campaign in Sicily was unfolding. To keep morale up – as well as hone skills – tactical training and parachute training both resumed in late July.

In spite of these disappointments, the battalion was on the eve of action but still without TFH, who remained in hospital.[36] By the time he rejoined the battalion, much had happened. Although the campaign in Sicily had its problems, it gradually succeeded in driving back the Axis forces. One of the problems was, of course, the escape of so many capable German troops across the Straits of Messina, which meant that an invasion of Italy would face a German army at full strength – with all that that meant in the first half of the 20th century. Churchill now pushed hard for follow-on operations against the Italian mainland. As he saw it, attacking the supposed soft underbelly of Europe had the potential to knock Italy out of the war, bring Turkey in, isolate the German forces in the Balkans and expose Austria to attack.[37] In spite of serious American reservations,[38] the British Chiefs of Staff, who were committed to clearing the Mediterranean and thus saving huge tonnages of shipping on the routes to the oilfields in the Persian Gulf and to India, carried the day.

---

[*]   Major-General George Frederick Hopkinson OBE MC (1896-1943) took over command of the 1st Airborne Division from Browning in 1942. He was killed on 9 September 1943 – one of only five British generals to be killed in action during the Second World War.

The invasion was to take place in two sectors. In Operation *Baytown*, the Eighth Army was to cross the Straits of Messina onto the toe of the Italian boot and from there push into Calabria. To the north, in a more ambitious landing, Mark Clark's Fifth US Army – with as many British troops as American – would land in the Bay of Naples. This operation – *Avalanche* – would threaten the Axis communications and lead to the rapid collapse of Italy, whose government was already making frantic, if discreet, soundings or peace.[39]

In the original planning, the great attraction of capturing the important port of Taranto in the heel of Italy had been recognised and an assault had been considered but rejected because of its formidable defences. However, with the signing of the armistice with the Italians on 3 September the picture changed. It was decided to carry the 1st Airborne Division to Taranto using British warships, seize the port and several nearby airfields, and follow up by shipping in V Corps and a number of fighter squadrons. The airborne division was warned for the operation – *Slapstick* – on 4 September and was to embark on or before 8 September. With such short notice, Operation *Slapstick* was soon nicknamed Operation *Bedlam*.

6th (RW) Para received its orders at 0200 hrs on 5 September 1943. It was to be ready to move almost at once and to be prepared to embark four hours later.[40] The expected postponement came, but by 9:00 a.m. on the 7th the battalion was moving off towards Bizerta. They drove through the shattered town, which had felt the full weight of Allied bombing, to an open hillside where the German Army in Africa had made its last stand. Here, the companies waited while the Commanding Officer gave out his orders to company commanders. Only B and C Companies, the advance element of Battalion Headquarters, the mortars and the MMG Platoon were to embark for Italy at once. A Company, the rest of Battalion HQ and the recently-formed Anti-tank Platoon would follow in the infantry landing ship *Prince Leopold*, under the Second-in-Command, Major Percy Davies.

By 1000 hrs on 8 September the first troops had embarked on HMS *Abdiel*,* a mine-laying ship commanded by Captain David Orr-Ewing, which was to carry them to Italy. Many of the first hours at sea were spent in issuing maps and orders. Slowly, the convoy drew towards Taranto and passed through the channel cleared by minesweepers. The *Abdiel* moved into Taranto Bay and dropped anchor about a mile from Castel San Angelo; the battleship HMS *Howe* anchored 200 yards away and during the evening, the Flag Officer Malta – Vice-Admiral Sir Arthur Power,† who was commanding the landing – visited the companies and met all officers of the Orders Group. Just before dark a lighter came alongside, the men picked up their weapons and shrugged on their loads, and prepared to disembark. False alarm: there was a shout of disapproval when the lighter pulled away empty and moved aimlessly, so it seemed, around the other ships in the harbour. It was another case of that well-known military condition, rushing to wait.

Through the ship's loud-speaker system everyone was kept informed of events on shore and at last, at about 2300 hrs, the men got ready to disembark once more. All available deck spaces had been allocated as parade grounds, but space was tight and a number of men had to be mustered below decks. Through the darkness, those on deck could hear the sounds of

---

*   The *Abdiel* was over 400 feet in length and 40 feet in the beam. She displaced 4,000 tons when fully loaded.
      She was also fast, capable of speeds up to 40 knots – although 15 knots was her usual cruising speed.
†   Later Admiral of the Fleet Sir Arthur John Power GCB GBE CVO (1889-1960).

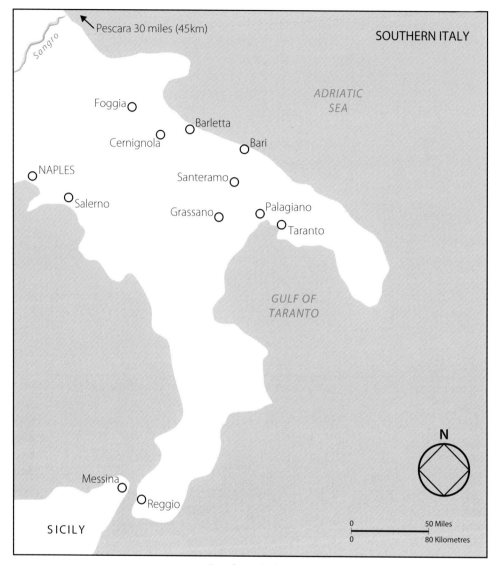

Southern Italy.

other units going ashore and marching away from the harbour, but no lighters approached HMS *Abdiel*. Then, just after midnight, chaos; the quiet of the night was shattered by a deep, roaring explosion and a violent shuddering of the ship. All the lights went out and the emergency lighting flashed on for only a short time. HMS *Abdiel* listed to port, righted herself for a few moments, listed again, and then began to sink rapidly. She had been hit by an un-swept magnetic mine which had risen from the sea bed, broken her back and split into two parts around the position of the wardroom. Both parts were completely submerged within two minutes. Captain John Pearson* later gave an account:

---

*   Later Major John Wesley Pearson OBE (1919-2009).

HMS *Abdiel*. (Author's collection)

… a searchlight swept the water and I caught a fleeting glimpse of two huge hulks slowly disappearing below the water… I then became conscious of many distressing calls for help around me… How far I swam after that I do not know, but my object was to reach the only light I could see, and that seemed miles away. After what seemed an interminable period I touched a floating drum to which I clung for grim death. I rested for a while, then paddled the drum about, and when a small Italian rowing boat loomed out of the darkness there were about 10 of us hanging on to one another around the drum.[41]

RSM Langford took to the water and, swimming about, helped several men to a raft, and rallied further men by blowing his whistle. Later he went after some others in distress, but his strength gave out and he was drowned. He was not the only loss; in this disaster, 6th (RW) Para lost its Commanding Officer, Lieutenant-Colonel John Goodwin; Major Trefor Evans; Captains John Mathias and Emrys Jones; Lieutenants Edwin Watkins, Alan Radford and Charles Egmore – who had taken over TFH's platoon when he went into hospital;[42] CSM William Harris; Sergeants Edwin Dale, William Birchall, Wilfred Smith and Fred Stock; and 45 others.[43] In addition, four officers and about 150 men had to be evacuated suffering from various wounds. Several of the military casualties were among the best swimmers in the battalion, but when their bodies were recovered it was found that their shoulder straps were buttoned over their webbing braces and they had struggled in vain to unbutton them and discard their heavy equipment.

Exhausted and bedraggled, the survivors who remained unhurt were taken first onto the battleship *Howe*, then to barracks recently occupied by Italian troops. Their part in the operation was over before it had properly started. The last to leave the jetty was Captain Stuart Stock RAMC – the battalion's Medical Officer – who had pulled many men from the waters of the harbour and brought them back to consciousness. The aftermath was if anything worse than the attack. The second ship carrying the remainder of 6th (RW) Para made it safely to port and disembarked the troops: Tony Crosland wrote that the sinking of the *Abdiel* had greatly dimmed his 'schoolboy enthusiasm for fighting … the sight and stench of those washed-up bodies, horribly and grotesquely swollen, limbs distorted, flesh decomposing: and the grim business of … burying them in a huge communal pit, trying hard not to be sick'.[44]

The battalion, under the temporary command of Pearson, began to sort itself out. There was no time to feel sorry for themselves – there was a war on. On 15 September a new Commanding Officer arrived, Lieutenant-Colonel Vernon 'Bill' Barlow of The King's Shropshire Light Infantry. Other officers and men were posted in and the companies equalised by cross-posting. The battalion rejoined 2 Para Brigade on 17 September and was immediately committed to operations in the area of Palagiano. Later in the month, receiving a rapturous welcome from the Italian civilian population, they moved northwards to Cernignola in support of V Corps which was concentrating in Foggia. A short while later, they moved again to Santeramo – and it was here, on 19 October 1943, that TFH rejoined a much-changed battalion.[45]

4

'The Boy Wonder'
The 6th Battalion (Royal Welch) the Parachute Regiment in Italy and the South of France[1]

In the aftermath of the sinking of the *Abdiel* a stream of miscellaneous articles — arms, ammunition and equipment — poured in from all directions. Clothing came from the sailors and marines and some of the more theatrically-inclined fusiliers appeared in bell-bottomed trousers, until reluctantly compelled to tuck the bottoms into their canvas gaiters. Cliff Meredith remembered that 'by 0630 hrs on the 11th we were ready, willing and able to fight'.[2] However, it was not to be so just yet. Almost 100 officers and men were drafted in; evacuated survivors came back in a steady trickle from North Africa and Sicily – some having hitch-hiked by pretty devious routes. John Pearson recalled that:

> With Major Len Holden and Captain Jack Masterton, I had been evacuated on HMS *Penelope* by circuitous means to 33rd General Hospital in Syracuse. We all had good medical treatment and nursing but the regime and hospital discipline were too irksome to accept for long. With a bottle of whisky, acquired from the OC of a Mobile Bath and Laundry Unit, we were able to 'buy' a trip back to Taranto on an American LCT, only to find we had been posted as deserters for leaving the hospital in the middle of the night …[3]

The battalion went from a strength of 17 officers and 414 men at the end of September, to 22 officers and well over 500 men by 28 October.[4] Among them was TFH, back from hospital. As soon as he was out of hospital and on two weeks' convalescent leave, then in his own words, 'I made a nuisance of myself in order to get back. Unknown to me, this turned out to be easy, as orders had been given for all red-bereted officers to be sent back to their units immediately and not held for drafting elsewhere. So off I went by ship, from Tunis.'[5]

Although there were many familiar faces, he found a much-changed battalion, for the sinking of the *Abdiel* and the first battle casualties in September had had a sobering effect. Battalions take much of their character from their leadership and the loss of the Commanding Officer and RSM in particular had had a marked effect. Goodwin was, by all accounts, a tough act to follow – and the battalion was lucky to get, in Bill Barlow, someone capable of doing so.

Major-General George Hopkinson had also been killed during an encounter with a German rearguard, shot by a sniper while observing a platoon attack at close quarters. Ernest Down, promoted to Major-General, had therefore taken over command of the 1st Airborne Division, and 'Lepro' Pritchard now commanded 2 Para Brigade. TFH found the battalion in billets at Santeramo, with A Company detached in the village of Grassano. Santeramo proved a pleasant spot in which to ease back into battalion life. In its cobbled streets, TFH found old friends, compared notes and took up a new job. From here on, he would command the battalion's Anti-tank Platoon.[6] Unlike a standard infantry battalion, a parachute battalion was not issued with the highly effective 6-pdr anti-tank gun, since it was too heavy to be dropped by parachute – nor could the ammunition have been carried. TFH did not, therefore, have to attend a technical course to qualify for this post. These heavier guns would come in to a drop zone by glider with the airlanding battalions, as would the 17-pdrs of the divisional anti-tank batteries. For its first hours on the ground, perhaps in contact with a more heavily-armed enemy supported by tanks, therefore, a parachute battalion relied on the weapon carried by TFH's Anti-tank Platoon: the *PIAT* (the Projector Infantry Anti-Tank). This weapon had entered service in time for the invasion of Sicily and was the British version of the American *Bazooka*. It was heavy, unwieldy and unsafe – but very effective at close ranges. George Macdonald Fraser said that 'it might have been designed by Heath Robinson after a drunken dinner of lobster au gratin'.[7] Fraser went on to describe the weapon from memory: four feet of six-inch steel pipe, with a padded butt at one end which went into the firer's shoulder as he lay in the prone firing position. Inside the pipe was a large, powerful spring which had to be cocked before each shot. This had to be done by the firer laying on his back and cocking the spring with the feet, 'gamely ignoring your hernia'. At the business end of the weapon, part of the end of the tube was cut away leaving a cradle, into which its two-and-a-half-pound bomb was laid.

The *PIAT*, with which TFH's Anti-tank Platoon was equipped. (Airborne Forces Museum)

The bomb was in effect a shaped charge which, propelled out of the tube by the release of the spring when the weapon was fired, would penetrate a vehicle or a bunker. 'You and the *PIAT* went ploughing backwards with the recoil, and the bomb went soaring away … the whole contraption weighed about a ton, and the bombs came in cases of three. If you were Goliath you might have carried the *PIAT* and two cases'.[8]

The battalion establishment allowed for four sections of seven men in the platoon – each section being three two-man teams and a section sergeant – plus the Platoon Commander, Platoon Sergeant, radio operator and orderly.[9] The men were among the biggest and strongest in the battalion because of the loads they would have to carry; they were also men with sufficient courage to face a German tank at less than 100 yards. The platoon could be split equally between the three parachute companies, or used together to form an anti-tank screen, or it could operate as a standard platoon for infantry duties in or out of the line. The Platoon Commander was also the Commanding Officer's adviser on anti-tank matters and integrated his coverage with whatever other anti-tank weapons, minefields and obstacles that were made available to the battalion. The men of the Anti-tank Platoon were, in TFH's words, 'a band of rascals of the very best sort; there was only one dud soldier but the rest – especially the NCOs and the Platoon Sergeant, Tromans – were first-rate.'[10] He went on to recall how this dud soldier had appeared one morning later on in the war looking very much the worse for wear, having clearly been badly beaten. TFH tackled Tromans and asked if, perhaps, the man had been found asleep on sentry duty. Tromans replied that this was indeed the case and that the other fusiliers, enraged at having their lives put at risk, had taken matters into their own hands rather than wait for formal military justice. 'This,' TFH remarked, 'exposed me to a practice which had been common in our army for very many years.'

*   *   *

TFH with two NCOs of the
Anti-tank Platoon in Italy.
(Farrar-Hockley family)

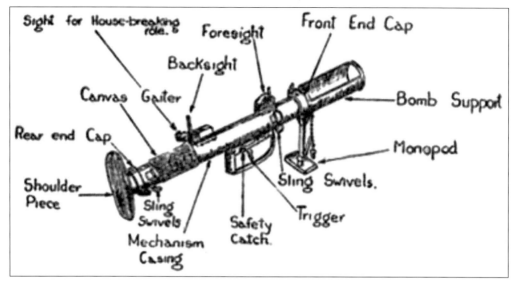

The *PIAT* and its bomb.

The object of the Allied armies in Italy continued to be to contain as large a German force as possible; their objective, in the Winter Campaign of 1943, was Rome. The actual capture of the city would be the task of the Fifth Army on the Allies' western flank. The task of the Eighth Army was to support the main effort by breaking through the Winter Line on the east, advancing to the great lateral road running across the Italian peninsula from Pescara through Avezzano to Rome, establish a bridgehead across the Pescara River and if possible, get into the Avezzano area to threaten the flank of the German forces defending Rome. Montgomery had decided to strike his main blow against the Bernhard Line on the coast rather than in the interior. V British Corps was to deliver it, with the 78th British Infantry Division, 8th Indian Division and the 4th British Armoured Brigade under command in the first phase.

There seemed little scope for 2 Para Brigade in this scheme of things. At the beginning of November, the brigade moved to Barletta, less B Company of 6th (RW) Para under Neill Boys, which went to Bari to quell trouble between various factions of Serbs, Croats and Muslims in the Yugoslav refugee camp there. In the weeks that followed, TFH and his platoon carried out various security duties, area reserve and even had to be prepared to provide labour in the Bari Docks in the event of an emergency. There was some relief when on 18 November the Commanding Officer was ordered to stage Operation *Hardman,* a diversionary seaborne operation synchronised with the Eighth Army's attack across the Sangro. In this operation, several times postponed until 27 November, the whole battalion embarked in a collection of caiques, schooners and fishing smacks skippered by Italian and Greek seamen. The flotilla sailed up the Adriatic coast to simulate a landing at Pesaro, but the sea was rough and many of the men were violently sick – which was the sum total of excitement throughout the whole affair so far as TFH could see. At 1800 hrs the strange array of craft turned for home. The skippers, reluctant to keep formation on the outward half, showed remarkable speed and seamanship on the return journey.[11]

Operation *Hardman,* 1943. (Airborne Forces Museum)

On 29 November, Major-General Down came and spoke to all the officers of 2 Para Brigade. TFH listened as Down confirmed what they all felt: that there was little prospect of action as an airborne formation, for aircraft were scarce and opportunity scarcer still. As a result, the brigade was being detached from 1st Airborne Division and organised as an independent infantry brigade for service under 15th Army Group, while the remainder of the division returned to England. Thus 2 Para Brigade did not jump into Arnhem with the 1st Airborne Division, with all that that might have meant.

*   *   *

In less than a fortnight, further drafts totalling five officers and 125 men had joined the battalion – bringing it up to a strength greater than ever before: 30 officers and 649 men. Plans were being made it seemed, for a quick move up to the German 'Winter Line': the War Diary recorded this period as one of 'feverish activity'.[12] This German line was a series of fortifications constructed by the *Organisation Todt,* of which the heaviest section, the Gustav Line, ran across Italy from just north of where the Garigliano River enters the Tyrrhenian Sea in the west, through the Apennine Mountain Ranges, to the mouth of the Sangro on the Adriatic. The centre of the line crossed the main Route 6 northwards to Rome and followed the Liri Valley. It was anchored on the mountains around Monte Cassino and Monte Cairo – giving the defenders observed fire on any attacker moving into the Liri Valley. On the western side of the Apennines there were two subsidiary lines providing depth to the defence: the Bernhardt Line in advance of the main Gustav positions; and the Hitler Line, five miles to the north. The Winter Line was fortified with concrete bunkers, artillery emplacements (some fully casemated), machine-gun emplacements, extensive belts of barbed wire, minefields, ditches and anti-tank obstacles. It was manned by up to 15 first-line German divisions, including a parachute division.[3]

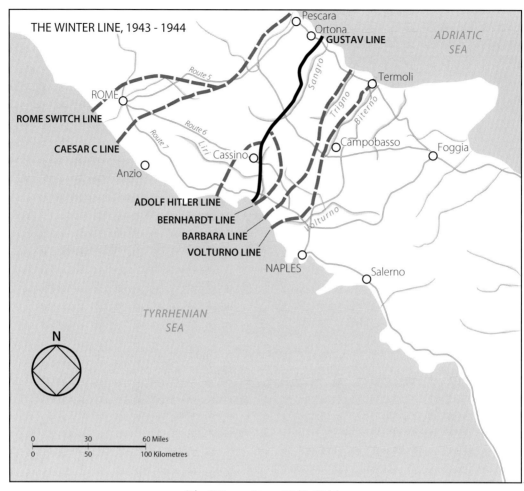

THE WINTER LINE, 1943 - 1944

Pescara
Ortona
GUSTAV LINE

ADRIATIC
SEA

Route 5

Sangro

Termoli

Trigno

Biterno

ROME

ROME SWITCH LINE

Route 6

CAESAR C LINE

Route 7

Liri

Cassino

Anzio

Campobasso

Foggia

ADOLF HITLER LINE

BERNHARDT LINE

BARBARA LINE

VOLTURNO LINE

Volturno

NAPLES

Salerno

TYRRHENIAN
SEA

N

0   30   60 Miles

0   50   100 Kilometres

The Winter Line, 1943-1944.

In the Adriatic sector the country presented almost unlimited difficulties for an army attacking up the peninsula. The so-called 'coastal plain', 15 miles or so wide, lying between the Maiella Range and the sea, is no plain at all, but a plateau whose flat surface is cut into a succession of deep steep-sided valleys by the many streams and rivers which run north-east into the Adriatic. Between the Sangro and Pescara rivers were the Feltrino, the Moro, the Arielli and the Foro; but smaller streams also lay across the attackers' path and on all of these, the Germans could delay the attack. It was an intensely discouraging form of warfare, rendered very much worse by the cold rains of early winter and the all-pervading mud. The weather in Italy is normally rainy in winter, with between 20 and 30 inches falling from November to March in temperatures of around 0 ºC on the coast to -10 ºC in the mountains. The winter of 1943-1944 was no exception; minor rivers surged and soil turned to mud. It seemed, to those involved, that Italy was either bone-chillingly cold and wet, or unendurably hot.

The shallow bridgehead established across the lower reaches of the Sangro after fierce fighting in mid-November was limited to the broad flat valley floor, but it was to form a springboard for the attack against the escarpment to the north. The persistent rain and the mud, in which everything stuck fast, forced Montgomery repeatedly to postpone the assault and also to abandon his original concept of a single great break-through operation carrying the Eighth Army straight to the Pescara. He now planned a more gradual advance with limited objectives. The main attack – the famous 'colossal crack' – finally went in on the night of 28-29 November, with the 2nd New Zealand Division taking part on the left flank. By dark on the 30th, after most violent fighting, the whole ridge above the Sangro was firmly in British hands.

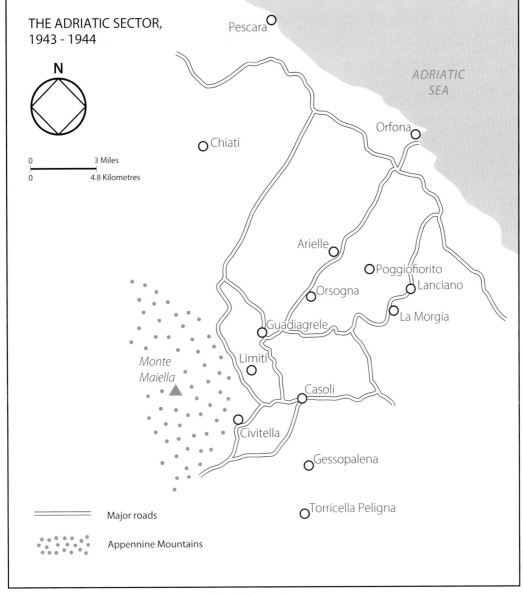

The Adriatic Sector.

'Lepro' Pritchard with the New Zealand Corps Commander, General Freyburg, at the Sangro River, 1944. (RWF Museum/Archives)

After a northward journey, first by train and then by road, TFH marched one evening in early December at the head of his platoon through a chill mist; the men hurrying over a heavily-cratered crossroads to reach the village of Salarola, in a salient of the line near Orsogna.[14] The quiet nasal voices of the men of the 2nd New Zealand Division, under the command of Lieutenant-General Sir Bernard Freyberg,* to whom the battalion now answered, warned them of the dangerous spots and of the enemy's daily routine. From now on for the next six months, in TFH's words, the battalion was 'plugging holes – and it was to be a wonderful maturing process for us as it was our first prolonged experience of battle.'[15] TFH went on to recall that, as 6th (RW) Para had a smaller establishment than a standard infantry battalion, Barlow used the four sections of the Anti-tank Platoon as a fourth company and therefore 'I had the experience of attending the Commanding Officer's Orders Group and so on.'[16]

This area of the front, around the little hilltop town of Casoli, consisted of barren foothills and steep valleys under what agriculture could be managed by the local farmers. Vegetation was sparse and roads narrow and winding. The small towns and villages, with their narrow streets and ancient stone buildings, seemed to cling to the sides and tops of the hills. Everywhere was under constant observation by the Germans, who held positions on the dominating upper slopes of the main Apennine Range.

---

*   Lieutenant-General Sir Bernard Freyberg VC (1889-1963) had won the VC on the Western Front in 1916. He commanded the British and Imperial troops in Greece and Crete in 1941 and later the NZ Corps in Italy 1944-1945. He was Governor-General of New Zealand 1946-1952 and Lieutenant-Governor of Windsor Castle 1956-1963.

A German position overlooking the Casoli area, 1943. (RWF Museum/Archives)

As 6th (RW) Para moved into the area, Barlow pushed C Company – under Leonard Holden – forward on to a saddle beneath the village of Guardiagrele, which was known to be held by a *Panzergrenadier* unit, while TFH and his platoon remained with the rest of the battalion, dug in on the forward slopes around Salarola. At 2100 hrs the first German shells began to fall: a slow, harassing fire which went on for seven hours, reminding them that the German Army was awake and in possession of the high ground. In the days that followed, the battalion was fortunate to lose only three men, including Holden, who was severely wounded and had to be evacuated. The Germans could also monitor the battalion's radio transmissions, as well as its movements. However, Captain Gwyn Bowen-Jones later recalled that, at the insistence of 'Huff' Lloyd-Jones, 'every radio transmitter in the 6th (Royal Welch) Parachute Battalion had a Welsh speaker manning the station.' As there was rather an acute shortage of Welsh speakers in the German Army, intercepted signals remained an enigma'.[17]

---

*   The same tactic was used successfully by the 1st Battalion of The Royal Welch Fusiliers who were engaged against the Japanese in Burma. It was again used in 1995 by the same battalion in the Balkan War when the author was in command.

6th (RW) Para advancing through the Casoli area, 1943. (RWF Museum/Archives)

Airborne artillery supporting troops in the forward area around Casoli. (Airborne Forces Museum)

On 11 December, 6th (RW) Para was relieved by 5th Para[18] and moved farther west to positions in front of Casoli, but still below the main Apennine Range. Casoli itself, which was in Allied hands, sits atop a conical hill and dominates the area around it, but it is itself still dominated by the higher ridges beyond. Through his binoculars, TFH could see troops of the German 2nd *Hochgebirges* (or Mountain) Division practising skiing, well out of Allied artillery range, on the snowy slopes below Monte Maiella. C Company, now under Major Eardley Michel, moved out to Gessopalana, and Lieutenant Frederick Ashby's platoon, with a *Vickers* machine-gun section, held the rock of La Morgia. B Company watched the flank and patrolled so often into the little town of Civitella that Lieutenant Douglas Atkins had a near escape from being elected Mayor. The Germans, watching from the church towers, knew that a change of units had been made and sent patrols to investigate – causing casualties to both sides. The battalion's patrols were helped by a local partisan group which had been founded by local lawyer Ettore Troilo, a furious antifascist, known as 'the Patriots of Maiella', or 'the Maiella Brigade'. The Polish intelligence officer of 2 Para Brigade, Lieutenant Stefan Havlena, often arranged meetings with both partisan and officers of the parachute companies to organise these offensive patrols.[19]

On 17 December, Anthony Crosland, who was now the Intelligence Officer, set out to discover whether the Germans were still in Guardiagrele. Helped by an interpreter, Crosland questioned local Italians in the houses of no man's land, who said the Germans were still there. Crosland therefore decided to confirm matters by making a covert reconnaissance with only a sergeant accompanying him. They lay up in a cottage till 0200 hrs and then struggled forward until, shortly before daybreak, they reached a point about a mile-and-a-half behind the German forward positions and nearly six miles from their own Battalion Headquarters.

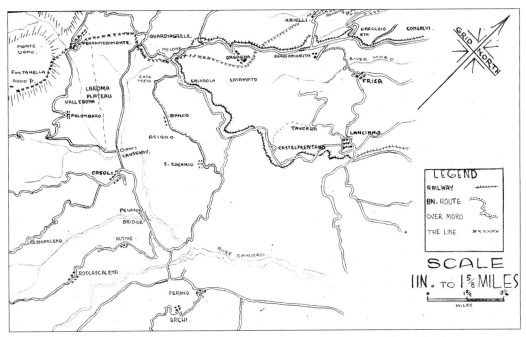

A sketch map of the position of 2 Independent Parachute Brigade on the Sangro
(War Diary, 2 Indep Para Bde).

From what they saw, it was obvious that the Germans were still in the village. After another day's lay-up and a return journey that was 'a nightmare', they made their way home but it was 0700 hrs on 19 December before they made it back for a welcome breakfast.[2] There was little chance, therefore, of pushing forward and Barlow ordered TFH with the Anti-tank Platoon to dig in on a hill 300 yards (275 metres) in front of Torricelli to cover the most likely approach for armour, should the Germans mount a local offensive. Snow fell daily and the bitter cold made any mobile operations impossible. At midnight on Christmas Eve the Germans rang the church bells of Torricelli. Within an hour, the battalion received news that it was to be relieved by the 2nd Battalion Royal Inniskilling Fusiliers.[21] Wrapped in greatcoats, packed in Jeeps and trailers, the men slid from corner to corner down the twisting road to their billets. For the first time in 12 days, TFH could get out of his clothes and lie down between dry blankets on the floor of a warm stable in the battalion concentration area, with the prospect of a long sleep and a late Christmas morning breakfast – but not before he had seen to his men. It was a well-established rule in the British Army that on operations, the first care of an officer was for his vehicles and weapons; then for his NCOs and men; and last of all for himself.

The mirage of a quiet Christmas was rudely shattered at 0500 hrs on Christmas Day when the officers, drivers and signallers were roused and briefed at Battalion Headquarters: 6th (RW) Para was to relieve the 24th New Zealand Infantry by nightfall.[22] It was a bitter morning and although there was no snow, an icy wind from the tops of the Monte Maiella and Maiore Grande blew along the roads. In Casoli, as the battalion drove through, the bells for early Mass were chiming from the white tower of St Mary Magdalene. The Jeeps skidded every now and again as they turned a sharp bend. Beyond the tiny village of Baiano the pitted road climbed steeply and brought the men to the collection of buildings occupied by the New Zealanders. Here they were made welcome by the Kiwis, who shared whatever extra food they had been sent for Christmas, until they left just after dusk. A Company held the forward edge of the position; B Company watched the deep valley on the left flank; TFH, with the Anti-tank Platoon, held the valley to the right. C Company was in reserve on the hill overlooking the hamlet of Baiano. Here they remained for the next 10 days, mounting the occasional patrol for intelligence purposes and exchanging fire with the Germans.

Severe blizzards at the end of the month made the slit trenches all but untenable and in the deep snow, tracks became highly obvious to the watching Germans above. Barlow therefore pulled the men back into fortified houses, cottages and farm buildings among the olive groves. The results of this change in tactics were immediately obvious: in more rest, better food, and consequently better health; higher morale – but stricter discipline. Camouflage and concealment had to be near-perfect and, above all, silence had to be maintained in standing-to, standing-down and changing sentries. Major Paddy Deacon of 4th Para was interviewed in later years for a TV documentary on the role of 2 Para Brigade in this battle and reported that during periods of rest from the line, he often spoke to TFH, usually in the makeshift Officers' Mess in Casoli. This period of the war in winter, under the Monte Maiella, was a terrible time for TFH and indeed for his battalion. The atrocious weather, the Germans' tenacity, and the impassable mountains and hills all represented huge obstacles for a lightly-equipped battalion up against well-entrenched and well-supported opposition. After the war, Deacon met TFH again and, remembering their experiences, TFH believed that this winter of 1943-1944 in Abruzzo was one of his most difficult periods of the whole war. Others supported this view: Anthony Crosland's diary recorded:

The severe weather conditions around Abruzzo in the foothills of the Appenine Mountains in the winter of 1943-1944. (Airborne Forces Museum)

So bad were the road conditions in the winter of 1943-1944 that mules were a regular method of resupply to troops in the line. (Airborne Forces Museum)

… the awful short gap between whistle and bomb-blast … under persistent shelling; the sight of a colleague with his head blown off; the immense psychological test which meant that it was not 'the physical specimens or the battle drill kings who came out best'; the enormous relief among the troops as they were finally relieved by another unit.[24]

TFH recalled that at this time, he had done a lot of patrolling and had been successful in laying ambushes. One winter night there was a lot of fresh snow and a very bright full moon. TFH had done two or three patrols already that week and did not want to go out that night. However, he prepared to do so anyway. At that point, Barlow arrived and asked TFH what his plans were. Having listened to him, Barlow sat back and said 'I don't think I want you to go out tonight.' TFH protested, saying that of course he was going. Barlow looked at him and replied, 'You are *not* bloody well going.' This taking of the responsibility away from him by the Commanding Officer greatly impressed TFH: 'He could judge that I'd had enough. I remember the glance between us and his tone, and I was greatly impressed that he could look into my soul and that he would take the responsibility.'[25] On the other hand, TFH later recalled that 'in a rifle company, the Platoon Commander was very much under the hand of his Company Commander. In the anti-tanks, however, I was given a degree of latitude. When we first came up into the line, I found that I had a lot of freedom and could use my own ideas; I had good NCOs to carry these through.'[26]

The battalion went back to Lanciano for a night's rest on 3 January 1944.[27] By this time it had lost six officers and men killed, three missing, and 68 wounded or sick.[28] On 5 January 1944, it moved to positions occupied by the 1st Battalion, the King's Own Yorkshire Light Infantry on the Orsogna–Ortona Road.[29] As the light faded, the Royal Welch Para Companies – their feet and legs wet through and chilled to the bone – began to march in through the snow. They soon made themselves comfortable in the cottages and farmhouses, barricading the windows and doors they did not need and stopping up the holes that remained before lighting their burners to make tea. In the darkness of the upstairs rooms or at the edge of the olive grove they sat, listening for movement, or watching for the dark silhouettes of a German patrol.

Until now the battalion had always been holding positions below the enemy, exposed to German artillery fire and unable to retaliate effectively. Barlow decided that the time had now come to gain the upper hand. On 7 January 1944 he moved C Company forward just after dark to the village of Arielli, where in a short, sharp encounter, they surprised and destroyed a German piquet. B Company then moved to cover the left of the new position while A Company remained in reserve in Poggiofiorito.[30] The effect of this move was to place the battalion on an elevated plateau, of which Arielli was the northern tip, but the whole area was still under observed enemy fire from artillery and from machine guns, 800 yards away across a deep valley. The German gunners registered one by one on the houses in B Company's area and then set out to destroy the buildings of Arielli. Fortunately the occupied houses were strongly built and thick-walled and had, moreover, been heavily reinforced with sandbags. Here Welshmen with mining experience came into their own, as bigger and deeper excavations were needed quickly. Short of a major attack, 6th (RW) Para was not going to be dislodgd.

From this position, the battalion denied the whole Arielli sector to the Germans and extensive patrolling was carried out to identify the closest German units. The task of capturing a prisoner, the plum job but certainly the most dangerous, was given to TFH and his Anti-tank Platoon. By this time, the platoon had salvaged a number of medium machine guns from wrecked tanks and carried these on patrols in place of some of the *PIATs* – giving them a great deal of extra firepower. TFH had already confirmed that enemy patrols visited a cottage on the ridge in front of B Company fairly regularly: 'I had been up there several times on reconnaissance so I knew where to put the men.'[31]

At 2100 hrs on 12 January, therefore, he led his platoon through B Company's position and up the ridge. They had no snow clothing, but the moon, which now rose, was soon obscured by cloud and by 2230 hrs TFH and his men were lying in ambush in three buildings and a

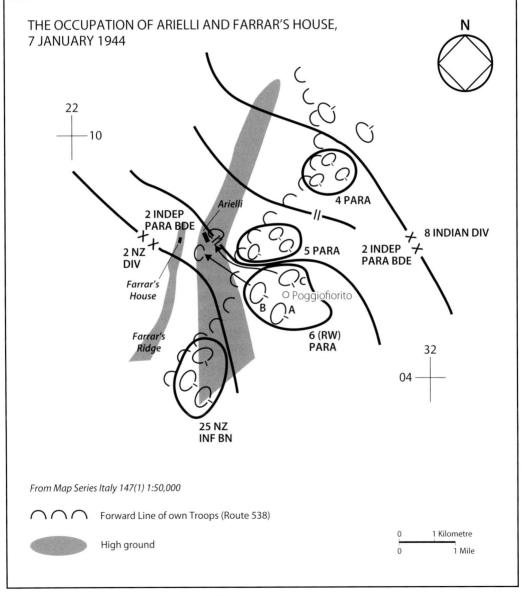

THE OCCUPATION OF ARIELLI AND FARRAR'S HOUSE,
7 JANUARY 1944

N

22

10

Arielli

2 INDEP
PARA BDE

4 PARA

8 INDIAN DIV

2 NZ
DIV

5 PARA

2 INDEP
PARA BDE

Farrar's
House

O Poggiofiorito

B   A

Farrar's
Ridge

6 (RW)
PARA

32

04

25 NZ
INF BN

From Map Series Italy 147(1) 1:50,000

Forward Line of own Troops (Route 538)

High ground

0   1 Kilometre

0   1 Mile

Arielli and Farrar's House.

A machine-gun position of 6th (RW) Para overlooking Gemmano in Southern Italy, 1943.
(RWF Museum/Archives)

The mountainous terrain around Arielli, in which the Germans so often held the higher ground.
(RWF Museum/Archives)

As the Allies advanced northwards, the Germans dropped all the bridges over every watercourse, no matter how large or small. (RWF Museum/Archives)

bunker. TFH thought they had a few hours to wait so decided to catch some sleep; not for long. At 2300 hrs the clouds cleared a little, and soon after midnight, Sergeant Tromans wriggled over to TFH and whispered that the Germans were coming. Those men who were resting were silently roused and the platoon stood-to. TFH could see nothing at first until movement among the trees drew his eye. Then he picked up dark smudges, well extended; the Germans had come right into their midst. All around him, fingers pushed safety catches forward and weapons were brought softly into the firing position as the German patrol moved from the shelter of the olive trees into the open and stopped by a haystack, from where its commander and another soldier went forward to the door of the cottage. The terrified tenant, an old Italian peasant farmer, had been visited earlier by TFH and told not to answer any knocking or calls from the Germans should they appear. In spite of his fears, the old man obeyed and so, apparently satisfied, the German officer called the others forward into TFH's net.

Silently, TFH drew the pin from a grenade and threw it among the Germans. As it burst, the Anti-tank Platoon opened fire. There was, as TFH recalled, 'a hell of a lot of firing for 30 to 40 minutes, then it all stopped.'[32]

The German patrol broke cover and ran. Some made it as far as a cut-off group under Sergeant Homer and were killed. Two more were shot and killed by Sergeant Tunstall and one of the *Bren* gunners. TFH called out 'comb your areas,' and the men began to search for the dead and wounded. Sergeant Tromans shot the German patrol commander as he very gamely fired back from the haystack; and to Sergeant Lavis fell the honour of capturing two of the enemy alive. When all the sections had come in and the dead had been searched and buried, TFH reported to Barlow on the radio and was called in. He led his men quickly back with their two prisoners, who were soon identified as being from *517 Panzergrenadier Regiment*. Next morning, congratulations came in from the corps and army commanders, as this was the only patrol across the whole front that had succeeded in taking prisoners. The ridge on which this action had taken place soon became known as 'Farrar's Ridge' and the cottage as 'Farrar's House'.[33]

There was little chance to bask in the glory of success though, for TFH and his platoon were ordered to maintain a standing patrol at the cottage for the next two nights in case the Germans should come back looking for revenge. On the second day, A Company was ordered to relieve him and take over the position at Farrar's Ridge and Lieutenant George Seal moved up with his platoon into Farrar's House and two small cottages immediately to the north. The following night, the remainder of A Company moved up into new positions to support Seal in his outpost. Shortly afterwards, Seal reported that two Germans were examining the haystacks and outbuildings of Farrar's House. Quite rightly, he held his fire and was ordered to continue to do so as long as possible. The German scouts soon left, but rifle shots were being fired at the windows of the cottage to provoke some response. Under cover of this fire, a German NCO with one or two men closed in. Suspecting that they intended to place a demolition charge against the cottage, Seal gave the order to fire, killing two of the Germans. Immediately, well-directed fire from a machine gun came in on two sides of the house. It was obvious that a strong patrol had moved in around the cottage and had every intention of fighting. The German officer commanding the patrol could be seen against the snow, unhurriedly moving from group to group of the enemy to redirect their fire. He gave his orders in a loud, clear voice, and Seal, who understood German, was thus able to shift his small garrison about to forestall each change of target ordered by the German. Effective fire support from the battalion's mortars brought a group of bombs down right on the roof of Farrar's House and all around it.[34] It was too much for the Germans, who broke contact and withdrew – leaving behind two dead and another prisoner, a Yugoslav conscript who was delighted to realise that for him, the war was over. From then on, as Major David Fleming Jones's diary records, things seemed 'much quieter. The locals seem much happier'.[35]

TFH had a narrow escape from death when he was sniped in Arielli, but at least rations and local food were getting better. Fleming Jones reported a dinner party on 13 February when 'Huff' Lloyd-Jones, Howells – the doctor – and Neill Boys arrived for a dinner with the company officers: 'Menu: Spaghetti, hamburger steaks, pancakes, savoury, pudding, vino, tea and brandy, nuts, fruit'[36] No wartime rationing here!

On 16 February, after five weeks in the same sector, the battalion moved to Limiti, which was to be its last position on the Adriatic.[37] Fleming Jones recorded 'Mess and quarters rotten. See Town Major and obtain a first class place complete with bath etc. The local baker lives here so we are well in. Farrar, Padre and I finish a bottle of whisky'.[38]

Initially the battalion was resting and reorganising – 'went to pictures with Farrar ... see *George Washington Slept Here* ...'[39] – which included taking a platoon of Italian paratroops under command of each company. Once this was completed, Barlow was once again determined to gain the initiative when on 25 February it relieved the 1/5th Punjabis of 8th Indian Division. On the 28th, he quickly pushed B Company up the hamlet of Limiti on the Laroma feature, over-watched by C Company above them and across the valley in Palombaro. When B Company was in position, Major Howard Cavanagh took A Company through and out to Carafico, a ridge running at right angles to Monte Mario. Reconnaissance patrols went out

Major Fleming Jones, 6th (RW)
Para. (RWF Museum/Archives)

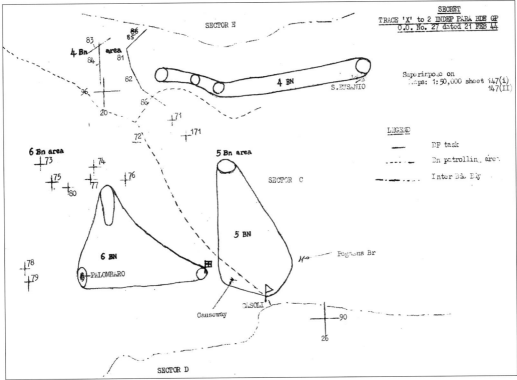

2 Para Brigade positions around Casoli, February 1944. (2 Para Brigade War Diary)

every night and one major attack, by 'Huff' Lloyd-Jones with B Company and a section of TFH's platoon, cleared the Germans from the village of Pissivini.[40] Another raid by Leonard Fitzroy-Smith with some of his own men and two of TFH's sections attacked Francesca with little result other than the severe wounding of one of TFH's best *PIAT* men. Finally, on a still, dark night, TFH and the Anti-Tank Platoon moved to the end of the ridge overlooking the road skirting the foot of the Apennines. From this position he could dominate the road and attack any vehicles on it, but the only target was a German cycle orderly in Pennapiedemonte, whose life TFH made miserable by forcing him to crawl down the hill under fire into the town with his messages.[41] There was still snow high up and the eruption of Mount Vesuvius in March meant that black ash came down with the snow – deep, black snow – coating every-thing. Even the food had ash mixed with it.[42]

So things went on, until 21 March, when the battalion was relieved and, after a night under the familiar shadow of Casoli Hill, moved into reserve. On 26 March, they started on a roundabout journey across the centre of Italy – via San Lorenzo – to the by-now infamous mincing machine of Cassino, under the command of the British 6th Armoured Division.[43]

*   *   *

On the day that the Eighth Army had landed at Taranto, the Fifth Army had landed at Salerno, south of Naples, in Operation *Avalanche*. Progress inland stalled almost at once and heavy German counter-attacks, combined with a dogged defence against the advancing land forces, made Clark at one point consider withdrawal;[44] but on 16 September, Eighth Army units advancing from the toe of Italy linked up with the troops in the Salerno Bridgehead. The advance north had resumed, but as the country grew more difficult, Fifth Army's progress became slower and slower until it was halted by the great mountain barrier that had stopped the Eighth Army in the east — the main ranges of the Apennines, which ran diagonally across Italy from south to north. The Winter Line, which hinged on the peak of Monte Cairo, above the Liri and Garigliano rivers, was fixed on these heights. Beneath lay the village of Cassino, at the entrance to the Liri Valley, dominated by the hill crowned by its famous monastery. Part of Cassino was captured at the beginning of February and in mid-March an intense Allied air attack was followed by a desperate, but indecisive, battle for the possession of the rest. Much of the Eighth Army was now brought across and concentrated with the Fifth between Cassino and the west coast, on a narrow front.

The advance party had arrived on 3 April and TFH had gone forward immediately on a reconnaissance with Fleming Jones.[45] The main body of 6th (RW) Para debussed on 5 April just short of a high, bare hill called Il Trocchio, but which the Americans, who had taken it at great cost, called 'Million Dollar Hill'. At dusk they were driven over a saddle to the base of the hill, which was being used by Allied artillery observers. Their way then lay along Route Six, which led to the foot of Monastery Hill and eventually through to Rome. Everywhere, total desolation met their eyes; no house stood with its four walls intact and the trees were no more than blackened stumps. Fleming Jones wrote that '… the ground around Cassino is like Flanders in the last war, very pock-marked'.[46] As they turned the corner at the foot of Il Trocchio, the vehicles gathered speed down the last stretch, which lay under German observed fire.

Monte Cassino. (Author's collection)

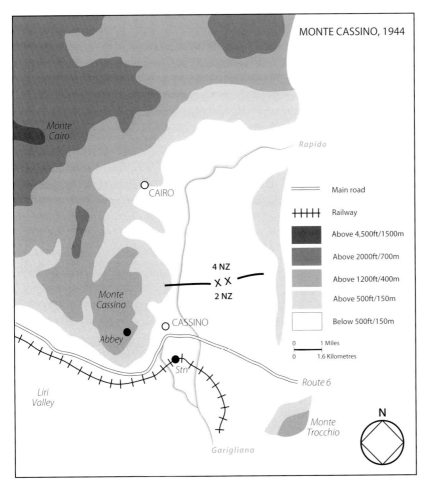

2 Para Brigade's area of operations, Monte Cassino, 1944. (Airborne Forces Museum)

Here, 6th (RW) Para took over a sector in the centre of the brigade's front, extending from Cassino Railway Station to Trocchio – relieving the 3rd Battalion Welsh Guards. 4th Parachute Battalion took post on their right in the station and 5th Para on their left. The tasks allocated to 6th (RW) Para were to reconnoitre the Garigliano River for a forthcoming attack and to prevent any enemy patrols from crossing it. B Company under 'Huff' Lloyd-Jones was on the river bank, A Company under Cavanagh was at the foot of Trocchio, and C Company under David Fleming Jones on the right – over-watching the approaches to the narrow flood plain.[47] As the War Diary recorded, 'The … position is dominated by the enemy held height of Monastery Hill on which stands the bombed ruins of the Benedictine Abbey… there could be no movement in company localities by day despite continual smoking by chemical generators and 25-pdr smoke shells'.[48]

By night, TFH and his men – along with other platoons – patrolled the river carefully, since the bank was reported as being heavily mined. Once the lie of the land was established, the men began the task of clearing and marking routes through these minefields and then collecting information on where and how the river could be crossed. This was dangerous work, as Fleming Jones's diary recorded, '24 April. Jerry Pearson's mine detecting party meet with disaster. All five wounded. Jerry loses both legs above the knee'.[49] By day they lay quiet, watching and planning for the night; the late winter days were cold and damp. Although the snow was fast disappearing from all but the highest slopes, the wind had a bite in it and the ground by the river was wet and marshy. After 11 days, the battalion was relieved by 3/15th Rajputs and tramped back up the track by the convent school to be driven to Venafro. Three days later, they took over a sector further north under the command of the 4th New Zealand Division. Here, the bare rock provided little cover, so that *sangars* had to be built up from loose stones. Supply came in at night by mule trains, but there were some positions that even mules could not reach and to which the loads had to be man-packed. Even so, the men got two hot meals a day, one just after stand-to in the morning; the other just before stand-to at night.

The days passed quietly enough on the whole. Shelling was light, since the only artillery available to the Germans was light mountain guns or tanks firing in the indirect role.* Aggressive patrolling was impossible at first because of the depth of the German minefields. However, by the beginning of March, Barlow had tracked down a French Moroccan *Tirailleur* officer who had laid most of the mines during the period when Vichy French forces had been allied to the Germans – and from then on, a vigorous patrol programme commenced. TFH recalled that at one point he went out as far as three-and-a-half miles in front of the line and encountered no Germans.[50] It was possible for a platoon at a time to be relieved and go back for a short rest with B Echelon in a tiny green space called the 'Happy Valley', for here the men did nothing but eat, sleep, and care for their arms and equipment. This time of stalemate came to a welcome end on 11 May 1944 when the long-awaited Allied attack on the Gustav Line began: 'The terrific artillery barrage is a revelation'.[51] 6th (RW) Para's part was a modest one: a series of simulated attacks, concentrations of fire and aggressive patrolling as a diversion. However this was but a brief interlude, for on 19 May the battalion moved back to the Salerno area to prepare for a parachute operation.

---

* The German 7.5 cm mountain gun, or *Gebirgsgeschütz-36*, had a range of 10,000 yards (9.25 km), compared with the standard 10.5 cm *Howitzer*, which fired out to 13,500 yards (12 km).

*   *   *

Down on the coast, in spite of the 'feverish activity re-equipping and preparing to re-assume our parachute role',[52] TFH revelled in a proper rest period arranged for the officers and men in the area between Salerno and Naples. To be able to relax after six months on the front line was a tremendous relief; Anthony Crosland recorded how a spell at the front made him appreciate 'what unadulterated bliss it can be to be clean, warm + well-fed'.[53] News of the Allied landings in Normandy on 6 June not only added zest to training when it was renewed, but also brought hope that at last, the end of the war in Europe was in sight, but not yet, for now it was back to parachute training.

After the first refresher jump in nearly a year – on 28 May – the men merely rolled up their parachutes and walked off with them tucked under their arms; those, that is, who were not injured due to strong and unpredictable winds on the drop zone. After the next jump they began practising once again the sequence of listening or watching for signals, running to a selected platoon or company rally point, reorganising and moving off either into the attack or to occupy a defensive position.[54] High winds and bad landings at this time robbed the battalion of Cavanagh and several others, who went off to hospital with broken bones, while Anthony Crosland remembered the old fears of parachute training as they re-asserted themselves 'in order of terror, first of jumping, secondly of flak, third of the Germans, fourth of fatigue and discomfort'.[55] TFH was one of those injured, but not seriously; by 3 June he was back on strength –[56] but the loss of Cavanagh meant that Leonard Fitzroy-Smith was promoted into his place and in turn, TFH was promoted to Captain.[57] This was a welcome step, but it meant

2 Para Brigade moving by road from Rome to Monte Cassino in 1944. (RWF Museum/Archives)

parting from the Anti-Tank Platoon to become Second-in-Command of B Company under 'Huff' Lloyd-Jones. The men were sincerely sorry to see him go, for he was known among them as 'The Boy Wonder' – and not in any sarcastic sense in the way of soldiers' humour; they meant it. As Cliff Meredith recalled, 'The men trusted his leadership qualities, but he was not popular with everyone and was several times pulled up for adjusting orders from above; but he was plucky, keen and determined.'[58] TFH himself recalled later that 'I felt I enjoyed the confidence of the fusiliers; we were a small unit that felt we had something!'[59]

'Lepro' Pritchard, who had been wounded near Cassino but stayed in command, was ordered on 30 May to mount an operation at 48 hours' notice, for the Gustav Line had been broken at Cassino on 18 May and on 23 May the Allies breached the Hitler Line and linked up with troops attacking out of the Anzio Beachhead; the Allies were advancing once more. He chose his own battalion to do it and appropriately, he named it Operation *Hasty*.[60] The assault group consisted of 60 officers and men, but TFH was not among them. The party dropped behind German lines at dusk, then broke up into small groups in order to harass enemy transport by laying mines on the main road and by shooting up trucks. The Germans reacted strongly, but on the sixth day the New Zealanders broke through and linked up.

*   *   *

On 15 July 1944 the battalion drove past Cassino – captured after so much bloodshed – along Route Six, through Rome and on to a camp above Ottavia, where 2 Para Brigade was concentrated for a new operation. Everyone expected to emplane without delay, but July turned to August and the brigade remained at Rome. On 26 July, all the Catholic officers and men attended Mass and a Papal audience at St Peter's; otherwise training and normal routine continued in an atmosphere of frustrated anticipation. It was not until the 13th that 'Lepro' Pritchard briefed the battalion and issued the operation order for something quite outside Italy: the assault landing in the south of France, Operation *Dragoon*. For this operation, the brigade would come under the command of a new formation – the Seventh US Army – and there was therefore yet more feverish activity learning to use American weapons, radios and vehicles in case the need should arise. TFH received the task of running a five-day course on weapons, which was widened to include German *Mauser* rifles, *Spandau* MG-42s, light MGs, light mortars, pistols and various grenades.[6]

Dragoon was an American strategic initiative aimed at the seizure of the port of Marseilles, the opening of new air bases and the landing of ground troops which, pushing north-east would trap the German armies in France between these forces and those advancing from Normandy in a vast pincer. Although its success came too late to relieve pressure on the Normandy theatre, it was a massive demonstration of American military power, technology and their ability to execute operations on a huge scale.

The US VI Corps – consisting of the experienced 3rd, 36th and 45th Infantry Divisions – would assault the beaches between Hyères in the west and Cannes in the east, centred on the resort of St Tropez. II French Corps would follow, breaking out of the bridgehead and capturing Marseilles. An enormous weight of naval gunfire – from 60 warships – would cover the landings, which would also be supported by the XII Tactical Air Command of the USAAF.[62] Against them were only six undermanned German infantry divisions and one panzer division – forming General Johannes von Blaskowitz's Nineteenth Army.

Defensive positions near Cassino, 1944. (Airborne Forces Museum)

Ahead of the seaborne landing, as in Normandy, an Airborne Task Force was to drop 15 to 20 miles inland. Its tasks were to prevent German reserves from counter-attacking the landings; to secure the roads for the advance of Allied armour; and to capture the German beach garrisons as they withdrew. This task force was composed of 2 Para Brigade – the only British troops to be involved in the operation – with an American Parachute Regimental Combat Team, the 517th, with three battalions: the 509th and 551st, which would land by parachute; and the 550th, which would land in gliders. This regiment also, like 2 Para Brigade, had a full complement of supporting artillery, engineers, anti-tank battery and support units. The Airborne Task Force was ordered to drop at 0430 hrs on 15 August – six hours before the seaborne landing. 6th (RW) Para was ordered to seize and hold the high ground north of the village of La Motte, which would be held by the Americans of F Company, 2nd Battalion 517 RCT. This task was allocated to B Company. The task of securing the hamlet of Les Arcs, with the farm of Clastron nearby, was allocated to C Company. A Company was to push along the main road to the little town of Le Muy.[63] This area, which dominated one of the three main roads to the coast, was to be held by the rifle companies supported by the three-inch Mortar, *Vickers* MMG and Anti-Tank Platoons. Artillery support would come from the US eight-inch cruisers *Tuscalora* and *Augusta* offshore.

This time there was neither cancellation nor postponement. During the late afternoon of 14 August the men were driven to the airfield and there they bivouacked. The battalion's

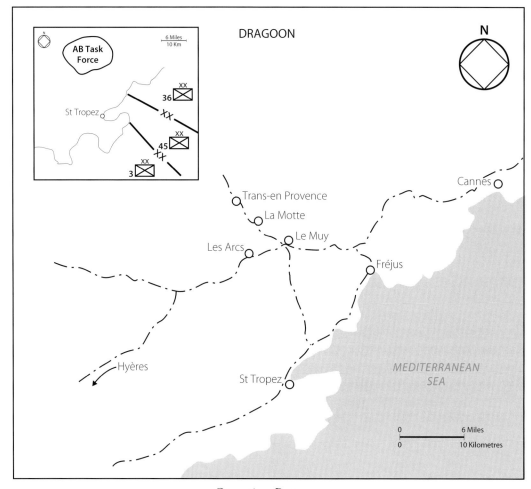

Operation *Dragoon*.

canteen – 'The Red Dragon' – served cakes and tea from the time the men arrived until they emplaned. At midnight they rose and breakfasted; by 0100 hrs, everyone was ready; by 0200 hrs, they were airborne. It was a three-hour flight across the sea to the landing zone. Here and there below them were guide-ships of the Royal Navy and USN marking the route; the aircraft-carrier HMS *Hunter* stood off the Italian coast to provide fighter protection. At 0430 hrs the *Dakotas* crossed the French coast. There was low cloud over the land, but just before 0500 hrs the drop began, in cloudy conditions and a heavy ground mist – but no AA fire.[64] Ian Chatham,* who was a young fusilier in B Company, recalled in a letter that 'I thought, and others thought the same, that we were going down in the sea. I heard a dog bark, and then I was in thick ground mist and into a tree!'[65]

---

* Gerald Ian Chatham (Ian), b. 1924 and commissioned into the RWF in 1945; the 6th Battalion War Diary on 15 February 1945 reported his successful completion of the War Office Selection Board. He retired as a Lieutenant-Colonel in 1976.

TFH himself recalled that:

> When we were within 30 minutes of dropping zone everyone stood up and began to make ready. I was, by arrangement, the last to go out as I had to make sure that the containers got away. We'd had trouble with this in the past — and it was very important for us that they should be released. The red light came on then the green. As I got to the door I threw the container switches but one jammed and I had to fiddle around with it. The crew chief, I think, for a moment thought that I was going to refuse and made an encouraging remark. I got the switch up and just had time to shoot him a furious glance before I jumped out. As I did so I saw below me what was, to all appearances, the sea and I was seriously concerned about this grey shimmering mass some way below me, to the point that I got out the mouth-piece of my inflatable life jacket. However, it proved to be a layer of low cloud. I was scarcely through that by more than four or five seconds when I hit the ground. Due to the switch jamming, I was some way beyond the end of my stick when I landed. I removed my parachute, got my weapon ready and using a compass began moving in the direction of our objective.[66]

As was often the case in airborne operations during the Second World War, identifying landmarks from the air proved difficult – and again, as was often the case, 2 Para Brigade ended up spread over a wide area with some men finding themselves miles from their objectives. 6th (RW) Para, however, came out relatively well. TFH's company was actually well-grouped among the vineyards, cornfields, and orchards. A few men were shot before they had even released their harness; others were engaged before they had gone 100 yards.

Cliff Meredith recalled that:

> 12 Platoon's task was to take a large farm or vineyard; we duly attacked it and the occupants promptly surrendered. After the surrender we found Cpl Williams of the Mortar Platoon hanging in a tree; he had been shot in the back. We were not amused. It is probably a good thing that the enemy had already surrendered.[67]

Most of the men, however, reached the rendezvous and set off to their respective positions while throughout the morning, stragglers kept coming in from the extremities of the drop zone. As soon as it was light, green smoke generators were lit to mark the battalion rally point; by 0715 hrs, 150 men had made it – 'including the CO, 2IC and all the company commanders – better than anyone had dared hope'.[68] Fleming Jones recorded that, 'Drop in Southern France at 0500. No flak. Make RV by 0630. Coy captures objectives by 1100 including 90 prisoners, much plunder, several cars and lorries …'[69]

It took TFH a while to rejoin the battalion. However, given his delay in getting out of the aircraft:

> I came across a lot of French people standing outside a farmhouse and I made them a speech in my best French telling them that the day of liberation had arrived and how splendid it was for them, etc. There was no answer and then one of the women nudged one of the men and said in French, "*Tell him to shove off!*" There had been a

The parachute drop at Le Muy in the South of France during Operation *Dragoon,* August 1944. (Airborne Forces Museum)

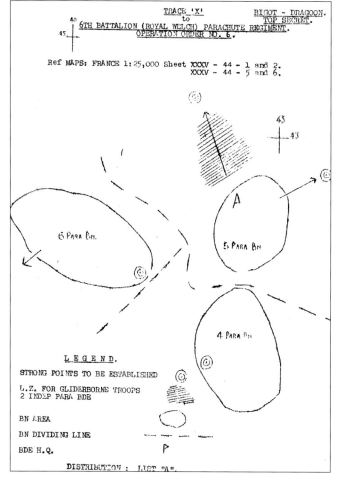

A sketch from Operation Order No. 6 showing the lay-down of 2 Parachute Brigade during Operation *Dragoon*. (6th (RW) Para War Diary, RWF Museum/Archives)

lot of noise of aeroplane engines, which was what had brought them out — and they thought we were SAS or whatever, and they didn't want to be involved. This incident brought me very rapidly to realise that the French were not all 100 percent ready to take up arms themselves.

I pushed on and shortly after dawn a shot passed my head. I took evasive action and found I was alongside a German ammunition depot. I then spent quite a bit of time dodging a party sent out to track me down. I made no valiant attempt to stand against them, but after evading tactics came upon an American airborne unit. Shortly after, I found B Company, who had been dropped accurately. The American navigators were spot on that day and dropped us well.[70]

C Company had to fight for Clastron, but B Company found their objective unoccupied, so pushed on and took an ammunition depot south of the village – killing two Germans and taking others prisoner. Ian Chatham related how 'on reaching La Motte, FH sent me up the church tower with his binoculars, the same again at Le Muy, eventually I came down leaving the binoculars, which became lost – FH was not pleased!'[71] By noon, as Fleming Jones's account confirms, all the company objectives were secure, 100 prisoners had been taken and very few casualties suffered. C Company had also captured a supply depot, 60-odd prisoners, much transport, and a great quantity of food.[72] Captain Arthur Masterton, Second-in-Command of the company, became the most popular man in the brigade when it was learned that his haul included a vast quantity of wines and brandy stamped '*Wehrmacht*'.[73]

There was little further action that day, as the American *Waco* gliders began to come in and crash-land on the rough landing zones. George Seal, who had now taken over Crosland's job as the Intelligence Officer, had sworn that the river along the dropping zone was dry; his surprise and chagrin at falling into four feet of muddy water can well be imagined, as can the stream of well-judged remarks from various wits among the fusiliers.

For the next three days there was little but desultory fighting – in the course of which TFH and his men gathered up small parties of confused Germans, with little fight in them. Meanwhile, the forces landed on the beaches were advancing fast. By the evening of 17 August the men 'had little to do except salvage the DZ for airborne equipment'.[74]

On the evening of 19 August, after a link-up had been achieved with the armoured cars of the US 117 Cavalry Reconnaissance Squadron, Barlow received orders to move the battalion to a defensive position near Fréjus. While this was being reconnoitred, TFH set off in his place at the rear of B Company as the battalion marched 16 miles to a holding position at Camp Gallienni, overlooking Fréjus. By the evening of 20 August, the battalion was in position with a company of 4th Para under command and the brigade Anti-tank Platoon, with its 6-pdr guns, in close support. From here, patrols were sent into Cannes; the French people were over-joyed to see them. Anthony Crosland recorded 'wildly cheering crowds', followed by 'a night of pure pleasure at liberated Cannes … a holiday on the Riviera' – and in later life he gained great amusement by recalling how his contribution to the liberation of France had been a drop on the millionaires' playground.[75] The locals, however, were still more delighted two days later when the Special Service Force of the US 3rd Infantry Division arrived – for with their arrival, the war in the South of France was over.

6th (RW) Para returned to Camp Gallienni and three days later embarked at St Raphael in a Liberty ship bound for Naples. The men were glad to reach Naples; none minded an airborne operation, but after the *Abdiel,* sea voyages were another matter. The battalion then returned to Rome on 31 August to find the camp at Ottavia just as they had left it 18 days before. They were given five days to get fully re-equipped and, in all respects, ready for a further airborne operation. TFH remembered that 'the Captains' Club got round the map and with the benefit of our combined strategic wisdom, tried to figure out where we were going. We reckoned Greece was a likely one.'[76]

5

'We have taken a heavy toll of the enemy' The 6th Battalion (Royal Welch) the Parachute Regiment in Italy and Greece, August 1944-February 1945

Greece had originally been invaded by the Italians, from their foothold in Albania, but their troops had been unable to subjugate the country. Indeed, the repulse of the Italians by the Greek Army was really the first victory of Allied arms over the Axis. As early as January 1940, the British Government had offered assistance to the Greeks; provided air force squadrons;[1] and embarked on a strategy of uniting the forces of Yugoslavia, Greece and Turkey against those of Germany and her allies Italy, Bulgaria, Romania and Hungary. However, the provision of ground and air forces in strength from Middle East Command was resisted by Sir Archibald Wavell – the C-in-C – as well as the Chiefs of Staff at home, as it would further stretch the resources of the Command, which were already deployed in Egypt, Libya, Palestine, Cyprus, Transjordan and Iraq.

In early March 1941 the German Army moved into Bulgaria and the Bulgarian Army took up positions along the frontier with Greece. A firm decision was therefore taken by the British Government to reinforce Greece, as a German ultimatum to surrender and join the Axis appeared inevitable. The Germans too had decided to move first into Yugoslavia and then into Greece. On 6 April, German aircraft bombed Belgrade. The day before, British, Australian and Polish troops began landing in Greece, but just as in Norway, they were no match for the German Army and the *Luftwaffe*. A painful evacuation reminiscent of Dunkirk was mounted in late April and Greece abandoned to occupation. By 1 June, Crete had also been lost.[2]

The Greek Army, which had fought so bravely and so well against the Italians, was quickly overwhelmed by the massive German onslaught – and after the surrender of Greece, the army was disbanded by the conquerors; the Greek Royal Family and Government fled to exile in England. Under occupation, resistance forces of various shades of opinion had emerged. Among these was ELAS (the People's National Army of Liberation) and the military arm of EAM, the National Liberation Front. These were communist organisations inspired and armed by the Soviets with a view to taking control of Greece after the war and thereby establishing permanent Russian bases on the Mediterranean.[3] Other factions, in particular the National Democratic Army (or EDES), supported the pre-war Royal Government. As in Yugoslavia, the British sent military missions to both sides. In May 1944, with the war running strongly

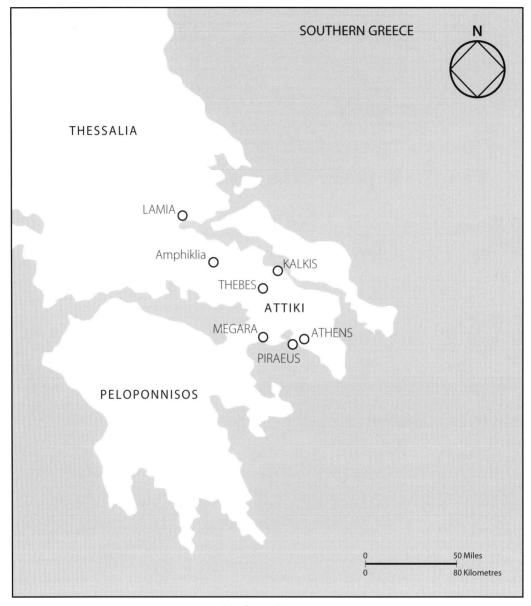

Southern Greece.

against Germany, the various factions signed an accord in Beirut which, in July 1944, ELAS appeared to have repudiated (probably in view of the obvious signs of a German evacuation of Greece) – undertaken to prevent their considerable forces in the Balkans from being isolated by a Soviet drive into Hungary, Romania and Bulgaria – and with it the chance to fill the power vacuum. In August, Churchill warned the British Chiefs of Staff to prepare forces to secure Athens and prevent a communist takeover.[4]

The result was Operation *Manna*. The German Army had not moved as fast as had been estimated and on 13-14 September, the troops for the operation were placed on 48 hours' notice to move. These troops were 23 Armoured Brigade, 2 Para Brigade and supporting units from Egypt, all under the command of Major-General Ronald Scobie;* the 15th Cruiser Squadron, with accompanying minesweepers; four British air squadrons and three Greek squadrons; and US transport aircraft.[5] In parallel, a comprehensive agreement was signed between the various Greek factions on 26 September. Under this agreement, all irregular forces in Greece would place themselves under the authority of the Greek Government in exile, which in turn would be under the orders of Scobie. No action in Athens would be permitted without British approval. This agreement, the Caserta Agreement, governed all future British actions in Greece.

*   *   *

Only 10 days after its return from the South of France, therefore, 6th (RW) Para was ordered to prepare for an airborne operation as part of Operation *Manna* and to concentrate for it on the airfields around Taranto.[6] The battalion was now organised into four companies: A, B, C as before – but with the support weapons platoons now grouped in S (or Support) Company.[7] TFH was given the job of moving the advance parties by road and then setting up the camp, but the party was also to include the whole of the intelligence section, which was to arrange facilities and gather information so as to be able to brief the main body as soon as it arrived.[8] TFH and his party got to Taranto in the early evening of 7 September; the rest followed by rail and after a thoroughly uncomfortable journey, the men detrained with some relief at San Panchrazio on 9 September, where they were guided to a camp near the village.

Once again, it was the old army story of hurry-up-and-wait; as the War Diary put it, 'in view of the delay which has arisen regarding the operation … the Bn may go at any time at short notice, but, on the other hand, the operation might not take place for several weeks'.[9]

Three weeks later, they were still there and heavy rain had begun to fall,[10] along with high winds. The dust turned to mud, while the winds tore at the tents and pulled the wooden pegs from the soaking ground. By the third day there was not a dry article of clothing or equipment in the camp. The whole battalion wearily packed up and moved a few kilometres down the road to drier billets in the villages of Torre San Susanna and Oria. B Company, with TFH still acting as its Second-in-Command, moved into the monastery of Oria.[11]

More delays and a move to Brindisi Airfield followed on 10 October: 'The Bn, from thinking the operation will never take place, now moves swiftly to take all action to ensure that all adm[inistration] and organisational arrangements are complete and that the Bn is launched smoothly and without feverish haste'.[12]

More last-minute changes followed – on 13 October the battalion actually emplaned before the operation was again postponed by 24 hours. At last, on 14 October 1944,[13] the bulk of the battalion took to the air. The flight that followed was extremely rough and it took three-and-a-half hours before the green lights went on for the drop onto the airfield at Megara, 40 miles (65 kilometres) west of Athens. The landing ground was hard and the wind was strong. Although the drop was completely unopposed, it was no surprise that there were casualties – among them Barlow, who broke a leg, and Wilfred Lawson, the Second-in-Command, who damaged an ankle. Barlow tried to continue in command by commandeering a bicycle, but eventually

---

*   Later Lieutenant-General Sir Ronald MacKenzie Scobie KBE CB MC (1893-1969), GOC III Corps.

A group of B Company, 6th (RW) Para, in Greece; seated centre is Major 'Huff' Lloyd-Jones, with TFH seated on the extreme right. (Airborne Forces Museum)

The drop into Greece in 1944. (Airborne Forces Museum)

the pain became too much and he had to be evacuated to have the leg set.[14] As there had not been enough aircraft available to lift the complete battalion, TFH and B Company had not jumped in, but landed with 5th Para at Megara on 15 October.

Fleming Jones, the Senior Company Commander, took command temporarily and led the battalion into Athens with 'Huff' Lloyd-Jones acting as Second-in-Command – thus putting TFH temporarily in command of B Company. As they entered Athens, the men received a truly rapturous welcome from the people – many of whom went to extraordinary lengths just to touch one of the soldiers: '… any British soldier was mobbed immediately he appeared and the clapping taken up on all sides'.[15]

Fleming Jones recorded: 'Nice landing. Crowds of Greeks on the DZ. Great "Well-come"… Terrific welcoming crowd and great excitement. Garlands and kisses from young and old'.[16]

TFH later recalled:

> After a difficult landing in high winds at Megara, we made our rendezvous and began the march into Athens. We had been warned that there was schism between those who supported the old government and the Greek Royal Family, and a strong vigorous group of communist-led guerrillas, the EAM-ELAS. When we got into Athens, the crowds gave us a colossal reception. I had one of those extraordinary wartime experiences. In the crowd I saw a sergeant in the Commandos who had been a friend of mine in ordinary days, and I just had time to say, *"Good Lord, Stefan, how good to see you – what are you doing here?"*
>
> We shook hands before the crowd separated us, and I've never seen him again. The Greeks were going mad and the difficulty was to contain and keep together our soldiers; there were a number of very attractive Greek girls trying to secure them for parties, which didn't help.[7]

Greek civilians crowd in the streets to welcome British paratroopers. (Airborne Forces Museum)

For the next few days the battalion was billeted first in two hotels – the officers in the Grande Bretagne and the NCOs and fusiliers in The King George – until, much to the disgust of the fusiliers, the brigade was concentrated in the Goudhi Barracks adjacent to the Royal Palace. From here, guards on key points were taken on until the brigade was dispersed around the city. 6th (RW) Para moved into a school in a suburb of Athens, where it came under the command of 'Arkforce', led by Major-General Robert Arkwright.* This was one of three temporary task forces formed to take over security duties and consisted of 23 Armoured Brigade Group, plus 6th (RW) Para. The other two forces were Pritchard Force, with HQ 2 Para Brigade, 5th Para and 9 Commando; and Jellicoe Force, consisting of 4th Para and the Special Boat Squadron.

The task forces were ordered to assume responsibility for law and order from the Greek security battalions which had been formed by the Germans during their occupation. These battalions were to be disarmed and disbanded – although some of their commanders were to face trial as collaborators. They were also to help provincial officials to re-establish government services; to assist with relief until other bodies could take over; and, of course, to show the British flag. A Company of 6th (RW) Para under Fitzroy-Smith moved to Khalkis, about 70 miles north-east of Athens; C Company under Michael Carr went to Amphiklia, on the Salonika Road beyond Thebes; B Company, with 'Huff' Lloyd-Jones back in command, left soon after for Thebes, north-west of Athens.[18]

Intelligence reports indicated that Greek resistance groups had the security situation well in hand. 6th (RW) Para was ordered therefore to work with them until Allied relief and the exiled Greek Government could properly take charge. However, on the ground, the picture was not so rosy. In Thebes, B Company soon realised that ELAS men, now down from the hills, were not committed to the Caserta Agreement – indeed many did not know of it. Ian Chatham recalled that '... we were outnumbered by hundreds of Albanians/Greeks – long beards, chests criss-crossed with belts of ammunition!'[19]

Under their leader, General 'Ares' Velouchiotis,† a Russian-trained communist, they were intent on setting up a government loyal to Moscow before the Provisional Government could return. TFH recalled that 'the communists wanted us to be on their side. They consisted of former regular officers won over from the King's service and some younger firebrands. They had not done much against the Germans though – in fact, they had made comfortable arrangements with them.'[20]

The civilian population, robbed by these men of what little the Germans had left them – and terrified by nightly raids or by the threat of arrest by ELAS and its secret police, the EP – looked to the British soldiers to help and protect them. A vast quantity of food had been left by the Germans in a dump in Thebes and this was taken over by the Swedish Red Cross, with B Company assisting by maintaining a guard to see that no thieving took place. In general, B Company got on well with the local officials and indeed with the ELAS commanders and soldiers. By 28 October, a new town prefect had been installed and commemorations were held marking the anniversary of the Declaration of War on Greece by Italy in 1941. On

---

*   Later Major-General Robert Henry Bertram Arkwright CB DSO (1903-1971), GOC 2nd Infantry Division.
†   Ares (or Aris) Velouchiotis (Ἄρης Βελουχιώτης), was the *nom de guerre* of Athanasios Klaras (1905-1945), the most prominent leader and instigator of the Greek People's Liberation Army. He died during the Civil War that followed the end of the Second World War, having committed suicide when isolated and surrounded by his enemies.

the following day, the distribution of food from the German dump began – although life appeared to be slowly returning to normal. Shops had re-opened for the first time in years, many tradesmen resumed their work and farmers began once more to bring vegetables and fruit into the market.[21]

On 4 November, the bulk of B Company was moved on to Lamia – and here a new phase of the occupation began. At Lamia lived both General Stephanos Seraphis,* the Military Commander of the ELAS, and General 'Ares', its political head.[22] 'Ares' was not yet ready to provoke open warfare against its rivals, EDES (from whom his party had captured and forcibly converted General Seraphis); nor could he afford to start a war with the Allies. He was therefore obliged to do as 'Huff' Lloyd-Jones told him.

TFH had been left in Thebes with one platoon of B Company. Here he was soon joined by Barlow, now fit again after his injury at Megara, and the Battalion Headquarters. In some ways this made life easier, as Barlow handled relations with the civil authorities. However, for any infantry officer, happiness generally increases in direct proportion to his distance from higher headquarters. On the surface, things were friendly enough: the soldiers outside Battalion Headquarters saluted the ELAS officers — when they remembered. Barlow and Colonel Pappazissis, the ELAS officer commanding the 36th Regiment, would ride in the hills on horses that had until recently been belonged to Italian or German officers.[23] Sometimes they stopped in a hamlet to drink the strong resinated wine and eat black olives, black bread, and *feta parnassou* — the sour goat's milk cheese which is now so popular, but was then a novelty. Then Pappazissis would sit back, smoke the cigarettes offered him with great enjoyment, and tell through his interpreter of the gallant doings of his regiment during the German occupation. On other days TFH's men would carry out training exercises in full sight of the town and its people, just to make the point that the men were experienced and practised in the use of arms.

Much of TFH's time was, however, taken up with the distribution of food supplies to needy villages. A special committee had been formed to decide on the policy for this in relation to the German dump, and had decided that 20 percent would go to ELAS and the rest would be distributed by the British.[24] The situation in some outlying villages was desperate – no food having been delivered for at least two months and the Germans having taken everything that might be of use to the British before they left. By the middle of the month, TFH could report that two-thirds of the villages within the Thebes jurisdiction had received at least some food supplies. TFH recalled his experiences in Thebes later:

> I took control of the town of Thebes, and was in effect the military governor, where we did a great deal of initial relief work before the official agencies came. There were two villages where they did not have a single blanket between them nor seed to put in for the following year's growth. We were able to obtain relief supplies and make sure that they went directly to them.

* General Stephanos Seraphis (1890-1957) was a regular officer of the Greek Army who had fought in the Great War. He had taken part in two attempted coups between the wars and been imprisoned. He was active in the resistance throughout the German occupation, but after the defeat of ELAS he was exiled. He returned to Greece on his release, but was killed in a traffic accident.

Our work in Thebes was continually hindered by the guerrilla brigade in the area – almost 5,000 in ranks. They were led by dedicated communist officers. They attempted to impose their rule on the villagers, which they had no mandate to do, and to impose a government in the town of Thebes, which we denied them. We succeeded in minimising their authority, pending some proper arrangements from Atens.[25]

We had first of all to stop the communists getting hold of the stuff and also ordinary crooks. Then we had to get it to people on a 'most need' basis. We also brought them seed for the next harvest. We also brought the Province back on its feet …[26]

TFH afterwards told me in conversation that bringing food to the starving people around Thebes was one of the best things he ever did,[27] but there were tense moments. On 14 November, the EP tried to arrest the former Mayor of Thebes on charges of collaboration; the British intervened and placed a guard on the man's house, which brought on a demonstration 300-strong.[28] Incidents like this made it increasingly clear that ELAS had no intention of disbanding, even though instructions had been issued to this effect and for it to be replaced by a new National Guard, 30 battalions each of 500 men, for which call-up instructions were being issued to all eligible males. The garrisons in the towns beyond Athens were therefore increased and TFH was joined by the bulk of S Company.

*   *   *

On 24 November 1944 the companies began to be relieved of their duties by other units. TFH's men rejoined B Company and moved back to Athens – as far as they were concerned, en route for Italy and further operations.[29] He himself was placed in command of the battalion's rear detail, to liaise with the incoming unit and tie up all administrative arrangements. As well as these mundane matters, however, he was to make sure that 11th KRRC were 'fully conversant' with the situation in Thebes[30] – he being the man who had been closest to the ground and therefore best placed to explain the intricacies of the local situation.

Back in the capital, great emphasis was at first laid on physical fitness, turnout and drill, but in the streets of the capital they detected an undercurrent of tension, unease – fear even – which had not been there when they left. ELAS's men openly carried weapons in defiance of orders against this. On 1 December, the six EAM ministers in the Greek Provisional Government resigned and on 3 December a banned demonstration collided with the police: 'A day of great excitement. Rioting breaks out in Athens and troops fire at KKE and EAM … a bad show'.[31]

Several demonstrators were killed and on Churchill's orders, British troops became involved for the first time in controlling those who had, only a few weeks before, welcomed them. Civil War loomed. 6th (RW) Para was ordered to seal off the central focus of demonstrations, Constitution Square. The battalion moved in from the Old Palace and by 1400 hrs, A and B Companies had cleared the square. B Company then cleared the main Stadium Street into Omonoia Square, with A Company working in parallel along University Street, until all crowds were dispersed. As Fleming Jones recorded, 'this was done with no great difficulty'.[32]

A Company was then left to control the cleared area.[33] The next day, Scobie ordered ELAS to evacuate Athens and Piraeus; their response was to try to seize the capital by force. Scobie

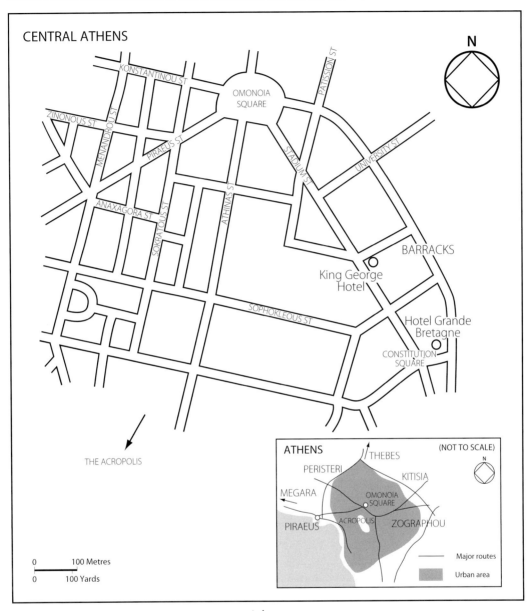

Athens.

issued a message to the people of Greece standing firmly behind the government, 'until the Greek State can be established with a legally armed force and free elections held'.

TFH was roused from sleep at midnight that night, for in spite of their promises to remain outside the city, ELAS troops were closing in for a military *coup d'état*. The first regiment of 750 men was already leaguered on the northern outskirts of the city, resting after a long forced march. Within half an hour, 6th (RW) Para was moving off in its Jeeps and three-ton lorries – a troop of armoured cars under command – on the road leading past the Averoff Prison with orders to surround and disarm the ELAS regiment, arrest its officers, and disperse its men.[34]

When TFH and his men had moved stealthily to their positions they found that the enemy with whom they had to deal were none other than their late acquaintances from Thebes. By the light of a flickering fire, Barlow once again faced Pappazissis while his newly awakened regiment, surrounded by the men of 6th (RW) Para with their bayonets fixed, looked on impotently. Pappazissis at first refused to disarm, but agreed to go to 23 Brigade Headquarters to meet the Brigade Commander. There he was told in no uncertain terms to give up his weapons or face the consequences. With tears streaming down his face, Pappazissis ordered his men to pile their arms. As dawn broke, the ELAS officers were separated from the men and sent off in lorries to one of the city prisons, while the 400 soldiers set off on the long march back to Thebes,[35] nearly 50 miles (80 kilometres) away – guarded initially by B Company until released. TFH later remembered this episode:

> There was a very unpleasant scene by firelight as we rounded them up and told them to hand over their arms. They did this with great ill-grace until my Commanding Officer, who had attempted to be friendly, gave an order to our soldiers to put a round in the breech of their rifles. Needless to say they all escaped later from their rather flimsy confinement...[36]

The task completed, 6th (RW) Para was relieved by the 2/5th Leicesters and was actually en route for the docks when the situation changed again. The battalion moved once more to Constitution Square to clear another big demonstration. This was done, but the embarkation was cancelled.

The leadership of the ELAS – their plan thwarted – had moved quickly to concentrate other troops on the capital until one after the other all the routes in and out were sealed. Scobie in response declared martial law. In Athens, 6th (RW) Para was redeployed and, late on 5 December, given orders to clear the centre of the city. Barlow had already left for Italy and until he could get back, the operation was in the hands of the Second-in-Command, Cavanagh.[37] Early on 6 December, the battalion formed up at the Tamion Building on Stadium Street, less B Company, which drove directly to Omonoia Square. Barlow's plan – for he was now back – was for A and C Companies to advance down Stadium Street and University Street, linking up with B Company in the square. The most opposition came from the EAM Headquarters in Stadium Street, but after a *Sherman* tank had blown the doors in, the garrison surrendered and were made prisoners. Fleming Jones recorded the incident: 'A long and tiresome day spent clearing the streets. We do an attack on the political HQ of EAM with tanks and take about 40 armed civilians prisoner ...'[38]

The enemy was by now bringing down mortar fire, as well as machine-gun and small arms fire and, soon afterwards, TFH – temporarily in command of B Company – was also hit, but stayed with the company. Ian Chatham recalled 'Much street fighting. FH was hit in the arm – asked me for a field dressing – I did not have one – told me to get one! Casualties were heavy and I remember men lying on the pavement near the first aid post'.[39]

With this task successfully completed, B and C Companies were ordered to reinforce 5th Para as it advanced to clear the area south-west of Constitution Square, towards the Acropolis. Although there was a good deal of sniping, this was successfully completed. However, as the day went on, there was more and more intense fire from ELAS – chiefly aimed at the police stations, which were heavily reinforced by British troops.

Operations against enemy strong-points continued over the next days: '7 December. A rather hectic day doing a hopeless job of street fighting against armed civilians who hide their arms while we are about and then shoot as soon as we turn our backs'.[40] Fitzroy-Smith was badly wounded leading A Company against one strongly-held position and the next day – 10 December – Carr, commanding C Company, was killed by a sniper. TFH's old Platoon Sergeant, Cliff Meredith, described the event:

> When … Major Carr was killed, he was up with my platoon (I was the Platoon Sergeant of 12 Platoon). He was shot in the throat and died instantly; when shot he was holding a grenade ready to throw, with the pin out. When hit he dropped the grenade; a fellow named Hawkes, who at the time was either a Cpl or a Sgt, picked it up and threw it away – thereby saving the section (No. 1 Section) from what would have been a disaster. He never received any recognition for that act. Athens was not particularly lucky for commanders of C Company.[41]

Most of the battalion, reinforced by tanks, was now concentrated in and around Omonoia Square, under heavy sniper and mortar fire. Here they felt relatively secure, if uncomfortable, but the position was vulnerable and everywhere overlooked – as TFH himself remarked, 'We were surrounded.'[42]

This was the situation as seen on 11 December when Churchill's envoy, Harold Macmillan,[*] arrived in Athens with the Commander-in-Chief of the Italian and Mediterranean theatre, Field Marshal Sir Harold Alexander. They found the British force essentially beleaguered in the heart of the city, with only six days' rations and three days' ammunition left. Accordingly the British 4th Infantry Division, en route for Egypt, was diverted to Greece, followed by two brigades of the 46th Division and a battalion of tanks.[43] Churchill himself arrived for a visit on 24 December, following which he persuaded King Georgios of Greece[†] to appoint a new government with Archbishop Damaskinos[‡] as Regent – firmly committed to a democratic future for Greece. These moves were to be vital in regaining the overall initiative in the campaign.

Meanwhile, the fight continued in the streets. Troops of 11th KRRC broke through the enemy cordon to reinforce the units in the city centre and a series of engagements, of growing intensity, followed. In particular, 2 Para Brigade began operations aimed at securing the temple-crowned Acropolis – a vital observation point above the city. 5th (Scottish) and 6th (RW) Paras crossed the start line for this phase of operations on 13 December. C Company met little resistance in the first street, but was engaged in a fierce battle for the second; B Company had to force its way forward, demolishing walls and doorways in order to make contact with the enemy. At nightfall the enemy withdrew – leaving 5th Para holding the Acropolis amid the ancient columns of the Parthenon.

---

*   Maurice Harold Macmillan, 1st Earl of Stockton OM PC FRS (1894-1986), known as 'Supermac', was later Conservative Prime Minister of the United Kingdom from 10 January 1957 to 18 October 1963.
†   Georgios II (1890-1947) reigned as King of Greece from 1922 to 1924 and from 1935 to 1947.
‡   Archbishop Damaskinos Papandreou (1891-1949) was the Archbishop of Athens and All Greece from 1941 until his death. He was the Regent of Greece until the return of King Georgios II in 1946.

The ELAS soldiers against whom they were fighting were often in civilian clothing, as Fleming Jones's diary makes clear, and there were women amongst them. They observed no rules: murder, torture, rape, arson, treachery; all were indulged in — there was even a case of flaying alive. The sign of the red cross was used to cover the transportation of arms and equipment in medical packs or ambulances, often with children or old people – especially those with missing limbs – made to carry ammunition and explosives. If the British overran their positions, they simply hid their weapons and came into the streets to greet them as long-lost brothers. The battalion took some time to learn the lessons, paying their tuition fees in casulties.

For the next three days, all companies mounted fighting patrols and it was in this period that Keith Murphy was wounded while in command of A Company and Frederick Ashby, who had taken over C Company from Carr, was also badly wounded.

On 17 December, command of C Company passed to TFH,[44] who recalled that: '... OC C Company was shot through the head, and I, while acting as OC B Company, had been wounded in the arm and chest but had recovered from that. Suddenly, at the age of 20, I was told by my CO to become OC C Company permanently. I felt a seasoned old soldier'.[45]

Taking over a new company is seldom easy, and never less so than when in contact with the enemy. There is no time for introductions or niceties. However, there is nothing like clear and present danger to form a rapid bond between an officer and his men – especially if that officer is known to be both brave and capable, as TFH certainly was. In this case things were easier than they might have been, since TFH had been a Platoon Commander in C Company until

British paratroopers involved in a fire-fight on a street corner in Athens. (Airborne Forces Museum)

Paratroopers enter an ELAS post through a window in Athens, December 1944. (Airborne Forces Museum)

he took over the Anti-tank Platoon, and as well as knowing the other officers, he also knew the senior NCOs and at least some of the fusiliers.

C Company had swept the area bounded by Piraeus, Sophokleous, Sokratous and Anaxagora streets with tank and mortar support and now TFH moved to occupy the hospital on Patission Street. Here he was counter-attacked almost at once, but the assault was beaten off with the loss of three of C Company's men. There was heavy machine-gunning down the street for much of the next day, but TFH's snipers were proving themselves more than a match for the opposition – killing and wounding 14 of the enemy.[46]

Things went on in this way for the next three days: heavy firing at close quarters, sniping, tanks and anti-tank guns being used to destroy buildings occupied by the enemy; dozens of grenades used. However, Fleming Jones felt that the tide was turning: 'Enemy activity quite energetic today but intuition tells me their effort is on the wane'.[47]

Christmas Day came and went with no respite, for the Greeks celebrated Christmas on 6 January – according to the old Julian calendar – and the communists did not celebrate it at all. 4th and 5th Paras had been pushing further into the city and companies of the National Guard also began to appear in the fighting, placed under the command of British battalions. On 29 December, TFH and his company managed to clear the area bounded by Athinas, Sophokleous and Menandrou streets as far north as Zinonos Street and even sent patrols up to

Konstandinou Street. TFH was given a company of the National Guard as well as his own men and, recognising their relative inexperience, he used them to clear buildings thoroughly once the platoons of C Company had made an initial pass.[48] This Greek company did well, finding explosives and ammunition and bringing in 120 prisoners; it was decided to leave them under TFH's command for the time being.[49] The next day, TFH's men cleared more of the blocks on the west of the square, south of Konstandinou Street, but there was no let-up in the intensity of fire. Indeed, field artillery was now brought in by the British, with 25-pdr guns being used in the direct fire role against enemy 75mm guns. TFH later recalled this phase of the battle:

> We had learnt the technique of mouse-holing – blowing a hole through houses to get at the enemy without going up the street. One morning we were mouse-holing through a chemist's shop and as we went through I saw one or two rogues taking cards of scissors etc. I stopped in the middle of this attack, very vexed, and said to my Sergeant, "*Get a hold of your soldiers and have all those goods handed back before we go on another step,*" which he rapidly did. The whole war seemed to stop for a moment as a reminder of the importance of discipline. We rapidly took our first objective, but then had to get out into the open street, where almost immediately I lost a number of men and the leading Platoon Commander, a South African called Stofberg.[*] He looked very grey and I saw he had caught a burst – of which several had hit him in and around the crutch. I opened his trousers and could see the rounds had passed through the fleshy inner part of his thighs and I said, "*Stoffy, it's all right – nothing vital's been hit,*" and I was happy to see the grey look pass from him![50]

On New Year's Day 1945 over 100 reinforcements arrived from Italy. They were much needed – especially those who were returning members of the battalion after having recovered from wounds. They were thrown straight into the fight. All that day and the next, enemy snipers were busy shooting at anything that moved – including their own civilians. Two women were shot in the street and a medical orderly sent by TFH to take care of them was also shot at, until TFH ordered heavy suppressive fire, which allowed the two women to be carried to safety. TFH and his company then used the opportunity, having made the enemy keep their heads down, to push forward and clear another two blocks of houses – killing four ELAS men and wounding 20.[51] The next day saw heavy exchanges of mortar fire, with 31 ELAS men killed and wounded, but many civilian casualties as well. On 3 January the slogging match continued. ELAS tried in vain to capture the hospital, but did force the American Mission to flee from the Kosmopolit Hotel

TFH, Dirk Stofberg and others in Greece.
(Farrar-Hockley family)

---

[*]   Dirk Stofberg was one of a number of South Africans seconded to the Airborne. He was wounded on 29 December [6th (RW) Para War Diary].

– which had been considered neutral territory. ELAS moved up in strength and had to be forced out inch by inch.[52]

On the evening of 3 January, orders were issued to a total of four British brigades – 10,000 men – to begin a new phase of operations aimed at destroying the Athens Corps of ELAS. Against them, surrounding the city, were at least 30,000 enemy troops, bolstered by German officers and NCOs left behind in the guise of deserters to foment trouble and delay pursuit. There were also, however, many genuine German deserters who stayed from a desire to remain in the fight, as well as a few Greeks who had been trained in the Soviet Army.

At 1800 hrs, TFH and C Company were relieved in place by C Company of 5th Para in order to prepare for the following day's battle. The battalion was reinforced with tanks, sappers, an entire Greek National Guard battalion, an anti-tank battery in the infantry role and a battery of light guns. The main body of the battalion, with A Company on the right, B Company in the centre and the reinforced anti-tank battery on the left – all supported by *Sherman* tanks from 46th and 50th Royal Tanks, *PIATs*, MMGs and National Guard – were to break into the enemy positions north of Omonoia Square. C Company, under TFH, was to work round and assault from the north to draw the enemy from the frontal attack and cut his lines of withdrawal.[53] The enemy territory to be captured was divided into 52 numbered blocks and assigned to each company. Tanks, sappers, machine guns, mortars and anti-tank weapons were all co-ordinated; timings were arranged; food, ammunition and medical support were laid on; communications were established – and then whatever sleep there could be was snatched.

Just before dawn on 4 January, A and B Companies stood-to behind doors and windows, mouse-hole charges already laid under the walls of the enemy-held houses. In the back streets, the *Shermans* squatted quietly. TFH and C Company, on the flank, were ready in the ruins of what had once been a fashionable shopping area along Patission Street – their *Shermans* shielded from enemy view by a single wall; the last fragment of a hotel. As the last stars faded, the chimneys and towers began to stand out sharply. At 0555 hrs the first tank started its engine, followed quickly by the others – the roar seeming to wake the streets into life. As the bell in the tower of Saint Nicolas's Church chimed the hour, the enemy positions were raked with intense fire from the windows opposite. The blast echoed and re-echoed from the Acropolis and Likavitos as the assaulting platoons moved into the attack.

At 0630 hrs, TFH led his men into the assault once more, passing through B Company's positions and the Piraeus exit from the square to link up with

All available methods of communication were used, including carrier pigeons. (RWF Museum/Archives)

C Company of the 5th Battalion, who had some hard going and made slower progress. They then turned at right angles and began straightening the line, clearing their way block by block. Barlow insisted on a methodical, thorough clearance with clear and definite bounds. Opposition was savage: six officers and 20 men were wounded on the first day, one officer and five men killed, and three tanks were knocked out. The method of systematic tackling of each block, smashing away with *PIATs* and explosives – and moving only through prepared mouse-holes – proved successful. Suddenly the attacking troops were clean through the main defensive positions. Darkness was coming on as TFH's men linked up with A Company and, with food, water and ammunition replenished, settled down for a watchful night with what little sleep could be had. The battalion was half-way to its objectives and although 6th (RW) Para's casualties were heavy, the enemy lost 50 killed, 14 wounded and nearly 200 prisoners on that first day. As the War Diary put it, 'We have taken a heavy toll of the enemy'.[54]

As dawn came on 5 January, TFH already had his men awake, fed and prepared for further fighting. The leading sections, doubling across the streets from their night positions, flung themselves into the doorways and gardens opposite. They met only a few terrified citizens, for the hard crust of resistance had been broken and the remnants of the communist forces, more intent on flight than on the fight, had withdrawn into the mountains during the night. The battle was won; the Athens Corps as a fighting force had ceased to exist. Soon after midday, Barlow issued new orders – giving the company commanders revised objectives up to two miles away. This sudden, rapid pace of advance 'seemed very strange'.[55] The British advance along the streets towards the northern suburbs was therefore something of an anti-climax, but around them flocked happy crowds who cheered and clapped as they passed, though here and there were weeping men and women recounting the death of some near relative at the hands of the communists. By 7 January, TFH and his men were occupying a defensive position on the western side of the city, with orders to prevent enemy re-infiltration. The attached Greek National Guardsmen at once began to search out any ELAS deserters or wounded left behind by their friends, as well as caches of weapons and ammunition.

'These Greek Nat Guards are very keen'[56], said the author of the War Diary – a polite way of saying that more than a few scores were being settled. Not surprisingly, on the afternoon of 13 January TFH and his men had a real sickener, even for men hardened by battle as they were. While carrying out a search in the suburb of Peristeri, they found the bodies of 80 civilians executed by ELAS in the German SS gaol for political prisoners, which had been more recently taken over by the communists:

> After we had driven the ELAS back out of Athens, we found places where they had butchered political opponents. Columns of people had been lined up and knives and axes had been used on victims. It was the most horrible and sickening sight and it made a deep impression on many of the soldiers.[57]

Fighting continued outside the city until 15 January, by which time British troops controlled all of Attica, for ELAS was no match for British formations in open country and had to agree to a truce on British terms. For a few days, 6th (RW) Para stayed in the suburbs until the Greek National Guard assumed responsibility for the area. The officers and men then moved into comfortable billets so that TFH and his comrades could once again enjoy the simple

comforts of a bath, a bed and a decent meal. An almost peacetime routine began immediately
– more than a little unsettling after so much moving and fighting:

> At that time there was a lot of political talk in the UK, including a certain amount
> in the TUC, that British soldiers were not fighting Germans but were taking on
> freedom fighters who had fought the Germans and had recovered Greece. The General
> Secretary of the TUC, Vincent Tewson,* and one or two others came out to Athens.
> The 2nd Para Brigade, officers and all ranks mixed, crowded into a theatre in Athens
> – the officers were told to remain silent – where Tewson said to us all, "*Well lads, I
> want you to answer these questions. Anybody can get up, irrespective of rank.*" He then
> asked what they thought about putting down the guerrillas. The officers left it to the
> soldiers, who made it clear that we had not been taking on a gallant lot of freedom
> fighters, but a group who did not enjoy popular support and some of whom were
> murderers of their own people. Tewson left satisfied.[58]

TFH stayed in Athens until the end of January when, with this peaceful interlude over, the
battalion embarked at Piraeus and sailed once more for Italy. 'As Athens glides past, there are
mixed feelings'[59], said the War Diary with typically British understatement.

Certainly it had been a job superbly done, as Scobie's Special Order of the Day made clear:
'... you have a far greater reward than any words of mine can express, in the grateful thanks
and warm friendship of the Greek people who will long remember what you have done for
them',[60] but it was also the worst fighting and the heaviest casualties that 6th (RW) Para had
so far endured, as TFH recalled:

> The 6th Battalion's strength was 528 all ranks throughout the fighting in Greece, but
> we lost 130 of that number killed or wounded badly enough to be taken to hospital
> — so it was quite tough fighting. We had about three weeks of intense street fighting.
> The enemy had the advantage of knowing Athens well, and they outnumbered us by
> about five or six to one, but it would be true to say that we had the advantage of better
> training and in the Parachute Brigade the quality of the soldiers was absolutely first
> rate. The fact that we did not give ground at all in our area was one of the main things
> which made them realise they were not going to get in.[61]

The tally of bravery awards proves this: DSOs for 'Lepro' Pritchard and Barlow – who
also received the OBE; three Military Crosses; nine Military Medals; and six Mentions-in-
Despatches.[62] Among these was TFH: a Military Cross and a Mention-in-Despatches –[63]
proof, if proof were needed, that he had led from the front. His MC citation reads as follows:
Battle of Athens, December, 1944 to January, 1945

> On the 6th December, 1944, Major FARRAR-HOCKLEY was wounded by a bullet
> in his forearm and had to carry his arm in a sling, but refused to be evacuated.
> As a result of officer casualties, Major FARRAR-HOCKLEY was put in command

---

* Vincent Tewson (1898-1981) was General Secretary of the Trades Union Congress from 1946 to 1960.

of a company ... in OMONOIAS Square, Athens. On the 24th December, 1944, his company was engaged on house-clearing operations astride PIRAEUS Road. Although there was heavy sniping, this officer had to expose himself to this enemy fire to successfully direct operations; he evacuated casualties and finally he himself had to lead the leading platoon when their officer was wounded. All this fighting he carried out in an inspiring manner and with complete disregard to his own safety.

On 4th January, 1945, when an attack was made to break the ELAS ring round the Square, Major FARRAR-HOCKLEY led his company round the right flank to attack buildings 49, 50, 51 and 52. This operation, owing to his disregard of personal danger, was most successfully carried out.

Major FARRAR-HOCKLEY is a most aggressive and courageous fighter who inspires confidence [in] all those around him.[64]

6

'... the continual scrubbing of operations'
The 6th Battalion (Royal Welch) the Parachute Regiment in Italy and Great Britain at the War's End, February-October 1945

The CPR Liner *Patricia Rathleen* docked at Taranto in the early hours of 1 February 1945. After disembarkation, a long journey in cattle trucks lasting three-and-a-half days – 'the train filled to the last square inch with men and materials'[1] – brought TFH and his companions to Rome. They then drove past the stately buildings in which Mussolini had intended to house the World Exhibition of 1940 and on down the Tiber to their barracks at Ostia Lido. Along the sea front the Germans had demolished the houses against an invasion. They had even stripped the fittings, including most of the doors, from the remaining buildings.[2] The accommodation was, however, comfortable, as the War Diary recorded: 'Apart from the shortage of electric light and the bomb damage at one end of the huge barracks, the layout and conditions leave little to be desired'.[3]

2 Para Brigade had been promised a period of several weeks in which to rest, refurbish and re-train. There were opportunities for local leave in Rome and Sorrento: sports and games – the battalion rugby team demolished a team put together by the rest of the brigade; fitness training; and parachute exercises. There was also a good deal of insistence on almost peacetime standards of drill and turnout – and the brigade represented the British Army at the Allied celebrations of the Red Army's anniversary in Rome. On St David's Day the English, Irish, Scots, and South Africans – now in the ranks of 6th (RW) Para – joined with the Welsh in homage to the patron of Wales:

> St David's Day is celebrated in style. No training is carried out. Extra foodstuffs have been saved and the Xmas issue has arrived. Leeks have been secured and a magnificent goat highly polished and decorated, and hastily 'trained' is on view. After a soccer defeat at the hands of 5 Para Bn – the first in the history of the Bn – the men's lunch commences. One selected man from each company eats the leek in traditional style with the drums beating and the goat and goat-major standing by. Officers and Sergeants have a rough and tumble soccer-cum-rugby match in the afternoon. The

Eden Hotel, Rome is the scene of most successful officers' dinner, where some 70 guests watch all distinguished visitors and new officers eat the leek.[4]

More training followed: individual cadres on support weapons and junior leadership; tactical schemes; and yet more jump training – the last much needed, as drafts of reinforcements continued to arrive. It was always assumed, however, that the brigade would return to operations. The Germans had succeeded in preventing an Allied breakthrough in the Po River Valley by building a strong series of defence lines and flooding large areas. This, and the winter weather, had made any large-scale operations impossible until now. Plans were, however, developed at Army Group level and focused on the city of Bologna and the Argenta Gap. Throughout March and April, 'Lepro' Pritchard and his brigade staff shuttled between the headquarters of Fifth and Eighth Armies – planning various options for the employment of the brigade. A generic operation order, which prepared the battalions for various eventualities,[5] was issued and in the end 33 separate contingency plans were made – but with no result.[6] In April the brigade group actually moved to the Foggia area, where the troops were briefed and prepared several times. The War Diary remarked with surprisingly good humour that the men were 'now fully accustomed to continual loading and unloading, packing and unpacking, issues and withdrawals'.[7] There was, however, 'a general feeling of disappointment in the continual scrubbing of operations'. The continual cancellation of planned drops was largely because the German armies, although numerous, were well aware of the progress of the war elsewhere and not inclined to give their lives in vain. Allied offensives, when they did develop, often met determined resistance from a few units for a short time, but once a breakthrough was made, the advance outpaced the requirement for any airborne operation.

The end was, however, in sight – and everyone knew it – not least because officers and men began to be given leave under the *Python* scheme. There were approximately five million servicemen and servicewomen in the British Armed Forces in 1945 and the demobilisation and re-assimilation of this vast force back into civilian life was one of the greatest challenges facing the British Government. Planning had therefore begun early and the scheme was made public on September 22 1944 – soon after the successful conclusion of the campaign in the South of France. Most servicemen and servicewomen were to be released from the Armed Forces according to their 'age-and-service number' which, as its name suggests, was calculated from their age and the months they had served. A small number of 'key men', whose occupational skills were vital to post-war reconstruction, were to be released ahead of their turn. Married women and men aged 50 or more were also given immediate priority.

The British Army's code name for the demobilisation scheme was *Python*. There were then two associated leave schemes: LIAP, or *Leave in Advance of Python*; and LILOP, or *Leave in Lieu of Python*. The latter was designed to compensate those whose tour of duty had expired, but who would be required to serve on – or indeed chose to serve on. The former was granted to those who met certain criteria, such as having been wounded or having been decorated for bravery or meritorious service.[8] Any soldier who proceeded on LIAP and who had served overseas for longer than four years remained on Home Service after his leave. However, those who received LILOP would have to return to their units overseas before eventual demobilisation.

On 27 April 1945, as Allied forces closed in on Milan, events accelerated. The deposed Italian dictator, Benito Mussolini, was captured by Italian partisans; the next day, he was executed in the small town of Giulino. On the 29th, Rodolfo Graziani* surrendered all Italian fascist Armed Forces to the Allies at Caserta and on 1 May, SS General Karl Wolff† and the Commander-in-Chief Army Group C, Colonel-General Heinrich von Vietinghoff‡ – after prolonged, unauthorised, secret (but unsuccessful) negotiations with the Western Allies aimed at trying to reach a separate peace not including the Soviet Union – ordered all German Armed Forces in Italy to cease hostilities. Vietinghoff signed the instrument of surrender, which stipulated that all German forces in Italy were to surrender unconditionally to the Allies on 2 May. Two days later, Field Marshal Montgomery accepted the surrender of all German forces in Europe on Lüneburg Heath.

VE Day was, however, not declared until 8 May. That day – and the following day – were treated as holidays. The only formal parade was held so that 'Lepro' Pritchard could speak briefly to the officers and men, but unlike at home the celebrations were restrained – almost muted – as if no-one could quite believe it was all over. It was a huge anti-climax to think that after three years, the tasks of 6th (RW) Para were finished, or so it seemed. They had fought many a hard fight since landing in North Africa: in the winter snows in the mountains of Italy; in the South of France; on the streets of Athens, but they came out of the war with a great reputation for efficiency and with their morale tremendously high – brilliantly led and bound together in an intimate comradeship.

*　*　*

TFH was still only 21 years old, but he had been exposed very early in his military life to that great teacher, WAR. Three years of operations in Italy, France and Greece had taught him more than some officers learn in a lifetime of service on the barrack square, or behind a desk in the Ministry. He had learned to endure hardship and discomfort. He had learned a great deal about comradeship and the bond that unites fighting men. It is often said of old soldiers that they never speak to others of their experiences, even their close family. There is a simple reason for this: only those who were there could possibly understand what it was like and what they endured.

He had learned a lot about leadership and developed his own powers of leadership: his will-power; his ability to communicate ideas and beliefs; his human touch; his professional expertise, loyalty and willingness to accept responsibility. He had also learned a great deal about courage – both physical and moral – which is inseparable from military leadership. War is supremely dangerous and competitive and, as Karl von Clausewitz tells us, '… the greatest moral strength in war is gained by those with the greatest courage …'[9] The leader can never be, in J.F.C. Fuller's words, just 'a prompter in the wings, but a key actor in the drama. He must experience danger'.[10] This because war is an heroic undertaking. If the leader is brave, and seen to be brave, he will influence the troops. They will trust his decisions even if it means hardship. This was evident in the experience of Farrar's House and to an even greater degree

---

*　Rodolfo Graziani, 1st Marquis of Neghelli (1882-1955), was an officer in the Italian Royal Army who had served in the Great War and later led military expeditions in Abyssinia and Libya before and during the Second World War. He was the only Marshal to remain loyal to Mussolini after he was deposed.

†　*Obergruppenführer* and *General der Waffen-SS* Karl Friedrich Otto Wolff (1900-1984).

‡　Heinrich Gottfried Otto Richard von Vietinghoff (1887-1952).

on the streets of Athens. Shared experience – especially where it involved hardship, danger and the loss of comrades – had been a powerful bond and it had engendered deep feelings of mutual trust and affection between TFH and his subordinates, as well as between TFH and his fellow company commanders, and with his CO, Barlow. No amount of *experience* can instil courage, because courage is an *instinctive* quality and one which different people have in different amounts. It is, moreover, a finite resource which with continued exposure to danger, will erode.[11] It is easy for anyone to be brave for a short time, but for a leader, what is most wearing is that he must be brave *all the time*.[12] There is an eternal debate about whether leaders can be grown, as it were, from seed, or whether they are born. Both are probably true, but TFH was without doubt a born leader. His example seems to show that the instinctive, or born, leader will be the more successful than one who has simply been trained since his powers of leadership – being instinctive – are deeply ingrained and more likely to survive the stress of battle.

It can be argued that the lower down the ladder of command one goes, the more that command and leadership are synonymous – and this is implicit in the nature of the officer training that TFH had had in the OCTU at Sandhurst. This correspondence of command and leadership results from two things: the primacy of the mission or task, and the level of delegated authority. The primacy of the mission at low levels means that the whole team at platoon or company level is in close contact with the enemy throughout the duration of that mission, and the primary task of the commander is in showing the physical and moral example required to accomplish that mission in the face of extreme danger. TFH had also learned, therefore, that a leader at low level must enjoy at least to some extent the personal friendship, as well as the trust, of the troops. In the British and Empire Armies, there was something of an inherited tradition about this:

> In other armies, such an association of all ranks on a common footing might be regarded as dangerous to discipline. In the British Army, an officer who had led his men to victory in a football match [would] be the more devotedly followed by them in a sterner field.[13]

He himself said something about this when interviewed in later life, remarking that: 'Our soldiers wanted us [the officers] to be a page or two ahead; they did not want us to be Napoleons … we lived a day at a time – sometimes 10 minutes at a time – and we had people who were not natural soldiers, but they did their best and I take my hat off to them.'[14]

TFH had also learned about decision-making, whether conscious or unconscious. The conscious method is through mental processes; the unconscious is intuitive. Some people are strong at one, and some at the other. Rarely are people good at both, and when forced to do the one they are least good at – usually when this requires an intuitive leap with little help at hand – problems ensue. This is probably what provoked Norman Dixon to remark, rather unfairly, that 'the apparent intellectual failings of some military commanders are due not to lack of intelligence, but to their feelings'.[15]

For a young officer like TFH, not schooled in the ways of staff colleges – and used to making decisions in the field – decision-making was first an intuitive process by him as the leader, based on his own situational awareness and his unconscious analysis from previous experience. Intuition is essentially the ability to arrive at decisions or conclusions without the explicit or conscious processes of reasoned thinking.[16] In the military sphere, its incidence can be defined as the sum of a person's intelligence and experience. It engages the subconscious and it works quickly; it is the converse of process, the long-drawn-out, staff-led business of reaching a decision through the ticking of every box, so beloved by training establishments. One noteworthy aspect of those with well-developed intuition is that their timing is excellent, as is their ability to recognise a change in the situation. One can see this development in TFH's conduct of his company's operations in Greece as a result of the hard schooling in Italy and France.

TFH had found his true vocation, that of military service: 'I enjoyed it every day. I had found something I loved, having been a lazy boy at school … I did like being in the army.'[17] War was his calling and fighting was his trade, in contrast to many others who were, at the time, very happy to return to civilian life. They were, as Shakespeare put it, '… but warriors for the working day' however much they had found comradeship and a sense of purpose in the war. But suddenly all comradeship and that purpose were gone – and for some, at least, there must have been a sense of vacuum or lost direction. One wonders how many of them, on a dull day back in some dreary office or drab works canteen, must have pushed back their chairs, looked into their memories and said to themselves, 'God, I *wish* the war was still going on.'

* * *

With the rest of 2 Para Brigade, 6th (RW) Para embarked on the troopship *Duchess of Richmond* at Naples on 17 June 1945. It was a pleasant, easy trip, with no cares about showing lights or smoking on deck. There was a programme of dances, concerts, cinema shows and lectures throughout the voyage – but no training parades. Gibraltar was reached on 21 June, where the interest in dances was heightened when a number of WRNS embarked.[18] As the convoy neared England there was a feeling of deep thankfulness in the hearts of all, touched too with memories of those who had been left behind and would never see home again. As the ship steamed into Liverpool on 24 June, where a band played to welcome them, the men cheered the summer rain which at first obscured the lights of the port. For what could rain matter? They were home again with the knowledge of a job supremely well done. TFH ended the war with a Military Cross; a Mention-in-Despatches; the Campaign Stars for Africa, Italy, France and Germany and 1939-45 for Greece; the 1939-45 War Medal; the Victory Medal;[19] and a fearsome reputation as a soldier.

Within a few days, TFH was sent away on his due leave, to be reunited with Pat and his family. As he was now over 21, there was nothing to stop them being married – and they were, almost immediately, on 7 July. With the help of the Griffin family estate agency and TFH's accumulated pay, they were able to buy the flat next to Emily at 18 Byron Road in Ealing. Here Pat was installed as TFH set off to rejoin 6th (RW) Para at the battalion's new home at Ashdown Park, Lambourn on the Berkshire Downs near Newbury. On 15 September, the battalion said goodbye to Barlow, who had commanded them since the *Abdiel* disaster and who had led them through so much. He was, without doubt, one of the formative influences on the young TFH, who remained devoted to him and his memory for the rest of his life.[20] He was succeeded by Lieutenant-Colonel John Tilly of the Duke of Cornwall's Light Infantry.*

---

*   Later Brigadier Alfred ('John') Tilly CBE DL (1910-2005).

The troopship *Duchess of Richmond*, formerly the pre-war passenger liner *Empress of Canada*.
Troopships were very much part of TFH's military life until after the Korean War, when in the
mid-1950s, air trooping was introduced. ((RWF Museum/Archives)

There had been other changes too. After more than three years of war, there were only four
of the original officers of the Royal Welch Fusiliers left standing: Major 'Huff' Lloyd-Jones,
Major Neill Boys, Captain John Neill, and the Quarter Master, Captain Rees Price.*

There was no hint of the battalion being wound up – quite the contrary. It was expected
that the brigade would be re-assigned to its old parent, the 1st Airborne Division, which was
earmarked for deployment to the Middle East as part of the Imperial Strategic Reserve,[21]
while the 6th Airborne Division would move to the Far East for operations against the
Japanese. However, the surrender of Japan following the explosion of the two atomic bombs at
Hiroshima and Nagasaki changed all such plans. With the war over in all parts of the world, it
was not considered necessary by the War Office to keep two airborne divisions in the order of
battle. Although the 6th was the junior of the two, it was the one to be retained. 1st Airborne
Division was therefore ordered to disband and 6th was assigned to the Strategic Reserve. 2
Para Brigade was ordered to join the 6th Airborne Division in place of 5 Brigade, joining 3
Parachute Brigade and 6 Airlanding Brigade. With the internal security situation in Palestine
already giving cause for concern, the division was ordered to the Middle East.

During this period, TFH also transferred from an Emergency Commission to a Regular on
28 April 1945, with his seniority backdated to 8 April 1944.[22] He also changed his cap-badge
from the Army Air Corps back to the Glosters, in which he had originally enlisted.[23] With
the Airborne Forces being reduced and there being at that time no permanent cadre for the

---

*   Rees John Price ('Posh', or 'Talkie') MBE (1902-1961) had been commissioned from the ranks as QM in
     1940.

Parachute Regiment, a change to more conventional soldiering was bound to come, but when interviewed in 1998, he was asked why he had not remained with the Royal Welch Fusiliers. 'Oh,' he replied, 'the Colonel of the Glosters remembered that I had had a good war, that I had an MC and that I had originally enlisted into the regiment. So before I knew what was happening, or rather before the Colonel of the Royal Welch Fusiliers knew, I found myself wearing the Back-Badge again instead of the Flash.'[24]

This does make sense: the Colonel of the Glosters at the time was Brigadier Alexander Pagan,* who had been Colonel since 1931 and knew his regiment intimately. The Colonel of the Royal Welch Fusiliers was Major-General Nigel Maitland Wilson, who was in poor health at the time and resigned the colonelcy in December 1946.[25] The senior serving Royal Welchman, Lieutenant-General Sir William Holmes, was in command in Palestine – and he too was on the point of retiring and emigrating to the USA. This was, therefore, one of those moments that seemed routine at the time, but which placed TFH on a very different path from that which he might otherwise have taken.

---

* Brigadier-General Alexander William Pagan DSO DL (1878-1948) was Colonel of the Glosters from 1931 to 1947.

7

'... this painful and thankless task'
The 6th Airborne Division in
Palestine, 1945-1946

In the years immediately following the Second World War years, British power was still dominant in the Middle East and its hub was the great military base of the Suez Canal Zone – the largest armed camp in the world and the centre of a network of other bases spreading out to Malta, Cyprus, Libya, Transjordan, Eritrea, Aden, the Persian Gulf States – and Palestine.[1] Palestine had passed to Britain as part of the dismemberment of the Ottoman Empire at the Congress of Versailles, but the British Government poisoned its own chalice even before picking it up through the Balfour Declaration,[2] which had established in principle the British Government's support for a Jewish homeland. This, and the arrival of a Zionist Commission in 1918, which in 1929 became the Jewish Agency,[*] began the process of igniting Jewish aspirations and arousing Arab suspicions. British rule was formalised under the League of Nations Mandate in April 1920, which divided the territory into two: Palestine to the west of the River Jordan and Transjordan to the east.[3] Jewish aspirations had led to civil disorder as early as 1921 and after the Arab Revolt of 1936, a Royal Commission had produced the radical idea of two States, with Britain retaining control of Jerusalem. The Arabs would have none of this and the British had no option, therefore, but to continue their administration. The next step was a Palestine White Paper, approved by Parliament, which attempted to use demography to prevent the establishment of a Jewish State in Palestine: an upper limit of 75,000 Jewish immigrants, plus 25,000 emergency cases.[4] In the closing stages of the war, Churchill's view had been that:

> The whole question of Palestine must be settled at the peace table, though it may be touched upon at the conference at Potsdam. I do not think we should take the responsibility upon ourselves of managing this very difficult place while the Americans sit back and criticise … . I am not aware of the slightest advantage which has ever accrued to Great Britain from this painful and thankless task. [5]

---

[*] The agency had no governing function, but was responsible for advising the government on issues affecting the creation of a Jewish national home and the interests of the Jews in Palestine. It thus exerted considerable influence over the Jewish population and its behaviour. By 1945, it had been made responsible for handling a range of Jewish affairs.

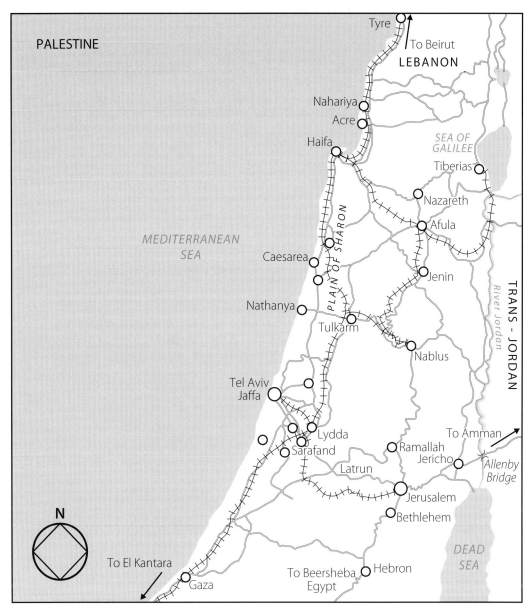

Palestine.

Immediately after the war, the new British Government, in an attempt to remain even-handed between Jews and Arabs, had restricted official Jewish immigration. This government had also announced the abandonment of plans to create separate Jewish and Arab States in Palestine. It had not been possible, however, to control illegal movements of population and the result had been massive Jewish immigration from Europe. This inevitably produced greater pressure for Statehood which, when frustrated, led to terrorism and atrocities between Jews and Palestinians. The *Haganah*, a secret Jewish underground militia, was able to mobilise large numbers of armed Jews at short notice, and did so as soon as the British withdrew. Its leaders did not always support terrorism and were able to exert some influence over the Jewish terror gangs – two of which were mainly instrumental in the insurgency. These were *Irgun Zwai L'eumi*, or IZL, which translates as the National Military Organisation; and *Lachemey Heruth Israel*, or Hebrew Fighters for the Freedom of Israel – more generally known as the 'Stern Gang'.[6] Their activities were officially condemned by the Jewish Agency, but even its own security organisation, *Haganah*, became involved at times with confrontation. *Haganah* was formed in the 1920s during anti-Jewish riots. It was organised and equipped on conventional lines, although part-time, and many of its members had served in the Allied armies. Within *Haganah* there was a small professional elite formation known as *Palmach*, organised into small commandos.

On 3 November 1945, Foreign Secretary Ernest Bevin,* exasperated by the legacy of the Balfour Declaration and exhortations from US President Truman, announced that only 13,000 Jews would be allowed to enter Palestine from Europe and that the Royal Navy would intercept any attempting to do so illegally.[7] This increased further the hatred of the Jews for the British, as well as their hatred for the Arab people. Given the political instability of the Arabs, the position of the British Army between these two was distinctly uncomfortable and the troops found their duties decidedly unpleasant.

Since 1944, large numbers of British troops had been required to maintain order, as the government had decided, contrary to Churchill's view, to hold Palestine as a base for forces in support of its interests in the Middle East.[8] As part of the army crack-down on terrorism, on 15 September 1945 the 6th Airborne Division was ordered to re-deploy from Britain to the Middle East.[9] This and other reinforcements raised the total garrison to 80,000 Empire troops and 20,000 policemen.[10] It was against this background that 6th (RW) Para moved to its first post-war operation – a foretaste of much that was to follow in the succeeding 40 years.

The Palestine garrison came under the command of the C-in-C Middle East, General Sir Bernard Paget;† the GOC-in-C Ninth Army, which covered Palestine and Transjordan until its disbandment, was Lieutenant-General Sir William Holmes,‡ late of the Royal Welch Fusiliers; thereafter, Palestine came under Lieutenant-General Sir Evelyn Barker.§ The GOC's command covered Transjordan as well as Palestine, since although Transjordan had been granted Independence in 1946 and its Hashemite ruler, the Emir Abdullah,¶ had been crowned King, Britain still retained treaty commitments, basing rights and supplied military assistance. Abdullah's personal vision was a Semitic kingdom embracing Transjordan and Palestine, in which Arabs and Jews (although with strict controls on immigration) would live together as equals.[11]

The troops in Palestine in 1945 consisted of three fighting divisions: the 1st Infantry, 1st Armoured and the 6th Airborne, as well as a number of non-divisional units and Empire troops from Africa. The 1st Armoured Division was later replaced by the 3rd Infantry Division,

---

*   The Rt Hon Ernest Bevin PC MP (1881-1951) co-founded and served as General Secretary of the Transport and General Workers' Union from 1922 to 1940 and had been Minister of Labour in the war-time Coalition Government.

†   General Sir Bernard Charles Tolver Paget GCB DSO MC (1887-1961).

‡   Lieutenant-General Sir William George Holmes KBE CB DSO (1892-1969).

§   Later General Sir Evelyn Hugh ('Bubbles') Barker KCB KBE DSO MC (1894-1983).

¶   Abdullah ibn Hussein, Emir 1921-1946, King from 1946 until his assassination in 1951.

which was disbanded in Palestine just before the final evacuation. The country was divided into three military areas: 215 Area in the north, with its HQ at Haifa covering the Galilee, the Jordan Valley, Acre, Safad, Nazareth, Beisan and Tiberias; 21 Area in the south, covering the districts of Lydda, Gaza, Jaffa, Tel Aviv and Samaria; and 156 Sub-Area, which covered Jerusalem. Area HQs controlled all static units, installations and infrastructure – leaving the field formations free to conduct internal security operations.[12] Also in the country were units of two Arab formations: the Transjordan Frontier Force and the Arab Legion. The Frontier Force had been created in 1921 by the then High Commissioner in Palestine, Field Marshal Viscount Plumer. This brigade-sized force was recruited chiefly from the settled Arabs of the towns and was a Colonial force with British officers, owing its allegiance to London.[13] The Arab Legion, by contrast, owed its allegiance to Abdullah. Both the Arab Legion and the Frontier Force were highly disciplined and effective – and the Legion was as well-equipped and trained as any force in the Middle East.[14] The military was, of course, subject to control by the civil authority – although in this case the High Commissioner was also a military officer, General Sir Alan Cunningham.*

*   *   *

The advance party of 6th (RW) Para under 'Huff' Lloyd-Jones, now Second-in-Command, left by train from Hungerford Station on 1 October bound for Liverpool. It sailed the next day on the troopship *Duchess of Bedford*. A and C Companies, under David Gilchrist and TFH respectively, moved off on the 10th and the remainder of the battalion on the 11th[15] – all by train. The whole battalion embarked at King George V Dock in Glasgow on the troopship *Cameronia*, which sailed for Palestine the next day. Anxious to develop the military standards of the many very young soldiers who had replaced the war veterans of the battalion released to civilian life on their return home in June, the Commanding Officer arranged a full programme of training for all ranks during the voyage, including PT, weapon training, and lecture periods. A Directive was issued to carry this forward on arrival:

> Owing to a great number of promotions within the battalion and reinforcements both in officers and men, the battalion will have to start building up virtually from scratch, on arrival in MEF.† It will not be an easy task and it will call for loyal co-operation and hard work from every single officer, NCO and man in the unit … . I want all commanders to bear in mind that our primary role is that of a parachute battalion and though we may of necessity be earthbound for some time, we must not lose sight of this fact during training … .
>
>   Unless the battalion is administratively sound, training can never be good, therefore I require all commanders to pay the greatest attention to detail in this respect. All officers must realise that the welfare and comfort of their men comes before their own, and act accordingly … .

---

*   General Sir Alan Gordon Cunningham GCMG KCB DSO MC (1887-1983) was noted for victories over Italian forces in the East African Campaign during the Second World War.

†   Middle East Forces. It was later renamed Middle East Land Forces (MELF).

> In the Middle East, hygiene and sanitation become of paramount importance.
> Commanders will stress to all ranks the necessity for absolute cleanliness in camp …
> the MO will inspect camp weekly …[16]

To the old hands, this sounded a bit like 'Janet-and-John go parachuting', but to be fair to Tilly, he must have felt very much in the shadow of Barlow, who had commanded the battalion through its most difficult days with huge distinction. In the eyes of the veterans, Tilly was a new boy. It did not matter what he had done; he had not been with them. Then he also had the burden, to which he alluded, of large numbers of new officers and men with no experience whatsoever. In effect, this was a new battalion and it had to be moulded very quickly into an effective fighting force.

That said, the tasks which would face the battalion in Palestine would be very different from those it had undertaken in wartime. The aggression and offensive spirit which had been so necessary in airborne assault operations had little place in routine internal security. Discipline, fitness, weapon handling and fieldcraft all remained important, but the junior officers and NCOs in particular had to learn to restrain their men; to use only the minimum necessary force required; to become mediators or negotiators in matters of dispute and even carry out some duties which might routinely fall to the police. The history, geography, culture, customs, religious sensitivities and politics had to be mastered – so too did skills familiar to the old pre-war India hands: the tactics for cordon and search operations, arrests and screening; road-blocks and checkpoints; terrorist recognition; riot control and crowd dispersal; and the use of intelligence to carry out carefully-targeted fix and destroy operations on terrorist cells. All officers and men had to master the regulations which governed their powers for opening fire, arrest and search – what would now be called the rules of engagement.

The ship passed Gibraltar on 16 October. For the old sweats, including TFH, it seemed only yesterday that they had called there on the way back from Italy. Malta was reached on the 19th, and on the 22nd the ship dropped anchor in Haifa Harbour. Disembarkation began early next morning and the battalion moved directly to No. 184 Military Transit Camp (MTC) in Haifa. On the night of the 24th, after the companies had carried out a hard day's training ashore, the men were allowed to investigate the delights of Haifa town. For many young soldiers, spending their first night in a foreign city after years of wartime austerity in Britain, it must have seemed like a different world.

The officers and men of 6th (RW) Para did not long enjoy the flesh-pots. After a few days, they moved south. The 6th Airborne Division was allocated responsibility for the southern sector of Palestine, which comprised the districts of Lydda, Gaza and Samaria. 2 Para Brigade was given an area in the Gaza District, a likely flash-point between Jews and Arabs because of its large Arab population. On 25 October, therefore, the battalion entrained at Haifa at 1900 hrs and at 0700 hrs the next morning arrived in Gaza. Here the battalion moved in to Nuseirat Ridge Lines just outside Gaza town for a period of settling in.[17] They did not receive a warm welcome from the Jewish press, which greeted the division as 'Gestapo' –[18] a greeting which was bitterly resented by those veterans of the war who had fought in France, Germany, Italy and Greece.

A second training Directive – covering the month of November 1945 – allocated one week each to individual, section and platoon, platoon and company, and company and battalion training. Individual training was focused on making good the loss of expertise in shooting and other skills through release and *Python*; collective training was focused on battle drills, internal security, house searching, and fighting in villages – all skills that the battalion had learned the hard way in Greece, but which had now to be re-taught by those veterans like TFH who remained in his company: Stofberg, his Second-in-Command; Rothkugel, another South African who commanded 10 Platoon; John Griffiths; Noel Brady,* who commanded 11 and 12 Platoons; and the senior NCOs of the company: Cliff Meredith, who was now the Company Sergeant Major, with Sergeants Aspey, Morgan, Shepherd and Oxley. In addition to programmed training, preparations for operations went on. There were visits to police stations and on 5 November, TFH – along with all his brother company commanders – took part in the brigade command post exercise, *Herod*. Tilly then issued a new Directive for operations, which identified that some of the key factors of modern war – the legal and media dimensions – had to be recognised and dealt with for the first time:

> Both Jews and Arabs have highly organised and efficient news and propaganda servic-
> es. It is essential, therefore that news of incidents be reported to and through our
> government before it is released by any other agency.
>
> In order that we beat the world press agencies at their own game, speed is essential
> at all levels… . The importance of rapid passing of information from the political
> point of view will be impressed on ALL RANKS.[19]

For the British Army, trying to maintain a line between Jews and Arabs was hard. Captain Peter Cavendish, who was General Hughie Stockwell's ADC when he became GOC 6th Airborne Division in 1946,† recalled that:

> It took about six weeks from arrival to change the British Army's attitude from pro-Jew,
> in sympathy with what they had suffered under the Germans, to very much anti. They
> were devious, arrogant people with no sense of humour. The Arabs were also devious,
> but were courteous and had an immense sense of humour. Senior commanders tried
> to be fair-minded – I remember Hughie [Stockwell] saying, "You've got to try," but
> it was hard.[20]

Toby Sewell, who served at this time in Palestine with 8th/9th Para, recalled that:

> … my experiences then resonate entirely with those of Peter Cavendish, and I have
> always had a lack of sympathy for Israeli positions. Then, they immediately treated the
> local people as second class citizens … while to me they were the instigators of much
> of modern terrorism. The Jewish Brigade we had at the end of the war in Italy were
> not a very attractive lot either.[21]

---

*   Brady was appointed Second-in-Command to TFH when Stofberg and the other South Africans departed on 28 November 1945. However, he did not stay long, as he was appointed Weapon Training Officer on 12 December. Captain Andrew Roberts took his place (War Diary).

†   Later Major-General Peter Boucher Cavendish CB CBE (b. 1925) commissioned 1945 into the 3rd Hussars, subsequently 14th/20th Hussars. He became Stockwell's ADC on 3 January 1948, having been commanding a squadron in Haifa. He retired in 1981 (*Army Lists*).

In Arab villages, after ponderous introductions and the ritualistic serving of mint-flavoured tea, the reassurance they brought sometimes made the visitors feel guilty of fraud. It was much harder to penetrate the cold suspicion encountered in the Jewish kibbutzes.[22] Gregory Blaxland remarked of these times, that: 'Gay, courteous and endearingly incompetent, [the Arabs] differed in every respect except bravery from their scowling foe [the Jews], and it was hard for the British to conceal which side they preferred'.[23]

On 1 December, 'Lepro' Pritchard – who was still in command of the brigade – put the battalion through its paces in his administrative inspection, followed immediately by a readiness exercise, *Scramble*. Training continued all month until Christmas, when: 'The battalion sat down to an excellent dinner and were waited upon, as is the custom, by the officers and sergeants. At night in the canteen, festivities were at their highest. C Coy won the competition for the best decorated dining hall'.[24]

With the holiday over, B Company was placed at three hours' notice to move for internal security (IS) duties on 28 December. On the 31st, rioting broke out in 57 Military Detention Prison in Gaza. A Company was called out to quell this, but it was necessary to open fire on the rioters,[25] which occasioned a Court of Inquiry to be called. On 5 January, A Company was sent to guard the divisional REME workshops, 15 miles southwards at Rafah – and there TFH was sent with C Company to relieve them on the 19th, only to be recalled on 23 February for possible operations.[26] On the following day, TFH was given orders to take C Company and to occupy the Arab village of Al-Jura after an attack was threatened by Jewish terrorists. Here he stayed, without incident, until relieved by the Anti-tank Platoon on the 25th in order to rejoin the rest of the battalion at three hours' notice to move for further operations; it was a false alarm. On the 26th, the battalion was stood down, less one company in turn remaining at one hour's notice to move.[27]

Parachute training meanwhile had also restarted with a practice parachute jump from *Halifax* aircraft for officers and senior NCOs on 19 January and further training for stick commanders during February. Tilly aimed to complete parachute conversion training by 15 March and to have revised the battalion's load tables for the *Halifax* Mark VII aircraft. HQs, *PIAT* teams, Rifle Platoons and detachments of the MMG and Mortar Platoons were all to carry out experimental jumps with equipment, but in spite of the short notice-to-move times and the training programme, all the traditional celebrations were enjoyed on St David's Day: 'Brigadier visited camp … Leek eaten, Goat, Goat Major and Drummer made rounds'.[28]

On 4 March an advance party consisting of a skeleton Battalion HQ and TFH's C Company moved to Gedera Camp just outside Jaffa, followed later by the main body. At Gedera, 6th (RW) Para was to be the brigade reserve for internal security duties with one company at three hours' notice to move; also to be prepared to carry out an airborne operation in an IS role. By the end of April, it was anticipated that three groups of war-enlisted men would be released and that reinforcements of fusiliers (but no officers or NCOs) would arrive. It was hoped that a fourth rifle company would be formed, although this was not possible in the event.* What was clear, however, was that considerable training for the new arrivals would be necessary. Tilly was in no mood for compromises:

---

*   On 13 April battalion strength was reported to have diminished to 28 officers and 537 men. See Field Returns of Offrs and ORs in WO 169/23227, 6th (RW) Para War Diary 1 January 1946 – 30 June 1946.

Due to moves and airborne training, loss of experienced NCOs and lack of officers; all officers and NCOs will have to work hard and carry out cheerfully the programme outlined …

All reinforcements will have to fire the War Course …

Specialists will have to be trained within the battalion to make up for wastage and to have at least thirty-three and one-third percent reserve. Cadres for drivers and cooks will have to be run by the bn… .

One-third of each coy (less HQ) will fire the *PIAT* during March. RE assistance to be obtained for instructing Pioneer Platoon in RE and demolition work. [29]

It was already obvious that the Jews in particular were well-organised and could rapidly call up reinforcements to take on troops engaged in searching settlements or arresting wanted men. It was clear that whenever an operation was mounted, the maximum available number of troops would have to be used in order to deter, or deal with, any Jewish counter-moves.

On 27 March, TFH with his company took part in Exercise *Dolgelley* – a parachute drop on a divisional DZ by C, HQ and Support Companies. However, the pace of internal security operations now began to increase and the emphasis to shift away from training towards commitments. On 30 March, A Company advance party left for guard duties at Latrun, followed by the main body on 1 April. At 2200 hrs on 2 April, heavy explosions were heard north and north-west of Gedera. C Company moved out to clear the area around the village of Isdud, but found nothing unusual. The area was patrolled for several days, without result. On 14 April, a Jewish strike was called and Tel Aviv placed out-of-bounds for 24 hours. A railway

Members of 6th (RW) Para emplaning a *Dakota* – probably for Exercise *Longstop* – in Palestine, 1947. (Airborne Forces Museum)

Members of 6th (RW) Para
waiting to drop from a *Dakota*
for Exercise *Longstop* in Palestine,
1947. (Airborne Forces Museum)

strike was called two days later on the 16th. Next, the battalion was warned for IS commitments in the Jaffa/Tel Aviv area.

TFH flew home on 19 April for a short leave and a course in Air Transport Support at the
School of Land/Air Warfare at Netheravon.[30] While he was away, disturbances broke out in
the area on 26 April: six men of 5th (Scottish) Para were killed that day and the battalion
prepared for deployment. On the 27th 'Lepro' Pritchard spoke to the whole battalion and on
the 28th TFH's fellow company commanders carried out a reconnaissance of their likely tasks
in Tel Aviv. On the 29th the battalion carried out road blocks and mobile road patrols as part
of a divisional system for controlling movement, especially at night – a hazardous and exacting
duty. These continued until 11 May, the day TFH returned from his course, and duties were
handed over to 4th Para. Intensive training began for a battalion exercise, *Stagger*, which was
to be held near Tiberias, but because of the security situation the exercise was cancelled.

On 31 May, 'Bubbles' Barker, the GOC-in-C Palestine, visited the battalion. That very
evening, six Arabs were arrested while attempting to buy weapons from fusiliers. Nothing,
however, stood in the way of really important matters: the King's Birthday Parade was held in
Jerusalem on the 13th – 'Parade successful but unpopular with Jews'. [31]

On 15 May, Field Marshal Montgomery had arrived in Palestine and addressed all officers
of 6th Airborne Division at Sarafand. He had already called on Cunningham – of whom he
had no opinion whatsoever as a soldier.[32] He makes it clear in his memoirs that he had come
rapidly to the view that the military was attempting to operate in a political vacuum and that
this was unacceptable. He demanded clear direction, and if that meant the forcible imposition
of British rule, then so be it. This would, of course, demand:

... a drastic revision of the way of life of the serviceman in Palestine; social activities would have to cease, the fullest precautions must be taken and, generally, everyone must be given a proper understanding of the task that lay ahead ... Before leaving Palestine I expressed my views very forcibly by cable to Whitehall.[33]

It was clear to everyone, therefore, that more trouble could be expected; 6th (RW) Para was warned to move to Tel Litwinsky, just east of Tel Aviv, if required. The advance party under 'Huff' Lloyd-Jones was ordered by wireless to move on Sunday 17 June with the rest to follow shortly thereafter, but TFH did not go with them, for he was posted on 21 June as Deputy Assistant Adjutant General on the staff of the Divisional Commander.[34] Thus ended TFH's service with the Royal Welch Fusiliers, although he never forgot his old friends and comrades and he remained a member of the association all his life – attending reunions whenever he could. It had been, in his own words, 'A most wonderful experience.'[35]

*   *   *

TFH arrived for his first experience of working on the staff of a formation at the headquarters of the 6th Airborne Division in Sarafand – not long after a new GOC, Major-General James Cassels,[*] had taken over command. A Divisional Headquarters in 1946 was a rather smaller affair than it later became. The GOC's staff was headed by the GSO1 (Operations) – a Lieutenant-Colonel who was the principal staff officer and responsible for the policy, the co-ordination and general supervision of all work, intelligence, security, the issue of orders, training and operations. At this time, the post was held by Michael Dewar.[†] There were two other lieutenant-colonels: a GSO1 (Air) – an appointment unique to the Airborne Division – and the Assistant Adjutant & Quarter Master General (AA & QMG), who was the officer ultimately responsible for all administrative matters within the division. This post was held by Peter Young,[‡] and then 'Bala' Bredin.[§] Under the AA & QMG were two more lieutenant-colonels: the Assistant Director Ordnance Services (ADOS) and the Assistant Director Medical Services (ADMS); and two majors: the Deputy Assistant Quarter Master General (DAQMG), who headed the Q branch and who was responsible for supply, transport and maintenance; and the Deputy Assistant Adjutant General (DAAG), who headed the A branch and was responsible for personnel matters such as postings, drafts, leave, discharges and re-enlistments, discipline, personal administration and pay.[36] It was this last post that TFH was to fill, working with a Staff Captain under him – a far cry from leading men in battle, which

---

*   Later Field Marshal Sir Archibald James Halkett Cassels GCB KBE DSO (1907-1996). He commanded 152 Brigade and then 51st (Highland) Division in NW Europe, 1944-1945. He was later a Divisional Commander in Korea, C-in-C BAOR and Chief of the General Staff.

†   Later Brigadier Michael Preston Douglas Dewar CB CBE (1906-1984). See *Who's Who* for full details of military service. He had served in Palestine during the Arab Revolt 1936-1939.

‡   Later Major-General Peter George Francis Young CB CBE (1912-1976). He was later Commander 44 Para Brigade (TA) 1955-1958 and GOC Cyprus 1962-1964 (*Army Lists; Who Was Who, 1971–1980*).

§   Later Major-General Humphrey Edgar Nicholson 'Bala' Bredin CB DSO MC (1916-2005). He served before and during the Second World War in Palestine, France and Belgium, North Africa and Italy; and later in the Cold War in Germany.

had been his bread-and-butter since he joined 6th (RW) Para in 1942. It was, moreover, a highly responsible position usually occupied by an experienced officer with staff training rather than a 22-year-old acting Major with nothing but regimental duty behind him. There was a Staff College in Haifa, but TFH was not sent there, and had to rely on his short course at Netheravon and learning on the job.

The division was the lowest level at which all arms and services, and their functions, were found represented on the staff and in the order of battle of the division's units. The divisional staff was large enough, therefore, to plan and conduct operations simultaneously and, as the official publication put it, '... assist [commanders] in the formulation of their plans, and the issue of orders to give effect to those plans. The first duty of the staff is to assist the commander by every means in its power; its second duty is to ensure the welfare, maintenance and comfort of the troops.'[37]

The Divisional HQ could expect to take up to five brigades under command, as well as its supporting divisional troops. Its fire support and engineer support were organic and the division could support itself logistically. All that said, a division in 1946 had very limited capabilities when compared to its modern equivalent: in firepower it equated to a 2014 infantry battle-group as organised and supported in Afghanistan. Moreover, a 1946 division had very limited communications, minimal ability to observe the battlefield other than visually, and no ability to engage an enemy beyond the range of the contact battle – even supposing an enemy could be observed. In a counter-insurgency campaign like Palestine, it had none of the electronic or airborne assets available to a modern division in Iraq or Afghanistan and was able to take the fight to the enemy, therefore, with ground troops only.

TFH found the division in the process of re-forming – and doing so while in contact with the enemy. The division's reconnaissance regiment had just been disbanded; gliders had been removed from the order of battle, which meant that 6 Airlanding Brigade was re-designated as an infantry brigade and removed from the division to be replaced by 1 Parachute Brigade; the Pathfinder Company was disbanded in September; and finally, 5 Parachute Brigade, which had been detached to the Far East, returned to the division in August – only to be disbanded in its turn in September.[38] Thus TFH and the rest of the staff found themselves dealing with three parachute brigades – 1, 2 and 3 Brigades – and the divisional troops.

Although parachute training continued at the Divisional Training School in Aquir, the main focus was on operations. The first major operation, during June, was *Agatha* – a large-scale search and screening operation designed to reduce the effectiveness of the *Palmach*. On 22 July came the attack on the King David Hotel in Jerusalem, with the death of 91 British civil servants and soldiers. It was followed by a large-scale search operation, *Shark*. Other operations were also mounted to try to limit illegal Jewish immigration and to contain sabotage of the rail network.

TFH's most serious operational involvements at this time, aside from his routine work, began almost immediately with a series of raids – co-ordinated at divisional level – on the headquarters of the Jewish Agency and other organisations suspected of complicity in terrorism. 1 Para Brigade was given six settlements in the north, 2 Para Brigade was allocated the headquarters of the agency itself, and 3 Para Brigade was tasked to move on two settlements in the south. In every case, searches for documents, weapons and ammunition were to be made and suspects arrested. Security was paramount. The operation was launched on 29 June and ended on

1 July. In all, 2,718 people were arrested and screened – of whom 636 were detained – 135 of them being probable *Palmach* members.[39]

Another series followed the *Irgun* raid on the Ottoman Bank's branches in Tel Aviv and Jaffa on 13 September. In the aftermath, a Jewish youth named Benjamin Kimchin was arrested, tried, found guilty and sentenced to 18 years in prison and 18 strokes of the cane. In retaliation, *Irgun* kidnapped the Brigade Major of 2 Para Brigade and three NCOs – all of whom were stripped and flogged. The reaction among British troops was one of fury and all units had to be confined to their barracks in order to prevent reprisals against the Jews. Five *Irgun* members were later stopped in a car at a road block and a fire-fight broke out. One terrorist was killed and the others, who were found to be in possession of rawhide whips as well as weapons, were arrested. They were tried and found guilty of terrorist offences; three of the four were hanged.[40]

Shortly after this, on 30 November, TFH's brief period on the divisional staff came to and end and he left Palestine for England;[41] casualties from the daily fighting and terrorist spectaculars on the day he left had reached 76 dead soldiers and 23 policemen.[42] Although he was not staff-trained, TFH clearly handled the job of DAAG with some skill. His annual confidential report, by the exacting Bala Bredin and supported by the GOC, describes:

… his abnormal drive and keenness which have resulted in his accumulating a wide military knowledge at a comparatively early age. His present job necessitates him alternating between carrying out the duties of DAAG and DAQMG. He can stand any amount of hard work … he has a clear brain, an immediate grasp of detail, expresses himself well on paper and is extremely loyal. Occasionally he is inclined to be over hasty, through over keenness, in his dealings with subordinate formations. I attribute this to his intense regard for exactness.[43]

*   *   *

6th (RW) Para also left Palestine soon afterwards – in January 1947 – and arrived in Britain on 2 February.* After two preliminary moves, it settled at Cambrai Barracks, Perham Down – at which point the RWF connection ended. In July 1948, the battalion was re-designated as 1st Battalion the Parachute Regiment, under which title it sill exists.

A month later, the Palestine problem was laid before the UN General Assembly, which in November 1947 decided on partition between Jews and Palestinians. As inter-factional fighting escalated, the British Army found itself under fire from both factions. It was with some relief that the army, therefore, withdrew through Jaffa and Haifa in July 1948.

However, the lessons learned in Palestine resulted in important changes of doctrine and practice in the British Army, as later campaigns would show. One commentator summed things up thus:

---

*   Those serving with the battalion, including TFH, qualified for the award of the General Service Medal (George VI) 1918 with clasp 'Palestine 1945-48'. *Medals Year Book, 1999*, p 89.

Operation *Bobcat*, Haifa 1947. (Airborne Forces Museum)

A group of *Hagganah* soldiers in Palestine, 1948. (Imperial War Museum)

The Jews had the highest quality of terrorists that the British Army faced in the post-war period, so the army probably set its standards by them, and it did them good … what was learned was applied much better elsewhere.[44]

6th Airborne Division as a formation was, however, a casualty of the withdrawal. In early 1948 it was announced that the division would be reduced to a single brigade.[45] This caused great gloom, as TFH himself remembered: 'It was thought to be the beginning of the end for airborne troops. There were, thereafter, repeated notices that the life of even one brigade might not last beyond a couple of years.'[46] Fortunately for TFH, these notices came to nothing.

8

'The most outstanding young officer' Great Britain and Jamaica, January 1947-July 1950

TFH returned home by air, rather than the regular trooping service, on 30 November 1946 – just in time for the birth of his first son Charles Dair (always known as Dair) on 2 December.[1]

He went first on *Python* leave until 11 December, after which he was posted as Second-in-Command of the Parachute Regiment Reserve Battalion.[2] This had been established at Beverley in East Yorkshire in late 1944, but moved to Piddlehinton in Dorset in 1945. It was transferred to Talavera Barracks in Aldershot around September 1946 under the command of Lieutenant-Colonel E.J. Coker, where it was renamed as The Parachute Regiment Training and Holding Battalion. Here TFH joined it, taking over from Major George Widdowson. The battalion's strength varied considerably, but had been as high as 90 officers and 2,000 men, a mix of newly-trained soldiers awaiting postings to service battalions and old hands looking forward to imminent demobilisation.[3]

Here he remained, weekly commuting to Ealing where Pat and Dair continued to live, carrying out routine administrative and training duties, until in September 1947 he was posted to another staff appointment – still in the temporary rank of Major – as GSO2 (Liaison) in the headquarters of the Royal Air Force No. 4 Group,[4] based at Heslington Hall, near Hull. No. 4 Group was the RAF's transport command, with 14 squadrons on 12 stations across England, under the command of Air Commodore Arthur Revington.* Its tasks were to provide air transport, including the *Dakota* aircraft used to support the Airborne Forces which were now reducing to one regular and one TA brigade. Because of this, the headquarters staff included a number of army officers charged with acting as the link between the army and the air force – carrying out all staff duties necessary whenever soldiers were to be carried, for administrative or operational reasons, in RAF aircraft. This was, however, a very brief interlude of less than six months, since the group was to be disbanded. In spite of this, TFH made a deep impression, as Revington noted in his annual confidential report, grading him 'outstanding':

> I unhesitatingly describe him as the most outstanding young officer I have ever met … everything he does, he does well … his opinions are sound beyond his years, and he has an infectious enthusiasm for everything he touches … for his own sake and that of the army as a whole, I hope his enthusiasm will not be thwarted by too

---

* Air Commodore Arthur Pethick Revington CB CBE (1901-1986) had served throughout the Second World War in Coastal Command and had twice been mentioned in despatches.

Dair's christening: TFH and Pat are in the centre, Neil Boys is standing next to Pat and next to him is Briony Smith; Anne Bennett, Dair's godmother, is holding him and behind her in WRAF uniform is Joan Winder; next to Anne is Henry Morning, then Pam, Beatrice and Ted's wife, Camille. The others are unidentified. (Farrar-Hockley family)

prolonged subservience to less capable officers merely because he is a few years their junior in age.[5]

On 10 March 1948 TFH was once again on the move, for it was back to regimental duty, but to a battalion with which he had never served: 2nd Battalion The Gloucestershire Regiment. It was time for TFH to make re-acquaintance with his regiment; a regiment with which he had last served as a Sergeant in the Young Soldiers Battalion in wartime – a very different matter from being a regular officer in a peacetime battalion, albeit one with a large cadre of National Service officers and men. 2 Glosters had been in the Netherlands at the close of the Second World War. From there they had moved into Germany: to Osnabrück, Bad Sassendorf, Werl and Soest; and then to Berlin. In late 1946 and early 1947, the battalion had staged through Gloucester before moving by troopship – the SS *Orbita* – to join the garrison of the Caribbean Area at Up Park Camp, Kingston, Jamaica with a company in Bermuda and a detachment at Airport Camp, Belize in British Honduras.[6] Troopships at this time had not improved much since the Crimean War, it seemed:

The wives of Major E.D. Harding and Captain E.L.T Campbell, for example, well remember sharing a cabin with 11 other women and children on the month-long voyage from Liverpool to Kingston, together with Captain A.H. Farrar-Hockley's wife [on the troopship *Empire Bure*] who travelled in equal misery.[7]

The battalion's role in the Caribbean was to be available for internal security duties – 'Military Aid to the Civil Power' – and other tasks such as hurricane relief throughout the area, which included both British Honduras and British Guiana on the American mainland, and Bermuda far to the north – as well as all the Crown Colonies throughout the Caribbean island groups. There was also a good deal of ceremonial: the King's Birthday Parade every year, as well as frequent Guards of Honour for visiting senior officers, government ministers or foreign guests.

Up Park was also the headquarters of the Area HQ and administrative troops, so room was tight. This was made worse by the modernisation programme of the brick bungalows of the camp, built before the Great War.[8] Because of this, each company took it in turns to spend a month at Newcastle – over an hour's drive away and 3,000 feet (1, 000 metres) up in the hills. Shortly after the battalion moved in, C Company was disbanded as a company; its manpower being shared out to the other three companies and the detachments. It remained in being as a cadre company with two wings: one at Kingston under the Company Commander, Captain P.W. (Sam) Weller; and one at Newcastle under the Weapon Training Officer (WTO), tasked

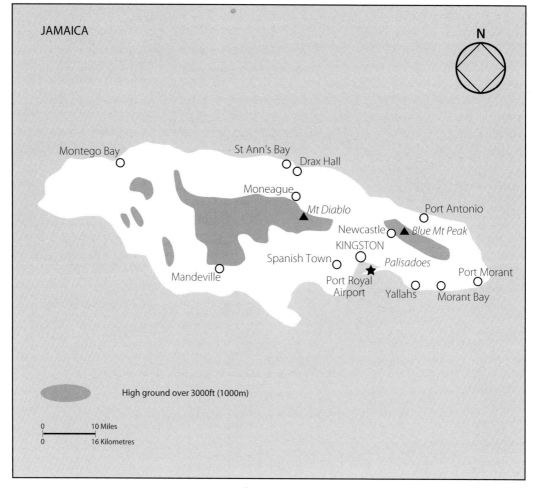

Jamaica.

with running individual cadre courses and collective training for the company at Newcastle. Being so high up, the climate in Newcastle was cooler than in Kingston and families could go on short leaves there to enjoy the facilities. The camp consisted of wooden bungalows raised on pillars about three feet (one metre) above the ground to allow air to circulate and to discourage insects and snakes.[9] It was here to Newcastle that TFH found himself posted as WTO[10] with Pat and baby Dair.

A view of Newcastle, Jamaica. (Farrar-Hockley family)

The Farrar-Hockley family bungalow at Newcastle, Jamaica. (Colonel Pat Beaumont)

It was back to being a Captain once more, with the consequent drop in pay.[11] With a young family, this could have been difficult – especially as prices in Jamaica were high on account of import duties. However, TFH's pay as a Captain – about £40 per month – was augmented by marriage allowance, ration allowance and a cost of living allowance of 2/3d [11p] per day.

TFH knew none of his fellow officers. The CO, Lieutenant-Colonel Robbie Berwell,* was relatively new in command; the Second-in-Command, who was TFH's immediate superior, was Major A.H. (Alan) Knight; the rifle companies were commanded by Majors Anthony Dillon, Peter Varwell, and W.V. ('Lakhri') Wood. The Adjutant was Captain Richard Reeve-Tucker; Support and Headquarters Companies were both commanded by captains: Stephen Farmer and John Pearson respectively. The last two members of the hierarchy who mattered to someone in TFH's shoes were the Quarter Master, Captain Roland Grist; and the Regimental Sergeant Major, WO I W. Murphy.[12] Berwell stayed in command only a short time – deciding to retire in November 1948 and being succeeded by Lieutenant-Colonel H.L.W. Bird.† TFH and Pat soon struck up firm friendships – especially with Alan Knight and his wife, Daphne, which was just as well, since neither TFH nor Knight found their Commanding Officer an easy man. Bird, however, seems to have recognised TFH's talents after only a short time – grading him 'outstanding' in his annual confidential report, recommending him for promotion and the Staff College and remarking that: 'His knowledge of his profession is that which one usually expects from a graduate of the Staff College'.[13] Brigadier Edwin Page,‡ the Area Commander, concurred.

2 Glosters, however, was to remain 2 Glosters for only a short period. With India and Palestine gone, the army was shrinking. Defence expenditure in 1947 had been set at £600 million, with the army's share being £270 million and with a manpower target of 339,000, down from 527,000, set for 1949. These targets were soon revised, however, to £222 million and 290,000 men – of whom 200,000 were to be regulars.[14] The infantry had already reduced to 113 battalions from a wartime high of 680, or one-seventh of the army – but it was now to shrink further, to 72 battalions not including Gurkhas and Empire troops, or 84 battalions in total.[15] To achieve this, all line regiments would be reduced to a single regular battalion.

For the regiments whose numbers were greater than 25 in the order of precedence, and whose two battalions therefore each represented a numbered regiment of foot (the Glosters were the 28th and 61st), this meant either the disbandment of that number or an amalgamation. The Glosters chose to amalgamate and keep both numbers in the title of the remaining battalion. This amalgamation took place on 21 September 1948 at Up Park Camp. The original 1st Battalion had served throughout the Second World War in India and Burma and afterwards had been stationed at Deolali in India[16] when Indian Independence and the reductions that followed were announced. It was here, therefore, that it was selected for reduction to a cadre; the officers and men were all posted to other units, or discharged – leaving only a small representative party to maintain the battalion's existence. This small party returned home to the

---

*   Later Honorary Brigadier R.J. Berwell OBE (1900-1988), commissioned into the 61st Foot in 1922 and served throughout the Second World War.

†   H.L.W. Bird OBE (1905-1973), commissioned 61st Foot 1925. Served with the RWAFF. Served on staff with BEF. Commanded 2nd Bn on two occasions and 1st Bn in November 1948-December 1949. Sub-area Commander at Seoul, Korea. Later commanded 149 Infantry Brigade (TA) at Oxford; retired 1957.

‡   Brigadier Edwin Kenneth Page CBE DSO MC (late the Cheshire Regiment).

The Amalgamation Parade of 1 and 2 Glosters, Jamaica. (GLRRM 05959)

Regimental Depot in August; it then moved to Jamaica for the amalgamation, arriving on 18 September, with their Regimental Colous.[17]

The Amalgamation Parade, in which TFH took part, was a simple one: the battalion, dressed in heavily starched, pressed, khaki drill jackets and trousers – no shorts, as the heat of the Caribbean summer had already passed – paraded in hollow square and the Colours were marched on. The Governor,* who was to take the salute, arrived – and as the Sovereign's representative, was given a royal salute. The 1st Battalion Colours were then marched on and the Governor inspected the parade, after which a special order of the day was read. The 2nd Battalion then took charge of the 1st Battalion's Colours and the 2nd Battalion Colours were marched off. With this symbolic act, the two battalions had amalgamated.[18] Some regiments no doubt found this process very difficult. One apocryphal story concerns an officer of the 52nd Foot, the 2nd Battalion, Oxford and Buckinghamshire Light Infantry whose 1st Battalion was the 43rd. This officer was in the habit of stropping his razor 52 times every morning. When he reached the 43rd stroke, he spat.

For the Glosters, there seems to have been no such bother as this was an amalgamation in form only, since the 1st Battalion had ceased to exist. There were no drafts to be absorbed; no newcomers to make welcome. Be that as it may, the battalion, now 1 Glosters, had only a brief spell of duty left in the West Indies. On 21 November 1949 the various detachments were all complete on board the troopship *Empire Windrush*, having handed over their duties to the 1st Battalion Inniskilling Fusiliers, and were steaming towards Southampton.[19] At the end of September, in preparation for this, TFH had handed over his duties as WTO and succeeded Reeve-Tucker as Adjutant. The Adjutant was not only the CO's personal staff officer, but the officer responsible for all matters related to personnel, administration, discipline and movements – roughly the same as his duties on the staff in Palestine – and his first task was therefore to organise the move home of the troops, the families and all the regimental property and baggage. TFH clearly did this very well, as Bird commented in his annual confidential report that as well as being outstanding as a trainer, he also excelled at the Adjutant's duties. He

---

*   Sir John Huggins KCMG MC (1891-1971) Captain-General and Governor 1943-1951.

remarked – as others had done before him – that in his opinion, TFH would rise to the highest ranks. This view was supported even on very short acquaintance by the brigade and district commanders.[20] It was their view that really mattered – exercising a levelling view as they did across the officers of the whole command.

On arrival, the troops entrained and moved to their new home, Roman Way Camp in Colchester, before dispersing for some home leave. Here, the battalion joined 29 Infantry Brigade under Brigadier Tom Brodie[*] and became acquainted with the other battalions and units in the formation: the 8th or King's Royal Irish Hussars; the 1st Battalion The Royal Ulster Rifles and the Bedfordshire and Hertfordshire Regiment; 45 Field Regiment, RA; 55 Field Squadron, RE; 57 Company RASC (later renamed 29 Ordnance Field Park); 249 Provost Company, RMP; 26 Field Ambulance, RAMC; and 10 Infantry Workshops, REME. The brigade had not long been formed and was still widely dispersed, from Durham to Salisbury Plain; its first training concentration had not been held until just before the Glosters arrived.[21]

The Farrar-Hockley family did not move into the military town at Colchester, for there was a severe shortage of officers' married quarters, and advertisements had been placed around the county asking for rented accommodation. The Farrar-Hockleys were given rooms in a wing of Polstead Hall, a Georgian House about nine miles north of Colchester.[22] Here, in January 1950, Pat once more became pregnant. Not long afterwards, TFH's father, Arthur Farrar-Hockley, died aged only 59. TFH of course went to the funeral in Peterborough, along with all his siblings. Not all were keen on going – especially Ted, who had almost to be dragged there. On the way back, and in spite of the solemnity of the occasion, the others had to resort to singing songs to get Ted to cheer up.

After two years in the Caribbean, 1 Glosters – although individually well trained – had to be reorganised and retrained collectively in conventional warfare ready for its new role. One rifle company, C Company, remained in cadre form under Major Paul Mitchell and CSM Ridlington – one of the measures adopted army-wide to reduce numbers. The remaining three companies – A, B and D – were under Major Pat Angier and CSM Harry Gallagher, Major Denis Harding and CSM Morton, and Major 'Lakhri' Wood and CSM Munro. Support Company, with the carriers, mortars, anti-tanks and machine guns, was under Major Sam Weller and CSM Baker. Reeve-Tucker became Signals Officer and Henry Cabral took up the appointment of Intelligence Officer.

Yet again, however, the CO did not stay long in command: in January 1950, soon after the return, Bird was selected to command 129 Infantry Brigade (TA) and his place was taken by Lieutenant-Colonel J.P. (James) Carne,[†] usually known as 'Joe' or 'Fred'. The relationship between a Commanding Officer and an Adjutant is usually a very close one, often leading to life-long friendships, and only surpassed by that between a Brigade Commander and his Brigade Major, or perhaps a general officer and his military assistant and aide-de-camp. Given that TFH did not much like Bird, this relationship was never going to develop between the two and Bird's departure was, therefore, fortunate for TFH. As things turned out, it was perhaps also fortunate for 1 Glosters, given what later transpired – although one cannot guess how Bird would have done in command at the Imjin. Carne, his replacement, was a remarkable

---

* Late Major-General Thomas Brodie CB CBE DSO (1903-1993) had seen service in the Second World War and in Palestine. He retired in 1955.
† Later Colonel James Power Carne VC DSO (1906-1986).

officer who, like Bird, had seen service in the Second World War and before; an officer whom even TFH, with his considerable battle experience, liked and admired from the first. He was a quiet, calm, softly-spoken man with a pleasant Gloucestershire burr in his voice. He had the knack of remembering names and faces immediately and of putting people at their ease. In a tight spot, he would appear as if from nowhere and put new heart into the men, who trusted him and admired him. TFH was a total contrast and complete foil for Carne. Both were capable but while Carne was steady, deliberate, calm and reserved, TFH was energetic, enthusiastic and full of vim[23] – but Carne's leadership and example were to prove to be among the most enduring influences on TFH's life.

9

'No-one but the Glosters could have done it.'
1st Glosters in Korea and at the Imjin River, July 1950-April 1951[1]

Wednesday afternoons in the peacetime British Army were traditionally given over to sports and games. So it was that on 26 July 1950, most of the officers and men of 1st Glosters were on the sports pitches. TFH, the Adjutant, was however in his office – thinking idly about the approach of summer leave. Not for long, for in walked the Chief Clerk, WO II 'Taffy' Evans, with a signal marked: 'Secret: only to be opened by the Commanding Officer, or the officer appointed to do so on his behalf'. TFH opened the envelope and read the message: 29 Infantry Brigade was to mobilise at once for service in Korea. Apart from reporting their requirements for officers and men to bring their battalions up to strength, however, COs were not to announce the news until a government press statement had been released.[2] The Brigade Commander, Tom Brodie, and some of his officers were in Normandy on a tour of the battlefields of 1944 and did not return until the following day.[3] TFH took the message to Carne, who was watching cricket. 'Well,' he said, 'not entirely unexpected. I'll come back to the office.' Not indeed unexpected, for the British Government had made a commitment in the UN Security Council to help South Korea repel the invasion from its communist neighbour in the North.[4] As 29 Brigade was being prepared for the new Imperial Strategic Reserve, which was announced in August 1950,[5] it was an obvious formation to send – second only to 27 Brigade in Hong Kong, which was also committed.

*   *   *

The Korean War had its origins in the division of Korea by an agreement of the victorious Allies at the conclusion of the Second World War. The Korean Peninsula had been ruled by the Empire of Japan since 1910, but following the Japanese surrender in September 1945, American administrators divided the peninsula along the 38th parallel, with US military forces occupying the southern half and the Soviets occupying the north.[6]

The opportunity to hold free elections throughout the Korean Peninsula in 1948 was missed, as in divided Europe, and this served to deepen the divisions between the two Koreas. In the North, a communist government was installed by the Soviets, while in the South a right-wing government took power. The 38th parallel was, *de facto* if not *de jure*, the border between two

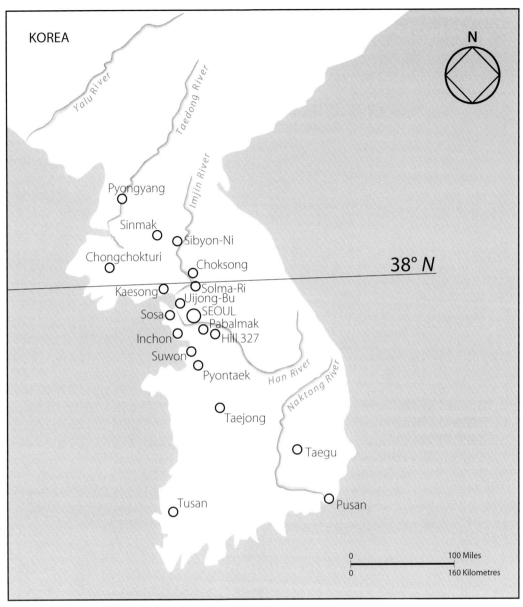

Korea.

Korean States. Discussions on reunification, however, continued in the months preceding the war, even as tensions grew. The North Korean dictator, Kim Il-Sung,* was determined to achieve reunification with the South by force and his Soviet backers became more and more closely involved in the North's planning for war.[7]

---

* Kim Il-Sung, born Kim Sŏng-ju (1912-1994), was the leader of the Democratic People's Republic of Korea – commonly referred to as North Korea, from its establishment in 1948 until his death in 1994.

There are differing views of the degree of both Soviet and Chinese support – ranging from backing if the North was attacked, to approval, to initiating a pre-emptive attack; but in April 1950, Stalin gave clearance for Kim Il-Sung's forces to invade the South, subject to Mao Tse Tung's agreement that China would send reinforcements if needed. Stalin, however, made it clear that Soviet forces would not engage in combat themselves, as he had no intention of initiating a general war with America and its allies.[8] Kim met Mao in May 1950; Mao was clearly worried about the possibility of US intervention, but nevertheless he agreed to support the North Korean attack.[9]

Several experienced Soviet generals, led by Colonel-General Terenty Shtykov and Marshal Alexander Vasilevsky, had been sent to the Soviet Advisory Group in North Korea and under their supervision, plans for the attack were completed shortly after Mao's approval was given.[10] Under the original plan, war would be initiated with a skirmish in the Ongjin Peninsula on the west coast of Korea. The North Koreans would then launch a 'counter-attack' against this 'aggression' that would capture Seoul, then encircle and destroy the South Korean Army. The final phase would destroy all remaining traces of South Korean Government authority and unite the country.

On 7 June 1950, Kim Il-Sung called for a Korea-wide election on 5-8 August 1950 and a consultative conference between 15 and 17 June 1950. On 11 June, the North sent three diplomats to the South as part of a planned peace overture that the South Koreans were certain to reject.[11] On 21 June, Kim asked permission from Stalin and Mao to open the war with a general attack across the 38th parallel, rather than the planned skirmish, because of fears that the South's intelligence services had learned of his plans and that preparations were under way to stop them. Stalin agreed.[12]

The Korean People's Army (KPA) crossed the 38th parallel behind massive artillery fire at dawn on Sunday 25 June 1950. The KPA claimed that Republic of Korea Army (ROK) troops had attacked them first, and that they would arrest and execute the South Korean leader, Syngman Rhee.* The KPA combined arms force was formed and trained on Soviet lines and included substantial numbers of *T-34* tanks, rocket launchers and heavy artillery pieces.[13] The ROK forces, by contrast, had almost neither tanks, nor anti-tank weapons, nor heavy artillery, and were completely incapable of stopping such an attack. Unsurprisingly, the ROK Army was routed within the first few days. On 27 June, Rhee secretly evacuated Seoul with his government. The city fell the next day. The South Korean forces, which had numbered 95,000 men on 25 June, could account for less than 22,000 men a week later. In early July, when US forces began to arrive, the remaining ROK forces were placed under operational command of the United Nations Command (Korea).[14]

The US administration under Democratic President Harry S. Truman† suspected that war in Korea might simply be a diversion – allowing the Soviets to launch a general war in Europe once the US Army was decisively committed in Korea. At the same time, '[t]here was no

---

* Syngman Rhee, (1875-1965) was the first President of the Provisional Government of the Republic of Korea, as well as the first President of South Korea.

† Harry S. Truman (1884-1972) was the 33rd President of the United States of America. He was Vice-President to Franklin D. Roosevelt and succeeded him on his death. He was subsequently re-elected and served as President until 1953.

suggestion from anyone that the United Nations or the United States could back away from [the conflict]'.[15]

In Truman's mind, Korea was where a stand had to be made – the question was, how? The first steps had to be taken in the UN Security Council. On 25 June, the day that the North launched its attack, the Security Council unanimously condemned the invasion of the Republic of Korea – passing UN Security Council Resolution 82. The Soviet Union, which as a permanent member had the power to veto all resolutions, had boycotted the council meetings since January 1950, protesting that the Republic of China – i.e. Taiwan – not the People's Republic of China, held a permanent seat in the council.[16] After debating the matter, the Security Council, on 27 June 1950 – and in the absence of the Soviets, who could have stopped all moves dead in their tracks – passed UNSCR 83, recommending that Member States should provide military assistance to the Republic of Korea. On 27 June, Truman ordered US air and naval forces to assist the South.

Truman still held back, however, from committing ground forces – and there were some among his advisors who believed that the North Koreans could be stopped by air and naval power alone.[17] The decision to commit ground troops and to intervene was made when a communiqué was received on 27 June from the Soviet Union, indicating that it would not move against US forces in Korea.[18] In spite of rapid post-war demobilisation, there were still substantial US forces in Japan under the command of General Douglas MacArthur.[*] Only the British and their Commonwealth partners had comparable forces in the area, but these were already heavily committed to operations in Malaya and to the defence of Hong Kong, Singapore and North Borneo.

As things turned out, the US provided 88 percent of the 341,000 international soldiers sent to Korea, with 20 other countries of the United Nations offering assistance.[†] Britain was second only to the United States in the contribution it made to the UN effort in Korea. 87,000 British troops took part in the Korean War during the three years of fighting and over 1,000 British servicemen lost their lives. This required a major effort, for in the aftermath of the Second World War and the introduction of the Welfare State, Britain was all but broke. Marshall Aid had eased some of the worst difficulties, but the continuing requirement to contribute to the defence of the West against Communism were heavy; the added burden of the Korean War – 'a distant obligation', as Prime Minister Clement Attlee called it – arguably destroyed Britain's chances of a strong, early economic recovery that might have rivalled

---

[*] Douglas MacArthur (1880-1964) was, with George Patton, the only US General of the Second World War to have been wounded in combat in the Great War. He was Chief of Staff of the United States Army during the 1930s and played a prominent role in the Pacific theatre during the Second World War. He received the Medal of Honor for his service in the Philippines Campaign, which made him and his father Arthur MacArthur, Jnr, the first father and son to be awarded the medal. He was one of only five men ever to rise to the rank of General of the Army in the US Army and the only man ever to become a Field Marshal in the Philippine Army.

[†] According to *United States Forces Korea* (United States Department of Defense), the totals committed at any one time from all partners were:
Republic of Korea, 590,911; Colombia, 1,068; United States, 302,483; Belgium, 900; United Kingdom, 14,198; South Africa, 826; Canada, 6,146; The Netherlands, 819; Turkey, 5,453; Luxembourg, 44; Australia, 2,282; Philippines, 1,496; New Zealand, 1,385; Thailand, 1,204; Ethiopia, 1,271; Greece, 1,263; France, 1,119.

that of Germany. The Chiefs of Staff were at first reluctant to contribute ground troops, but by the summer of 1950, the political imperative to support their American allies was irresistible; the decision was made on 24 July.[19] 27 Infantry Brigade, which was stationed in Hong Kong under the command of Brigadier Basil Coad,[*] was sent to Korea immediately. It was later joined by Australian, Canadian and New Zealand units, and became a Commonwealth infantry brigade.

*   *   *

For TFH as Adjutant of the 1st Glosters, the most pressing problem was manpower. To bring the battalion to its wartime establishment required the formation of a fourth rifle company and an Assault Pioneer Platoon under Captain H.J. ('Spike') Pike – as well as bringing the existing companies and departments up to full strength:[†] in particular, the Anti-tank, Mortar and Signals Platoons; and the Regimental Aid Post had to be expanded. An additional problem was that some National Service officers and men, who were close to their discharge date, could not be sent to Korea unless they volunteered.[‡]

Most of the officers and men were to be recalled from Classes A and B of the Regular Reserve;[§] the Glosters would receive not only their own reservists, but also men from the other regiments in the Wessex Brigade Group:[¶] the Royal Berkshires, the Devons, the Dorsets, the Royal Hampshires and the Wiltshires. TFH and his staff had to go through the entire nominal role of the battalion man by man to determine who would go to Korea, who needed to be replaced and what blank files needed to be filled. Eight days later, the first reservists began to arrive.[20] Lofty Large, who was one of these reservists, remembered that:

---

[*]   Later Major-General Basil Aubrey Coad CB CBE DSO DL (1906-1980) held battalion, brigade and divisional commands during the Second World War and immediately after.

[†]   The post-war infantry battalion establishment of 35 officers and 914 men had been reduced in 1948 by reducing the fourth company and the Pioneer Platoon to cadres.

[‡]   The requirement for a peacetime force larger than that made possible by voluntary recruitment led the post-war Labour Government to move towards establishing a National Service system in 1946. The National Service Act was passed in July 1947 after considerable opposition from some Labour and Liberal politicians. The Act was to come into force at the beginning of 1949. The Act initially required a period of one year to be served in the Armed Forces followed by a liability for a possible five years in the Reserve. Financial crises, the advent of the Cold War and the Malaya emergency led to the National Service Amendment Act in December 1948 –increasing the period of service to 18 months. This enabled National Servicemen to be used more efficiently and effectively, particularly overseas. The demands of the Korean War led to the length of service being extended to two years – surpassing even the Service Chiefs' original wishes. Liability to further service in the Reserve was reduced with each of these extensions. The period of service remained at two years until the end of National Service in 1962.

[§]   Class A reservists were men liable for call-up, who could be brought in without the issue of a Royal Proclamation. Section B reservists could not be called in before such a Proclamation was issued.

[¶]   Brigade Groups had been formed by the Director of Infantry in October 1946 – grouping regiments together for recruiting, training and the allocation of manpower. The Brigades were the Guards, Motorised Infantry (later Green Jacket), Light Infantry, Gurkha, Parachute Regiment, Machine-gun (disbanded in 1947), Highland, Lowland, North Irish, Welsh, Home Counties, Yorkshire and Northumberland, Lancastrian, East Anglian, Wessex, Mercian, Midland and later, Foresters.

There had been a pep talk by the Adjutant, Captain Farrar-Hockley, and an interview with the Commanding Officer, Colonel Carne. The interviews were conducted individually in the CO's office, where Joe Carne shook hands and welcomed each man to the unit, asked a few questions – which showed he had seen our record documents – and wished us the best of luck for our future with the battalion. There were 30 of us. Joe Carne saw every man and made every one feel welcome under his command.[21]

The Glosters' manpower problem was less pressing than some others, who needed a reinforcement of 75 percent of their strength. In the case of the Bedford & Hertfordshires, the problems were so acute that their place in 29 Brigade was taken at very short notice by the 1st Battalion of the Royal Northumberland Fusiliers, which was stationed at Warminster in Wiltshire.[22] As the officers and men arrived, TFH and the Regimental Sergeant Major, E.J. (Jack) Hobbs, sorted them into their companies and departments – seeing fair play among the predatory company commanders. Thereafter, an intensive programme of training was needed to shake down the amalgam of regular soldiers, National Servicemen and reservists – forming them into cohesive companies and platoons. Major Digby Grist remembered that 'the battalion was like a disturbed ant-hill'.[23]

There were also the attached arms and services to be taken into account: the usual detachments of REME mechanics, RAMC doctor and orderlies, Army Physical Training Corps (APTC) instructor, Royal Army Pay Corps (RAPC) paymaster and clerks, and Army Catering Corps (ACC) cooks; plus a Royal Signals rear link detachment. Once this was completed, Carne and his Second-in-Command, Major Richard Butler, put the battalion through a rigorous series of live-firing exercises on Stanford Training Area in Norfolk, helped by a special team which included US officers and men. With them were detachments from other units in 29 Brigade: the 8th Hussars; 70 Field Battery of 45 Field Regiment RA; and 55 Field Squadron RE. There were new units too, as the brigade had been reinforced by C Squadron of the 7th Royal Tanks, 11 Light Anti-Aircraft Battery RA, and service support units that included a Mobile Bath and Laundry Unit![24] These exercises were so realistic that the Gun Position officer (GPO) of 70 Field Battery, 'almost went grey' when he discovered how close his shells were dropping on an 'attack' o Frog Hill.[25]

With this training period over, the battalion dispersed for a short embarkation leave – after which the Chief of the Imperial General Staff, Field Marshal Sir William 'Bill' Slim,[*] inspected the troops. The advance party, led by Richard Butler and including Digby Grist, then left for Korea by air to join US units in the line and gain first-hand experience of the conditions of the war.[26]

The main body moved to Southampton and on 2 October embarked on the troopship *Empire Windrush*.[27] The outward voyage was devoted to physical training, weapon training,

---

[*]   Field Marshal William Joseph 'Bill' Slim, 1st Viscount Slim KG GCB GCMG GCVO GBE DSO MC KStJ (1891-1970) saw active service in both the First and Second World Wars and was wounded in action three times. During the Second World War he commanded the Fourteenth Army and then 11th Army Group in India and Burma. After the war he became the first British officer who had served in the Indian Army to be appointed Chief of the Imperial General Staff. From 1953 to 1959 he was the 13th Governor-General of Australia.

FM Slim visits 1 Glosters before departure for Korea; from left are Slim, Carne, TFH, and Sam Weller. (GLRRM 05488.2)

tactical lectures – as Robert Holles remembered, 'There had been no rest from the Bay of Biscay to the China Sea'.[28]

TFH's outward voyage was, however, interrupted. At Suez, as the ship was preparing to pass through the canal, he was summoned home by air. Pat had given birth to their second son, Kerin, on 3 October but the child had died only a week later, on 10 October. TFH hurried home to be with Pat, who was not unnaturally deeply upset (although people did not show their feelings as they do nowadays). A hasty funeral was arranged and held before TFH left once more, again in a hurry, to rejoin the ship a week later at Colombo.[29]

It was not until 10 November that the ship docked at what was left of the port of Pusan in Korea, to be met by a reception committee of Korean girls in dazzling silk kimonos and a group of South Korean officials.[30] TFH however cast a critical eye over the broken, filthy train sitting in the marshalling yards of Pusan that was to carry the battalion to its destination: Suwon. By 0400 hrs the following morning, the train had been cleaned up and packed with soldiers and their gear. With a heave and a strain, the engine slowly steamed away from the station.

*   *   *

While 29 Brigade had been in training and transit, the Americans had been fully engaged. The Battle of Osan was their first significant engagement of the war, involving Task Force (TF) Smith – a small forward element of battalion size from the 24th Infantry Division. On 5 July 1950 T.F. Smith attacked the North Koreans at Osan, but without weapons capable of destroying the North Korean tanks. The attack failed and out of the 540 men engaged, 180 were killed, wounded, or taken prisoner. The KPA continued its advance south – pushing back US forces at Pyongtaek, Chonan and Chochiwon – forcing the 24th Infantry Division to retreat to Taejon, which the KPA captured, inflicting severe losses on the 24th Division: 3,602 dead and wounded, and 2,962 captured –[31] including the Commanding General, Major-General William F. Dean.[*]

---

[*]   William Frishe Dean, Snr (1899-1981) had served in the Second World War. He received the Medal of Honor for his actions on 20-21 July 1950 during the Battle of Taejon. Dean was the highest ranking American officer

By August, the KPA had pushed back the ROK Army and the Eighth (US) Army to an area around Pusan, which enclosed about 10 percent of Korea in a line partially defined by the Nakdong River. In the resulting Battle of the Pusan Perimeter, from August to September 1950, the US Army withstood sustained KPA attacks while the USAF and the US Naval Air Forces disrupted the enemy's logistic supplies with up to 40 ground support sorties every day – destroying bridges, halting daylight road and rail traffic, hitting logistic depots, petroleum refineries and ports. Meanwhile, US Headquarters in Japan dispatched a continuous stream of soldiers, equipment and supplies to the beleaguered defenders of the perimeter. Tank battalions deployed to Korea directly from San Francisco to Pusan – which was, by a fortunate chance, the largest port in Korea. By late August, the Pusan Perimeter had 500 combat-ready medium tanks available. By early September, ROK Army and UN forces outnumbered the KPA by 180,000 to 100,000.

Against the rested and re-armed UN forces, the KPA were increasingly undermanned and poorly supplied; and they lacked naval and air support. To relieve the Pusan Perimeter, MacArthur devised an amphibious assault at Inchon on the western coast, well over 100 miles (160 kilometres) behind the KPA lines. On 6 July, he had ordered Major-General Hobart R. Gay,[*] Commanding General of the 1st (US) Cavalry Division, to move his division to Korea; the division embarked at Yokohama in Japan to reinforce the 24th Infantry Division inside the Pusan Perimeter. This was the pre-cursor to the move on Inchon, which had to receive approval from the President. Once he had this, MacArthur activated X (US) Corps, under General Edward Almond,[†] which consisted of 40,000 men of the 1st Marine Division and the 7th Infantry Division along with 8,600 ROK Army soldiers.[32] The attack was launched on 15 September and was completely successful. As soon as the build-up had reached sufficient strength to break out from its bridgehead, the 1st Cavalry Division began its northward advance from the Pusan Perimeter to link up with the 7th Infantry Division at Osan – thus threatening to trap the main KPA force in southern Korea.

On 25 September, Seoul was recaptured by South Korean forces. American air raids were causing heavy damage to the KPA, destroying many of its tanks and much of its artillery. North Korean troops in the south, instead of withdrawing north, rapidly disintegrated – leaving their capital of Pyongyang vulnerable. On 29 September MacArthur restored the government of the Republic of Korea under Syngman Rhee. On 30 September, Secretary of Defense George Marshall sent a crucial private message to MacArthur, which said: 'We want you to feel unhampered tactically and strategically to proceed north of the 38th parallel'.[33]

On 1 October 1950, the ROK Army began its pursuit of the KPA north of the 38th parallel and MacArthur issued a statement demanding the KPA's unconditional surrender. Six days later, on 7 October – with UN authorisation – his forces followed the ROK Army northwards.[34] X Corps landed at Wonsan in south-eastern North Korea and Riwon in north-eastern North Korea, already captured by ROK forces. The Eighth US Army and the ROK Army drove up western Korea and captured Pyongyang on 19 October 1950. By the end of the month, UN forces had captured 135,000 KPA prisoners of war.[35]

---

captured by the North Koreans during the war.
[*]   Lieutenant-General Hobart Raymond 'Hap' Gay (1894-1983).
[†]   Edward Mallory 'Ned' Almond (1892-1979) had served in the Great War, the Second World War and the occupation of Japan.

* * *

The Glosters' train made a slow, uncertain progress on its 200-mile journey up the Korean Peninsula through Taegu and Taejon, and past the Naktong River. 'At each small station platform the train was surrounded by hordes of ragged children and emaciated old women, begging for food, fighting each other to collect the scraps of biscuits and chocolate which were showered from the carriage windows'.[36]

On the third day, 14 November, the train heaved itself into the remains of Suwon Station to be greeted by the smiling faces of Richard Butler, Anthony ('Jumbo') Wilson, Sergeant Reid and the rest of the advance party. From there, the men were moved into the buildings of the Agricultural College, which was their first base in Korea. Here, the battalion prepared itself for the war as autumn turned to winter and the weather turned colder, much colder, and windier. Carne soon had the battalion out on a short refresher exercise called *First Frost* but even before this was over, orders came in on 24 November for another move: this time to Kaesong for anti-guerrilla operations.[37] These operations turned out to be nothing more exciting that guarding key points and bridges until 30 November, when a series of sweeps and searches were launched around Sibyon-ni – which reminded TFH of his days in Palestine – until C Company met a North Korean unit on the Tusan Road, where the battalion suffered its first dead and wounded.[38]

It was at Sibyon-ni that news came in of a major change in events: the entry of the Chinese 'Volunteer' Army into the war. The UN forces' success thus far had, ironically, very nearly been their undoing. As early as 20 August 1950, Chinese Premier Zhou Enlai told the UN General Assembly that 'Korea is China's neighbour ... The Chinese people cannot but be concerned about a solution of the Korean question'.

China in effect warned that in being seen to safeguard Chinese national security, they would intervene against the UN Command in Korea.[39] Truman however interpreted the message as 'a bald attempt to blackmail the UN', and dismissed it.[40] Chinese leaders had debated in early October whether or not to send Chinese troops into Korea. There was considerable resistance among many leaders, including senior generals. However, Mao and Zhou strongly supported intervention; they carried the day. On 8 October 1950, Mao Tse Tung re-designated the PLA's North East Frontier Force as the Chinese People's Volunteer Army, or PVA –[41] thus beginning the fiction of an impromptu, spontaneous action by Chinese soldiers, out with the control of the Chinese Government or the Communist Party. To commit Chinese forces openly as an expeditionary force of the nation would have caused a great many difficulties – including the danger of a formal state of war with the USA.[42]

The PVA's 13th Army Group crossed the Yalu River, the border between North Korea and China, in secret on 19 October and launched its First Phase Offensive on 25 October – attacking the advancing UN forces near the border in a move designed first and foremost to prevent the UN forces from closing up to the border and destroying what was left of the North Korean armies.[43] The overall plan was for a first operational echelon of four armies to advance to blocking positions: the Forty-second Army to cross the border in the west, at Manpojin; behind it would be the Thirty-eighth Army, moving on Huichon. The Fortieth Army would move from Sinui-ji towards Pukchin and the Thirty-ninth would follow it. The second operational echelon, the Sixty-sixth and Fiftieth Armies, would remain behind these forces and support armoured elements operating on the west coast.[44] This move, made solely by China, changed the attitude of the Soviet Union. Twelve days after Chinese troops entered the war, Stalin gave approval for the Soviet Air Force to provide air cover. After mauling the ROK II Corps at the Battle of Onjong, the first engagement between Chinese and US forces took place on 1 November 1950. Deep inside North Korea, the PVA Thirty-ninth Army encircled and attacked the US 8th Cavalry Regiment from the north, north-west and west – over-running the defensive position in the Battle of Unsan. This surprise attack resulted in the UN forces retreating to the Ch'ongch'on River, while the Chinese, unexpectedly, disappeared into the mountains after their victory. Because of this, the UN Command was not convinced that the Chinese had intervened directly. Indeed, on 15 October 1950, Truman and MacArthur met at Wake Island and here, MacArthur speculated there was little risk of Chinese intervention in Korea, as their window of opportunity for aiding the KPA had closed. He was very, very, wrong.

*   *   *

At 0800 hrs on 30 November, the Glosters were relieved and ordered north[45] as part of a new UN offensive called, with deep irony as it turned out, *Home-by-Christmas*. The battalion group arrived just south of the North Korean capital of Pyongyang, where they left their train and climbed aboard a convoy of American trucks driven by black soldiers for a dusty, hair-raising drive over the Taedong River and on northwards, stopping only for a short lunch of tea and 'compo' rations – * during which TFH recalled sitting with Jack Hobbs, 'exchanging pieces of [tinned fruit] cake and [processed] cheese, almost unidentifiable as such for their covering of dust …'[46]

In the late afternoon of 30 November the battalion was dropped in a pleasant valley under pine-clad hills. Here, the men began to dig their first defensive positions and prepare for the arrival of the Chinese, for already, the offensive had turned bad: the Chinese had been waiting in ambush with their Second Phase Offensive. On 25 November on the western front, the PVA 13th Army Group attacked and overran the ROK II Corps at the Battle of the Ch'ongch'on River and then hammered the 2nd (US) Infantry Division on the UN right flank. For 1 Glosters, however, preparations continued undisturbed until at noon on 2 December, orders came in to withdraw. The main body of the UN force had already withdrawn and 29 Brigade was to act as rear guard. The realisation dawned that the Glosters were on their own, without transport, and in the dark. Snow was falling as Carne gave the orders for the companies to begin falling back on foot.[47] This was the start of the Eighth Army's retreat – the longest in US Army history – and it was made possible by successful, but hugely

---

* Composite, or 'Compo' rations came in boxes for four men (a tank crew) or 10 men (an infantry section) and in some cases, individual boxes. Each wooden case contained enough food for the required number of men for one day. Each day's ration consisted of: breakfast, usually compressed bacon and an oatmeal block; a mid-day snack of hard-tack biscuit, margarine, jam and processed cheese; and supper of tinned meat and vegetables, or stew, or meat pudding plus tinned fruit, rice or sweet pudding. There was also dried soup, tea, condensed milk, boiled sweets and chocolate, cigarettes and, the most essential: hard lavatory paper stamped with the Ordnance mark! Bread and fresh food were provided as a supplement, because Compo was calorie-based, not vitamin-based, having been developed between the wars from Arctic sledging rations. If eaten without fresh supplements it would therefore, in the medium term, cause scurvy.

costly, rear-guard action by the Turkish Brigade near Kunuri which delayed the PVA attack for two days (27-29 November). Casualties mattered far more to the UN forces than to the Chinese. For one thing, the Chinese simply did not value individual lives in the same way as Western armies did – nor did they invest anything like the same amount in the training, equipment or welfare of their soldiers. For another, they had almost limitless manpower close at hand. By 30 November, the PVA 13th Army Group had managed to expel the US Eighth Army from north-west Korea.

After a thoroughly unpleasant march, 1 Glosters Battalion Group reached its new concentration area where, with a brew of hot tea inside them, the men got what sleep they could in their blankets on the cold ground; but the withdrawal was not over. On the night of 4-5 December 1950, the main body of I (US) Corps had crossed over the Taedong River towards its new defence line – leaving 29 Brigade as rear guard. 29 Brigade too had to cross the river which it did, out of contact with the enemy advanced guard; the Glosters crossing last of all. As each company reported in to TFH at Pyongyang Airfield, the men climbed aboard American trucks and drove off southwards. As they did so, the last bridges over the river were blown on Carne's orders by the Sappers. Thus the UN forces abandoned the North Korean capital, captured in triumph just a few weeks before.

The Glosters concentrated once more at the small town of Sinmak, about 30 miles north of the 38th parallel, and then moved into a defensive position at the extreme west of the UN line on the bare hills above Chonsoktu-ri in what the troops called 'the Valley of Death'[48] – but there was still no contact with the enemy. On 11 December, the corps moved further south, beyond the 38th parallel, with 29 Brigade again acting as rear guard. The Eighth Army had retreated from the north faster than it had advanced. UN morale hit rock bottom when Commanding General Walton Walker was killed on 23 December 1950 in a road traffic accident.* However, in north-east Korea, X Corps had managed to damage the PVA 9th Army Group badly and had, by 19 December, established a defensive perimeter at the port city of Hungnam. X Corps was forced, however, to evacuate Hungnam almost immediately in order to reinforce badly-hit US formations further south.[49]

A week later, the Glosters were back once more at Kaesong, but from there they moved to a leaguer position just north of Seoul. Here they went into Corps Reserve as the battle at last stabilised. For a while, almost peacetime conditions prevailed, with baths, a cinema, a NAAFI mobile canteen, regular mail – and preparations for Christmas. Military duties continued at low intensity, but there was word of yet another withdrawal south of the Han River since the Chinese armies were building up along the Imjin. To be on the safe side, Christmas was celebrated on 24 December:

> All day the cooks slaved with their ovens improvised out of petrol-drums let into the clay, roasting the turkeys which had been thoughtfully provided with the previous day's rations. The Sergeant Major made a rum punch from tins of American fruit-cocktail and carefully conserved rum rations. Oranges were also provided. The feast was to be followed by a 'party', and a supply of tinned beer …[50]

---

*   Walton Harris Walker (1889-1950) served in the Vera Cruz expedition and in both World Wars.

In the event, the 25th was quiet – as was the following week. Major Richard Butler, the Second-in-Command of the Glosters, was invalided home sick around this time and Digby Grist, commanding Support Company, took his place. Grist recalled that: 'I don't think there's an instruction book on how to be a Second-in-Command in a battalion on active operations; if there is I haven't found it'. TFH had therefore given him some advice: 'Just keep out of the Colonel's hair and yet in touch with the situation … You have your own set-up at F Echelon* which takes quite a load off the back of Battalion Headquarters'.[51]

Then, early on 1 January 1951, the Chinese attacked across the Imjin in their Third Phase Offensive – also known as the 'Chinese New Year's Offensive' – and fell on the 1st (Republic of Korea) Infantry Division.[52]

The Corps Reserve was alerted at 0545 hrs and after several changes of plan, occupied a new defensive position that night. On 3 January, the Chinese attacked the positions of 1 RUR and 1 RNF, but made no progress in spite of inflicting at least 100 casualties on the RUR – indeed their attack was thrown back with great loss, as the corps main body completed its move. The Chinese favoured night attacks in which UN positions were encircled and then assaulted by superior numbers of troops. The attacks were accompanied by trumpets and gongs, which were used both for tactical communications and to disorientate the enemy. That night, 3-4 January 1951, 29 Brigade was also ordered to pull back south of the Han. They did so – leaving another capital city behind them; taking up new positions to the south of Pyongtaek. The Chinese New Year's Offensive had again overwhelmed the UN forces, allowing the PVA and KPA to capture Seoul for the second time. These setbacks prompted MacArthur to consider using tactical nuclear weapons against Chinese or North Korean territory. There was a sudden, great, fear among Western Powers that the most modern military forces of the civilised world might be defeated by the peasant infantry of China.[53]

Following the death of General Walton Walker, Lieutenant-General Matthew Ridgway[†] had assumed command of the US Eighth Army on 26 December – just in time to see the PVA and the KPA offensive. UN forces retreated to Suwon in the west, Wonju in the centre, and the area north of Samcheok in the east; here, under Ridgway's leadership, the front was stabilised and held.[54] The Glosters, along with the rest of the UN forces, watched as hordes of ragged, frightened, weary refugees moved through their positions in a seemingly endless stream of human misery – but the PVA had by now outrun its supplies and thus was unable to press on beyond Seoul as food, ammunition, and equipment had to be carried forward at night, on foot, and bicycle from the border on the Yalu River to the three battle lines. Finding that the PVA had pulled back to shorten the line of communication, Ridgway ordered a reconnaissance-in-force on 5 February 1951, which became Operation *Roundup* – a full-scale X Corps advance under the UN Command's airsuperiority.

---

*   Grist is mistaken; he means A Echelon. An infantry battalion was organised into F Echelon, the fighting companies and support platoons; A Echelon, the transport and supply elements under the Quarter Master that provided immediate replenishment and reinforcement; and B Echelon, which held the bulk of the battalion's reserves of spare parts, spare equipment, ammunition, rations, vehicles and so on – as well as the field record office.

†   Matthew Bunker Ridgway (1895-1993) held several major commands and was most famous for resurrecting the UN war effort in Korea. His long and prestigious military career was recognised by the award of the Presidential Medal of Freedom on 12 May 1986 by President Ronald Reagan.

29 Infantry Brigade, in reserve, moved steadily forward during Operation *Roundup*; first to Suwon, then to the tiny hamlet of Kumnyangjang-ni and then to the village of Pabalmak. On arrival there on 11 February, Carne was told to relieve a battalion of the 1st (US) Cavalry Division. This relief was completed by noon on 12 February; the Glosters finding themselves in possession of a bare, nameless, hill from which they watched an American attack on the nearby Hill 350. That night, Chinese patrols probed the Glosters' positions but were repulsed. Opposing their further advance in front of the Han River lay a strong force of Chinese infantry, well dug in on the slopes of a hill named Hill 327 and re-christened 'Gloucester'. On 13 February, Carne was told that this was to be the Glosters' objective while immediately before their attack, a regiment of the 1st (US) Cavalry Division would attack the feature immediately to their east – code-named 'Cheltenham'. Preparations were temporarily interrupted that night by a local Chinese counter-attack, but on the 14th, preparatory air-strikes and artillery fire began as the weather deteriorated into lashing rain, hail and mist.[55] At 1030 hrs on 16 February the assaulting companies of the Glosters moved forward: D Company on the left under Major 'Lakhri' Wood and C Company on the right under Major Charles Walwyn, as the Americans on their right made slow progress in the face of heavy Chinese fire. Carne, TFH and the battalion's tactical headquarters moved between, and slightly behind, the two leading companies.

There was still no sign of life from the defenders of Hill 327 as the leading companies closed to just 100 yards from the objective. The supporting mortar, artillery and tank fire began to shift ahead of the assault, onto the reverse slope of the hill. Then, from nowhere, or so it seemed, came a hail of rifle fire and grenades.[56] Walwyn was wounded almost immediately.

Men of the Glosters moving up before the attack on Hill 327, supported by *Centurion* tanks of the 8th King's Royal Irish Hussars. (IWM BF 454)

Carne held C Company back and told D to work round to a flank, which they did – gradually clearing the Chinese from their bunkers and gaining the summit. C Company under its Second-in-Command, Mardell, also pushed on and they too reached the summit soon after D Company. There still remained many bunkers to be cleared one by one: difficult, as the crest of 'Gloucester' was almost a knife-edge.

By late afternoon the leading companies were approaching the secondary objective: a feature code-named 'Bristol', but it was soon clear that the Chinese had had enough. They had fled – leaving weapons, ammunition, food and equipment where they had been dropped. The final objective, code-named 'Dursley', was taken – again without opposition – by B Company under Major Denis Harding. As night fell, the Glosters began to dig in, but not for long. The next morning, A Company under Major Pat Angier, with a squadron of *Centurion* tanks from the 8th Hussars, probed forward and by 18 February the battalion had advanced 6,000 yards without further enemy contact. As dawn came up, the river lay broad and calm beneath them. Here the Glosters dug in once more until on 23 February, they were relieved by a brigade of the 25th (US) Infantry Division and moved by rail to Inchon.[7]

*   *   *

At about the same time, the PVA counter-attacked once more with its Fourth Phase Offensive and achieved some initial success. However, the offensive was blunted by IX (US) Corps at Chipyong-ni in eight days of grim, close-quarter fighting. Surrounded on all sides, the UN force faced more than 25,000 Chinese communist troops – a force ratio of around 15 to 1.

Centurion tanks firing in support of the attack on Hill 327. (IWMBF 385)

1 Glosters attacking Hill 327. (GLRRM 06956.21)

Before this stand, UN forces had usually retreated in the face of such odds to avoid becoming encircled and thus cut off, but this time they stood and fought. Thanks to Ridgway's influence, the defence was far more cohesive than had been the case before and massive artillery and air power caused huge casualties to the Chinese.

29 Brigade remained in reserve at Inchon during Operation *Ripper*, which began on 7 March 1951 and which once more expelled the PVA and the KPA from Seoul. This was the fourth time that the city had changed hands in one year and it was little more than a ruin; the pre-war population of around 1.5 million had been reduced to 200,000 and the people were suffering from severe shortages of food, fuel, water, medicines and shelter.[58] Chinese and North Korean soldiers began to surrender in their thousands.[59] On 21 March 1951 – ironically, this was 'Back-Badge Day', when the Glosters celebrated their victory in Egypt in 1801 – the Glosters began a move to the Imjin River, where they were to dig in above Uijong-bu under the command of the 3rd (US) Infantry Division. This move was part of a sequence of operations which included *Courageous* (23-28 March 1951) and *Tomahawk* (23 March 1951), which slowly depleted the PVA and KPA forces. UN forces advanced to 'Line *Kansas*', which in the west, where 29 Brigade was located, followed the Imjin River north-east to the 38th parallel.

The Glosters' position on Line *Kansas* covered a rough road leading south through the hills, which had been used less than three months earlier as a main axis of advance by the Chinese. This road had been improved and strengthened by the UN engineers earlier in the campaign. Here they remained until 1 April when they moved further north, up this road, to the Imjin River itself: the forward edge of Line *Kansas*. Here they relieved a Filipino battalion, but there were so few troops to cover the line that there was a gap of three miles between the Glosters' left and the nearest ROK battalion, and two miles from the Glosters' right to 1 RNF. The Glosters, isolated as they were, were ordered to deny the use of the road to the enemy.[6]

Carne laid the battalion out with A Company forward left on what was known as the Castle site – a high point west of the village of Choksong. D Company – temporarily under the command of Captain M.G. Harvey, since Wood was away with a leave party in Japan – was placed on a hill south-east of this same village. B Company watched the approach to the right flank; C Company was in depth above Battalion Headquarters, which was located where the road crossed a small stream as it entered the hills. The open valley mouth facing the river was held by the Corps of Drums under WO II Phil Buss – the Battalion Headquarters' Defence Platoon – and a prominent hill to the west of this position was held by Carne's only remaining troops, the Assault Pioneer Platoon under 'Spike' Pike. Each rifle company also had a section of two *Vickers* medium machine guns; a mortar fire control party to direct the fire of the battalion's platoon of six three-inch mortars; and a forward observation officer from the Royal Artillery who could bring in artillery fire and air support. The Artillery Battery Commander, Major Guy Ward, stayed with Carne in his tactical headquarters, from where he

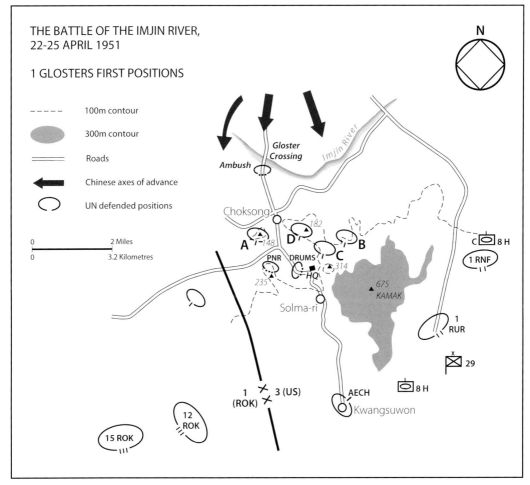

The Battle of the Imjin River, 22-25 April 1951: 1 Glosters' first positions.

could co-ordinate fire support across the whole of the battalion area – calling if necessary not only the whole of 45 Field Regiment and 170 Mortar Battery in support of 29 Brigade, but also whatever guns of 3rd (US) Infantry Division were in range and uncommitted.

This was the best that Carne could do with limited resources: a frontage of seven miles (11 kilometres) and a depth of five miles (eight kilometres). This was more than twice what a battalion would usually expect to hold given the weapon ranges and tactical doctrine of the day. The gaps between the Glosters' companies would be covered by direct fire; the gaps between the Glosters and their flanking units would have to be covered by observed indirect fire or by aircraft. The real difficulty was night. In 1951, infantry brigades and battalions had none of the technology available to a modern formation and relied therefore on illumination from mortar or artillery star-shells to assist the Mark 1 human eyeballs on general issue to all soldiers – nor was there much in the way of defence stores: barbed wire, pickets, and mines. It was eight days before the first truck-load of kit reached the Glosters, and 17 days before the second load.

A vigorous patrol programme of the sort that TFH remembered well from his days in Italy soon established that the ford across the Imjin, known as 'Gloster Crossing', was intact – it was in fact an underwater bridge, marked by buoys,[61] used for centuries by the Koreans – and that the Chinese had established a defensive position to cover it on the far bank. These defences, however, proved to be unoccupied. It seemed that, weakened by the weight of UN firepower

Looking east from Point 235 towards Point 314, Imjin River. (GLRRM 05449.6)

Imjin battlefield looking south-east over D Company towards B Company. (GLRRM 05475.3)

Bend in the Imjin River with A Company's position on the left. (GLRRM 05475.7)

Positions overlooking Gloster Crossing on the Imjin River. (GLRRM 06956.27)

and the severity of the winter weather – and unable to maintain their supplies – the Chinese main body had withdrawn in secret as early as March, unobserved and un-pursued.

At this point, on 11 April 1951, President Harry Truman relieved MacArthur of his command for reasons that are well known and need not be rehearsed here. Ridgway was appointed Supreme Commander, Korea in his place and General James Van Fleet[*] assumed command of the US Eighth Army. Ridgway issued orders to hold Line *Kansas*. However, the Chinese Commander-in-Chief, Peng Teh-Huai,[†] had no intention of remaining on the defensive. Having replenished and refurbished his forces and with winter past, he gave orders for a new offensive: the Fifth Phase Offensive, also known as the 'Chinese Spring Offensive'. This attack involved three field armies with approximately 700,000 men, whose first fury was to fall upon I (US) Corps, of which 29 Brigade formed a part. From 13 April onwards, reconnaissance units began to infiltrate between UN positions – gathering intelligence and seeking out weaknesses.

---

[*]   James Alward Van Fleet (1892-1992) served in both World Wars. He commanded one of the assaulting regiments on Utah Beach on 6 June 1944.

[†]   Later Marshal Peng The-Huai (Peng Dehuai) (1898-1974) had enlisted in the army of a warlord as a private soldier, fought for the Kuomintang against the Japanese and later joined the Communists. He served as China's Defense Minister from 1954 to 1959.

In parallel with these Chinese preparations, UN task groups were being pushed forward to make contact with the enemy by reconnaissance-in-force. Digby Grist had been summoned to the forward headquarters of 1 Glosters on 19 April when TFH had called him up, saying: 'The Colonel's got a job for you. You're to bring your gear up as you'll be here for one or two nights'.[62] His task was to lead two companies of the Glosters which, with two squadrons of the 8th Hussars, on a 12-mile (20 kilometre) foray. 'All that day Guy [Lowther] with his tanks and the Gloucesters [*sic*] on foot searched for the enemy. Not a trace!'[63]

However, on 21 April the main Chinese advance began. Moving towards the Glosters was the Sixty-third Army with three divisions – the 187th, 188th and 189th – whose orders were to open the road towards Seoul which the Glosters were tasked to deny them. To their right, facing 12th and 15th ROK Regiments on the Glosters' left flank was the Sixty-fourth Army's 192nd Division. The Glosters were about to be attacked by up to four divisions – a comparative force ratio in men of around 70 to 1 and in guns and mortars of around 8 to 1.[*]

Allied intelligence sources picked up indications of the impending attack and word was passed down the line. The forward units were therefore not caught unprepared when, on 22 April, the first signs of enemy movement were seen north of the Imjin. Carne and the IO, Henry Cabral, went forward to observe what was developing. TFH, who had been back to Brigade Headquarters, joined them: 'It was no great push as yet: only very small parties … but how very odd that, after concealing their hand for so long, they should alert us by sending down daylight patrols …'[64]

Whenever the enemy appeared, heavy artillery fire was brought down, but the dug-in companies were told to lie low and maintain concealment. As evening approached, the sense of anticipation grew. As TFH recalled, Carne thought that what was coming was 'the real thing'.[65] Hot food and more ammunition were brought up before dark and at dusk, an ambush was set on the crossing, commanded by Lieutenant Guy ('Guido') Temple.

Three hours later, the Chinese made their first attempt to cross the river at the ford. Temple's platoon destroyed this and the next three attempts,[66] but after a lull, faced by two Chinese battalions, they came under enormous pressure even though every Allied gun and mortar within range was engaged.[67] At Battalion Headquarters, Captain Richard Reeve-Tucker, the Signals Officer, came in with a message from Temple: 'They're still trying to cross in hordes, Sir', he said to Carne.

'In another five minutes he [Temple] reckons they'll be out of ammunition'.

Carne looked at TFH and Guy Ward. 'Tell him to start withdrawing in three minutes', he told TFH.

'Guy, I'm going to ask you for one last concentration, and then start dropping them short of Gloster Crossing as soon as the patrol is back at the first cutting south of the river'.[68]

The patrol in fact exhausted their ammunition and then threw rocks at the Chinese.

Unknown to Carne, a second Chinese regiment of three battalions was crossing the river one-and-a-half miles (two-and-a-half kilometres) downstream at an unknown, unmarked, underwater bridge. Two of the battalions from this regiment swung eastwards and attacked A Company on the Castle site, while the third attacked D Company:

---

[*] A Chinese division at this date consisted of three regiments of infantry, up to eight batteries of light guns and up to 16 batteries of medium guns and mortars – about 9,000 men and 144 pieces or ordnance.

… hundreds of Chinese soldiers clad in cotton khaki suits; plain, cheap, cotton caps; rubber-soled canvas shoes upon their feet; their shoulders, chests and backs criss-crossed with bandoliers of ammunition; upon their hips, grenades… .Those in the forefront of battle wear steel helmets that are reminiscent of the Japanese.[69]

At the same time, the left flank company of 1 RNF had also been attacked and forced back – opening a gap through which yet another Chinese battalion moved, swung south-west-wards, and attacked B Company of the Glosters. Not long after midnight, therefore, the three forward companies of the battalion were all being hard pressed by a force which outnumbered them at least six-to-one.

Before dawn, Carne moved the command post up to the ridge held by C Company, where RSM Jack Hobbs had built a bunker some days before for just this purpose. It was obvious to Carne that the situation was desperate. As the sun rose, Corporal Walters, one of the signallers who was also TFH's driver/operator, told him that Pat Angier wanted to talk to him.

Angier said, 'I'm afraid we've lost the Castle site. I'm mounting a counter-attack now but I want to know whether to expect to stay here indefinitely or not. If I am to stay on, I must be reinforced as my numbers are getting very low'.[70]

TFH passed this news on to Carne, who was already considering options, but would the Chinese continue to attack in daylight – given the threat of Allied air power? If they did, it would not be long before the Glosters were surrounded.

He spoke briefly to Angier and told him: 'You are to stay there at all costs until further notice'.[71]

This was a harsh order, which Carne knew would condemn many men to death, but unless it was carried out, the Chinese would reinforce their foothold without hindrance and then turn on each company of the Glosters one by one – destroying each in detail.

Angier's response was calm and firm: 'Don't worry about us, we'll be all right'.

The most that TFH could do was to organise a re-supply of ammunition in two *Oxford* carriers, which he sent forward with Henry Cabral. A Company pressed home their counter-attack: Lieutenant Philip Curtis was killed while bombing the Chinese out of a bunker where they had installed a medium machine gun; he was later awarded a posthumous Victoria Cross. Soon afterwards, Angier too was killed. By the time that the Second-in-Command, Captain Terry Waters, got forward, the chance to re-take the Castle had passed. D Company too was under huge pressure and without considerable air support, it would soon be over-run. At 0730 hrs, Brodie gave Carne permission to withdraw the forward positions and, as soon as it became clear that there would be no air support, Carne told A and D Companies to pull back into positions immediately north-west and west of Battalion Headquarters. B Company was ordered back to the hill below the mountain of Kamak-San to the east of the road. Every avail-able gun and mortar fired to cover this move – and the effect on the massed concentrations of Chinese infantry was terrible: their dead and wounded lay in heaps. As TFH later recalled, 'Throughout, the gunners were absolutely excellent. I have never seen such a slaughter as they caused'.[72]

By noon, the Chinese had had enough and a strange calm fell over the battlefield:

The operations map was fitted back into its place … I put my hand to the telephone to tell the remainder of the battalion how our new line stood, taking it from its rest without looking down. For I was looking at the tiny group of marks upon the talc; and as I looked I realised that this was what the Chinese would attack next – to-night![73]

TFH recalled a series of incidents, each clear in their own way, but unclear in their continuity, order and context:

> Colour-Sergeant Buxcey organising his Korean porters with mighty loads for the first of many ascents to the new 'A' Company positions … Captain Bob Hickey, the doctor, working at the Regimental Aid Post, one hand still wet with blood as he turns round… The ambulance cars are filled; the Jeep that Bounden drives has been out time and again with the stretchers on its racks … I remember watching the slow, wind-tossed descent of a helicopter that came down for casualties for whom the winding, bumpy road back south would have meant certain death … Captain Carl Dain, the counter-mortar radar officer came in to say *"I'm sending my vehicles back, except for my Jeep. I've decided to stay with you to make up your numbers of Forward Observation officers …"* That morning the Padre, Sam Davies, said a funeral service for Pat Angier, whose body had been brought back on one of the Oxford carriers by Lieutenant Cabral … but we did not forget the others.[74]

Later that morning, Digby Grist was taking a hard look at what support would be needed for when battle was joined once more. News came in that the rear headquarters and A Echelon – about five miles (eight kilometres) to the rear, was being attacked. Carne sent Grist back at once. Grist made it, but through an ambush, which meant running the gauntlet of fire.[75]

Of the forward companies, B Company had been least engaged and Harding had managed to withdraw to his new position unobserved, so that when the Chinese began to work their way forward again, he was able to slow them down with effective ambushes and heavy artillery fire. The Chinese again pulled back and waited for night. Well they might, for the day's fighting had knocked the fight out of the Chinese 187th Division. It had been intended that the 188th Division would by now have made a passage of lines through the 187th and be enveloping the rest of 29 Infantry Brigade. Instead, the 188th would have to take on the destruction of the Glosters. If they succeeded, the general scheme of manoeuvre could still be achieved by the Chinese.

Just before midnight, renewed Chinese attacks were mounted on B and C Company's positions, repeating the pattern of the previous night: 'Wave after wave of men armed with grenades and sub-machine guns stormed the positions under cover of medium machine guns and mortar fire, were halted by the fire of the defence – small arms, mortars, guns – and driven back with heavy loss'.[76]

After two hours, there was a pause – probably to allow the Chinese to effect an echelon change by bringing up a fresh regiment. At 0245 hrs the attack was renewed. Although the Glosters had inflicted huge loss on the enemy, attrition was beginning to tell on their own numbers – and the attritional odds favoured the Chinese. The Chinese commanders were prepared to sacrifice any number of men to achieve their objective; there was, by contrast, a limit on the casualties that the British could accept and still maintain a cohesive defence.

At 0300 hrs, Paul Mitchell, commanding C Company, rang TFH – who was drinking a cup of coffee to keep himself awake – on the field telephone: 'I'm afraid they've overrun my top

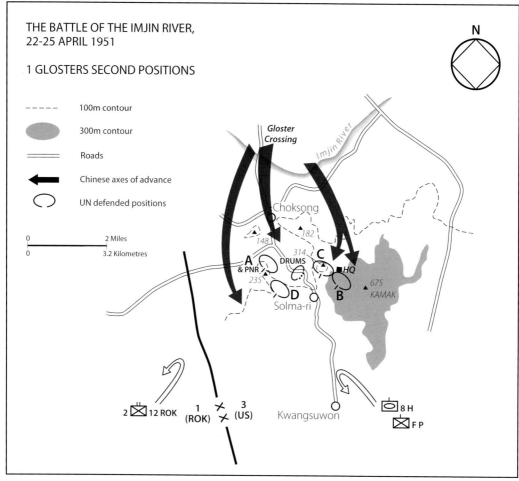

THE BATTLE OF THE IMJIN RIVER,
22-25 APRIL 1951

1 GLOSTERS SECOND POSITIONS

N

- - - - -   100m contour

⬭   300m contour

=====   Roads

◀   Chinese axes of advance

◯   UN defended positions

| 0 | | 2 Miles |
| 0 | | 3.2 Kilometres |

Gloster
Crossing

Imjin River

Choksong

182

148

314   C

A
& PNR   DRUMS   ◼HQ

235   *675*
KAMAK

D   B

Solma-ri

2 ⊠ 12 ROK   1
(ROK)   ✗   3
(US)   Kwangsuwon   ◻ 8 H

⊠ F P

The Battle of the Imjin River, 22-25 April 1951: 1 Glosters' second positions.

position and they're reinforcing hard. They're simply pouring chaps in above us. Let me know what the Colonel wants me to do, will you?'[77]

Carne knew that with the enemy on C Company's position – which was, in effect, the vital ground* – he had to make some rapid changes in the lay-down of the battalion. 'Pack the head-quarters up' he said to TFH, 'and get everyone out of the valley up between "D" Company and the Anti-tank Platoon position. I'm going to withdraw C Company in 10 minutes; and I shall move B over to join us after first light'.[78]

What Carne intended was to shift B and C Companies from the east to the west of the road and close in around Hill 235 – later to be called 'Gloster Hill' – which was still held by the Assault Pioneer Platoon.

---

*   In British doctrine, the vital ground is ground whose possession makes a position tenable or untenable.

Only one-third of C Company's men made it to the new position, but by dawn most of the battalion had re-deployed. TFH and his signallers burned any papers that were not essential and smashed any equipment that was too heavy to move.

Carne made a round of the positions at about 0700 hrs on 24 April, escorted by two regimental policemen and his driver. There was something of a shooting match as he did so and when he returned to the headquarters, his rifle over his shoulder as he filled his pipe, TFH said to him, 'What was all that about, Sir?'

'Oh', Carne replied, 'just shooting away some Chinese'.[79]

Now it was B Company's turn. In contact with the enemy it was a slow and painful process and only 20 men made it. At first, TFH thought the company had been completely wiped out, for the men had had to fight their way through Chinese who had infiltrated into the rear.[80] The sight of them was more than welcome. TFH had meanwhile been in touch with the Brigade Headquarters and he had some cheering news: the Filipinos were on their way forward – and on the following day, an infantry brigade with tanks would come up to relieve the encircled battalion, but before that happened the Glosters had to stay where they were. TFH organised a party to go down to the old headquarters site and collect ammunition, food and radio

Signallers working during the Imjin battle. (GLRRM 05478.2)

batteries, under cover of a smoke screen fired by the gunners. By 0900 hrs, the party had made it back, heavily loaded.[81]

The relief column, however, made little progress as the Chinese had already infiltrated in strength. Tanks from the 8th Hussars were sent forward in support, but even so, the column could not break through. As if to confirm to Carne that he had scaled a mountain of dung and failed to take a fly-swat, Brigadier Tom Brodie came through on the radio to tell him that if the Glosters did not hold their position, the rest of 3rd (US) Infantry Division – including 29 Infantry Brigade – would be cut off by the Chinese advance. Carne answered, 'I understand the position quite clearly. What I must make clear to you is that my command is no longer an effective fighting force. If it is required that we stay here, in spite of this, we shall continue to hold. But I wish to make known the nature of my position'.[82]

As TFH recalled:

> I heard the Brigadier's voice in the head-phones again. I could tell he did not like committing us to such a desperate task. He said he realised how things stood with us, but the job had to be done; and we were the only ones who could do it … Biting on the stem of my empty pipe, I began to reflect on the day's events and the coming battle[83]

Carne and Harding on the Imjin position. (GLRRM 06956.16)

Carne had about 350 fighting men available, including lightly wounded. He had little ammunition, radio batteries were running out and once darkness fell, the enemy would be able to traffic the road below them. Brodie knew all this, but insisted that the Glosters remain where they were in order that the Chinese should commit forces against them that might otherwise reinforce their attacks elsewhere. Lieutenant-General Frank Milburn, commanding I (US) Corps, knew it too; not that this made Carne's task any easier. TFH made what use he could of the remaining radio battery power by arranging an emergency re-supply by *Auster* aircraft that night, and a full replenishment by *Fairchild* the next morning.

The afternoon passed slowly and as darkness drew in, so Carne closed the battalion's perimeter in more tightly around the summit of Hill 235.[84] A Company was on the north-west, D on the east, B and C south and the support platoons to the south-west. Headquarters was sited between A and Support Companies. The summit was generally bare of cover and the ground rocky. Digging was not practicable, so the men made rock *sangars*. They were apprehensive, fearful yet determined – and above all, confident in their CO, who had been among them a good deal all day: quiet, unshakeable, implacable. He was, as Digby Grist remembered, 'a very special sort of man. We in the Gloucesters [*sic*] already knew this and the whole world was to know it before long. He was a man of deep thought and few words'.[85]

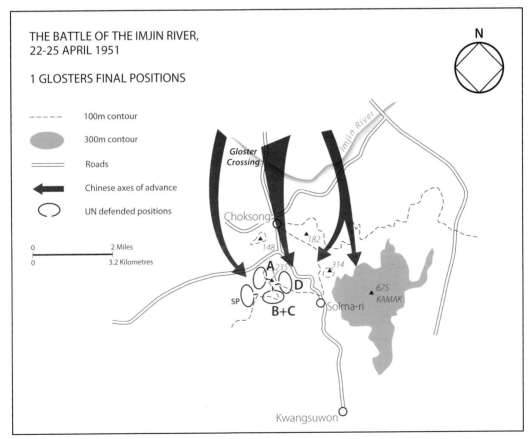

The Battle of the Imjin River, 22-25 April 1951: 1 Glosters' final positions.

The summit of Gloster Hill after the battle; A Company's final position is on the far left of the hill top. (GLRRM 05449.7)

Intelligence sources later said that the Chinese lost 4,000 men during the crossing of the Imjin up to the night of 24 April – but they were ready to lose more.

At 2045 hrs, the Glosters detected a new approach. Immediately the artillery began firing on pre-registered defensive (DF) fire tasks but even so, hundreds of Chinese infantry got into the Glosters' perimeter – blowing bugles and whistles, shouting commands, as they tried to overwhelm the defence. Slowly, though, they were driven back or killed. Three hours later, they were back again, blowing trumpets and bugles.

'It will be a long time before I want to hear a cavalry trumpet playing after this', said Carne to TFH.

'It would serve them right, sir', he replied, 'if we confused them by playing our own bugles. I wonder what direction they'd go if they heard 'Defaulters' played!'

TFH called Drum-Major Buss and asked him if he had a bugle; of course he did, in his haversack.

'Well play it, Drum-Major', TFH said.

So Buss played 'Reveille', 'Defaulters', 'Cookhouse', 'Officers Dress for Dinner', 'Orderly Sergeants to the Regimental Sergeant Major' and all the rest.[86]

As the notes died away, at last, there was a silence. Surprised, confused, perhaps fearing a counter-attack, the Chinese paused – but it was a long night, 'one of the longest in the history of war'.[87]

The Chinese were back again, mostly from the north, soon after dawn. A Company, attacked seven times in all during that night,[88] was driven back at last – reduced to a single officer and less than 30 men. TFH went forward to take command of what was left:

> … there is nothing left for me to do at Battalion Headquarters just now. Here we are … the gallant little body of A Company that has had two nights of battle as I have never seen before … we have been pushed off Point 235 … we must go back to it.[89]

TFH knew that if the counter-attack was to succeed, it would have to be put in before the Chinese had had time to establish themselves. He made an immediate impact on the men, re-manning trenches, getting casualties evacuated and re-establishing fire superiority over the enemy. The enemy, although checked, did not remain inactive for long and they were now only 40 yards away. Three more Chinese attacks were beaten off; then, gathering up the men and a few volunteers who came forward to join in, TFH led them forward at the run in his planned counter-attack – a distance of only perhaps 30 yards. The Chinese did not stand and fight, but fled. In later life, when he was a Lieutenant-General, his ADC asked him how exactly he had motivated the men to return to the attack. He said that there was no need for shouting; he had simply passed on quiet words of encouragement – explaining that the situation would be better for everyone if they could get back onto the company position. The men were obviously fearful, some disorientated, but no heavy hand was needed – just the knowledge that they were going to do this together.[90]

Quickly, TFH disposed his few men to cover all the likely approaches, as he was sure the enemy would soon be back. At 0745 hrs, the Chinese flooded forward once more. TFH asked the Forward Observation Officer, Captain Ronnie Washbrook, to bring down fire right on their own heads. It worked, but the Chinese immediately began to regroup: 'Looking at my watch, I see that what seemed an hour's action took but three minutes …'[91]

With some aircraft now available, Washbrook brought down a series of napalm strikes, followed by cannon runs, on the northern slopes. Six pairs of F-80 aircraft attacked, forcing the Chinese to pull back.[92] In later life, he was asked how he had felt, with his deeply held Christian convictions, in the aftermath of the napalm strike – having seen many hundreds of the enemy burned to cinders. He recalled that in spite of the horror of the moment – and the results of the strike were indeed horrible and deeply affecting – he had felt chiefly satisfaction that the position had been held. The enemy were soldiers – and like all soldiers, took their chance in war. He never, he said, lost any sleep over the matter.[93]

Soon afterwards, TFH was summoned back to Battalion Headquarters. When he got there, Carne told him that news had come in from Brigade Headquarters. The whole division was under huge pressure and was falling back towards Uijong-bu. There would be no relief column after all. The Glosters were to fight their way back with as much artillery fire support as could be given. Carne therefore gave rapid orders, then looked at the RMO, saying 'Bob, I am afraid we shall have to leave the wounded behind'.

Hickey replied without hesitation, 'Very well, Sir. I quite understand the position'.[94] He remained with the wounded, along with Padre Sam Davies and the RAP staff – who were all taken prisoner.

The withdrawal was scheduled for 1000 hrs; everything that might be of use to the enemy was to be destroyed before then. Just before the due time, Carne said to TFH, 'Let Sam Weller

Chaplain Sam Davies conducting a service just before the Imjin battle opened. TFH is in the
left centre, identifiable by his bald head. (GLRRM 05456.3)

[the Support Company Commander] know that I have just been told by the brigadier that the
guns are unable to support us – the gun lines are under attack themselves. Our orders are quite
simple; every man to make his own way back'.[95]

This is hard indeed to credit. Even if the whole of 45 Regiment had been attacked, there must
have been other guns within range – and it was known that the Glosters were isolated. TFH
passed the word, and soon officers and men were hurrying down the slopes in the sunlight.
They had held an impossible position for three nights and two days against enormous odds.
Brodie wrote in the Brigade Headquarters' log, 'No-one but the Glosters could have done it'.[96]

Carne later said of the affair that 'I hope I never have to fight a battle again like that one.
But if I did I would get the same men'.[97]

A Company was to be the first to move, but there were so few men that TFH rejoined
Battalion Headquarters – leaving the company to its one remaining subaltern. There was little
food, no water and precious little ammunition and everywhere, men were destroying equipment that would have to be abandoned, so as to deny it to the enemy. At 1000 hrs, A Company
moved off, followed by the other companies in turn. The long ridge two miles (three kilometres) south of Gloster Hill was held by the Chinese and this blocked the Glosters' direct line
of retreat south or east towards the main UN positions and the initial direction of travel was,
therefore, south-west.

TFH had stayed as long as possible with Hickey and now he ran down the hillside – catching
up with the rear of Support Company and Battalion Headquarters. They turned towards the
saddle at the head of the valley; once over this, they should find cover. The valley narrowed
and suddenly, from high up, machine-gun fire blurted out – but not into the moving column;

The Regimental Aid Post after the Imjin battle. (GLRRM 05449.3)

this was fire that quite clearly was meant to send a message: 'you are exposed; we are concealed and you are in our sights'.[98]

The column moved on; the fire came down again – closer this time:

> I knew there was but one course open to me if the men with me were to remain alive for more than five minutes. Feeling as if I was betraying everything that I loved and believed in, I raised my voice and called: "*Stop!*" They stopped and looked towards me, their faces expectant. I shall never know what order they anticipated. Then I said: "*Put down your arms!*"
> … After all that we had done, after all the effort we had exerted in fulfilling our task, this was the end: surrender to the enemy![99]

Was their sacrifice necessary? Lieutenant-Colonel Roy E. Appleman had serious doubts when he later interviewed various senior officers, including Brodie, and the corps and divisional commanders. He concluded that:

> It is clear that Brodie did not appreciate the seriousness of the Gloster position on the 24th, nor did he inform the 3rd Division of it. I had an interview with Brodie on

the Gloster affair in Sep 1951 at his then CP in Korea. He refused to answer some of my questions, but he did say at the very end that he would assume 50 percent of the responsibility of not keeping higher command well informed ... I know that Gen. Ridgway had made it clear ... that a UN force should not be sacrificed under any circumstances, and that if such appeared a possibility then an American unit should be chosen to bear the risk.[100]

TFH himself concluded in the official history that: 'If the Glosters had been kept in position deliberately because they were destroying and delaying a substantial portion of the Chinese 63rd Army, their loss might have been justified. Actually, they were lost by oversight'.[101]

10

'We have many ways of killing you slowly'
Prisoner of War, April 1951-August 1953

TFH and his small group waited in the sunlit valley, exchanging cigarettes and matches. They did not have long to wait, for soon Chinese soldiers came running towards them:

> They were all short men by our standards … They wore the ragged yellow-khaki cotton uniforms we were accustomed to seeing them in … None had a badge of any sort, but I noticed the leader … had a mark in the centre of his cap above the peak, which had obviously been made by a badge.[1]

After the battle and the shock of capture, reaction was already setting in and the men all felt hungry, thirsty and exhausted. TFH noted soon afterwards that 'there was a difference in the way that the majority – officers and men – behaved. I studied this for quite some time before I realised what it was: they were suffering from a form of mental shock …'[2]

Soon they were told to move and shortly afterwards joined a second group of about 50 under Guy Ward, the Battery Commander; Drum-Major Phil Buss; and Provost Sergeant Peglar. Already, TFH's thoughts had turned to escape: with Sam Weller, Henry Cabral, Peglar and the Intelligence Sergeant, Crompton, he began to make plans. Peglar had managed to conceal a compass, which he passed to TFH, who had hidden several maps inside his clothing. First, however, the Glosters' wounded had to be recovered from the hillsides and brought down for evacuation. With this done, the column of captives moved slowly away through the hundreds upon hundreds of Chinese dead – killed by air strikes, artillery fire or the Glosters' small arms.

After about an hour, a third party came into view under Bob Hickey, the Medical Officer; Chaplain Sam Davies; Medical Sergeant 'Knocker' Brisland; and George Baker, the Company Sergeant Major of Support Company. There were more wounded too, with whom the Chaplain and the RMO had elected to remain rather than escape.[3] After half an hour, the whole group was marched back past the site of Battalion Headquarters, which had been broken up and looted. It was later ascertained that a total of 21 officers and 509 men of 1 Glosters were captured, along with five officers and 59 gunners of the Royal Artillery and another two officers and 22 men from attached arms and services – that is 80 percent of the Glosters' strength.[4] By now they were moving through dense bodies of Chinese soldiers moving forward, but moving cautiously and ever fearful of UN air attack. Because of this fear, further movement

Chonsong PoW Camp, 1952. (GLRRM 04727.1)

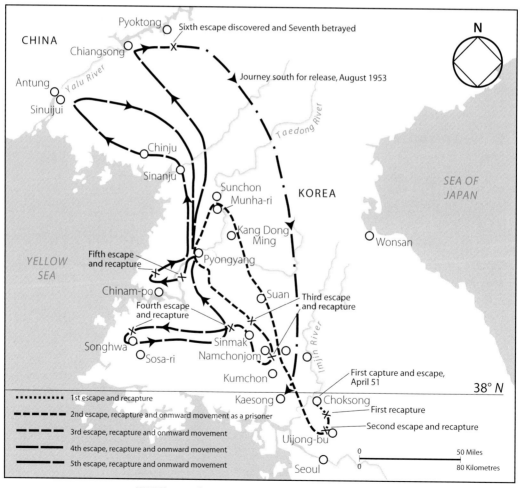

TFH's travels as a Prisoner of War, 1951-1953.

was made under cover of darkness and as the column approached a road junction alongside the Imjin River, it became tangled up with a mass of people, vehicles and mules; this was it! TFH, Crompton and Sergeant Clayden slipped off the road and into the river.

TFH spent seven hours in the cold river, at one point nearly drowning, until he managed to crawl ashore on a deserted beach some miles downstream on the north bank of the river. Of his companions, there was no sign. Clutching an old blanket that he managed to drag from a dead mule, he crawled into a hole, wrapped himself up and slept until daylight woke him. He was not far from Castle Hill and Gloster Crossing. He was soon discovered by a passing Chinese patrol, but feigned death and was ignored. Realising that the area was too open, TFH decided to cross the river before dark and then try to strike across country over the mile or so of enemy territory that lay between him and the new UN defence line. Scouting around, TFH noticed a mass of footprints which clearly indicated an underwater bridge; this was the place. Waiting for twilight, he stripped off his clothes and made them into a bundle. The water, although cold, came only just above his waist – and to his relief, he reached the far shore easily. Two minutes later, he was dressing under the cover of the river bank.[5]

Four hours later he was back at the place where he had been captured and pushed on over high ground covered with thorny scrub through which he struggled, 'cursing, sweating, and growing progressively angrier',[6] until he reached a valley, and then rice paddy – but between TFH and his objective, Chinese soldiers were digging weapon pits, which he could dimly see in the darkness. A long detour was out of the question and TFH quickly decided to work his way through the Chinese position. Wriggling on his stomach through the mud, he reached the far side of the rice paddy and crawled into some scrub on the hillside. Day was fast approaching. Breaking into a run, TFH crossed another paddy and then followed a stream looking for a place to ford it. He soon found a crossing, but it was guarded. In the waning dark, TFH decided to bluff the sentry and cross anyway; it worked. Soon he was climbing another hill, heading south and then east. Another sentry – another bluff; TFH hawked, spat and mumbled as if he were a Chinese or Korean soldier stumbling around in the early dawn. The sentry let him pass and as full daylight came he climbed a high hill which was scarred with the wreckage of an abandoned Chinese position. Beyond this, another hilltop provided cover and a fine observation site with a view of nearly 10 miles. Here TFH lay up for the day.

His route onwards lay due south, through hamlets in which he could see only Korean peasants. In the early afternoon, therefore, TFH cautiously made his way into one of these villages and disguised himself with an old rice sack, removing and hiding his uniform jacket and blackening his face with mud. Thus disguised, and carrying a walking stick made from a fallen branch, he moved in a leisurely fashion along a road – following a field telephone cable which he confidently assumed would lead him to UN positions (perhaps the 1st ROK Division). With all the detours, ups and downs, he was still, however, a mile from his estimate of where the UN lines lay. After a short rest in a deserted village he pushed on again for what he hoped would be the last stage of his journey.

It soon seemed that it was not to be: 'A figure came running down from the trees … it was a Chinese; in his hand he carried a long barrelled pistol that looked like a *Mauser*. It was pointing in my direction'.[7] But TFH's disguise held good and the Chinese spoke no Korean. TFH could not believe his luck. He pushed on until he was perhaps no more than 600 yards from UN positions when at last his luck ran out. No more than 15 yards away was a North

Korean soldier, pointing his weapon straight at TFH's chest. 'I knew beyond a shadow of a doubt that I was recaptured!'[8]

TFH was marched by his captor, a 2nd Lieutenant, into a village and from there – under guard by two majors – back along the line of communication. Over the next couple of days, the guards lost their way, saved TFH from summary execution, fed him in a desultory fashion when they remembered, until at last they reached their destination: the Divisional Headquarters, whose telephone cable TFH had mistakenly identified as friendly. Here, although dejected by recapture, he was delighted to be reunited with two Glosters: Privates Fox and Graham. These two had also made attempts to escape, but had been recaptured.[9] They were soon marched off again, generally moving south-east, and as they walked the three exchanged stories of the battle and their capture. TFH was already thinking of escape once more – an idea with which the two young soldiers enthusiastically agreed. That night, the group was quartered in a small village and here they remained for five days, joined by a Puerto Rican prisoner named Morales.

UN artillery fire was frequent – a cheering sound because it indicated that friendly lines were still close. What TFH did not know until much later was that on 15 May 1951, the Chinese had commenced the second phase of their Spring Offensive and attacked the ROK Army and the US X Corps in the east at the Soyang River. After gaining some initial successes, they were halted by 20 May. At the end of May, the US Eighth Army itself counter-attacked once more and regained Line *Kansas*, just north of the 38th parallel. Here, Ridgway halted further UN movement north and thus began the stalemate that lasted the whole of TFH's captivity until the Armistice of 1953.

On the evening of the fifth day, the march was resumed amid this fire and two days later, the party halted at a village which the men dubbed 'Mother Reilly's' after a good-natured old Korean woman who lived there.[10] Here they were given a little food and joined by a South Korean Sergeant who had been captured while on patrol. At dusk, they moved off once more. At the next billet, TFH talked to Fox and Graham and they decided that they must escape within the next day-and-a-half. Morales too was eager to escape and the four made ready. That night, a chance came. The watch was slack and the four slipped away from the village – free again, but within half an hour, Morales had disappeared. There was no time to linger; the three Englishmen pressed on.

Their plan was to hide by day and move by night, returning first to 'Mother Reilly's' to get food and then striking across country towards friendly lines, through country with which TFH was familiar from the end of 1950 and the beginning of 1951. Another night's travel brought them to the immediate objective, but it was occupied by enemy troops. The three therefore made for a large, abandoned Buddhist monastery that lay nearby and which TFH had marked earlier as a possible hiding place. It had been raining for some time and the men were wet and cold. In a room which seemed to belong to the caretaker they found the embers of a fire. Soon afterwards, they found the caretaker in person. At first, the old lady was far from pleased to see them but, once they were established as Englishmen, she became both friendly and fearful. She disappeared and returned soon after with a teenage girl and a young boy, carrying the ingredients for a substantial meal. For the next two days, the men were hidden in an underground wood store: warm, dry, well fed and even able to smoke: 'three thoroughly contented men'.[11]

On the third night, TFH decided to make a reconnaissance prior to moving on. At the same time he wanted to give the old woman a note for the UN authorities, should they return, which would show that she had sheltered them and perhaps gain her some reward. As he was talking to her, there was a heavy knock on the door. TFH was hastily shoved into a tool shed from which, through a crack, he watched as four Chinese soldiers forced their way into the house. Obviously suspicious of something, they began to ransack the place and it was only a few moments before TFH was found, dragged outside and furiously questioned before being tied up. The house was ransacked and the old caretaker badly beaten. Fox and Graham, however, remained undiscovered and eventually TFH was marched off at the double down a stony track. 'There was one real snag in this', recalled TFH, for in an effort to move quietly while making his earlier reconnaissance, 'I had left my boots in the temple',[12] and thus ended TFH's second escape attempt. Fox and Graham were luckier. They made a clean break from the temple area and made good progress for several days until they were captured by North Korean soldiers. They were interrogated, but to their surprise, given food and allowed to rest. After further questioning they were given safe conduct passes and escorted through the North Korean lines to safety, without either being made to sign or to make any sort of confession or pro-communist statements.[13] They were fortunate indeed.

TFH was first taken back to 'Mother Reilly's' and after another two days, back up the line of communication to the Divisional Headquarters. With no boots, TFH's feet soon became cut, blistered and sore. From the Divisional HQ, TFH was sent straight to the Army HQ and here he was pushed into a dark cell. Stumbling over a group of sleeping South Korean prisoners he called out, 'Is there any room in here?'

Out of the darkness came a reply: 'Over here ... who is it?' Thus TFH met yet another English prisoner – a young Northumberland Fusilier named Derek Kinne.[14] To his surprise, Morales was also there – he had sprained his ankle on the hillside soon after their escape – and the three exchanged accounts of all that they had seen. Morales had told Kinne that 'I'm goddam glad I got recaptured by these Chinese. They're better than the North Koreans'. Kinne could not help wondering if he was right.[15]

Here, however, TFH underwent his first real interrogation at the hands of a Chinese who called himself Chen. This was Chen Chung-Way,[16] who spoke excellent English with a slight American accent. TFH and Kinne both refused to answer any questions other than to give their number, rank and name. Chen switched tactics, embarking on a long series of political lectures, each lasting up to nine hours. At least it allowed TFH to rest and he was even given medical treatment for his lacerated feet, but at last, TFH allowed himself to be drawn into an argument: 'I could take no more. A great flood of words burst from me, which no protest of his could dam ... we were in the midst of a heated argument ... I walked back through the darkness with my guards, calling myself all sorts of a fool'.[17]

Indeed, TFH had already given Kinne 'a rocket' when the young man had recounted how he too had argued with Chen, challenging the status of the Chinese as volunteers.[18] However, meeting TFH had sharpened Kinne's eagerness to escape: 'More important to me than anything else', he wrote, 'was that the arrival of this officer brought into the foreground once more the question of escape'.[19]

This question clearly preoccupied Kinne throughout his captivity thereafter: Lofty Large, another prisoner, remembered that he 'made an absolute fetish of escaping ...'[20]

The consequences of this were that TFH was identified as being politically aware and therefore a target for possible re-education. Morales and Kinne were sent away and the next three nights passed with a series of political lectures – but the time came when TFH was once more marched away, still in his stockinged feet, to the obvious regret of Chen. Progress on the road was slow because of TFH's lack of boots and because his injured feet were causing him great pain. On the second day, the guards allowed Kinne to drop back and help him; the elderly NCO in charge of the guard detail also found some rags with which to bind TFH's wounds; and finally, on the second night, he produced a pair of rubber and canvas Chinese boots: 'It was, at least, a change for the better: I did not have to avoid every stone on the path'.[21]

Food was reduced to a few spoons of maize, millet or barley, so that TFH and Kinne had to resort to chewing the inside of pine-bark to keep up their strength.[22] Movement along the Chinese lines of communication was mainly by night, because of the fear of air attack,* until about two hours into the fourth night when the group found themselves on the veranda of a Korean house. Here a long lecture on rules and regulations began until TFH, who had a carrying voice, protested that they were tired and that he was injured. Someone in the next room heard his voice and called his name: 'I knew at once that it was the Colonel'.

It was another in a series of reunions in which stories and news were exchanged well into the night. It appeared that the series of forced marches made by TFH and his companions had been necessary in order to catch up with this party, the last column marching north after the Imjin River battle and the subsequent UN counter-attack to Line *Kansas*.[23] Ironically, it had been known by those at home that Carne was a prisoner long before TFH was sure of it, as the New China News Agency had reported it in early June 1951.[24] The next day, TFH began to assess the lie of the land. The village formed an L-shape around the base of a mountain and consisted of the usual mud-and-straw walled houses, with cattle sheds and outhouses. The Korean peasants – mostly old men, women and children – were clearly anxious to avoid contact.[25] Rations and facilities were limited and all the officer prisoners spent the daylight hours in an open dugout – an old gun position – except for Colonel Carne, Denis Harding, and any South Korean prisoners – all of whom were isolated and kept under guard. The Chinese sought, in particular, to limit the influence that Carne and Harding could wield on other prisoners. Derek Kinne's account makes it clear that throughout their time as prisoners, Carne and Harding did everything they could to resist their captors and stiffen the resolve of others. Lofty Large recalled his first reunion with Carne, which sheds light on how he was able to maintain this influence:

> He was standing apart from his column, greeting all the men in my column as they passed. As I approached him I was very surprised when he said, *"Well done, Large. Chin up, we'll be OK soon"*.
>
> What a man, how could he remember the names and faces of nearly all his battalion, even new arrivals like myself – who certainly had not looked like this the last time he had seen us.[26]

Among those in the dugout, TFH found many friends that he had thought dead: Bob Hickey, 'Spike' Pike of the Assault Pioneers, 'Jumbo' Wilson, Geoff Costello, RSM

---

*   However, as TFH himself pointed out in his paper 'A Reminiscence of the Chinese People's Volunteers in the Korean War' (*China Quarterly*, June 1984), the Chinese had plenty of Russian-supplied modern aircraft and the *Mig-15* was more than a match for the in-service American fighters; Chinese ground-based air defence was highly effective and for a time at least, they succeeded in reducing UN mastery of the air to parity – especially in the north-west. See also Large, *One Man's War in Korea*, p 81.

Jack Hobbs, Company Sergeant Majors Harry Gallagher and Ridlington, and 'Muscles' Strong – the PT Instructor. Ironically, both Hobbs and Gallagher had been prisoners of war once before, both taken on the Dunkirk perimeter in 1940;[27] there were others who had spent time in Japanese prison camps during the Second World War – men who, although mentally prepared for the coming ordeal, must have found the prospect of another spell in such hands all but unendurable. There were also men from the 8th Hussars, Northumberland Fusiliers and the Ulster Rifles – as well as a young Filipino Lieutenant named Thomas Battilo and a US Marine Corps pilot, Captain Byron Beswick. Byron had been badly injured by burning fuel when ejecting from his *Corsair* aircraft after being hit by anti-aircraft fire.

TFH spent three days in this place, during which he was able to have at least some treatment for his injured feet, before the march was resumed. The recovery period had not been enough though and after another two days, Hickey and Doug Patchett – the RMO of the 8th Hussars – decided that surgery was essential, for as Kinne remembered, 'the pus ran constantly'.[28] They gave TFH what little morphine they had and then set to work with a razor blade, the others holding him down, while as TFH recalled, 'I regret to say I swore a good deal'. From then on, TFH had to be half-carried until the next staging area was reached in a gold-mining camp. Here, Hickey managed to persuade the North Koreans to move the injured prisoners on by road transport. Kinne and TFH were both able to get aboard the trucks, but as usual this had its drawbacks as the North Korean and Chinese drivers frequently lost their way, as TFH later remarked in his paper on the Chinese People's Volunteers that 'A feature of excellence was night navigation…'![29]

Lofty Large recalled that many of these trucks were captured American or British vehicles, but most were Russian and ran on diesel: 'The smell of diesel fumes was strange to me, and it seemed nearly always there was, mixed with the smell of diesel, the smell of death. The stench of death was everywhere along those roads'.[30]

Food was also very scarce and Kinne was caught foraging one night in the guards' accommodation. Kinne's first reward was a thrashing from the guards; his second another rocket from TFH:

> "*Damn it, Kinne*", he said, "*Haven't I told you you're not to go off scrounging unless you let me know you're going and I give you the all clear?*"
>
> "*Yes, Sir.*"
>
> "*Well, what the hell do you mean by it? Any scrounging will be done as an organised effort, then you won't get caught. If you do this again I shall place you in close arrest.*" I didn't know what to say; I almost felt like laughing. The idea of placing me in close arrest in a town slap in the middle of enemy territory seemed incredible. And yet I saw what he meant – and close arrest was a serious thing. Serious enough to keep me from laughing, to make me reflect on this queer business of whose authority was right and whose was wrong.[31]

However, by supper-time, they were friends again – had there been any supper to have, that is. In one town they came upon a group of eight prisoners, including two Britons, who were working as slave labour for the North Koreans; all were close to starvation. TFH tried hard to persuade the Chinese guards to take these men with the group, or else evacuate them to a proper camp. Although the men remained where they were when the party moved on, it later transpired that they had been moved and that they survived the war.[32]

On the last day but one of the journey, Kinne was eyeing one of the guards' packs, which he knew contained food that should have gone to the prisoners, but which had been stolen. TFH crawled over to him.

'Kinne', he said, 'when you take a risk, go flat out. If you decide the risk's worth it, it's all or nothing. When I slide back the opening in the wall, I'll hold the bowl and you get the sugar out. Ready? Now!'

This foraging operation succeeded and taught Kinne a lesson that he never forgot.[33] Finally, after a journey partly by truck and partly on foot, the injured were reunited with the rest of the group for a longer and much-needed rest.

When the main body resumed its northward march, about 40 men – sick and able-bodied alike – were separated out and sent to a village called Munra-hi. TFH and his group now joined this party. The village consisted of around 40 houses close to the Taedong River. Here they were surprised to find the rest of Sam Weller's group and another reunion took place. The days were spent in a pine wood about a mile from the village and at nights the group was crammed into a school building which was just big enough to allow everyone to lie down. Food improved, but sickness – especially dysentery – continued to increase. Moreover the group was addressed by a Chinese named Tien Han, who informed them that they were now to be treated as 'war criminals'; interrogations soon followed. TFH was sure that the fact he had engaged in a political argument had been reported and sure enough, at his first questioning he was asked where he had received his political training. However, the guards soon tired of interrogations and these were replaced with long lectures on the Chinese Revolution.

The upside of this period was that under the care of a female doctor and a proper medical orderly, TFH's feet began to heal fast and he was soon making plans for another escape attempt along with Bob Hickey, Thomas Battilo, Cooper and finally Byron, once his burns had healed up sufficiently. Bob, however, had to withdraw as he was given the responsibility of looking after the sick and injured – a duty he felt he could not abandon. However, one evening most of the group were assembled by the Chinese and taken away on a night march to another camp –[34] leaving TFH, four other able-bodied men (Guy Ward, Chaplain Sam Davies, Duncan Palmer – an American pilot – and Sergeant Fitzpatrick of the Royal Artillery), all the sick and two men in close arrest, Carl Livesey (an American) and Sergeant Sharp of the Glosters. After five days, the reason for their separation made itself clear: the group had been selected for re-education.

Each morning, they were lectured by 'a very ugly, lisping Chinese called T'ang',[35] whose demeanour was smiling and friendly – until one morning when Hickey, Byron and Thomas Battilo were dragged up the hillside having been recaptured after an escape attempt. These three spent the next three weeks in solitary confinement. The men talked among themselves, considering whether, as had happened before, they were being indoctrinated prior to being released as a gesture; it seemed possible, but unlikely. They argued about whether or not they should listen to the Chinese lectures.

TFH's view was simple: '... we should listen to as much as they cared to give us, provided we were not required to write anything, sign anything, record, or broadcast, or give lectures ourselves'.[36]

The others agreed – and while this relatively easy life continued, further escape attempts were put on hold. This situation continued through much of the summer. The Chinese lecturers changed, as did the guards – and some of the group were sent northwards.

TFH, husbanding his strength, was determined to make another escape attempt before the end of summer, but he was laid low by a fever – during which he was cared for by the others, both physically and spiritually. In particular he found the presence of the Chaplain, Sam Davies, a matter of great importance; captivity had not eroded his strong sense of Christian belief – rather, adversity had made it stronger. At one point, he wrote that the fever left him as the Chaplain said prayers and laid hands on him. It appears that TFH had contracted malaria – not surprising given the amount of time he had spent in low-lying swamps where mosquitoes bred – and from this, blackwater fever had developed. The cause of blackwater fever is unknown, although it is a mutation of malaria and it is thought that quinine may contribute to it. Within a few days of onset of this condition the symptoms include chills, high fever, jaundice, vomiting, rapidly progressive anemia, and dark red or black urine. In the 1950s, this disease was far more common than it is nowadays and in those days, death followed in very many cases without intensive care – including dialysis, drugs and intravenous fluid.[37] TFH was very tough, certainly, but also very lucky; his recovery was little short of a miracle.

Once the fever had abated, TFH began to do some basic physical training exercises to build strength, helped by a diet that was greatly improved from the early staples of rice and kaoliang (a plant in the sorghum family whose grains resemble maize) by the addition of potatoes and other vegetables; even simple things like a fried pancake became wonderful. Lofty Large remembered the food well:

> Eating rice, sometimes sloppy rice, was not as easy as it sounds. Practically no one had any spoons or other eating utensils. We had no plates or mess-kit. So we had to do what we could with what we had. Like many of the others I used the inside pocket of my tunic for a plate. George Baker tore it out for me. For a long time I used my cap badge as a spoon. Have you ever seen a Glosters' cap badge? Well, it makes a bloody awful spoon.[38]

After almost three months in Munha-ri, in late August, the men were abruptly told one evening to pack up and prepare to move. Everyone was tremendously excited. They were sick of Munha-ri and its never-ending lectures, its petty restrictions, its dull routine and its bullying guards. To their surprise, they went not north, but south. Moving always by night they passed through Pyongyang, where they noticed Russians and some other Europeans – who ignored them. Turning south-east, they began to approach the front: a prospect that seemed to terrify their guards, even more so whenever UN aircraft were heard. Lofty Large recounted his experiences of these long marches:

> A shout which sounded like 'Suselah-Ah'. That meant 'take five'. The one I always longed for was 'Sweejo-Ah'. That meant we had reached our destination for the night, and would be herded into a small area, to be surrounded by guards and allowed to sleep. Many of us often fell asleep during the five minute breaks. I remember once falling asleep on a pile of loose rocks, in pouring rain… .

... I remember the songs. The Glosters had been stationed in the West Indies ... and (strangely to my ears) there often came floating through the darkness the sound of several voices (some melodious, some otherwise) singing the calypso type of songs of the West Indies... .[39]

After 10 days on the road, they reached their destination: the courtyard of a house in a small village where the men were crammed into two small rooms. During the day, as had become usual, they were moved out onto an open hillside and for the next five days they were largely ignored. Here, TFH's thoughts turned once more to escape. One evening, he managed a whispered conversation with Duncan Palmer, whom he had identified as a prospective partner. Duncan was unwilling to try an escape at that moment, as he thought it possible that peace negotiations were under way and that the Chinese might therefore release some prisoners to show good faith. If this turned out to be impossible then, he said, he would be willing to try. TFH decided to give him three days to make up his mind and then, if necessary, go it alone. Two evenings later, the local Regimental Commander broke the news that peace talks, which had begun as early as 8 July 1951 and continued sporadically, had been broken off; it was enough. That night, TFH and Duncan agreed to move. TFH, being an experienced escaper, was by now well aware of the main problems facing them: not getting away from the camp, for that was the easy part, but remaining free thereafter. First, North Korea was a police State in which all civilian movement was strictly controlled; secondly, they did not know the language; thirdly, they were physically different and stood out; fourthly, contact with civilians was risky; and last, food had either to be saved from the meagre rations in the camps or else gathered from standing crops and eaten raw.[40]

The next night, the two of them slipped away from the village – foraging for food in the maize fields, resting by day and moving by night, 'filled with that splendid feeling which I had lost months before at the monastery: freedom!'[41]

On the fourth night they had to swim a broad river – which although it can be identified on modern mapping, appears to have no English name – on the far side of which was an obviously well-used track; this was no place for them to hide. Avoiding a village and some cultivated fields they climbed a hillside covered with old trenches and dugouts. TFH thought these were probably relics from the North Korean retreat to the Yalu River. Here, they decided to rest and dry their clothes as best they could. Duncan took off all his clothes except for a thin flying-suit and spread them out to dry, while TFH decided to risk an approach to a nearby house to try to get food. The nearest village proved to be full of Chinese troops, so TFH selected an isolated house. His initial approach clearly frightened the family, but once TFH had made them understand that he was English, the fear turned to smiles. The farmer spoke to his wife, who scooped up all the food they had from a cooking pot – nine cobs of boiled maize – and thrust it into TFH's hands. Back in the abandoned trenches the two men ate their corn. TFH was on the point of saying that they must now move, when the sound of voices reached them: it was a group of Chinese soldiers looking for firewood. The two men lay still, unseen for the moment, but Duncan decided to make a run for it. TFH urged him in a whisper to stay still, but off he went. He nearly made it, but tripped over a tree root and fell. In the confusion, TFH slipped away into thicker cover from which, 10 minutes later, he saw the soldiers return with Duncan and then move off with him to the village. A few moments later, TFH realised that Duncan had left all his clothes on the hillside. It was September and soon the Korean winter would return. Without warm clothes, Duncan could die of cold. TFH worked his way towards the village, trying for hours to find a way to get the clothes to Duncan without being caught. At last he realised that there was nothing for it but to surrender once more. His third bid for freedom had ended.

Ten minutes later, TFH was standing in front of some very surprised Chinese soldiers who, after a short time, realised that the two men were together and that they were escaped prisoners. After an interrogation and a night in a barn, the two were marched to Namchon-jom, a town on the western railway. That night they were put on a truck and joined a heavy stream of traffic on the main western highway. Beyond a town they managed to identify as Sinmak, the truck left the highway where they dismounted, marched up a hillside and were locked up in two small, securely guarded bunkers. The slightest movement resulted in being poked through the bars by a sharp steel rod; it was an unpleasant night.

Two days of confinement passed, with thin, watery meals twice a day until they were moved to another village and another set of bunkers, dug into a hillside. The next morning, on his visit to the latrine, TFH realised he was ill. After a few paces, he vomited; his throat was sore and swollen and his foot, after having been repeatedly poked with the sharp steel rod, was turning septic. He asked the guard, a good-natured fellow, for a doctor. He seemed to understand, but during the exchange, TFH managed to get an idea of his surroundings and decided to try tunnelling out of the bunker. For two days he worked carefully on his tunnel, scattering the dug earth on the dugout floor and using stones to hide the entrance. A medical orderly then appeared, who dressed his foot but could do nothing for his throat, but the man seemed very interested in TFH's eyes – why, TFH could not then fathom.

Returning to his dugout, he was horrified to find two Chinese inspecting the inside – but somehow, amazingly, they did not find the tunnel. That night, TFH returned to work. He watched the routine of the garrison carefully to determine patterns. Each evening, for example, the Chinese garrison all gathered for political indoctrination, which ended in a patriotic song. He later wrote more on this subject, saying that:

> On average, the soldiers were occupied in one way or another for about 12 hours a day. The remaining 12 hours were given to an afternoon rest period – one or two hours – eight hours for sleep, with a couple of hours of 'free time', when a soldier played games, had to undertake maintenance of his clothing and personal equipment or a share in domestic chores … Had an officer of the North American or Western European armies circulated … he would have been struck by the time and effort devoted to political education, rare in his experience, and to the wide range of weapons and equipment among units.[42]

On the fourth evening, while political education was in progress, TFH silently hacked out the last few inches of earth and slipped out into the gloom. The sentry on guard at the dugouts was very close – so close TFH could hear him hawk and spit, but shortly afterwards he moved away – only 20 feet, but enough – and began to talk to a comrade. Moving very cautiously, TFH crossed the open ground around the dugouts and entered the cover of a field of maize; then he was in bushes, then more open ground. He leapt from the bushes and ran as fast as he could, his sickness forgotten, heading for a hillside to the north – he was free again![43]

TFH knew it could not be long before the tell-tale signs of his escape were discovered – and sure enough, he heard the alarm raised by the firing of shots. After no more than 10 minutes there were voices and flashlights – but he was not discovered. He decided that his best course of action was to head west towards the coast. Fifteen days, he thought, would get him to the coast. Another two nights brought him back to Sinmak and on the way, his reflection in a pool of water explained the medical orderly's interest: the whites of his eyes were yellow, indicating that as well as tonsillitis, he probably also had jaundice. Travelling by night, he managed to avoid the built-up areas around Sinmak and the busy roads crammed with military traffic.

When he had calculated his escape, TFH had estimated that he would need 15 days to reach the coast and another three days to find a boat; having learned to sail a small boat as a boy was about to become a very useful skill indeed. He then needed perhaps three days more to sail to freedom – a total of three weeks therefore. He felt that with his poor health and thin diet, this was the maximum period he could hope to remain active. To achieve this, he must cover at least 10 miles each day – and by travelling at night, he was simply not doing this. Once he was clear of the main militarised area, he therefore changed tactics: hiding up and sleeping by night, he would select a covered route from a position of observation and then travel by day. This worked – and although the terrain was rough, his strength was reduced, his shoes were in poor shape, and there were frequently rivers to cross, he began to make good progress. After 12 days he began to look for signs of the sea and on the morning of the 16th day, there it was below him! He began to think of where to enter the sea and how he might find a boat but, crossing some flat fields of beans only half a mile from the coast, he collapsed unconscious.

Some hours later, he woke in a house, on a bed. He had been found by a friendly Korean family who, at huge risk to themselves, had taken him in. These good people fed him and cared for him for six days 'as if I was one of their own'.[44]

Communication was hard, but eventually TFH managed to explain that he needed a boat, and gave the old man – who was the head of the family – all the money he had, which, soaked with water and sweat, he had kept concealed, sewn into his clothes. Then early in the afternoon, only a few hours before he intended to move, disaster struck. A North Korean soldier appeared and, offering an apple, engaged one of the children in conversation. It was not long before the child spoke the word for an Englishman – '*Yungook*'. TFH watched all this in horror from his hiding place and, as the man ran off to fetch help, he made a break for the sea. Before he could escape, he was surrounded by Chinese soldiers and, only a quarter of a mile from the sea, his fourth bid for freedom ended.

TFH was taken first to the village of Sosa-ri, where he was briefly interrogated and then marched off to the nearest military headquarters – not an easy journey for a man in such a weakened physical state. Here he was again interrogated, but refused to give any information other than that he was an escaped prisoner. He was offered the chance to write home and did so, but when he again refused information, he had to watch his letter being torn up in front of his face. Following this he was again marched off, but only two miles, at the end of which he was pushed into a locked room in the courtyard of a farm. There was straw on the floor and the smell of unwashed bodies. Although he could see nothing in the darkness, his foot touched another body: "'*Hell! Is there any room in here?*" I asked. To my complete surprise, a very young, English voice replied: "*Is that another Englishman?*" A minute later I was shaking hands warmly with Mike'.[45]

Mike turned out to be Michael Halley, a South African fighter pilot serving in the RAF, who had been shot down. Lying side by side, Mike passed on all the news he had – as well as an infestation of body lice. Next morning the two were put into a bunker with a group of wretched, ragged, South Korean prisoners – a situation they were glad to leave, but their main preoccupation was escape, as soon as possible. However, after supper the following night, TFH was taken to another house where, until just before dawn, he faced a group of three Chinese officers. Throughout the night, a melodramatic sham trial proceeded in which TFH was indicted as a war criminal, shown the nature of his crimes, and had explained to him the Chinese version of the events of the war. All attempts to argue with his captors were silenced and in the end he gave up trying. In spite of threats, however, he refused to write or sign anything that looked like a confession.

The next day, the situation changed. The two were given as much kaoliang and egg-plant soup as they could eat and were then taken back to the headquarters in which TFH had been interrogated five days before. Here, they were surprised to be treated kindly by the local Commander, but that night they were put on a Chinese truck bound for Pyongyang. They reached the city at dawn where, after a pause of half an hour – during which they were fed – their journey continued, but the driver rapidly became lost and it took all morning to reach their destination, which was less than two miles from their breakfast halt. Here, in a village, they were stripped of all their clothes and possessions and locked in a cell with two cell-mates, 'a Chinese boy of 15 and one of the filthiest men I have ever seen'.[46]

Loud protests eventually secured the removal of these two and over the next days, the two men did their best to clean themselves up, delouse, and make fresh escape plans. On the fourth day, however, Mike was removed. The next night, TFH too was moved on.

In the company of a surprisingly friendly Chinese officer, who shared his food and borrowed a padded greatcoat for his captive against the growing October chill, TFH was taken to Chinju. Here he was again locked in a cell, but well fed, and later taken into the village to be locked up in the local police cells. However, no transport could be obtained and, waiting under guard at a crossroads, TFH met up with his next companion – a young American F-80 pilot who had lost a leg while getting clear of his damaged plane; he got around on crutches and with the aid of a small handcart. This was Lieutenant-Colonel Thomas Harrison – Tom – of the US Air Force, who had been in Chinju since he was shot down six months before. The next day, the two were taken away to the town of Sinuiju, on the south bank of the Yalu River and right on the border with China, therefore. Here, the two men were handed over to the North Korean police, who searched them thoroughly – taking away their shoes, the draw-strings of their underwear and even Tom's crutches. They were then put into a cell. In the cell were 21 men and boys, sitting cross-legged in absolute silence. No-one stirred as the two entered – and clearly they were terrified of the guards. Room was made for the newcomers, the door clanged shut and the key turned in the lock.

The rules of this prison soon became clear. At 5:00 a.m. every morning the prisoners were roused from sleep and in absolute silence, adopted a sitting position, heads bowed. At dawn, one man was permitted to remove the blackout from the window and prisoners were permitted to use the latrine, a square hole in one corner of the room behind a flimsy screen. Two or three hours later, food would be distributed: half a bowl of millet, kaoliang or maize per man. TFH and Tom were allowed a little rice and sometimes fish – as well as the basic ration, which they tried to share with their fellows. At dusk, the blackout was replaced and the second meal of the day – identical with the first – was brought. At 10:00 p.m. the prisoners were ordered to lie down and sleep. This routine never varied and any deviation, however slight, was rewarded with savage punishment.

Every third or fourth day, six men or women were allowed out of the cell to wash – and on these occasions, some whispered conversation was possible. A boy who spoke a little English explained that none of the prisoners knew their crime; they had usually been denounced by an unknown enemy, had not been tried and never would be. They would stay in prison until moved elsewhere, or were released through the influence of friends, or they died. On the second wash day, one of the guards actually engaged the two in conversation and told them that there was another UN prisoner in the next cell. Some words were exchanged and their comrade turned out to be a young Australian; they did not discover who he was for some time. Fifteen days passed in this soul-destroying way until at last, the two were taken out, given back their belts – everything else had been stolen – and told to prepare for a journey. As they left, a long, miserable column of Korean civilian prisoners emerged – wired together ready for a long march either to another prison or a labour camp.

After much argument the two managed to secure shoes, but nothing else. Their hands were then bound with wire and they were put on a truck, which for the next four days headed east, then turned south and later south-west until they found themselves back in Pyongyang. Here they were taken to a police station, but were fed and not put in the cells. They even managed to talk to a young English-speaking prisoner who told them that peace negotiations had re-started at Kaesong. At dusk they were put into a Jeep and driven out of the city to a large farm complex guarded by North Korean soldiers. Here they were placed in a barn, where they met not only a freckle-faced young man wearing an American flying suit, but also their Australian comrade from Sinuiju Prison. These two were 1st Lieutenant Jack Henderson, who had been shot down in the summer, and Flying Officer Ron Guthrie – also a pilot – who had bailed out of his damaged *Meteor*.[47]

This place turned out not to be a PoW camp, but a North Korean interrogation centre. The food ration was very meagre, the weather was turning cold and the men had no proper winter clothing – especially Jack, who had only a thin flying suit. Tom was soon under intensive interrogation and, when he refused to co-operate, his food was stopped altogether. All those not under interrogation were made to work at construction or labouring, which rapidly sapped their remaining strength. It was not long before the three able-bodied men decided once more to escape – but there was Tom to consider. Tom, however, once he heard their plans, was in no doubt: as the most senior officer, he ordered them to escape. TFH decided to begin a breach of their prison wall that very night.

However, before he could begin work, TFH was called for interrogation. At first the questions were bizarre: 'Give us the organisation, means of recruitment and training, method of dispatch, and system of communication of the British Intelligence Services throughout Europe and the Far East'.[48]

TFH made the mistake of smiling at the insanity of this line of questioning and was immediately rewarded with threats and blows. With a warning to think over his response, he was taken back to the barn. Once there, he lost little time in starting to cut a hole through the upper part of the barn wall, which was made of mud and wattles, using an old screwdriver and a rusty table knife that he had picked up outside, supplemented by an old razor blade. He decided that night to take the hole to a point which, were it to be discovered, could be explained away as a fall of mud from the wall. Although, in the light of day, the excavation seemed glaringly obvious, the guards failed to spot it. The next night, TFH began again. Once he began to cut the wattles, there was no stopping. After about two hours, TFH had removed enough of these to make an escape hole, and set about the outside layer of mud. However, he was dismayed to discover a second layer of wattles. Although the barn was cold, he was now perspiring freely; after another hour, he was through. The three escapees wriggled through the hole – Ron knocking over an old cast-iron stove as he did so. This fell with a crash loud enough to rouse the whole village, but there was no reaction. Another lucky break came when they found a pile of padded clothing in the courtyard and soon, warmly dressed, the three were free men once more.

By morning, they had covered about 12 miles and they rested in cover on a hilltop over-looking Pyongyang. Here, eating some raw diakons – a long, crunchy white radish – they made a plan: they would head for the coast, then turn north and find a small boat. While the daylight lasted, they carefully planned a route for the next night's travel and at dusk, moved off following a small river. They met a young civilian, who saw them, but they managed to evade him. They avoided the next village and, descending back to the river, came to grief. TFH, who was leading, heard the unmistakeable sound of a rifle bolt close by and as the moon came out, he saw a sentry covering their approach. Signalling to the others to crawl away and not be caught, he walked boldly up to the sentry, who, rather at a loss, led him to the nearby guard-post, while the other two men slipped away.

In the guard-house, TFH tried bluff: seeing a picture of Joseph Stalin on the wall, he pretended to be a Russian. It almost worked, but for the arrival of a Russian-speaking Police Captain. TFH left the guard-house with his arms tightly bound; his fifth escape attempt ended. After an almost sleepless night, the Commander of the interrogation centre arrived: *"Ah"* he said, greeting me with a friendly kick, *"so it is you they have caught. I wondered which one it was"*.

He was taken to the next village, where a Police Lieutenant-Colonel and the civilian inter-preter of the interrogation centre, known as Kim, were waiting. Kim, his face twisted with rage, told TFH that 'You have been very foolish. You must be killed for this, I think'.[49]

From now on, TFH entered a new and far more brutal phase of his captivity. Under initial interrogation he refused to give any information about his two companions. When he continued defiant, he was told that if he refused to co-operate, then his captors would adopt more severe measures. He answered, 'I have told you how things stand. I have nothing more to say'.[50] He was then taken down a passage to a thick steel door and into a cell. Here he was ordered to strip to the waist:

> My mind could not conceive the truth that my senses offered. We were standing in a small square room, with cement-faced walls and a concrete floor. High above us, from a wooden ceiling, ropes trailed from metal rings. There were two more such rings in the left-hand wall. Under the right wall was a large barrel of water.[51]

As he stripped off his shirt, blood on the floor and walls, the bare lights and the equipment told him that although this was the middle of the 20th century, he was in a torture chamber. His wrists were tied and he was told to kneel. Once on the ground he was repeatedly beaten around the head and kicked. Through the blows, he could see the looks of enjoyment on his captors' faces, but this was merely the opening gambit. Next, he was firmly tied to a tiny chair and the chair was then kicked over so that TFH was on his back, unable to move. Cold water was thrown over him from the barrel and a towel placed over his face. More water was then thrown over the towel – which clung firmly to his face – and then, whenever he inhaled, he drew the wet towel more deeply into his mouth. As the water content increased, less and less oxygen could get through and TFH began to drown. He was being subjected to an ancient form of torture which today is called water-boarding, but which had long been practised in China.

With his captors holding his head firmly to prevent him struggling, more water was poured on until, at last, TFH passed out. When he came to, the chair was upright and the water was pouring from his nose and throat. His captors had known just how far they could go – and still bring him round – by applying a lighted cigarette to his back. The interpreter, Kim, again asked for information on his companions, which he refused, and after 10 minutes the whole terrifying process was repeated. When he was eventually dragged from the room, he had been tortured three times in this way. Scarcely able to walk, he was thrown into a police cell where, tightly bound, he spent the night. They came back for him on the second day and once again the alternate questioning and water-boarding went on. On the third day he was left alone. They came again on the fourth day but not on the fifth, and then once more on the sixth. In between times he was given a small amount of maize to eat each morning, but no water. He was not permitted to use the latrine so that his clothes were soon fouled. The ropes which bound him cut into his flesh; his joints seemed on fire and the biting of body lice became an almost unbearable torment.

When he was again taken to the chamber on the evening of the sixth day, he was close to breaking-point:

> I could not disguise from myself that my resistance was weakening. Now I was reduced to the state where I said that I would endure it for one more time; and when that time came, for one more time again … That day Kim had said to me: "*If we do not find them, I think you will be tortured to death. We have many ways of killing you slowly.*"[52]

By the next day, TFH realised he could take no more. He still had strength to pray, though. In spite of severe danger and imminent death, his faith, he later wrote, was never stronger. Within an hour, things began to get better.

It did not seem so at first. The door of his cell opened and Captain Li from the interrogation centre came in, looked him over, and told him that tomorrow he would be shot. Such was TFH's condition, he was actually glad. Two of his ribs were broken, he was covered with cigarette burns, he had enteritis and body lice and he was severely weakened – but once Li had gone, the Korean policemen untied him. He was able to move and to restore some circulation. Shortly afterwards, another policeman gave him cigarettes and matches, and later a sleeping mat – simple acts of kindness that reduced TFH to tears. When Li returned the next morning, TFH was calm and prepared: 'I went over my life, realising how lucky I had been to have had so much happiness … I hoped my family would be informed of my death without too much delay, so that there would not be prolonged anxiety'.[53]

Li led him out into a fine November morning and he saw, standing at ease on a mud square, a file of armed soldiers. Li motioned him towards the soldiers and he went, reciting the 23rd

Psalm to himself as he did so. To his surprise, Jack Henderson came out of a nearby building; was he also to be shot? Apparently not, for the party continued walking towards Pyongyang. During a short halt, TFH and Jack managed to exchange a few words and TFH learned that Jack and Ron Guthrie had been caught two days before, beaten up repeatedly and made to kneel for hours with a heavy board held up by the arms behind their backs. Just then, Li returned and, tapping his pistol and looking directly at TFH, said: 'You understand if you try to escape again, I shall shoot you'.[54]

It seemed that death had been postponed, at least for now. TFH's debriefing report after his eventual release makes the following comment:

> It is impossible to explain in the few words above, the mental reactions of Source [i.e. TFH] during the seven days of torture and ill treatment. There were long periods when Source, who is not deeply religious, indulged in prayer, and considers the assistance he got from this a great comfort and strength to him ... It is a wonder that his health and mind have not suffered a permanent injury, but ... he managed to continue resisting the enemies [sic] actions, and his determination to live kept him going in spite of a considerable deterioration in health.[55]

A long, hot march followed for the two weary, hungry men until they reached a small coal-mining town. Here they boarded a Jeep and were driven to a disused coal mine, where Li handed them over to North Korean soldiers. Inexplicably, as he left, he gave them all the cigarettes he had. The two men were then taken to a group of huts where, as they approached, there was a great shout: 'Welcoming words greeted us; on all sides friendly faces appeared; Henry Cabral, 'Spike' Pike, Mike [Halley], Ronnie [Washbrook] our Gunner, Tom, Ron – and new friends, British, American, French. It was almost a second homecoming as we were borne inside'.[56]

*   *   *

The prisoners' accommodation was a series of cold, unheated huts and the food meagre: three meals a day of corn and rice and a little thin diakon or cabbage soup. Sometimes there was a little tobacco, but to TFH, it seemed like comfort. Here in the coal mine, he caught up with news from his regiment: how many had been offered better treatment by the Chinese and North Koreans in exchange for their co-operation; how Lieutenant Terry Waters, attached to the battalion from the West Yorkshires, had ordered some of the men to go along with this in order to save their lives – but being an officer, had himself refused and, as a result, died of his wounds. The story of Waters' courage and example affected TFH deeply. To the end of his life, the memory of it could reduce him to tears.[57]

After only a few days, all the prisoners were taken out and searched, all winter clothing removed, and the men marched away; they knew not where. Many of the men were too weak to walk and TFH soon realised that as a result of his experiences, he was one of them. Those not able to walk were put on a cart, but he became worse – lapsing into the fever that he had last suffered at Munha-ri in the summer – indicating that he had recurring malaria, which can continue for many years. The lack of food – the Lieutenant in charge of the escort sold most of the rations on the road – and the biting cold soon began to take its toll: Ronnie Washbrook

Gloster PoWs on the march from the Imjin to the Yalu River, over-watched by their Chinese guards. (GLRRM 05449.8)

and 1st Lieutenant Harold Hintz, an American officer, died and TFH fell into a coma from which his friends managed to revive him. Henry Cabral too died in a village – only one march away from their final destination.

After a halt of two days, the men were put on a truck for the final 23 miles of their journey, which was to end at the town of Chiang-song on the Yalu River and, like Sinuiju, right on the border with China. Later, TFH could remember little of that time other than arriving in a courtyard of mud huts and lying under a blanket by a tiny brazier, where a Chinese voice told him: 'You are lucky to have come this day ... Tomorrow is Thanksgiving Day'.[58]

In the days that followed, the men at last received proper medical care, clean clothes, padded winter suits and decent food: rice, bread, bean curd, a little meat, potatoes and tea. There were even powdered eggs and milk for the sick men in the camp hospital. Even so, more men died. Of the eight who had left the coal mine unable to walk, three had already died. One by one, all the rest died too until only TFH was left. His recovery was long and difficult, but he ate all he could get and forced himself to begin walking a little each day. By Christmas Day he could visit others in the camp's hospital wards, share a prayer and sing a carol.

The day came when TFH was asked to pay the bill for his hospital treatment. The first demand was to send greetings to Mao Tse Tung, which TFH and all the others refused. Next they were asked to fill in and sign a form commending the doctors and nurses. TFH, in the hope that their names might reach the international Committee of the Red Cross, wrote a short statement attesting that two doctors and a nurse had indeed attended them. To this were attached the names, ranks and numbers of all the patients. A few days later, he was asked for a day-to-day account of his treatment and to be photographed with the staff. This too he refused. As a result, although he had been told he should remain in the hospital for another six weeks, he was discharged the following day.

On 15 January 1952, TFH and Sergeant John McCracken, a Scot who had emigrated to America and who was now serving in the US Army, boarded a truck bound for a camp at Pyoktong. McCracken had spent time there the previous year and it had an evil reputation. Every day, 15 to 20 men had died from cold, or ill-treatment, or under interrogation. After initial processing, TFH was taken to an unheated hut, but was given padded blue clothing, a greatcoat, a blanket and food. The next day he was allowed to sit in the sun, where he watched the guards taking lessons in political indoctrination, reading and writing – and even exchanged some words with an English-speaking Chinese who was most likely a Commissar. He was, however, kept away from other UN prisoners and his one attempt to speak to another European ended in him being locked in his hut. He was surprised, therefore, when that after-noon – a Saturday – he was fed and taken to a waiting truck with four others, who all turned out to be Americans. One of them, Philip Teague, he had already met at Kang-dong. The others, Captain Charlie Martin, Lieutenant William Wright and Major David MacGhee, were all discharged hospital cases.

An hour's drive through the snow brought them to their new camp: a schoolhouse in Pyn-chong-ni, 10 miles east of Pyoktong and four miles south of the Yalu. Here, the first prisoner TFH met was Anthony Perrins, whom he had last known as Intelligence Officer of the Northumberland Fusiliers; he was at last back with his friends. Here he found Colonel Carne and nearly all the surviving officers and senior NCOs who had been captured at the Imjin River, along with others who had been captured earlier, at New Year 1951. He soon found that he was not the only one who had been tortured. Here at Pyn-chong-ni, the men received food and treatment that was bearable; the next day – being Sunday – there was no early reveille; no compulsory political study – and meals that included meat: pork soup in the morning and pork stew in the afternoon; luxury indeed, since on other days there was only rice, or bread, with either diakon soup or beans. Every 10 days there was a small issue of sugar, tobacco and paper – and a good deal of bartering followed. Little things like paper loomed large in the lives of prisoners; mail was an especially important, if rare, event and one which the Chinese and North Koreans controlled strictly. TFH recalled later that 'I think I got four or five letters from my wife during the whole period [of captivity], even though she wrote every day'.[59]

The camp kitchen and hospital were run by the prisoners – as was the social centre of the camp, the small barbers' shop, where in a small hut heated by a stove, there was a monthly haircut and a weekly shave – as well as all sorts of talk, controversy and rumour-assessment. Everything else, however, was run by the Chinese. Reveille was at dawn and it was followed by physical training exercises, washing and barrack jobs. There was then a tiresome wait of more than two hours for breakfast. This was followed by a morning of political study – lectures from the Chinese, a short break and then another study session ending at 4:00 p.m. Supper was at 4:30 p.m. and was followed by a third period of study – making a total of around nine-and-a-half hours a day. The final episode of the day was an evening address by the Camp Commander, before lights-out at 9:00 p.m. It was a dull, repetitive and irksome regimen, but the dullness on the surface concealed the fact that the prisoners were absolutely in the power of 'evil, political extremists who could – and did – reach into the camp to take out those they wished to exploit …'[60]

As one of their captors, a convinced communist and principal interpreter to the camp Commandant, known to the prisoners as Wong, remarked: 'No one knows you are here. If you resist us, we shall put you in a deep hole where you will remain for 40 years – and your bones will rot. The world will forget you'.[61]

The political study included topics such as starvation in America, or the unaided defeat of Germany and Japan by Russia. The prisoners' hilarity caused much rage among the Chinese – dangerous, given that the camp authorities could reach in and select any man for torture or execution at will. Even so, it was obvious that the programme was a shambles. Word trickled in from outside that peace talks had continued and that the Hanley Report on the treatment of prisoners of war had caused international outrage.* This report, the *United States Senate Subcommittee on Korean War Atrocities of the Permanent Subcommittee of the Investigations of the Committee on Government Operations*, concluded that '…two-thirds of all American prisoners of war in Korea died as a result of war crimes'.

The Chinese made feasts of the American Thanksgiving and Christmas Day 1951; official photographers arrived to record the jollity for propaganda purposes and every effort was made to get prisoners to write letters of thanks to the communist hierarchy. The press representatives were astonished to find that none of the prisoners could read or write! As a result, the senior American officer, Colonel Brown, was arrested, charged with heading a resistance movement and put in an open cell – without greatcoat or bedding – in 40 ° of frost. Two other officers who protested this treatment were also arrested, as was the senior British officer and also Denis Harding, who had just been discharged from hospital after a bout of pneumonia. Their 'trial' took place on 8 February 1952. All read confessions prepared by the Chinese, but all refused to incriminate their fellows in any way. In an attempt to extract co-operation, Harding was strung up from a beam for 24 hours, then left naked in the open air, then strung up again – all without success. Shortly afterwards, sentences of six months' imprisonment – solitary confinement – were handed down to the three senior officers and three months each to the two who had protested.[62] Although the Chinese rarely executed prisoners like their Korean counterparts, mass starvation and diseases, compounded by torture and ill-treatment, had swept through the Chinese-run PoW camps during the winter of 1950-1951. More than 40 percent of all American PoWs died during this period. The Chinese defended their actions by claiming that all Chinese soldiers during this period were suffering mass starvation and diseases due to logistical difficulties, which were caused by UN attacks – a line they continued to take in the winter of 1951-1952. The UN PoWs pointed out that most of the Chinese camps were located near the easily supplied Sino-Korean border and that the Chinese withheld food to force the prisoners to accept their programmes of forced communist indoctrination programmes.[63]

In late February 1952 a flu epidemic struck the camp and half a dozen men went down with pneumonia – TFH was one of them. He was fortunate, for at this time the Camp MO, known as 'the dirty doctor', was replaced by a young man who was clearly more capable and interested

---

*   Colonel James Marin Hanley (1904-1999) served in the US Army during the Second World War and in the Korean War was head of the army's War Crimes Section. After the war he also contributed to the much larger US Senate Report No. 848 of 1954 by Senator Joseph McCarthy.

in his charges. Under his care, TFH recovered and, there being no period of convalescence allowed, returned to the lectures on the twilight of World Capitalism. The prisoners were so uncooperative, however, that by Easter 1952 even the Chinese had to admit defeat and the compulsory study was quietly dropped – under the guise of spring-cleaning, in order to save face.

The Chinese again made a special event of Easter, with extra food – even some *saki* – and of course the inevitable photographers. It made a wonderful change from the poor, basic diet of rice and diakon soup. A British lawyer named Jack Gaster had been invited to China and North Korea by the regime and had clearly seen a stage-managed event, being quoted in the *Shanghai News* that: 'The food I have seen our men eating would make a British housewife's mouth water'.[64]

This sort of encouragement to their enemies – along with that of Mrs Monica Felton – was deeply resented by the prisoners; that their own people should help to hide what was happening from the rest of the world was almost worse than the treatment itself,* but the best part of the Easter festivities was the escape of two Australian pilots and three Americans. The men were caught within a few days, however – as TFH himself remarked, 'It was very hard to escape from a North Korean prison because we looked so different – blue eyes and a fair skin meant we were easily identifiable outside'.[65] The men were later put on trial, charged with a host of farcical offences. Farcical, until sentences of between four and 10 months' imprisonment were handed down.

In spite of this, TFH was determined to make another escape attempt with a large party: Sid Cooper, Jack Hobbs, CQMS Day of the Royal Marines, CSM Harry Gallagher, 'Muscles' Strong, CSM Morton and 2nd Lieutenant Sheldon Foss, an American artillery officer. The escape attempt had been put on hold when news came in that peace talks had re-opened, but it was accepted that if there was no resolution to the war, then the party had to make a break in late July or early August 1952 in order to make the best of the good weather and the available food in the countryside. TFH decided to try a daylight escape based on deception. The plan was to impersonate a water-carrying detail – the red arm-bands worn by the detail were counterfeited – and then give the guards the slip either under cover of a washing detail, which would cause confusion about who was who; or by taking advantage of bad weather, when the guards would seek shelter. The party members were all carefully briefed and each assembled a pack-load of supplies and gear. TFH was even given a compass by Carl Livesey. Over a period of days, the loads were smuggled out of the camp and hidden in a field of maize and beans. After a tense wait, on 28 July there was heavy rain all day and late in the afternoon the party assembled in the guise of fetching water, but it was too wet for the Chinese and the attempt had to be shelved.[66]

It was 4 August before the party had its kit together and was ready for another attempt. The day before, extra food had been given out to honour a Chinese festival which the British and

* Jacob (Jack) Gaster (1907-2007) was a far-left lawyer and MP. He served in the British Army during the Second World War. He travelled to North Korea as part of an international legal delegation. The team produced a report that was widely criticised as being pro-North Korean. Monica Felton (1906-1970) was a far-left feminist who visited North Korea in 1951 – after which she published her anti-war, pro-North Korean book *That's Why I Went* in 1954. As a result, she was sacked from her job as Chairman of Steneage Development Corporation.

Commonwealth officers turned into a celebration to honour the accession of their new Queen, Elizabeth II; the Chinese were furious. The next day, the party gathered all the food they could and donned their red arm-bands. Once at the river, TFH and Gallagher went into the maize field and began to hide the last items of baggage – but they were seen by one of the sentries. Both pretended to have been answering a call of nature, but soon afterwards, Gallagher and Morton were arrested. TFH made it back into the camp and spread the word among the rest of the party – and for a while, nothing happened. At about 8:00 p.m. Sam Weller too was arrested and no sooner had TFH and the others dispersed what they had of their escape kit, his name too was called and he was taken away. Taken in front of the Chinese Company Commander, he was invited to confess to planning an escape, but said nothing and was taken to the cells in the nearby North Korean police station. He found an old nail and scratched his name on the wall, under those of previous prisoners – thus TFH's fifth escape attempt was over before it had properly started.

By now, TFH was generally known by his captors and fellow prisoners alike as a 'thorn in the side of Chinese efforts toward peace and quiet'. He was, as Lofty Large recalled:

> ... another escape-o-maniac, but, like young [Kinne] he only had to see a half chance and he was through it! The problem with that method is you are always on the run in an even weaker state than necessary due to solitary confinement and almost nil rations.
>
> I think the Adjutant [i.e. TFH] was the best chance we had of anyone escaping. He could navigate, had some knowledge of the area and where he was starting from, was switched on mentally and had been physically very fit. Had he played it cool long enough to build up his resources and given himself a fair chance I feel sure he would have cracked it. But, like [Kinne] he was a marked man ...[67]

In solitary confinement, TFH's routine began at dawn with reveille. Prisoners were supposed then to sit cross-legged without moving for the rest of the day, but TFH sat as he wished, able to adopt the right position if he heard the guard approaching. There were two visits to the latrine allowed; a little, poor food; but no washing, smoking or talking. After 10 days, TFH was moved to a gaol that had been built under Japanese rule. Here the conditions were even more spartan than before, but he had the companionship of a young USAF Corporal and two officers – and he could see the outside world. The Americans had been in the gaol since the spring of 1952, charged with using chemical or biological weapons. The Corporal, Abbot, had been repeatedly interrogated and beaten, but had refused to confess to anything. As well as the Americans, TFH became aware that Padre Sam Davies was also detained close by and the two were able to talk through a small gap in the wall.

Sam Davies recalled in his memoir of the war that: 'Tony Farrar-Hockley was just the neighbour needed for such an occasion – a soldier of great resourcefulness and courage, and altogether a man of great versatility... I confided to him my fears about the future. "Steady on, Padre", he said. "In the words of Mr Micawber – 'Something'll turn up'".[68]

Religion being anathema to the communists, Chaplain Davies had been subjected to continuous persecution from the moment of his arrest. Davies later said that he was regarded by the Chinese as 'some sort of special reactionary 'Commissar" attached to the troops and that he had been given 18 days in solitary confinement at one point for 'illegal religious activities and a hostile attitude'.[69] His faith, however, was more than a match for his captors. TFH advised him to feign 'repentance' and allow the Chinese to save face. By this means he could get out of solitary confinement: 'You are no use cooped up here, whereas as Chaplain in the compound you are of very great use'.[70] Davies did as he was advised; it worked. Thereafter he was able to practise his ministry with at least toleration from the Chinese.

TFH was kept in this prison for more than a month: 'Sometimes the days passed swiftly in meditation; sometimes they dragged intolerably'.[71]

In September 1952, he was at last told what charges he would face, but he was able to tell the pre-agreed deception story learned by all members of the party. As a result, although Weller was kept in solitary confinement, TFH, Morton and Gallagher were all released. There had been several more escape attempts while TFH had been in solitary confinement. In fact, during the year there were 41 attempts. None succeeded as far as can be ascertained, although two men managed to cover more than 100 miles before they were recaptured. Otherwise, TFH found the usual routine still in place: arrests, trumped-up 'charges', poor food and little of it – but no weakening in the indomitable spirit of the prisoners. Not long afterwards, however, there was a major change in the life of the camp: the prisoners were divided into two groups and separated into Numbers 1 and 2 Companies.[72] This was in line with the general Chinese practice of keeping men in small groups, where they could be controlled and, if possible, subverted politically rather than in large compounds. TFH's group was put into an annex to the main camp, in which there were several groups of eight to 10 men and one larger group of about 30, constituting No. 4 Company.[73]

Then one morning at the end of October 1952, TFH's platoon was told to pack their gear and prepare to move. TFH was collecting his kit when a Chinese guard, known as Chang, came up to him and said; 'You are not going with the others. Pack your kit and go below to the schoolhouse'.[74]

Not sure what this would mean, TFH said goodbye to his comrades and went down the hill. Here he joined No. 1 Company, in which he had many friends, which was now re-housed in the schoolhouse. He was not left alone for long. That evening, he was again told to pack his kit and taken to the camp headquarters. Here, he was reprimanded for failing to obey regulations and told that he was to be taken elsewhere; he did not know where. After a chilly wait of two hours he was put onto a truck, where there was another wait – and then the journey was cancelled. TFH was locked up for the night, without his kit and with no bedding.

A week later, he was still there. After four days he had managed to get his kit back and then in the evening of the seventh day, the Chinese changed their minds and, with a dire warning on the consequences of future disobedience, he was returned to No. 2 Company – now housed in a different building about a mile west of Pyoktong. This compound was roughly U-shaped, the base formed by the main living accommodation; the kitchen and a small common-room formed the left arm; and a library on the right. Here he was met by the Company Commander and Chang, 'a short, plump individual. This Chang was a graduate of St John's University in Shanghai, spoke excellent English and was in many ways a cultivated man'.

He was also usually polite and amicable with the prisoners, but for all these qualities, he was 'the most dangerous man on the Chinese staff … an unprincipled opportunist, who readily lent himself to the beating-up of members of the escape party…'.[75] TFH's interview was, however, short and he soon found himself back among friends – although he was surprised to be given a billet with the Turksh contingent.

Although the nights were now becoming cold, daytime temperatures through November continued mild and in the wake of the Helsinki Olympic Games, the Chinese decided on a Prisoner-of-War Command Olympics as a propaganda stunt. After much discussion, it was decided that the British officers would take part so as to be able to re-establish contact with other groups. Having never been noted for prowess at sports and games, TFH was not selected for the party, which returned with 'many cheering messages from our men in other camps', and a thoroughly entertaining account of the antics of the Chinese.[76]

At some point – possibly around this time – TFH and the other prisoners were given small notebooks, about three-and-a-half inches by two-and-a-half inches, of poor-quality paper with some Chinese script; the inevitable picture of Chairman Mao; and a small coloured map of Korea: in all, nearly 100 pages of valuable paper. These were probably meant for recording the results of political education. TFH, however, used his for quite a different purpose. Neatly written in ink and filling the entire book is *Set at Hazard* – a murder-mystery play in three acts set over the Christmas holiday in a country house belonging to Mrs Allington. Whether or not this was ever performed is not recorded.[77] TFH's love of amateur dramatics was, however, still very obviously alive and he must have passed many hours pleasantly enough composing the play.

Thanksgiving came round once more, with again improved food – a matter of huge interest and importance to the prisoners. The same extra allowances were made at Christmas and New Year, but the prisoners paid for this with a diet of potatoes and cabbage – occasionally beans – thereafter; but for all that, conditions had improved. There were even a few non-political books brought in, with newspapers. Christian worship was also tolerated. There was no Chaplain, but two officers who were lay assistants led Catholic and Protestant worship on Sundays. Padre Sam Davies was allowed to visit on Christmas Day. TFH was delighted to be able to receive Communion and join an inter-denominational carol service in the evening, which even the Chinese attempt to introduce a lecture on Communism could not spoil.

At midnight on New Year's Eve, TFH and Sid Cooper saw in 1953 – on the promenade in front of their accommodation – a new plan for escape already forming in their heads. Until now, no attempts had been made in winter as the prisoners would be too weak to survive the harsh conditions. However, some men were thought now to be fit enough to try to escape down the frozen Yalu River to the sea, disguised in white clothing. February was set as the date for departure. Two pairs of British officers – one of them TFH and Cooper – and one American pair, began to prepare. The biggest challenge was food, since more than usual would be needed to combat the cold weather. This had to be found and then carried. By various efforts, with some close shaves bordering on discovery, dried meat and dried beans were accumulated. As the date set for the escape approached, the pairs drew lots for who would go first; TFH drew last place. After a delay of a day because of what seemed like an unusual degree of alertness among the guards, the first two pairs tried to slip away. They were immediately arrested and the Chinese guards then came looking for more. TFH just managed to get rid of his pack before the Chinese burst in. Finding nothing, they went off, grumbling – but it was clear that TFH's sixth attempt to escape had been betrayed from within the camp. TFH firmly believed, and reported in his debriefing later, that the source was Major Clifford Allen – a black American.[78]

For four days, nothing happened. Then a Chinese named Chen Chung Hwei arrived and sent for TFH. He told him that he had 'positive information' that TFH was responsible for

The camp at Pyoktang, sketched by Major Guy Ward. This drawing was first published in *The Illustrated London News*, 5 January 1954.

'Life in a Chinese PoW Camp', drawn by Major Guy Ward. This drawing was first published in *The Illustrated London News*, 5 January 1954.

arranging the escape attempt and that if he confessed, he would be spared further punishment. TFH kept silent. He was harangued for half an hour, but then allowed back to the compound. TFH felt sure, however, that Chen had a good source of information and he dispersed his escape kit, helped by Jack Hobbs and CSM George Baker. The next night, TFH was summoned again and told to pack his kit. He was interrogated for eight hours that night by Chen, then allowed two hours' rest, and then handed over to another Chinese called Kung. Instead of being taken back to his cell, TFH was stripped of his padded jacket and thrust into an outhouse. It had been snowing for some hours and the temperature was well below freezing; this was doubtless some sort of softening-up process. TFH did not dare try to sleep for fear of frostbite and passed a thoroughly miserable night. He remained in the outhouse all next day. There was no breakfast and only a meagre supper just before dusk. Soon afterwards, Kung arrived and demanded to know if TFH had decided to confess. TFH made no reply and was left for a second night; this was worse than the first. TFH was, by now, shaking with cold – his hands and feet were swollen and blue. TFH refused both breakfast and supper in an attempt to draw attention to his condition. At first he thought this had failed and he was bound to lose fingers and toes from frostbite. However, a medical orderly was summoned who examined him, gave him some foul-tasting medicine and gave instructions for him to be moved.

The contrast could not have been more marked. He was taken to a room with a heated floor; so hot he had to lie on top of his clothes. When he woke up next morning he found his shirt was badly scorched! From then on, things improved. TFH got at least some of his kit back and Kung – who had failed to break him and could not reappear without severe loss of face – did not return. Two meals came in each day and some exercise – as well as visits to the latrine – was possible. Apart from the dreary routine, TFH could do little but watch the

A Korean village scene of the sort that TFH would have encountered during his several escape attempts. (GLRRM 05451.1)

Chinese guards going about their duties or being put through political indoctrination. After a week, during one of these visits, TFH was surprised to encounter Denis Harding who, although his six-month prison sentence had expired, had been kept in solitary confinement until he signed an undertaking to 'co-operate' – whatever that meant. This was part of the continuing pattern designed to separate those who wielded influence among the prisoners – and so tighten control. TFH's case was not a particularly serious one, though, for in spite of their information, the Chinese had failed to catch him in the act of escaping – but he had to be kept confined for enough time for face to be maintained. Eventually, TFH agreed to confess to having broken a minor regulation related to the daily roll-call and on Easter Sunday – 5 April 1953 – he was released.

TFH immediately noticed that the camp had now, for the first time, been securely fenced in. He also found, however, that truce talks were expected to begin again soon and also that an agreement had been reached for the exchange of seriously ill or wounded prisoners. Armistice negotiations, which had begun after the UN halt on Line *Kansas* in the aftermath of the Imjin River battles, had continued sporadically, with breaks planned or unplanned for two years: first at Kaesong in southern North Korea; then at Panmunjon, right on the 38th parallel. A major area of negotiation was the matter of PoWs and their repatriation. The PVA, KPA and UN Command could not agree on a system of repatriation because many PVA and KPA soldiers refused to be repatriated. The UN Command advised that only 70,000 out of more than 170,000 North Korean and Chinese prisoners desired repatriation. This was unacceptable to the Chinese and North Koreans, if only for reasons of face – so important in the Orient.[79]

With the latest round of these negotiations imminent, conditions in the camps had vastly improved: better food, washing facilities, tobacco and matches, and razors. News came too of a previously unknown camp nearby, housing No. 3 Company, which was made up of hard cases among the non-commissioned ranks requiring special attention. These men were now, suddenly, allowed to visit the other companies for sports and games and recreation. TFH was delighted to see Sergeant Smith and Corporal Bailey of the Glosters, and they him – confounding the Chinese assertions that British soldiers hated their officers! These men brought news of savage treatment meted out to some of the men. Some had been manacled and confined in boxes, no more than six feet by three, for up to six months. Corporal Walters, TFH's radio operator, had been confined in this way and forced to stand to attention for more than 40 hours, until he collapsed. Lofty Large described this sort of treatment in detail:

> Men were put in those boxes for two or three weeks. In at least one case it was for a month. They were handcuffed with their hands behind their backs. They usually had dysentery, but they never came out of the box or had their handcuffs removed for anything. They ate and drank like a dog. The guards kicked or banged the box often, to keep them awake … There were also cages. These were the same as the boxes, only the guards could watch you didn't get any sleep.[80]

Derek Kinne, whom TFH had not seen since the late spring of 1951 but who had made several escape attempts, had endured similar treatment in a box. He had also been hung from a beam for hours on end and so savagely kicked and beaten that he was no longer able to walk properly and had had his hands bound so tightly in the Chinese manner that he found using his hands difficult – yet none had given in to demands that they collaborate.[81]

The next change in the course of events was that the prisoners were allowed to listen to the radio news from Peking, in English – unless there were things their guards did not wish them to hear. From this news, the men heard of the exchange of at least some of their more seriously ill comrades. It was obvious that the peace talks were making progress and as they did, so the prisoners' conditions improved. Sports and games were encouraged, food increased in quality and quantity and the prisoners were able to hold a celebration in honour of the Coronation; but there were constant attempts to use these improvements for propaganda purposes. The senior British and American officers also began to draft orders for behaviour in the event of a truce: a correct attitude was to be maintained; there should be neither fraternisation nor violence. These orders were read out at all camps and became known to the Chinese. Possibly as a result, TFH was re-arrested in late June.

Four nights of interrogation by Chen followed, until 'to my delight, he was forced to retire when an abscess burst in his mouth. Moaning, spitting pus and blood, he hurried away …'[82] The questioning, however, continued all night: questions about the Coronation celebrations, escape preparations, the prisoners' behaviour in the event of a truce; the inquisitors appeared to be fishing on the basis of not much hard evidence and TFH was not asked to confess to any particular crime. It was not until 19 July that TFH realised what the interrogation was really all about: a chance meeting with another prisoner, Lieutenant Guy 'Guido' Temple, made TFH aware of an attempt to murder the Camp Commandant. Temple and another prisoner had managed to slip out of the camp a few days earlier and had made a thorough reconnaissance of the area – returning to the compound of their own volition. This puzzled the Chinese exceedingly – pushing them to the conclusion that the two had made contact with non-existent secret agents in the hills. TFH's arrest, it seemed, had originally been aimed at finding out more about Temple's absence, but at about the same time, a Korean had made a bungled attempt to shoot the Commandant and had been immediately shot by the guards. Chinese logic determined that TFH had sent Temple out to make contact with the assassin and show him, by a photograph, the identity of the Commandant. It began to look as if TFH would only be saved by the conclusion of a truce, even though the Chinese had no evidence other than imaginings for their case.

The next day, TFH was formally charged with being an accomplice to the attempt: 'I had never seen Ding [i.e. Ding Fang, the Commandant] more angry; nor more frightened', TFH recalled.[83]

Ding harangued TFH for more than an hour, chain-smoking and trembling throughout. TFH was threatened with dire penalties if he did not confess and also incriminate Harding. TFH made no answer and was sent back to his cell for several days. Then, on 27 July, a Chinese whom TFH had never seen before came into the cell carrying a long paper rolled up in his hand. He ordered TFH to read it. TFH did so, expecting to find a sentence of imprisonment. Instead, it was a formal notice stating that a truce would come into effect at 1100 hrs that morning – in 15 minutes' time. Later, TFH was told that two officers had signed confessions and that they, and Weller, who had not confessed to anything, had received long prison terms – making the point that the Chinese would keep selected people as long as they wished even after a truce came into effect. TFH still said nothing. He had one more interview with Ding, who was clearly mortified at the thought of all his prisoners being taken away and he having achieved nothing.

In the Armistice Agreement which had been shown to TFH, signed on 27 July 1953, a Neutral Nations Repatriation Commission was set up to handle the matter of PoWs and this had unlocked the stalemate. What TFH would later discover was that this agreement restored the border between the Koreas near the 38th parallel and created the Korean Demilitarized Zone (DMZ), a two-and-a-half-mile (four-kilometre)-wide fortified buffer zone between the two countries. Tension, incidents and threats from the North continue to this day. On 5 August 1953 the first prisoners were exchanged and TFH was released from close arrest.[84] Back in the compound he found a new Company Commander, who said to him: 'No trouble from you, now there is peace in Korea. Soon you will go home ... No trouble from you and you will be all right'.[85]

He found, too, a new atmosphere among the prisoners: impatience to leave and doubt that the Chinese would keep their side of any bargain. However, each day the radio news gave details of exchanges at Panmunjon. It was also known that a delegation from the International Committee of the Red Cross was to visit and the Chinese were clearly anxious to discover what the prisoners would say to them – fearing loss of face. Soon cigarettes and other comforts began to appear in large quantities, along with Red Cross parcels that had clearly been with-held for months, if not years.

On 17 August, TFH and his companions left the camp for the last time in several trucks. Not far down the road, just outside No. 1 Company's compound, the men were told to dismount from their vehicles and go inside. There, TFH had his first sight in many months of Lieutenant-Colonel Carne: 'He was very thin; his face was drawn and his eyes tired ... . He had been in solitary confinement for 19 months'.[86]

TFH joined a long line of men anxious to shake Carne's hand. After a delay of two days, the men were moved on. It turned out that the Red Cross had been due to visit and, intent on avoiding such a visit, the Chinese had accelerated the repatriation programme. On 19 August, the convoy of trucks carrying the men left Pyn-chong-ni, heading east. The journey was uneventful and by late afternoon the men were boarding a train for a move south. By the following evening, they were at Pyongyang, where they changed trains. The next afternoon they drew up at Kaesong Station, having crossed country that TFH recognised from his earlier escape attempts.

Their destination was a staging area in a series of tented camps south-east of Kaesong. Here, the men were held for eight days – the result of the Chinese stratagem to avoid contact with the Red Cross. However, on the eighth day, exchanges began. Each night, around 10 men of all nationalities would be taken out. The days seemed to drag interminably and what was worse, the food began to deteriorate once more. One of the few consolations was a Sunday church service for the Protestants. TFH was much struck by Psalm 126 – which describes the delight of the Jews after the end of the Egyptian captivity – and felt that he 'ought to remember the words; and to remember all my many prayers that had been answered during my captivity'.[87]

One evening, an officer of the 8th Hussars came running into the dining hall, shouting that names were being called and that TFH was one of them. He collected his belongings, said goodbye to his friends and was taken to join some of the Glosters' NCOs and men in a holding area. At dawn the next day, after a final speech reminding them of their good treatment in the hands of the Chinese, the men were put on trucks and told that they would be exchanged at 0900 hrs. At 0845 hrs, the last check-point was passed and the trucks entered the exchange zone, in the area in which the truce negotiations had been carried out.

Before I could realise it, we had pulled up … and a pair of steps had been put against the back of the truck. An American began to call out our names and a Chinese checked them against a list.

I did not need my bundle of belongings any more. It remained by the seat on which I had been sitting. I suddenly realised that it was a very hot morning as I came down the steps into the sunlight to be clapped on the back by an American soldier who led me towards a wooden arch marked: 'Welcome to Freedom.'

It was nine o'clock on the 31st August 1953.[88]

11

'I'm finding this very difficult' Home Service, December 1953-March 1956

On 20 December 1951 the troopship *Empire Fowey* had brought the reconstituted 1st Glosters back from Korea in time for Christmas, where they were met by cheering crowds and newsreel cameras, a message from the King, another from Ridgway, and speeches from the Mayor and Lord-Lieutenant of Gloucestershire.

By an odd chance, the Chinese had released the names of many of their prisoners on the previous day.[1] The battalion had been re-formed under Digby Grist from those 169 survivors who had made it back from the Imjin,[2] wounded men returned to duty and those on leave in Japan. Within a few days, Grist had about 250 all ranks and insisted that the battalion be returned to duty. Ten days after the Imjin River battle, the Glosters were operational again – guarding bridges on the Han River. Soon afterwards, on 8 May, General James Van Fleet presented the US Presidential Citation to the battalion – the highest award of distinction that a unit can receive from the American military – the ribbon of which is still worn on the sleeves of the Glosters' successor regiment today.[3]

The Chinese offensive that had fallen on the Glosters at the Imjin had been halted at the 'No-Name Line', north of Seoul. On 15 May 1951, the Chinese commenced the second phase of their Spring Offensive and attacked the ROK Army and X (US) Corps in the east at the Soyang River. After gaining some initial successes, they were halted by 20 May. At the end of May, the US Eighth Army counter-attacked once more and regained Line *Kansas*, just north of the 38th parallel. Here Ridgway halted further movement north and thus began the stalemate that lasted until the Armistice of 1953.

At this point, the Glosters returned to the Imjin River battle site to find unburied bodies lying everywhere – and thus the harrowing task of identifying the dead from their identity disks or personal effects. It was about this time that the Glosters acquired their second nick-name – as Digby Grist recalled, speaking to a Canadian officer: 'We reckon you Gloucesters [*sic*] are gloomy. You want to snap out of it!'[4] Easier said than done – but the opportunity to lighten the mood came with the formation of the Commonwealth Division under Major-General James Cassels* in August 1951. The division was ordered to advance across the Imjin. Only two weeks later, the battalions of 29 Brigade began to be relieved. The 1st Welch were to

---

* Later Field Marshal Sir Archibald James Halkett Cassels GCB KBE DSO (1907-1996). He had served throughout the Second World War and was later Director of Operations in Malaya and Chief of the General Staff.

The Colonel-in-Chief of the Glosters – HRH Prince Henry, Duke of Gloucester – arriving to greet the returning prisoners of war from Korea with Lieutenant-General Sir Edward Wetherall, Colonel of the regiment. Pat Farrar-Hockley is on the extreme left of the picture. (Farrar-Hockley family)

take over the Glosters' positions, but it was to the 1st Royal Leicesters that Grist, his officers and NCOs were detailed to help ease the new unit in until their departure.

Back in England, the Glosters had moved to Warminster in Wiltshire as Demonstration Battalion at the School of Infantry. In February 1952 the battalion had lined the route for the funeral procession of King George V in London and in April it had received new Colours in Gloucester. The battalion sent a representative party to take part in the Coronation in June 1953.[5] All the while, Carne, TFH and the rest were still prisoners in the hands of the Chinese.

* * *

After their release at the end of August 1953, the prisoners were first reunited with each other. In a letter to a friend soon after his release, Carne wrote that:

> All of us are pretty fit considering everything, although some have lost weight particularly Denis Harding, Sam Weller and Pike. I was alone for the last 18 months, but all our officers, and the sergeants, were first class in captivity as far as I can make out. Much respected by our allies.[6]

They were then taken straight to Japan for debriefing[7] in order to extract as much information from them as possible that might be useful either militarily or for future war-crimes trials, should these ever be possible. TFH's two-part debriefing document runs to 50 pages and ends with this comment by Major A.N. West-Watson, who commanded the debriefing unit and who personally conducted TFH's interrogation:

> Source [i.e. TFH] has during his captivity, displayed a courage and high sense of duty which it would be difficult to surpass. His continual enthusiasm for escapes, in spite of all the punishment received when captured, must have been an inspiration to all United Nation PW with whom he came into contact. Since his release he has been of considerable assistance to this Unit, in assisting the interrogation of many other ex-PW, and in supplying a vast amount of useful information.[8]

Carne and TFH also went together to the British Embassy on 7 September. A Top-Secret memo from the Ambassador recorded that Carne had outlined the treatment he had received at the hands of the Chinese and that he had been given a series of messages to communicate to the British, which seem now far-fetched:

a)   The Chinese would like the early unification of Korea but if this is not possible, they want a buffer zone larger than the present one which should be policed by Chinese and British forces. They would accept a British command and, at a pinch, only British forces.
b)   They would like the United Kingdom to undertake the reconstruction of both North and South Korea.
c)   The price the Chinese would be prepared to pay for the good offices of the United Kingdom would be:-
    i)   Cessation of the war in Malaya;
    ii)   The renewal of the lease of the New Territories at Hong Kong when it expires in (?) 1985;
    iii) The possible grant of the mandate of Formosa to the United Kingdom provided the UK would maintain a sizeable pacific Fleet;
    iv)   The settlement of the Indo-China question.
    … He was asked how, assuming that the Chinese really wanted him to communicate all this to HMG, they expected to get a reaction from us. Colonel Carne said that the Chinese had urged the early appointment of a fully-accredited Ambassador to China with whom they could discuss matters.[9]

The Ambassador concludes with the remark that 'This does not make sense'. One has to agree.

TFH embarked on the troopship *Empire Orwell* and sailed from Japan on 12 September.[10] He seems to have tried to get Korea out of his system during the voyage by writing poetry, as a number of drafts and typed fair copies survive in his papers. Some are very personal in nature and directed to Pat; others visualise the English countryside; others are clearly religious, like this one, which echoes Newman's 'Lead, Kindly Light' and 'The Pillar of Cloud':

Be very dear to me:
Thus I would have you be,
Closer than a friend.
Be a high tow'r of strength –
A kindly path whose length
Leads by a friendly tread
Far from the past … .[1]

More practically, he had on at least one occasion to break up a fight when some men were trying to throw another overboard – on the ground that he had collaborated with the Chinese. TFH, having been so close to breaking point himself during his torture, had a good deal more sympathy and understanding for what the man might have done, and why, than did many others – but there was another aspect to the matter of return: his family's feelings.

After the Imjin battle, Digby Grist had written to Pat telling her that TFH had not rejoined what had been saved of the battalion and had therefore been posted as missing. His words that TFH had been, 'All through the three nights and days of this huge Chinese attack … as ever, an inspiration and a goad',[12] were of little comfort. On 17 May, Grist was able to write again with more hopeful news. Privates Fox and Graham had rejoined after their escape and had brought word that TFH had been seen, alive, on 7 May.[13] Pat forwarded the letter to the Director of Personnel Administration in the War Office and after a delay – during which time

The *Empire Orwell* docks at Southampton with returning PoWs, TFH among them, 1953.
(GLRRM 05481.1)

he too had received and reviewed Fox and Graham's accounts. He was not, however, prepared to list TFH officially as a Prisoner of War; only as 'Missing – believed Prisoner of War'.[14]

This meant that TFH's pay stopped and Pat therefore lost her income and her entitlement to quarters or hirings. Feeling sure in herself that TFH was still alive, but fuming at the attitude of officialdom in the face of sacrifice in war, she packed up at Polstead Hall and went back to Ealing, where TFH's family did their best to keep her occupied and supported. In August, TFH's remaining personal effects that had not been lost or fallen into enemy hands, which he had left with A Echelon, were sent to Japan and then back to Pat via Liverpool.[15] It was not until December, just in time for Christmas, that the emotional roller-coaster slowed, when the Chinese released an official list of prisoners on which TFH was named.[16] At least his pay re-started and Pat had something to live on and some hope of seeing him again. Thereafter, Pat wrote almost daily – although very few of her letters ever reached TFH and even fewer of his arrived in Ealing. One letter at least was received in June 1952, giving the address of Camp 2. This and subsequent instructions from DPA express hope that letters are coming in and that letters to prisoners were being handed over at the site of peace negotiations in Panmunjon.[17] From then until the date of TFH's release there was only a letter from Captain Bob Hickey to his parents, asking them to get in touch with Pat and tell her that TFH was alive and well.[18] On 30 August 1953, however, came the telegram announcing his release and a letter confirming that he was well, would go to Japan and then home by ship – arriving in about eight weeks.[19]

The ship docked at Liverpool on 14 October.[20] Although the long voyage had delayed the reunion with Pat and Dair, it did at least allow time for readjustment, medical attention and plenty of good food. There was time, too, for the released prisoners to talk over their experiences with comrades who had shared the same hardships and for Pat and the other wives to prepare themselves for the emotional shock of reunion. Then there was Dair, who did not remember his father at all and for whom there would be a big change in his life and the pattern of his relationships. Air travel is a wonderful thing, but too often in modern operations, soldiers have been pulled straight from combat and within a few hours, dumped into normal life. The contrasts are too stark and can cause huge difficulties in adjusting to changed circumstances – especially in terms of family relationships, where each partner has learned to be alone and has made changes to their lifestyle which they can resent having once more to abandon. In both Iraq and Afghanistan 50 years later, the army reintroduced a period of decompression, which essentially did the same job as the troopship voyages used to do.

Once back at home, the released prisoners rejoined their old battalion – at least on paper. It would have been a thoroughly awkward business, for example, for the sitting CO to be sharing an office with Carne, but they were all together on 21 November 1953 when the City and County of Gloucester paid tribute to them as the whole battalion marched through the city – welcomed by one of the biggest crowds ever seen there. For the last time, Carne led the parade. He was, by now, an almost legendary figure – having been awarded the DSO for bravery and distinguished conduct at Hill 327, the US Distinguished Service Cross and then the VC for his actions on the Imjin. While in captivity, Carne had managed to carve a small Celtic cross out of stone and during the Thanksgiving service in Gloucester Cathedral that followed the march, he handed this cross into the care of the Dean.[21]

The list of honours and awards to the Glosters, published shortly after this, was a truly staggering tally which has never since been surpassed. In addition to Carne's VC, the second VC

– Curtis – was a posthumous award, but there were two more DSOs, a George Cross, an OBE, six MCs, three MBEs, two DCMs, 10 MMs, 13 BEMs and 55 Mentions-in-Despatches.[22] The two DSOs went to Harding and to TFH for their actions at the Imjin River.[23] TFH's citation, recalling his command of A Company and their almost hopeless but successful counter-attack, reads as follows:

> Throughout this desperate engagement, on which the ability of the battalion to hold its position entirely depended, Captain Farrar-Hockley was an inspiration to the defenders. His outstanding gallantry, fighting spirit and great powers of leadership heartened his men and welded them into an indomitable team. His conduct could not have been surpassed.

He was also twice mentioned in despatches (once for the action at Hill 327 [24] and the second time for his conduct while a prisoner)[25] and also received the British and UN Campaign medals – making 10 medals and three MiDs for active service and for braverysince 1942.

For TFH, like everyone else, there was a period of medical assessment in the Aldershot British Military Hospital. A report detailed the various conditions from which released prisoners were likely to suffer as a result of their deprivations:[26] malaria, dysentery, hepatitis, malnutrition and its frequent result, pneumonia, arthritis, osteoporosis caused by calcium deficiency, cirrhosis of the liver, frostbite, and the physical effects of torture. TFH himself had had malaria and blackwater fever – and it appears that he also developed hepatitis.

There was also the difficult job of re-establishing relationships with his wife and son after a long absence – especially long in terms of the lifespan of a young child. The reunited family stayed at Byron Road, Ealing and Dair later recalled how when his father returned he was, inevitably, a stranger. His mother had seemed rather detached – perhaps the result of losing her second child and then being left alone with all the pain and stress of not knowing what was happening to her husband (if he was alive even) and if she would ever see him again. Fortunately, Bryony was also living at Byron Road and this provided welcome company, but TFH was not for a long while his old, ebullient self. He woke up in the night, shouting and in a muck sweat as he relived his experiences in his dreams; at other times he sat, staring into the fire, for hours with tears in his eyes.

'I'm finding this very difficult', he would sometimes say – and no wonder; he was undoubtedly suffering from what is now known as Post-Traumatic Stress Disorder.

TFH as a Captain in the Glosters immediately after his return from Korea. (Farrar-Hockley family)

Dr William Shadish concluded from various studies that at least 80 percent of ex-prisoners suffered from some sort of mental illness which would manifest itself in various ways and that TFH's symptoms were typical: anxiety, restlessness, insomnia, memory loss, nightmares and 'survivor guilt'.[27]

The experience of Korea changed him and stayed with him forever. He would never, ever, waste food or throw food away. Even when he had recovered, he was always a rather distant father – not unloving by any means and always a good friend – but he was not to be interrupted while working and there was not much hugging.[28] What pulled him through? A combination, probably, of the love of his family, the strength of his Christian faith and a sense of purpose generated by the return to hard work in the arms of his other family, the British Army. He also continued to use the effort of writing to get Korea out of his system. He and Pat went to Denmark for a long leave, taking young Dair, to stay with Pat's cousin Mary Morning, who was married to a Dane and lived in Copenhagen. Here and in Ealing, with Pat acting as typist and editor, he wrote *The Edge of the Sword*, which was published the following year to immediate acclaim. It was written very rapidly and this was probably made possible by the detailed debriefing TFH had gone through in Japan. Although he was not permitted to keep a copy of the interrogation document – it was classified – he had an excellent memory and had retained the experience. When one compares the report with the text of the book, the similarities are immediately obvious. The book was reprinted again in 1993 and once more in 2007.

*   *   *

In February 1954, TFH was posted once again to a staff appointment: this time as Staff Captain 'Q' in the headquarters of Eastern Command at Wilton Park, Beaconsfield under the command of Lieutenant-General Geoffrey Bourne – later famous as Templer's predecessor in Malaya and the architect of the plan that delivered a successful campaign there. The Commands,* which were headed by a 3-star General, were responsible for the administrative command of all units in their area of responsibility; for civil-military liaison; for inter-service co-ordination; and for military aid to the civil authorities – but not for the training of combat units assigned to deployable divisions or corps.[29] Under them there were a number of districts, commanded by major-generals, which were usually contiguous with TA divisions, regular formations and garrisons. Eastern Command at this time consisted of Home Counties District, which was also 44th Division; East Anglian District, which was also the 54th Division; and South Midlands District, also 48th Division. In addition, there were elements of the Strategic Reserve such as 19 and 29 Infantry Brigades. For TFH, having previously been both a DAAG in a Divisional Headquarters and a GSO2 in an RAF Group Headquarters, this was something of a come-down. However, with reductions in the army and reversions in rank all round, it was inevitable – and he was, after all, still very young. The Staff Captain 'Q' was one of a team of three, responsible for mundane matters such as works services in barracks and married quarters. TFH's colleagues here were Major Brian de Saulles of The Queen's, and Captain Robert Owen of the Argylls. It was a soft landing, in fact. His immediate superior,

---

* At this date, these were Eastern, Western, Southern, Scottish and Northern. London and Northern Ireland were free-standing districts. The Commands were merged into UK Land Forces between 1968 and 1972.

the AQMG – Lieutenant-Colonel W.P.M. Allen of the Middlesex Regiment – remarked that he had maintained his drive and enthusiasm, even though he was 'very much more suited by temperament and previous experience for a staff appointment with a field force formation'.

He also remarked, as had Bredin in 1st Airborne Division, that 'His chief failing is a certain impatience with the staffs of other HQs and formations who do not work at the same high tempo or to the same high standard which he sets himself'.[30]

The Brigadier General Staff, Richard Anderson,* agreed and described him as 'A most promising young officer who is well above the average of his rank. He has a forceful character and a pleasant personality'.

The Chief of Staff, Major-General John Cowley,† concurred and recommended him for a place at the Staff College. This appointment only lasted seven months, however, for TFH had already been selected for a place at Camberley.

On 23 September 1954, he was sent to the Royal Military College of Science, Shrivenham for a short course of one month in Military Science and Technology and then on a five-day briefing at the School of Infantry in Warminster.[31] His report from the Commandant at Shrivenham described him as 'certainly the most outstanding officer on the course'.

Acknowledging that TFH had little technical background and found some of the technical subjects difficult, the Commandant mad it clear that TFH had worked extremely hard to overcome this lack:

> A most outstanding officer with a very charming but forceful personality. He is an extremely good speaker who took a leading part in all aspects of the course. From the beginning he established himself in a dominating position … He is capable of much original thought, and his style of writing is refreshing though at times somewhat bizarre.[32]

This was the precursor to his attending the Army Staff College, Camberley – for which he had been recommended repeatedly in his annual confidential reports and for which he had now been selected – having passed the required examination at some point, which is not recorded in his documents. This was a crucial moment in his professional career. The family moved to a married quarter at 5 Queen Elizabeth Road, Camberley. Dair – who was now nine – was away at his prep school, Beaudesert Park, but there had been a very recent addition: on 14 October 1954 the Farrar-Hockley's third son and second surviving child, Hilary – sometimes known as 'Hils' – was born. Against the background noise of a very young baby, therefore, TFH settled down for a year of very hard graft.

*   *   *

---

*   Later Lieutenant-General Sir Richard Neville Anderson KCB CBE DSO (1907-1979); had served on active duty before and during the Second World War. He was later GOC 17th Gurkha Division and GOC-in-C MELF and GOC-in-C Northern Ireland.

†   Later Lieutenant-General Sir John Guise Cowley GC KBE CB AM (1905-1993) – later Master-General of the Ordnance.

Even before sitting the examination, there were certain qualifications required of a Staff College candidate: 'Good service in the field. Three years' service as Adjutant. Good service on the staff or as an instructor for two years'.[33]

With a peacetime establishment of 290,000 – of whom 19,000 were officers – the army sent 140 senior captains to the Staff College each year; 15 percent of those eligible, therefore.[34] At the time, the Staff College at Camberley followed a one-year-long curriculum based on military history from the Napoleonic Wars to the Second World War; military strategy; Soviet military studies; and the study of brigade, division and corps level operations in all phases of war, logistics, and imperial policing. There was also much attention to the conventions of service writing, and to learning by rote the long tables of unit and formation organisations.[35] The syllabus was partly geared to the needs of an army still heavily engaged in the security of the Empire – especially in the Middle East, Malaya, Kenya, Cyprus and Hong Kong – as well as the demands of a continental army to confront the Soviets (trying desperately to hold on to the legacy of the Second World War in terms of campaigning and military strategy at a very large scale, in the face of the continuing reductions in defence spending).

The college was organised in three divisions – A, B and C – of which A and B were accommodated in the college at Camberley and C (of which TFH was a member) was housed three miles away at Hawley. Central lectures and exercises meant time on a bus, therefore. Each division was headed by a Colonel and divided into six syndicates of 10 students: seven British officers and three Allied, Empire or other service students under a Directing Staff Lieutenant-Colonel. The year's course was divided into five terms and at each term-break there was a re-shuffle of syndicates to ensure that students were assessed by a number of Directing Staff officers. The students may have been in the top 15 percent of the army, but the DS were even more highly selected and, as a body, were a by-word for enforcing rigorous staff duties and discipline.

The emphasis throughout the course was on thorough appreciations of a given situation, leading to the 'right' answer, as laid out in the Directing Staffs' 'Pink' (so-called because the notes for the staff were always printed on pink paper). This regime endured at Camberley almost to the end of its existence; it was certainly alive and well in the late 1980s. John Masters recalled the same during his time at the Staff College in Quetta, where he was ticked off severely in his final interview for being scruffy, failing to attend to minor conventions of service writing, and being opinionated – that is, daring to differ from the received view of things. This could be dangerous, for as he wrote: 'There was no more important phase of a professional career, except command in battle'.[36] The last phrase is telling, and might not have been universally shared by selection boards. Fortunately, TFH had the benefit of both.

Those officers who did not attend the Staff College were unlikely to be promoted beyond Major. They were almost guaranteed to reach that rank as a result of the Hore-Belisha Reforms before the Second World War, but there was always the danger that those who went through the Staff College would become more process-driven, more predictable, less dangerous to an enemy than those who spent their time in the field – and so lose their trust in intuition. However, even before the Second World War, and certainly in the 1950s, '… it had become impossible for an officer to reach a senior post without having the psc [passed staff college] qualification'.[37]

TFH's division at the Staff College, Camberley. (Farrar-Hockley family)

Under Deverell as CIGS from 1936 to 1937, 100 percent of the 168 brigadiers and above were psc – and this figure had declined only slightly to 95.2 percent under Gort (1937-1939).[38] A survey of 1945 divisional commanders shows that the trend had survived the war.[39]

These tendencies, to rely on the 'right' answer and to denigrate the experience of field command can be seen in TFH's report endorsed by the Commandant, Major-General Charles Jones,* which says his:

> Farrar-Hockley has a very strong and forceful personality and tremendous determination. He is honest, straightforward and sincere and possesses plenty of energy and self-confidence. He has a good brain and accepts responsibility with ease. His views, normally sound, are always put over clearly and with great conviction and he is certainly not easily swayed by others: indeed he is rather too prone to stand up for his own opinions even when they have been proved false. In all work and activities he has shown himself to possess powers of leadership well above the average and on occasions he can be rather too dominating. Without doubt he is a high class officer, full of zeal and sparkle but at present he is inclined to apply, without sufficient consideration, lessons he has learnt in war. This and his dogmatism may earn him hard knocks in the future but he is resilient and imaginative and should go a long way in the Service both in command and on the staff.

---

* Later General Sir Charles Phibbs Jones GCB CBE MC (1906-1988).

It was clear that TFH had managed to put the experience of his Chinese captivity behind him and that he was once more his old self: enthusiastic, very hard working, hard on himself and on others, and with no time for anything other than total commitment from anyone. However, the experience of war and captivity in Korea, on top of the experiences of the Second World War and Palestine, had given TFH some very firm views and qualities. He knew the importance of thinking ahead, anticipating the future and having an outline intention – or perhaps vision – in mind, linked closely to his belief in always seeking to gain, maintain and exploit the initiative. In doing so, improvisation and rapid problem-solving were crucial skills. He believed strongly in communicating and keeping everyone informed of a changing situation – especially retaining key points of detail. He gave, and expected, complete trust in those around him; right or wrong, he would stick with them. This, with his strong emphasis on care of the men as an officer's primary responsibility at all times and in all places, was a key element in his ability to inspire men to achieve astonishing results in spite of great adversity – but above all, TFH had become strongly unorthodox in much of his thinking.

Doctrine books and tactical manuals were the starting point for a plan; not a substitute for it. TFH knew well that no plan ever survives contact with the enemy and therefore, one had to think outside the box; no hidebound thinking for him. This sort of approach, his strong personality and his willingness to argue a point were bound to put up backs in some – especially some of his superiors – and this to a great degree explains many of the comments made about him by reporting officers.[40] This could have stopped his career dead on more than one occasion, in spite of all his achievements. However, TFH had one other quality which helped him in this regard, as in many others: he was lucky. Of course, by planning ahead and preparing carefully, as he emphasised, one can to a degree make one's own luck – but there are times too when the random nature of luck takes a hand, so much so that one cannot afterwards explain how or why such-or-such a thing turned out as it did.

TFH with a group of fellow Staff College students on a TEWT, 1955. (Farrar-Hockley family)

TFH and the cast of the Staff College pantomime. (Farrar-Hockley family)

Somehow during the course of the year at Camberley, TFH found the time to help Derek Kinne write his account of the Korean War and his time as a prisoner, published by Frederick Mueller in 1955: *The Wooden Boxes*.[41] He also returned to amateur dramatics by playing a leading role in writing and producing the Staff College pantomime – a hallowed tradition at Camberley. Far more impressively he began work on editing the papers of General Sir Ian Hamilton, a task entrusted to him by the Hamilton family, which were published by Hollis & Carter in 1957.[42] This task was a great compliment to TFH by the Hamilton family, showing that they placed complete trust in both TFH's abilities as a writer and in his discretio.

In November 1955, TFH was once again posted to a staff appointment – this time back to the Airborne Forces after an absence of nine years – in the prestigious job of DAA & QMG of 16 Parachute Brigade. Brigade Majors and 'DQs' were much sought-after posts: reserved – with some other posts in the War Office and military assistants, to senior officers – for the top 10 percent of the Staff College students. TFH had clearly attained this level, passing out with a 'B' grade: No-one ever – ever – was given an 'A' grade.

12

'Our destination was a matter for speculation'
16 Parachute Brigade in the Middle East: Cyprus, Suez and Jordan, 1956-1958

TFH, once again promoted to the temporary rank of Major, joined the headquarters of 16 Independent Parachute Brigade Group in Aldershot on 14 November 1955[1] – under the command of Brigadier Mervyn ('Tubby') Butler – as its DAA & QMG in succession to Major T.J. Barrow. A Brigade Headquarters in those days was a small affair, with only five staff-trained officers including the Commander and the officer commanding the Signals Squadron. TFH's contemporaries included the Brigade Major, Miles Marston of the Argyll and Sutherland Highlanders, and the GSO2 Air, Major Frank King – later a full General – who was responsible for all aspects of training and operations related to parachuting. Working under TFH were two staff captains: one for 'A' and one for 'Q'.[2] The family moved into a married quarter, near the Prince Consort's Library, at 6 Knollys Road. Hilary was just over a year old and Dair, now aged 10, was still at his prep school.

16 Parachute Brigade and its counterpart in the Territorial Army, 44 Parachute Brigade, were all that now remained of the wartime airborne corps.[3] The title of 16 Brigade perpetuated the two airborne divisions – 1 and 6 – but the brigade's direct lineage was, ironically, to the old 2 Independent Parachute Brigade with which TFH had served from 1942 to 1946. The brigade was concentrated at Aldershot – close to the RAF bases of Odiham, Benson and Lyneham – and consisted of three parachute infantry battalions: the 1st, 2nd and 3rd Battalions of The Parachute Regiment; the 1st having been re-designated from TFH's old battalion, the 6th (Royal Welch) – the 1st Guards Independent Parachute Company, 33 Parachute Light Regiment RA, 9 Parachute Squadron RE, 216 Headquarters and Signals Squadron (including a Brigade Headquarters Defence Platoon, Light Aid Detachment REME and a Postal Section), 16 Parachute Field Ambulance, 63 Parachute Company RASC and 16 Brigade Ordnance Field Park.[4] The Parachute Regiment at this time had no permanent cadre and was maintained by seconding officers and men from infantry regiments after they had completed initial training and a period of regimental duty. Those who had not qualified as parachutists had to undergo a period of selection and then drop training at the hands of the staff of P Company – an extended version of the programme that TFH had undergone in 1942, conducted by a smaller version of the old Parachute Holding and Training Battalion

with which he had served in 1948 – in order to confirm their suitability for service in the brigade. TFH himself, having not jumped since 1947, had to carry out refresher training and qualifying jumps before taking up his new post.

Once British forces had withdrawn from Korea, and the Cold War had begun in earnest, the army effectively divided into two streams. First, there were the armoured and motorised divisions and brigades which formed the garrison of Germany – Britain's contribution to NATO's Northern Army Group facing the Soviet threat to Europe. Secondly, there were the light, more easily transportable formations – 17th Gurkha Division in the Far East; and the Strategic Reserve in Britain consisting of the 3rd Infantry Division and 16 Independent Parachute Brigade Group which, with 3 Commando Brigade Royal Marines, provided the rapidly deployable forces for interventions outside Europe. Some units – especially line infantry battalions – could of course spend time in both streams, as well as undertaking garrison duties in what remained of the Empire overseas, but as nuclear deterrence made open war in Europe less likely, it was in the Middle and Far East, and in Africa, that the East-West confrontation resulted in actual conflict.

One of these conflicts was in Cyprus, which erupted as Korea stabilised and the insurgency in Malaya was brought under control. The island, originally part of the Byzantine Empire but later conquered by the Ottoman Turks, had been acquired by the British Empire from Turkey in 1878 through a leasing arrangement. When Turkey joined the Central Powers in 1914, Britain terminated the lease and annexed the island as a Crown Colony, although in 1915, Britain actually offered the island to Greece in return for Greece's entry into the war – an offer which was declined. Under British rule, Cyprus escaped the ethnic cleansing of Greeks and Turks from each others' territory which followed the Greco-Turkish War between 1919 and 1922. Its Greek population, however – 80 percent of the island's total – had never forgotten its identity; and since the Ottoman Empire began to break up in the 1820s, had wished for reunion with Greece, or *Enosis*.[5] There had been significant troubles in 1930 and 1931 when British troops had been deployed. Throughout the Second World War and after, Greece was in no position to press any claim to the island – being either allied to Britain, or under German occupation, or torn by civil war. From the late 1940s however, Greek Cypriots again revived the old dream, but the membership of NATO by both Greece and Turkey added a new dimension to the old enmities. Turkey, meanwhile, saw itself as the guarantor of the rights and freedoms of the Turkish minority and tensions between the communities, resulting from the campaign for *Enosis,* almost provoked war between the two countries.

For Britain, Cyprus had become, belatedly, a vital component in its security architecture in the Middle East. Once both Palestine and the Suez Canal Zone had been evacuated, Cyprus, which lies about 40 miles (65 kilometres) south of Turkey, 50 miles (80 kilometres) west of the coastline of Israel, Syria and Lebanon and 250 miles (400 kilometres) from Egypt – but 500 miles (800 kilometres) east of Greece – provided a perfect location for the basing of land, sea and air forces, as well as for intelligence gathering in the region. Britain's oil interests in Iran and Iraq, the free navigation of the Suez Canal and her relationship with the Baghdad Pact required Britain to remain engaged. As an official government statement put the matter: 'Britain can no more consider relinquishing our sovereignty over Cyprus at the present time than over Gibraltar … Britain's experience in Egypt [i.e. in the Canal Zone] had shown that bases without sovereignty cannot always be relied on'.[6]

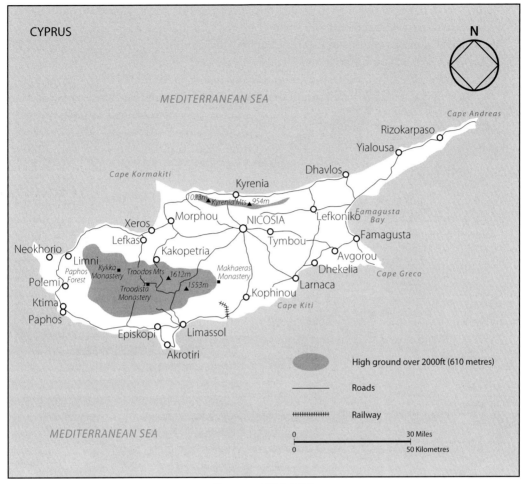

Cyprus, 1956-1958.

The campaign for *Enosis* took a new turn in 1950 under the leadership of the Patriarch of the Greek Orthodox Church in Cyprus, Archbishop Makarios. Makarios summoned George Grivas, a retired right-wing Greek Army officer who had collaborated with the Germans against the communists during the Second World War – a tension of which TFH had had personal experience. Grivas realised that he would never defeat the British in conventional military operations and therefore adopted what is now termed an 'asymmetrical approach' – doing what the weak have always done when faced by the strong: avoiding trials of strength unless on very favourable terms; exploiting the vulnerabilities of the occupier – especially in the minds of the home population; using propaganda; and adopting indirect methods of attack. He turned to insurgency, terrorism and guerrilla warfare in order to convince the British that the benefits of remaining were not worth the costs – especially as the majority of the population favoured Independence from Britain.[7] Grivas formed the organisation known as *EOKA* – a Greek acronym for 'National Organisation of Greek Cypriot Fighters' – to conduct the campaign and to gather support, by compulsion if necessary, from the population. The *EOKA* Campaign was launched on 1 April 1955 with a series of bomb attacks, murders of off-duty policemen and soldiers, attacks on Turkish villages and communities, and the intimidation of those Greek policemen and other officials who remained in their jobs.

By the autumn, the British Government recognised that strong measures were needed. In particular, greater numbers of Security Forces were required. It was, and is, generally accepted that to secure the population during an insurgency and separate the insurgents from the people – thus denying them support from the population, or the ability to coerce, or freedom of manoeuvre – there has to be a certain density of Security Forces. Achieving this density is a key factor in tipping a counter-insurgency campaign towards a decision. Historical norms say that total government forces should number around one for every 50 of the population in insurgent-affected areas. Achieving this ratio of forces had been a key contributing factor to success in Malaya, as well as to failure in Palestine. Field Marshal Sir John Harding, who had recently retired as Chief of the Imperial General Staff, was appointed as Governor with roughly the same powers and unity of command as those given to Field Marshal Templer in Malaya. He had direct access to the Prime Minister in London and complete control over all aspects of both civilian and military administration. Harding continued an existing policy of social and economic reforms designed to convince the people that they would be better off with Britain than under Greek rule. He also entered negotiations with Makarios, but without making any headway, so that in November 1955 a State of Emergency was declared. Harding took lessons from Malaya and Kenya and established a committee structure to co-ordinate security activities. He built up the intelligence-gathering architecture and rebuilt the police – including a Special Branch and a CID – using Greek Cypriots and British officers.[8] Military and police operations, coupled with the use of the death penalty for convicted terrorists, made rapid headway.

Field Marshal Harding visits 16 Para Brigade on operations in Cyprus. (Farrar-Hockley family)

The position of most Turkish Cypriots was one of support for the British in their efforts to maintain security and destroy *EOKA;* the majority of junior ranks in the Cyprus Police were, interestingly, Turks.[9] Those few Greeks who remained in the police did so at considerable risk to themselves and their families. This is not to say that the Turkish population did not cause problems for the British; nor could the Security Forces show partiality. On occasions this caused surprise and resentment when Turks were subjected to the same sort of measures – searches for weapons and so on – as were the Greeks. At the same time the understandable, but stubborn, refusal of the Turks to co-operate in any way with measures which might help the Greek Cypriot population and restore stability – even when it was in their own local interest to do so – diverted the police and army from the business of fighting insurgency and terrorism.

Concurrently, there were other developments in the region. As well as the evacuation of the great garrisons from the Suez Canal Zone after the Revolution in Egypt that brought Gamal Abdel Nasser to power, there was instability in Jordan. Differences between the new King, Hussein, and Sir John Bagot Glubb, Commander of the Arab Legion, had been apparent since 1952. Jordanians were growing impatient with being effectively a British possession, reliant on a bilateral treaty and a subsidy which gave Britain powers over defence arrangements, the promotion of Arab officers and the funding of the Arab Legion. A Free Officers' Movement, similar to that which had brought about the Revolution in Egypt, was operating in the Arab Legion by 1954. Egyptian influence was spreading – and Soviet influence with it. The Israelis threatened the West Bank and British interest in maintaining an armoured brigade in Jordan once the Canal Zone was evacuated did little to satisfy Jordanian desires for more self-government.[10] British policy in the Middle East remained focused on four objectives: first, to maintain oil supplies from the region; secondly, to maintain its Middle East influence via the Baghdad Pact incorporating Iraq, Turkey, Iran and Pakistan; thirdly, to prevent war by this means – and particularly to reduce the state of perpetual hostility between Israel and its Arab neighbours; and last to prevent Soviet intervention in the area. The influence of Russia in the Middle East was perceived to be growing, and a series of Egyptian arms deals with the Warsaw Pact between July 1952 and September 1955 promoted antagonism from Britain towards Egypt.[11]

*   *   *

16 Para Brigade had deployed to Cyprus in 1951 and from there had moved to the Suez Canal Zone, not returning to Britain until 1954. In December 1955, 1 and 3 Para had been placed on standby to move to Jordan, but had been allowed to disperse for Christmas leave. When they returned in January, the battalions had been deployed rapidly to Cyprus so as to be close by in case a non-combatant evacuation operation, or NEO, was required to rescue British civilians in the event of a breakdown of order in Jordan. The sacking of Glubb – who was seen as too conservative and too evidently the instrument of British indirect rule – by King Hussein in March 1956 settled the immediate unrest in Jordan, but 1 and 3 Para had, in the meantime, become involved in counter-insurgency operations in Cyprus; and in February 1956, took part in the arrest of Makarios.

A month later, in response to Anglo-American moves to depose him, Nasser nationalised the Suez Canal Company – but not the canal – seized control of its assets, funds, offices and rights, and declared martial law in the Canal Zone.[12] British Prime Minister Anthony Eden

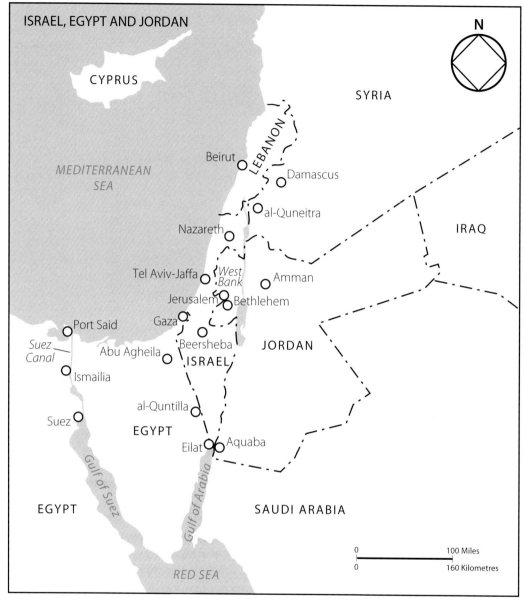

Egypt, Israel and Jordan.

quickly made it absolutely clear that military action would have to be taken, and that regime change was a firm requirement. Nasser could not be allowed, in Eden's words, to 'have his hand on our windpipe'.

The military aim articulated by the Egypt Committee on 30 July stated: 'While our ultimate purpose was to place the canal under international control, our immediate objective was to bring about the downfall of the current Egyptian Government'.[13]

High-level planning for a military option against Nasser began almost immediately. On 31 July 1956, Lieutenant-General Sir Hugh Stockwell, GOC-in-C I (British) Corps – who had commanded 6th Airborne Division in Palestine just after TFH had left – was appointed to command land operations against Egypt in what was likely to be a joint and combined undertaking with the French.[14] In spite of Mountbatten's later account, in which he urged an immediate amphibious operation against Port Said, there appeared to be no possibility of an early attack on Egypt. September seemed the earliest possible date. This was not least because neither Britain nor France had striking forces available at this sort of readiness. Of the Imperial Strategic Reserve, both 16 Para Brigade and 3 Commando Brigade RM were deployed in Cyprus, 3rd Infantry Division needed a large amount of shipping which had to be assembled, and the French were heavily engaged in Algeria. From an early date, therefore, the British (and French) Government's problem was 'how to fill up the time before our striking force can be got ready'.[15]

Initial analysis and planning established that Alexandria had to be seized as the main operating base and the force could switch to an advanced base at Port Said later. At no time did the military planners consider the occupation of the whole of Egypt, or the overthrow of Nasser, or the capture of Cairo. A detailed plan – Operation *Musketeer* – was made, briefed and accepted on this basis and the forces assembled and made ready. However, after considerable delays, a conference in London, and interventions by the French, a whole new plan – *Musketeer Revise* – had to be worked up (based on an idea floated by the French at a meeting between Eden and Prime Minister Guy Mollet on 10 September) that an economic blockade backed by air and naval action only, aimed at destroying the Egyptian Army from the air, would suffice. Ground troops could then land in limited numbers, facing little or no opposition.[16] The landing force objective was to be at Port Said, followed by the occupation of the canal and then a drive on Cairo as a subsequent operation.

On 27 April, Butler, Marston and TFH went out to Cyprus for a month's reconnaissance.[17] TFH made another short visit in May to settle matters relating to accommodation and logistic supplies, while 1 and 3 Para took part in Operation *Pepperpot*, in Paphos Forest, searching out the bases of several *EOKA* cells.[18] On 23 June the headquarters, 2 Para and elements from other brigade units all returned to Cyprus for counter-insurgency operations in various areas including the Troodos Mountains, Paphos Forest, Kyrenia and Nicosia. These operations were a continual round of village cordon and search operations, road blocks, curfews, law enforcement and riot control. At one point during Operation *Lucky Alphonse,* Grivas's headquarters was captured – providing a major intelligence coup – but he himself escaped.[19]

However, the prospect of operations in Egypt was still very real and the planners were aware that specialised preparations were required. The two parachute battalions in Cyprus had to be relieved and given refresher training, since they had not jumped for 11 months. This took place in August, when the whole of 16 Brigade returned to Britain to conduct mission rehearsals and combat training; this training had included battalion-sized drops on the Imber DZ on Salisbury Plain and brigade field firing exercises using air and artillery support. While at home, the battalions also had to absorb a number of reservists who had been recalled to the Colours for the operation and who required considerable training.[20] Two of the Royal Marines Commandos had to be taken to Malta for amphibious training, which they had not done for 10 months. Then RAF Transport Command had to be prepared and retrained to drop the parachutists; the landing craft for the Royal Marines had to be taken up from trade – many were being used in the Irish Sea for transporting pigs – and moved to Malta.

On 9 August, 16 Brigade moved back once more to Cyprus to await orders. It was not allowed to sit around, however, and was once again committed to rehearsals, training and operations against *EOKA*. On 2 October, the brigade was deployed on Operation *Sparrowhawk* in the mountains around Kyrenia, with Butler's tactical headquarters at Ayios Amvrosios along with its interpreters, detainee cages, screening teams, trackers, dogs and handlers – all of which TFH had to assemble and co-ordinate – along with a platoon of policemen, Special Branch officers and Intelligence Corps personnel. As well as many arrests, this operation resulted in one of the largest hauls of weapons ever recovered during the entire emergency in Cyprus.[21] As a result of information gathered, a second *Sparrowhawk* operation was launched in West Kyrenia from 11 to 16 October.

Ten days later, the brigade group was again deployed on Operation *Foxhunter,* in Paphos Forest around Morphou, when orders were received to prepare immediately for operations in the Canal Zone, less 1 Para, which was to remain committed to counter-insurgency operations in Cyprus. TFH recalled how, until 48 hours before the actual assault on Egypt, the bulk of the brigade was so dispersed and closely engaged in internal security operations that the assault force was only just assembled in time.[22]

*　*　*

Once the order to launch the operation was given, hostilities were to open with an air offensive. At the same time, the assault fleets from Malta and Algeria were to sail, as would the follow-up forces from the United Kingdom and Algeria. The air offensive had to be sustained throughout the six-day transit of the fleet, and until such time as the amphibious forces were in position off Port Said. The assault would be a combination of parachute landings by both British and French brigades – the British at Al Gamil Airfield and the French south of Port Said to block the approaches from the south and a landing across the beach. Naval gunfire support would be available, and close air support would be provided by the Fleet Air Arm. The second echelon of the assault would be a British parachute battalion brought in by sea, which was to advance south down the causeway which bypassed Lake Manzala. Frank King later recalled some of the planning undertaken by the staff:

> For our part we had sufficient aircraft to drop a force of about 800. It was clear therefore, that if we were to succeed, we must achieve complete surprise. From this initial deduction, two decisions emerged: first, to drop directly into the objective and second, to arrive at an unsocial hour, i.e., at dawn.
>
> It was normal practice to employ a small (about 40-man) pathfinder group who dropped some 30 minutes before the main force and, by laying cloth markers, lighting flares and setting up an electronic beacon, not only guided the main force to the drop zone, but indicated precisely where the drop was to begin and end – but this would clearly not be possible on an occupied airfield; surprise would be lost and the pathfinders mopped up before the main force arrived. Recourse was therefore made to a *Canberra* pathfinding aircraft of Bomber Command. A cross was marked on a large-scale air photograph of El Gamil. The *Canberra* crew were confident that they could lay a flare or smoke bomb precisely on that point. This then would become the marker for our drop and the *Canberra*, by circling the DZ, would guide the main force in.

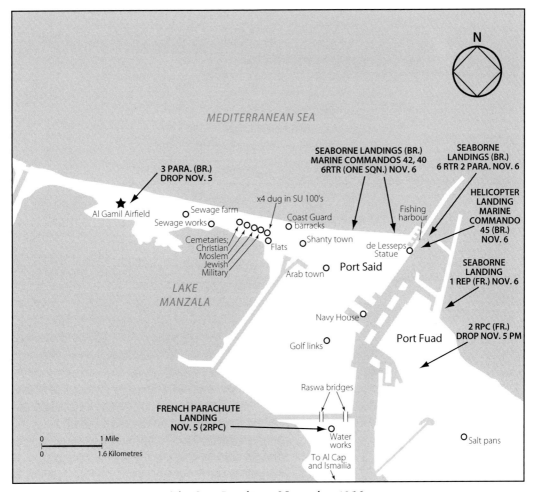

The Suez Landings, November 1956.

El Gamil was a long, narrow airfield with beaches and sea on its northern edge and a large inland lake to the south. This predicated an approach on an east/west axis, but a mile or so to the east was a dock area which intelligence indicated to be bristling with anti-aircraft defences. No pilot was willing to fly straight and level at low altitude over this area. On the other hand, approach from the west at dawn and in tight formation gave a heading directly into the rays of the bright rising sun; few pilots fancied this. By courtesy of a local hospital, large quantities of gentian violet were procured and aircraft canopies were liberally coated. It worked and was gratefully adopted.[23]

There was also, however, a secret deal with the Israelis. A common military operation by France and Britain with Israel had been rejected early on for two reasons. First, there was still strong anti-Israeli feeling in Britain – and especially in the British Army from the Mandate period in Palestine. Secondly, the British Army simply did not regard the Israeli Defence Force as being capable of conducting a traditional high-intensity war. Britain's treaty obligations to Jordan in the event of war with Israel further complicated matters. Under the terms of the

The drop at Suez, 1956. (Airborne Forces Museum)

Paratroopers collect equipment from containers in Suez, 1956. (Airborne Forces Museum)

Jordanian-British Treaty of 1948,[24] an operational plan, *Cordage*, envisaged operations from the air and the sea to neutralise the Israeli Air Force and attack military installations and lines of communication. The dilemma of course was that Britain could either aid Jordan, or launch Operation *Musketeer* and so collude with Israel – but not both. In the event, action against Egypt was judged more important, but the deal with Israel was so secret that it was not revealed to the British military below Chiefs of Staff level. This deal was a final attempt after months of diplomatic wrangling to provide a *casus belli* with at least the appearance of legitimacy. The Israeli attack, Operation *Kadesh*, was to be made on 29 October – following which Britain and France could intervene, with the supposed intention of separating the combatants and creating a demilitarised zone of 10 miles each side of the canal. The political and intellectual acrobatics needed to justify this corrupt and shady excuse for action were considerable: 'We were all flummoxed,' said the then Air Commodore Thomas Prickett, 'because *Musketeer* had been developed on the basis of seizing the Suez Canal. It was now to be implemented by separate forces – something it had never been intended to do and really needed a new plan. It was thus obviously bogus from the start.'[25]

The Israelis launched their attack as planned. The Anglo-French ultimatum was issued on the 30th, and was due to expire on the 31st. This demanded that Israel and Egypt should each stand back 10 miles from their own side of the canal, or in the event of their refusal, the Allies would invade Egypt to enforce these terms. The Israelis accepted the terms while Egypt refused them, even though Nasser agreed to a ceasefire. *Musketeer* was ordered, and in the circumstances it was directed solely against Egypt.

Port Said was defended by an Egyptian brigade of three regular infantry battalions supported by anti-tank guns, and a large number of anti-aircraft guns used in the ground and air roles. The garrison's ranks had been swollen by troops drifting in from Sinai, so that the total fighting strength was about 4,500. On top of this, the Egyptians had issued arms and ammunition to all and sundry in the town; British troops later picked up 57 three-ton lorry loads of arms and ammunition around the Arab quarter.[26] The risks were clear from an analysis of the force ratios: the Allies could get in only 1,400 parachutists to oppose this garrison, and this light force must hold on until the seaborne force linked up. It was agreed therefore that the operation would commence the next day, with the parachute insertion 24 hours in advance of the arrival of the seaborne assault force. The troops were to push hard to secure the canal, but there would be no move on Cairo.[27] Frank King again:

A fair inference at the time was that an airfield of that size probably contained at least 2,000 men. We were anxious to get the whole force on the ground in about four-and-a-half minutes. This meant a very tight formation with following aircraft, slightly above the leaders so as not to run down parachutists already in the sky. The meteorologists were adamant that there would be stiff cross-winds. This meant that given the narrowness of the drop zone, unless we restricted dropping heights to 700 feet and below, many soldiers might drift onto the beaches, which were mined, or into the sea. So 700 feet became our ceiling. But this too raised problems. A year or so before the brigade had had several fatal accidents when parachutes had failed to open. Thus reserve chutes had become very much the fashion and a substantial proportion of our soldiers had never jumped without one. But they only worked if the dropping height was above 1,000 feet, since below that height, by the time the soldier realised that his main chute was playing truant, it was too late to deploy the reserve. A firm decision was made – no reserve chute – which was not received with universal enthusiasm. However, when each man was issued with his operational load – food, water, medical gear, digging equipment, ammunition, grenades and many other items – only the strongest would have welcomed any additions.[28]

The seaborne assault against Port Said was programmed for 6 November, but there would be no naval gunfire available; only air support. 3 Para, under Lieutenant-Colonel Paul Crook, was ordered by Butler to make the drop. Butler gave an initial briefing to Crook on Thursday 1 November and held a final, formal orders group at 1600 hrs on Saturday 3 November – after which the brigade's camp outside Nicosia was locked down. With 3 Para would drop the Brigade tactical headquarters – Butler with a protection group, signals detachment and one or two staff officers; a fire direction party from 33 Light Regiment to call in air support or naval gunfire and an air contact team from the RAF; a troop of sappers; a detachment from the field ambulance, including a field surgical team; and a detachment from the RASC Company to co-ordinate re-supply. Peter Woods, a reporter from *The Daily Mirror,* had managed to persuade someone, somewhere, that he was parachute-trained and so managed to get a seat on one of the aircraft. As it turned out, he had never jumped before, injured himself badly on landing and spent the whole operation in 3 Para's Regimental Aid Post. On Sunday, the officers and men were briefed: A Company and the sappers, under Major Mike Walsh, would take the western end of Port Said Airfield – including the control tower – and then prepare a nearby bridge for demolition; B Company, under Major Dick Stevens, would block the main road from Port Said to the airfield so as to stop the Egyptians interfering; C Company, under Major Ron Norman, was to form the reserve for the unexpected but were also to reconnoitre the south side of the drop zone and block off the native shanty town; a hastily formed D Company, under Major Geoff Norton, was to clear stores from the drop zone and relieve A Company in place once they had blown their bridge, so that A Company could be re-tasked. At the same time, a battalion group from the French 2nd *Régiment Parachutistes Coloniaux* was to drop near the water-works on the south side of Port Said.

At 0415 hrs on 5 November, the first aircraft taxied onto the runway for the three-hour trip to Port Said. Egyptian anti-aircraft fire caused some damage to the aircraft on the approach and some casualties in the air. However, the first lift was on the ground in 10 minutes. The Egyptian defences, sited to cover the beaches, recovered quickly from their initial surprise and soon artillery shells, rockets fired from multi-barrelled launchers, mortar bombs and small-arms fire were all arriving among the assaulting troops. However, within half an hour, the airfield had been secured and its defences silenced – and the companies of 3 Para moved against the shore defences. Rolling these up involved vicious, close quarter fighting among the sewage farms and cemeteries that backed the shoreline until darkness and shortages of ammunition halted the advance.[29] As early as 1300 hrs, French officers had been in contact by telephone with the Egyptian Brigade Commander, Colonel Hassan Rushdi, and at about 1615 hrs Rushdi opened negotiations for a ceasefire. At 1630 hrs, Butler arrived at the French headquarters, followed at about 1700 hrs by the Military Governor of Port Said, General El Mogih. Surrender terms were dictated to the Egyptians and they were given until 2130 hrs to comply. The news of the surrender talks had been relayed by radio to Stockwell on his command ship, the *Tyne*, and he quickly dictated the terms of surrender. The shooting stopped, and air attacks were put on hold – [30] but at about 2215 hrs, before the ceasefire could be fully implemented, the local Egyptian Commander had got through to Cairo and had been told to go on fighting. He was further told that London and Paris were under attack from the Russians, so that he would be well advised to be on the winning side! So the operation had to be re-started. Approval was given to launch the amphibious assaults the next morning, though with severe restrictions on supporting fire so as to keep damage and casualties to a minimum.[31] At first light, 3 Para returned to the attack – over-running a section of Soviet *SU100* assault guns, capturing the coastguard barracks and clearing blocks of flats which were being used by Egyptian snipers and artillery observers.[32]

At 0450 hrs, the amphibious and helicopter-borne assault came in under covering fire from 3 Para's machine guns and anti-tank weapons. These weapons also proved highly effective in demolishing parts of a shanty town being used by Egyptian troops – thus enabling a link-up to be made with 3 Commando Brigade. At nightfall, 2 Para came ashore with a supporting squadron of tanks. The parachute brigade had succeeded in all its tasks: capturing the airfield, which was operational again within four hours of the landing; clearing Egyptian forces from their defences; capturing quantities of equipment; and preventing Egyptian reinforcements from moving up and interfering with the amphibious assault.

Hughie Stockwell had been ashore for some hours and had almost got lost on the return to his command ship, but had one final piece of drama to deal with:

> All I wanted at that moment was a whisky and soda. But Ken Darling [the Chief of Staff] appeared holding an urgent signal, so urgent that he insisted on my taking it before doing anything else. I looked at the slip of paper. It read 'Cease-fire at midnight'.
>
> It was difficult at that moment for me to take in the words, let alone grasp the full impact of that brief signal. I was cold and tired and wet, yet also exhilarated after seeing my soldiers in action all day at Port Said. We were on the verge of complete success. Wednesday, November 7, would have found us well established on the Ismailia-Abu Seir line. By Thursday night we surely would have been down to Suez. Lives had been lost, but Britain had shown her worth. Now, just as we were reaping the reward of all the effort and the months of preparation, we were to be thwarted of our prize.[33]

Trying to make the best of a bad job, Stockwell urged Butler to get as far down the canal as he could by midnight. Butler did not need much urging, and he was able to get as far as El Cap, about three miles short of El Qantara, where 'we would have been clear of the narrow causeway that bypassed Lake Manzala'[34] – and so, in Stockwell's words:

> ... that, for the moment, was that. It had been an exciting and successful battle and everyone had given of his best. The soldiers acquitted themselves quite splendidly. Considering the frustrations and delays in getting to grips with the job and the continually changing plans, orders and counter-orders, it was remarkable how well it all went ... it was a military success. The cease-fire coming when we were all on the crest of the wave and in sight of achieving our military aim made stopping all the more galling. But ... the whole Suez operation had been bedevilled from start to finish by the lack of a clear political aim.[35]

By the time the ceasefire came into effect, four paratroopers had been killed and 36 wounded. It was not until 10 November that the troopships carrying the 3rd Infantry Division arrived off Port Said, having overtaken the slow-moving transports. After two days of uncertainty, 3rd Division was ordered to disembark on Monday 12 November[36] and relieve the Parachute and Marine Brigades. That same day, 16 Para Brigade embarked on the troopship HT *New Caledonia* and returned to Cyprus. As it turned out, this was to be the last ever combat parachute drop made by British Airborne Forces up to the time of writing.

TFH's part in operations in both Cyprus and Suez had been in the background, working as a staff officer, in contrast to his previous experiences. However, without good staff work, the moves of the brigade would never have been accomplished – nor the troops launched successfully into battle. The brigade group had frequently been split between three countries, its accommodation in four sets of camps and barracks, with frequent moves – twice at only 48 hours' notice. TFH himself has left no memoir of this time and there is little to draw on in official accounts. However, in such episodes, silence is golden. When things go well, no comment is passed; it is only when matters run awry that notice is taken. He had scarcely had a day off, let alone a weekend, and had managed only two weeks' leave in the previous year. Butler summarised his work in his annual confidential report:

> The various administrative problems connected with these moves and the operational tasks required to be carried out placed a very considerable burden on Farrar-Hockley, and he has discharged his duties most efficiently, speedily, with cheerfulness and with tremendous drive... . he is always looking for ways of helping units in the Brigade Group... He is ruthless in his quest for complete efficiency, which is the standard he sets himself ... His powers of organisation are quite exceptional ... and is certainly outstanding as a DAA & QMG. Not only that but I consider him well-fitted to command a battalion now, despite his youth. He is the finest captain I have served with in the Army.

High praise indeed – and fully endorsed by Hughie Stockwell,[37] because without such work, the morale, efficiency and well-being of the formation could not have been maintained. No surprise therefore that TFH was recommended for the award of the MBE, which he received in the Birthday Honours of 1958 –[38] in addition to the clasps for Cyprus and Near East to add to his General Service Medal 1918.

* * *

16 Brigade Headquarters remained, for the time being, in Cyprus. In late January and early February 1957, TFH was at home in Aldershot on leave;[39] the headquarters then returned to Aldershot in March. In June 1957, TFH ceased to be the DAA & QMG and took up the appointment of Brigade Major,[40] handing over to Major Robin Carnegie of the 8th Hussars. At the same time he was also promoted to the substantive rank of Major. As Brigade Major, TFH's role had not changed much since it was defined in the pre-war *Field Service Regulations* as being:

i.   To assist [his] commander in the execution of his functions of command.
ii.   To assist the fighting troops and services in the execution of their tasks.[41]

This rather general guidance was supplemented by specific responsibilities laid on the G, or General Staff, branch – to which the Brigade Major's post was assigned. These were laid down in the *Field Service Pocket Book* as:

i.   To obtain and communicate information about our own troops, the enemy, and the theatre of war.
ii. To prepare plans and issue orders for operations.
iii. To arrange for communication, cipher, censorship. The provision and distribution of maps, secret service, guides, interpreters and propaganda.
iv. The organisation, training and efficiency of troops.
v.   To draft despatches.[42]

Even more so than the DAA & QMG, the Brigade Major had a very close, special relationship with his Brigade Commander. It is a partnership that engenders many close and lasting friendships which endure throughout and beyond the military service of those involved, but it also benefits the junior partner through the mentoring of the senior, with all the implications for that officer's development which this brings. His report for 1957, again from Butler, reflected this and said much the same things as that for 1956 – although Butler remarked, as others had done before, that '… he is inclined to be intolerant … This trait leads him on occasions to do too much himself. With a view to the future, he must accustom himself to running a system in which he decentralises a good deal more'.[43] Butler also used the well-worn cliché that TFH did 'not suffer fools gladly'. One wonders why he should have done. However, there was a thread running through his reports since Korea, indicating more than just complete self-confidence: perhaps a degree of arrogance which, if not checked, might impact on his further progress whatever his experience and qualities. It might also have been a subconscious fear, left over from Korea; fear of relying on others who might let him down. His later entry in the *Dictionary of National Biography,* by Professor Brian Holden Reid, identified this: his 'not always comfortable personality: he was irrepressible, not easily intimidated, incorrigibly stubborn, defending what he thought was right tenaciously …'[44]

*   *   *

In the aftermath of Suez, 1957 was a relatively quiet year for 16 Parachute Brigade, but in 1958, the tempo of operations in the Middle East stepped up again. 1 Para was committed to operations in Cyprus, but *EOKA* was fundamentally weakened by this stage; the focus of British force projection shifted back to Jordan. In the post-Glubb era, King Hussein turned to the United States in place of Britain as his principal source of foreign aid, but he did so without a bilateral treaty. In April 1957, Jordan had received an emergency aid grant of $10 million from the United States to help bolster the country against the threat of Nasser-style revolutionary Nationalism as practised in Egypt, which had quickly removed monarchical government there and had the potential to do the same in Jordan. From the American point of view this would have two undesirable consequences: first, threaten oil supplies and the navigation of the Suez Canal; and secondly, increase the pressure on its client, Israel.

Hussein had, in fact, first turned for support to neighbouring Iraq, which was much larger, more populous and far wealthier from its oil revenues than Jordan. Iraq, also a monarchy under a Hashemite King, Hussein's cousin Faisal II, had until then generally supported Jordan in the Arab world and its government had taken Iraq into the Baghdad Pact in 1955 as a means of ensuring continued Western – especially American – support against the Soviet Union and its clients in the radical Arab movements. In July 1958, Lebanon was threatened, not for the last time, by civil war between Maronite Christians and Muslims. Tensions with Egypt had grown too, in 1956, when pro-western President Camille Chamoun – a Christian – did not break diplomatic relations with Britain and France during the Suez Crisis. These tensions were further increased when Chamoun showed interest in joining the Baghdad Pact, which Nasser saw as a threat to Arab Nationalism. In response, on 1 February 1958, Egypt and Syria announced the integration of their two countries to form the United Arab Republic (UAR). This development – which produced a large and powerful bloc – was greeted with enthusiasm by the advocates of Arab unity, but it made the position of conservative or moderate monarchist regimes potentially fragile.

To counter-balance it, Jordanian-Iraqi negotiations were quickly concluded and, on 14 February 1958, Hussein and his cousin – Faisal of Iraq – issued a joint Proclamation uniting the Hashemite kingdoms of Iraq and Jordan into a federation called the Arab Union. Faisal was to be Head of State and Hussein his deputy. The Arab Union was short-lived. Lebanese Sunni Prime Minister Rashid Karami and other Lebanese Muslims clearly wished to join the newly-created United Arab Republic, while Christians wanted to keep Lebanon aligned with the West. A Muslim rebellion, covertly supported by the UAR through Syria, caused Chamoun to complain to the UN Security Council. The UN sent inspectors but failed to uncover any evidence of significant intervention from the UAR. Hussein, fearing that an anti-Western revolt in Lebanon might spread to Jordan, requested Iraqi assistance. Instead of moving toward Jordan, however, on 14 July 1958 the Iraqi Army's 19 Motorized Brigade under Brigadier Abd al-Karim Qasim moved into Baghdad, murdered Faisal and other members of the Royal Family, and seized control of the government.

Hussein, overcome by rage, shock and grief, at first threatened to send the Jordanian Arab Army – the re-named Arab Legion – into Iraq to avenge Faisal's murder and restore the Arab Union. His ministers, however, advised against this, for in Iraq the army and police supported the coup. Qasim's first moves were to take the new Republic of Iraq out of the Arab Union and the Baghdad Pact. Jordan was isolated as never before and Hussein appealed both to the United States and to Britain for help. The United States began an immediate airlift of fuel supplies. The coup in Iraq, along with continuing internal instability, had also caused Chamoun in Lebanon to call for American help. Eisenhower responded by authorising Operation *Blue Bat* on 15 July 1958. This was the first manifestation of the Eisenhower Doctrine, under which the US announced that it would intervene to protect friendly governments wherever it considered them to be threatened by Communism. The operation involved much of the US Sixth Fleet, including three aircraft carriers, the 2nd Provisional Marine Force and the US Army Task Force 20 (1st Airborne Battle Group and the 187th Infantry Regiment of the 24th Infantry Division) – a total of approximately 14,000 ground troops, which remained in Lebanon until 25 October 1958.

At the same time as the US moved into Lebanon, British troops were ordered into Jordan. The intervention was conducted under the command of Headquarters Middle East Land

Forces, which was allocated 16 Parachute Brigade Group, less 1 Para – which was committed to operations in Cyprus – but with 1st Battalion The Cameronians (Scottish Rifles) added subsequently. The brigade had moved once more to Cyprus between 13 and 15 June in anticipation of a crisis in the region. Here, Brigadier Tom Pearson, who had taken over command from Butler, planned a series of contingencies with TFH and the staff, which included an airborne assault in Lebanon and the same in Jordan,[45] or an administrative move. In all cases, operational plans had to be made and orders issued; staff tables and loading plans had to be worked up based on the desired order of arrival; accommodation, feeding and all aspects of administration planned. At this point, the loyalty of the Jordanian Arab Army was not assured, and so an opposed landing was considered a definite possibility. On 17 July, the brigade was ordered to move by air – using US *Globemaster* transport aircraft – to Amman, but an opposed landing was not, after all, on the cards and the troops would not drop. Even so, the troops began landing before diplomatic clearance had been obtained from the Jordanians – before, even, the government was aware of their coming.[46] The staff, including TFH, were in position at Nicosia Airfield that night. 3 Para, now under Lieutenant-Colonel Michael Forrester, later reported:

> Our next move, to Amman, came at even shorter notice than the move from England. In the evening of 17th July, we were warned to be ready to move the following afternoon and our destination was very much a matter for speculation. However, during the night our future was clarified, our load tables re-written, and shortly after dawn we were ready to follow the 2nd Battalion to Amman.[47]

Before dawn on 18 July, the airlift of the main body began. By late afternoon, the forward elements of the brigade – its tactical headquarters, the Guards Independent Company and 2 Para Group – were all in position and Pearson had reported that 'every effort [had been] made by JAA to provide Adm[inistrative] assistance. All ranks confined to airfield. Internal sit[uation] quiet'.[48] Ironically, perhaps, the aircraft overflew Israel because clearances for alternate routes over Arab countries could not be obtained in time.

On 19 July, Pearson was formally designated as Commander British Forces in Jordan and issued a Directive on relationships with the British Embassy and the Jordanian Government. Because of the potential for an attack by armoured elements of the Jordanian Arab Army, the deployment of a squadron of tanks was asked for by the British Defence Co-ordination Committee (Middle East), but on 20 August this was refused by the Chiefs of Staff;[49] ironically, a British armoured regiment had been stationed in Jordan until 1957. A squadron of RAF ground attack Hawker *Hunters* did, however, arrive. In the meantime, TFH, Frank King and Robin Carnegie continued to manage the fly-in of the rest of the brigade. 3 Para again reported that: 'We flew in throughout that day and night and awoke to find ourselves allotted one building and a patch of sand on the edge of Amman Airfield ...'[50]

The Cameronians arrived by ship on board the aircraft carrier HMS *Bulwark* on 7 August. The last unit to arrive was 17 Field Battery of 33 Light Regiment, which staged through Aqaba and arrived in Amman on 22 August – bringing Butler's strength to 216 officers and 2,850 men at Amman, and a detachment of 22 officers and 216 men from 3 Para at Aqaba.

Once the force was complete, a temporary base had to be built and training exercises conducted. 3 Para again:

> Thanks to the generosity of the Jordan Arab Army [*sic*], our patch of sand became a sea of bivouacs with the main essentials of battalion life conducted from our building which had previously housed a company of the Royal Bodyguard. At this stage our 'Q' staff were sorely overstretched with the RQMS folding up the barracks in England; the QM handing over … in Cyprus, and the MTO combining his normal duties with those of QM at Amman.[51]

The overstretch at battalion level was mirrored and magnified at brigade level and both TFH and Robin Carnegie found themselves dealing with issues in Cyprus, Jordan and at home. The tasks given to the brigade now included the protection of British and friendly nationals' property, or their evacuation if needed; support for the JAA or the Jordanian Government if required; security of the airfield; the security of the Aqaba Docks; and the planning and preparation of defensive positions to protect key points and defilades in the event of outside attack.[52] However, although for some weeks the political atmosphere in Jordan was explosive, the government kept order through limited martial law. The JAA continued its unflinching loyalty to the King, and the Israeli frontier remained quiet.

Once the administrative chaos of a series of moves at short notice had been resolved, there was time for some light relief:

> Within a few days we had hired furniture from the Winter Palace Hotel in Jericho … Away from the dust bowl of Amman, the days slipped pleasantly by: days spent swimming from the smooth sandy beaches [of Aqaba] with its backcloth of green palms, exploring the wonders of the coral reef, or guarding the valuable cargoes … on the wharf … excursions were made to the craggy peaks of the mountains which towered over and dominated the town.[53]

There were trips to ancient Petra, sports and games with the Jordanians and between British units and plenty of field firing exercises. King Hussein himself visited the brigade to express his thanks. The only incident that gave TFH and Pearson any lost sleep was when four men from 3 Para strayed across the Saudi Arabian border on 30 September and were arrested and held by the Saudis until following diplomatic interventions, they were handed over at Aqaba a month later. By this time, it was felt that the situation in Jordan no longer required the presence of British troops; in fact, it might begin to prove counter-productive if they stayed longer. The brigade therefore began its withdrawal on 25 October, through Cyprus, with the first troops landing back at Lyneham on the 27th.[54]

TFH's time with the Brigade Headquarters was now drawing to a close. His annual report – once again a grading of 'outstanding' and once again supported by the next level of command – remarked on his 'abundant commonsense' and his willingness to 'shoulder heavy responsibilities'.

Pearson made a point of saying that he had never had to question TFH's wisdom, even when he had taken decisions in the Commander's absence. TFH seems to have heeded Butler's advice about trusting his juniors, as Pearson remarked that TFH was 'never reluctant to give

HM King Hussein of Jordan visits 16 Para Brigade during the intervention in 1958. Peter Malone is on the right of the picture. (Airborne Forces Museum)

junior staff officers work of importance and he takes great pains to make them more proficient in their work by sympathetic instruction'. However, there was still a tendency – noted by Pearson – to assume that his point of view was always right.[55]

TFH had also made a career choice during the course of 1958. In January, the War Office had announced that the permanent cadre of the Parachute Regiment was to be re-established. Secondments would continue, but officers could now belong to the regiment full-time. Although TFH's prospects with the Glosters were excellent, he decided after much reflection that he would return to his original choice of arm. Perhaps, too, the prospect of garrison service in Germany and elsewhere no longer looked appealing when compared with the opportunities for deployment anywhere with the Strategic Reserve. He himself never set out his reasons in detail, but whatever they were, on 30 May 1958 he changed his cap-badge for the third time.[56] Not that he ever forgot the Glosters; the ties forged in Korea were far too strong for that. For their part, the Glosters' view of TFH in the late 1950s, as expressed by Bill Morris and Bill Reeve-Tucker, who knew him well, was that of an almost legendary figure: brilliant, full of spark and enthusiasm, capable and energetic, a firebrand – but the Glosters were too small for him. No-one was surprised therefore when he returned to the Airborne Forces – from whence anyway he had come – and although there was some sadness, there was no resentment at his going.[57]

In the ordinary course of things, TFH would now have commanded a company. However, he had already done so, twice, in wartime and had nothing to prove in the matter of leadership at low level. Pearson had also remarked that his heavy workloads as DQ and as BM had curtailed his natural desire to read, research and reflect on his profession. He was thus nominated to attend a six-month course at the Joint Services Staff College and after that, to take up an instructional post at the Royal Military Academy Sandhurst.

13

'The complete professional' Education and Training at Latimer and Sandhurst, 1959-1961

The years following the Suez expedition were years of considerable upheaval in the army – the size and shape of which had been under scrutiny as early as 1955 when the then Defence Minister, Selwyn Lloyd, had imposed further retrenchment in the Defence Estimates. Lloyd had tried to reduce National Service from two years to one. Harding as CIGS, and then Templer,* had successfully resisted this on the grounds of commitment levels. As a sign of things to come, however, a new pay code with revised terms for Short Service regular engagements was introduced to encourage Regular Service. Over the next two years, the pressure began to build for an end to National Service in peacetime. The Navy and the RAF had no wish to keep it, and the army clung to it only because of the size of its commitments. Its tradition was in professional, regular, service; training conscripts took time and manpower, and the cost of maintaining a large force – even at National Service pay scales – meant that there was little left in the pot for much-needed modernisation, but commitments remained the sticking point.

Assessments pointed to a requirement for 200,000 British troops worldwide, later revised under political pressure to 185,000. Against this, the most optimistic forecasts predicted that recruiting would not sustain an all-regular army of more than 165,000. When, after Suez, Harold Macmillan became Prime Minister, he appointed the tough and capable Duncan Sandys at Defence. Sandys believed firmly that conventional armies were all but outmoded for modern war and that nuclear deterrence was the way of the future – in spite of the evidence which Suez had provided to the effect that war, under the umbrella of nuclear deterrence, was still possible. Not surprisingly, he was soon head-to-head with the Service Chiefs. Macmillan, desperate to reduce the drain on the economy which military commitments produced, instructed Sandys on 24 January 1957 to undertake a complete review of defence. He was to review policy, deployments, organisations, funding, and even pay and conditions of service. At one stroke, the Service Ministers and the Chiefs were sidelined.

Sandys's work – the Defence White Paper of 1957 – might have been expected to address some of the shortcomings in the services that Suez had highlighted, but these problems were subordinated to the development of a nuclear deterrent independent of the USA, whose support,

---

* Field Marshal Sir Gerald Walter Robert Templer KG GCB GCMG KBE DSO (1898-1979) fought in both World Wars. He is best known for his time as High Commissioner in Malaya between 1952 and 1954. He was CIGS from 1955 to 1958.

after Suez, seemed dubious; and a compensating reduction in other forces. Sandys aimed to reduce defence spending from £1,600 million to £1,420 million, end conscription, and compensate for reduced manpower with greater mobility – the use of staging posts like Aden and Gan rather than overseas bases – and tactical nuclear weapons. Of the three services, the army came off worst. Templer and the Army Council were unshaken in believing that an army of 165,000 would never meet its commitments. There were some noisy exchanges between Templer and Sandys, but much as Temper disliked and distrusted Sandys both personally and professionally, Sandys had Macmillan's backing and, although the Army Council regarded the White Paper as a disaster, it had no real option but to accept it.

Most of the reductions would be through the ending of National Service, but there would be reductions too in the numbers of regular officers and NCOs. These were planned to be spread over a four-year period from 1958 to 1962, using annual quotas. As far as possible, these reductions would be voluntary and accompanied by generous redundancy payments. Politically, it was recognised that the army's problem was different from that of the other services. Not only did it have to take account of its regimental and corps structure, but it needed to shed more than twice the number of personnel as the Royal Navy and RAF combined. The requirement, for example, for the first year – 1958-59 – was for 1,380 officer volunteers and 1,819 NCOs: a total of 3,199. The actual number applying for redundancy that year was 25,800. Not everyone who applied would therefore get redundancy, and some of those who wished to stay were nominated for redundancy whether they liked it or not.

It still remained to be seen whether recruiting would fill the ranks with regular soldiers, for the economy was picking up, jobs were plentiful in civilian life, and in the aftermath of National Service, army life did not enjoy a particularly rosy image –but the High Command of the army was faced with some difficult decisions. An army of 165,000 was only two-thirds the size it had been before the Second World War. Not only would individuals be made redundant, but also entire formations would go; and so too would some of the famous regiments – especially in the infantry. The Parachute Regiment, as it turned out, escaped untouched by these moves and TFH had therefore made a good move when he transferred, but these major changes in organisation formed the backdrop to his service over the following five years as National Service – which was all that TFH had ever known since he first joined the army – gave way to a smaller, all-professional force.

*   *   *

The Joint Services Staff College had been founded in 1938 and it had moved to Latimer House, near Buckingham, in 1947. Latimer, originally the home of Lord Chesham, was a beautiful country house built in 1838 on the site of a much older manor house. The task of the college was to train officers to fill joint command and staff appointments – especially on operations – by studying modern war on a joint service and multinational basis, and widening their knowledge of inter-service issues. The Commandant was always a Major-General or equivalent. Senior Directing Staff included Royal Navy, British Army, Royal Air Force and civil servants of equivalent grades. Officers attending the course were often lieutenant-colonels and TFH was junior both in age and rank for the course. It was a requirement that previous confidential reports had identified that course members had the potential to rise at least two ranks. The course lasted six months and was attended by up to 60 officers from all three services and the Commonwealth. As well as a programme of lectures, seminars, discussions in syndicate and directed reading, the course included table-top exercises in which operational problems were studied by groups of officers from a variety of service, and national, cultures. The majority of those officers who passed the course went on to joint, central staff, combined, or international appointments.[*]

TFH attended the 21st course held at the college, from 13 April to 16 October 1959. After almost three years of hectic coming and going, it was a welcome interlude. As always, however, he threw himself into the course, achieving a grade of 8 – the top grade being 9 – and being recommended to return as a member of the Directing Staff. While on the course, he came under the influence of Colonel Rex Whitworth of the Grenadier Guards.[†] Had the Second World War not intervened, Rex Whitworth might have become an historian by profession. In spite of having taken a First in Modern History at Balliol College, Oxford he had been turned down by the Foreign Service and taken up a Travelling Fellowship with Queen's College. Although 1938 was a hazardous time to be in Central Europe, he travelled widely – strengthening his French and German – before being called home to be commissioned in the Grenadier Guards in 1940. Having served with distinction throughout the war, he had recently published a well-regarded biography of Field Marshal Lord Ligonier. He later continued his historical work, publishing – among other works – a biography of William Augustus, Duke of Cumberland. Whitworth was a serious, academic historian of a type that TFH had never before encountered. Without doubt, he left a deep impression and helped to shape the future direction of TFH's development as an historian and as a writer.

TFH also began corresponding with Basil Liddell Hart at this time. Liddell Hart proposed TFH as a member of the IISS [1] and thereafter they corresponded on the career of Sir Ian Hamilton, Kitchener and the War Councils, and even contemporary NATO strategy – Liddell Hart opining in the latter discussion that 'I would not agree that the NATO view of defence is based on the potential of atomic weapons. Rather, the widespread defence is forced on us by our paucity of numbers; the acceptance of gaps – wide gaps'.[2]

This correspondence sparked an interest in the interplay of conventional forces and nuclear weapons that was to remain with TFH for the rest of his service.

The language of TFH's course report contains few surprises:

> … much experience, plenty of self confidence, and power of original thought. He expresses himself very clearly and forcibly … Misuse of these great abilities might well arouse hostility in less gifted colleagues on a joint staff and so arouse resentment and lack of co-operation. I believe however … he is quite intelligent enough to know how to deal with people whom he has to persuade.[3]

From Latimer, TFH was posted to Sandhurst in October 1959.[4] With his huge wealth of experience, he was a natural choice to instruct at either Sandhurst or the Staff College, or both.

---

[*]   'Joint' appointments are those in a national, tri-service context. 'Combined' appointments are those in a multinational – alliance or coalition – context.

[†]   Later Major-General Reginald Henry ('Rex') Whitworth CB CBE MA (1916-2004). He was Commander Berlin Infantry Brigade and GOC Yorkshire District.

As he was still a Major, it was to Sandhurst he was sent – charged with the heavy responsibility of helping to form the next generation of young officers for the army.

The RMC, which had ceased to function in 1939 and, during the Second World War, had operated as an OCTU – which TFH had of course attended – never re-opened. Instead, a new establishment was formed: the Royal Military Academy Sandhurst. The new Sandhurst took the place of both the RMC and the former RMA Woolwich. For the first time, the training of all regular officer cadets would be in one establishment (National Service and Short Service commissioned officers were trained at Mons Officer Cadet School in Aldershot or at Eaton Hall until the latter closed down in 1960). Instead of Gentleman Cadets, there were now Officer Cadets enlisted into the army; and no longer paying fees, but drawing pay. They still, however, had to pass into Sandhurst through an examination set by the Civil Service Commissioners. The fact that this was achieved under a Labour Government should be no surprise. Such a government might be expected to dismantle an establishment open only to the sons of those who could afford to pay fees. However, there seems to have been little or no opposition in Parliament and the Reform would, therefore, probably have gone through even under a Conservative administration. The RMA Sandhurst received its Charter from the War Office on 29 July 1946. It was to produce a different type of officer for a modern army. It was Hughie Stockwell, the former GOC of the 6th Airborne Division and the Land Forces Commander at Suez, who as Commandant from 1948 to 1950 had set the curriculum and the tone which held sway when TFH arrived.[5]

The training regime for the 18-month course at Sandhurst centred on the function of an officer to command and lead his men both in barracks and in battle. It also included military training, in order to equip the officer with the same skills as his NCOs and men, and technical and liberal studies to complete his education. Its aim was 'to produce a young officer with a sound education in appropriate military and academic subjects, with a wide interest in the current problems of world affairs, and the enthusiasm to continue to increase his knowledge by his own initiative'.[6] Montgomery, writing in the first edition of the new Sandhurst magazine, said that its task would be, quite simply, 'to produce officers who will be fit, morally, mentally and physically, to lead the British soldier'.[7]

What Sandhurst would not do, however, was to take the place of the arms and services schools in giving specialist training. Gone was the old emphasis on equitation, drill, and the like which had been the rule before the Second World War. The curriculum now included – on the military side – Leadership, Tactics, Weapon Training and Shooting, Signals, Physical Training and Military Writing; and – on the educational side – Sciences, Mathematics, Modern Languages, Current Affairs, Military History and English. The military studies of the academy were in the hands of the Assistant Commandant, Brigadier Cecil ('Monkey') Blacker,* who was therefore an important person in TFH's life. The educational side of the curriculum was in the hands of civilian lecturers rather than military instructors, under the guidance of the Director of Studies. One thing which was held in common with the old RMC was the quality of the officers and NCOs who were posted to the Directing Staff. None but the best were accepted – and in the aftermath of the Second World War, Korea, Malaya, the Mau

---

*   Later General Sir Cecil Hugh Blacker GCB OBE MC (1916-2002), who was Vice-Chief of the General Staff and Adjutant-General in the 1970s.

Mau and Suez, many had combat experience. Another common thread from the old RMC was the Cadet Government: each company consisted of seniors, intermediates, and juniors. The senior intake provided the under officers, and the intermediates the sergeants and corporals, responsible for daily supervision of the cadet companies.[8] Sports and games were important too, and included rugby, soccer, cricket, rowing, sailing and cross-country running.[9]

Hughie Stockwell had had decided ideas on the style of the place. His ADC, Peter Cavendish, recalled that:

> When Hughie took over … we drove over from Aldershot at about 3 o'clock, had a chat, went to tea at Government House, and then went back to Aldershot. On the way back in the car, Hughie said *"Right, now we're in charge of Sandhurst. Boy,* (he always called me 'boy') *we've got to think how we make it spark. They're a dull lot at the moment, and officers are supposed to have drive, initiative, and get-up-and-go!"*[10]

He was right; it *was* dull – but it had been brilliantly organised. The basic curriculum was sound if unspectacular, and the staff officers and NCOs of the best. What Stockwell had sought to do was produce the future leaders of the army by enlivening the curriculum – changing the style (not the content) by encouraging the staff to develop a generation willing to take risks. Stockwell brought in parachute training courses – the foundation of the famous Edward Bear Club; he also introduced leadership lectures to the whole academy under the title of 'Battle Experience'. These were given either by resident staff members or by visiting speakers. Sandhurst should produce students who were not just qualified academically as officers, nor necessarily tactical wizards; what mattered was leadership. The training regime was, therefore, the vehicle by which this was to be developed. Implicit in this was that the Regular Commissions Board would already have selected cadets who had innate, in-born qualities of leadership. It was perhaps fortunate for the British Army that an experienced field commander like Stockwell was in command at the beginning of the new Sandhurst. The model that Stockwell established has endured to the present, even while the Sandhurst course and curriculum have undergone constant change and evolution – and it was one that TFH understood at once, and with which he could identify.

By the time that TFH joined the staff at Sandhurst, Hughie Stockwell's 18-month course had been extended to two years. TFH assumed the appointment of Chief Instructor in Old College, which was under the command of the highly experienced Lieutenant-Colonel David Lloyd Owen.* Lloyd Owen had served with the Long Range Desert Group during the Second World War and had later been Gerald Templer's Military Assistant in Malaya. He had also published an account of his war service, *The Desert My Dwelling Place*, in 1957. He was also just as highly decorated as TFH and was not at all intimidated by his exceptional subordinate. This mattered: Lloyd Owen, with Whitworth, was a second key influence on TFH's personal and professional development at an important time.

---

*   Later Major-General David Lanyon ('Luigi') Lloyd Owen CB DSO OBE MC (1917-2001). He was commissioned into The Queen's; he had commanded the Long Range Desert Group and was later GOC Near East Land Forces.

Another key influence was Peter Young,* who had been appointed as Reader in Military History at Sandhurst in 1959 and who arrived at the same time as TFH to establish a new department.[11] He had already written two books, both autobiographies – *Bedouin Command* and *Storm from the Sea* – while he was still in the army, but with his lifelong interest in history (and with the position at Sandhurst) he went on to write particularly on the English Civil Wars and the Napoleonic Wars. As well as military experience and academic rigour, Young was possessed of a great presence and a powerful persona – especially as a speaker. Moreover, at that time, Military History and War Studies were not popular subjects outside the army. Apart from Oxford, Sandhurst was the only academic institution with a faculty of Military History. It was, in due course, the forcing-house for many eminent historians and political scientists including David Chandler, Michael Orr, Tony Heathcote, Richard Holmes, John Sweetman, Eric Morris, Keith Simpson, John Pimlott, Anthony Brett-James, Paddy Griffith, Christopher Duffy and Duncan Anderson. As well as being able to contribute to the formation of the next military generation, therefore, TFH himself was also formed and moulded to a considerable degree by these influences. However, TFH had very firm views about the training and development of future officers. Having been through a wartime OCTU himself and seen so much combat, he considered that fitness was a paramount requirement, as was flexibility in tactical thinking and professional knowledge; an officer must always be better trained and informed than his subordinates, as well as capable of doing any of their jobs as well or better than they could do so themselves.[12] He had no time for the gifted amateur – on whom, magically, the ability to command in battle would somehow descend without the need for tiresome study and practice. He made a number of changes therefore to the way that the curriculum was taught, most of which were later taken up in a study into officer training carried out by the Director of Army Training in the early 1970s that resulted in merger of Mons and Sandhurst – making the new academy even more tightly focused on leadership training and development and encouraging higher education among officers by recruiting more graduates.

Because of these influences and the access to the library, along with a structured routine in his working life, TFH's literary career certainly progressed during and after his time at Sandhurst. He later contributed the article on the Somme, 1916, to *Great Battles of the British Army as Commemorated in the Sandhurst Companies* under David Chandler's editorship in 1991 and also contributing a section from *The Edge of the Sword* to the small book *Serve to Lead,* which was given to every cadet on the day he joined. He also completed his own third book, which he had been working on while at the JSSC, *A Short History of the Second World War* published by Frederick Muller; and he contributed to *The Red Dragon* – the Royal Welch Fusiliers' short wartime history published in 1960.

TFH's professional life focused on his duties in Old College, one of three colleges forming the academy; the other two being New College – housed in red-brick Edwardian buildings – and Victory College, at that time housed in a collection of Nissen Huts behind the New Buildings. The Old College consisted of four companies: Blenheim, Dettingen, Waterloo

---

* Brigadier Peter Young DSO MC (1915-1988) served in the wartime Commandos – eventually commanding a Special Service Brigade. Subsequently, he went on to command a regiment of the Arab Legion before leaving the army to join the academic staff at Sandhurst. In later life he founded The Sealed Knot and was the author of a number of well-respected books.

A company of Sandhurst cadets on parade outside the Old Building, 1962. (Author's collection)

and The Inkerman – each commanded by a Major with a Captain as Second-in-Command, a Company Sergeant Major and a Company Quarter Master Sergeant. Each company had three platoons, commanded by a Captain with a Colour-Sergeant of the Guards as his deputy. The cadets were grouped as juniors, intermediates and seniors for instruction or education but on exercises, companies took to the field as a formed body with the more senior cadets filling the command appointments. TFH's task was to ensure that the military syllabus was correctly taught across all companies and intakes by the different members of staff. He was also responsible for running the exercises and field training events other than those managed by the weapon-training or signals wings, and for all central lectures and presentations.[13]

In the ordinary course of things, TFH had little interaction with individual cadets. Peter Crocker, who was a cadet during TFH's time at Sandhurst, recalled that the Chief Instructor was a fairly remote figure; it was the Company Commander, Platoon Officer and Drill-Sergeant who figured much more largely in everyday life. TFH could not, however, be missed: a stocky, barrel-chested man with piercing blue eyes – the original thousand-yard stare – with a fearsome reputation for courage in battle. He was, said Crocker, 'the complete professional, but punchy too, and very aggressive.'[14]

Captain Peter Cronk, who had joined Dettingen Company as a Tactics Instructor, shared the office with TFH and the two became friends. Cronk recalled that:

> Somebody came to the office one day and asked if I had taken the Practical Promotion Exam [i.e. from Lieutenant to Captain] and if not why not! I was detailed to go to Lasham Airfield the following week to take it. I ascertained from Tony what it entailed and considered that I was just about able to cope with most of the problems.

However I was completely ignorant about an 'Appreciation'.* Tony said: "*1645 tomor-row. Here. It will take 45 minutes. Alright?*"

By 1730 the following day I was confident enough to present myself at Lasham and make a reasonable enough effort at passing the exam. Tony F-H had given me a really concise and clear tuition on 'appreciations' and in the event I passed top of the 250-odd candidates who attended the following week![15]

Charles Messenger, later a highly accomplished historian and writer himself, was a cadet in Dettingen Company from 1959 to 1961 and saw a good deal of TFH. He remembered him, and a number of episodes involving him, well:

He wore more medal ribbons than any other member of staff, including the Commandant. We had all read *The Edge of the Sword* and so were well aware of his exploits in Korea and looked up to him as a real fighting soldier.

In my last term, Waterloo Company won the inter-company drill competition, unheard of for an Old College company. That night there was a Band Night, not just for Old College, but for New and Victory as well. After dinner, we decided to invade New and Victory Colleges en masse to celebrate this singular success. The result was a riot, with cadets even being thrown out of first floor windows. The situation appeared totally out of control when a single figure appeared, resplendent in Parachute Regiment mess kit and a great rack of medals. "*Get back to your lines,*" he roared. Such was our respect for Farrar-Hockley that we obeyed immediately. Order was restored in an instant.

When he spoke, it was with drive and total conviction. He said what he meant … In our final term at Sandhurst we had one brief opportunity to command real soldiers on exercise. Bored and impatient to be commissioned, we initially did not take the exercise seriously. TFH saw what was going on and gathered us together. He told us in his usual forceful manner that 25 percent of the last intake that had passed out from St Cyr [the French equivalent of Sandhurst] had already been killed in Algeria and it was time we grew up. Just one of his many talks that we took to heart … He was a great man.[6]

Each summer term, the intermediate and senior cadets were formed into a battalion, under the Cadet Government, and taken on a camp. This camp was one of TFH's big responsibili-ties. In 1960, Lloyd Owen and TFH laid on a camp in Northern Ireland in the form of a long tactical exercise, preceded by an airlift and a parachute insertion by a platoon of cadets who had qualified on the Edward Bear course. The format of the exercise – with long moves on foot, a variety of tactical problems, and of course the method of insertion – has TFH's finger-prints all over it.[17] In the following November, an even more testing exercise was mounted by TFH and Lloyd Owen in the harsh terrain around Santa Margarida in northern Portugal.[1]

---

* Now called the 'Estimate', it is the process by which the task or mission and the object resisting its success – usually the enemy – are analysed; the factors of time and space, resources and environment considered; and the required effects, such as surprise or deception measured. From this process, one or more courses of action are identified which will in turn be developed into a plan and orders.

TFH and Pat enjoying a prawn cocktail. (Farrar-Hockley family)

TFH also, of course, inherited responsibility for the Edward Bear Club: the parachute training club which ran courses to qualify cadets in military parachuting, which had been running since it was founded by Captain Richard Worsley – later General Sir Richard Worsley – in 1950. The main event was always a Royal Military Academy Course at RAF Abingdon during the summer. Charles Messenger again recalled how, while on this course:

> I remember Para Farrar, as we called him, joining us for a jump from a *Beverley*. He borrowed a parachute smock and wore his ordinary shoes. Once on board, he handed sweets around and when it came to the jump, he strolled nonchalantly up to the door and just stepped out. He showed how easy it all was.[19]

TFH was able to witness several notable events during his time at Sandhurst. In December 1959, Hughie Stockwell, who knew TFH well, took the Sovereign's

Edward Bear – or, judging by his medal bar, a poke at TFH by the Edward Bear Club. (*Wish Stream*, summer 1950)

The Sovereign's Parade
at Sandhurst, 1963.
(Author's collection)

Parade.[20] In July 1960, the same duty was performed by the Prime Minister, Harold Macmillan
– a veteran of the Great War.[21] Finally, in July 1960, the Queen visited Sandhurst to open the
National Army Museum – the brainchild of Sir Gerald Templer – in its first permanent home.[22]
As well as the Queen, the staff and cadets played host to four field marshals, 50 generals and
two admirals; the Secretary of State for War; the High Commissioner for Pakistan; and the
legendary lady of SOE, 'Odette'.* TFH at least could look Odette in the eye, for he was one
of the few present who, like her, had been captured by the enemy, imprisoned, tortured and
condemned to death – but had somehow survivd.

TFH's superiors at Sandhurst, as had become habitual, thought very highly of him – and
he again earned an 'outstanding' report for 1960 from Lloyd Owen. The report was fully
supported by Blacker, who recommended him strongly to command a battalion, saying that:
'This is a remarkable officer, who would fill any job open to him with distinction and force'.
However, Blacker also remarked that 'firm handling will be needed if his considerable talents
are to be put to their best use'.[23] The Commandant agreed, as did the GOC-in-C Southern
Command – another airborne soldier from the Second World War, Lieutenant-General Sir
Nigel Poett.†

---

* Odette Sansom Hallowes GC MBE L d'H (1912-1995) was captured while on an SOE mission, tortured and
  sent to Ravensbrück Concentration Camp where she survived only because the Germans believed her to be
  related to Churchill – and therefore useful as a bargaining chip.
† Later General Sir Joseph Howard Nigel Poett, KCB DSO (1907-1991). He had commanded 5 Parachute
  Brigade and 6th Airborne Division in North-West Europe. He was subsequently GOC-in-C Far East Land
  Forces.

In spite of this consistent approbation, TFH could not escape a nagging feeling that somehow, somewhere, something had gone wrong. He was 36 and after 18 years' service, his career had stalled. How? He had commanded troops in battle with complete success and he had decorations to show for it. He had filled every staff job exceptionally well. He was a graduate of the Army and Joint Services Staff Colleges and he had published work to his name. In fact he need not have worried, for the Parachute Regiment had its eye on him to command a battalion – but he had not served at regimental duty since he was a Captain in 1 Glosters, and he needed a tick in that box. The Military Secretary therefore asked the Commandant at Sandhurst to release him before his two-year tour was over so that he could become Second-in-Command of 3 Para and thereafter, all being well, its Commanding Officer. Blacker was not keen to stand a gap in the key post of Chief Instructor and pointed out with some justice that:

> As College Chief Instructor, Major Farrar-Hockley is occupying a key post … I could not release him before the end of April [1961], and then only if an infantry major, suitable to become chief instructor, replaced him… I am quite ready … to accept this dislocation if it is really necessary for Farrar-Hockley's future. His interim report at regimental duty can, however, only cover two months if his name is to be considered in July for command in 1962. This seems to be a case in which perhaps excessive inconvenience and dislocation are being caused in order to comply with the strict letter of the law with regard to recommendations for command.
>
> The Commandant, myself and Farrar-Hockley's College Commander – all officers of reasonably wide experience – are prepared to give him, on his work at Sandhurst, the clearest and strongest recommendation for command which we can give…[24]

The Deputy Military Secretary replied in January in essence, albeit politely, telling Blacker to do as he was told in a smart and soldierly manner. However, he did promise that the Parachute Regiment, with whom he had consulted, would immediately replace TFH. He could scarcely disagree with Blacker's argument about reporting, however, and said that:

> The Selection Board would most certainly accept recommendations from the RMAS for command especially in a case such as this, but I think you should write an interim confidential report on Farrar-Hockley when he leaves in April and make it quite clear… why you recommend him for command.[25]

Accordingly, TFH left Sandhurst after only 17 months on 25 April 1961 and assumed the appointment of Second-in-Command in the 3rd Battalion of the Parachute Regiment, just a few miles down the road at Aldershot.

14

'… failure seemed unthinkable, success somehow assured' The Persian Gulf and the Campaign in the Radfan, 1961-1965

TFH was posted to 3 Para as Second-in Command on 20 June 1961.[1] He was also granted the brevet rank of Lieutenant-Colonel, with effect from 1 July 1961.[2] In the British Army, a brevet commission (now long since discontinued) was only by courtesy. Officially, both titles were used: 'Major and Brevet Lieutenant-Colonel so-and-so'. Originally the term designated a promotion given on occasions such as a Coronation, or the conclusion of a war, but after the Crimean War it was limited to cases of distinguished service in the field and on the principle of seniority – and brevet commissions were confined to ranks between Captain and Lieutenant-Colonel. The brevet conferred rank in the army, but not in the regiment. When an officer served with his regiment, only regimental rank counted; if the regiment was with a larger formation, then brevet rank could be used to determine command of temporary units formed for special purposes – thus it was possible for a regimental Major to hold a brevet Lieutenant-Colonelcy with seniority over the commission of his own Commanding Officer. Appointment to a brevet also counted towards the requirement to have served for a sufficient time in a lower rank to be eligible for promotion to a more senior one.

3 Para was in barracks in Aldershot, as part of 16 Parachute Brigade, under the command of Lieutenant-Colonel R.C. ('Roly') Gibbs* – an immensely capable commander who had served with distinction in the Second World War and in Palestine; had held temporary command of 16 Parachute Brigade in Cyprus; and who later went on to serve in Aden to command British Forces in the Middle East and, eventually, to be Chief of the General Staff. He was exactly the sort of Commanding Officer to place above TFH, who with a lesser man could have been highly intimidating. As Gibbs's obituary put it, 'Many who fought with him considered that the awards he was given should have been repeated many times over for the sustained acts of courage and leadership that he displayed'.[3]

TFH was not above a spot of leg-pulling however, no matter how revered the CO was; as both David Charles and Hew Pike† – then a Platoon Commander – recalled:

---

*   Later Field Marshal Sir Roland Christopher Gibbs GCB, CBE, DSO, MC, KStJ, DL (1921-2004). He was Chief of the General Staff – the professional head of the British Army – from 1976 to 1979.

†   Later Lieutenant-General Sir Hew William Royston Pike KCB DSO MBE (b. 24 April 1943), GOC 3rd Infantry Division and DC-in-C Land Command.

There are many stories illustrating TFH's conviction, and clarity of mind. In Parachute Regiment circles, one of the favourites dates back to the time when 'Roly' Gibbs, FM to be, was commanding 3 PARA and TFH was his Second-in-Command. Quite a team! After addresses by the Commanding Officer to the battalion, 'Roly' would saunter off, leaving the field to the Second-in-Command, who would begin by pronouncing that "What the Commanding Officer *really* meant was …"[4]

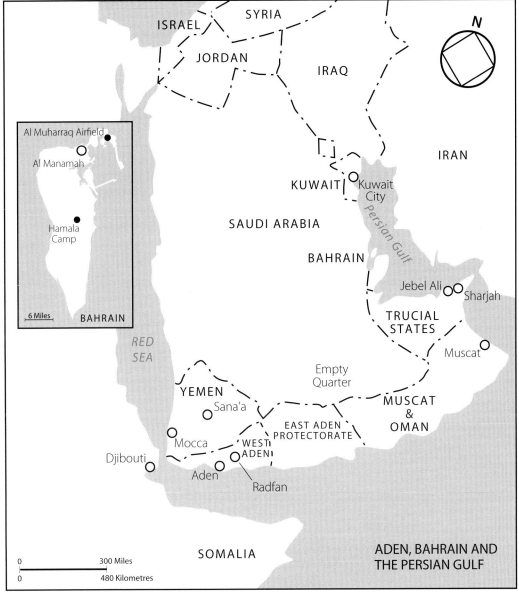

Bahrain, Aden and the Persian Gulf.

In October 1961, the battalion moved at short notice to Bahrain as part of Operation *Vantage* – an operation to support the newly independent State of Kuwait against territorial claims by Iraq. On 25 June 1961, Britain had relinquished its authority in Kuwait, and Abdul Qasim, the same who had murdered King Feisal in Iraq and precipitated the British intervention in Jordan, announced that Kuwait would be incorporated into Iraq – seeking, perhaps, Kuwait's predicted oil assets as well as its sea port. The military threat was seen, by Britain, as imminent: a large naval task force of two carriers with escorts deployed to the Gulf – and the whole of 24 Infantry Brigade from Kenya, strongly reinforced, was flown in; so too was 2 Para from Cyprus, now commanded by TFH's old friend, Frank King. This was enough to deter aggression. Iraq did not attack and the British forces were later replaced by the Arab League. Iraq recognised the Independence of Kuwait in 1963.[5]

Although the troops deployed to Kuwait did not remain there for long, 3 Para spent the next year in Bahrain. Here it came under the command of British Forces Arabian Peninsula, the old Middle East Command which, under the overall authority of a 4-star General Officer, was divided into two subordinate commands split by the Suez Canal. These were British Forces Arabian Peninsula, which was headquartered in Aden, and the rump of the former Command, which was based at Episkopi in Cyprus – and which in 1961 was renamed Near East Command.

Near East Command was an inter-service organisation, exercising command over three military districts: Cyprus; British Troops Malta, Libya and Tripolitania; and Cyrenaica Area. British Forces Arabian Peninsula, which in spite of its change of terminology was still in official circles being referred to as 'Middle East Forces', was divided into three subordinate military districts. These were the Aden Colony and the Aden Protectorates; the Persian Gulf Sheikhdoms and Sultanates – Sharjah, Bahrain, Oman and the Trucial States – the garrisons of Eritrea and British Somaliland being long gone; and a reserve infantry battalion based at Nairobi in Kenya. In times of peace, the garrison of Aden consisted of only a single infantry battalion and the garrisons of the Persian Gulf another one or two battalions and/or a Royal Marines Commando – plus of course the local levies such as the Trucial Oman Scouts and the Aden Protectorate Levies.[6] Once the insurgency in Aden developed, however, the garrison there grew rapidly to a full brigade under the headquarters of 24 Infantry Brigade, and was, at times, increased to two brigades.

Bahrain itself is a small island some 10 miles (16 kilometres) wide and 30 miles (48 kilometres) long. The climate is cool and wet in winter but very hot and dry in summer, with high humidity. Daytime temperatures can exceed 50°C, with humidity above 80 percent. Here, the officers and men of 3 Para were accommodated in a tented camp next to the main air base – hard lying in that climate. In the mid 1960s, Bahrain had not begun to benefit from the huge oil revenues of the Gulf and it was still ruled as a feudal, desert kingdom. The task of the resident battalion there was to act as a contingency force for any emergency which might occur throughout the command. Here the battalion remained until 6 May 1962,[7] carrying out training in desert operations and preparing for various eventualities – none of which actually appeared.

TFH and Gibbs clearly got along famously. Gibbs wrote in TFH's confidential report for the year, describing him as 'an outstanding officer in every respect' and recommending him for command of a regular battalion, that he:

… combines more practical knowledge and experience of soldiering than any other person of his age that I know. He also benefits by a detailed, extensive and ever-increasing knowledge of military history … In war his record shows him to be a leader of outstanding merit. In peace he is an excellent organiser and trainer. His knowledge of tactics is very sound; he knows what he wants to achieve and his methods show thoroughness, originality and efficiency. His staff work is first class … He is a practised and excellent speaker who can talk to any audience.[8]

Gibbs then went on to address head-on the adverse criticism that TFH had often encountered before in his reports, putting this into perspective:

He has a forceful personality. His judgement and opinions are quickly reached, soundly based and forcibly put over. He has such a frank and forthright manner that people are inclined to consider him blunt, and he is indeed fearless of stating his opinions. He has however such an excellent sense of humour and of fun that it would be difficult to take offence. He is trusted and respected by those above and below him.

Gibbs's views were strongly supported by the Brigade Commander and by the GOC Aldershot District. This was the sort of report that TFH needed, the final tick in the box as Blacker had hinted at Sandhurst, to ensure his succession to a regular command.

HE Sir William Luce, the British Resident in Bahrain, inspects 3 Para at The Queen's Birthday Parade. (Farrar-Hockley family)

On 10 July 1962, not long after the return from Bahrain, TFH was appointed Commanding Officer of 3 Para, with the substantive rank of Lieutenant-Colonel.[9] He was 38 years old and was only a month short of 20 years' commissioned service – years in which he had seen and done more than many soldiers dream about.

* * *

The lower down the ladder of command one goes, the more that command and leadership are synonymous. There comes a point – somewhere between company and battalion command – where command ceases to be just leadership and is balanced by two further elements: control of people and resources; and decision making.[10] That is not to say that leadership ever disappears as an essential attribute of command; it is reinforced by the other aspects. TFH knew all about leadership and no-one – not even his sternest critic – would ever have called that into question. He had what Montgomery described as: 'The will to dominate, together with the character which inspires confidence. A leader has got to learn to dominate the events which surround him; he must never allow these events to get the better of him …'[11]

Most armies have, in their doctrine, a list of qualities required of a leader and these lists usually include such attributes as courage – first and foremost, moral and physical – determination, discipline, selflessness, intelligence, vision, willpower, professional knowledge and a sense of humour. TFH had all these, but just as important, he was *known* to have them; his formidable reputation went before him. Because of his extensive experience on the staff, he also understood perfectly well the business of control of people and resources and of decision making. He knew which decisions lay with him; which were properly the preserve of a higher authority; which could be delegated; and which were not really command decisions at all, but were control measures that could be handled by the staff. He was, moreover, a highly intuitive leader and decision-maker. Gibbs had pointed this out when he spoke of TFH's ability to make up his mind rapidly. Intuition is really the product of experience and intelligence and is a function of the subconscious. If well-developed, it can certainly be trusted (provided it can be tested by the application of its converse – process) against the constraints of time, space, environment and resources. The trouble with many decision-makers is that they have had intuition beaten out of them at service schools and colleges and they rely, therefore, wholly on process. With the loss of intuition go unpredictability, unorthodoxy and the ability to improvise.

Being a Commanding Officer in a British infantry battalion in the early 1960s was about as close to being God as it is possible to be on earth, without actually being God. The CO – the 'Old Man' – was an absolute ruler with extensive powers of discipline, the authority of a magistrate, the full weight of the Army Act and 300 years of certainty behind him. There is still no other command quite like it – possibly because beyond it, one passes from the closeness of the regimental family to the command of a formation. A CO sets the tone of the battalion, just as a headmaster does in a school; the standards, efficiency and professional capability of the unit all derive from him. He chooses to a large degree who will be its officers and NCOs – and they in turn owe him loyalty. There would have been a good chance, too, in many infantry battalions of that time that the CO would know personally a great many of the officers and men – and would have done so for years. This was not the case for TFH, of course, but he had had the advantage of serving with 3 Para for more than a year and so getting to know the officers, sergeants and corporals, as well as – probably – the best and worst among the paratroopers;

for a CO can never know everyone in his command in the way that a Company Commander does; it is just too large.

A CO then was also very much a father-figure to the young officers and the men, some of whom would never have had anyone quite like that in their lives. There was always therefore a desire within a battalion to please the CO, something quite different from sycophantism. A few words of praise from the CO meant a very great deal, even if it was just in the annual confidential report that a CO would write on every officer; he was the end of the line. 'The CO says' provided a judgement which was the end of the matter and no-one would look beyond it. For his part, a CO had to be very careful with his utterances, as the slightest throwaway remark could result in a great deal of work, if interpreted as 'the CO wants so-and-so done'!

In his turn, the CO also needed a father-figure – someone with whom he could discuss problems and, if need be, bare his soul. This had to be someone outside the operational chain of command. The responsibility fell to the Colonel of the regiment or, in the case of the paras, the Colonel Commandant. The Colonel was the tribal chief of his regiment; the head of the family. He was also someone who had, in his turn, commanded troops and faced all the difficulties that any CO had to face. TFH was fortunate to be able to turn for advice, wisdom and guidance to the formidable General Sir Gerald Lathbury, who had commanded 1 Parachute Brigade at Arnhem.[*]

Behind the CO was that other formidable person, the CO's wife. She too would exercise leadership, but in a different way, for no-one would give orders to army wives if they wanted to live and thrive! In the early 1960s, the army was, compared to modern times, relatively unmarried. The company commanders, the sergeant majors and senior sergeants would very often be married men – so too the more senior captains and the older corporals – but young officers and soldiers were usually single. For one thing, even with marriage allowance and ration allowance, they were simply not paid enough – before the days of the military salary – to be able to get married; and for another, the demands of soldiering in the twilight of Empire took them away from home for long periods. When a battalion moved station, it would be expected that the wives and families would move too – to follow the drum – with all the stress and sheer hard work required to pack up one married quarter; be subjected to the humiliating nit-pick of a march-out inspection; then move into a new one – perhaps on the other side of the world – and set up home again. If the battalion was sent on operations unaccompanied, then the wives and families would stay in their home station and somehow keep themselves occupied. Before the days of mobile phones and the internet, there were only occasional telephone calls and airmail letters to keep husbands and wives in touch. The CO's wife, with the battalion's families' officer, would therefore have to keep a close watch on the welfare, health, safety, schooling, social life and happiness of the families – and look cheerful about it too. Some of the junior ranks' wives might have jobs, but it was rare indeed for an officer's wife to work in those days. She was expected to make supporting her husband's career and keeping house a full-time job.

All this fell to Pat, who, by all accounts, performed to as high a standard as TFH himself did. Hilary remembered Pat doing her duty: 'Endless hours in mum's car after school as she visited wives from Scott Moncrieff Square to Chetwode Terrace!'

---

[*] General Sir Gerald William Lathbury GCB DSO MBE (1906-1978) was later Governor of Gibraltar. He was Colonel Commandant from 1962 to 1965.

Of course, Pat also had the task – while TFH himself was in station – of looking after him, looking after the two boys and their education, and taking her turn in the usual round of the social life of a garrison town. TFH threw himself into command; he just loved it, but because it absorbed him, he needed organising – and when he was not absorbed by command, he would often be improving his knowledge of military history in preparation for his next piece of writing; but TFH also joined in with the Wives Club activities – in particular, cooking. He loved cooking and somewhere along the road he had become very good at it – possibly an unconscious reaction to the years of deprivation in Korea – but whatever the reason, when the Farrar-Hockleys entertained it was usually TFH who did the cooking rather than Pat, who was, in TFH's words, a good, plain cook. As Hew Pike recalled, 'His [i.e. TFH's] pastry was a speciality and I guess that not many COs have had the temerity to demonstrate cooking skills to their Regimental Wives Club, but he would do so, whilst sometimes almost asphyxiating his audience with the *Hexamine* field cooking tablets that he insisted on using'.[12] Susan Hickman recalled that 'I well remember Tony giving the Wives Club a cookery demonstration, and I still use his chicken pâté recipe and his curry/apple soup!'[13] TFH himself – in an interview in 1983 – said modestly: 'I quite enjoy cooking. I believe in the quality of life and also in the quality of food. So much food in this country is desperate although it has got better in recent years'.[14]

The Farrar-Hockley family had moved into the CO's house, the red-brick Edwardian Blenheim House, which was next to the Officers' Mess in Farnborough. Dair was now at TFH's *Alma Mater,* Exeter School, so only home during the vacations and occasional exeats. Hilary was at Miss Seed's pre-prep school in Knolly's Road, where a strict regime was the order of the day – her standards being exemplary – and no-one was surprised when she was later made MBE for services to education. Hilary recalled that 'She had to put up with me and Alistair Mackie, as well as being saluted by the entire officer corps, based in Aldershot, from the GOC downwards. Christmas nativity plays at the Smith Dorrien Theatre!'[15] Not everyone loved Miss Seed's as Hilary did. Brigid Keenan called it 'Miss Seed's, the awful place we were sent to in Aldershot, though Miss Seed liked me and put me in charge of making her 'Camp' coffee'.[16] Miss Seed eventually retired in November 1969 and TFH was enlisted to help the wife of the battalion's families officer, Mrs Tricia Norrie Giles, in writing to as many former victims – and parents – as could be traced to raise money for a proper presentation to her.

Part of the task of organising the CO while the CO organised the battalion was also taken on by his orderly, known in years gone by as the soldier-servant, who would see to the CO's kit, polish his leather, and so on. This was Corporal Ted (or Eddie) Olive, who had joined TFH when he became Second-in-Command. The two were to serve together for the next 40 years. Olive did not drive the CO's car, however; this was done by Corporal Barnett. The CO's orderly was a key man in another respect too. Together with the Regimental Sergeant Major, he would be able – once he and the boss knew each other well enough – to speak very plainly; to give God the unvarnished truth about how he was going about his business, or telling him what was really going on and what others really thought when everyone else was being highly deferential. That dose of reality from these two NCOs has saved many a CO from making a total fool of himself.

TFH was, as usual for a CO, supported by a team of staff officers and company commanders. His Second-in-Command was Major Peter Ballion; the Adjutant, Captain Jeremy Hickman; IO, Lieutenant Ian McLeod; the Quarter Master, Captain Jack Crane; the Mechanical Transport Officer (MTO) and Technical Quarter Master, Captain Tom Duffy; the Chaplain,

TFH talking to Major Tony Ward-Booth in the Radfan. (Airborne Forces Museum)

Fred Preston; and the RSM, Arthur Channon. A Company was commanded by Major Michael Walsh,* who had succeeded TFH at Sandhurst as the Parachute Regiment's representative; B Company, Major Peter Walter; C Company, Major Tony Ward-Booth; D Company, Major Steve Ellwood. For this team, TFH was an awe-inspiring figure: 'A CO who had done it all,' in Michael Walsh's words.[17] They found him to be a strict disciplinarian with an absolute insistence on the highest of standards: 'Inspect something every week', he told Walsh, 'it keeps people on their toes'. As his superiors had several times remarked in reports, TFH also had a tendency to do everything himself rather than delegate and to keep subordinates, even when detached, on a tight rein. He did everything brilliantly, but it could at times be frustrating.

3 Para remained in Aldershot with 16 Parachute Brigade for the rest of 1962 and throughout 1963 under the command of Brigadier Michael Forrester – 'Smiling Death' – whom TFH had now known for nine years at the Staff College; on the Brigade Staff when Forrester was himself a CO; and now with 3 Para. Forrester was a hard man to please; very tough, certainly brave – and TFH impressed him. In his first confidential report, Forrester summed up the qualities that so many other reporting officers had noted down the years. He made no comment on TFH's unorthodoxy or his supreme self-confidence – remarking however that he inspired confidence in all who came into contact with him, but also saying that: 'While he expects and exacts a high standard from his subordinates, he should be on his guard against allowing the

---

* Later Major-General Michael John Hatley Walsh CB DSO (b. 1927). He commanded 1 Para in Aden and was awarded the DSO. He was later GOC 3rd Infantry Division and then 3rd Armoured Division after its conversion; and Director of Army Training. Following his retirement from the army, he was the Chief Scout of the United Kingdom and Overseas Territories from 1982 to 1988.

deep understanding which he shows of them, together with his intrinsic sense of loyalty and fairness, to colour his impression of their abilities'.[18]

This sounds either like a warning that the weak should be allowed to go to the wall and the devil take the hindmost, or else perhaps a note of caution to a young CO – regardless of his war service – not to be indulgent. Hew Pike, who had been recruited into the regiment by Mike Walsh – now his Company Commander – saw TFH at first hand at this time and had a somewhat different view of what TFH was doing, and how he was doing it:

> To a subordinate, his humour and generosity of spirit were always a source of relief, often of gratitude too. He was always interested in others, and consistently supported those who served him well – his loyalty often surfacing at critical moments in life, whether personal or professional, when TFH would appear on some pretext or other, for a fatherly walk in the woods, during which the real object of the conversation might only emerge towards its conclusion.
>
> He loved his soldiers, too – guarding their welfare assiduously – which they understood and appreciated. He was also quite a supporter of the 'lame duck'. I was always a little surprised at his patience with easily the worst soldier in my platoon, whom he nicknamed 'Loopy' but for whom he seemed to have quite a soft spot. He gave people a chance, and all merited that chance …
>
> His padres could expect kindly yet characteristically frank critiques of their performance in the pulpit, from a man with a fine singing voice and a seemingly near perfect memory for *Hymns Ancient and Modern*. One newly-joined Padre to the Parachute Brigade recalls being taken into his office and given a talk of which any Bishop would have been proud.[19]

In the following year's report, Forrester noted that 3 Para was 'very well trained, organised and administered. Esprit de corps and morale are high and All Ranks go about their duties with enthusiasm and sense of purpose'. He went on to pick up his thread from the year before:

> It is understandable in one with such all round ability that he should at times have appeared to be doing more than his share. There may have also been signs, on occasions, due to his untiring efforts to bring on others, that he was allowing his enthusiasm for their progress to colour his estimate of their ability. In recent months, however, he has successfully countered these tendencies with beneficial results.[20]

It was far more likely that TFH merely masked the way he was exercising command, for he was most unlikely to change his approach – he was far too honest for that – and in any case, TFH's views of how he lived a Christian life (by the unthinking permeation of all his daily actions, no matter how small-seeming, with the message of the Christian gospel) would simply not permit him to do otherwise. Comments like these, which at worst give the impression that the Brigade Commander was encouraging his COs to scramble to higher rank on the backs of their subordinates, say much more about Forrester than about TFH. For TFH, loyalty was a three-way business: it worked upwards, of course, but it worked downwards and sideways too – but he could be a formidable, and terrifying, proposition too, as Brian Holden Reid remarked:

… more than able to instil fear into those who served under him in his relentless search for military efficiency. Yet his abrupt, decisive, commanding manner concealed a very kind man. He was very forgiving of military failure, for his long and varied experience had taught him that men would always make mistakes and that they should be given the chance to learn from them.[21]

In any case, the next superior reporting officer – Major-General John Metcalfe –* had, like Forrester, been commissioned into The Queen's, but some years earlier. He knew just what Forrester was like and was having none of it – especially as he had commanded regular troops during the Second World War while Forrester had commanded pre-war Territorials; there was always a certain tension there. His report, which in those days was not disclosed to TFH, said that: 'I know him well. He is a man of the highest principles, religious faith and abounding self-confidence. He has great powers of original thought and habitual independence of mind … He is a great leader and sets a fine example'. Inevitably, perhaps, Metcalfe also cautioned against TFH's tendency to think himself infallible – but this was a very minor tut-tut; and in army reporting at that time, what the first SRO thought carried rather more weight than the opinion of the originating officer.

Far from taking offence at Forrester's remarks, TFH embarked on a tease. 3 Para's ARU (Annual Report on a Unit) Inspection was due. TFH could have taken the battalion into the field, but what would a sham battle prove, scripted as it would be, when he himself knew all too well what the real thing was like? Whatever one might think of Forrester, he too had seen plenty of action during the Second World War and after, but Forrester had been commissioned into The Queen's – one of the smartest regiments in the army and one whose parades were a by-word. TFH 'seemed to have decided, not the Brigadier, on a particularly complicated drill parade as an appropriate demonstration of our prowess. He did love his drill'.[22]

The soldiers of the Parachute Regiment did *not* love drill – they had not enlisted to be guardsmen – and there was a deal of grumbling.[23] What no-one knew was that in February 1943, TFH had successfully completed a drill course at the Guards' Depot, Caterham.[24] TFH seems to have taken this parade mounted. Hilary recalled TFH lifting him onto the horse after the parade – a highly unusual thing for a parachute battalion CO to do, but then TFH had gone riding in Greece wearing his red beret, so why not in Aldershot? His support for 'the lame duck' did not, it appears, extend to the barrack square. As Brian Holden Reid remarked in TFH's *DNB* entry: 'He once erupted in fury and literally threw an unkempt young subaltern off the parade square and confiscated his sword. Yet he recognised his fundamental talent, and this bumbling, disorganised young man would eventually rise to equal him in rank'.

A spell at home, even in command of a battalion, allowed TFH to pick up his alternative career as a writer and military historian. His first major historical work, *The Somme,* was published by Pan Books in 1964 in time for the 50th anniversary of the outbreak of the Great War – and re-issued in 1966. He was encouraged to write the book by both his old mentor at Sandhurst, Peter Young, and by Basil Liddell Hart, whom he had befriended. This was a first class book: concise, well written and showing independence of judgement.[25] It was this book

---

*   Major-General John Francis Metcalfe CB CBE (1908-1975) had commanded a battalion in Burma during the Second World War and a brigade in Malaya during the Emergency.

which, although superseded by later research – particularly in the archives of Germany after the collapse of Communism – brought him membership of 'the select company of soldier-historians and analysts who dominated the post-war British Army: Michael Carver, John Hackett, W.G.F. Jackson, and Richard Clutterbuck'.[26]

*   *   *

In early April 1964, 3 Para returned once more to Bahrain as the resident infantry battalion. A parachute battalion was chosen for this task in case a need arose to re-intervene rapidly in Kuwait. This time, the battalion's base was the hutted Hamala Camp, situated in open desert 12 miles (20 kilometres) from the main town of Manama and although not luxurious by any means, was a good deal more civilised than the tents by the airfield. The battalion was to remain here for at least 18 months and a limited number of families came too – about 90 in total – with married quarters provided near the camp.[27] The Farrar-Hockleys moved into a first floor flat near the naval base at Juffair.

TFH worked the battalion hard, believing that in a station like Bahrain, this was the best way to maintain morale as well as effectiveness. The companies were deployed in rotation between Hamala Camp, Muharraq Airfield and a tented training camp which was established in Jebel Ali in the Trucial States. This was reached by a flight to Sharjah and then a short drive across the desert to Dubai, on to Abu Dhabi and so to Jebel Ali. There was then no road at all, so this was across the sand, where now there is a five-lane highway.[28] At Jebel Ali it was possible

TFH as CO 3 Para, 1964. (Airborne Forces Museum)

to carry out live-fire tactical training, or link up with the Royal Navy's Amphibious Warfare Squadron for amphibious exercises on the coast. Using the three *Beverley* aircraft based in Bahrain, it was also possible for the companies to drop into a DZ two miles away from Jebel Ali Camp at regular intervals. There were also expeditions further afield – to Kenya, Buraimi Oasis and Bandar Abbas in Iran – the latterby dhow.[29]

However, the main focus of attention for the battalion other than Kuwait, as the regional reserve, was Aden. Aden was originally established by the Royal Navy as an anti-piracy station to protect shipping on the routes to British India. With the opening of the Suez Canal in 1869, it fulfilled a second important function as a coaling station. However, after India had become independent in 1947, the possession of Aden made far less sense than before – even though by 1960, Aden was, after New York City, the busiest port in the world. The British sought to create a federation between Aden Colony and the surrounding Protectorates – the Federation of South Arabia – to act as a stabilising influence in the region, maximise trade and provide one of a chain of military bases near the Gulf oilfields. In 1962, therefore, the British Government had announced that Aden would be maintained as a permanent British garrison – East of Suez – although it also announced that the Federation would be granted Independence. As well as a Royal Naval station, Army and Royal Air Force contingents would support the newly-formed Federal Regular Army (FRA) and the irregular forces of the Aden Protectorate Levies.[30]

The Emergency, which broke out in 1963, was inspired by the growth of Arab Nationalism spreading down the Arabian Peninsula from Nasser's Egypt, under-written by the Soviet Union. Its doctrines found a ready audience in Yemen, to the north of Aden. Supported and inspired by the Yemenis, anti-British guerrilla groups with varying political objectives began to coalesce into two larger, rival organisations: first, the Egyptian-supported National Liberation Front (NLF); and secondly, the Front for the Liberation of Occupied South Yemen (FLOSY), who attacked each other as well as the British. Hostilities broke out into the open on 10 December 1963 with an NLF grenade attack against British High Commissioner in Aden, Sir Kennedy Trevaskis, at Khormaksar Airport. The grenade killed a woman and injured 50 other people. On that day, a State of Emergency was declared in both the Colony of Aden and throughout the Protectorates. The NLF and FLOSY campaigns against British forces in Aden relied largely on grenade attacks; and another such attack was carried out against the RAF station at Khormaksar during a children's party – killing a girl and wounding four children. Other attacks were targeted against off-duty British soldiers and policemen. Much of the violence was carried out in the Crater – the old Arab quarter of Aden – but the Federation was also threatened by the tribes in the Radfan area of the country. They too were backed by Yemen – trained and equipped by the Egyptians.[31]

The Radfan, an area of some 300 square miles (768 square kilometres), lay to the east of Thumier and bounded on the north by the Halmayn Mountains; on the east by the Wadi Bana; to the west by the north-south road from Aden to the Yemeni border; and to the south by the desert which stretches to the sea. Its defining and dominating feature, from which its name derives, is the mountain (or Jebel) of Radfan. Seen from the air, the Radfan looks arid and barren, but there are two fertile areas: the Dhanaba Basin and the Wadi Taym. In these areas, where such water as there is from the innumerable smaller *wadis* that drain into the two catchments irrigates the thin soils, dense cultivation supports a remarkably large population. The *wadis* and plateaux are terraced for cultivation; wells and cisterns preserve water; and the villages of the 10 tribes which constitute the Radfanis watch each other, engage in blood feuds lasting centuries and unite only when outsiders threaten them – thus the history of feuding and communal violence among the Radfanis was a way of life.

Like the Pathans of the North-West Frontier, every man was armed and trained in shooting and field-craft from an early age. Maybe there were bad shots among the Radfanis, but no-one ever reported them. Like the Scottish Highlanders of the 18th century, they resisted any attempts by central government to impose its authority. So long as their warlike tendencies were directed against their own kind, no-one much minded and, for most of its history, the Radfan had never been visited by Europeans. In January 1964, when the FRA penetrated a remote part of the Radfan, an elderly tribesman approached a British officer and asked, 'Surely you must know my old friend Colonel Wahab?' The officer regretted that he had not had the pleasure. Subsequent investigation revealed that the Colonel had been a member of the 1901 Anglo-Turkish Boundary Commission which had managed to penetrate the western part of the territory. Few others had bothered since then, although A Squadron 22 SAS under Peter Walter had certainly done so two years previously.[32]

Much of the area lies above 2,000 feet (700 metres), but the peak of the Jebel Radfan rises to 6,000 feet (2,000 metres). The ground is so cut with *wadis* and gorges that a distance of one mile (1,600 metres) on the map is often three times that distance on foot. Maximum daytime temperatures would often reach 115° F (46° C), but with very low humidity and a considerable drop in temperature at night to near freezing. One officer who was in the Protectorate at this time recorded his impressions thus:

> The full impact [of the heat] hits you as you step from the aircraft to be met by a blast of hot air that makes you wonder who has left the oven door open. To this heat is soon added dust and not long after that the squalor that seems indigenous to every Arab town. How can people whose religion enforces cleanliness tolerate such filth all around them? How can they clean themselves and do nothing to their surroundings?[33]

The pro-communist government in Yemen had long coveted the territories which comprised the South Arabian Federation. Many Radfanis served as mercenaries in the Yemeni Army, but the Yemenis principally saw the Radfanis as the means of waging insurgent warfare against the Federation – using weapons supplied from Yemen. From late 1963 and into early 1964, the Qutaibis – the main tribe of the Radfan –began an uprising, spurred on by the governments of both Egypt and Yemen.[34] In January 1964, battalions of the FRA had carried out some low-level operations in the Rabwa area and built a road through the Rabwa Pass into Wadi Taym. However, once these battalions were withdrawn for other duties, dissident tribesmen reoccupied the pass, destroyed the new road and threatened the main Aden to Dhala road. Soon ambushes, mines, tolls on travellers and theft of goods became regular occurrences. One traveller robbed would tell a dozen others of his experiences, and so fear was spread by word of mouth. As a result, the GOC Middle East Land Forces, Major-General J.H. (John) Cubbon* – known to the troops as 'the red ant' – decided to mount a

---

*   Major-General John Hamilton Cubbon CBE DSO (1911-1997) was commissioned into the Cheshires but commanded 6th (RW) Para soon after TFH had left it; and 1 Para when it was redesignated.

new, punitive operation using British troops to clear the insurgents from their main base east of the main road, about seven miles south of the border with Yemen. The mountainous, bare and largely trackless terrain made the movement of heavy equipment, guns and motor transport very difficult. Military operations relied therefore on air-mobility and cross-country marching under lod.

Cubbon delegated the conduct of the operation to the Commander Aden Garrison, Brigadier R.L. (Louis) Hargroves –* known as 'the black rat' – who formed 'Radforce'. His plan called for several phases: On 29 April, a patrol of A Squadron 22 SAS was to infiltrate by night to secure and mark a DZ. On 30 April, the 1st East Anglian Regiment,† with the armoured cars of D Squadron 4th Royal Tanks and the FRA Armoured Squadron, would mount a diversion and clear the Rabwa Pass.

Major-General John Cubbon, GOC Middle East, with TFH, Captain Jeremy Hickman and RSM Arthur Channon in Bahrain. (Farrar-Hockley family)

On the same day, 45 Commando RM would infiltrate to the left, through the hills, supported by the 1st and 2nd FRA Infantry Battalions to capture high ground overlooking Danaba – a feature code-named 'Rice Bowl'. Shortly afterwards, B Company of 3 Para under Major Peter Walter, which had been sent from Bahrain and placed under the operational command of 45 Commando for this operation, was to drop at midnight onto a DZ in the Wadi Taym from which they would advance to capture the key feature codenamed 'Cap Badge' – occupying it until 45 Commando completed their sweep towards it from Wadi Boran.

So it was that in late April 1964, British Army trucks were rumbling up the Dhala road towards the village of Thumier – situated in the foothills of the Radfan Mountains, north of Aden – [35] in numbers never before seen in the territory. Thumier Airstrip could not take *Beverley* transport aircraft, so the vast majority of movement had to be by road. By the end of the month the strike force was assembled: the force HQ; a squadron of armoured cars; two battalions of the FRA, plus two troops of armoured cars; J (Sidi Razegh) Battery; 3rd Royal Horse Artillery under Major Peter Cronk, who had shared the office with TFH at Sandhurst,

---

*   Brigadier Sir Robert Louis Hargoves CBE DL (1918-2008) was a noted businessman and was prominent in politics as a supporter of Margaret Thatcher after his retirement from the army.
†   Formed on 25 August 1959 by the amalgamation of the Royal Norfolk and Suffolk Regiments in the East Anglian Brigade. It became 1st Battalion the Royal Anglian Regiment in 1964.

A patrol of 3 Para in the Radfan. (Airborne Forces Museum)

with six 105 mm guns; A Squadron 22 SAS under Major Peter de la Billière;* and a company of the 1st East Anglian Regiment. In addition there were the men of 45 Commando, Royal Marines based in Aden under the command of Lieutenant-Colonel Paddy Stevens, who had established a camp just east of the road. On the eve of the operation they were joined by the men of B Company 3 Para from Bahrain, with four rifle platoons instead of the usual three. Several days were spent in shooting, navigation training, fitness, night patrolling and heli-copter familiarisation – and then, the operation was ordered.

The troop from 22 SAS which was detailed to mark the drop zone in the boulder-strewn landscape was landed by *Scout* helicopters at last light on 29 April, but failed to reach their objective before daylight and so lay up in cover. However, the patrol was seen by a shepherd and, surrounded by hostile tribesmen, became embroiled in a fight for survival. The patrol managed to break clean after dark and withdraw – losing their Troop Commander, Robin Edwards, and a Trooper killed and two more men wounded. The two dead men were muti-lated and decapitated – their heads exhibited in Sana'a in the Yemen.[36] A second attempt was made by the SAS to mark the DZ but the helicopters carrying the patrol were engaged by small-arms fire, damaged and forced to return to base. The intensity of fire during this battle showed that the paras would be in a fight as soon as they landed – and probably unable properly to regroup and consolidate. The drop was therefore cancelled at the last minute by

---

*   Later General Sir Peter Edgar de la Cour de la Billière KCB KBE DSO MC MSc (b. 1934).

Sketch by TFH of B Company's action in the Radfan. (Farrar-Hockley family)

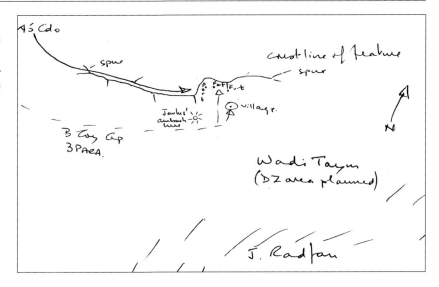

Cubbon.[37] Instead, it was decided to capture the feature by a night approach march and attack. 45 Commando had secured a number of high features without a fight and closed up to the enemy. The plan from here on was modified: two companies of 45 Commando would advance directly by night to the high ground ahead of them, securing at least a foothold by daybreak on the features of 'Sand Fly' and 'Coca Cola'. By dawn on 1 May, both features had been occupied and the East Anglians and the FRA had cleared the main road. 45 Commando was ordered to hold its positions, while the East Anglians moved up to occupy 'Coca Cola' so that the marines could push on.[38]

From here, the plan called for 45 Commando to occupy the 'Gin Sling' and 'Cap Badge' features from the west while B Company made a wide encircling movement up to and across the DZ planned for the drop, coming up behind the enemy by dawn.[39] On the night of 4 May, the marines and paras set out into the darkness. All were heavily laden, principally with ammunition and water. It was one of those marches which demand much of the infantryman: rough country, up and down, all of 10 miles (16 kilometres), carrying 27,000 rounds of small-arms ammunition between them – as well as rations, water and radio batteries. For the officers navigating, there was the problem of maintaining direction across steep and broken country – and several times, both the marines and B Company lost their way, but recovered skilfully. For every 100 yards they advanced, they were forced to climb or descend 300. Bearings were lost in the darkness and had to be rediscovered. If one of the heavily laden men fell, there was a constant fear that he had broken a limb – raising the question of whether he should be carried, which would mean abandoning important loads – or be left behind, perhaps to be found by a band of merciless tribesmen. They knew that they were marching against the clock and that daylight would expose them to fire from every direction.

As the sun rose, Peter Walter saw that they were still far from their objective. Paddy Stevens admitted freely later that he had underestimated the time it would take to complete the move.[40] Skirting the crests and resting in shadows, Walter managed to avoid a meeting engagement on the line of march. At last, he saw the village of Habil Sahaba, a fortified village tucked into the base of the escarpment, and the stone watch-towers which were his target. He had hoped to surprise the towers' garrisons by night, but now he had to close on them in daylight. Still

Troops of 3 Para advancing under fire from tribesmen in the Radfan. (Airborne Forces Museum)

half a mile away, Radfani tribesmen began firing – and as bullets ricocheted among the rocks, the paratroopers were forced down behind the rocks and buildings of the deserted settlement of Wuli, 1,500 yards south-east of Habil Sahaba.

Under cover, the men were neither safe from fire nor closing on their objective, so Walter – having brought fighter ground attack aircraft onto the target – led a dash with the majority of the leading platoon to clear the positions surrounding the central watch-towers; two other platoons were deployed to clear the village. No sooner had the leading parties moved off than a group of tribesmen, believing them to be the entire force, came in to attack them from behind. The fourth platoon – with supporting elements – had yet to close up and its Commander, Captain Barry Jewkes, saw what was happening. He immediately attacked, and the Radfani were all killed.

The noise of this action, combined with that of clearing the watch-towers and the village, drew the entire weight of the local forces down on the paratroopers. A prolonged struggle ensued for possession of the battleground. The British force had the valuable support of their two mortars, but ammunition for these weapons was limited to what the men had been able to carry. Every man in the force had two bombs in his load, but mortars fire rapidly and this stock would soon be exhausted. Although the artillery at Thumier was out of range, the radio was used to bring RAF Hawker *Hunters* in to strike at Radfanis positioned in caves and *sangars* in the rocks. These aircraft were also able to suppress the fire from snipers spread out on the overhanging heights. However, Walter 'did not have the firepower for close support to assault the hillside in front which was, in any case, immensely steep. His orders were therefore to keep pressure up on the enemy while 45 Commando worked along the crests'.[41]

Late in the afternoon, the paras were relieved to see the marines of 45 Commando driving the Radfani snipers from the heights, having been working steadily forward since first light. Barry Jewkes was killed soon afterwards while moving towards the village – with Sergeant Baxter and three others – to deal with snipers. Baxter was hit in the chest by a sniper and while Jewkes was attending to him, he was shot dead. Soon, Fred Preston, 3 Para's Chaplain, appeared in a *Belvedere* helicopter: 'As the casevac party was in a fluster, he took charge, loaded the 10 wounded paratroopers, sent them out with the casevac team, and remained to give Jewkes and one other fatal casualty, Private Michael Davis, a temporary, shallow burial'.[42]

B Company stayed on for a few days – patrolling the area – before the area was handed over to the East Anglians and the marines and paratroopers withdrew to Aden, where Davis and Jewkes were properly buried, and then back to Bahrain.

*   *   *

No-one in Aden believed, rightly, that a day of warm skirmishing had conquered the Radfani tribes – even though they had suffered a tactical defeat. A new Brigade Headquarters was brought from Northern Ireland to continue the campaign of pacification. This was 39 Infantry Brigade, commanded by Brigadier 'Monkey' Blacker,[43] who had been Assistant Commandant at Sandhurst during TFH's time on the staff there. 39 Brigade was part of the 3rd Infantry Division and therefore assigned to the Strategic Reserve. TFH had gone to visit B Company while it was detached under 45 Commando, and while there he had met both Hargroves and Cubbon. According to one account, TFH lobbied for the rest of 3 Para to be brought into action, telling Hargroves that the battalion was 'already acclimatised and battle-ready, having completed a training course in the Kyrenia Mountain Range in Cyprus'.[44] According to TFH's own account, however, it was Cubbon who had taken the initiative, saying that:

> *"I think we may need your battalion down here because there are all sorts of problems up in the Radfan and we've got nothing like enough troops." … I went back to Bahrain to be told by the Brigade Commander, "You are to take a force down as speedily as possible. But we must leave one company here." So I decided to bring Peter Walter's company back …*[45]

As a temporary stop-gap, the regimental band was left in Bahrain to show the flag; the men taking up rifles in place of their musical instruments until Peter Walter's company returned to take over. The debriefing of the SAS patrol that had been pinned down near Shab Tem showed that a considerable insurgent stronghold was located in the area of Hajib – a village 6,000 yards down the eastern side of the Bakri Ridge, on high ground, protected from the north, east and south by escarpments. The insurgents, 300-strong and uniformed, were well dug in and equipped with mortars, machine guns and radios. The advance through the area of Hajib, the Danaba Basin and the Sha'ab i Dharfi feature was to be the task of 3 Para.

The battle-group which assembled in the Wadi Rabwa close to Thumier comprised 3 Para, less B Company; I (Bull's troop) Parachute Light Battery, 7th RHA, under Major David Drew and J (Sidi Razegh) Battery, each with four 105 mm *Howitzers*, supplemented by two five-and-a-half-inch medium *Howitzers* under Major Tony Stagg; No. 3 Troop of 9 Parachute Squadron RE, transport and medical elements and a rifle platoon formed by the RAOC heavy

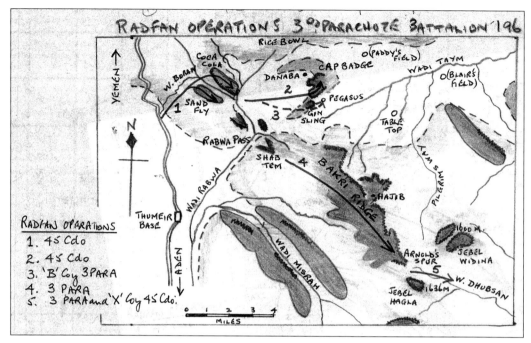

A sketch map of 3 Para operations in the Radfan.

drop detachment, which was attached to A Company, to take the place of one of its platoons which had been previously detached to Peter Walter's company.[46, 47]

None of the big *Belvedere* helicopters of the RAF were available to carry heavy loads forward and at best there would be two *Scout* helicopters of 653 Squadron, Army Air Corps, to carry a few light loads and make reconnaissance flights. In the near future, 815 Naval Air Squadron, with its *Wessex* helicopters, on board HMS *Centaur* was expected to join the force. The official post-operation report noted a distinct failure of communication between the army and the RAF, which had led to the *Belvedere* force being stood down for a complete week for repairs and rest. TFH must have been aghast at such a thing, which would never have happened had 16 Parachute Brigade been tasked to command this operation, but 39 Infantry Brigade was far less experienced and not nearly as well structured for joint operations. There was just a chance that Land Rovers might be able to crawl up the track leading out of the Wadi Rabwa – otherwise, everything had to be backpacked from the start. The 105 mm guns had to remain in the *wadi* – considerably shortening the range of any covering fire they might be able to offer forward.

Blacker's plan involved three phases: First, he would occupy and dominate the Bakri Ridge; then he would push 3 Para along the Wadi Dubsan; and finally, the East Anglians would take Wadi Misrah and clear Jebel Huriyah. The objective of the forthcoming operation was partly punitive, but partly also designed to show that the British and FRA could and would take the fight to the Radfanis whenever and wherever they wished, should the Radfanis continue to choose violence.

On 16 May, Blacker gave TFH orders to the effect that he was to be prepared to move forward from his reserve position in the Wadi Rabwa and occupy the Sha'ab i Dharfi feature. The advance was to begin as soon as possible, but because no helicopter lift was available, at least part of the force would have to act as porters.[48] TFH was concerned as much by the lack of intelligence as by the physical difficulties of the operation. Writing a few days afterwards, he remarked that 'hard, local intelligence was difficult to come by for the original operation, as planned; as distinct from long-term, somewhat general material from covert sources. When the SAS patrols found difficulty in getting in *ab initio*, it became apparent that resistance would be strong'.[49] After a reconnaissance flight with Blacker, Francis Graham-Bell – commanding 653 Squadron AAC – and Lieutenant-Colonel Alastair Thorburn of The King's Own Scottish Borderers,[50] TFH, forming his own plan and orders, decided that in view of the terrain, the lack of lift and the loads to be carried, he would make the approach march over two nights. He had, however, already warned the battalion that this would be no easy task and that casualties were probable, not just possible. As Mike Walsh recalled, 'This was a wise move, for the majority of the battalion had not been in action before'.[51]

Indeed, it was a much younger and less experienced battalion than the 3 Para that had dropped into Suez. The officers and men were largely untested in battle – with some notable exceptions – however they were undaunted by the prospect of action, even though TFH had told them to accustom themselves to the prospect of losing their lives. They were well trained and acclimatised to desert – although not to altitude. In their training, TFH had stressed many old North-West Frontier tricks: the importance of holding high ground at night; of not being caught in the open in daylight; of picketing; and of carrying enough water, ammunition and radio batteries to maintain the basic essential functions of a fighting unit.[52]

That first night, 16-17 May – which was Whit Sunday – TFH advanced the Anti-tank Platoon, armed with rifles and machine guns, to the deserted village of Shab Tem, which had been selected as the forward road-head for dumping supplies.[53] From this outpost he sent forward three patrols in bright moonlight to seek routes up to the far ridge. They discovered only one – and even this involved crossing several steep-sided ravines. Moreover, next day it became evident that the track out of the Wadi Rabwa had been blocked by a landslide and it could not be used by laden vehicles moving up to Shab Tem; this would impose a delay of 24 hours. The Quarter Master, Jack Crane, and the MTO, Tom Duffy, therefore sent several empty vehicles across the worst break in the track and organised the manhandling of loads over to them: ammunition, water and food. If there should be a severe battle, these would be their sole source of replenishment.

On the night of 17-18 May, with the stocking up of supplies still in process, reconnaissance patrols were sent out. These indicated that only one of the three possible approach routes, a camel track to the right of Bakri Ridge, was feasible – and it was this route that TFH took with the main column.[54] The battle-group moved with A Company leading, followed closely by the mortars and machine guns, then TFH's tactical headquarters and the Battery Commander's party; then C Company and the sappers with their heavy loads in the rear.[55] By first light, they were on the ridge. On the next night, 18-19 May, an ambush patrol under 2nd Lieutenant Hew Pike moved off to stop any enemy withdrawing before the main body closed up and captured at least one prisoner. Pike's patrol became involved in a running fight with the insurgents, but established a position dominating the objective. Pike later recalled that:

> We were … engaged on hard terrain above us by tribesmen, who had these very long *Martini-Henry* ancient rifles. They were good shots – very warlike and courageous people, tough people … this was enough to get us to initiate the fire and manoeuvre

drills that everyone is taught at Sandhurst … as we engaged the enemy positions in the dark (basically firing with the others moving and so forth) we moved forward up the mountain. And at the end of that we found they had all disappeared down a cliff and buggered off: vanished.[56]

As dawn broke, Pike was reorganising when up came TFH. Sitting on a sandbag, TFH congratulated Pike on his navigation and tactics, but seemed a little put out that no prisoner had been taken – a highly deflating experience for a young officer after his first battle.

While this had been going on, the Anti-tank Platoon under CSM 'Nobby' Arnold cleared the Al Dahri Ridge, taking three prisoners.[57] The main body continued to advance: 'I found myself', wrote TFH later,

> … in front of the battalion with the two leading Company Commanders. I had with me my long-standing orderly, Corporal Ted Olive, who is an old and dear friend of mine. I told him to go to an OP 500 to 600 yards ahead and that I would send somebody up to support him. I saw this lone figure going on ahead and I thought to myself: *"What am I going to say to his wife, who was just arriving in Bahrain, if he is hit."* However, nothing happened.[58]

Over the next three days, intensive patrolling was carried out to clear the western slopes of the Bakri Ridge and the numerous *wadis* throughout the Sha'ab Khulila, Sha'ab Wahida and the Sha'ab Suma'an.[59] Many insurgent positions were discovered and engaged; several insurgents were killed and wounded, and prisoners taken; and weapons, ammunition and supplies were found and seized or destroyed. These weapons included British, French, German and Russian small arms dating from 1897 to the present. There were also many tons of flour, grain, coffee, nuts, kerosene and cooking oil. C Company and the Royal Engineers were deployed as fighting porters during these days – each officer and soldier carrying up to 180 lbs (a truly immense load made up of a box of ammunition, a box of batteries, or a jerry can of water and his personal weapon); possibly TFH remembered how the Chinese had used porters at night in Korea. It was very hot and progress was slow, only about half-a-mile an hour, up and down the broken, precipitous slopes. Just before dawn, TFH halted on a knoll crowned by two deserted houses. The porters shed their loads and returned to Shab Tem. As the battalion, less C Company, made camp, there was a brief flurry of fire from a flank – sending bullets whistling over them. Two of the battalion's mortars fired a random response onto the flashes and, as the moon came up, quiet returned.

The next day, 22 May, the Army Air Corps *Scout* helicopters flew a series of loads forward from Shab Tem, while the paratroopers watched the silent and apparently deserted landscape from five concealed observation posts. During this resupply, TFH managed to speak to Graham-Bell, saying, 'I know that you've been very busy and I have refrained from asking for any helicopters … but when I do ask for them, I shall want them quickly. I will not ask for them unless I mean business'.[60]

The next phase of operations now went ahead and was planned as a three-pronged advance, with 45 Commando and the 2nd Battalion FRA clearing south-east down Wadi Misrah from Thumier; 1st East Anglians with a troop of armoured cars clearing northwards up the Wadi Nakhalain to block the insurgents' escape routes; and 3 Para was given the task of clearing south-eastwards along the Bakri Ridge towards the Wadi Dhubsan. In the event, the operations of 45 Commando and 1st East Anglians were not pushed through because of heavy flooding in the *wadi* bottoms. 3 Para began to move on 23 May. At nightfall, C Company reappeared to take on the role of an advanced guard – Ian McLeod leading – while A Company and the engineers humped the loads. The column set off, wending its way through the deep ravines, finally securing its initial objective on the top of the Hajib escarpment as dawn approached. Here, they were about half-way to the final objective: 7,000 yards in a straight line, but 10,000 on the ground.

The Bakri fighting bands were uncertain as to what to do next. They did not like operating at night, preferring to use darkness to regroup and rest. This had become apparent as a result of 45 Commando's operation. All of them were crack marksmen and they therefore preferred to wage guerrilla war by day among the rocks and caverns with which they were familiar, sniping and closing in when any British position looked vulnerable. They had now lost a good deal of territory. Moreover, the Wadi Dhubsan had never previously been penetrated by government forces – and in it lay the Radfanis' principal grain stores. By contrast, the British could operate better by night, lying up in the heat of the day.

When the battalion group began to expand their positions, at first on the flank and then towards the heights overlooking the Wadi Dhubsan, the Radfani resistance hardened; and their resistance became at times ferocious. C Company began to clear a complex of villages at the south end of the Bakri Ridge to secure the start line for A Company to move onto the Alfara Ridge at the head of the *wadi* leading down into the Dhubsan. The surface of the Bakri Ridge was arid and uninviting – a series of grey shale terraces which the eroding wind and weather had shaped into some giant's staircase – and the considerable opposition in the first two villages was silenced by the guns of J Battery and the battalion's mortars; but the company was then held up by a saddle of ground – beyond which stood stone watch-towers with thick dry stone walls, connecting tunnels and escape routes leading into dead ground: relics of old inter-tribal wars. These towers were beyond the guns' range, and too robustly constructed to be destroyed by mortars. The RAF *Hunters* were therefore called down by the battalion's Forward Air Controller, Captain Keith Riddell of the Royal Artillery. These aircraft ran in twice onto the towers with bombs and 30 mm *Aden* cannon – the empty cases falling onto the heads of the waiting paratroopers. Unbelievably, no-one was wearing a helmet. The watch-towers fell silent; C Company cleared the position and A Company moved onto the Alfara Ridge.

As A Company began to advance, their left protected by the Anti-tank Platoon, groups of tribesmen opened fire from two villages ahead. Most estimates agreed that there were about 40 men with at least five light machine guns. The guns, firing at extreme range, dropped shells onto the Radfanis as the paras advanced rapidly, in spite of enemy fire. The British force now looked down into the Wadi Dhubsan. This area, hitherto a safe base for the Radfani's operations, was to be entered as a demonstration of power and the grain stocks held there were to be destroyed. Blacker told TFH that: 'The aim is not to slaughter tribesmen, but to teach them that we will come wherever we need to if they misbehave.' In the event, the final assault was delayed by heavy rainstorms.

On 24 and 25 May, therefore, the stores remaining in the Wadi Rabwa were brought forward to a new dump on the Hajib escarpment by helicopter and the sappers worked round the clock to extend the track from Shab Tem in order to bring forward the guns of I and J Batteries. X Company of 45 Commando was also moved forward by helicopter and placed under TFH's command for the final phase of the advance. There were two tracks into the Wadi Dhubsan: the best, which ran south, then east and then doubled back westwards into the *wadi*, was an obvious choice and TFH thought it certain that this would be strongly ambushed. The alternative route was poor going, winding 3,200 feet (1,000 metres) down the mountain into the valley. TFH decided to make a personal reconnaissance and when he did so, he found a route involving a descent of 30 feet (10 metres) by rope down a cliff face, along a boulder-strewn stream bed and directly into the *wadi* in the rear of the village of Bayn Al Gidr. TFH decided that this was the way to come – choosing a conscious paradox: that the bad going made for a good route *because* it was bad and would, therefore, be less likely to be contested by the enemy. Looking down it, he said to Graham-Bell – indicating the sheer cliff on the right, 'We will rope our way down there tonight'. He paused a while in thought and then added, 'Whatever happens, the most important thing will be to get the casualties out. Don't forget it. That's the most important thing'.[61]

Beginning at 2200 hrs on the night of 25 May, while C Company picketed the Jebel Haqla to the right, the main column (led by TFH's command group and the Machine-gun Platoon) used ropes to abseil down the rock face – descending in the darkness into the village.[62]

By first light on 26 May, the battalion's medium machine guns were in position to cover the assault. A Company moved forward rapidly, taking the high ground overlooking Bayn Al Gidr. Sentries posted by the tribesmen around the village rapidly woke the garrison, which promptly fled to a man. By 0600 hrs, the upper *wadi* had been cleared without a shot being fired. X Company of 45 Commando was now advanced down the right side of the *wadi*, tasked with clearing the enemy as far as Hawfi. Very quickly, groups of tribesmen were seen hurrying into the *wadi* from the south – returning from their ambush positions on the better of the two approaches in the upper slopes on the route that TFH had rejected. Fire was opened by at least 50 insurgents, the shots echoing along the sides of the *wadi*. TFH had been talking to Blacker,[63] who had arrived by helicopter at 0600 hrs, and once the meeting was over TFH flew in to Bayn Al Gidr, where he was given map co-ordinates of the marines' position. He decided once more on personal reconnaissance and took a *Scout* helicopter to check on their progress, accompanied by the IO, Ian McLeod.

Taking off, TF's *Scout* flew towards the map reference given to him on the radio, which was in fact wrong. The reported map reference was 500 yards in front of where X Company actually was. Major Jake Jackson, the pilot, sought the shelter of the cliffs as they skimmed the Wadi Dhubsan, over the Battalion Headquarters and support elements on the valley floor. They crossed a deserted tract and, suddenly, approaching the map reference point, the ground and cliffs on either side were milling with turbaned tribesmen – shaking their fists and firing their rifles. The noise of the engine obscured the sound of their shots, but then the men in the *Scout* heard a sound like the opening of beer cans: 'Fuel began to flood down over the visor of the chopper', as TFH recalled:[64]

> 'Can you keep flying?' asked TFH, 'This is the last place to put her down.'
> 'I've got power,' said Jackson.
> Coolly, he turned the *Scout* towards the head of the *wadi*, but then either the engine or the rotors started to make a clattering noise. As they swept forward, the advanced element of Battalion Headquarters on the valley floor swung into sight.
> 'Down there,' said TFH.

They landed safely and Jackson switched off the engine. Around them, a fire-fight was in progress. Fifty tribesmen had moved into position and more waited behind them – no doubt those seen by the *Scout* earlier on. There were now some casualties to be evacuated, including Ian McLeod, who had been shot through the wrist in the *Scout*. Later, TFH gently rebuked McLeod for suggesting that they had been 'shot down'. 'Not shot down ... forced to land, old chap; forced to land', he said with a grin.[65]

The Regimental Sergeant Major – Arthur Channon – then led a party from the headquarters to the damaged helicopter, but was wounded on the way, for the Bakri riflemen were shooting with accuracy at 800 yards' (750 metres') range. Even as Padre Fred Preston helped carry the wounded back, the heels of his boots were clipped by bullets. The shooting-down of TFH's helicopter made the front pages of almost every newspaper in Britain the next morning. That day, Dair was on parade with the Exeter School Cadet Corps – receiving their annual inspection from no less a personage than Field Marshal Sir Richard Hull, then Chief of the Imperial General Staff. Knowing Dair was there in the ranks of the Corps of Drums, Hull sought him out to tell him that all was well and that his father was uninjured.[66]

Back in the Radfan, it was a tiresome morning and afternoon. A Company cleared to the north but in the end, the difficulty of breaching the tribesmen's well-concealed defences was overcome by C Company. Ordered to outflank them by marching round from the Jebel Haqla, they did so rapidly – surprising the Radfanis' left flank and forcing them to abandon their positions – supported by five *Hunter* strikes, mortar and artillery fire. At least six insurgents were killed; and 11 rifles, two-and-a-half tons of food and 18 cans of fuel were found and destroyed for the loss of one marine killed and six men wounded. The battalion then formed a defensive perimeter for the night, within which lay the crippled *Scout*, as this was to be denied to the enemy and repaired if humanly possible.

653 Squadron made repeated flights to resupply the battalion, evacuate the wounded and bring up two REME aircraft technicians to work by torchlight through the hours of darkness to repair the helicopter before dawn. Graham-Bell came forward early to assess the problem, bringing a bottle of whisky for TFH, whom he found in cover under a brisk fire from insurgents. Graham-Bell dashed forward at some speed and flung himself into cover where:

> ... between gasps I handed over the whisky ... I noticed that Tony had stood up so I did likewise and we continued talking. It suddenly dawned on me that this was a trifle unwise and I asked: *"Aren't we rather exposed here?"*
>
> *"Oh yes,"* replied Tony, *"I thought that, if they were still in their positions, our standing up would draw their fire."*[67]

Next morning, as the Radfani grain stores were set alight, Jackson climbed into the *Scout* and tried the starter motor. The engine fired, the rotors turned – and when the helicopter lifted, hovered and then rose rapidly into the air, there was a hearty cheer from the paratroopers, who knew that this heralded their own extraction.[68] Jackson disappeared through the smoke billowing up from the grain stores.

The officers and men of 3 Para began the long climb out of the *wadi* to the heights of the Alfara Ridge. From there, they were airlifted by *Wessex* helicopters of the Royal Navy to Aden town and the delight of a cold beer – leaving behind the unfortunate marines of X Company,

A 3 Para soldier observes a *Hunter* fighter-jet attack near the Wadi Dhubsan, May 1964. (Airborne Forces Museum)

who were left holding the Bakri Ridge – and from there to Bahrain on 31 May. Follow-up operations continued however, and on 7 June, D Company of 3 Para was flown from Bahrain to join first the 1st East Anglians, then the 1st Royal Scots and finally the 1st King's Own Scottish Borderers – taking part in operations in the Wadi Thaym and Wadi Bana areas until 22 June.

TFH left a personal account of the fighting in the Radfan, on which this chapter is based; it was the result of an order from Cubbon, who insisted that every Commanding Officer should write his own account directly after any operation and before he left the theatre of operations.[69] The account, however, is sketchy, compresses much of the detail of the action and plays down the severity of the fighting, the terrain and the conditions endured by the officers and men. His formal after-action report, probably compiled by the Adjutant, is fortunately much more detailed. Cubbon was under no illusions, however, and later wrote of this operation that 3 Para's '… speed and hard fighting over high and seemingly inaccessible mountains astonished the enemy as well as the rest of 39 Brigade'.[70]

One matter, however, exercised TFH greatly and this was the death of Barry Jewkes. Jewkes was recently married and had left a widow and young child. His widow, a German lady, was quite literally shattered and without the means to support herself and her child unless she returned to live with her parents in Germany. Jewkes was on secondment from the Lancashire Fusiliers – a regiment which had a charitable fund designed to pay for the education of the children of officers killed on active service. Unfortunately, when he went across to the paras, Jewkes had not kept up his subscriptions to the Regimental Association: 'By diplomacy and some cunning, TFH paid the missing sum from his own pocket – thus ensuring that the boy subsequently attended an excellent public school and later joined the army.'[71]

Hew Pike recalled more of his memories of TFH during this operation in his funeral eulogy:

> TFH's sheer confidence and authority were formidable. I doubt that anyone here ever witnessed him ruffled, let alone rattled. In his mind, there always had to be a way to resolve difficulties – a way forward. His calm, phlegmatic temperament did indeed seem to "rise superior to every misfortune", in Gibbon's memorable phrase, "and derive resources from adversity". He had the power, through his presence, to command confidence whilst communicating energy.
>
> His addresses to his battalion – discursive and without a note – were always memorable, often spellbinding. Ranging across the bigger picture one minute, plunging into the minutiae of soldiering the next. His masterly oration to us all when we emerged from the mountains of the Radfan dwelt on the broad significance of the battalion's task, it is true, but did not omit the professional details either – the use of fighting porters for want of helicopters, even the improvised use of tinned compo margarine by the Machine-gun Platoon when the rifle oil ran out. Resourceful soldiering par excellence, he reminded us.[72]

Although 3 Para had only been committed for 10 days in the Radfan Campaign, they were 10 decisive days in the true sense of the word. A battle is only decisive if, either it concludes a war or a phase of operations, or else it sets events on a course of action from which there will be only one possible result. In this case, the operation had demonstrated that British troops could go anywhere at any time – dominating the Radfan and destroying the Radfanis' food supplies at will. The result was political negotiation in London with the dissidents and their allies.

As a result of the action – and in addition to the new General Service Medal 1962 with the clasp 'Radfan', which everyone engaged received – 3 Para won two Military Crosses, one Military Medal, one British Empire Medal and several Mentions-in-Despatches. TFH himself was awarded a bar to his DSO – that is, a second award of the decoration. The citation, written by Blacker and strongly endorsed by the succeeding levels of command, explains why:

> … Lt-Col Farrar-Hockley's battalion was called upon to perform an extremely difficult 10-mile advance … the whole operation was fraught with tactical and administrative difficulties of considerable proportions, and included two tough battles as well as several skirmishes. The performance of this battalion during this very testing period was superb, and was largely due to the inspiration and exceptional leadership of its Commanding Officer.
>
> … he launched a brilliantly executed attack which finally drove the enemy from their position. This was only one example of the extraordinary energy, drive and resource with which this officer inspired his battalion … Whether personally leading patrols into enemy country, or by his own example drawing forth exceptional efforts from his men, or improvising ingenious methods of supply, Lt-Col Farrar-Hockley's leadership and bravery were of an order far beyond the call of duty.[73]

To some people, TFH said that the Radfan had been the most challenging operation of his career – an extraordinary statement given his severe experiences in Italy, Greece, Palestine and Korea. Perhaps it was because this was the first time that he, TFH, had been in charge and fully responsible for the operation rather than being someone else's subordinate.[74]

*   *   *

3 Para remained in Bahrain for the rest of TFH's period of command, without further operational deployments. He was clearly very concerned about the possibility of anti-climax affecting the officers and men. Mike Walsh, who was now Second-in-Command, was given the task of organising a testing series of exercises including parachute drops with the Trucial Oman Scouts. At Christmas, TFH was determined that a special effort should be made. After the carol service on Christmas Day, every unmarried officer and soldier – regardless of rank – was invited to have dinner and spend the day with one of the limited number of families. Mike Walsh remembered that his married quarter was filled with 24 cheerful souls from the battalion orderly room.[75]

Pat Beaumont remembered TFH at this time 'for his kindness, consideration and Christianity' and went on to recall several episodes which illustrated TFH's approach to his command:

> When rogue soldiers came to him on CO's orders, if he felt that they had some quality that he could influence, he would sidestep the *Manual of Military Law* and ask the soldier if he would accept his award … I recall he sentenced a soldier found guilty of drunkenness to three months as barman in the Officers' Mess! He personally supervised his employment as barman and general dogsbody, making sure he worked his fingers to the bone. Over a period of time this soldier was promoted through the ranks – finally becoming a Company Sergeant Major.
>
> Our freefall team would display regularly for the Ruler. Inevitably they would receive a gold Omega or Rolex at the end of each event. TFH ensured that the team were allowed to keep one only in the Paymaster's safe to take home at the end of the tour and somehow, through the Political Resident, had the rest returned to the Treasury and the sum generated in lieu was given to charities … [76]

TFH, having taken a formal leave of the Ruler of Bahrain, handed over command on 14 March 1965 to F.H. (Jim) Scobie. Scobie had a most unenviable series of tasks: to fill the shoes of a commander of TFH's stature and then to carry the battalion through the post-Radfan period. Knowing TFH's fondness for ceremonial, Mike Walsh arranged a proper formal parade to say farewell to TFH – at which he was presented with two drums (one side and one tenor) along with a 3 Para tie, which it had also been Walsh's task to invent and have manufactured. TFH himself gave the battalion a silver cup for the inter-company rugby competition. Later, Barry Jewkes's parents presented a silver cup from his old regiment which had been used for rugby and, with TFH's consent, his cup became the Champion Company Cup.

The Commander Land Forces in the Gulf, Brigadier M.W. Holme, describing TFH as 'a most friendly, helpful and delightful colleague in Bahrain' and recommending him strongly – as did the superior reporting officers – for command of a brigade, summed him up in terms that strike a familiar chord with anyone who has read a number of his annual confidential reports:

> With all [his] qualities, it might be thought, and anyone with only a passing acquaintance of him might think, that he is a hard calculating military machine, but this is not so, for he has a most pleasant, cheerful and sympathetic nature, with a good sense of humour, and most important of all, he abounds in good practical commonsense ... Like all strong and competent people, he likes to get his own way, which is of course nearly always right, but just occasionally he could, with advantage, demonstrate more clearly his consideration for the views and interests of others.[77]

His battalion never forgot him – and the last word on TFH as a CO must go to one who served under him; who remembered, as they all did:

> ... the man of deep and penetrating intellect, at home in the world of ideas, and of scholarship. The man of rigorous conviction and unremitting standards, the man of generous spirit, warmth, and humour – whose reflective, knowing smile would lighten the atmosphere of even the most serious discussion.
> ... the Christian soldier and leader, the soldier of exemplary moral and physical courage, the soldier of indefatigable endurance and resilience, the soldier of irrepressible, contagious confidence and authority – in whose company, failure seemed unthinkable, success somehow assured.[78]

15

'A benevolent hurricane' Confrontation in Borneo, 1965-1966[1]

Leaving the command of an infantry battalion can be a huge anti-climax. Post-command blues are quite usual, for one day a Lieutenant-Colonel could be the master of all he surveyed, and the next he could be fighting for a seat on some crowded commuter train – heading for a dark and gloomy office in London where he would do well to get someone to make him a cup of tea. TFH was, once again, lucky. Instead of a staff appointment in Britain or Germany he was posted to the headquarters of British Forces Borneo as personal staff officer to the Director of Operations,[2] in yet another theatre of war where his very considerable experience would once again be put to the test. Confrontation with Indonesia was in full swing and although TFH had no experience of operations in the jungle, he had plenty in the conduct of both conventional war and counter-insurgency in difficult environments. The campaign in Borneo contained all these challenges.

After a short period of leave, during which he and Pat could see something of the two boys, TFH was off once more. Pat was able to go with him, though, and settle into a delightful bungalow close to the headquarters – only a stone's throw from a secluded beach where the family swam and Peppie (the family's black poodle) loved to explore the thick vegetation along the shoreline. Ted Olive and his wife accompanied them, taking over a brick-built married quarter close by and supervising the work of the Chinese domestic staff.[3] Hilary was now at St Peter's School in Exmouth; Dair remained at Exeter School until the end of the summer term and in September, having been awarded an army scholarship, he went to Sandhurst. Michael Walsh delivered him into the loving embrace of a large Drill-Sergeant on the steps of the Old Building.[4] Both were able, however, to fly to Brunei and then be flown to Labuan for holidays.

* * *

The roots of what later became known as 'Confrontation' – or *Konfrontasi* – lay in the way that the Republic of Indonesia had come into existence, as well as in the complex character of its President, Sukarno.[*] The Republic had emerged from the Japanese occupation of the Dutch East Indies; collaboration with the Japanese by indigenous groups as a means of ending European Colonialism; and then resistance by those same groups to the return of Dutch

---

[*] Sukarno – like most Javanese people he had only one name – also known as Bung Karno (1901-1970), was the first President of Indonesia.

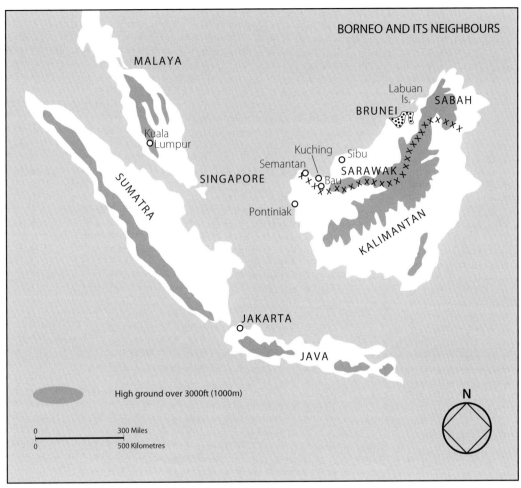

Borneo and its neighbours.

colonial power. The British and Indian Armies had fought a campaign against them during 1946 to return the territories to their Dutch allies and had then withdrawn at the end of the year;[5] after another two years of intense fighting, the Dutch were forced to hand over control of most, but not all, of the territories. Political turmoil, however, was the order of the day throughout the 1950s. Sukarno, who had been in the forefront of nationalist activity before the war, had no love for the West. He was by far the most charismatic figure on the Indonesian political scene, and it was he who emerged as its leading politician and first President.

After Independence, most of the island of Borneo became the Indonesian region of Kalimantan. However, three territories in the north remained under British control: the Protectorate of Brunei, the Crown Colonies of Sarawak, and British North Borneo – later known as Sabah. Sarawak and Sabah had only become British Crown Colonies after the Second World War and they were, as a result, economically and politically at a low stage of development. Brunei, ruled by its autocrat, the Sultan, was a small Malay State whose economy rested on its considerable oilfields, which were operated by Western companies. In spite of the presence of Malays in all three territories, their ties with Malaya proper were weak – relying as much as anything on their common relationship with Britain. Nationalist political forces were emerging it is true, but without any real consensus on the future direction of that Nationalism.

The first stage of Confrontation began in 1959 when the Indonesian Government demanded the cession of the last remaining Dutch-controlled area in the region, Western New Guinea (which had been agreed under the original Independence deal, but not implemented), to Indonesia. The strategy of Confrontation included large-scale purchases of modern weapons and equipment from the Soviet Union – and this rang immediate alarm bells in Western capitals.[6] Diplomatic pressure in the UN was also used to drive a wedge between the Dutch and their American allies, who were always unwilling to be seen as being on the side of Imperialism. This worked so successfully that the Kennedy administration finally decided, in the autumn of 1961, to coerce the Dutch into accepting a *de facto* Indonesian annexation of Western New Guinea – not least because in the wake of Indonesian arms deals with the Soviets and the emergence of Indonesia as a 'Guided Democracy', the administration was concerned that Sukarno would move fully into the communist camp in South-East Asia.

Meanwhile, in 1957, Harold Macmillan's defence review in Britain had made fundamental changes in British posture in the Far East. Over the next four years this restructuring, along with the formal end of the Emergency in Malaya; the new Malaysian Government's ambivalent attitude towards the pro-Western security apparatus of the region – the South-East Asia Treaty Organisation (SEATO) – the increasing desire of Singapore for Independence and self-government; and the state of the British economy all conspired to bring into question Britain's ability to maintain its military commitments outside Europe.

In May 1961, Prime Minister Tunku Abdul Rahman of Malaya* began, somewhat abruptly, to pursue the idea of merging Malaya and Singapore into a single State. Uncertain at first, British policy makers welcomed this idea of a Greater Malaysia as a means towards a new British policy for the region. The British North Borneo territories were now to be included in this new State, both to make it more viable and to relieve the British from the responsibility for their collective security and administration. In the short term at least, British bases in Singapore would remain, until such time as local defence structures were capable of defending the new State. In the event, Brunei rejected membership of the new confederation when it took shape in September 1963. Indonesia, for its part, refused to accept Malaysia and when Sukarno launched his undeclared war, it was in Britain's interests to prevent this new friendly State – operating within the British economic orbit and staunchly rejecting Communism – from being dismembered.[7]

Greater Malaysia did not, however, command majority support in any of the Borneo territories, but support for joining a Greater Indonesia was also weak. More people supported either continuing the status quo or merging the three British territories as a distinct entity rather than being submerged in a greater union. The British assembled a Commission of Inquiry to establish the wishes of the people in the Borneo territories and this commission reported in March 1962: it provided just enough political justification, just in time, to proceed with the Greater Malaysia project.

---

*   Tunku Abdul Rahman Putra Al-Haj ibn Almarhum Sultan Abdul Hamid Halim Shah (1903-1990) was Chief Minister of the Federation of Malaya from 1955 and the country's first Prime Minister after Independence in 1957. He remained as the Prime Minister after Sabah, Sarawak and Singapore joined the Federation in 1963 to form Malaysia. He is widely known simply as 'Tunku' or 'The Tunku' – a princely Malay title.

Brunei had rejected unification because the Sultan had no wish to lose control of his oil revenues. On the other hand, Tunku Abdul Rahman had argued against Brunei's resistance on the ground that the Sultanate could not survive on its own; this stance ignited internal conflict within Brunei. In November 1962 the Brunei People's Party (*Partai Brunei Rakyat,* BPR), led by Sheikh Azahari bin Sheikh Mahmud,* won a landslide victory in elections to the newly-created Legislative Council. Azahari's manifesto commitment was clear: the federation of the three British North Borneo territories into a Republic with a socialist economy. The Sultan, not surprisingly, vetoed any moves in this direction. On 8 December 1962, the insurgent group *Tentera Nasional Kalimantan Utara* (TNKU), or North Kalimantan National Army – the military wing of the BPR – attacked government, police and oil installations in Brunei.[8] The BPR turned for help to a neighbour which, since 1955, had presented itself as a leader in the Afro-Asian struggle against Imperialism: Indonesia. The British Far East Command had little trouble in putting down the TNKU insurgency, chasing the survivors into the jungle and restoring the Sultan's government.[9] The revolt, however, was the spark that ignited a greater problem.

The Indonesian Government now engaged actively against the new Malaysia. On 20 January 1963, Subandrio,[†] Foreign Minister and head of the *Badan Pusat Intelijen* (BPI) – or Central Intelligence Agency – publicly declared that Indonesia would follow a new policy of Confrontation; this time against Malaysia, which was no more than '... the henchman of Neo-Imperialism and Neo-Colonialism pursuing a policy hostile to Indonesia'.[10]

MI6 reported that the *Tentera Nasional Indonesia* (TNI), the Indonesian National Army, was moving combat troops into Borneo as well as providing support for TNKU and other dissident groups in Sarawak who opposed the Malaysia project. Ironically, many of the officers among the Indonesian force had been trained at the British Army's jungle warfare school at Johore Bahru in Malaya. This convinced the British Government that Indonesia meant to oppose the creation of Malaysia by force of arms. This realisation transformed the situation.[11]

The formal Proclamation of Malaysia was achieved on 16 September 1963 – merging Malaya, Singapore, Sabah and Sarawak. This gave Sukarno and Subandrio enough justification to claim that Tunku Abdul Rahman threatened Indonesia's interests in the status of Borneo. They escalated Confrontation, unleashing mob attacks on the British Embassy in Jakarta and stepping up cross-border incursions in Borneo. Confrontation from here on was fought by the Indonesians on three levels: a diplomatic battle to win the support of world opinion through diplomacy and propaganda; a political battle to win the support of domestic and regional opinion through diplomacy, subversion, propaganda, and political measures; and a military battle fought mainly, but not entirely, along the border between Kalimantan and the North Borneo territories, to influence the other two levels of engagement.

* * *

The strategic and operational initiatives in the land campaign in Borneo lay with Indonesia. As the aggressor, it had the choice of deciding where, when, how and with what forces it

---

*   1928/29-2002: better known as A.M. Azahari.

†   Subandrio (1914-2004) was Foreign Minister and First Deputy Prime Minister of Indonesia.

would strike. The Indonesians used a combination of regular units, volunteers drawn from radical political groups and renegade or dissident volunteers from Malaysian States – especially communists – to launch armed incursions across the northern border in Borneo. The over-arching scheme of manoeuvre was first to identify an area whose people could be portrayed as appealing for fraternal assistance from Indonesia to free them from the yoke of Colonialism; then to establish control in that area, which could be declared a 'liberated area'. This would, it was suggested, fatally undermine the credibility of Malaysia. This was the extent of Indonesian military strategic and operational design. There was actually no consensus among Indonesian leaders about their war aims, how they should be achieved, nor how far the conflict should be pushed. The AURI – the Mobile Brigades of the Police Field Force – and BPI, supported by the PKI, generally tried to escalate the conflict. The Navy and Marine Corps were more cautious. The Army High Command tried not to be seen to be undermining the national struggle against Colonialism, but rightly regarded the British and their Commonwealth part-ners as much more dangerous adversaries than the Dutch – and they worried too that esca-lating the conflict would radicalise the country, playing into the hands of the PKI. This is not to say the TNI did not fight. The army had more than enough strength to commit units, as well as volunteers to operations in Borneo, and did so; but it also carefully held back its strongest units while keeping those units that were committed to battle under tight control. The Indonesian Government always denied that its armed forces were involved in military operations and insisted that volunteers or irregulars conducted all incursions across the border – not that this fooled anyone.

The British were well aware of the strategic confusion and operational muddle that charac-terised the Indonesians' conduct of the war, but tended to assume there was more support for the desire to expel them from the region than there really was. This, with the commitment of Indonesian regular troops to ground incursions and the activity of Indonesian naval and air forces, obliged the British and their Commonwealth allies to deploy considerable resources to defend Malaysia. The first Commonwealth Ground Force Commander in Borneo, Major-General Walter Walker,* had used these troops to conduct aggressive – but small-scale and, above all, covert – pre-emptive strikes across the border into Kalimantan to disrupt Indonesian forces, deny them safe haven and keep them on the defensive. These operations, code-named *Claret*, were gradually escalated in size and scope in response to Indonesian pressure and reinforcements.

Claret operations, which were to be part of TFH's bread and butter during his time in Borneo, were never admitted during Confrontation or for many years afterwards, but were conducted from about July 1964 until July 1966 and were instigated by the Director of Operations after clearance by the British and Malaysian Governments. Their purpose was to seize the initiative and put the Indonesians on the defensive, instead of allowing Indonesian forces to be safely based in Kalimantan and attack when and where they chose.[12] However, it was important not to permit Indonesia to present evidence of what it might call neo-imperialist aggression – thus *Claret* operations were highly classified and never publicised, although it seems that

---

*   Later General Sir Walter Colyear Walker KCB CBE DSO (1912-2001). Walker had served on the North-West Frontier; in Burma during the Second World War; and in Malaya. He was later to become well known for his right-wing political views.

some British journalists were aware of what transpired.[13] British casualties on *Claret* operations were publicly reported as being in Brunei, Sarawak or Sabah. These operations involved both Special Forces and conventional infantry battalions. While Special Forces conducted reconnaissance patrols into Indonesian Kalimantan in order to find and observe Indonesian forces,[14] conventional forces were tasked to act on this information by ambushing or attacking the Indonesians under a policy of 'aggressive defence'.[15] *Claret* was largely successful in regaining the initiative by Commonwealth forces, inflicting significant casualties on the Indonesians and keeping them on the defensive – without escalating the war – until they were suspended towards the end of the campaign.[16]

*   *   *

TFH arrived in Borneo on 12 April 1965 and took up his new appointment on 26 April. Walker had just moved on – in March 1965 – and he found himself working for the newly-appointed Major-General George Lea.[*] Above Lea was the Commander-in-Chief Far East Forces, but politico-military authority lay with the Emergency Committees in Sarawak and North Borneo – including their Governors, who were the Commanders-in-Chief for their colonies. In Brunei, there was a State Advisory Council answerable to the Sultan. After Malaysian Independence in 1962, supreme authority was vested in the Malaysian National Defence Council in Kuala Lumpur, with State Executive Committees in Sabah and Sarawak. Military direction was from the Malaysian National Operations Committee, of which the Commander-in-Chief Far East was a member. When TFH arrived, this was Admiral Sir Varyl Begg,[†] who handed over in June to Air Chief Marshal Sir John Grandy.[‡] Grandy quickly established good working relations with Hull, Lea and the Commonwealth senior commanders so that TFH had an unique view of senior relationships at very high level during the conduct of operations.

The Director of Borneo Operations, based on Labuan Island, was also Commander British Forces Borneo – and all British, Commonwealth and Malaysian forces in Borneo were under his ultimate command. Beneath him and his staff was a Land Forces Commander, who was the GOC 17th Gurkha Infantry Division. This was Major-General Peter Hunt,[§] with Charles Linford[¶] as his Colonel GS – or Chief of Staff. This one-on-one command arrangement could be uncomfortable at times – especially as many key staff officers were responsible to both generals for specific parts of their briefs. Below 17th Division were, initially, the headquarters of 3 Commando Brigade in Kuching with responsibility for the western part of Sarawak – or the 1st, 2nd, 3rd and 4th 'Divisions' – as the administrative districts were known; and 99

---

[*] Later Lieutenant-General Sir George Harris Lea KCB DSO MBE (1912-1990). He served with the Airborne Forces during the Second World War and was at Arnhem. He also commanded 22 SAS Regiment in Malaya.

[†] Admiral of the Fleet Sir Varyl Cargill Begg GCB DSO DSC KStJ (1908-1995). He had served at sea in various theatres throughout the Second World War and the Korean War.

[‡] Later Marshal of the Royal Air Force Sir John Grandy GCB GCVO KBE DSO KStJ (1913-2004). He was the only officer who fought and commanded a squadron during the Battle of Britain to reach the post of Chief of the Air Staff. He implemented the final stages of the RAF's withdrawal from the Persian Gulf and the Far East.

[§] Later General Sir Peter Mervyn Hunt GCB DSO OBE DL (1916-1988), Chief of the General Staff from 1973 to 1976.

[¶] Charles William Linford MC, late the Royal Irish Fusiliers; no further details found.

Gurkha Infantry Brigade in Brunei responsible for the East, or 5th Division – plus Brunei and Sabah. The 1st Division contained the capital of Sarawak, Kuching, which was only 25 miles (40 kilometres) from the border), and half the population. Much of this division was under cultivation and accessible by road, but eastwards lay the 2nd Division, which was inhabited mainly by Iban tribes. The 3rd and 4th Divisions were true wilderness and the small 5th Division covered the eastern approaches and the Sultanate of Brunei.

These Brigade Headquarters between them controlled five British and Gurkha infantry battalions deployed in rotation from Malaya, Singapore and Hong Kong, and an armoured car squadron. In January 1965, the first two infantry battalions from Britain arrived and, after six weeks' jungle training, deployed on operations; one of these was 2 Para. The two new battalions allowed the Director of Operations to increase the number of brigades. The 2nd and 3rd Divisions of Sarawak, with some 442 miles of the border, became Mid-West – later Central – Brigade with its headquarters in Sibu. The new Brigade Headquarters was that of 19 Airportable Brigade under David Fraser, with TFH's old OCTU comrade, Toby Sewell, as his Brigade Major – covering the approaches to where the main oil reserves lay and there-fore the area of greatest threat.[17] Mid-West Brigade area had two infantry battalions and a Malaysian artillery battery. During the year, a Singapore battalion arrived to provide security for Kuching Airfield and a second British armoured squadron also cme in.

Early in 1965, both Australia and New Zealand agreed to deploy their forces into Borneo to supplement the rotation of British and Gurkha units. These units were chiefly those serving with 28 Commonwealth Brigade in Singapore. Tours were of varying length: Gurkhas gener-ally did six months; British battalions based in the Far East did four months; while those deployed from Britain normally did a year, less training time, split into two periods of five months and deployed in a different area for each half of their tour.

The air component based in Borneo consisted of detachments from squadrons stationed in Malaya and Singapore. These included *Pioneer*, *Beverley* and *Hastings* transport aircraft and around 12 helicopters of various types. After a struggle, the Director of Operations wrested control of the air forces committed to operations in Borneo away from HQ Far East Forces. Support helicopters – *Belvederes* and *Whirlwinds* from the RAF, *Wessex* and *Whirlwinds* from the Navy – increased to around 40, but there were never enough, given the challenging jungle terrain of Borneo and the lack of roads straddling the border, which forced both Indonesian and Commonwealth forces to conduct operations on foot. Both sides relied heavily on air transport for troop deployment and resupply to forward operating bases – so much so that in late 1964, another 12 *Whirlwinds* were deployed. Meanwhile, the Army Air Corps (AAC) was creating air platoons or troops of three *Sioux* light helicopters in many units, including some infantry battalions, as well as operating *Auster* and *Beaver* fixed wing aircraft and some of the new *Scout* helicopters, which could carry troops. As well as transport, the air force provided vital fire support to ground operations from both carrier and land-based aircraft including *Javelins*, *Sea Vixens* and even *Vulcan* bombers.

Finally, there was a significant contribution from Special Forces. One squadron of around 60 men from 22 Special Air Service Regiment under the command of Lieutenant-Colonel John Slim,* son of the famous wartime commander of the XIV Army in Burma, deployed to Borneo

---

*   Later Colonel John Douglas Slim, 2nd Viscount Slim OBE DL FRGS (b. 20 July 1927).

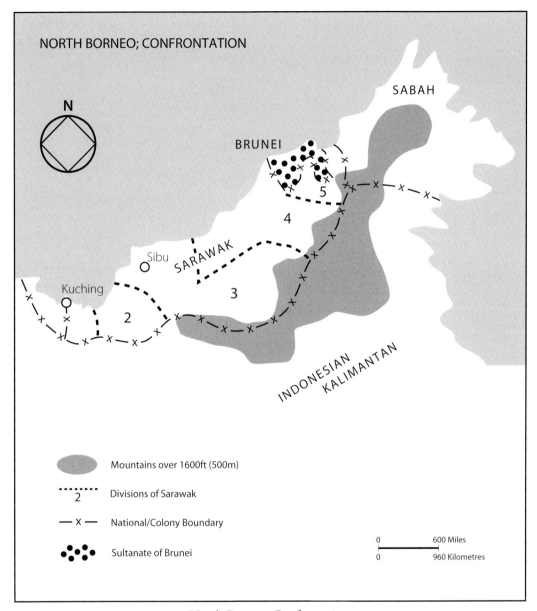

NORTH BORNEO; CONFRONTATION

N

SABAH

BRUNEI

5

4

Sibu   SARAWAK

Kuching

3

2

INDONESIAN KALIMANTAN

Mountains over 1600ft (500m)

2   Divisions of Sarawak

— x —   National/Colony Boundary

Sultanate of Brunei

0 ————— 600 Miles
0 ————— 960 Kilometres

North Borneo: Confrontation.

in early 1963 in the aftermath of the Brunei Revolt to gather intelligence in the border area. Thereafter, a Special Forces' presence remained until the end of the campaign. Faced with a border of nearly 1,000 miles, they were thinly spread and heavily tasked. Tactical headquarters of 22 SAS deployed to Kuching in 1964 to take control of all Special Forces – although the requirement to provide at least one squadron in Aden was a considerable constraint, solved by the creation of new units for Borneo. The first to be employed was the Guards Independent Parachute Company, which already existed as the pathfinder force of 16 Parachute Brigade.

A Company 2 Para, Nibong Village; Borneo, 1965. (Airborne Forces Museum)

Soldiers from 2 Para being landed by *Wessex* helicopter on a jungle HLS in Borneo, 1965. (Airborne Forces Museum)

The Joint Force Headquarters at Labuan, Borneo. (Farrar-Hockley family)

Next, the Gurkha Independent Parachute Company was raised. Sections of the Special Boat Squadron (SBS) were also sent from Singapore. Finally, parachute battalions, when deployed, formed patrol companies (C in 2 Para and D in 3 Para). Special Forces' operations mainly consisted of covert reconnaissance and surveillance missions by four-man patrols. However, some larger-scale raiding missions took place, including amphibious operations by the SBS – thus by the time of TFH's arrival, or very soon afterwards, there were more British military personnel deployed in Far East Command than in the British Army of the Rhine: Britain's foremost NATO commitment.[18] Confrontation posed not only the problem of fighting what became known in military doctrine as a 'low intensity', undeclared, war against a volatile but disorganised enemy with both conventional and unconventional forces in the field; but also the problem of maintaining a credible deterrent threat that would stop the conflict from escalating to open war. This was not easy. The TNI included 132 infantry battalions, an air force equipped with modern Soviet-supplied jet aircraft and a navy that deployed Soviet-supplied submarines, frigates and patrol craft armed with missiles. The Indonesian forces in Borneo in early 1965 were commanded by General Maraden Panggabean,[*] Commandant of the Inter-Regional Command, Kalimantan; he had previously been responsible for conquering Dutch New Guinea. The ground forces were composed of three full battalions facing Kuching in the West – that is, eight regular and 11 volunteer companies; a marine battalion facing East Brigade with six regular and three volunteer companies; and a battalion with five regular and three volunteer companies facing Central Brigade. During 1965, this force was increased to 50 regular infantry companies and about 20 irregular companies, with the main effort against West Brigade.

---

[*]   Maraden Saur Halomoan Panggabean (1922-2000).

il.

Faced with this level of Indonesian forces, the British Government had had no option but to reinforce Far East Command strongly enough to allow it to win any contest.[19] There was quality as well as quantity, for because Borneo was the most important theatre of operations – eclipsing Aden at this point – it received the best troops and the best commanders: paratroopers, Gurkhas, marines; and Brigade Commanders like Harry Tuzo,[*] David House,[†] and David Fraser.[‡] The officers and men were, too, all regulars now that National Service had ended – and this meant that the constant turnover which units had experienced in Malaya was no longer a factor.[20] All this made Far East Command the most costly British overseas military commitment, draining the Strategic Reserve and drawing resources away from NATO in the Central Region. The British economy struggled to support the independent nuclear deterrent – major contributions to NATO's collective security in the West – and these forces deployed elsewhere to protect its interests. Analysis had concluded by 1961 that British economic interests in Southeast Asia were too small to warrant the large and expensive military forces stationed in the region to protect them and that the government must reduce them. However, the same analysis indicated that the most vital British interest of all was to maintain as much influence on American policy and strategy as possible. This clinched decisions to maintain military forces in Southeast Asia and remain committed to SEATO.[21] Trying to do this through Greater Malaysia, as a client, was one of the factors that had provoked Confrontation with Indonesia – just at the time that the Americans found themselves being dragged into the war in Vietnam.[22]

*   *   *

TFH's role in all this was a difficult one. His task was to be the principal staff officer to the Director of Operations and, as such, to co-ordinate the operations of 17th Division; the Special Forces; the police, naval and air forces; tactical air transport; and supporting arms such as artillery, engineers and intelligence – a task which inevitably brought him into conflict with Linford and Hunt. Commonwealth operational design focused on carefully co-ordinated military, intelligence, police and political operations to deter or defeat incursions. Operating from a network that eventually grew to 27 company-sized forward locality bases strung out along the border – sited to guard against incursion along vulnerable routes – Commonwealth infantry battalions, supported by artillery, armoured cars, engineers, and airpower (above all, helicopters), controlled their tactical areas of responsibility aggressively in order to prevent Indonesian incursions from disrupting the area. TFH's responsibilities also included *Claret* operations, in which a critical factor was intelligence and, in particular, signals intelligence (or Sigint). The Royal Signals were able to intercept all Indonesian tactical military communications from listening stations, such as that at RAF Chia Keng in Singapore; those in cipher were decrypted by Intelligence Corps analysts based at Government Communications

---

*   Later General Sir Harry Crauford Tuzo GCB OBE MC (1917-1998). He was GOC Northern Ireland and Deputy Supreme Allied Commander Europe.

†   Later Lieutenant-General Sir David George House GCB KCVO CBE MC (1922-2012). He was later GOC Northern Ireland during the Troubles and held the office of Black Rod.

‡   Later General Sir David William Fraser GCB OBE (1920-2012). Known as 'Fraser the razor', he was a distinguished military historian and prolific author, as well as a successful General.

Headquarters (GCHQ) in Cheltenham.[23] This complete penetration of the enemy and his intentions was as thorough as that which *Enigma* had provided during the Second World War and was crucial in gaining and maintaining the initiative. Major Anthony Vivian* was the GSO2 Intelligence in Headquarters 17th Gurkha Division, but like many others, he reported to two masters: Linford and TFH. Vivian had the specific task of collating all Sigint received and, as he recalled, 'I had a little hut in which all Sigint was tabulated. At noon each day – it was a seven-day-a-week operation – everyone trooped in for the daily briefing and I stood up and told them what the Indonesians were doing! I then saw TFH every evening to update him.'[24] Vivian was thus well aware of the tensions in the chain of command. Hunt was, he recalled, 'laid-back, but sharp.' TFH on the other hand was 'pushy, taking things on that he should not have done and sometimes taking decisions that should have gone to one of the generals.' He was aggressive, insistent on following-up, wanting to get involved, believing that wherever there was a problem, there was also an opportunity – and sometimes over-using George Lea's authority. The danger here was that intelligence sources would be compromised and thus his eagerness had to be restrained.[25] Wherever possible, signals intelligence had to be corroborated by other sources. Field Marshal Edwin ('Dwin') Bramall,[†] then a Lieutenant-Colonel commanding the 60th Rifles in Borneo, wrote a summary of his battalion's two tours of duty for The King's Royal Rifle Corps Annals, in which he remarked that 'there were plenty of freelance agents [amongst local people visiting relatives across the border] ready to give information, if the money was right and they approved our methods ... by picking and paying well, we gained more than we ever lost'.[26]

Whatever the frictions, TFH had his usual galvanising effect on the staff. 'He descended on my headquarters ... like a benevolent hurricane and has kept us all on our toes ever since', wrote George Lea.[27]

Anthony Vivian remembered that:

> He liked to be the best. He had a sort of aura and was a very inspiring, impressive chap to follow. He energised the staff and insisted that they carry out proper military training, including PT, but he did not tolerate fools and you did not get on the wrong side of him. When he got annoyed with me I reminded him that, like me, he had been a Royal Welch Fusilier! One day I realised that I had lost my headquarters pass so I went to TFH and owned up. He looked at me and said "*Well find it. I'll give you a day; otherwise the fine is £20.*" I went off feeling rather sheepish. Then I remembered that it must have been in the pocket of a jacket that had gone to the laundry. I went over, and there it was. As I came out, who did I bump into but TFH, out for a run. Of course he guessed straight away what had happened and simply roared with laughter![28]

In spite of the high level of resources employed, armed clashes – although frequent – were small in scale. With few roads and little open country, mobility was a challenge for both sides and aircraft were often the most manoeuvrable element of any force – and thus a crucial

---

*   Later Brigadier Anthony Chester Vivian CBE (b. 1933). He commanded British Forces in Belize 1980-1982 and was United Kingdom Military Representative in SHAPE.
†   Field Marshal Edwin Noel Westby Bramall, Baron Bramall KG GCB OBE MC JP DL (b. 1923) had served in the Second World War. He was CGS between 1979 and 1982, and CDS from 1982 to 1985.

force multiplier. Indeed, patrols and patrol bases came to rely almost entirely on the support of the *Wessex* helicopter fleet for re-supply. The largest ground battle of the war pitted less than 200 troops on both sides against each other. The terrain and climate of Borneo were defining factors: rugged, jungle-covered mountain ranges along a 1,000-mile frontier; oppressive humidity; and very little modern infrastructure in the way of roads, settlements, airstrips or fixed communications. Along much of the frontier there was little or no habitation for up to 80 miles (130 kilometres) inside British-held territory. The main routes for travel lay along rivers, on the banks of which lay scattered the long houses of the various tribes: Iban, Kenyas, Kayans, Ukits and Punans – all with their own languages, customs and taboos. It was essential to enlist the support of these tribes both as trackers and to gather intelligence on the movements of the Indonesians.[29]

With an area of 287,000 square miles (743,330 square kilometres), Borneo is the third-largest island in the world – and is the largest island of Asia. The interior of the island is predominantly mountainous, with peaks up to about 8,000 feet (2,400 metres) and the highest point is Mount Kinabalu in Sabah, with an elevation of 13,435 feet (4,100 metres). These jungle-covered mountains rose to knife-like ridges and precipices, with the rivers in the valleys capable of becoming raging torrents after just a few hours of heavy rain. There was always a temptation – especially when trying to penetrate secondary jungle with poor visibility – to use tracks and paths, but this had to be avoided because of the danger of mines, or ambush. The coast is a low, largely marshy, belt 10 to 50 miles (16 to 80 kilometres) wide, which includes large areas of mangrove swamp. Borneo lies on the Equator and therefore has a tropical climate, hot and humid, along the coast. Here temperatures remain fairly constant throughout the year and average about 80° F (27° C). The high mountainous areas have a cooler climate. Annual rainfall averages from 100 to 160 inches (2,540 to 4,060 mm) with the bulk of the rain falling during the monsoon season from late October to February. Tropical rain forests, with dense undergrowth, therefore cover most of Borneo.

The most important element in the physical defence of the border was the network of forward patrol bases occupied by infantry companies, supported by mortars or artillery, usually 1,000 to 1,500 yards (i.e. up to one kilometre) from the border itself and providing 'a springboard from which patrols could operate and a haven to which they could return … also to provide protection for border villages and a focal point for gathering intelligence'.[30]

Bramall described these bases as having to be:

> … prepared to withstand attacks by a battalion group supported by mortars, and much attention therefore had to be paid to field works, fields of fire and defensive devices to hinder an assault. All troops slept protected by overhead cover, or at least by thick blast walls, and all were within easy reach of their fighting trenches. All trenches were linked by telephone to a central command post … the important thing was to maintain constant vigilance because, with the border so close, the risk of surprise attack was considerable.[31]

For the troops deployed in these jungle patrol bases, life was exhausting – an unrelenting series of patrols through close country, moving for eight hours a day and then lying up where they came to rest; laying ambushes, or avoiding them, or fighting their way out of them if they were caught; mapping unknown ground; struggling to communicate hundreds of miles using HF crystal or valve radio sets; clearing landing zones; mounting surveillance on the most likely border crossing points; carrying out 'hearts-and-minds' activities among the native people by giving out medical aid in return for tracking duties or information. A company could usually expect only a week or 10 days' rest during its entire tour of duty. All that said:

> Despite the full complement of mud and rats, which always characterises such forti-
> fications, the British soldier quickly adapted himself to the very primitive conditions.
> Safely out of the orbit of battalion office and the RSM, he seemed cheerfully prepared
> to live in the jungle indefinitely.[32]

As *Claret* operations continued and developed during 1965, the permitted depth of penetration into Indonesia increased from an initial limit of 5,000 yards to 10,000 and then to 20,000 yards. Infantry companies, however, generally remained within range of artillery support. By mid-year, the programme of *Claret* operations had, in effect, established a quarantine zone up to two miles deep on the Indonesian side of the border. In response, although they remained publicly silent on the subject, the Indonesians laid down thousands of anti-personnel mines opposite Western Brigade in particular.

Indonesian offensive operations were not, however, entirely stopped by *Claret*. A signifi-cant attack was mounted against Plaman Mapu, the base of B Company 2 Para, which was identified as a target because it was less than one mile (one kilometre) from the border and lacked support from any other Commonwealth base. 2 Para had arrived in March 1965 and its three companies were allocated bases 20 miles apart, heavily fortified and with all trees and undergrowth cleared for fields of fire. Each company base had a section of three-inch mortars and MMGs; A and D Companies also had a 105 mm pack *Howitzer* manned by gunners of the Royal Artillery positioned with them. The CO of 2 Para was Lieutenant-Colonel Ted Eberhardie, who had served in what was now Indonesia as the IO of 5 Para Brigade during operations in Java in 1945 and 1946. Eberhardie had very definite ideas about how operations were to be carried out. Here in Borneo, there was no Special Branch intelligence available and if no Sigint was received, the only way of picking up Indonesian incursions was by putting out large numbers of small patrols, with native trackers, to watch, listen and report back. If needed, artillery fire could be called in to support a patrol and reinforcements deployed rapidly by helicopter. Eberhardie made everyone travel light: no heavy packs; just the bare essentials of food, water and ammunition. Under the tutelage of Captain Huia Woods, a Maori who had become the battalion's Education Officer, every platoon had a fully trained tracking team of three men. Patrols would be out for 10 days at a time and companies always had two platoons deployed, with one resting and in reserve at the base.[33] One veteran, CSM John 'Patch' (or 'One-eye') Williams, recalled that:

> We really hammered it in the jungle for that period, really did give it stick ... we all
> had to learn 10 Dyak words a day; like food, water, enemy, tracks, wounds, everything
> — so that every single soldier had at least 50 words in Dyak. We were tested on them
> every day. We realised that a hearts and minds campaign was more effective in the long
> run ... Because we felt we hadn't got down to really showing our soldiers what they
> should expect, we set up our own little battle school. We pushed each platoon in turn,

with all its officers and NCOs, through this mini-battlefield. We made it as realistic as possible and used live ammunition. Unfortunately, two men were killed in separate incidents, which was very sad and everybody was unhappy. But everyone knew that those who'd been killed had done the wrong thing; they hadn't kept their heads down. Their deaths pressed the point home very quickly. It really switched on the young men, young NCOs and officers who had never heard bullets whizzing round their ears. It showed them how to react, which was later to prove an essential factor …

… As the CSM I made sure the first thing we did when a patrol came back in was give everyone a tot of rum; then they had a shower, de-loused, got new gear, read their mail, had a couple of big hearty meals, because this was the first cooked food they would have had in the period, then a reasonably good night's sleep. But they still had to do their sentry-go and everything else. The next day they were briefed and got themselves ready for the next 10-day patrol which started that night. So the pressure was very much on. It was killing. Our goal was to get the guys to the peak of physical fitness, maintain it, then ask them not to eat cooked food, drink tea, smoke or speak for 10 days. Not only to the young soldiers but across the whole board, it was a new discipline in all sorts of ways.[34]

From the beginning of 2 Para's tour, the Indonesians were active across the whole of the battalion's front. In late April, Indonesian troops landed at Pontiniak and marched north-west to Balai Karangan – south of Kuching and opposite Plaman Mapu – where B Company 2 Para was located. Most of B Company's officers and men were, as usual, out on patrol and Plaman Mapu was held only by the company headquarters cooks, clerks and signallers; an under-strength platoon of young soldiers, newly arrived from training; and a mortar section. The base was commanded by the Company Commander – Major Jon Fleming – with Captain Nicky Thompson, CSM 'Patch' Williams and CQMS Goodall. Fortunately, there was also an artillery FOO to make good the lack of a co-located *Howitzer*. The Indonesian attack began at 0500 hrs on 27 June 1965 and was made by two full companies, with support weapons, and a third company in reserve. The Indonesians penetrated the perimeter unseen during heavy monsoon rain and overran a mortar pit. Counter-attacks were launched by the para-troopers and the hand-to-hand fighting went on for nearly two hours. Effective mortar and artillery fire was brought down by the gunners to support the base, while Eberhardie deployed a whole company to reinforce the base and another three platoons to cut off the Indonesian withdrawal. Two companies of Gurkhas were also flown in to follow up the retreating enemy. 'Patch' Williams recalled the effect of the attack:

They should have massacred us. They really thought they'd win through on their superior fire power. They came straight in firing their *Kalashnikovs*. Although the conditions underfoot didn't help us they did more to thwart them because they were coming up a slight incline. Had they had a dry purchase they'd have overrun us on the first assault. But eventually they stopped because Mick had gathered the fire of the other section and was hitting them as well so they fell back down the gully again. I then got someone else on the gun which had been hit four times by bullets. The radio set by my side had been shattered, but I didn't realise then I'd been hit and was blind in one eye. It was still pitch black with mud everywhere. I then raced around, picked up some wounded, took them down to the CP and then took a resupply of ammunition and spread it to the rest of the guys around me. By this time I think there were, on the position, only about 15 of us standing.

The enemy then tried to launch a further attack which we managed to beat off. We'd lost one mortar but the FOO was now firing the remaining one straight up in the air and bombs were landing about 30 yards away on the enemy, which was where we wanted them. I asked for volunteers to take a patrol out and clear the lines and, God bless them, to a man they said they'd go. So I selected three and off we went. We cleared the position around the perimeter and then came back in, by which time the first of the helicopters had arrived with the quick reaction force. Then it all started. There was so much activity it was untrue, people coming in, helicopters, the doctor. They couldn't believe what they were seeing. The lads standing, cuts and wounds, no shirts, just their trousers and boots, with mud everywhere. It must have been a sight.

There was this swathe cut through the jungle, with lots of blood and a trail of equipment, everything discarded by the Indonesians fleeing back to the border. The blood trail was there for three days. [35]

Although the fighting had been close and bitter – and the bulk of the paratroopers were young recruits – only two men of B Company were killed in the fighting, with seven others wounded. It was this engagement that earned 'Patch' Williams his nickname. The Indonesians announced that two of their soldiers were killed and claimed a major victory, although it later transpired there had been around 300 Indonesian casualties – the dead having been thrown into a nearby river by their comrades.[36] Unsurprisingly, TFH went out to the battalion immediately, for neither Hunt nor Lea was impressed by the way in which the Indonesians had been allowed to penetrate the area in such strength, undetected; Eberhardie was definitely in line for the sack. TFH, however, managed to calm things down once he had established the facts and briefed the two generals.[37]

The exhausting war of patrols, ambushes, incursions and raids along the Borneo border was changed during 1965 by three decisive events: First, the British had developed, in *Claret*, an effective method of maintaining military control of the vital border area without provoking an escalation in the fighting; secondly, the Indonesians made a grave error by expanding the military conflict into mainland Malaya; third, the political situation in Jakarta was completely disrupted by an armed uprising that backfired disastrously. The internal divisions in Indonesia, along with the strain that the conflict placed on the fragile Indonesian economy, brought about a crisis in Jakarta by mid-1965. The army feared Sukarno's flirtation with Communism; the PKI feared that a shadowy 'Council of Generals' was plotting Counter-Revolution. On the night of 30 September-1 October forces which included infantry from the Presidential Palace Guard, air force special troops, PKI agents and volunteers tried to decapitate the Army High Command in Indonesia by mass assassination. The conspirators seized and murdered six senior generals including General Achmed Yani, Chief of the General Staff, at an airbase outside Jakarta. However, they missed the one who really mattered: Suharto,* Commander

---

* Suharto (1921-2008) was the second President of Indonesia – holding the office for 31 years from 1967 until his resignation in 1998.

of the Army Strategic Reserve, whose primary mission was to suppress unrest and rebellion. In circumstances that remain unclear, Suharto and his forces defeated the coup and placed Sukarno under *de facto* house arrest. This, in turn, ignited months of violent political confusion in Indonesia – leading to the destruction of the PKI; massive loss of life; and by the spring of 1966, the replacement of Sukarno by a new coalition led by Suharto and supported by the Army High Command.

In retrospect, this marked the definitive turning point in Confrontation; the British and their allies had outlasted the regime that had unleashed the conflict,[38] but this was not at all clear at the time – and for the rest of 1965, the strain did not abate at all.[39] What was perhaps the best-known *Claret* operation took place on 21 November 1965 against this back-drop. A company from the 2/10th Gurkhas encountered an Indonesian platoon in an entrenched position inside Kalimantan, opposite Bau. The position was sited so that it could only be approached from one direction, along a ridge so narrow that only three men could move up it in line abreast. An hour-long fire-fight followed, which has since become known as the Battle of Bau – during which the Gurkha Company attacked the Indonesian position. At least 24 Indonesians are believed to have been killed in the attack, while the Gurkhas suffered three men killed and two wounded. Cpl Rambahadur Limbu subsequently received the Victoria Cross for his actions in this attack, with a misleading citation to disguise the fact that the operation took place inside Indonesia.

A similarly successful operation – although different in character – was mounted by the KRRC, who laid an ambush on a track crossing the border which had been shown to be used by the Indonesians. The ambush party took the best part of two days to move stealthily into position and once there, waited another two days before anything happened:

> Then suddenly … at about 11 o'clock in the morning, a scout, moving cautiously, came into view in the ambush area, wearing the usual black leather boots, peaked cap, camouflaged smock and American equipment of the Indonesian regular forces.[40]

The initial fire-fight killed seven Indonesians, but the rest fought back fiercely. The ambush commander, Lieutenant Michael Robertson – who was awarded the Military Cross for his actions – called in artillery, mortar and *Energa* grenade fire (as did the enemy) before breaking contact and withdrawing successfully with only one man wounded. It was later learned that a total of 14 Indonesians had been killed, and others wounded.

At the end of 1965, TFH was promoted to Colonel and his position upgraded to Colonel GS [41] – on the same level therefore as Linford in 17th Division – and he insisted that the rate and pace of *Claret* operations should be maintained. In March 1966, another Gurkha battalion – the 1/7th – was involved in some of the fiercest fighting of the campaign during two raids into Indonesia. Minor actions by Indonesian forces also continued in the border area, including counter-battery fire against British gun positions. The final Indonesian incursion took place in May and June of 1966 when signs of a substantial force crossing into Central Brigade were observed. This force was around 80-strong – mostly volunteers, with some regulars. They moved fast towards Brunei – pursued by 1/7th Gurkhas; almost all were killed. It was exploited by a final *Claret* operation: an artillery ambush by 38 Light Battery RA.[42]

There were occasions on which *Claret* operations were either unfeasible or were not approved. Brigadier David House, commanding Central Brigade, faced such a problem in dealing with an Indonesian camp close to the border and called a meeting to thrash out the problem. As it happened, TFH had been to the area and knew the problem; he had also had a discussion with the crew of a 105 mm pack *Howitzer* – the Commander of which, a Sergeant – was present at the meeting. At TFH's prompting, the Sergeant stood up and said:

> Sir, I think I can help. Those men below are from the Indonesian Army and they don't trust their own air force. The next time there is a supply drop to them, let me fire a round. The troops will think the aircraft has dropped a bomb and they will shoot at it. The air force will then refuse to drop any more supplies and the base will have to pack up.

On the excellent principle of never confusing the quality of advice with the rank of the giver, House accepted the scheme. It turned out exactly as the un-named Sergeant had predicted.

*   *   *

It was not until May 1966 that it became clear that the new regime in Jakarta was looking for a political resolution to Confrontation – and August before it was achieved through the Bangkok Agreement. This obliged the British to begin drawing down their forces – effectively ending the argument that Confrontation kept them too busy to make any contribution to the US effort in Vietnam.[43] Confrontation had forced the British to consider, earlier and more intensively than they expected, whether or not they could still remain a military power on a wider stage. Those considerations revealed how completely the British depended on American support to play any real strategic role in the region – or anywhere else, for that matter. This dependency prompted the British to try to make changes in their global defence posture by persuading the Americans to underwrite arrangements whereby a four-power inner circle of Western allies – the USA, Britain, Australia and New Zealand – could co-ordinate activities and share resources for the collective security of Southeast Asia.

The British General Election in March 1966 brought Harold Wilson's Labour Government a larger majority, but with a further increase in the strength of the left in his party. Wilson was not, therefore, able to move closer to the US – and at the same time, economic pressures forced Defence Secretary Denis Healey to search for yet more economies in defence spending. The defence budget post-Confrontation was reduced from £2.4 billion in 1964 (£95.33 billion at today's prices in terms of economic power) to £2 billion by 1970 (£61.28 billion at today's rates in terms – again – of economic power).[44] In spite of this, the British Government still tried to maintain forces in the Far East – 40 percent of the total forces overseas, amounting to 10 percent of the defence budget. Moreover, this included a nuclear deterrent maintained in Singapore as a commitment to SEATO.[45] Cuts in programmes and weapons procurement, savings in administration and reductions in forces in Africa and the Persian Gulf – especially withdrawing from Aden – made it possible to cut 16 percent of the defence budget for a reduction of only 4 percent in capability.[46]

*   *   *

TFH laying a wreath at the Remembrance Sunday service in Labuan. (Farrar-Hockley family)

TFH's tour in Borneo came to an end as the campaign began to wind up – in April 1966 – and he handed over his post to Colonel (later Field Marshal) Nigel Bagnall:* the two took an instant dislike to each other.[47] George Lea, with whom TFH obviously got on very well and who was a great foil and restraint on TFH's more extreme flights of enthusiasm, wrote in his confidential report that:

> I have derived the greatest pleasure and inspiration both from his company and from the outstanding quality of his staff work. His sure hand at the helm of the joint operations staff of my headquarters has enabled me to travel, as I must, with a feeling of complete confidence that everything is under control at the Labuan base ... He has taken infinite pains to raise the quality of staff work in the headquarters and there are many young members of the staff who are bruised but better practitioners from hi teaching.
>
> He both believes and indulges in plain speaking and it has been a matter of the greatest interest and importance to me to see that he has the delicacy of touch and the sense of occasion not to allow this to impair his personal relationships.[48]

---

*   Field Marshal Sir Nigel Thomas Bagnall GCB CVO MC (1927-2002) served in the infantry and in the Paras before becoming a Cavalry Officer. He served in Palestine, Malaya, and Cyprus – and he and TFH should have had much common ground. Bagnall later commanded I (BR) Corps and NORTHAG. He was CGS from 1985 to 1988.

The Commander Far East Forces supported Lea's recommendation for promotion to Brigadier and another grading of 'outstanding', but with some reservations:

> It is indeed a tribute to his intelligence and to his attractive personality that he can possess and use such immense driving force without building up against himself reaction and obstruction from those less well endowed with brains and personality. At the same time, there are occasions, as seen from the point of view of the higher headquarters, when he would do well to pause, consider and consult before seizing his pen. For this reason I consider that his next staff tour should be at the Ministry of Defence…[49]

Borneo had given TFH an insight into how military force could contribute to the resolution of a political problem. Instead of the progressive escalation that is often inevitable, military force – carefully targeted – had produced conditions that promoted sensible negotiations by rendering Confrontation ineffective while using only such force as was necessary.[50] It also gave him insights into the workings of a tri-service, multi-national, political/military command engaged in operations far from home; it had exposed him to some of those who would go on to the very top of the army over the coming years; it had given him yet more operational experience in a different environment; and it provided the context in which he would operate in his next appointment as the Brigadier in command of 16 Parachute Brigade.

16

'He must take off his maroon-coloured spectacles'
The Brigadier, 1966-1970

In the British Army, a Brigadier is the lowest-ranking of general officers and a Brigade the lowest level of organisation that can be called a formation – having under its command units of all arms and being, therefore, capable of independent action, if only for limited periods. TFH took command of 16 Parachute Brigade in Aldershot on 22 April 1966 with the temporary rank of Brigadier,[1] succeeding his old friend 'Roly' Gibbs. The brigade – no longer 'independent' – consisted of its headquarters staff; the headquarters and Signals Squadron – 216 – which with the Defence Platoon was responsible for the administration and security (as well as the communications) of the headquarters; three parachute infantry battalions: 1, 2 and 3 Para under Mike Walsh, John Roberts of the Welsh Guards and Tony Ward-Booth respectively; the Guards Independent Parachute Company under Major Sir Nicholas Nuttal of the Royal Horse Guards; 7th Light Regiment RHA – re-designated as 7th Parachute Regiment in 1966 – with its three batteries of 105 mm pack *Howitzers*; 9 (Parachute) Squadron RE; 23 Parachute Field Ambulance RAMC; and attached parachute companies of military police, REME, RAOC (an ordnance field park and a heavy drop company), and RCT.[2] 16 Brigade had an exact mirror in the Territorial Army, 44 Parachute Brigade (TA), and together they came under the administrative authority of the Headquarters Airborne Forces, also in Aldershot. On 1 February 1965, the brigade's units had started to move to new barracks which had been constructed in Aldershot to replace the old Stanhope Lines. This was Montgomery Lines, opened on 7 April 1965 at a cost of £3 million. Field Marshal Viscount Montgomery of Alamein himself took the salute at the parade to mark this occasion. As things turned out, the quality of the buildings was appalling – and by the time the parachute brigade left Aldershot 30 years later, the barracks and married quarters were in a state of near collapse.

TFH's real superior was, not HQ Airborne Forces, however, but the GOC 3rd Infantry Division which commanded the army's contribution to the Strategic Reserve: 5, 19 and 24 Airportable Brigades. Headquarters 24 Brigade had been detached to Aden and the other two brigade HQs had also been deployed, in turn, to South Arabia and Borneo; 16 Para Brigade was therefore assigned to keep the Strategic Reserve at divisional size. At the time, the GOC was Major-General Tony Deane-Drummond,[*] who, although originally a Royal Signals

---

[*] Anthony John Deane–Drummond CB DSO MC (1917-2012) spent most of his career with Specialist and Airborne Forces. He served in Operation *Market Garden* and was captured at Arnhem, but successfully escaped. After the war, he commanded 22 SAS in Malaya and Oman.

Field Marshal Montgomery visiting the headquarters of 16 Parachute Brigade at the opening of Montgomery Lines. 'Tubby' Butler, the Colonel Commandant, and TFH are to his left. (Farrar-Hockley family)

Officer, had seen a great deal of service with Special Forces – including the command of 22 SAS.

16 Parachute Brigade could operate independently, outside the framework of a division, but only for a limited period. It was also designed for strategic effect and rapid response – that is, it could be air-transported anywhere at very short notice. However, it had serious shortcomings. Once on the ground, it lacked tactical mobility and protection against any enemy equipped with armour and air power; it could not move rapidly without vehicles or helicopters; and it could not maintain its own line of communication. In short, it could do only certain tasks once committed: hold a lodgement until heavier forces arrived, as it had done at Suez; show a presence, as it had done in Jordan; take part in internal security operations, as it had done in Aden; or engage in combat with a lightly armed enemy, as it had done in the Radfan and Borneo.

As with every brigade in the British Army at that time, 16 Parachute Brigade contained no capability above that already available within its subordinate units, and the Commander's functions in combat were limited to planning and sequencing the operations of his units to achieve an effect greater than the sum of the parts. Even when reinforced, the Brigade Commander could conduct only close operations in contact with the enemy. He had no ability to see anything beyond the range of the immediate contact battle, and if he had, he lacked the means to do anything about what he had seen. Interestingly, TFH wrote to Field Marshal Montgomery early in 1967 enclosing proposals for a parachute division in the army which would address these shortcomings. The division would consist of two brigades, each with a heavy mortar battery and a logistic regiment; and in the divisional troops the SAS regiment; the current parachute artillery regiment; a light armoured regiment which would include the Pathfinders, a reconnaissance squadron and a guided weapons squadron; and a heavy drop company RAOC. However interesting – and the overall uplift of forces was relatively modest – TFH got precisely nowhere with these proposals.[3]

As things stood though, the brigade was small enough for its Commander to know all his officers well – certainly down to Company Commanders, and many of the senior NCOs. TFH in fact could do better than that, for as a parachute officer of long standing, he knew a great many people personally – especially the Commanding Officers: two of whom had been his Company Commanders in the Radfan. In return, he would be easily recognised by the 3,500 or so officers and men. Moreover, whatever the parachute brigade lacked in top-end capability, it certainly did not lack courage, motivation, commitment, professionalism, endurance and the ability to improvise. Generally, formations do not, in the British Army, generate the sort of loyalty that regiments do. There were a few exceptions at divisional level, like the 7th Armoured Division – the Desert Rats. However, unlike most brigades, whose units rotated in and out every couple of years, 16 Parachute Brigade stayed together and thus it had a strong sense of community and shared experience.

As things turned out, 16 Brigade did not deploy on operations while TFH was in command – an unusual experience for him. This was, in part, because of the lack of opportunity, since the major operations of the time – in Aden and Borneo – were both winding down. It was also in part because, although these operations were winding down, much of the combat power of 16 Brigade was dissipated as units were committed piecemeal to them. During 1966, 1 Para was detached to British Guiana until Independence in February; D (Patrol) Company of 3 Para under Major Peter Chiswell was deployed to Borneo – the Parachute Regiment's final involvement there – from January to July;[4] and 2 Para was stationed in Bahrain, deploying to Aden and the Radfan at various times and in varying strengths, throughout 1966 and 1967. In January 1967, 1 Para also deployed to Aden and remained there until two days before the final British withdrawal on 29 November.[5] Mike Walsh, CO 1 Para, remembered that whenever companies or battalions returned from operations and their members were awarded decorations, TFH would insist on those honoured being in his office, in drill order, at noon to be officially notified by him in person and presented with the appropriate medal ribbon.[6]

Operational commitments were therefore declining and as things turned out, 1968 was to be the only year that the British Army did not incur deaths on operations somewhere in the world since 1939. We have the benefit of hindsight in this: as far as TFH and his staff were concerned, they could be called on to go anywhere at any time – and there were always contingency plans to be made or updated in conjunction with the staff of the 3rd Division and the Director of Military Operations in Whitehall. The brigade's relationship with the Directorate of Land / Air Warfare in Whitehall was also important, for it was this directorate that oversaw developments in doctrine, training and equipment for air support to land operations. TFH obviously milked this relationship for all that it was worth in terms of resources, causing

Headquarters staff, 16 Parachute Brigade, 1967. Ted Olive is in the rear rank, second from the right. The front rank, from left, is: Maj C.N. Last (OC 216 Signal Squadron), SSgt Ward, Maj Tony Ward-Booth (DAA & QMG), WO1 (Superintendent Clerk) Simpson, TFH, Sgt Robinson, Major Ted Ashley (BM), Cpl Nicholl, Capt David Taylor. (Farrar-Hockley family)

Deane-Drummond to raise an eyebrow and remark that he should 'be careful that the official contact that his formation has with MOD (DL / AW) on air matters is not abused'.[7]

TFH was insistent that the Brigade Headquarters must think ahead, that although any actual plan developed might not be entirely fit for whatever purpose might arise, it would serve as the basis for development. It was *planning* that mattered, just as much as the plan itself. 'Wherever there is a problem or a crisis, there is an opportunity,'[8] he would frequently remark.

There were contingency plans for a re-intervention in Malaysia. TFH thought there was a good chance that 'the glue would come unstuck'; to support the government of King Idris in Libya, where Britain had important oil interests and a major training area (Idris was indeed later overthrown in 1969 by a military *coup d'état* led by Muammar Gaddafi); in Oman, where an intervention was quietly later made to support Sultan Qaboos against the Dhofari rebels sponsored by neighbouring Yemen; and for various scenarios related to the Nigerian Civil War that broke out in July 1967, with the attempt by the Biafra region to break away. These Nigerian scenarios included humanitarian relief, or an inter-positioned peacekeeping force, rather than actively taking one side or the other in what was, however distressing, an internal problem for a Commonwealth Member State. Peter Chiswell, who after commanding his company in Borneo took over as Brigade Major, remembered that 'TFH was a wise judge on which contingency might become a reality. He gave clear instructions and his personal interest was invaluable. He also made life fun and was a joy to work for with his dry sense of humour.'[9]

TFH clearly found the policy aspects of this planning troubling. He disliked what he saw as an inability by politicians to make decisions and stick to them – to put things off until a problem had become a crisis – and then once a decision had been made, to interfere in details that should be left to qualified professionals.[10]

Much of this planning involved conferences, war-games and table-top exercises at divisional level – and here, TFH was always very free with his opinions. Deane-Drummond remarked, with a touch of exasperation, that:

> At times he states opinions more appropriate to a Divisional Commander and he needs to be gently reminded that at present his command is only a brigade … As a senior officer, he must learn to weigh up his statements and his instructions before issuing them … [11]

There were regular field training exercises too – including a brigade exercise in Scotland, on which TFH insisted that no-one would deploy unless they parachuted, or were at least trained, qualified and prepared to do so. During this exercise, Peter Chiswell recalled how TFH had a second unlucky episode in a helicopter – on the day before Dair was due to pass out of Sandhurst – in July 1967:

> … he and I, with two other officers, were flying in a *Scout* helicopter when suddenly the helicopter started to dive. We had struck a cable strung across a valley. The pilot recovered control before we hit the ground. No-one was killed! TFH and the pilot in the front received nasty cuts to their faces, but otherwise we were all OK. We were all, however, very shaken. In a quiet voice TFH said, "*Well done the pilot. Peter, we will stay here, please find some help.*" After a long walk at night I eventually found help.[12]

TFH was as much concerned with what we now refer to as the moral and intellectual components of fighting power, as with the physical. He ran a series of study periods for his officers on the theme of leadership. Much time in these studies was taken up with considering correct conduct, moral courage and the responsibilities of the leader towards the led, and they had a great influence on those that attended them. Underpinning this was TFH's personal commitment to the Christian religion, which was one of the most important things that defined who and what he was. Although he never preached, it was clear that he personally 'ate, drank and slept' Christianity and that for him personally, to deny the teachings of Jesus Christ was unacceptable.[13] Telling the truth at all times, speaking plainly, putting the soldiers before oneself and being loyal in three directions – up, down and sideways – rather than just upwards, were inviolable principles. Many people recall that TFH cared deeply for the welfare of his men and for their families. Deane-Drummond commented on this, saying that:

> he has the knack to win the hearts of his soldiers, who have great affection for him … He is surprisingly sensitive to criticism of the infantry in his command… he is such a first-class officer that they accept anything he says … he is a champion of the underdog, and this sometimes tends to distort his opinion on individuals.[14]

It was perhaps this tendency to champion the underdog and to stick up for those beneath him that gave him, undeservedly, the reputation of holding pronounced left-wing political views. He did not hold such views and, in fact, on many controversial issues of the day – and this was, after all, the 1960s – he took a decidedly conservative line. As he grew older, this tendency became more marked. TFH was no radical; however, he was never prepared to accept received wisdom simply because he was told to do so by his superiors. He had an extraordinarily retentive memory, great powers of analysis, and a quick mind. He was also sceptical and not, therefore, inclined to accept anything at face value. As long ago as Korea, his interrogators had found him stubborn and willing to defend what he believed was right to the last. It was this questioning, argumentative attitude that most probably gave rise to the belief that he was inclined to the political left.

One advantage of not being deployed on operations was that TFH could pursue his literary career. If things were quiet and he decided to stay at home and write, the staff – under Peter Chiswell – had clear instructions not to disturb him unless there was a matter requiring a decision from the Brigade Commander; but if there *were* such a thing and they did *not* disturb him, then there would be trouble! During his time in Aldershot he wrote *The Death of an Army*, published by Barker in 1967, which followed on from *The Somme.* In the latter, he had not accepted Liddell Hart's highly unfavourable view of Haig's generalship – nor the idea that the battle had been an unmitigated disaster because of the huge cost in casualties. *Death of an Army* is undoubtedly a great piece of narrative, highly readable and evocative; the reader senses strongly the terrain and atmosphere of the battlefield. The book is, however, very much focused on the tactical details and manoeuvres, as one might expect given TFH's experiences. He was critical of Sir Horace Smith-Dorrien's generalship, but gave little justification for this view, and few insights into the feelings and impressions of the commanders and senior staff officers. His chief concern seems to have been to show that regimental esprit, high-quality training and sheer guts could stop a numerically superior enemy, but unwittingly contribute to the smaller army's destruction.[15] *Death of an Army* needs to be read with good maps to hand, for the publisher did not provide enough – and this was a lesson that TFH took strongly from this particular book.

TFH was also in considerable demand as a speaker. His personal files for these years show him visiting all sorts of units and places to give talks – from St Peter's School in Lympstone, to C Battery of the Honourable Artillery Company in London; or to the regular monthly meetings of the Military Commentator's Circle, usually dinner and a guest speaker at the RAF Club. He also contributed articles widely: here, a piece for the Outward Bound Trust Annual on his experiences in Korea; here contributing and editing entries in Chambers's *Encyclopaedia*, for example. He also made a contribution to Purnell's *History of the Second World War* – on the move of the Eighth Army after the break through the Mareth Line to Enfidaville in 1967 – at the request of the editors, Basil Liddell Hart and Barrie Pitt.[16] This did not interfere too much with another advantage of not being deployed, which was that TFH could spend more time at home with Pat and with the boys too – although Dair was now a subaltern in 3 Para and Hilary was away at school. The Farrar-Hockleys lived in the Brigade Commander's house – The Warren, in Heath End – on the road from Farnham to Aldershot, where Sgt Ted Olive was based as TFH's batman. Here Pat ran a tight ship, supported TFH in his command, and marshalled the wives – especially those whose husbands were deployed on operations (a situation with which she was all too familiar). Pat also acted as TFH's researcher and typist for his writing; in return, TFH did much of the cooking. Cooking did not end at home, though, for he continued to give classes to the brigade wives' clubs. His choice of steak *tartare* on one occasion was *not* a success: Parachute Regiment wives in the late 1960s were not *quite* ready for minced raw beef and raw egg!

While TFH was in command of the brigade, he lost perhaps his most important link with the past. In 1957 his mother, Bea, had gone to live with his sister Pamela in Johannesburg, South Africa. TFH had managed to see her once or twice, while travelling to and from Borneo, but otherwise their contacts were regular letters and a weekly phone call. On 15 April 1968, at the age of 80, Bea died in St Margaret's Nursing Home in Pretoria.[17] The news came through by telephone on a day when TFH had a house full of visitors. It was Dair who answered the phone and then took TFH outside into the garden to break the news. He was visibly much moved and although with an effort he quickly regained control of himself, it was some time before he mastered his grief. Bea's funeral followed very soon afterwards and TFH was not able to get to South Africa in time for it. Bea was cremated in line with her own wishes and subsequently TFH's sister Pam, with whom Bea had lived in South Africa, brought her ashes home. TFH was there when she was finally interred in the Griffin family plot in Gunnersbury Cemetery, Ealing – her name inscribed along the curb-stone.[18]

Private grief had to be set aside for duty, however, for within a week of his mother's death, TFH had to concentrate fully on the highlight of his command: a review of 16 Parachute Brigade by Her Majesty The Queen and HRH The Duke of Edinburgh on 24 April 1967.[19] This review was entirely TFH's own idea and he organised the thing, as he was wont to do, himself. His concept was to show the Queen the role of every unit in the brigade and the review was to have a dramatic start, with a mass drop by 540 parachutists – and an additional company group in helicopters – landing on Laffan's Plain near Rushmoor. This area had been used extensively for training by heavy armoured vehicles. It was 'very rutted and in a hell of a state', to quote Mike Walsh. TFH had 9 Squadron RE working for weeks with graders and heavy plant – flattening the ground to make it safe for an airborne landing. There were a range of other displays and, of course, a Guard of Honour, but it was the landing that took up most planning and rehearsal time. The air movement plan was extremely complex, involving both RAF Abingdon and Brize Norton, with a flight-path in to the London control zone and then over Farnborough from the east. There were three live rehearsals on 17, 19 and 21 April and then, the weather having stayed fine, the real thing. Mike Walsh was the first to jump and although – in spite of the sappers' efforts – there were some injuries, Walsh himself landed safely (to TFH's great relief) and the demonstration was a huge success. The Queen and the Duke, clearly relaxed and enjoying themselves greatly, stayed to lunch with the brigade and almost the entire who's who of the Airborne Forces' senior officers at the time. After the visit, the Queen immediately sent a message of thanks, which was followed up by a letter from the Queen's Private Secretary, Martin Charteris, in which he said:

> It really was a magnificent demonstration and I am sure you realised at the time how deeply impressed both Her Majesty and the Duke of Edinburgh were by it. the Queen told me to follow up her message with a letter to emphasise how interested she was in all you had to show her ... It was a memorable day.[20]

The parachute drop for The Queen's
review of 16 Parachute Brigade.
(Farrar-Hockley family)

TFH drives with The Queen and the Duke of Edinburgh during the Royal Review of 16
Parachute Brigade, 1967. (Farrar-Hockley family)

The Queen talking to TFH during her inspection of 16 Parachute Brigade. (Farrar-Hockley
family)

After his first year in command, Deane-Drummond cautioned TFH against being too
impulsive and urged him to 'take off his maroon-coloured spectacles – although I know how
difficult this must be'.[21] TFH clearly took these comments to heart, for in his second report,
Deane-Drummond commented that 'As I always expected, he has grown into his job and has
rounded off the minor limitations he had on first taking over'.[22] Grading him once more as
'outstanding', Deane-Drummond asserted that he would reach the highest ranks of the army.
The GOC Southern Command, General Sir Geoffrey Baker,* agreed: 'In my opinion he is
the most remarkable soldier of his vintage in the army today: a professional of outstanding
skill and proven courage who has operational experience; at the same time a deep thinker and
writer'. Both reporting officers recommended him for command of a division in the future and
as a result, the Military Secretary directed that he should be included in the Major-General's
Pool 1 for command.[23] In his final report, in July 1968, the new GOC Southern Command,
Sir John Mogg,† made much the same recommendations.[24]

TFH had clearly given much thought to what would follow command. It was usual for
post-command brigadiers to spend a year at the Imperial Defence College (later the Royal

---

*   Later Field Marshal Sir Geoffrey Harding Baker GCB CMG CBE MC (1912-1980). He had served in the
      Second World War and was Director of Operations and Chief of Staff for the campaign against *EOKA* in
      Cyprus. He was Chief of the General Staff before his retirement.
†   Later General Sir Herbert John Mogg GCB CBE DSO (1913-2001). He was Deputy Supreme Allied
      Commander Europe prior to his retirement.

College of Defence Studies). However, TFH had decided to pursue an alternative: a Defence Fellowship at Oxford. Having been undistinguished at school and uninterested then in going to university, TFH had come late to scholarship, but once he had been bitten by a love of military history, that love became part of what defined him and he clearly now felt the gap in his formal education and saw the Defence Fellowship Scheme as a way of making up for his lack of academic qualifications. In November 1967, with the approval and support of Deane-Drummond, TFH submitted his application to the Military Secretary.[25] He had already discussed his potential area of study with the Rector of Exeter College, Oxford, Sir Kenneth Weare,* who as early as November 1967 had written to say that Exeter would be happy to sponsor TFH and that his proposed thesis was 'one of the best projects I have ever heard of'.[26]

In February 1968, his request was approved by the Selection Board.[27] When, therefore, he handed over command of the brigade on 24 October 1968[28] to Ted Eberhardie – who had not, after all, suffered any career foul in Borneo – the Farrar-Hockleys, less Dair, moved to a new house: Pye Barn, which TFH bought in the village of Moulsford in Berkshire – having sold his property in Ealing. Although he could not know it then, this was to be TFH's home for the rest of his life. However, at this early stage it could not be called a house; it was a Tudor barn, complete with at least one ghost – a grey lady with long, flowing hair, who could be seen on the stairs from time to time. The barn had to be converted from the ground up – and as well as hiring contractors, TFH and Ted Olive did a great deal of the work themselves at weekends and during leave periods. It became, in time, a very comfortable family home and their base of operations whenever they were in Britain. It was particularly important to Pat as a stable base in a military culture which, at that time, still demanded that wives should follow the drum. There was, however, an early incident in late 1968: TFH found himself being thoroughly ticked off by Moulsford Parish Council when he landed a helicopter on the village recreation ground near Pye Barn on a Sunday, without first asking, and being told that this was simply not on.[29] On a subsequent occasion he *did* ask, and received permission – and while waiting with two police officers for the helicopter, he gave them a demonstration of how to prepare a smoke grenade for LZ marking. Unfortunately for TFH's dignity, the grenade cooked off – immersing him, genie-like, in a cloud of orange smoke while the two policemen danced about helplessly, somewhere between consternation and hilarity.

Exeter is the fourth oldest college of the University of Oxford and is still located on its original site in Turl Street, where it was founded in 1314 by Walter de Stapeldon, Bishop of Exeter, as a school to educate clergymen. From its foundation, Exeter was popular with the sons of the Devonshire gentry – Stapeldon himself was a Devonian – and the college's illustrious alumni included, among many others: the Anglo-Saxon and Norse scholar – and novelist – J.R.R. Tolkien; the historian Corelli Barnett; the playwright Alan Bennet; and the Nobel Laureate Sydney Brenner. Exeter had also given birth to the pre-Raphaelite brotherhood: William Morris and Edward Burne-Jones had both been scholars of Exeter.[30] As an old boy of Exeter School, the choice of Exeter College by TFH was, therefore, natural.

The Defence Fellowship Scheme, which had been established in 1967 by General Sir John Hackett[†] when he was Deputy CGS – with the full support of Denis Healey, who was then

---

*   Sir Kenneth Clinton Wheare Kt CMG MA DLitt LLD (1907-79), Rector of Exeter College 1956-1972.
†   General Sir John Winthrop Hackett GCB CBE DSO MC (1910-1997). He had served in Palestine before

Secretary of State for Defence – provided around half a dozen fully-funded places each year for colonels and brigadiers to pursue an area of research which would contribute to the development of defence policy and strategy; but which would also provide an opportunity for the fellow to broaden his perspective. TFH was one of the second group selected for this scheme and had chosen to study the effects of National Service on British society between 1938 and 1957, with a particular view to investigating what benefits it conferred; what problems it imposed on the nation in the military, economic and social spheres; and whether National Service was likely to be relevant to the needs of the country and its army in the foreseeable future.

He had been led to this area of study by an incident during the time that he had commanded 3 Para in 1964, when the battalion had taken part in a training exercise in the Gulf. After the exercise, the battalion was given some local leave and TFH was driven to their destination by an officer of the host nation:

> The journey was expected to take some hours and the officer … kindly arranged that we should stop en route for lunch. When we made this break, no instructions were given to the soldier driver so I suggested that I should give him some change in order that he might go away to get himself something to eat. *"Oh, that is not necessary,"* his officer remarked. *"In any case, I expect he has some food with him."*
>
> *"Well, what about getting him a cup of coffee?"* I asked. *"We shall be here for an hour or so. It will give him a chance to stretch his legs."*
>
> *"Why should he want to do that? He has to do his military service. He might as well do it sitting in the car as out of it."*
>
> … there were several other instances of this attitude which seemed to me to reflect a contempt for the time of men collectively and as individuals. I wondered whether it was a consequence of conscription, in use in this particular state for generations, and was led on in the train of thought to consider whether the British Armed Forces had developed such an attitude during the generation of National Service which had come to an end …[31]

This thought led on to a consideration of how much conscription influenced the life of a nation – especially as there was a dispute in public opinion about whether or not National Service should have been ended. TFH did not only consider the period from 1938 onwards, which encompassed his own life and military experience, but went back over the many centuries of English history during which military service in the militia had been obligatory – beginning with the Anglo-Saxons; on through the medieval period; into the Stuart age and the upheavals in the three kingdoms, in which control of the militia had been a key factor. He went on to look at the arguments in favour of introducing compulsory service after the Anglo-Boer War and the various studies undertaken as a result of that war; at the period from 1916 to 1919; and finally at the Second World War and afterwards.

---

the Second World War, and then in the Middle East and North Africa during the war before commanding 4 Parachute Brigade at Arnhem, where he was badly wounded and captured. He again served in Palestine after the war and was later C-in-C BAOR. He became Principal of King's College London after his retirement.

The final part of his thesis, which analysed the post-war data and outlined his conclusions, was divided into three major sections: first, a survey of the literature of early compulsory service to determine whether or not military obligation had influenced the development of modern British society; secondly, why, having abandoned compulsion, did Britain re-adopt it when it was widely believed that this was inconsistent with civil liberties; last, what were the discernable consequences of conscription in the modern age and what were the practicalities of employing it again in the foreseeable future? This section was based on discussions with many public and private authorities and some 3,000 interviews with former national servicemen and conscripts. He concluded that there were considerable objections to Compulsory Service because of the increasingly rapid advance of technology – even then – which made short periods of service untenable. There were objections too because of the increase in defence land that a larger, conscript, force would need for training purposes; and that there would be a big effect on equipment procurement programmes. Next came the considerations of cost – which would be two-and-a-half or three times the then budget for defence. He also considered how selective conscription might apply and concluded that this would cause anger, however it was applied. By the same token, if conscription were applied universally and the Armed Forces took up to 100,000 conscripts – plus a few more going into the Emergency Services – what was to be done with the surplus of 400,000 young men who would be liable for call-up ?

In spite of all these objections, his interviews and questionnaires revealed a strong level of opinion in favour of some sort of National Service – 72.4 percent of those questioned; a positive attitude towards young men being trained in arms against the prospect of having to defend the nation – 57.4 percent; but a very strong vote in favour of National Service including non-military obligations, as well as military ones – 77.46 percent. In the end, however, he concluded that although the time might come, because of a war of national survival – or an inability to recruit through voluntary enlistment; that conscription could be reintroduced – that time was not now. Should it be required because of either of the two reasons cited, then there would have to be a dramatic shift in the way that the Armed Forces were organised, trained, equipped and led – but as things stood, even at the height of the Cold War, 'The simple fact is that National Service has not been reintroduced because there is no requirement for it'.[32]

There was, of course, time for family, leave and recreation during these years at Oxford – although leave was much taken up with the Pye Barn project, with Ted Olive still on hand to help and to drive the car if needed. This car, a Dodge *Dart,* had been bought by TFH in Borneo and brought back home by ship.[33] On 14 June 1969, Dair married Victoria King, (TFH's PA/researcher for five years – and daughter of his old friend, Frank King) at Bagshot Park – then the depot and home of the Royal Army Chaplains Department. When Dair and Victoria went to Malta, TFH and Pat were able to visit for a short holiday. Shortly after, Dair had had to spend some time in the naval hospital following a viral infection. TFH himself became ill in October of that year, having contracted pneumonia, from which he did not fully recover until December. While recovering he was somewhat surprised to receive an invitation that, had he accepted it, would have ended his military career: this was to become Visiting Professor in Military and Strategic Studies at Acadia University in Wolfson, Nova Scotia in succession to Dr Martin Blumenson. Although touched by the compliment, TFH said no. A second interesting invitation also came in at this time – and one which TFH could certainly accept. This was from General Sir John Mogg, who was about to become Adjutant-General of the Army. Mogg was conscious of the need to plan ahead for the needs of the army in the 1970s and 1980s. He therefore wrote to a number of officers ranging in rank from Major to Brigadier – that is, those who would be running the army in those years – whose opinions he valued, or whom he believed to have sound and imaginative ideas. TFH, not surprisingly, was on Mogg's list.[34]

The original Defence Fellowship had been agreed for one year, from October 1968 to September 1969. In March 1969, TFH realised that he could not complete his thesis in the time available and asked for an extension of one term, to the end of 1969, which was agreed; subsequently he asked for, and got, another extension until March 1970 because of his illness. [35] It was not, however, until December 1974 that the Academic Studies Steering Group got round to considering TFH's thesis and awarding him the symbol 'df';[36] Oxford University was rather quicker in awarding him the degree of BLitt. TFH was justly proud of this degree, not least because at this time, the British Army contained very few officers who held a degree of any sort.

Part of the reason for requesting the second extension was that TFH had not solely been writing his thesis. He had also been engaged on two more books of military history, as well as some lesser projects. He was, for example, asked to advise on how the official history of 28 Commonwealth Brigade should be tackled when it closed down in December 1969; and he reviewed General Matthew Ridgway's account of his time in Korea for the *R.U.S.I. Journal*.[37] However, the first of the major pieces of writing was *The War in the Desert*, published in 1969 by Faber. In this book, TFH realised the potential that he had shown in *The Edge of the Sword* of making military history accessible to the lay reader. The book was an immediate success and has remained popular ever since. The second book was *Airborne Carpet: Operation Market Garden*, published by Macdonald & Co in 1970. This, thanks to the patronage of Basil Liddell Hart, who contributed the foreword[38] – and in spite of their academic disagreements on matters related to the Great War – was accepted as a contribution to the series of books in Purnell's *History of the Second World War* (a response to the massive rise in interest in the war from the mid-1960s onwards). The book was very short – only 160 pages – and again suffered from the want of good maps. However, it was generally regarded as an excellent introductory account of the operation from the British point of view.

On 6 March 1970, his Defence Fellowship completed, TFH took up his next appointment[39] while the family stayed at Pye Barn. He had been selected for a post in MOD Operational Requirements –[40] a complete departure from all his previous experiences, but in November, this was abruptly changed by No. 2 Board and he was ordered to take up the post of Director of Public Relations (Army), or DPR (A) – a post for a rising Brigadier who, when he reached higher rank, would need to have an acute awareness of the media and its role.

17

'Believe me, it isn't a carnival' Director of Public Relations (Army) and the beginning of the campaign in Northern Ireland, March-August, 1970

A system of military-media relations, in which the national media was visibly part of the war effort and reporters were embedded in military units and commands, had been very much part of military life in the Second World War – although in practice, the relationship was based on negotiation rather than orders from the army to the media, even though things were heavily weighted in the army's favour. As a reflection of the increasing importance of the media, the War Office had instituted the post of DPR (A) in 1937. By 1970, however, DPR (A) was not a department of the General Staff, but part of the central Defence Public Relations Staff under a civilian director, Mr J. Groves, who ultimately reported to the Chief of Defence Staff.[1]

This formal military-media apparatus had, however, become much less a feature of defence in the twilight-of-Empire campaigns that occupied the army – and TFH, in the second half of the 20th century – than it had been during the Second World War. However, the experiences provided by these conflicts put the British initially ahead of their contemporaries around the world in dealing with the impact of television. It was the campaign in Northern Ireland, so very close to home, that crystallised things in Britain – even though Vietnam was now doing the same thing, to a far greater degree, in the USA. Formal training in giving media interviews while on operations, for example, was introduced at the Royal Military Academy in the early 1970s – chiefly as a response to the ever-present TV cameras following any incident in Northern Ireland.[2]

British troops had been on the streets in Northern Ireland for only five months when TFH took up his post and although initially they had been welcomed in Nationalist areas, things had turned sour. It was perhaps ironic that TFH had spent so much time in planning for contingencies that never happened while in command of 16 Parachute Brigade, only to find himself involved in a contingency that had *not* been foreseen; which would engage him closely for the next two years; and which would involve 16 Parachute Brigade, in whole or part, for years to come.

*　*　*

The sectarian violence which has been so much a feature of Irish history since the 16th century had broken out again in 1968. The origin of this outbreak, it can be argued, lay in the partition of Ireland in 1921 and the refusal of the Irish Republic to accept the status of Northern Ireland as part of the United Kingdom – and in so doing, providing a continuing impetus to the Nationalist minority in the North; while at the same time, the Protestant majority in Northern Ireland clung to a siege mentality – feeling themselves threatened by both the Republic and the large Catholic minority at home. The repression and discrimination that resulted from this feeling of threat and the atmosphere of enmity it generated gave rise to three Irish Republican Army (IRA) campaigns in the north – none of which met with any real success, but which rather served to harden Protestant opinion. To protect itself from the IRA and to keep Catholics subjugated, the Northern Ireland Government – which was Protestant-dominated, independent and devolved from Westminster – maintained a permanently armed police force, the Royal Ulster Constabulary (RUC); and an armed police reserve, the B Specials. Both were regarded with fear and loathing by many Catholics. Protestant determination to maintain the status quo also showed itself in abuses based on religious discrimination in jobs, education, housing and the electoral system.

It was these abuses which led in 1967 to the formation of the Northern Ireland Civil Rights Association (NICRA), which was non-violent and at this time; not associated with the IRA or its political wing, *Sinn Féin*. It was also viewed by many as a healthy sign, in that Northern Ireland's Catholics were for the first time trying to win rights *within* the United Kingdom rather than seeking to undermine the State. It was also true, however, that many Republicans joined NICRA early on with the long-term goal of subverting it. The Civil Rights Movement, by means of mass demonstrations, marches and other peaceful activities, sought to focus public attention onto – and thereby correct – anti-Catholic discrimination. So successful was this that in November 1968, the Northern Ireland Prime Minster, Terence O'Neill,[*] announced a programme of reforms involving a points system for housing; the appointment of an ombudsman; the abolition of the company vote in local government elections and its replacement by one-person-one-vote, as elsewhere in Britain; a review of the Special Powers Act; and finally, the end of the notorious Londonderry Corporation. Protestant reaction was predictably hostile. Many were already suspicious of O'Neill because of his earlier moves to establish better relations with the Republic. Violence against Catholics and attacks by Ulster Volunteer Force (UVF) terrorists against Republican activists increased.

The beginning of the campaign that was to absorb TFH's energies as DPR (A) and afterwards can be accurately dated to the NICRA march in Londonderry on 5 October 1968 which, although banned by the government, went ahead anyway. It was then attacked by the RUC and the resulting riot was recorded by the world's press and TV cameras.[3] In January 1969, a legal civil rights march from Belfast to Londonderry was attacked by a Protestant mob at Burntollet Bridge.[4] Marches, counter-demonstrations and riots continued all through the spring and into the summer, watched closely by the media. The Stormont Government continued to ban civil rights marches but allowed Protestant counter-demonstrations to go

---

[*]   Terence Marne O'Neill, Baron O'Neill of the Maine PC (1914-1990) was the fourth Prime Minister of Northern Ireland and Leader of the Ulster Unionist Party (1963-1969).

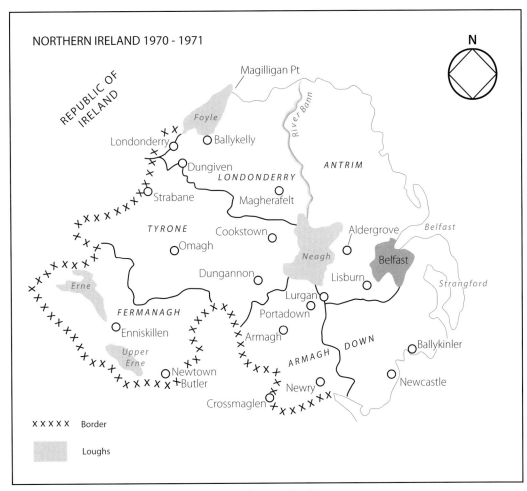

NORTHERN IRELAND 1970 - 1971

Northern Ireland.

ahead, with the result that confrontation became inevitable. There were Protestant bomb attacks and sabotage incidents from April to June; in July and August, a new surge of violence broke out. By now, even the most moderate Catholics had lost all faith in the RUC's impartiality, and this was fuelled by cases like the Samuel Devenny murder.[5] The RUC found it more and more difficult to control rioting and was forced to use baton charges, CS (or tear) gas, and even gunfire, which further fuelled the explosive situation. By early August the force, which was only 3,000-strong, was exhausted and forced out of Catholic districts. These, like the infamous 'Free Derry' with its huge mural, became No-Go areas. Prime Minister James Chichester-Clark,* who had succeeded O'Neill in May, called out the B Specials, who were poorly equipped, poorly trained and anyway, regarded by Catholics as no more than uniformed thugs.

---

*   James Dawson Chichester-Clark, Baron Moyola PC DL (1923-2002) was the penultimate Prime Minister of Northern Ireland and eighth Leader of the Ulster Unionist Party (1969-1971).

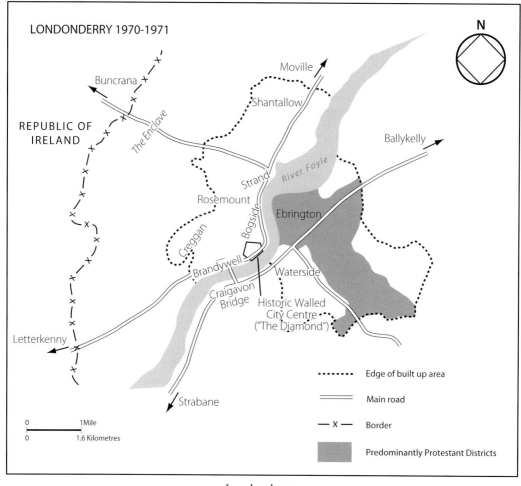

LONDONDERRY 1970-1971

N

Moville

Buncrana

Shantallow

REPUBLIC OF
IRELAND

The Enclave

Ballykelly

Strand

River Foyle

Rosemount

Bogside

Ebrington

Creggan

Brandywell

Waterside

Craigavon
Bridge

Historic Walled
City Centre
("The Diamond")

Letterkenny

Strabane

0   1 Mile
0   1.6 Kilometres

········· Edge of built up area

═══════ Main road

— x —   Border

Predominantly Protestant Districts

Londonderry.

The crisis came to its climax at the annual Protestant Apprentice Boys' march in Londonderry on 12 August 1969, which the government allowed to go ahead, in spite of pressure to ban it. As the march passed the Catholic Bogside, it was attacked. This attack developed into three full days of savage fighting throughout Londonderry which left 10 people dead, 1,600 injured – of whom half were police officers – hundreds of homes burned out and damage to commercial property estimated at more than £8 million.[6] In Belfast, Hastings Street and Springfield Road Police Stations were attacked. On 13 August, the Stormont Government asked British Prime Minister Harold Wilson for troops, as the police were on the point of collapse.[7]

The garrison of Northern Ireland under its peacetime district structure consisted of 39 (Airportable) Infantry Brigade – which had deployed to the Radfan in 1965 – with two infantry battalions based at Holywood outside Belfast and Ballykinler in County Down, and an armoured reconnaissance regiment at Omagh in County Tyrone. These troops were immediately called out and supplemented by a further 3,600 men from Britain. The troops gained admittance to the No-Go areas without opposition and indeed were warmly welcomed. This lull did not last long, for by mid-September, troops were being deployed routinely in Belfast

Makeshift troops' accommodation in Northern Ireland during the early period of the campaign
– 3 Para. (Paradata)

against Protestant rioting and were frequently attacked by UVF gunmen. One report on a Protestant attempt to storm the Catholic Unity Walk flats in Belfast described matters thus: 'It is difficult to describe this utterly incredible scene in a British city: a howling drunken mob, half-bricks and broken flagstones bouncing down the street, petrol bombs, and now automatic weapons joining the fray.'[8]

The situation was aggravated in October following the Hunt and Cameron Reports,[9] which called for the disbandment of the B Specials and the complete reorganisation and retraining of the RUC, with the army maintaining order in the interim. These proposals infuriated Protestants while their other major proposal, the establishment of the Ulster Defence Regiment, alarmed Catholics.

What of the IRA? In the initial stages of this conflict, the organisation had been taken by surprise. Unable to carry out its self-declared role as the protector of the Nationalist community, it had been dubbed 'I Ran Away'. However, it had been active in setting up the early No-Go areas like 'Free Derry' in Londonderry's Bogside and by early 1970 it began to reappear.[10] In December 1969, the IRA had split into the Provisionals and the Officials as a result of violent differences of opinion on how to respond to the events of 1969. In January 1970, *Sinn Féin* held its conference in Dublin and here a political split mirrored this paramilitary divide – resulting in the formation of Provisional *Sinn Féin*.[11] Soon afterwards, having seized control of the Catholic No-Go areas, PIRA launched an active terror campaign against the people, the Security Forces and the State of Northern Ireland. The Officials too engaged in guerrilla warfare until 1972 when they declared a ceasefire and transformed themselves into a wholly political organisation – later known as the Workers' Party. In its early months, PIRA was not a particularly effective insurgent movement, but it learned rapidly and it became the most formidable insurgent enemy that the British Army had faced since Palestine; and the first recognisably modern terrorist/political/criminal nexus to confront Britain's intelligence and security apparatus.

It was just as well that PIRA was not particularly good at its business in the early days, for neither was the British Army. Its initial tactics for inter-positioning between the two factions and its responses to civil disorder had been essentially those of Aden, which it had left only 18 months before. Intelligence gathering was negligible, media handling was poor, equipment was basic and leadership had not yet been devolved much below battalion level. By early 1970, troop strength stood at 7,300 divided between two Brigade Headquarters – 8 Infantry Brigade in Londonderry having supplemented 39 Brigade in Belfast. 16 Parachute Brigade was also, for a time, deployed in the Province. Officially, the army was acting 'in support of the civil power', maintaining the political line that this was not a counter-insurgency campaign, but a police action to contain civil disorder. This was the situation, then, at the time TFH took up the poisoned chalice of DPR (A).

* * *

If TFH had hoped for a quiet few weeks to find his way around his new job, he was sadly disappointed. On Thursday 26 March 1970 the Police (Northern Ireland) Act became law. The Act provided for the disarmament of the RUC (which in the event never happened) and the establishment of a professionally-trained and qualified RUC Reserve. The Act also established the Police Authority of Northern Ireland, which was meant to include representatives from across the community – although none of the main Nationalist parties ever joined it. While the changes laid out in this Act were being implemented, the army would maintain primacy for upholding law and order in all areas of Northern Ireland affected by violence. This, potentially, could last for years – although there was a determination from the beginning that as soon as possible, the RUC would resume responsibility for routine law enforcement and for public order.[12] Then, on Sunday 29 March, there were serious disturbances in Londonderry following a march to commemorate the Easter Rising of 1916. The army later established a cordon around the Bogside. Two days later, there were riots in the Springfield Road area of Belfast following an Orange Order parade. For the first time, the army used snatch squads and CS tear gas to arrest Catholic youths. The confrontation was intense, with 38 soldiers and an unknown number of civilians injured.

1 April 1970 was the day that the UDR began operations. Roy Hattersley,* then Minister of State for Defence, visited Northern Ireland to mark the occasion – having been briefed by TFH among others. Initially Catholics formed 18 percent of the UDR's membership. However, it was later to become almost exclusively Protestant. TFH was much involved with the Head of DS 7 in the MOD over getting the right publicity, stressing the balancing of the UDR to reflect all communities; covering the collection of weapons from the former B

---

*   Roy Sydney George Hattersley, Baron Hattersley FRSL PC (b. 1932) was MP for Birmingham Sparkbrook for 33 years from 1964 to 1997. He served as Deputy Leader of the Labour Party from 1983 to 1992.

Riot control in Northern Ireland, 1970. (Queen's Regimental Archive)

Specials; and generally demonstrating that there was no substance to fears that the UDR would be dominated by ex-Specials. TFH arranged a series of informal briefings for the press, necessary because it was already clear that many former Specials *had* in fact joined the new force following the official disbandment of the Specials on 30 April – including many of the Divisional and Sub-divisional Commandants.[13] Media coverage of the UDR story was, however, overshadowed by continued serious rioting in the Ballymurphy Estate in Catholic West Belfast, which continued for several days until on Friday 3 April Major-General Ian Freeland* – the GOC Northern Ireland – warned that those throwing petrol bombs could be shot dead if, after a warning, they did not stop using them. If arrested, those using petrol bombs could face a sentence of 10 years in prison.[14]

Predictably, this tough line from Freeland sparked a reaction from the media in which TFH was caught up. The BBC's *Panorama* programme immediately lodged a request for a recorded interview with Freeland, on which TFH minuted his Minister asking for clearance.[15] The broadcast went out on 6 April on BBC 1, with the interviewer trying to make Freeland enter into political commitments on things like how long the army would stay on the streets; and on getting tough (or, in BBC parlance, 'intimidating') with disorder. It was clear that a lot

---

*   Later Lieutenant-General Sir Ian Henry Freeland GBE KCB DSO DL (1912-1979). Freeland had served throughout the Second World War and in Kenya during the Mau Mau Revolt.

of what Freeland had said was later edited in order to make the broadcast more sensational, but by today's standards, Freeland said little enough and dodged the traps pretty well. This was not, however, the view at the time – and Freeland was rapidly and roundly abused from all quarters. Unhappily there had also been a press conference a few days before at Holywood Barracks by the Minister for Defence Administration, where the topics had been matters like future troop strength, plans for the forthcoming Easter weekend, and the presence of the Royal Scots – a regiment which was viewed as unacceptable in Catholic quarters on account of its religious and ethnic make-up.[16] Immediately after the broadcast, Freeland had to write to Home Secretary James Callaghan* apologising for any embarrassment caused by his interview and saying how grateful he had been for Callaghan's words of support.[17] All this was picked up by the weekend broadsheet newspapers. On 12 April, *The Sunday Times* published a piece entitled 'The Straight Shooter' on Freeland; the *Telegraph* took a harder and more supportive line towards the army in 'Truths that General Freeland Told'; while *The Observer* concentrated on 'Disorder in Ulster'. TFH had clearly spent much time talking to journalists and editors in advance of these pieces and warned both ministers and his superiors that *The Times* piece in particular would be negative, using words like 'despair'.[18]

The result of this hiatus was direction from the Under-Secretary for the army to TFH on press facilities in Northern Ireland –[19] the immediate vehicle for the new rules being a request from Columbia Broadcasting of New York to TFH to film an item on the UDR.[20] No objections were raised, but from here on there were to be 'normal safeguards' and a strict procedure for clearance of any remarks between the GOC NI and CGS. The GOC was to be informed of any media requests; he in turn was to inform the MOD immediately and clear all requests through TFH. The object of any interview and the main questions were to be provided in advance; any statements were to be cleared; and the likely areas for supplementary questions were also to be submitted so that briefings and preparation could be thoroughly carried out.[21] The army was, it seemed, belatedly waking up to the power of the press.

Evidence of this can be seen in the tension between the Secretaries of State for Defence and Home Affairs – whose responsibilities both involved the army. A draft letter from Hattersley to Home Secretary Callaghan on the army's policy regarding arrests, which TFH had helped to write, pointed out in response to demands for a tougher approach that recent violence was designed to provoke just such a heavy-handed response in order to use this for propaganda purposes. The army's default position, to use only minimum force necessary to contain the trouble, was designed to see that this aim was frustrated. Hattersley certainly did not think that large numbers of arrests were a good thing unless convictions could be assured.[22] A visit by Northern Ireland MPs was another area in which TFH had to take a hand, as Captain Percy Orr – the Unionist MP for South Down – had said he would tell the press that he would be demanding guarantees of security for Northern Ireland in the light of comments from the government of the Irish Republic which had followed recent violence.[23] This sort of mischief-making was a distraction that everyone, TFH included, could well do without.

---

*   Leonard James Callaghan, Baron Callaghan of Cardiff KG PC (1912-2005) was Prime Minister of the United Kingdom from 1976 to 1979 and Leader of the Labour Party from 1976 to 1980. Callaghan is to date the only politician to have served in all four of the Great Offices of State – having been Chancellor of the Exchequer from 1964 to 1967, Home Secretary from 1967 to 1970, and Foreign Secretary from 1974 to 1976.

At the same time, there was a great deal of discussion about the force levels that would be maintained in Northern Ireland – and for TFH, how this would be presented. In April, Hattersley determined that the steady state would be eight battalions – a mix of resident units on two-year tours and roulement units doing four-month tours.[24] However, there were immediate reserves in case of need: one *Spearhead* battalion with its leading elements at 24 hours' notice to move anywhere in the world; an additional *Spearhead* battalion dedicated to Northern Ireland; and a Northern Ireland reserve battalion earmarked in BAOR. As well as infantry battalions and Royal Marines Commandos, RA regiments and engineer squadrons were used in the infantry role. The Irish regiments – Irish Guards, Royal Irish Rangers, 5th Inniskilling Dragoon Guards and The Queen's Royal Irish Hussars – were not to be deployed; nor were Gurkha units to be used.

Thursday 18 June 1970 saw a General Election across the United Kingdom – the first in which 18-year-olds could vote. Against the predictions of the pollsters, Edward Heath's Conservative Party replaced Harold Wilson's Labour Government after six years at Westminster. Peter Carington[*] became Secretary of State for Defence, while Reginald Maudling[†] was appointed Home Secretary and given responsibility for Northern Ireland. The relationship then between the Unionists in Northern Ireland and the Conservatives was a strong one. Indeed, the official title of the Tory Party was 'Conservative and Unionist'; there were likely to be few concessions to Republicans from this administration. In Northern Ireland, the Unionist Party held eight of the 12 Westminster seats and among the new entry were several men who would be prominent in Northern Ireland for decades to come: Ian Paisley was elected for North Antrim;[‡] Frank McManus,[§] a Nationalist Unity candidate, gained Fermanagh-South Tyrone; Gerry Fitt,[¶] founder of the Social Democratic and Labour Party (SDLP), took West Belfast; and Bernadette Devlin,[**] leading light of the Civil Rights Movement, took Mid-Ulster.[25]

Meanwhile, headquarters staffs in both London and Lisburn were focused on contingency plans to cover likely trouble-spots during the coming marching season. Orange Order parades were expected on 1 July, marking the anniversary of the Battle of the Somme in 1916, at which the 36th Ulster Division had suffered devastating losses; as well as the anniversary of the

---

[*]   Peter Alexander Rupert Carington, 6th Baron Carrington KG GCMG CH MC PC DL (b. 1919) served as Defence Secretary from 1970 to 1974, Foreign Secretary from 1979 to 1982 and as the sixth Secretary General of NATO from 1984 to 1988. He had previously served in the Cabinets of both Harold Macmillan and Sir Alec Douglas-Home.

[†]   Reginald Maudling (1917-1979) held several Cabinet posts, including Chancellor of the Exchequer.

[‡]   Ian Richard Kyle Paisley, Baron Bannside PC (1926-2014) founded the Democratic Unionist Party (DUP) in 1971. In 1979 he became a Member of the European Parliament. He opposed all attempts to resolve the conflict through power-sharing between Unionists and Nationalists, and all attempts to involve the Republic of Ireland in Northern affairs. His efforts helped bring down the Sunningdale Agreement of 1974 and the Anglo-Irish Agreement of 1985. Paisley and his party also opposed the Northern Ireland Peace Process and Good Friday Agreement of 1998. In 2007, following the St Andrews Agreement, the DUP finally agreed to share power with *Sinn Féin*. Paisley became First Minister.

[§]   Frank McManus (b. 1942) also sat in the House of Commons. He is a brother of Father Seán McManus – the Irish-American lobbyist and Catholic Priest – and Pat McManus, a member of the IRA killed in an explosion in 1958.

[¶]   Gerard Fitt, Baron Fitt (1926-2005).

[**] Josephine Bernadette Devlin McAliskey (b. 1947), usually known as Bernadette Devlin, is an Irish socialist and Republican. She sat in the House of Commons from 1969 to 1974.

Williamite victory over James II at the Battle of the Boyne in 1690, according to the old Julian calendar. Around the anniversary of the Boyne in the new style – 11, 12 and 13 July – Ulster Protestants and their Scottish cousins, who came over in large numbers for the events, were expected to march in Belfast, which was by far the biggest city in the Province with a population of 400,000; and Londonderry, which had only about 56,000 inhabitants. However, there was also felt to be potential for trouble in towns as far apart as Magherafelt, Dungannon, Lurgan, Dungiven, Cookstown and Armagh.[26] Later estimates put the numbers expected at 365 bands, 35,000 marchers and 60,000 spectators. As one officer put it, 'Believe me it isn't a … carnival … The Ulster crowds are celebrating a victory. Of course they enjoy it but there is a grimmer underlying tone to this than an English carnival!'[27]

Freeland concluded that he could not enforce a ban on marches with this level of participation and the CGS, Sir Geoffrey Baker (with Cabinet approval), decided to put in place a reinforcement for Freeland consisting of an armoured car squadron and five major units: four infantry battalions and an artillery regiment in the infantry role; as well as two independent infantry companies, an additional engineer squadron, a field ambulance and a transport squadron – which would provide drivers for the infantry battalions' *Humber* one-ton armoured vehicles, or 'Pigs'. TFH was involved in the major effort of drafting press releases, briefing editors and journalists, briefing and preparing the Army Board and Ministers, and crafting the presentation of this reinforcement. Various formulae had to be prepared, as the size of the reinforcement could easily change right up to the last minute. More to the point, there were any number of traps and awkward questions that the press could pose: Why not ban marches altogether? What was the effect of cancelling a major exercise in Kenya? What would be the effect on Britain's commitment to NATO caused by the withdrawal of units from the British Army of the Rhine? And the use of the high-readiness Armoured Reconnaissance Squadron which was assigned to the Allied Command Europe Mobile Force? Did the Maltese Government have a view on the withdrawal of a Royal Marines Commando from the island? And what about the use of Protestant Scottish battalions?[28]

It was as well that Freeland had more forces available, for matters began to escalate almost at once. 26 June 1970 saw five people, including two young girls aged nine and four years, killed in a premature explosion at their home in the Creggan Estate in Londonderry. Their father, a PIRA terrorist, had been making an improvised explosive device for use against the army. The explosion also killed two other terrorists. The girls were the first females to die in this latest episode of Ireland's 'Troubles'. On the same day, newly-elected MP Bernadette Devlin was arrested and subsequently jailed for six months for riotous behaviour during the Battle of the Bogside – a serious own-goal for the Security Forces. There was rioting by local residents in Londonderry following the news of the arrest, which spread to Belfast. By the following day, this had developed into sectarian violence.

In this atmosphere, the likely trouble that the Orange Order's parades could produce did indeed come to pass. On Saturday 27 June the New Barnsley Orange Lodge insisted on marching along the Springfield Road in West Belfast, led by its band and banners. This had been a major flash-point the year before and local Nationalists warned the RUC that trouble would follow if this march went ahead. The police declined to ban it and the Ballymurphy Estate erupted in some of the worst rioting since the summer of 1969. That night, as men from the 3rd Battalion The Queen's Regiment struggled to keep the factions apart using tear gas and – for the first time – the *Neptune* water cannon,[29] groups of Protestant rioters began to make incursions into the Catholic Short Strand enclave of East Belfast. Catholics in the area believed that they were going to be burnt out of their homes and claimed that there were no troops on the streets to protect the area. IRA gunmen took up sniping positions in the grounds of St Matthew's Catholic Church and engaged in a prolonged gun battle with Protestants in what was the most significant IRA operation to date. Across Belfast, six people were killed – of whom five were Protestants shot by the IRA.

In response to the violence, Home Secretary Reginald Maudling paid a visit to Northern Ireland. As he boarded the flight home he was reported to have said: 'For God's sake bring me a large Scotch. What a bloody awful country!'

TFH, meanwhile, was writing to Baker's Military Assistant – warning of the international press reaction to the weekend's events in Northern Ireland. This was, he said, 'commonly critical of the army's activities during the violence over the weekend'.

Amongst a range of questions, two were pressed particularly: First, why were soldiers simply standing about under a hail of missiles? Secondly, as Freeland had warned petrol bombers that they would be shot, why had none *been* shot? TFH cited especially Max Hastings in the *London Evening Standard*; and the *New York Herald Tribune*, which had reported that 'The British Army took a beating in Belfast this weekend … Nobody seems to have any orders for action … The mobs ran riot'. TFH then turned his ire on Brigadier Michael Bailey, the Assistant Chief of Staff and spokesman for Headquarters Northern Ireland, who 'appeared at a loss to explain convincingly what new steps the army could take to deal with a deteriorating situation'. [30]

Shortly afterwards, following an informer's tip-off, troops from the Black Watch and the Life Guards were tasked by Freeland to search the Lower Falls area of West Belfast and recover paramilitary weapons.[31] The search began at about 3:00 p.m. on Friday 3 July and concentrated on Balkan Street, where an Official IRA cache was believed to be hidden. A column of six *Saracen* and *Saladin* armoured vehicles carried the troops, who cordoned off the street and in the search uncovered 19 weapons. As the troops left the area, a small crowd of youths on Raglan Street pelted them with stones. The troops replied with CS gas. The stone-throwing then escalated into a full-scale riot and a number of streets were hastily barricaded to prevent the troops from entering. The local Official IRA Commander, Jim Sullivan,* feared that the troops would launch a bigger raid and told his men to move weapons out of the area. At about 6:00 p.m. PIRA terrorists attacked the soldiers using home-made grenades and several soldiers suffered leg wounds. As more troops were sent into the area, Sullivan ordered his men to confront the troops. One source later said: 'The way we looked at it, we were not going to put up our hands and let them take the weaponry. We didn't want the confrontation, but we couldn't surrender'.[32] According to one source, up to 70 Official IRA men were involved. During the exchange of fire with the Officials, troops fired more than 1,500 rounds while hundreds of local youths also pelted the troops with stones and petrol bmbs.[33]

The army also fired 1,600 CS gas canisters, including heavy grenades launched by catapults – some of which went through the roofs of houses. Journalist Peter Taylor described the

---

* Jim Sullivan (d. 1992) was Second-in-Command of the Belfast Brigade of the Official IRA. He was Secretary of the Central Citizens' Defence Committees established in the city after the burning of many homes by Loyalist mobs in the 1969 riots. In 1973, he was elected to Belfast City Council.

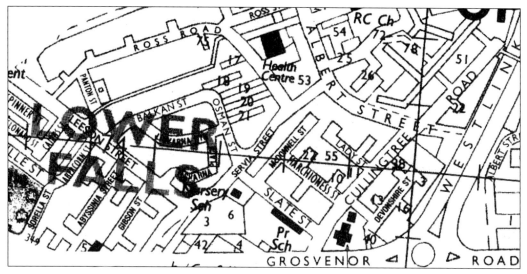

The area of the Lower Falls search operation, July 1970.

effect of the gas: 'The clouds of choking and suffocating gas drifted up the narrow alleyways and back streets of the warren that is the Lower Falls. The gas got everywhere, in through windows, under doors and into the residents' eyes, noses, throats and lungs'.[34]

At about 10:00 p.m. – four hours after the violence began – Freeland ordered that the area was to be put under an indefinite curfew and that anyone caught on the streets would be arrested. Soldiers announced the curfew through loudspeakers on vehicles and in helicopters within an area which was bounded by the Falls Road in the west, Albert Street in the north, Cullingtree Road in the east and Grosvenor Road in the south – about 3,000 houses altogether. However, during the curfew this area was extended in the south-west as far as Dunmore Street. Shortly after the announcement, around 3,000 troops moved into the area – supported by armoured vehicles and helicopters – and began to surround the zone with a hastily-erected barbed wire entanglement.

Shooting and rioting continued for a number of hours after the curfew began.[35] Three soldiers were shot and wounded in Omar Street. The Provisional IRA pulled out – leaving the confrontation to the Officials – allegedly because it believed the clash would end badly and it would lose the few weapons it had. The last shots were fired around dawn on Saturday 4 July, but even while the shooting continued, troops were conducting a house-to-house search for weapons in at least 1,000 houses. Any journalists who remained inside the curfew zone were arrested. Unsurprisingly, there were scores of complaints of soldiers hitting, threatening, insulting and humiliating residents. Pubs and businesses were also searched and it is claimed that several were looted by the soldiers. Two civilians were killed, one by being run over by an armoured vehicle, and an IRA man was shot; he died later. The IRA also shot dead a Polish photographer. According to one account: 'The soldiers behaved with a new harshness … axing down doors, ripping up floorboards, disembowelling chairs, sofas, beds, and smashing the garish plaster statues of the Madonna which adorned the tiny front parlours'. [36]

At the Northern Ireland Cabinet meeting on 7 July, the mood was a mixture of defiance and denial. It was reported that during the search operation, 'little structural damage had

Two views of the search in the Lower Falls. (Queen's Regimental Archive)

been reported, apart from the pulling up of floorboards'; ministers concluded that there was a 'smear campaign' being mounted against the British Army.[37] The British Minister of State for Defence, Lord Balniel, also defended the actions of the troops, saying that: 'I am deeply impressed by the impartial way they are carrying out an extremely difficult task'.[38]

Back in Belfast, at 5:00 p.m. on Saturday 4 July, troops announced by loudspeaker that people could leave their homes inside the curfew zone for two hours to buy food and other supplies. However, no-one was to leave or enter the designated area. During this two-hour period, the local MP – Paddy Devlin – was arrested by the army for doing just that. By noon on Sunday 5 July, however, there was a feeling among locals that the operation was being wound down. Another account said that 'the British knew that most of the 'more attractive' armaments had been spirited away 'before the cordon was fully effective'.'[39]

The curfew was broken when 3,000 women and children from Andersonstown marched to the British lines with supplies for the people inside the curfew area.[40] The soldiers tried to hold back the crowd at first, but eventually allowed people to pass.

In spite of the versions of events already cited, the search uncovered about 100 firearms, 100 home-made grenades, 250 lbs of explosives and 21,000 rounds of ammunition. Among the firearms were 52 pistols, 35 rifles, six machine guns and 14 shotguns – [41] most of which belonged to the Official IRA. Whatever satisfaction the army could draw from having seized these weapons was, however, more than offset by the damage to its image and reputation among Catholics – even those who believed in the Union. Among the troops deployed had been a lowland Scots battalion, recruited largely from Glasgow, many of whose men were extreme Protestants from a city where inter-sectarian hatreds were every bit as violent as in Belfast. The questions that had been asked earlier about the deployment of battalions like this seemed justified – but the damage was done. Even if only half the allegations were true, these men had relished the opportunity to bash the 'Fenians'. TFH later made his own enquiries into the search operation and concluded that 60 searches at least had led to serious abuse. However, he was never able to gain enough evidence to press charges.[42] The first result of this operation was, therefore, a major change for the worse in relations between Catholics and the British Army – many who had not been Republicans now became so – and between the British and Irish Governments. The second result was a heightening of the enmity between the two factions of the IRA. The Officials blamed the Provisionals for starting the confrontation with troops and then leaving them to fight alone against overwhelming odds – resulting in the loss of much of their weaponry. Over the following year, the two factions clashed violently – shooting, beating and kneecapping each other's members. The third result was that PIRA's position was strengthened. Its thugs could beat or even kill anyone who fraternised with the British – and Heaven help anyone accused of collaborating. During the next two years, PIRA would thrust Northern Ireland into the armed conflict that would endure for the next 30 years.

The fall-out from the media coverage of this operation, which had been intense, landed on TFH's desk in Whitehall – even though, with a devolved government, Stormont still took the lead. On 7 July, TFH wrote to the Permanent Secretary to the Under-Secretary of State on the subject of television features – about which he had evidently been approached by both the independent Thames Television and the BBC. TFH recommended that assistance should be provided, since 'If we accept the production teams officially, we shall be able to maintain a measure of control. GOC NI is willing to assist'.[43] However, only two days later – on 9 July

1970 – a letter to TFH and to Mr D.A. Nicholls (the Head of Defence Secretariat (DS) 6 in the MOD from Headquarters Northern Ireland) on the subject of the army's publicity profile in Northern Ireland directed that in order to minimise the army's exposure to 'tendentious criticism' by both sides, press releases, interviews and statements would from here on be done by one of two Stormont ministers – Brian Faulkner and Roy Bradford – who were considered 'photogenic' and who spoke with a local voie.[44]

On Friday 17 July 1970, Chichester-Clark flew to London with Robert Porter (then his Minister of Home Affairs) to meet Maudling. Five days later, a ban on all parades and public processions until January 1971 was announced by the Stormont Government. However, on 30 July there were further riots in Belfast and on the 31st Daniel O'Hagan – aged 19, a Catholic – was shot dead by the army during serious rioting in the New Lodge Road area of North Belfast. In response to the growing disorder, the army rapidly realised that its weapons, tactics and procedures needed modernisation. On 2 August, troops first began to use so-called rubber bullets – baton rounds, fired from the US-manufactured *Federal Riot Gun* – in Londonderry during rioting there. These rounds were intended to be fired at the legs of rioters or at the ground in front of rioters so that the bullet would ricochet, losing some of its force, and then hit the target. Often, however, the rounds were fired directly – resulting in a number of deaths and many injuries.

Against the background of these events, TFH was asked by Baker for his views on the structure and role of the DPR (A)'s department, which he set out in a short paper. 'The present organisation', he wrote:

Protestant violence in the Shankill area of North Belfast, 1971. (Farrar-Hockley family)

... is viable but, in its present form, unlikely to yield the offensive and enterprising policy that is needed if, at the very least, we are to stir the public from its present apathetic and ambivalent attitude to the Armed Forces.

... the feeling in Fleet Street and the BBC and ITV is that what they are getting is information strictly tailored for political advantage ... they do not understand why they do not deal with a service officer at the top of PR. In a curious way, editors are rank snobs: they like to deal with an admiral, general or air marshal. They also hold to the belief, however mistakenly, that a uniformed officer will be more able to give a picture in the round.

He went on to recommend that the Defence Public Relations Staff should be headed by a 2-star military officer with a civil deputy; and that defence advertising – by contrast – needed an administrator and co-ordinator to act with the Home Office, FCO, Central Office of Information and the Treasury.[45] Shortly after this, TFH left the post of DPR after only five months – on 25 August 1970 – having been selected for promotion to Major-General at the remarkably young age of 46.[46] He handed over rapidly to Brigadier A.J. (John) Archer, who had been withdrawn early from the Imperial Defence College.

The period from August 1969 to August 1970 had marked essentially a transition for the army in Northern Ireland, from impartial peacekeeping to confrontation with a substantial minority of the population, while still using the coercive techniques of imperial policing. The lessons of Malaya and Cyprus were largely ignored, or forgotten, chiefly because the threat was seen as civil disobedience rather than insurgency. That said, the campaigns in Malaya and Cyprus – which stressed a counter-insurgency philosophy based on winning the hearts and minds of the population – relied as much on the coercive aspects of this policy as on the persuasive aspects; there were carrots aplenty, but some stick too. However, in Northern Ireland, the army would have to change its ways – and change fast – if disaster was to be avoided.

18

'They will not stop at murder on the streets.' Commander Land Forces, Northern Ireland, August 1970-October 1971

On 26 August 1970, TFH took up a new appointment: that of Commander Land Forces (CLF) in Northern Ireland. As such, he had command of all regular army and UDR units. He was, effectively, the Divisional Commander – relieving the GOC, now a Lieutenant-General, of the day-to-day responsibilities of the campaign on the ground. This left the GOC, as Director of Operations, with overall operational command of all three services for internal security operations and military aid to the civil power; as Director of Operations, the GOC also fulfilled the second major area of his responsibilities: that of managing the military-political interface – sitting on the Northern Ireland Cabinet Security Committee with the Prime Minister, RUC Chief Constable Arthur Young,* and Burrows, the London government's representative. The GOC also reported directly to the CGS in London and operated under a Directive from him.[1]

Freeland summarised matters thus in a letter to TFH just before he took up his post: 'Your job will be to command the soldiers and conduct the army's operations in detail. There are grey areas, such as the UDR and the TAVR which need special consideration …'[2]

TFH therefore exercised operational control over the two infantry brigades: 39 Brigade – with four major units and one armoured car squadron – covering Belfast, Lough Neagh and the area northwards, east of the River Bann (i.e. County Antrim); and 8 Brigade – also with four major units – covering Londonderry and the Province west of the Bann: Counties Tyrone, Fermanagh and Armagh. The Province Reserve, 3 Queen's, was under TFH's direct command and was responsible for an area south-east of Lough Neagh – essentially, County Down. It was, however, usually committed to operations in Belfast when it was not needed elsewhere.[3] In addition, there were reinforcements at critical periods. As well as HQ 16 Parachute Brigade, which had deployed for a time in early 1970, HQ 5 Airportable Brigade was also deployed from Bulford to Belfast in October 1970.[4] TFH had also a small number of force troops units: 34 Field Squadron Royal Engineers, with a wide range of responsibilities from construction, to road closures, to explosive ordnance disposal; a field ambulance, base workshops REME, transport squadron and an Army Air Corps composite squadron with 10

---

* Colonel Sir Arthur Edwin Young KBE CMG CVO OStJ KPM (1907-1979) was the first head of the Royal Ulster Constabulary to be styled Chief Constable. Young was instrumental in the creation of the post of Chief Inspector of Constabulary.

Sioux light helicopters and four *Scouts*. For day-to-day tasking, the RAF detachment of eight *Wessex* medium helicopters was also under his tactical command. Finally, there were the two major units on standby – the NI Reserve Battalion in BAOR and the NI *Spearhead* Battalion in England, with an additional armoured car squadron also available. Plans also existed to reinforce the Province – if needed – by another two Brigade Headquarters, 15 major units, two armoured reconnaissance regiments and eight *Wessex* helicopters. [5]

There was, too, the UDR, whose strength was at this point about 4,000 – of whom nine officers and over 600 men were Catholics and many of them were allowed to keep their weapons at home.[6] There had been over 7,000 applications to date and recruiting was buoyant.[7] Its projected 10 battalions were to be distributed across the two brigade areas – covering static tasks and some internal security duties in the less confrontational areas in order to allow the regular troops to concentrate where they were needed. Each battalion, which had a regular CO and a strong cadre of regular officers and NCOs, had a varying number of companies depending on the local population base. Of these, some companies were to be part-time and some full-time – effectively Provincial Regulars – using an old, tried-and-tested army formula from the days of Empire. Although it would take time for them to reach full operating capability, their local knowledge would be invaluable in developing an intelligence base and a better understanding of the pattern of life and social make-up of the Province.

In spite of this relatively large span of command, TFH was not the GOC's Deputy Director of Operations. This role was fulfilled by the highly capable Chief of Staff, Major-General Tom Acton.* This was a potentially awkward situation – although Acton was a much older man and far above TFH in seniority. Matters eased when Acton was relieved in 1971 by a Brigadier. Moreover, TFH had no separate staff of his own. He and the GOC shared the same headquarters – the staff of which all, therefore, served two masters. TFH had seen the pitfalls of this sort of one-over-one command, with its division of responsibilities, in Borneo. He was determined to stick to his brief and leave politics to his chief – with some relief. They did not, however, see eye-to-eye on some matters – especially on the conduct of the campaign, which TFH believed would be a long one but which Freeland, by contrast, believed would be short-lived and could be handed back to the police within a year or so.

TFH did have one staff officer of his own – his aide de camp, or ADC. A Major-General is usually the lowest rank for which an ADC is provided – the tasks of this officer being to organise the General's programme, movements, transport (Ted Olive – his orderly in 3 Para – had joined him, along with Sgt 'Piggy' Watson, who had driven him), administration and welfare. He would also accompany the General to all visits and meetings and take notes. The ADC usually came from the General's regiment and when TFH was asked who he wanted, he chose his son, Dair – still serving with 1 Para in Malta.[8] Nowadays, such a choice would be regarded as odd and, no doubt, occasioned a deal of comment. Back then things were more relaxed, and TFH's choice is not hard to understand. For most of the time that Dair had been growing up, TFH had been abroad; he was, moreover, proud of his son for following him into the Parachute Regiment. On the other hand, the ADC was often used by other officers to sound out the General's thoughts on a particular issue. Having TFH's son as the aide made this a trickier proposition – not that being the General's son meant that Dair had an easy time.

---

*   Major-General Thomas Heward Acton CBE (1917-1977).

The *Humber* 1-ton APC, or 'Pig' which, replaced by the AFV 430 series in BAOR, became the mainstay of IS operations in Belfast. It was up-armoured and fitted with various modifications over the years and remained in service until around 1990. (Author's collection)

In fact, those in the headquarters at the time thought that Dair was worked harder than any other ADC they had known.

This was an excellent chance, though, for TFH and Dair to regain some lost time together. TFH and Pat had moved to a married quarter inside the secure compound in Thiepval Barracks, Lisburn – although Pat was often away from the Province. Dair and Vicki had a civilian hiring nearby, but Vicki too was often in England – not least because she was expecting her first child. On 8 July the following year, TFH and Pat became grandparents when Dair and Victoria's first boy, Piers, was born in Aldershot.

* * *

When TFH arrived, the army's main operational focus was on first, riot control in towns and secondly, border patrols and operations against the IRA in rural areas. He was briefed on the policies on processions and searches; on the Special Powers Act; on the use of gas; and water cannon and dye in the water as a means of identifying rioters for retrospective arrest. The Special Powers Act gave the army power to make arrests; to search premises; to stop and search suspects and their vehicles; to require answers to reasonable questions; to detain suspects for interrogation for up to 48 hours on police authority; and to require the production of identity documents on demand.[9] He was also told of a number of special, or non-lethal, weapons that were in development: an 'incapacitating round', CS bursting grenades and a liquid form of CS agent. Briefing him were those staff officers who would be close to him throughout his time in this command: the Brigadier GS, M.E. (Mervyn) Tickell; and three GSO1s: Lieutenant-Colonels M.N.S. (Mervyn) McCord and C.M. (Clive) Brennan of the Royal Irish Rangers; and C.D. (Chris) Piggins of the Royal Fusiliers.[10] TFH found common ground with Tickell – a Sapper who had won an MC during the Second World War and who was later a Major-General; and with McCord, later a Brigadier, who had served with the Ulster Rifles in Korea at the time of the Imjin battle. He also quickly got to know his key subordinates: Brigadier J.A.C. (Alan) Cowan of the Royal Anglians, who commanded 8 Brigade; and Lieutenant-Colonel Ken Dodson, the CO of 3 Queen's. He already knew, and trusted, Brigadier F.E. (Frank) Kitson of the Royal 60th Rifles, who commanded 39 Brigade.

By far the most outstanding of these three was Kitson.[*] Kitson had seen active service with the Rifle Brigade and subsequently the Royal Green Jackets in Malaya, Oman and Cyprus; and in Kenya on loan to the Special Branch of the Kenya Police. He had also recently completed a Defence Fellowship at Oxford, where he and TFH had become friends.[11] At Oxford, Kitson had carried out 'an examination into the steps which could be taken in order to make the army ready to deal with subversion, insurrection and peace-keeping operations[†] during the second half of the 1970s'.[12]

It was published in 1971, while he was still in Northern Ireland, under the title *Low Intensity Operations*. Kitson had developed clear ideas on what was required to win in an insurgency. His writing stressed that military actions alone would not solve the problem, but political activity without the legal use of force was also doomed to failure. 'It is', he wrote, 'fatally easy to underestimate the ability of a small number of armed men to exact support from exposed sections of the population by threats … neither government pronouncements, nor the natural loyalty of a people, will avail if terrorists are allowed to build up their organisation unchecked'.[13]

He also laid out the framework of requirements for success: a mix of political and economic measures combined with the forces of the law; a good co-ordinating machinery; establishing the right political atmosphere; developing intelligence; and operating within the law, but changing the law as required to suit circumstances.[14] Kitson was intelligent, experienced, and courageous. He was prepared to speak his mind and stand up for what he thought right. He could also be difficult, intolerant of stupidity or laziness, and was notoriously bad company at parties. He was the right man in the right place at the right time. He made TFH think about what the army was doing right and what it was doing wrong – and how to do better.

* * *

Almost immediately after taking up his new post, TFH was exposed to the secret planning for two eventualities – the first of which was the imposition of direct rule from Westminster in place of the Stormont Government. In the worst case, a breakdown of law and order was feared

---

[*]   Later General Sir Frank Edward Kitson GBE KCB MC DL (b. 1926). He was subsequently Commandant of the Staff College and Commander-in-Chief United Kingdom Land Forces.
[†]   At the time, this meant 'keeping the peace', rather than its later meaning of UN Chapter VI 'blue-beret' operations.

in the wake of such a contingency, accompanied by 'guerrilla warfare, indiscriminate violence by both sides, and the interruption of essential services'. The most likely course of events was, however, seen as a continuation of current trends.[15] Top-level planning in London, at this stage, had identified major tasks only and it was followed by more detailed efforts within HQNI, which began in February 1971. These plans looked at – among other things – force levels, legislation, border control, the UDR and safety of service families. Consideration was given to taking the RUC under army control, restructuring the intelligence architecture, re-shaping command and control, maintaining essential services, and making best use of public relations and psychological operations. It was also suggested that the Territorial Army should be used for border security.[16] This was a highly contentious issue, as the TA had only recently begun to expand after its dramatic reduction under the Labour Government in 1967-1968. It was, moreover, very mixed in terms of its ethnic and religious make-up in Northern Ireland – its members and their families very vulnerable to attack within communities – and there was a strong feeling that it should be kept out of internal security. This was, in the end, the line taken and maintained: the TA was never, in Northern Ireland, part of 'the Security Forces'.[17]

The second planning issue was the use of internment without trial for suspected terrorists. This was a measure that had been used twice before since 1919, with considerable success when it had been put into effect on both sides of the Irish border. The Stormont Government was keen once more to press ahead with the measure, with a planning figure of 300 internees, and intending to use HMS *Maidstone* – an old submarine depot ship which had been used to quarter troops in Belfast – until such time as proper facilities could be constructed. The CGS and VCGS were not at all keen on the idea and military planning went ahead cautiously.[18]

In the near term, though, TFH was immediately involved in the process of determining what force levels would be needed over the coming year. There was uncertainty as to what would happen following the release of Bernadette Devlin, which was planned for 23 October; and the overall concept of operations remained that of keeping a strong deterrent presence on the ground at all times – especially in urban areas. Freeland thought that both factions of the IRA were better co-ordinated than was widely believed; that the likelihood of Protestant violence was high; that the Devlin release was overstated as a threat; but that hooliganism was on the increase. He thought that if pushed, either by Protestants or by the Security Forces, the IRA would defend its territory aggressively. He also considered that marches could trigger trouble, but so too would the implementation of local government Reforms which would harden Protestant attitudes.[19] The cry of 'No Surrender' – the Protestant motto since 1690 – now meant maintaining the status quo and, above all, making 'croppies lie down'.

What then should the force levels look like? The troops currently available included about 3,700 UDR personnel at any one time, but for limited duties. The RUC had 3,600 constables and 300 reservists and its capability was increasing. In particular, the Special Patrol Group – which in spite of its name was chiefly organised for public order – had formed four sections of 30 men in Belfast and two sections in Londonderry, shortly increasing to three. However, the military view remained that 'the RUC are not able to shoulder much more of the burden than a year ago'.[20]

Given that situation, there had to be a permanent deterrent presence on the 'peace lines' – i.e. the interfaces between the two ethnic communities – with enough troops in reserve to control major disorder. There was still, at this point – in practice as well as in the view of government – no insurgency in Northern Ireland, but rather a major civil disorder problem.

Freeland did consider withdrawing troops from the streets altogether, leaving most things to the police and acting as mobile reserve, but 'the lack of police makes this unachieable'.[21]

The requirement for troops was therefore stated as nine battalions from November 1970 to Easter 1971 – rising to 10 at Easter. Two of these would be deployed in Londonderry, one on the border, four in Belfast with an additional city reserve battalion, and one battalion as Province reserve. These units would be found from the resident armoured reconnaissance regiment, the three resident infantry battalions, two roulement battalions from BAOR, an armoured reconnaissance squadron and an infantry battalion from England, and two RA regiments in the infantry role. If, however, Freeland did get through the danger-period without serious trouble, he felt that this total could quickly be reduced to eight major units. This was the proposal that was sent through to London and, in due course, accepted.[22] Slightly later, it was also concluded that the blanket ban on marches and demonstrations should be lifted, since it was unsustainable, but that considerable restrictions would remain on the numbers and types of march to be allowed in order to reduce the potential for trouble.[23]

Once he had digested all this and then found his way around, as it were, TFH wrote to his major subordinates – setting out how he saw things:

Soldiers of the Parachute Regiment on the streets of Belfast in 1971. (Paradata)

INTENSIFICATION OF OPERATIONS

It is now clear we are in for a prolonged period of raiding and bombing outrages along the border and in the countryside; outbreaks of hooligan violence in Belfast and probably Londonderry and other sensitive towns, many or all of which will be backed and organised by IRA elements ... as you know, the GOC has decided that we must take tougher measures to combat disorder and violence. What are these measures to be? So far as the border and countryside is concerned we shall be undertaking a greater number of operations to accomplish the following: snap, short term, widespread road checks by day and night; area searches for arms, explosives, ammunition and documents; cordon and search operations on areas known to be used for training – these will be more effective when we have had time for preliminary clandestine reconnaissance and surveillance; ambushes in response to hard intelligence; night patrolling in sensitive towns ... we must make maximum use of our helicopters.

In towns and cities we must make quicker and more effective use of our IS weapons such as the baton round and water cannon ... the baton round, fired in volleys, must at once be followed up by snatch squads... ensure that we arrest troublemakers of whatever age.[2]

TFH with Bryan Webster, CO 1 RRF in Northern Ireland, 1971. Webster was later TFH's Chief of Staff in South-East District. (Maj-Gen Bryan Webster)

This was TFH 'getting a tremendous grip on things', as Bryan Webster,* then commanding the 1st Fusiliers, remembered.[25] Peter Butler, who was the GOC's military assistant, also remembered TFH as 'one of the most dynamic officers I have ever met. He always seemed to have a multitude of things on his mind ... He seemed never to rest.'[26]

Clive Brennan, then a GSO1, recalled similarly that TFH would and could absorb masses of information about people and places. This, with his penchant for getting out and about, meant that he rapidly knew a great deal about the Province and the major players.[27] Malcolm Ross-Thomas, who was the GSO2 Intelligence and Security – there was, incredibly, no GSO1 – saw a great deal of TFH and remembered later that:

> I saw a lot of TFH as the Chief of Staff would not allow non-infantry officers to be on duty in the operations centre at night; there were therefore only four of us that could do it. TFH was the most energetic man I ever met and he never seemed to sleep. After his morning meeting, at which he would dish out jobs to the staff, he would be off out on the ground. He would return late in the afternoon and send for the staff to report on progress on their tasks before tackling his in-tray. He would then go home but come back to the ops room at night, sometimes in a dinner jacket straight from a party, then change into combat kit and go out again. He would return about 1:00 a.m. – with Dair falling asleep – before going home again. When I went for breakfast after finishing my spell of duty he was always up and about having read every newspaper, demanding to know what I thought about such-and-such an article in, say, *The Irish Times*![28]

TFH wrote to his old friend David Lloyd Owen early in his tour – giving his early impressions and saying that:

> The situation here is one of those that looks as extraordinary at close quarters as it does from a distance. An unpleasant aspect of the problem is that the greater majority of those taking part in active plotting and rioting are not doing so because they want to achieve an end, but because they enjoy violent behaviour on a tribal basis.[29]

In public, TFH quickly effected a sea-change in the perception of the campaign, stating in a television interview in November 1970 that the army was facing 'organised terrorism' which had orchestrated the recent riots. In his view, therefore, the problem of major civil disorder was about to become an insurgency. The army was not, yet, facing 'a well-oiled machine' however, and TFH thought that for now, the IRA was not particularly good at its business.[30] In another broadcast on 5 February 1971, which followed a search operation in the Republican New Lodge area of North Belfast (during which five soldiers had been wounded) he bluntly identified the IRA leaders by name – singling out Francis Chard, Billy McKee, Leo Martin, Liam Hannaway and Kevin Hannaway.[31] He said that the army had carried out the search because 'we have good evidence that it harbours ... IRA Provisionals' who had openly paraded their

---

* Later Major-General Bryan Webster CB CBE. Commissioned into the Royal Fusiliers in 1951 and served in Korea and the Suez Canal Zone. He later commanded 8 Infantry Brigade in Londonderry.

activities 'with some braggadocio'.[32] He went on to say that the army faced 'a long haul ahead and [is] nearer to the threshold of a harder operation'.[33] This was the first time that any senior military officer had warned of a long struggle against a nascent insurgency and it probably made him few friends – especially among Edward Heath's new government, which did not wish to hear such uncomfortable truths so soon after taking office.[34] Naming the IRA leaders was not, however, intended as a direct threat, but was more of an attempt to assert that the British Army was in control and knew who was who;[35] it turned out to be a mistake, since (probably unbeknown to TFH) British intelligence agents were negotiating with several of those whom TFH named in an effort to control some of the wilder excesses of their campaign. The Provisionals regarded this broadcast as more than ample proof of British bad faith.[36]

What TFH was seeking to do was to bring more clarity to the mission of the army in the developing campaign. Military training at this time conditioned units either for conventional war in Europe, or for late-colonial internal security duties in Hong Kong, Aden (until it was evacuated), or the West Indies. TFH thought that this was both out of touch and out of date and he was concerned to focus training and operations onto counter-insurgency and counter-terrorism through the closer integration of intelligence and operations; the use of the techniques, described by Kitson, aimed at separating insurgents from the people; embracing new technologies, techniques, tactics and procedures; and above all, changing the mind-set.[37]

The development of actionable, tactical intelligence was thus a high priority and TFH followed closely Kitson's use of covert surveillance using the 'Bomb Squad'. The unit was formed during the summer of 1971[38] and had its genesis in the success of IRA bombings. At the start, with the support of both Kitson and TFH, a few civilian cars manned by soldiers in plain clothes would cruise around or park up in odd places keeping a lookout for suspicious behaviour. The unit was based in Palace Barracks, Holywood and gradually extended its operations beyond watching for bombers – using its people to infiltrate marches in order to give the Security Forces warning of what was likely to happen. As this developed, its name was changed to the Mobile Reconnaissance Force, or MRF, and was led by Captain Arthur Watchus.[39] The unit followed somewhat the philosophy which Kitson had developed in Kenya.[40] By mid-1972, it consisted of up to 40 men and a small number of women from across the army. MRF teams of up to nine men were allegedly – but after the departure of both Kitson and TFH – tasked with tracking down and arresting, or killing, suspected members of the IRA; they also ran a number of front companies to gather intelligence, such as the Four-Square Laundry in Belfast.[41]

The SAS was also being used in covert operations, but this did not get off to a very good start, for as early as 2 October 1970 TFH was writing to Brigadier Fergie Semple –[*] Director of the SAS Group – in the aftermath of the use of a troop of 22 SAS. In his debriefing at home, the Troop Commander had obviously said that the troop had been given a task which was unworthy of the SAS and Semple had complained. In response, a clearly furious TFH wrote a letter back that would have had a heavy impact on the Troop Commander's future – if he had one:

---

[*]   Brigadier Roderick Ferguson ('Fergie') Semple MBE MC (1922-2003).

The task for which we asked for an SAS party was a clandestine watch with intermit-
tent patrols to investigate certain areas, it needed a delicate touch. When the troop
arrived, they were inadequately equipped having, for example, not a single pair of
binoculars with them. I regret to say that it was my strong impression that the enthusiasm of the Troop Commander was somewhat dampened by the weather at the time.
As things stood, I was obliged to modify considerably my original requirement and
to put them to a lesser task.

I forbore to make any official complaint … My suggestion is that you should now
come over … [42]

In fact, there was more that TFH could have said, but did not: the troop had arrived bearing
all the marks of service in the Oman – sun-tanned and wearing desert boots – and when
they went to pick up their hired cars, they all presented driving licenses bearing addresses in
Hereford.[43]

Perhaps as a result of early frustrations, TFH pioneered one initiative which later became a
valuable tool for establishing evidential trails on the movements and activities of IRA men: the
development of the infantry close observation platoons. These were based on battalion reconnaissance platoons but given extensive training in the insertion, operation and extraction of
covert observation posts in both urban and rural terrain.[44]

As well as using the MRF, Kitson also pushed the co-ordination of intelligence, for he
had a close relationship with the Assistant Chief Constable of the RUC in Belfast – Sam
Bradley – and Kitson's experiences as a Military Operations Officer in Kenya and a Company
Commander in Malaya told him that intelligence and operations had to be fused at the
lowest practicable level if timely action was to be taken and results achieved. Kitson particularly wanted the decentralisation of Special Branch. As things stood, Special Branch intelligence was passed up to RUC Headquarters at Knock and then, depending on the agenda
of the Stormont Government, passed back selectively to HQNI and so on down the line.
Not only did this compromise the principle of timeliness in intelligence, but also it fractured
the unity of effort and unity of command. Unofficially, moves were made in this direction,
but it was not until the end of the year that any real progress was made at higher levels.[45] In
tandem, TFH was also pushing for more military intelligence officers on long tours across the
Province and for the establishment of a proper Intelligence Corps unit as part of the headquarters, which was successfully established as 12 Intelligence & Security Company under
Roger Patton – a Lieutenant-Colonel rather than a Major.[46] Developing a modern approach
to complex counter-insurgency was not going to happen overnight, and it was as well for the
army and the campaign in Northern Ireland that both Kitson and TFH began the process at
such anearly date.

Since the Falls battle, the matter of searches had been a tricky one. When Frank Kitson
proposed an operation in the Catholic Ardoyne area in North Belfast, it prompted the
response from London that although small-scale, routine searches should continue; no major,
large-scale operation was to be mounted without approval from Whitehall.[47] Chichester-
Clark wanted an over-ride for this rule in cases where time was of the essence, which was
duly agreed.[48] TFH's views on this can be imagined: he was wholly opposed to interference
from on high in tactical matters; however, the sensitivities being what they were, he had to
swallow his irritation.

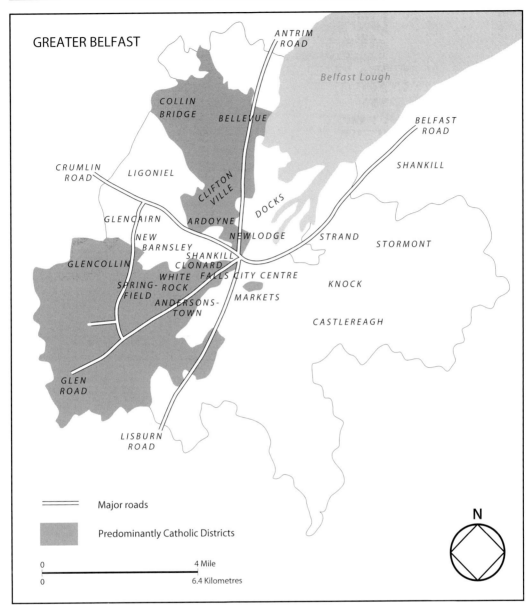

Belfast.

More intensive operations along the border quickly followed TFH's instructions. These included large-scale road checks, sweeps and searches to hit IRA units holding explosives and weapons in rural areas; the spiking and blocking of border crossing points on minor roads; and searches in the towns of Newcastle, Newry and Bambridge. In order to maintain this level of activity, and being thoroughly air-minded, TFH rapidly realised that helicopters were essential – just as they had been in Borneo. In mid-December he sought to pre-empt any moves to reduce the numbers of RAF helicopters available for tasking – signalling the Director of Military Operations in London that the presence of six *Wessex* had allowed a high tempo of road blocks and snap searches which denied the IRA the use of training areas and impeded their ability to move weapons and munitions. TFH believed that he needed to be able to move at least two platoons of infantry and a company command group – 70 men – and so could not reduce below a minimum of five aircraft.[49]

More operations on the border were, however, risky since the border was almost completely unmarked and, in places, extremely difficult to determine. On 25-26 January 1971, two *ferret* scout cars of TFH's old battalion, 3 Para – which was now commanded by his old Brigade Major, Peter Chiswell – and two Land Rovers from 4 UDR crossed into the Irish Republic by mistake at Mullan Bridge on the border of Fermanagh and Cavan. The paratroopers, new to the area, were detained for about 45 minutes by the *Garda Síochána* and the matter quickly reached Irish Government level, where there was a deal of unhappiness. TFH, who naturally took a close interest in his old battalion, had to hold an enquiry. He was determined to see that no soldier would suffer for a simple mistake in difficult circumstances, but the risks of this happening again had to be minimised.[50]

From the beginning of 1971, violence had begun once more to grow in Belfast and Londonderry. On 29 January, Edward Heath in Cabinet expressed his frustration to Defence Secretary Carington at the continuing riots and acts of lawlessness, 'which he believed to be the work of subversive organisations'. The government, he said, was not really aware of the Directive under which GOC Northern Ireland was working – nor the way that units were briefed for tasks. Descending to the lowest tactical level and interfering in matters which were not his concern, he went on to express the view that a 'quicker reaction to trouble was needed to nip riots in the bud … '

The army, however, seemed reluctant to act and the public could not understand why fire was not returned promptly – nor why vigilante groups were tolerated in the so-called No-Go areas.[51] The reaction of CGS, GOC Northern Ireland and TFH himself to this was expressed in a note to Carington, drafted by one of his officials: 'Senior officers are undoubtedly irritated to say the least with what they feel to be the wilful refusal of the government to understand the reasons for their restraint. The situation is ironical: many of the politicians … are eager to see rougher tactics and it is the army who argue for minimum force and moderation'.[52]

Indeed, after the Falls battle, Freeland *had* tried restraint; however, at the same time, both factions of the IRA had increased their tempo of operations against the army. The Provisional IRA in particular planned for an 'all-out offensive action against the British occupation'.[53] Chief of Staff Seán Mac Stíofáin' decided they would 'escalate, escalate and escalate' until the British had had enough, and left.[54] The PIRA Army Council therefore approved offensive operations against the British Army from the beginning of 1971, which included the use of well-trained snipers, as well as mob violence and the relentless bombing of commercial targets – especially in Belfast. A major search operation in the Catholic Clonard area of West Belfast by 2 Royal Anglian on 3 February led to stoning, petrol bombing and 54 arrests; further operations on the 4th and 5th resulted in exchanges of gunfire and a *Saracen* armoured personnel carrier being set on fire by petrol bombs. This operation had been initiated by TFH himself,

---

*   Seán Mac Stíofáin (1928 -2001) was born John Stevenson in London and became associated with the Republican Movement in Ireland after serving in the RAF. He was the first Chief of Staff of PIRA – a position he held between 1969 and 1972.

A typical street scene in Belfast in 1971. The wire mesh is part of a protective anti-rocket screen around a police station. (Author's collection)

against the advice of Clive Brennan and the staff: 'Clive,' TFH had said somewhat testily, 'with you I sometimes feel I am heading into a very strong wind.'[55]

Brennan's advice was, however, the right advice on this occasion. The following day, Gunner Robert Curtis of 94 Locating Regiment RA became the first British soldier to be shot and killed by the Provisionals. He was followed soon afterwards by Lance-Bombardier James Lawrie of the same regiment; Private Colin Wootton of 3 Queen's was critically injured.[56] Brothers John and Joseph McCaig, and Dougal McCaughey, were all Fusiliers serving with the 1st Battalion, The Royal Highland Fusiliers at Girdwood Park Barracks in North Belfast. On 10 March, the three had been granted a short leave pass and, having been lured away from safety by three girls, they were murdered by the IRA. Their bodies were found by children at 9:30 p.m. that night —[57] an episode that would have made TFH recall the murder of British soldiers in Palestine by *Irgun Zwei L'eumi* in 1947. The murders were closely followed by another – that of Chief Inspector Cecil Patterson, the regional head of Special Branch in Belfast. The following day, Home Secretary Reginald Maudling made a statement in the House of Commons in which he said that security arrangements for off-duty soldiers were being reviewed, and that: 'The battle now joined against the terrorists will be fought with the utmost vigour and determination. It is a battle against a small minority of armed and ruthless men whose strength lies not so much in their numbers as in their wickedness'.[58]

The insurgency had arrived, and a joint Army-RUC internment working party was established shortly afterwards.[59]

Ironically, Baker – the CGS – had visited Northern Ireland on 7 and 8 January 1971 and been briefed by Chichester-Clark, Freeland and TFH. He had visited various areas and in his follow-up letter had noted a relaxation in tension. As a result, he hoped that it would not be necessary to reinforce the Province during Easter. There had also, clearly, been a discussion about tour lengths, with all those involved coming out in favour of the existing four-month tour for roulement units, with the notable exception of Frank Kitson, who had pressed for much longer tours. In the same vein, Baker felt unsure about whether two years was too much for the resident, accompanied, units – thinking aloud that maybe 18 months would be better.[60] These ideas were rapidly dispelled by events on the ground and as a result of the rise in the tempo of operations in January and early February, both *Spearhead* battalions were committed to Northern Ireland and a selective call-out of the UDR was initiated – permitting TFH, for the first time, to mount major internal security operations simultaneously in both Belfast and Londonderry.[61] The rise in violence also prompted a visit from Carington on 28 and 29 January. He had arrived on the afternoon of 28 January for briefings and discussions with Freeland and TFH before going on to call on Chichester-Clark. The following day, TFH had taken him round Belfast and in a letter shortly afterwards, Carington said that he had been 'glad to have the opportunity to see something of the situation at first hand', having visited 3 Queen's in West Belfast, 1 RRW in the Lower Falls, and 2 Royal Anglian in the Ballymurphy.[62]

TFH was, as Malcolm Ross-Thomas had noted, on the ground a good deal himself; he made a point of knowing his way around the Province and the people.[63] As early as September 1970, he was writing to the Moderator of the Presbyterian Church, asking him not to move the Reverend Mr Courtenay from the Henry Taggart Memorial Church in Springfield as he had done 'such excellent work in resolving differences and has earned the trust of people of different sects'. In this instance, the answer was a lemon. Dr Freer, the Moderator, wrote back rather sharply – saying that he was not going to have his clergy doing social work for Catholics, and that TFH had better mind his own affairs.[64] Sometimes, TFH's movements had a more exciting outcome than during Carington's visit. One Sunday night around this time, TFH needed to visit troops in Belfast. His two armoured Land Rovers were pre-positioned, with their drivers and an RMP close protection team. At the last minute it emerged that the MI5 head of station and Mervyn McCord would be joining them. This increased the requirement for escorts and so Ted Olive and Sgt Prentice – TFH's cook – volunteered. This slightly unorthodox mobile patrol made its way down the Springfield Road until the unmistakeable rat-tat-tat of a *Thompson* sub-machine gun could be heard, followed by the thump of rounds raking the top side of the vehicle. In typical fashion, Sgt Watson accelerated away to lead the vehicles into Springfield Road Police Station. In the follow-up, the gunman was shot and arrested. TFH, rightly, decided to call it a night, but on returning home, the vehicles had to be positioned in such a way that Pat could not see the strike marks. TFH may have had no qualms about facing IRA fire, but his wife was quite anoher matter.[65]

Another reason for Carington's visit was that Freeland had asked to retire slightly early. As Sir Arthur Young, the Chief Constable of the RUC, had also recently retired, there was concern in Whitehall that this coincidence of departures might be seen as either a sacking or a change in policy. Carington wrote to Freeland, however, that: 'You have had many difficulties to face and your motives have been misconstrued and maligned by disaffected people of every sort … I would not want you to leave Northern Ireland without saying to you how highly all of us who have worked with you have come to esteem your judgement and courage'.[66]

Troops dismounting from a stripped-down Land Rover on the Crumlin Road in North Belfast. The presence of the wicker basket and the dreaded army-issue cardboard suitcase indicate that this is a shift change at an observation post or static guard. (Farrar-Hockley family)

Freeland had never expected to have to deal with the situation that had developed in Northern Ireland on his watch. He had gone there from the post of DCGS, which had been abolished, in order to complete his pensionable service as a Lieutenant-General. He had found the task difficult, not least because of the tight-rope he had to walk between serving the Northern Ireland Government, which was responsible for law and order, on the one hand; and serving the CGS as the commander of a military district on the other. His task had been further complicated by the desire of the government in Westminster to push Reforms that would undermine the Republican Movement through fair treatment for Catholic citizens, while the Stormont Government had absolutely no wish to go down this road at all; nor had he found Young's successor, Graham Shillington,[*] easy. As Carver described him, he was respected, pleasant, but ineffectual. No wonder Freeland was anxious to leave.

Freeland was replaced by Lieutenant-General Erskine Crum,[†] a clever officer with a thorough theoretical understanding of counter-insurgency, if little in the way of relevant operational experience. He was extensively briefed, but on 16 February, after the shortest period in command, he suffered a severe heart attack. He died a month later, on 17 March, aged 52.

---

[*]   Sir Graham Shillington (1911-2001) was Chief Constable 1970-1973.

[†]   Lieutenant-General Vernon Forbes Erskine-Crum CIE MC (1918-1971) had served in North-West Europe during the Second World War and then on Mountbatten's staff in the Far East. He had latterly served in a number of posts related to the Household Division and at the Imperial Defence College.

In his place, on 2 March, came Lieutenant-General Harry Tuzo, whom TFH had known as a Brigade Commander in Borneo, and with whom he had been exchanging friendly correspondence on the performance of Royal Artillery units in the Province from both operational and public relations points of view; TFH was always meticulous about helping non-infantry units to perform well.[67] Tuzo was an experienced Gunner who had seen a great deal of action in North-West Europe during the Second World War, and then commanded a regiment in Kenya and a Gurkha brigade in Borneo. He had been appointed Chief of Staff of BAOR as a Major-General and then Director, Royal Artillery – a post from which he expected to retire. Crum's death propelled him to a new command at a critical time. As his obituary in *The Independent* put it: '... for the next two traumatic years he was to need every ounce of his diplomatic, negotiating and military skills, for these were terrifying times for the Province ... Those who had judged Tuzo not C-in-C material had not seen him under fire'.[68]

Michael Carver,* who was about to be CGS, was involved in the selection of Tuzo, whom he firmly recommended from a list of eight possible runners: 'He seemed to me', wrote Carver, 'to have the right qualities of toughness, resilience, breadth of outlook and rapidity of mind'.[69] This being so, one wonders why the army had decided to dispense with his talent and make him retire at what was, clearly, the height of his powers, while promoting an inexperienced Guardsman who, as it turned out, was in poor health but concealing the fact. Tuzo was pitched in at the deep end, as the security situation was deteriorating – and very soon afterwards, Northern Ireland's Prime Minister, James Chichester-Clark, told Edward Heath in a highly confrontational telephone call that he intended to resign that same evening as he was 'disappointed in the results of our discussion on Tuesday'.

Heath had agreed extra forces for Northern Ireland and did not understand Chichester-Clark's position, but Chichester-Clark was adamant that what was needed was not simply more troops, but 'an effort to kill or capture IRA men'. However, all his suggested methods had been ruled out as being too oppressive or likely to upset the minority. A long and bad-tempered argument followed about what was and was not being done – especially in the light of continuing No-Go areas, which London appeared to be condoning; and irritation at the armed demonstrations which had accompanied several IRA funerals, which had raised Unionist demands for a tougher line.[70] Heath said he thought Chichester-Clark's position and reason for resigning were 'absolutely unjustifiable'.[71] Chichester-Clark, however, went ahead and quit.

Chichester-Clark was replaced by Brian Faulkner.† His first encounter with the British Cabinet in London took place on 1 April – a meeting also attended by Tuzo and the newly-appointed CGS, Michael Carver, who had assumed the appointment that very day.[72] Also present were Alec Douglas-Home,‡ Maudling and Carington. Tuzo took the opportunity to

---

*   Later Field Marshal Richard Michael Power Carver, Baron Carver GCB CBE DSO MC (1915-2001), subsequently Chief of the Defence Staff. Carver had seen service during the Second World War with the Royal Tank Regiment, and later in the Mau Mau Uprising in Kenya and the UN mission in Cyprus.
†   Arthur Brian Deane Faulkner, Baron Faulkner of Downpatrick PC (1921-1977) was the sixth and last Prime Minister of Northern Ireland from March 1971 until his resignation in March 1972. He was also the Chief Executive of the short-lived Northern Ireland Executive during the first half of 1974.
‡   Alexander Frederick Douglas-Home, Baron Home of the Hirsel KT PC (1903-1995) served as Prime Minister from October 1963 to October 1964. He is notable for being the last Prime Minister to hold office while

outline the army's scope and scale of activity, as well as the increasing range and brutality of the IRA's atrocities.[73] However, the major discussion item was internment. Faulkner, although he had been one of those pressing most strongly for a tougher line on the IRA, said that he opposed internment unless it could decisively end the IRA's ability to operate and could be implemented on both sides of the border. Tuzo, in the meantime, briefed the meeting on the progress of planning and the preparations for a camp to be constructed at Long Kesh – a programme that would take four or five months to complete.[74] It was, however, not until 25 May that TFH, through the Director of Military Operations in London, was able to issue a signal warning 48 Engineer Squadron for a five-month tour of duty – during which it would construct Long Kesh Internment Camp.[75]

Another area of study and planning for TFH was the matter of the border and whether or not it could effectively be closed. Many crossings had been closed after the IRA booby-trapped the Crossmaglen Crossing Point in August 1970 by erecting spikes or concrete blocks. The locals simply by-passed these obstacles, or else destroyed the spikes. TFH and the staff concluded that even if very large amounts of manpower and resources were devoted to it, closure would never be effective without something akin to the Iron Curtain – not an example that anyone was keen to follow. The effort was, therefore, discontinued for the time being.[76] In later years it was picked up again in response to the intense campaign of violence mounted by PIRA from across the Irish border in South Armagh and Fermanagh.

All this gave TFH little time to continue his parallel career as a writer. However, he did maintain contact with the academic world. In September 1970, for example, he took part in a conference at Lancaster University with Walter Walker, organised by Lieutenant-General Sir Napier Crookenden –[*] the GOC-in-C Western Command and a fellow airborne soldier of great distinction – in which he gave a speech drawn from his Defence Fellowship: The Army in British Society. In the same month he lectured at the JSSC Latimer, encouraging others to take up the opportunity offered by the Defence Fellowship Scheme. In October he took part in a 40-minute film on leadership, sponsored by *The Financial Times* and the Industrial Society.[77] He also gave lectures and speeches at regular intervals – one of which, at the Staff College, gave rise to a correspondence that sheds light on TFH's continuing commitment to the Christian faith. Major Ian Dobbie[†] was writing his Commandant's paper on the value of the Christian faith to leaders and wrote to TFH asking him to expound on some remarks which he had made. What those remarks were is impossible to say, for TFH never wrote a script and always spoke from memory, using slides as a prompt. However, his almost prophetic response to Dobbie – uncomfortable reading for many now – was as follows:

---

being a member of the House of Lords, prior to renouncing his peerage and taking up a seat in the House of Commons for the remainder of his Premiership.

[*]   Lieutenant-General Sir Napier Crookenden KCB DSO OBE DL (1915-2002) served in the Second World War as Brigade Major in 6 Airlanding Brigade and then leading his regiment in the Battle of the Bulge and then the Rhine crossing. He was Director of Operations in Malaya 1952-1954 and commanded 16 Parachute Brigade 1960-1961. He was Director of Land / Air Warfare 1964-1967 and was the last GOC-in-C Western Command.

[†]   Later Brigadier William Ian Cotter Dobbie (b. 1939).

The army is coasting on a tradition of morality which is no longer underpinned except on a random basis … every foreseeable campaign we are likely to be involved in, great or small, abroad or at home, will involve people who hold strong beliefs. Our danger is that the leadership of the Armed Forces will believe in a number of things in general but scarcely anything in particular … Does the army recognise the need to retain the old-fashioned form of morality? If it does, then … steps must be taken in training and worship to bring future commanders to a personal Christian faith. If it does not, we should say so and face the consequences.[78]

Speaking engagements had to be minimised, however, for from March 1971 onwards the disagreements between the two wings of the IRA intensified, with more kneecappings, beatings and shootings. However, this brought little respite to the British Army, as the summer marching season got under way. By July, the Provisionals in particular were in a reckless mood. Tuzo thought that 'to gain an advantage they will not stop at murder on the streets'.

Intelligence had told TFH that their plans to attack marchers and troops during the summer season were in place. Since March, there had been an average of two bomb explosions every day and on one day in July, 20 bombs destroyed shops, banks, public houses and the offices of the *Daily Mirror* newspaper in Belfast; another four soldiers had been murdered, including two men from 2 Para in Andersonstown in July; and 30 wounded along with four civilians – at least one of whom was an IRA terrorist – shot dead by the army.[79] Favourite targets for attack were the British Army garrisons around the Bogside and Creggan in Londonderry – especially the Bligh's Lane base. Perhaps most humiliating of all, on 16 July, Gerald Fitzgerald – a wounded IRA man – was removed at gunpoint from the Royal Victoria Hospital by his co-terrorists even though he was under armed police guard.[80]

Because of all this, planning for internment was advanced. However, informed guesswork thought that any swoop would only get about 25 percent of the really important members of both wings of the IRA who were known to be around and who were under some sort of surveillance.[81] When Tuzo had taken command, he had issued new orders to TFH and his other major subordinates in which he had listed his priorities as being first, to bring to justice all those who broke the law; secondly, and explicit within the first point, to uphold the *rule* of law; and third, to recover arms, explosives and ammunition. He stressed that intelligence, and the closest co-operation with the RUC, were both crucial to achieving success.[82] As violence mounted, criticism of the army and RUC grew louder. Protestants in the Province and many elsewhere in Britain felt that the Security Forces were not doing enough to crack down, while at the same time, Catholics accused them of atrocities, harassment and over-reaction. A paper by Mervyn McCord, prepared for TFH, summed up the success rate in meeting Tuzo's directives: since January, the army had made 1,167 arrests, of which only about half – 548 – had led to convictions.[83]

Tuzo therefore proposed a plan to reduce this level of criticism and, at the same time, put pressure on the IRA and gain some hard intelligence. His proposal was the arrest of up to 100 selected individuals. However, no-one could agree on what would be done with these men subsequently.[84] A discussion took place on 19 July, with the idea that the plan might be put into effect after the Apprentice Boys' march in Londonderry. Frank Kitson, who was about to go on leave, was told by TFH that some arrests were imminent.

'I thought this was crazy,' recalled Kitson, 'as we had nowhere to keep them. I told TFH that they had not so far done anything illegal and it would make things harder for us if we do bring in internment.' TFH agreed but said that no alternative could be identified. He made no attempt to explain any of the background to Kitson – he never did so, assuming responsibility for things even when he disagreed as the only loyal and honourable course of action – but he did agree that nothing would be done until Kitson came back from leave.[85] However, Kitson had only been gone a few days when pressure from Faulkner, who was being goaded by Ian Paisley, led to the proposed operation being adopted and put hastily into effect by TFH and his subordinates on 23 July. Kitson read of the operation in the Sunday newspapers and while he was doing so, was telephoned by the CGS, who asked him to come by for a drink after church. On the doorstep, Carver said, 'What's going on in Belfast?' Kitson replied, 'I thought you were going to tell me!'[86]

Kitson was saddled with an operation with which he had not agreed and whose consequences he would have to manage when he got back. This operation was *Linklater*, approved personally by Maudling. Its avowed aim was to harass both wings of the IRA, to disrupt activity, and to 'show we know who the leaders are' so that they would understand that they could easily be arrested if internment were to be introduced. It included a large number of searches of selected IRA men's houses and work places.[87] On 23 July, 105 houses searched, three men were detained but two of these were quickly released without charge. Among the finds were subversive literature, radio equipment and some explosives. There were more searches on 26 and 27 July which recovered a few weapons and documents.[88] Maudling's statement, however, over-egged the pudding:

> The army's operation in Northern Ireland this morning marks the beginning of a new phase in the battle against the IRA ... Its significance is the stress it lays on the fact that the function of the Security Forces is not merely to contain disorder and violence, but to search out the men and the organisation responsible. This will be pursued. In this new phase the Security Forces will act with the utmost vigour.[89]

In the end, 20 people were prosecuted amid rioting and shooting at the troops. In the week that followed, there were more than 90 attacks of various kinds, with three or four explosions or arson episodes every day. The operation was therefore a let-down, giving both Protestants and Catholics the idea that the army was ineffective, while also generating a good deal of trouble – but not enough trouble to make anyone think twice about the results of introducing internment.

Tension mounted as the date of the Apprentice Boys' march approached. The Northern Ireland Government considered banning it, but with opposition from Paisley and other hard-line Protestants strong, Faulkner felt he could not ban the march unless he got internment in exchange. Carver and Tuzo had already agreed that neither the march should be banned, nor internment brought in – and Faulkner had said publicly that he would not consider internment unless recommended by the GOC and Commissioner Shillington. Carver and Tuzo continued to hold this line, but out of the public eye, Faulkner became more and more insistent that the situation was deteriorating. On 30 July, the British Ambassador in Dublin had met Irish Prime Minister Jack Lynch,* to warn him that internment was probably immi-

---

* John Mary 'Jack' Lynch (1917-1999) was the Taoiseach of Ireland twice from 1966 to 1973 and 1977 to

nent. Lynch said he could not put this into operation in Eire, for with the mood in his country over events in the North, no Irish Government would survive such a measure. The two also discussed Direct Rule: Lynch said that he preferred this to a General Election, which would result in a government in Stormont led by Ian Paisley![90] The matter came to a head in early August, when Faulkner went to London to press his demands: internment, or else London would have to accept immediately the imposition of Direct Rule on Northern Ireland and with it, winding up the Stormont Parliament and Government. After a long discussion, Heath and his Cabinet agreed to Faulkner's demand for internment, along with a six-month ban on all marches, which was presented as 'a decision for the Stomont Government'.[91]

Fearing a leak, Tuzo decided to implement the operation, *Demetrius*, on 9 August. In preparation, three more major units which had been given notice to move some time before were sent to reinforce the command, raising Tuzo's total force to 17 battalions. Bizarrely, TFH handed over his command as CLF on 3 August to Major-General Robert Ford,[*] just a few days before. Why this happened remains a mystery. Those who could shed light on it are all

Troops on Operation *Demetrius* – internment – in Belfast in 1971. (Author's collection)

1979.

* Later General Sir Robert Cyril Ford GCB CBE (b. 1923). He served in the Second World War and in Palestine. He was later Adjutant-General of the Army.

now dead, but to change the commander who had overseen all the planning and replace him with someone who did not know the ground, but who would be responsible for the operation, seems highly odd. There was no hint of any clash of personalities; TFH's relationship with Tuzo was good, and Tuzo – who liked a hands-off approach to his subordinates – was not given to having rows or disagreements of any sort.[92] However, TFH and Carver, the CGS, were known to dislike each other intensely even though they had never served together. TFH probably regarded Carver as no better than a politician; Carver doubtless thought TFH was a loose cannon. The only explanation for his early move that makes any sense in the context of the time and what followed later – both for TFH personally and for the Province – is that because TFH was due to hand over within weeks and because the operation had been brought forward, it was thought better to put in place immediately the officer who would own the consequences in the medium to long term.

TFH therefore had to stand on the sidelines – no doubt silently fuming – and watch; Malcolm Ross-Thomas recalled him telephoning most days asking what was going on, and having to be politely refused details.[93] On 6 August, Lynch and US President Richard Nixon were briefed.[94] In the initial seizures, 326 men were arrested from an initial list of 520 names compiled by the RUC – on what basis they would not say. All those arrested were taken initially to Girdwood Park in North Belfast or Ballykelly Barracks near Londonderry for initial screening – following which more than 100 were immediately released – and from there to RMP Magilligan at the eastern end of Lough Foyle, since the construction of Long Kesh had not been completed. The operation was followed by severe rioting, shooting and bombing in both Londonderry and Belfast. 2 Queen's, brought over from Germany as one of the reinforcing battalions in Belfast, were attacked from all sides. On 9 August, for example, A Company pre-empted three incendiary devices and exchanged 50 rounds of rifle-fire with snipers in one afternoon; subsequent searches turned up not only weapons, ammunition and explosive devices, but also home-made javelins made out of welding rods and hundreds of petrol and nail bombs.[95] Frank Kitson had returned some measure of order to Belfast by 12 August, but violence grew in Londonderry with barricades erected in the Bogside and Creggan districts. On 19 August, an operation was mounted to remove them which partially succeeded. In the aftermath, Tuzo agreed to let local leaders have these barricades removed through negotiation – a move which failed and which led directly to the establishment of permanent No-Go areas, which during 1972 had to be removed in one of the army's biggest operations since 1945, *Motorman*.

Worse, the intelligence on which the arrests were based turned out to be at best partial and outdated, if not downright wrong. Even worse still, news of the operation had leaked and many wanted men had made good their escape across the border. The source of the intelligence had been largely Special Branch, which was clearly not as good as it thought itself to be, even when guided by professional intelligence officers like David Eastwood, who had been seconded from the Intelligence Services.[96] The vast majority of those arrested had been Catholics and thus the operation was represented by Republican propaganda as a repressive, one-sided measure. This no doubt contributed to the fall in Catholic membership of the UDR from about 18 percent to three percent; it may also be significant that the paramilitary Ulster Defence Association (UDA) was formed in August 1971.[97] One useful product of internment was, however, the 'Freds': a few IRA men who escaped internment in return for helping the Security Forces with information. A few were given safe houses, looked after by the MRF, and

A typical vehicle check point in Northern Ireland in early 1972. This one is on the bridge at Strabane in County Londonderry. (RWF Museum/Archives)

run by a staff officer from Headquarters Northern Ireland – from where they were loaned to units who took them round in vehicles to point out people on the streets and give intelligence on them. This proved especially effective in helping to arrest the IRA's Quarter Masters and thus recover stores of arms and explosives.[98]

In public at least, TFH's view was that the operation had yielded a reasonably good level of intelligence and had forced the IRA leadership into hiding. Forty-eight hours of rioting, a propaganda attack by the Republican media and a few weeks of bombing and shooting were, he said, a price worth paying.[99] He was partly right, in that the house searches which accompanied the arrests did produce documents and other useful material; and the IRA leadership certainly did have to disappear. This they could easily do, since internment was not being applied across the border and whatever the IRA and *Sinn Féin* leadership thought of the Irish Government, they made it a strict rule never to antagonise Dublin by engaging in any operations against the Irish Security Forces. In private TFH was, however, well aware that the intelligence had been out of date and he would have preferred a more selective programme of arrests; some who were there at the time were surprised that TFH went along with such an ill-founded operation – but he would have had no choice.[100] What was perhaps most surprising was that internment and Direct Rule had not been introduced simultaneously, since Direct Rule would have been welcomed by the Catholic population and drawn the sting from internment. What happened was the worst of all worlds: internment allowed the IRA to take control of the Catholic population through fear of the Stormont Government allied with intimidation of any waverers; and it led to a further deterioration of the security situation – and thus to the introduction of Direct Rule anyway – but by then the trust of the Catholic population had finally been lost. One possible explanation for this costly error was the small Commons majority of Heath's government at a time when he was negotiating Britain's entry into the

Troops in riot gear deal with disorder in Londonderry in early 1972. (RWF Museum/Archives)

EEC. The loss of the Unionist Party's votes at Westminster would have led to failure and this Heath was not prepared, perhaps, to risk.

A little later, the methods of deep interrogation carried out by the Interrogation Wing of the Joint Service Intelligence School on 11 of those picked up during the operation came under scrutiny in the Compton and Baker Reports.[101] These methods – which included the use of stress positions, hooding, continuous white noise, sleep deprivation and the denial of food and water – had been those developed in Malaya, Kenya and Aden; but they had not been briefed to, nor approved by, ministers either in Northern Ireland or Whitehall. Carver, the CGS, always denied that he had any knowledge of the matter and there is no indication anywhere that either Tuzo, or Shillington, or Ford, or TFH were any the wiser. The use of these five techniques, as they were termed, was later forbidden by what became known as the Heath Directive. However, the combination of internment and interrogation, and the rumours and allegations they spawned, further antagonised Catholic opinion in the North and that of the government and people of the Irish Republic: 'It was a far cry from the days of August 1969 when the army had been welcomed in the Catholic areas as an alternative to the RUC and the B Specials. We were now Enemy Number One'.[102]

By the time TFH left Northern Ireland, there had been nearly 7,000 violent incidents including at least 1,000 bomb attacks, causing 50 deaths. Soldiers and policemen had come under fire on 1,500 occasions, and 261 police station attacks had been logged. By the end of 1971, search operations had recovered 700 weapons and 1,600 grenades or other explosive devices; fifty-nine soldiers and policemen had been killed and another 180 people, IRA men and civilians, had also died.[103]

*   *   *

The besetting problem that had confronted TFH and others, and which continued to confront the British Government and army for years to come, was how to defeat a guerrilla army strongly supported by part of the population and able to use the exceptional human camouflage thus provided without further alienating that same population. It was what another deep-thinking Parachute Regiment officer, Rupert Smith,* later dubbed 'war among the people'. Even to begin to answer this required a clear political agenda aimed at addressing the grievances which allowed insurgency to thrive; and the Unionist Government in Stormont in 1970 and 1971 was not interested in such Reforms. Without such Reforms, the use of military force was always at worst counter-productive, at best dealing only with some symptoms of the problem.[104] Because of this, TFH in particular had a task that was constantly changing, balancing the requirements of two masters – London and Stormont – with different agendas. Difficult as it was to issue frequent changes of orders to his subordinates, TFH evidently decided that the uncertainty engendered by such veering and hauling would stop with him and his subordinates would be allowed to get on with the job rather than ponder the machinations of policy.

Although in 1971 the army had begun to refine its tactics at street level to devolve responsibility down to platoon and section commanders – and to introduce new training and new weapons – many in it had yet to change their mindset from that of Aden, Kenya or even Cyprus. It was, admittedly, difficult to do this while in contact with the enemy and while also having to manage its other major commitment, that to NATO; nor would the British Government admit that it had an insurgency on its hands, rather than just a problem of public order allied with organised criminality. It is also easy for us to be clever with the benefit of hindsight, but it has to be admitted that the army behaved with considerable severity in Northern Ireland in the early days of 1970 – sometimes with justification, but sometimes without – and that it made many enemies for itself by so doing. Nor was the army helped by the conflicting agendas of Westminster and Stormont which, acting together, might quickly have removed the causes of grievance from the Catholic population. The lessons were learned, eventually, and there is equally no doubt that the campaign in Northern Ireland changed the army and brought it into the era of modern conflict, but in the short term it was the IRA that proved itself better able to adapt to a volatile situation. There was enough understanding of complex counter-insurgency around at the time for the issues to be addressed and for the army to undergo the required transformation over the following years – a process that TFH was active in bringing about – Frank Kitson having laid them out very clearly in his definitive report, so much ahead of its time, *Low Intensity Operations*.[105]

TFH's early departure was protested by some – partly on personal grounds but also because it gave a message that the army was not serious about the campaign. Officers in comfortable peacetime billets could be in post for up to three years, but where continuity was really needed in order to understand the situation in a complex counter-insurgency, people in key posts could be moved after only a short time. Simon Winchester, writing in *The Guardian* on the day that TFH left, was particularly damning:

---

*   Later General Sir Rupert Anthony Smith KCB DSO OBE QGM (b. 1943). He later commanded 1st Armoured Division during the Gulf War and UNPROFOR in Bosnia 1995-1996. Subsequently he became Deputy Supreme Allied Commander Europe.

All who met him found his energy astonishing, his personality endearing, and found in his directives and disrespect for diplomacy a welcome change from most soldiers. The misgivings at his departure will be largely directed at Whitehall … [who] have ruined the continuity of military policy in Ulster, or at least the military strategy that Farrar-Hockley has managed to build up.[106]

In time, common sense did win the day. Nearly all headquarters staff officers were sent to Northern Ireland on two-year tours with only roulement units doing short tours – and those units were provided with continuity NCOs who knew their areas well. Having achieved this in Northern Ireland, the army however forgot it in subsequent campaigns and did not embrace the principle again until the war in Afghanistan.

TFH was never directly involved in Northern Ireland again – and indeed as things turned out, he had earned his last campaign medal. However, his membership of the Parachute Regiment – in the aftermath of the later events in Londonderry which became known as 'Bloody Sunday' – meant that the IRA would always have him in their sights. There was one other, personal, result of TFH's involvement in Northern Ireland, both in the MOD and in the Province: a hardening of his mistrust of politicians, no matter what their colour. TFH could not dissemble – it was simply not in his nature – quite apart from the fact that what was being done by both factions in Northern Ireland in the name of his religion appalled him. He gave clear military advice to his political master and expected in return that there would be a consistency of approach, a statement of strategic objectives and then a reasonably hands-off policy to allow the military the freedom of action to proceed. However, in a campaign so close to home and at such an early stage, his advice was often too blunt and his reaction to fudging the issues caused more than a little irritation by those whose responsibility it was to confront issues and take decisions, but who seemed incapable of doing so. Although he was still destined for the highest ranks – and had been marked out as such for many years – it was probably here that it became clear that he would never be allowed to hold a post like CGS, VCGS, or C-in-C of either BAOR or UK Land Forces – nor indeed probably any Army Board job. To the CGS of the day – who controlled all senior appointments – he was an uncomfortable presence, an outsider to the system and not properly house-trained; a man of the frontier, rather than of the drawing room. On the frontier, therefore, he would remain. Had TFH set out his thoughts on this, such a path would probably not have displeased him.

19

'The enemy are not supermen' GOC 4th Armoured Division, October 1971-October 1973

Since 1945, and certainly since 1953, TFH had always belonged to that part of the British Army which had been committed to expeditionary operations outside the NATO area. He had no background in, nor experience of, armoured warfare and it was perhaps surprising that on leaving Northern Ireland he was appointed to command the 4th Division, one of the three armoured formations making up I (BR) Corps – the United Kingdom's biggest contribution to NATO – in the British Army of the Rhine.

By the late 1950s, BAOR had evolved from being a post-war army of occupation to a partner with German, Dutch, Belgian and US formations making up the Northern Army Group – facing the Russian and Warsaw Pact Armies across the Inner German Border. During the late 1950s and early 1960s, I (BR) Corps had gone through an extensive programme of re-formation, reduction and re-equipment. The *Chameleon* trials resulted in the strengthening of the brigade level of command and the integration of all arms at that level, as well as the acceptance of battlefield nuclear weapons; the close co-operation with air forces; and the realisation that regular, large-scale, field training events were necessary in order to exercise properly the divisional and corps commanders and their staffs. Without large bodies of troops deployed, then the frictions of movement and logistics; of getting orders into the hand of the recipient in a timely manner; of crossing obstacles; and of planning and conducting a battle from a small, mobile, tactical headquarters could not properly be realised.[1]

When TFH was appointed to his new command, the corps consisted of the 1st, 2nd and 4th Divisions, each with two brigades made up of two armoured regiments and two mechanised infantry battalions – plus the divisional reconnaissance, light helicopters, artillery, engineer, supply, transport, maintenance, medical, air defence and provost units from which detachments were sent to the brigades to make them complete fighting entities.* By 1970, under the arms plot, armoured regiments could expect long tours of residence in Germany – at least eight years – while infantry battalions usually did from four to five years before changing role and moving to other duties. All other arms and service units were permanently stationed in Germany, rotating personnel through on a normal two-year posting cycle.[2]

There was, too, under Heath's Conservative Government, a respite from the almost continuous cycle of defence cuts. A Strategic Command had been formed, with all combat units

---

* The exception was 11 Mechanised Brigade of the 1st Division, which had three infantry battalions and one armoured regiment.

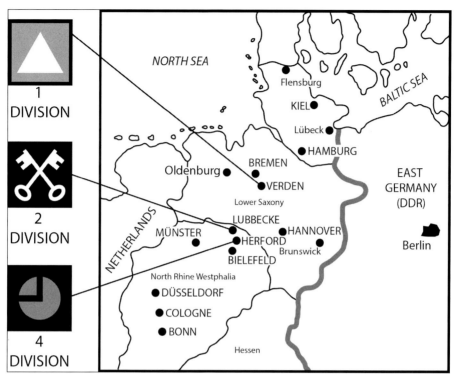

A map showing the locations of the 1st, 2nd and 4th Divisions and the divisional areas in Germany, taken from the Corps Headquarters' Christmas card.

in Britain under its direction; and the old Territorial Commands had been abolished and replaced by a single Headquarters Land Forces, with districts responsible for home defence. Several infantry battalions earmarked for disbandment, amalgamation or reduction to a single company – including the Glosters – were reprieved; and the TA, which had all but disappeared under the previous Labour Government, was being expanded. Overall, 4.5 percent of Britain's gross domestic product was to be spent on defence.[3] BAOR was the largest and most expensive of Britain's overseas commitments and in the wake of the Soviets' crushing of the Prague Spring in 1968, there were few who argued with its size and cost, for this was the very height of the Cold War and even though the West depended ultimately on nuclear deterrence, the huge size of the Group of Soviet Forces in Germany and its client armies – 20 Soviet divisions in Germany, 11 divisions in other European satellite countries and up to 60 client country divisions[*] – demanded a heavy presence of NATO ground troops.[4] It was for this reason that NATO developed and maintained a range of nuclear weapons, from the 155 mm artillery shell, through short-range missiles, aircraft-delivered bombs and inter-continental ballistic missiles. As TFH himself wrote:

---

[*] The mobilisation potential of the Soviet Army was more than 200 tank, motor rifle and airborne divisions. At that time, the mobilised strength of the US Army – NATO's strongest member – was 40 divisions: a figure which declined to 26 after the Vietnam War. Even allowing for the American overmatch in technology, the odds were heavily in the Soviets' favour.

In Europe, the NATO Supreme Allied Commander is painfully aware that, in the event of war, because his reinforcements and supplies are so few, his front would quickly be broken open at one or more critical points … NATO strategy will continue to be inextricably interconnected with nuclear weapons in the face of Warsaw Pact strength in conventional forces.[5]

*   *   *

After leaving Northern Ireland, TFH enjoyed a short period of leave at home. During this time, Peter Chiswell recalled meeting him:

In September 1971 TFH invited me to lunch, where he gave me the astonishing news that MOD wanted 3 Para to fly as soon as possible to Ghana to occupy the Ghanaian Army whilst the Metropolitan Police, escorted by elements of the SAS, tried to identify the leaders of the plot to assassinate the Prime Minister.* My request for transport aircraft to enable us to parachute back to a DZ near Aldershot was met. The weather however was unkind with strong winds; we air-landed nearby and enjoyed a brief rest at home before flying to Accra.[6]

In early October, TFH and Pat moved house once more to the GOC's residence, Taurus House, in the quiet town of Herford in North Rhine-Westphalia – not far from the Corps Headquarters at Bielefeld – and in the centre of the North German Plain where any battle with a Soviet invader would be fought. With them went Hilary, who had left Exeter School the previous year. He had joined the Potential Officers' Troop at the depot of the Royal Corps of Transport in Aldershot and then gone before the army's Regular Commissions Board, hoping for a place at Sandhurst. However, he was deferred and told to return in a year's time. He therefore joined Pat and TFH in Herford, filling in time by doing various jobs around the station and otherwise enjoying life in Germany. They were joined, of course, by Ted Olive as orderly; Sgt Gordon ('Piggy') Watson as driver for the staff car and the Dodge *Dart* that Ted Olive had driven over from England; and Sgt Peter ('Wink') Prentice of the Army Catering Corps, who had been with them in Northern Ireland, as chef. Because of TFH's recent service in Northern Ireland, Watson was trained in close protection and carried a pistol at all times. Shortly after their arrival, the staff were surprised to hear a loud explosion from the GOC's outer office: Watson had had a negligent discharge. Before anyone else could move, TFH came straight out and took charge. Watson must have expected the sack, but TFH remained true to his usual rule, that anyone can make a mistake once.

TFH took up his command on 10 October 1971,[7] relieving David Fraser, whom he had last known in Borneo. The division had been commanded in the recent past by two of TFH's former superiors, Vernon Erskine-Crum and Michael Forrester. Now, his immediate superior, the Corps Commander, was Lieutenant-General Sir Roland 'Roly' Gibbs – to whom TFH had been Second-in-Command in 3 Para. The two were already, therefore, good friends and struck

---

*   The Prime Minister was Kofi Busia, who was deposed the following year by a military coup. 3 Para carried out a series of joint exercises with the Ghanaians while 'showing a presence'.

up an immediate rapport. Although he too had commanded a parachute battalion, Gibbs had a good deal of experience in mechanised warfare from Normandy onwards. Within his own headquarters, TFH was supported by his Colonel GS, Desmond Rice,* responsible for all matters related to intelligence, operations, training and security. Next came another Colonel, Jimmy Hellier[†] (often known as 'Zebedee') – the DAQMG – responsible for administration, personnel, supply, transport and maintenance. Hellier was a highly competent organiser and logistician who had served in the Merchant Navy during the Second World War and then joined the Royal Signals. The Commander Royal Artillery, initially Brigadier Arthur Stewart-Cox[‡] and from March 1973 Brigadier Edward Burgess,[§] commanded and co-ordinated all fire support and air defence for the division; Burgess was another extremely competent officer who rose to the highest ranks of the army.[8] The Commander Royal Engineers was Colonel

Chris Popham.[¶] TFH also had, as usual, an ADC. Initially, for a short period, this was Captain Barney Rolfe-Smith, who had joined him in Northern Ireland; Rolfe-Smith was succeeded by Captain Desmond Bowen,[**] who after a short career in the army joined the Civil Service and rose to top of his profession. TFH was, therefore, supported by as able a team as any GOC could wish for.

TFH's two subordinate armoured brigades were the 6th, at Soest, and the 20th at Detmold. 6 Brigade had only just moved into the area from Barnard Castle, having been withdrawn to Britain in 1968 as an economy measure. Here it took the place of a Canadian armoured brigade group which had moved south to Laar, where it joined a US Division. 6 Brigade was commanded by Brigadier David Alexander-Sinclair,[††] an experienced officer of the Rifle Brigade and contemporary of Frank Kitson who had served in Malaya, Cyprus and Kenya. 20 Brigade in Detmold was

TFH as GOC 4th Division, 1972.
(Farrar-Hockley family)

---

*   Later Major-General Sir Desmond Hind Garrett Rice KCVO CBE (b. 1924).

†   Later Major-General Eric James Hellier CBE (1927-2011).

‡   Later Major-General Arthur George Earnest Stewart Cox CBE DFC (1930-2003). Stewart Cox had won the DFC in Korea and was later GOC Wales.

§   Later General Sir Edward Arthur Burgess KCB OBE (b. 1927); was later Deputy Supreme Allied Commander Europe.

¶   Later Major-General Christopher John Popham CB (1927-2005).

**   Desmond Bowen CB CMG was later Director-General Policy in the MOD, as well as holding senior NATO appointments.

††   Later Major-General David Boyd Alexander-Sinclair CB (1927-2014).

commanded by Brigadier John Stanier,* who was succeeded in 1972 by Richard Lawson.† Both TFH's Brigade Commanders were thus also extremely capable, high-flying professionals – and Lawson, like Alexander-Sinclair, had combat experience (in Aden, Nigeria and the Congo). From what little correspondence remains, TFH enjoyed a close relationship with Lawson and Alexander-Sinclair, who both remained friends long afterwards, and a workable but somewhat chilly personal relationship with Stanier.

Life in BAOR in the 1970s was busy, but structured. Every year, the infantry regiments would fire their classification and conduct field firing at Sennelager while the armoured, armoured reconnaissance and artillery did the same at Bergen-Hohne. There would be low-level tactical training on one of the training areas, such as Soltau-Lüneburg, or Haltern, or Sennelager.

Concurrently there would be command post exercises and study periods for the regimental, brigade, divisional and corps headquarters staffs. Then, in the autumn, with the harvest in, there would be brigade, or divisional – or even corps – exercises with one formation being exercised while another provided the exercise control and enemy force. These exercises, involving all arms, would cover hundreds of square miles of land and were on a scale which it is now impossible to comprehend, but they made the officers and men used to living and working in the field for long periods; taught them road-march discipline; camouflage; how to cross rivers and minefields; how to construct defensive positions; and how a major tactical operation involving many moving parts had to be carefully planned, properly supplied, closely controlled and regularly exercised. Battle-group live-fire training was also being developed in the army's newly-acquired training area in Canada, at Suffield in Alberta, where troops would spend up to six weeks during the summer months. This training area was acquired in addition to the existing area at Wainwright when the Revolution in Libya brought Colonel Muamar Gaddafi to power – denying the British Army the extensive desert training area it had previously used there.

As well as the routine round of training there was plenty of time for sports and games, with a full programme of inter-unit matches throughout the command in boxing, athletics, soccer, rugby, cricket, hockey, cross-country running, and equestrian sports. Then there was adventurous training: sailing on the Dummer See, the Möhne See and at Kiel; skiing – Exercise *Snow Queen* – in the Harz or in Bavaria; and expeditions around Europe or in the Canadian Rockies following the end of the military training package at Suffield. TFH himself had no time for, nor interest in, skiing other than to present prizes at the Divisional Ski Meeting.[9] What he did insist on was keeping current in military parachuting – jumping with the German Army near Oldenburg and taking Desmond Bowen, Ted Olive and Sgt Watson with him. TFH was always number 1 in the stick, and Ted Olive number 2. This was a more-than-usually uncomfortable experience, for not only did the Germans jump from large helicopters – without the benefit of slipstream, this was akin to a balloon jump

---

*   Later Field Marshal Sir John Wilfred Stanier GCB MBE (1925-2007). Subsequently Chief of the General Staff. He had the dubious distinction of being the first officer after the Second World War to become the professional head of the British Army without having heard a shot fired in anger on active service in that war or any subsequent campaign.

†   General Sir Richard George Lawson KCB DSO OBE KCSS (b. 1927) served as GOC Northern Ireland during the Troubles and later succeeded TFH as Commander-in-Chief Allied Forces Northern Europe.

6 Armoured Brigade mounts the annual Staff Colleges Demonstration at Sennelager in 1973.
(Author's collection)

– but also the drop zone was a marshy area criss-crossed by deep drainage ditches which could make landing hazardous.[10] TFH had, too, come to enjoy cricket. Although he had never had any aptitude for ball games, he was an enthusiastic – if low-scoring – batsman and a fearless fielder in the slips and even captained the Divisional Headquarters side, as Dwin Bramall, GOC 1st Division (a highly accomplished cricketer and captain of *his* Divisional Headquarters side) recalled.[11]

There was, too, a vibrant social life. As well as the 55,000 troops on the corps – along with the army and lines of communications units and all their families – there was a 10,000-strong RAF presence at the airfields of Gutersloh, Laarbruck, Brüggen and Wildenrath; military hospitals – with a full staff of British doctors and nurses – at Iserlohn, Münster, Rinteln, Bad Eilsen and Hannover; and a host of expatriate civilians working for the various garrison, station and liaison staffs; the NAAFI; British Forces Broadcasting Service; Services Kinema Corporation; SSAFA; the Salvation Army; and the British Forces Education Service. TFH himself continued to give cookery demonstrations to regimental wives' clubs and to speak about leadership – especially in the context of the Christian faith – often at the nearby Church House in Lübbecke.

In 1970, in an effort to boost morale and retention, a military salary was introduced in place of the old system of pay and marriage allowance. In general, pay rose as the military was brought more on a par with civilian counterparts and monitored by an independent Armed Forces Pay Review Body. A Lieutenant could now be paid around £5/15/- a day and a Major,

£9/10/- per day (£77.60 and £141.70 in terms of purchasing power at today's values).* There were now, however, deductions: for income tax and NIS; for single men's accommodation and food; or married quarters. However, there was also an additional bonus in the shape of a local overseas allowance, paid to make up the difference in the cost of living between Britain and Germany.[12] There were, too, some very welcome perks in the shape of duty free tobacco, alcohol and other goods; cheap petrol; duty and tax-free cars; and some free leave travel – even though some items such as tea, coffee and spirits were still rationed. All in all, quarters were good, the standard of living was high, and one result was that the army became much more married than it had been a decade before when TFH was in command of a battalion. With this large expatriate population – not to mention the other Allied nations and the German civilian population, but no television – there was a constant drumbeat of weekend parties, curry lunches, sports fixtures, dining-in nights and club activities.

Desmond Bowen recalled that TFH, while relishing being in command and in charge, was somewhat out of place in this life in BAOR. This was an army that he did not know and which he felt was a little too comfortable and predictable, cosy even – something of a stately dance of orchestrated exercises and activities. What he wanted was that his division, and this army, should prepare for war. As a result, he often demanded surprise inspections or call-outs and other shocks to the system. This made him an uncomfortable, somewhat disruptive, presence for the staff and his subordinates.[13] Many people remember his formidable intellectual powers, his quickness of mind, his alertness and scepticism, his drive for efficiency and battle-readiness. They also remember his towering presence and commanding but sometimes abrupt manner, but they also remember his deep faith and the undoubted fact that his aggressive exterior concealed a very kind man who could be very forgiving of failure, provided that the same mistake was not repeated.

As well as the demands of this very full life, as GOC, TFH had to manage the relationship with the host nation. This had long passed the stage of occupiers and occupied, but there could be tensions. Where troops were barracked in towns, the pressures of heavy traffic and the behaviour of Thomas Atkins off-duty did not go down well. Herford was a case in point, with the Divisional Headquarters and its signal regiment – plus an armoured reconnaissance regiment, in the town – and a corps signal regiment (the 7th) just outside. Bad-tempered visits from an irate *burgomeister* were all too common. However, around Soest, where the units were garrisoned outside the town and where the shortage of married quarters led to many families taking hirings in German villages, the communities were far more integrated and the relationship harmonious. Matters would be exacerbated further when large-scale exercises caused damage to buildings, fences, fields and stock – all of which had to be paid for. Both TFH and Pat made a great effort to learn German in order to better fulfil their responsibilities in Anglo-German relations – taking lessons from a Jugoslav expatriate with the wonderful name of Herr Fartić –[14] and holding regular dinner parties for senior German officers from flanking formations, as well as prominent civilians in the local administration and business community.

*   *   *

---

* The actual daily rates of pay in 2014, for comparison, are £83.05 for a newly-commissioned Lieutenant and £155.68 for a newly-promoted Major (AFPRB Report for 2014, Cmnd 8828).

TFH arrived at Herford in the immediate aftermath of a divisional field training exercise, *Forefront V*, which meant that he had a period of familiarisation with his command before embarking on any major tactical exercise. His arrival did, however, coincide with a major revision of the General Deployment Plan (or GDP) by the Corps Commander's staff. This was the corps' part in the defence of Europe against a Soviet attack, as part of the Northern Army Group. In essence, the various national corps lined up from north to south in a layer-cake configuration. The British corps was flanked by Dutch and Belgian corps and it is doubtful if these would ever have made it into position before a full-scale Soviet attack developed. The Belgian corps consisted of two divisions and a parachute regiment, of which only one division – the 17th – was stationed in Germany. The Dutch corps,

TFH and Pat on holiday, about 1972.
(Farrar-Hockley family)

although numerically strong and well equipped, had only a single brigade deployed forward. There was, moreover, no operational depth to the defence, for the army group reserve – III (US) Corps – was stationed in continental USA and would need weeks to deploy through the ports of Bremerhaven and Wilhelmshaven.

What the revised GDP stressed was a more mobile, less static, concept of defence. A strong screen force would be deployed forward consisting of armoured reconnaissance regiments supported by anti-tank guided missiles, artillery, armed helicopters and RAF aircraft. This force would identify and make contact with the enemy, reporting back on major thrust lines which would enable the defence to focus on major killing areas in which the Soviet armoured masses could be engaged from blocking positions in the first phase of the main defensive battle; and then counter-attacked in later stages as the Soviet second operational echelon came forward.[15] These were early days, however, and it was not until the Reforms instituted by General Sir Nigel Bagnall – as Corps Commander and then Army Group Commander – in the 1980s that a truly coherent operational plan emerged. In the 1970s, everyone knew that ground forces were there to trade space for time, and create a Soviet target array suitable for the inevitable nuclear strike which was NATO's only hope of survival.

The revision of the corps GDP was briefed to the Corps Commander in November 1971 and then to TFH and his fellow divisional commanders and their senior staff officers on 15 December.[16] What had driven the review was a series of improvements in the capability of the corps through the introduction of new equipments. By July 1972, all armoured regiments had been issued with the new *Chieftain* main battle tank in place of the older *Centurion;* and in addition, each regiment had a troop of *Swingfire* wire-guided, long-range anti-tank missiles mounted in AFV 438 armoured vehicles. All artillery regiments had been issued with Field

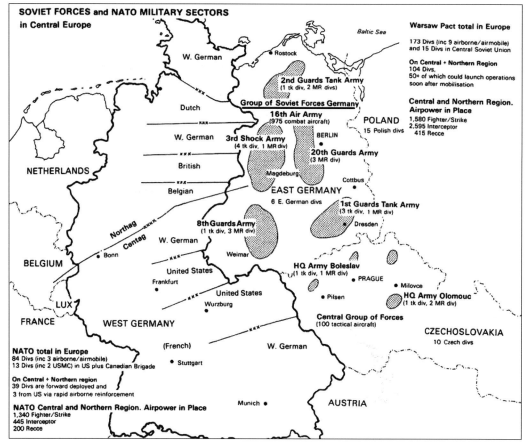

SOVIET FORCES and NATO MILITARY SECTORS in Central Europe

Baltic Sea

W. German

● Rostock

2nd Guards Tank Army
(1 tk div, 2 MR divs)

Dutch

Group of Soviet Forces Germany
16th Air Army
(975 combat aircraft)

POLAND
15 Polish divs

W. German   **3rd Shock Army**
(4 tk div, 1 MR div)

BERLIN
●

20th Guards Army
(3 MR div)

British

Magdeburg ●

Cottbus
●

NETHERLANDS

Belgian

EAST GERMANY

6 E. German divs

1st Guards Tank Army
(3 tk div, 1 MR div)

Northag

● Dresden

Centag

8th Guards Army
(1 tk div, 3 MR div)

BELGIUM   ● Bonn   W. German   Weimar

HQ Army Boleslav
(1 tk div, 1 MR div)

● PRAGUE

● Milovce

United States
Frankfurt
●

HQ Army Olomouc
(1 tk div, 2 MR div)

LUX

United States
Wurzburg
●

● Pilsen

FRANCE   WEST GERMANY

(French)   W. German

Central Group of Forces
(100 tactical aircraft)

CZECHOSLOVAKIA
10 Czech divs

NATO total in Europe
84 Divs (inc 3 airborne/airmobile)
13 Divs (inc 2 USMC) in US plus Canadian Brigade

● Stuttgart

On Central + Northern region
39 Divs are forward deployed and
3 from US via rapid airborne reinforcement

NATO Central and Northern Region. Airpower in Place
1,340 Fighter/Strike
445 Interceptor
200 Recce

Munich ●

AUSTRIA

Warsaw Pact total in Europe
173 Divs (inc 9 airborne/airmobile)
and 15 Divs in Central Soviet Union

On Central + Northern Region
104 Divs,
50+ of which could launch operations
soon after mobilisation

**Central and Northern Region.
Airpower in Place**
1,580 Fighter/Strike
2,595 Interceptor
415 Recce

Soviet Forces and NATO military Sectors in Central Europe.

Artillery Computing Equipment, or FACE, a first-generation automated fire control system.[17] In the following year, the corps-level artillery brigades – 1 and 7 – had also received the USD 501 surveillance drone, the M107 175 mm self-propelled gun and the M 110 eight-inch SP *Howitzer*.[18] The three divisional artillery groups each had two close support regiments of *Abbott* 105 mm SP guns for close support to the brigades, and during 1972 these were enhanced by a general support regiment with two batteries of M 109 155 mm SP guns and a battery of M 110. At the same time, the armoured reconnaissance regiments received the *Scimitar* and *Scorpion* tracked vehicles in place of the wheeled *Saladin*. The army air corps regiments were issued with the SS11 anti-tank missile and its thermal sight for their *Scout* helicopters – giving TFH and his fellow divisional commanders a mobile anti-armour reserve for the first time. During 1973, the aircraft themselves would be replaced by the *Gazelle* reconnaissance heli-copter and the *Lynx* anti-tank helicopter. The Engineers too received a major boost. The M2 rig, the world's first self-propelled bridging vehicle, was brought into the corps-level engineer brigade – making it possible to establish a tactical crossing over a major river in a fraction of the time it had previously taken. The Sappers also received a new medium girder bridge for use on the lines of communication; and the bar mine and mine-layer, which allowed major minefields to be laid mechanically from armoured vehicles rather than laboriously by hand.[19]

For the Royal Signals, improvements were made in the *Bruin* trunk communications system. The infantry, now mounted in the tracked AFV 432 vehicle rather than the *Saracen* or *Humber* one-ton 'Pig', received the new IWS – the first image-intensifying night sight – and the first issues of disrupted pattern camouflage uniforms.[20]

These were significant enhancements, raising the fighting power of TFH's division far above what it would have had when he had last served in a Divisional Headquarters in 1947. However, TFH still lacked some key capabilities which put him no further ahead than would have been the case at the end of the Second World War: the infantry had no proper fighting vehicle – just a battle-taxi – and their arsenal lacked anti-tank weapons, heavy machine guns, grenade launchers and flame throwers. At divisional level, TFH's only reserve was the aviation regiment, for he lacked a third brigade. Nor had he any real visibility over the battlefield, beyond the range of the contact battle. The Corps Commander had stay-behind OP parties for real-time information on a local level, but the drones and reconnaissance aircraft still took film or photographs that had to be brought home and developed – and were thus always out of date. Last, the necessary stocks of ammunition were simply not there. The corps had, at first and second line, no more than four days' supply at intense rates – further evidence, if any were needed, of the trip-wire nature of the defensive plan.

Notwithstanding these shortfalls, TFH set about familiarising his command with its new equipment and training the staffs and units for the potential struggle against the Soviets. He was often on the road or in a helicopter, visiting units in barracks or in the field. In February he held an initial study period on the revised GDP, followed by a Command Post Exercise (CPX) *Keel Haul*, in March. The corps CPX, *Summer Sales*, took place in June with 6 Brigade providing the administration and exercise control. The division's second study period, Exercise *Quadrant 72*, was historically-based and over two days considered campaigns that offered lessons applicable to the conduct of a war on the North German Plain: a defence, followed by a fighting withdrawal and then a counter-attack. These were the Retreat from Mons in 1914, the North African campaigns of 1941 and 1942, and Operation *Market Garden* in 1944.[21] It was attended by the Corps Commander and the Chief of Staff of BAOR, Major-General David House,[*] as well as brigade and regimental commanders and staffs from across the division.

Both TFH and his friend in the 1st Division, Major-General Dwin Bramall, made great efforts to improve relationships and co-ordination with the *Bundeswehr*. There were joint TEWTs and studies in which the experience of the older German officers in Russia was tapped: how to get tanks into action at night; how to do real damage to massed armoured formations; how to be in the right place at the right time; and how to co-ordinate all arms for the most effect.[22]

Collective training was heavily curtailed by the demands of Northern Ireland. TFH was always without a percentage of his command, as infantry battalions in particular went away for their two months' training and four months' deployment, followed by block leave. The aftermath of 'Bloody Sunday' in late January and early February 1972 – and Operation *Motorman* in late July 1972 – required 4,000 reinforcements to raise the army's strength in Northern Ireland to 27 infantry battalions, two regiments of tanks and four armoured engineer vehicles

---

[*]   Later Lieutenant-General Sir David George House GCB KCVO CBE MC (1922-2012). He was GOC Northern Ireland and subsequently held the office of Black Rod.

in order to dismantle and occupy the No-Go areas of Belfast and Londonderry. During the course of the year the corps had to find 14 infantry battalions, five artillery regiments, two regiments and seven squadrons of armour, five transport squadrons as APC drivers, three engineer squadrons and four aviation squadrons to support operations in Northern Ireland.[23]

The constant movement of infantry battalions in particular, in and out of their mechanised role, troubled TFH since their core skills for general war were clearly being eroded. On the other hand, there were advantages to be gained from operational experience in terms of the capabilities of individual officers and soldiers. All units in BAOR were subject to a round of periodic inspections and tests: NATO demanded an operational evaluation and a regular call-out to test readiness, *Active Edge*, which replaced the old alerting exercise, *Quick Train*, in 1973.[24] The national chain of command imposed an annual administrative inspection and a Fitness-for-Role inspection – the format for which was very much the GOC's call. TFH, with his emphasis on the unexpected, warned a number of infantry battalions that he would inspect them with the specific intention of finding out whether or not deployments to Northern Ireland had an adverse effect on their ability to fulfil their NATO role. 2 Queen's was one of these, and it was reported in the Regimental Journal that the inspection was one of the strangest ever seen, for in addition to testing the battalion's ability to move rapidly into the field with all its equipment and take up a tactical position, it included a ceremonial parade – the first the battalion had had for six years – during which TFH personally drilled the battalion. This would have come as no surprise to those who knew him, of course. 2 Queen's clearly did well, for TFH wrote to the CO, Lieutenant-Colonel (later Major-General) Mike Reynolds,* that 'My inspection showed me that a unit of high quality, such as yours, can contend simultaneously with two demanding roles'.[25]

One result of the high level of deployments was that the planned corps exercise, *Springing Tiger*, was cancelled and divisional exercises were curtailed. TFH was, however, determined to press on with whatever collective training he could and in October he ran a divisional exercise, *Forefront VI*, which began with training at battle group level – controlled by the Brigade HQ – and then continued with brigade training controlled by the Divisional HQ and with a parallel observation exercise for the divisional reconnaissance, aviation and artillery regiments.[26]

The tempo continued during 1973. Winter might curtail a full-scale deployment but in January, TFH held a logistic exercise to test the capabilities of his service support units: the divisional transport and supply units, and the field workshops and field ambulances. This ran into the Corps Commander's CPX, *Winter Sales*, in February – during which Carver, the CGS, paid a visit and met the brigade commanders and other officers. Desmond Bowen recalled that this was the only time he ever saw TFH looking at all anxious.[27] After a break, TFH's own CPX to test the Brigade Headquarters, *Keel Haul*, took place in April with the Divisional HQ acting as control; in May the tables were turned when Exercise *Main Brace* tested the Divisional Headquarters, with the brigades as lower controllers. This exercise prepared the headquarters for its part as a player in the Corps Commander's CPX *Summer Sales* in early July.[28]

---

* Later Major-General Michael Frank Reynolds CB (b. 1930). He had served in Korea – where he had been badly wounded – Cyprus and at Suez. He later commanded the ACE Mobile Force (Land).

Formation training was again curtailed that summer – this time by the deployment of six out of TFH's eight armoured battle groups to Canada on Exercise *Medicine Man*. However, in September, 6 Brigade took part in a two-week tripartite exercise – *Sealed Knot* – with the Germans and Belgians; followed immediately by a 7th German *Panzergrenadier* Division exercise, *Big Ben*, involving part of 20 Brigade. After only a week to draw breath, both brigades were again in the field for TFH's divisional exercise, *Forefront North*, in the first fortnight of October. This coincided with the annual *Reforger* exercise, which tested the deployment of US reinforcing units from continental USA to Germany and was held in heavily wooded country around Bergen-Hone.[29] The exercise was the culmination of TFH's theme while in command: that a division had to be trained, ready, and tactically proficient in rapidly adopting – and holding – a defensive position, repelling a series of heavy attacks and then switching rapidly to the counterattack.

The demands of life in BAOR did not stop TFH from continuing his parallel career as a writer (quite the reverse) and Pat continued to be his chief collaborator and researcher – distracted only when they became grandparents for the second time, with the birth of Dair and Vicki's daughter, Charlotte, on 28 September 1973. Having finished his administrative tasks or reports when home from field training exercises, he was always very disciplined about setting aside time to read and write.[30] The long drives to visit or inspect units provided time that he used to the full – reading source material, or dictating, or correcting drafts. In 1972, *Arnhem: parachutisten vallen uit de hemel* was published by Standaard in Antwerp. This was very largely a Dutch version of his earlier book on Operation *Market Garden*. The following year he published his biography of the German parachute commander, Kurt Student.[31] Desmond Bowen, who spoke German fluently and could act as interpreter,

A *Chieftain* tank from 6 Brigade on Exercise *Forefront North*. (Author's collection)

AFV 432 vehicles from 6 Brigade on Exercise *Forefront North*. (Author's collection)

Infantry from 6 Brigade on Exercise *Forefront North*. (Author's collection)

recalled TFH visiting and interviewing Student at length – discussing in particular how the British and Germans had drawn completely opposing lessons from the invasion of Crete: the Germans deciding to abandon air assault, while the British – who had been on the receiving end – embraced it.[32]

However, by the early 1970s, TFH's historical studies had begun to shape his approach to the way he exercised command and conducted himself professionally. In *The Death of an Army*, he had shown that a small force highly motivated, well led and trained could stop a numerically superior enemy but in so doing, offer itself up for destruction. Would BAOR, to which he had come as a stranger, succeed in stopping a Soviet attack while avoiding destruction? He had his doubts.[33] These were reinforced by a survivability study in which TFH took part, led by the Defence Operational Analysis Establishment. This study identified the potential of the Warsaw Pact's firepower to destroy headquarters and other installations using conventional, nuclear or chemical weapons. It recommended a range of responses and improvements: to camouflage, concealment and movement; to deployment procedures; to ground, air and NBC defence; to the physical protection of vehicles; to reductions in the infra-red signature, radio traffic and noise from headquarters; and finally to the size and siting of command installations.[34]

Building on his studies while in command of the division, TFH wrote later about how a land battle might develop in the Central Region:

> ... the Russian forces travel forward in column, tanks behind one another, under the protection of strong air defences. NATO air and ground observation units, combining with electronic intelligence, warn that a Soviet division is approaching an area defended by one or two battle groups, roughly, nine battalions attacking two ... Slowed by the fire of the defence, the enemy vehicles, tanks and infantry in armoured carriers, will be among the NATO forces in, say 20 minutes from [the] first engagement.
>
> ... Assume that the defence had chosen its ground cunningly, uses its weapons skilfully and enjoys continuous support from its own artillery and intermittently from the air to the point it has reduced the attack advantage to about two-to-one. It then engages in a close-quarters battle ... It is a diminished defence that has to deal with the next attack, and the next, and the next. Though the enemy are not supermen, are delayed by the problems of obtaining information as to losses and shifting defence locations prior to mounting the next attack, their weight on the ground and in the air and the depth of their resources will day by day break the limited resources of those who oppose them.[5]

A decade after his time in command of the 4th Division, TFH felt that NATO's continued investment in technological advances, which maintained and extended a considerable superiority in equipment capability, modified this scenario considerably. However, in the mid-1970s, nuclear release was still the only eventual recourse to avoid defeat.

TFH explored these ideas in the two biographies which were the product of these years. The first had been his biography of Student, later translated into German in 1983. The second was his best book on the Great War, *Goughie. The Life of General Sir Hubert Gough*, published in 1975 by Hart-Davis MacGibbon. This book is a sustained defence of the Fifth Army Commander, attacked by overwhelming German forces on the opening days of the *Kaiserschlacht* in April

A group of soldiers from the 4th Division on a field training exercise in 1974. (Author's collection)

TFH being ceremonially driven out of the barracks in Herford at the end of his tour of command (Farrar-Hockley family)

1918. TFH argued that Gough had done well to hold a reasonably coherent line – even though driven back – and had been unjustly made the scapegoat for the failures of others, which had produced the conditions that allowed the German attack to penetrate as far as it did.[36]

Forefront North was TFH's last act in command of the 4th Division. On 10 October 1973, his two years having passed (so it seemed, in a flash), he handed over his command to Major-General Michael Gow[37] and returned to the Ministry of Defence in London once more for a new appointment as Director, Combat Development (Army).

'A marriage between technology and military thought'
Director Combat Development and GOC South-East District February 1974-July 1979

TFH took up his new post on 2 February 1974 after a period of leave;[1] the family had moved back to Pye Barn and TFH commuted by car to London most days – which was then still possible without undue delay – driven by Ted Olive. Combat Development no longer exists as a Directorate of the Ministry of Defence – having been subsumed first by the joint Assistant Chief of Defence Staff (Concepts) and later by ACDS (Operational Requirements). In TFH's time, the role of the Directorate, which had been formed in 1967 under a Brigadier, was laid down as 'to keep military thought abreast of, or if possible in front of, technology, so that when new techniques become available we have a considered view of how to use them'.

This was expressed in the *Army Combat Development Guide* –[2] the key document that not only expressed the tasks of the Directorate, but also provided the essential framework for the Operational Analysis Establishment, the Arms and Service Schools, the Staff and Defence Colleges, the Royal Military College of Science and the equipment procurement departments of the three services. The various Defence Research Establishments also worked closely with the Directorate. TFH had a detailed interest in the various war-games run at Fort Halsted and, in particular, how it modelled the passage of orders and information between headquarters and units. He found that Fort Halsted worked on the assumption that information was always passed immediately and with 100 percent certainty. When he pointed out that this was not the case, it was accepted and, as a result, Halsted modified their games to include elements of variable delay and uncertainty.[3] He was also interested in research into sleep deprivation conducted at DOAE West Byfleet – probably as a result of his experiences in Korea.

These establishments received their funding from elsewhere and answered to other masters. TFH held no control over them, even though they directly affected his work, or were affected by it. The department therefore had to tread a difficult line: trying to prophesy what future warfare, both conventional and insurgent, might look like in order to drive the component elements of capability – doctrine, manpower and structures, training, equipment procurement, logistics and command and control – in the same direction. As Director Combat Development, TFH was responsible for the formation of tactical concepts up to 15 years ahead and for recommending how equipment should evolve to meet these tactical concepts (or vice-versa); the development of tactical doctrine based on current organisations and equipments; the dissemination of doctrine throughout the army and to the other services and allies where appropriate; and representing the army on inter-service equipment matters. He also sat on a plethora of other boards and committees: operational requirements, army logistics, equipment procurement, military priorities, among others – making one line of his job description ring rather hollow that, 'to be effective, forward thinking must be carried out by a Director who is free from other day-to-day responsibilities'.[4]

The Directorate came under the authority of the Vice-Chief of the General Staff within the Army Department of the Ministry of Defence – initially Lieutenant-General Sir David Fraser, from whom TFH had taken over the command of the 4th Division – and then from 1975, Sir William Scotter.* It was small: beneath TFH there were two Colonels, J.R.C. Pitcairn of the Royal Artillery and P.D. (Paddy) Blyth of the Royal Anglians; and two Lieutenant-Colonels: G.W. Preston-Jones of the Royal Engineers and J.P. (John) Cross of the Royal Artillery.[5] There were six grade 2 staff officers, two warrant officers, four military clerks and seven civilians – a total of 26 personnel.[6] The two Colonels headed a division of the Directorate: Division 1, which was responsible for co-ordination, quadripartite and bilateral talks, briefs, and the Army Combat Development Committee, which was headed by a Major, John Stevens of the Royal Signals; Division 2 looked after tactical concepts; and Division 3 looked after tactical doctrine for operations in Europe and also outside the NATO area. Among the civilians was Linda Wood, a typist. Shortly after TFH's arrival, his secretary left (giving very little notice) and TFH asked Linda to take on the secretarial role, which with some trepidation, she did – thus beginning a relationship that was to last the rest of TFH's life. John Stevens also acted as MA and he recalled that:

I had arrived in the Directorate during the summer holiday season when TFH was on leave … I was told that our mission was to familiarise ourselves with emerging technologies of our individual specialisations and produce papers giving our predictions of future military developments and capabilities up to 20 years ahead – well beyond the current developments being managed by OR branches.

I was somewhat apprehensive of the first meeting with my new boss – I had read *The Edge of the Sword* many years before and been deeply impressed by his bravery and resilience. I had heard of his fearless reputation over the years since and rather wondered how we would get on. On meeting him my first impression was that he was a very good listener and appeared much less fearsome than his reputation suggested. He was one of the few senior officers I met who, when he talked to you, gave you his full attention, listened and responded to your conversation.[7]

It was undoubtedly TFH's combination of operational experience, intellect and original thinking that had brought him to this post,[8] but this did not mean that he would be listened to: established structures are very conservative and dislike deviation from the accepted norm.

---

*   Later General Sir William Norman Roy Scotter KCB OBE MC (1922-1981). He had served with the Gurkhas during the Second World War and then transferred into the British Army after Indian Independence. He was subsequently C-in-C BAOR.

Unsurprisingly, his perspective on the job of the Directorate was chiefly influenced by his own extensive experience of operations. However, his historical researches were also a factor. Major – later Major-General – Rob McAfee* recalled that:

> He was unusual among senior officers of that era, in that he allowed his reputation to speak for him. Many of his BAOR contemporaries fought their way up the pole by inventing 'new' concepts, developing personality cults and affecting familiarity with German politics. TFH was refreshingly straightforward and devoid of 'side' and preferment – he was a soldier through and through.[9]

This was, however, a time when army policy on training and education had shifted away from historically-based study – probably a reaction to the fixation on studying the Second World War that had lingered at Staff Colleges for decades. Instead, the focus shifted to training (rather than educating) officers, to concentrating on technical skills and the role of emerging technologies. Given the imbalance of conventional forces in the European Central Region, this is perhaps understandable, however misguided. In particular, training focused on the use of tactical – as well as strategic – nuclear weapons, their delivery means, and how these could be used in combination with conventional forces. Moreover, the GDP that TFH had trained his division to fulfil in Germany had become a substitute for doctrine – or indeed any flexibility of thought in conventional tactical matters. What need of doctrine, many said, when we have a GDP?

In State-on-State war, TFH certainly accepted and supported the concept of stable deterrence against the Warsaw Pact. His time in Germany had also convinced him that only harnessing technology would overcome the Soviet threat if deterrence failed, without recourse to the catastrophe of a nuclear war. TFH saw war as first and foremost a human activity, from which the man on the ground could never be excluded, but 'he ploughed a lonely furrow, for whatever the preferences of individuals, army policy generally shifted away from historically based study … Many of its premier staff and training courses stressed technical proficiency and technological solutions'.[10] TFH's view, completely contrary to this, is summed up in the *Combat Development Guide*: 'A tactical concept is a marriage of technology and military thought – equipment and ideas; as the two evolve, so concepts change'.[11]

Under TFH, the Directorate sought to outline the concept of British Army operations worldwide beyond the next decade, and thereby guide the development of doctrine and equipment. This work included general war in Europe, counter-insurgency and intervention. The army's primary commitment was to NATO in Europe, but it had to be balanced against the continuing requirements for overseas garrisons and counter-insurgency – especially in Northern Ireland – as well as the possibility of operations outside Europe, short of general war, such as the campaign in Borneo. Technological possibilities were already emerging: guided weapons – both anti-armour and anti-air; surveillance and target acquisition; automatic data processing; encrypted speech transmission to speed up tempo and eliminate the need for

---

*   Major-General Robert W.M. McAfee was commissioned into the RTR and was Brigade Major 6 Field Force 1977-1979. He commanded 6 Armoured Brigade 1988-1990 and was the last COS of I (BR) Corps. He commanded NATO's Multinational Division (Airmobile) 1995-1998.

cumbersome codes like *Slidex* and *Griddle*; lasers; cluster munitions; a vehicle charging system for radio batteries which would save time and manpower; hovercraft; biological and chemical agents and protection against them; and greater strategic, operational and tactical mobility.[12]

The mechanism for disseminating concepts and receiving new ideas was the Army Combat Development Committee. This was chaired by the VCGS with TFH as his deputy and it included representatives from across the War Office, most major arms and services, and other services and allies as required.* Under this committee, TFH was responsible for co-ordinating and instructing a series of sub-committees and working groups. Of these, the study of counter-revolutionary warfare and counter-insurgency post-1975 was probably the most pressing. This group was tasked with looking at the lessons of Northern Ireland and of potential new insurgent techniques, new equipments, the effectiveness of existing techniques and how these could be improved. This was a subject close to TFH's heart from his time as CLF Northern Ireland and although the group was led by the Director of Infantry, TFH maintained a close interest. It is perhaps surprising therefore that its findings were conservative to the point of being unimaginative: the control of urban and rural road movement by road blocks, observation posts, vehicle check points and snap VCPs was thought to be adequate; the protection of key and vulnerable points, and convoys, was weak; revised procedures were needed for searches and for identifying wanted men; and training was needed in evidence handling so that convictions could be obtained in the aftermath of incidents or searches. Better selection and training was also identified as a need for both infantry search teams and Royal Engineer teams – the latter carrying out high-risk clearance and search operations. New drills and weapons for crowd control were identified to replace the old methods which still reflected late-Colonial practice.[13] There was nothing here about winning over or protecting the civilian population; about police-military co-operation; about terrorist recognition; or about the control of incidents. All this came later.

Another area of interest was air mobility. One achievement of which TFH was always very proud was his championship of the *Chinook* helicopter, for he was, in large part, responsible for the purchase and introduction into service of this remarkable aircraft. He was also keenly interested in the development of anti-armour technologies – partly no doubt as a result of his command of 4th Armoured Division and his study of the Soviet threat – but also, perhaps, because he had long ago been Anti-tank Platoon Commander in 6th (RW) Para and remembered how ill-equipped infantry battalions were in the face of German armour. Things had scarcely improved: the 84 mm *Carl Gustav* and the American 66 mm light anti-tank weapon *were* little more use than a *PIAT*. The 120 mm *WOMBAT*, although effective, had a massive signature and was unlikely to survive long in the face of Soviet tanks and artillery. He therefore encouraged studies into anti-tank guided weapons and into the development of composite, or *Chobham*, armour for tanks. This latter technology, which was highly advanced and effective, was later handed over by the government free of charge to the Americans.

---

*   The membership was laid down as: Headquarters BAOR; FARELF; the Directorate of Land / Air Warfare; the Directors of Infantry, the Royal Armoured Corps and the Royal Artillery; the Engineer and Signals Officers-in-Chief; the Staff College and the Royal Military College of Science; within MOD Military Operations (1), Operational Requirement, Army Staff Duties (1), the Master-General of the Ordnance's staff, Defence Secretariat (6), Defence Intelligence (16), ADOSR, and Q (Doctrine and Training). The Defence Liaison Staffs of the United States, Canada and Australia were also invited on occasions (T.N.A. WO 32/21264).

Electronic warfare was also high on the agenda and TFH had early on told John Stevens to begin work on a paper. The early draft included reference to the ranges of VHF and UHF radios and, among other issues, TFH homed in on these – wanting to know what these were. It had to be explained to him that range was affected by many factors including weather, terrain, siting, power and frequency. 'I was impressed,' said John Stevens, 'by what a good listener he was and how quickly he appreciated the issues once they were explained. He was able to analyse papers very rapidly and identify soft spots or the lack of information.'[14]

EW was, at that time, shrouded in secrecy and dominated by the Royal Signals. TFH felt that once the relative capabilities of NATO and the Soviets were identified and the huge mismatch revealed, the army generally needed to be far more aware of the threat and the counter-measures. He was determined therefore that DMO would be the responsible Directorate for many aspects of EW as a General Staff matter – not one to left to specialists. John Stevens recalled that:

> Having outlined the investment in systems on the other side, and our own miniscule resources, we were invited by the US to visit their exercise area in the SE of the zone to see deployed systems being used there. We travelled over and spent a couple of days looking at the equipment deployed quite close to the [likely] Forward Edge of the Battle Area, and were very impressed. . . The bottom line we concluded was that a credible capability could be created, but it required properly trained manpower and the development of new equipment at a time when both were in very short supply. It required more disclosure to the rest of the army of what it was all about, and convincing the General Staff that it really did matter and that we needed the capability ourselves if we were not going to be involved in future operations lacking a vital part of the intelligence picture.[15]

As a result, TFH directed a phased plan to the future which included the formation of an EW regiment within the Royal Signals – this at a time when there were, as usual, reductions being made in army manpower. An EW squadron from Blandford and two static squadrons under GCHQ were therefore formed into 14 Signal Regiment; not only was this achieved remarkably quickly, but also it was unusual for DCD to focus on something so current. The army therefore has TFH to thank for the retention and development of this capability.

DCD (A) was also the sponsor of defence seminars and studies involving the academic world; having done a Defence Fellowship helped here. One particularly important example, on Contemporary European Defence Problems, took place at All Souls, Oxford in April 1975 under the chairmanship of Professor Michael Howard. As well as TFH, the military participants included the Director of Defence Policy in the MOD, Air Commodore D.C.A. Lloyd; the Deputy Chief of Defence Staff (Intelligence), Air Marshal Sir Richard Wakeford; and Lieutenant-General Sir James Wilson, GOC South-East District. Key academic contributors included Professor Laurie Freedman, Michael Edmonds and John Garnett. There were also delegations from Germany, France, Italy, and the FCO;[16] a similar seminar, on British Defence Policy, took place at Southampton University the following yar.

On 9 February 1974, TFH was invited to join the Regimental Council of the Gloucestershire Regiment by Brigadier Tony Arengo-Jones, who was then Colonel of the regiment. Doubtless the regiment had an eye on him – as a former Gloster and a General – with a view to him

TFH visiting Romania while DCD (A) with Secretary of State for Defence Roy Mason. TFH is on the extreme right of the picture. (Farrar-Hockley family)

becoming Colonel at some future date, for he had remained in close contact with the many friends from his Korea days for whom he had huge affection and respect. These included Denis Harding and of course Joe Carne, whom he always called 'Colonel', and for whom TFH's car, driver, house and indeed he himself were always available. This was followed almost immediately by his appointment, in June 1974, as Colonel Commandant of The Prince of Wales's Division – the administrative grouping of the nine regiments of Wales, Mercia and Wessex – that under a Brigadier and a small staff, ran recruit training; officer selection; officer and NCO postings at regimental duty; and NCO promotions in both Regular and Territorial battalions.* This was largely a figurehead role, although Officer Selection Boards were held three times a year, but with the appointment to the Regimental Council, it put TFH back in touch with the two regiments in which he had served before transferring to the Paras: the Royal Welch Fusiliers and the Glosters.[17]

Goughie was published in 1975 and TFH had a good deal to do with correcting proofs and indexing the book. The reviews were uniformly favourable, as were the many letters he received. Two in particular must have meant a great deal: Peter Young summed the book up in

---

*   At this point the division consisted of 1st Devon and Dorsets, 1st Cheshires, 1st and 3rd (V) RWF, 1st, 3rd (V) and 4th (V) RRW, 1st Glosters, 1st Worcesters and Foresters, 1st Royal Hampshires, 1st Duke of Edinburgh's Royal Regiment (Berks and Wilts), 1st Staffords, 1st and 2nd Wessex Volunteers, and 1st, 2nd and 3rd Mercian Volunteers. The Divisional Headquarters was at Litchfield and its two training depots were at Litchfield and Crickhowell in South Wales.

a single word: 'Superb!' Frank Kitson, writing on 8 July 1975, said that 'I think it will establish you as one of the foremost biographers of the age'.[18]

However, TFH had little time for beginning major new writing projects in these years, although he did produce an Adelphi Paper on the Arab-Israeli War of 1973 co-written with Dr Elizabeth Monroe* – a noted Middle East historian who had written *Britain's Moment in the Middle East, 1914 – 1956* and who had established the Middle East Study Centre in St Anthony's College, Oxford. This followed the theme of a small, highly trained force facing a numerically far superior enemy. It concluded that Israeli intelligence was patchy at best regarding the deployment of new Soviet weapons to Egypt, which the Soviets wished to evaluate in combat, even if that risked their capture and exploitation by Western intelligence agencies. Many of these systems – the T62 and 64 tanks, the SA6, SA7 and ZSU 23-4 anti-aircraft systems and the *Sagger* wire-guided anti-tank missile – achieved technological surprise but the training and efficiency of the Israeli soldiers (especially in armoured units) remained more than a match for the Arabs. That said, the Israelis shed a great deal, if not all, of their complacency; reintroduced more formal discipline which had been missing ever since the days of the *Hagganah*, and re-armed. Their final conclusion noted 'a recognition at last that war is unlikely to make things better for either side, and would most likely make them worse'.[19]

TFH also produced a short historical book, *Infantry Tactics 1939 – 1945*.[20] He concluded the introduction to this book with a statement that summed up his view of the primacy of the human factor in war; the result of 30 years of field command on operations: 'The greater the risk of injury or death, the greater the need for leadership'. Soldiers did not follow their commanders simply because they had been ordered to do so: 'They obey only because they have confidence in the judgement and courage of the leader to carry them through the crisis'.[21]

Even though he produced less major published work than in previous years, TFH was in great demand as a speaker. In May 1973, for example, he spoke at the Berlin Brigade annual study period. In September 1973 he presented a paper on the utility of military force for the maintenance of internal order in modern societies at the annual conference of the IISS – a subject that caused fluttering in the MOD's dovecotes: DPR Army set up a meeting to discuss responses to potentially awkward questions in order to prepare TFH with the right lines to take.[22] Seldom, if ever, did TFH write a script or keep notes for these talks – and posterity has, therefore, no record of them. John Stevens, acting as MA, often travelled with him to look after the technical aspects, having previously prepared a pack of 35 mm slides at TFH's direction. These slides were the basis of the talk and he would use them as prompts, speaking forcefully and succinctly for as long as he was scheduled and then taking a range of questions which he always answered carefully.[23] Travel plans had, however, to be treated with care as TFH was aware of the threat from the IRA against any senior officer who had served in Northern Ireland: bookings for trains, aircraft, hotels and so on were always made in the name of 'Mr Brown'.

In 1975, he made his first visit to Korea since 1953 when he was invited to attend the Republic of Korea Armed Forces Day on 1 October. In all, he spent five days in the country

---

* Elizabeth Monroe (1905-1986). After serving on the staffs of the League of Nations and Chatham House, she obtained a Rockefeller Travelling Fellowship in 1937 for study in the Mediterranean area. After that, she headed the British Government's Middle East Information Division during the Second World War; she was the Middle East Correspondent for *The Economist* for 15 years before settling down at St Antony's College.

Visiting Korea for Armed Forces Day, November 1975. (Farrar-Hockley family)

with Dair acting as Honorary ADC. As well as visiting the Armed Forces Headquarters, the UN Cemetery in Seoul, the Ministry of National Defence, the National War Cemetery, and the British Memorial he was also invited to call on President Chung Hee. In South Korea, the government and people continued to be very much aware of the sacrifices made by the Allied nations during the Korean War: TFH was, therefore, a highly honoured guest.

In an interview with *Soldier* Magazine, TFH acknowledged that he could not escape tours of duty in the MOD, but insisted that he had 'thoroughly enjoyed his job as Director of Combat Development (Army)' which he held for three years. 'I always prefer doing duty with troops but that's not to say I pined at my desk in the MOD. On the contrary, I found it a very interesting and rewarding experience'.[24] One suspects, however, that after three years in London he was glad to escape. This he did in May 1977 when he was appointed to command South-East District, in the rank of Lieutenant-General,[25] in succession to Sir James Wilson.* It must have been a tremendous relief, for some of those close to him said that he had come to the conclusion that this post was to be the pinnacle, and end, of his career – and after the assassination of Airey Neave he had seriously considered resignation and going into politics.[26] At that date it was also automatic that a Lieutenant-General would receive a knighthood in recognition of at least 30 years' of service to his country; TFH was made a Knight Commander of the Most Honourable Order of the Bath (Military Division) in the Queen's Birthday Honours list, 1977.

---

*   *Lieutenant-General Sir (Alexander) James Wilson KBE MC (1921-2004) retired from the post. He had served during the Second World War and had, for a time, been Private Secretary to the C-in-C of the new Pakistani Army.

* * *

The Farrar-Hockleys moved back to Aldershot once again – taking up residence in Wellesley House, behind the garrison church and close to the enormous equestrian statue of the Duke of Wellington (which gave the house its name) – while TFH joined his new headquarters in Knollys Road, opposite the depot of the Parachute Regiment, where in the GOC's office was another reminder of the great Duke: his desk. Pat clearly missed Pye Barn, but she was too good a General's wife – and too good a regimental wife – to complain; at least in Aldershot there were many regimental families whom she knew, and others that needed her help. In this respect, the Guild of St Helena was especially important to her. The objectives of this body were to promote the Christian faith among the members and ex-members of the Armed Forces and their families, and among the civilians attached to those services and their families; and to relieve in cases of need the wives, widows and dependants of members and ex-members or the Armed Services, and of civilians attached to those services.[27] Although generally a reserved person devoted to her role and to her husband, Pat could be very forceful at times and was one of the few people who could put TFH in his place, or tell him that he was *not* going to do something. From time to time she would formally inspect Wellesley House, usually before some major visit. As Captain Mike Motum, who later joined TFH as his ADC, recalled: 'More than once I saw her rubbing her finger on top of a cupboard, checking for dust in a manner from which any Sergeant Major could learn: "*Dust, Sgt Olive, dust!*" I can hear her now!'[28]

Hilary was now at Henlow, having been selected for RAF officer training for the administrative branch, and in due course he went to Cranwell. From Henlow he was a frequent weekend visitor to both Aldershot and Pye Barn. After one weekend pass, TFH offered him a lift back to Henlow in a *Gazelle* helicopter which landed – this time with prior clearance from the Parish Council – at Moulsford, collected the two and then decanted Hilary at Henlow. The arrival of a 3-star officer had, of course, occasioned the call-out of the duty officer to the HLS. Hilary recalled his dismay at seeing that this officer was his own Flight Commander – 'who was not best pleased when Officer Cadet Farrar-Hockley, not Lieutenant-General Farrar-Hockley, got out of the aircraft. I was made to pay for that ride.'[29]

Nearby, too, was TFH's nephew, John – son of his half-brother Ted – who was in training at the RAMC Centre, Mytchett.

Aldershot had been a Military Command from 1944 to 1967, when it disappeared in the reorganisation that led to the centralisation of all the commands in Headquarters Land Command, at Wilton. Michael Carver had been the last GOC-in-C of Southern Command and thoroughly approved of the removal of this level of command, which would increase:

> the standing and local value of the District Commanders … All that Command Headquarters, many of the routine jobs in which were held by retired officers, appeared to do was to act as an unnecessary buffer between District Headquarters and the Ministry of Defence – disagreeing with one or the other just for the sake of expressing a separate opinion.[30]

The headquarters staff was relatively small and, being non-deployable, contained a good percentage of retired officers and civilians as well as serving officers and soldiers. TFH's Chief of Staff was Colonel Bryan Webster, whom he had known as CO 1 RRF in Northern Ireland,

The headquarters staff, South-East District, 1978. On TFH's right are Brian Webster and Tim Smyth-Osbourne. His PA, Nan Smith, is in the front row on the extreme right. Mike Motum is in the rear rank second from the right. (Mike Motum)

and his AQ & QMG – also known as the Colonel Administration – was Colonel E.T. (Tim) Smyth-Osbourne of the Coldstream Guards. He also had the advantage, now that he was back in a command appointment, of being given an ADC, Captain D.H. ((David) Keenan,* of the Parachute Regiment. Wilson had dispensed with his Fusilier ADC six weeks before the hand-over and so TFH arranged for Keenan to cover the gap and learn the job before he himself arrived (important because there was no Military Assistant; only a civilian Private Secretary –the fiercely protective Mrs Nan Smith) and although the PS knew a very great deal and provided wonderful continuity, the ADC still had to do much more than was usually the case.[31] Finally, Sergeant Arthur Sullivan from the Royal Corps of Transport joined the staff as TFH's driver.

South-East District differed from all the other districts – except Scotland – in that it was not commanded by a Major-General, but by a Lieutenant-General. This reflected the size and importance of the command. It covered the whole of the Home Counties: Kent, most of Surrey, East and West Sussex, Hampshire and the Isle of Wight, Berkshire, Buckinghamshire and Oxfordshire. Within TFH's span of command were major conurbations containing millions of people, from the Medway towns to Southampton and Portsmouth; Reading, Basingstoke and Oxford; the southern shore of the important seaway of the Thames Estuary, the Solent and

---

* Later Brigadier David Herbert Keenan OBE. He served in the Falklands War and commanded 7/10 UDR in Northern Ireland. He was Commander BMATT Zimbabwe 1994-1996 and did the same job, as well as being Defence Attaché, in South Africa.

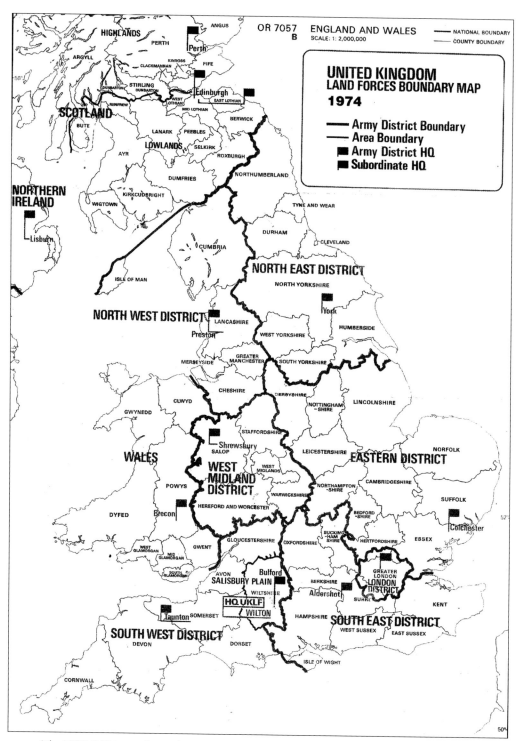

The UKLF District boundaries as established in 1974 [UKLF official publication].

the English Channel with the ports of Tilbury, Dover, Folkestone, Ramsgate, Southampton and the great naval bases of Portsmouth and Gosport; the airports of Gatwick, Lasham and Southampton, and the RAF stations of Brize Norton, Abingdon, Manston, Farnborough, Waltham and Odiham, and the US airbase at Greenham Common, near Newbury; the Atomic Research Establishment at Aldermaston; along with the extensive infrastructure of roads, motorways and railways that connected them. As well as the naval and air stations, TFH himself exercised command over a number of large garrisons: Aldershot of course, but also Dover / Shorncliffe, Chatham, Deal, Thatcham and Bordon. Among these were not only field units, but major training establishments like the RMA Sandhurst, and the Staff College at Camberley; the Northern Ireland Training and Advisory Team, with its ranges and training areas at Lydd and Hythe; the Guards Depot at Pirbright; the Rifle Depot at Winchester; the Schools of Electrical and Mechanical Engineering at Bordon and Aborfield; the Royal Engineers' Schools at Chatham and Minley; the Parachute Depot, RCT Training Regiment and the Army School of Catering in Aldershot; the RAMC Training Centre at Mytchett; and The Duke of York's Royal Military School at Dover. It was arguably the greatest concentration of military personnel anywhere in Europe west of the Iron Curtain. Not only did this vast area have to be secured in the event of a major war on the continent, but it was also the highway through which would pass the majority of the reinforcements of units, formations and materiel for the British Army of the Rhine. It was, therefore, vital ground. An extra *frisson* was added by the growing requirement to co-operate with, and support, the various civil police forces to defeat or deter the threat of IRA terrorism on the British mainland. In February 1972, an Official IRA car bomb had exploded outside 16 Parachute Brigade's Officers' Mess – ironically killing the Catholic Chaplain, Gerry Weston, five female staff and a male gardener; and injuring 15 others.[32]

TFH had relatively few Regular troops under his direct operational command, as most of the units and establishments served other masters, and his responsibilities were chiefly administrative. In the case of the other services, his function was that of co-ordination although for home defence matters, he was *primus inter pares*. His two resident Regular brigades were first, 2 Infantry Brigade – commanded by Brigadier Maurice Atherton and based at Shorncliffe – with a home defence role. Atherton was also the Deputy Constable of Dover Castle and of the Cinque Ports, and TFH often visited him at his residence in the castle, going on ghost walks and attending parties. There was, however, no more 16 Parachute Brigade, for it had been disbanded at the end of March 1977 just before TFH had taken over command. In its place was TFH's second brigade-sized formation, 6 Field Force under Brigadier Mike Gray,[*] based in Aldershot and designated as the UK Mobile Force. It was the shadowy remnant of 16 Parachute Brigade. TFH had been aware that the reduction of the parachute capability at brigade level was imminent since the Defence Review of 1975,[33] which cut £600 million from defence over three years. This was an event that evoked huge sadness, but also a strong feeling that the loss of a large chunk of the army's ability to intervene outside the NATO area was a grave mistake. At the same time, the army had been carrying out a series of trials known

---

[*]   Later Lieutenant-General Sir Michael Stuart Gray KCB OBE (1932-2011). Gray had seen service in Malaya, Cyprus, Suez, Jordan, Aden and Northern Ireland and was well know to TFH. He was himself later GOC South East District.

The IRA bomb attack on the Officers' Mess in Aldershot. (Parachute Regimental Museum)

as *Wide Horizon* – the aim of which was to use advances in communications and information technology to cut out the brigade level of command. In practice, it was soon found that this level of command was essential and brigades came back by stealth, under the guise of Task Forces in Germany, and Field Forces elsewhere. A single battalion group remained in the parachute role within 6 Field Force for contingency operations, known as the Parachute Contingency Force, with another battalion held on a next-for-duty basis – carrying out very limited jump training. These two battalions and some supporting arms remained in Aldershot, with a Gurkha battalion and a light-role infantry battalion of the line. The third parachute battalion joined 5 Field Force – a light infantry formation based at Münster in Germany with the unglamorous task of protecting nuclear missile and artillery units there. The brigade's former supporting arms and services units which joined 6 Field Force retained only sub-units in the parachute role.[34]

This was particularly galling for TFH, not only because he had commanded the brigade and had looked forward to seeing more of the officers and men as their District Commander, but also because he was, in that same year, appointed Colonel Commandant of the Parachute Regiment in succession to 'Roly' Gibbs – the greatest accolade that any regiment can bestow on one of its senior officers.[35] The following year, TFH received the additional, and very rare, honour of becoming Colonel of another of his regiments – the Glosters – whose Royal Colonel-in-Chief was the Duke of Gloucester. Not long before, between 1968 and 1970, the Glosters had been scheduled for amalgamation with the Royal Hampshires, but had been reprieved by Edward Heath's Conservative Government. This had been greeted with great relief, but to raise the strength of the regiment from the company of 120 men to which it had been reduced prior to the proposed amalgamation, back up to 650, was a tall order. For many years, the Glosters received large numbers of surplus recruits from elsewhere in the Prince of Wales's Division – in particular the Royal Welch Fusiliers and the Royal Regiment of Wales.

Although not in any sense in the chain of command, and being in consequence so useful as a father-figure to the commanding officers (as TFH himself knew from his time in command of 3 Para), the Colonel of a regiment had a major say in the selection of young officers for commissions; the commissioning of warrant officers; and the functions of the regiment's institutions, its associations and their events: the Regimental Headquarters, the museums, chapels and memorials. He would also be consulted on the appointment of commanding officers and company commanders, but only after the relevant selection boards had conducted the appropriate selection procedures. Much of the business of the Colonel was therefore wrapped up with morale and the moral component of fighting power – and without the focus of 16 Brigade and its role for the officers and men, these had taken a hard knock. TFH took his responsibilities as Colonel Commandant and Colonel of

TFH with the Duke of Gloucester, Colonel-in-Chief of the Gloucestershire Regiment. (Farrar-Hockley family)

both regiments with great seriousness and would never delegate his duties to the Divisional Brigadier (Lennox Napier in The Prince of Wales's Division) or the Regimental Colonel (Jim Burke in the Parachute Regiment) unless it was absolutely unavoidable.

TFH visited every Regular and TA battalion and the depots of his regiments once a year without fail. As Colonel Commandant of the Parachute Regiment, TFH personally sponsored a reunion for his old comrades in 2 Independent Parachute Brigade, which was run by the CO of the Para Depot, Lieutenant-Colonel Graham Farrell. The reunion was timed for a period in which the Junior Parachute Company would be on leave so that their accommodation could be used – and in addition to demonstrations by the battalions, there was a memorable dinner (with much singing) on the Saturday and a church service on the Sunday morning followed by lunch.[36] He visited the Glosters in Ballykelly, where they were undertaking a resident tour of two years in Northern Ireland – having served repeated tours in the Province since 1969 and narrowly missing TFH's tenure as CLF when they deployed to Belfast in December 1971.

One of TFH's few hates was profanity and he often said that he could think of no situation when swearing at or in front of soldiers was permissible. While visiting 1 Glosters in Münster and being taken round by the CO, Lieutenant-Colonel (later General Sir) John Waters,* he

---

*   Sir Charles John Waters GCB CBE (b. 1935) was Commander 3 Infantry Brigade in Northern Ireland,

TFH visiting 1 Glosters at Ballykelly in Northern Ireland, here talking to LCpl Phillips of A Company. The Commanding Officer, Lt-Col H.T. Radice, is centre rear of the picture.
(Farrar-Hockley family)

came upon a platoon being motivated to their task by Sgt Joe Courtney – motivation that included more than a few expletives. TFH took rather a dim view to say the least, telling Waters that he would not have soldiers sworn at in this way. When pressed on this perhaps untenable position, he did admit to one situation where this had been permissible: at one point while a young officer in Italy with 6th (RW) Para, artillery fire began landing very close by. Cliff Meredith had pointed out in highly robust and colourful language that this was friendly fire and they should get out of this as soon as possible; this unusual occasion was the exception that proved the rule.[37]

Bryan Webster remembered clearly how TFH made an impact on everyone in the headquarters, and indeed throughout South-East District: with his infectious enthusiasm for every aspect of military life and his ebullience he was impossible to miss; he was also very much in charge. He walked to and from home every day, took plenty of exercise, was a light drinker – rarely touching spirits – and smoked no more than a couple of ounces of pipe tobacco each week. Of course, he set about visiting subordinate units and formations, and getting to know the patch, with a vengeance;[38] he would not have briefs written on officers – a waste of staff time in his view – for he insisted on knowing everyone personally which, with his remarkable memory, he did. However, not long after taking over, TFH found himself dealing with something quite unexpected: Military Aid to the Civil Ministry, or MACM, in the shape of a

Deputy Commander Land Forces in the Falklands War, GOC 4th Armoured Division, Commandant of the Staff College, GOC Northern Ireland, Commander-in-Chief UK Land Forces and finally DSACEUR.

short-notice commitment for the three services to provide cover during a major national firemen's strike.

This strike, over pay and conditions, began in early November and providing cover involved some 10,000 men and women from all three services, but chiefly the army, who were deployed nationwide.[39] Infantry battalions and regiments from other arms and services provided the spine of the organisation, reinforced by specialist teams from the Royal Engineers, Royal Air Force and Royal Navy who were trained and equipped for rescue work inside burning buildings, or dealing with hazardous materials. Without their skills, the operation could not have succeeded. The troops were equipped with 700 vintage *Green Goddess* fire engines – venerable relics from the Second World War which had, at one time, belonged to the now-disbanded Civil Defence Corps, but which had been held in care and maintenance by the Home Office. 'If there's one thing wrong with a *Goddess*, it's her rolling rear', commented one reporte:

> It was something Peter Darlington, of the Royal Welch Fusiliers, could have done without … on the first call of the day. He had problems enough trying to keep up with the police car ahead after just one 20-minute practice drive without feeling the back of the vehicle "wafting around like a tipsy trailer". For example, it had a disconcerting habit of trying to get into reverse gear every time he sought second gear. "*She's a solid old machine all right,*" he said, "*and despite her age, she has less than 2,000 miles on the clock. But that back end doesn't half wobble.*"[40]

Within his own district, TFH saw this as *his* operation and he held his subordinates very much to account for the delivery of the required service. He set up an operations centre and insisted on a briefing every morning, after which he would head off to visit at least one unit somewhere in his huge area of responsibility.[41] Usually, a unit of around 500 military personnel would replace 2,000 firemen, with fire officers to provide technical advice and the

Soldiers from 3 Queen's on fire-fighting duty with a *Green Goddess*, 1977.
(Queen's Regimental Archive)

Soldiers from 3 Queen's fighting a big fire during the firemen's strike of 1977.
(Queen's Regimental Archive)

Soldiers from 1 RWF on fire-fighting duties, 1977. (RWF Museum/Archives)

police providing escorts through traffic, and interposing between troops and strikers to ensure there was no contact between the two that might lead to unfortunate consequences. Units were usually deployed not in fire stations, but in TA or Cadet centres, in living conditions that were basic to say the least, and variously described by the press as 'squalor'[42] and 'Cockroach Hilton'.[43]

The operation, which carried on over Christmas and into 1978, had the highly beneficial effect of tightening good relationships with the police and fire officers, as well as with the other services; and indeed did wonders for civil-military relations generally. Local people welcomed the troops and showered them with food, drink and hospitality. However, the deployment is probably best remembered for the uproar in the press about army pay. In the wake of the then Labour Government's policy on service pay, and in the context of severe price inflation, pay had fallen dramatically. A married soldier serving a three-year engagement was paid about £44 per week. Tax, National Insurance and quartering charges reduced this to £20,[44] which was not enough for a family to live on and far less than firemen were being paid *before* their strike – never mind after it. One interview with a Commanding Officer, Lieutenant-Colonel (later Major-General) Morgan Llewellyn* of 1 RWF was particularly hard-hitting and led to Llewellyn being dubbed 'Colonel Fury'[45] – although anyone less suited to such a nickname is hard to imagine.

There was massive support for this view – from the ranks, from the families, from the population at large and from the chain of command. The Adjutant-General, Sir Jack Harman, and the C-in-C UK Land Forces, the now General Sir Edwin Bramall, both came out strongly in favour. In response, the then Secretary of State for Defence, Fred Mulley,† gave a mealy-mouthed answer:

> We all understand that the Services have slipped behind. I share [Llewellyn's] concerns, but the Services are well aware that the 12-month rule stands and must apply to them: that they are like others who have been hit by the pay policy. They accept this.[46]

The result of this row was a large pay award of more than 30 percent in the last year of the disastrous Labour administration – 1978-1979 – which was, however, only partly implemented. It was fully implemented only when Margaret Thatcher's Conservative Government took power in 1979. We do not know TFH's view on this issue as he has left no letters or diaries, nor did the headquarters complete the required unit historical report for the period. However, given his championship of the underdog, it is reasonable to conclude that he would have taken the same view as Bramall, Harman and others. The end of the strike was not the end of MACM, however, and by the winter of 1978-1979 – 'the winter of discontent' that

---

* Later Major-General Richard Morgan Llewellyn CB OBE OstJ DL (b. 1937). Was later Commander 48 Gurkha Brigade, GOC Wales and Chief of Staff UKLF. He was also Colonel of the Royal Welch Fusiliers. After he retired, he was ordained in the Anglican Church in Wales.

† Frederick William Mulley, Baron Mulley PC (1918-1995) became Secretary of State for Defence in 1976. He is best remembered for falling asleep during the Queen's Jubilee Review of the Royal Air Force at RAF Finningley in 1977 when there was considerable noise around him. Having a small sleep during an exercise was thereafter referred to by members of the RAF as having a 'Fred Mulley'.

'Now then, men . . . this is a block of flats and I'm an old
lady in distress—who's going to rescue me ? . . . Men . . . ?'

Mac's view of the army during the firemen's strike. (*Daily Express*)

preceded the election of Margaret Thatcher's Conservative Government – the district was involved in 18 different contingency plans; Rob McAfee remembered that:

> Mike Gray [Commander 6 Field Force] tried to avoid him and when diplomatically 'unavailable' I would be summoned to HQ South-East District to receive a wigging, or possibly instructions, intended for my Commander. I only fell out with him once, again for reasons mentioned in your chapter. His COS phoned me one day to say that the GOC would like a company of soldiers for a fortnight to undergo sleep deprivation trials. Our battalions were probably up to their necks in aid to the civil community tasks, or maybe I just considered the trial a bloody waste of time. I told his COS as much, but within half an hour I had TFH on the line, who told me to do as I was told – so I did![47]

While the firemen's strike was going on – just before Christmas 1977 – Major Roy Giles, the Deputy Assistant Military Secretary, was the district duty officer. Giles was telephoned at home by the police – telling him that the sail training ship *Winston Churchill*, crewed by teenage girls, had run into trouble in very rough weather in the Channel and was aground on a sandbank. The Coastguard had put out a call to ships for assistance, but the only vessel close by was the flat-bottomed army landing ship HMAV *Audemer*, which was being taken by a scratch crew of five from the military port at Marchwood, Southampton to Chatham, where it was to be broken up at the end of its life. *Audemer* had responded: Giles relayed the news to TFH, who asked to be kept informed. Meanwhile, *Audemer*'s Captain and crew had run in close to the *Winston Churchill* – which being flat-bottomed and of shallow draft they could do – and attached a tow, but being flat-bottomed and of shallow draft, they did not have the power to pull the ship free. The Captain solved the problem by paying out the tow line, dropping every anchor, and then using the *Audemer's* powerful winch to pull the *Winston Churchill* clear – effectively using the *Audemer* as a kedge. This was a dangerous task, brilliantly executed and acknowledged as such by the Coastguard. When TFH heard the news, he was determined that the ship and its crew should receive the proper recognition for having saved lives at sea. For the rest of his time in command, Roy Giles pursued the possibilities of the award of various levels of the Order of the British Empire, the George Medal and the Albert Medal – all met with official obstruction. Faced with this mean-spirited response, TFH eventually did the only thing possible: the crew was re-assembled at Chatham with what still remained of the ship – a mast and not much more – where TFH presented each man with the GOC's Commendation, finishing by nailing a final commendation certificate to the mast.[48]

In the New Year of 1978, with the firemen's strike over, TFH and his command returned to business as usual. TFH demanded exercises to test the response to an emergency at Gatwick, building on the relationships that had developed with the police; and study periods and TEWTs on every topic imaginable: 'South-East District ran more study periods than anyone else, usually with the most enormous and elaborate cloth models,' recalled Bryan Webster.[49]

One of the many, but memorable, study days was held at Deepcut and looked at the British contribution to the Korean War – in particular the Imjin River battle. David Keenan recalled one particular day when he and TFH went, for reasons that were not immediately clear, for a long walk over Watership Down. Once they returned to the headquarters, TFH told him to send out a Flash signal to all his immediate subordinates, mainly 1-stars, telling them all to be at Watership Down (with the appropriate maps) at 0830 hrs the following morning – and to warn the Officers' Mess to provide a field lunch for 80. 'That night I had phone calls every few minutes, brigadiers knocking on my door, all demanding to know what was going on.' What was going on was a snap, totally paperless, TEWT. It turned into a long, very hard day in which it rapidly became clear that many of these quite senior officers' professional knowledge was woeful – and TFH 'put them through Purgatory'. At 1530 hrs, TFH summed up their shortcomings and then told them all to be back at 0830 hrs the following morning, with every Lieutenant-Colonel and Major under their command – 'and no excuses, mind' – and that they would act as directing staff. Uncomfortable as it was, it reminded everyone very firmly that they were all, first and foremost, soldiers.[50]

In the same way, TFH felt sure that in the event of war with the Soviets, NATO would be taken by surprise. Britain could expect the early arrival of *Spetznaz*, Special Forces, bent of sabotage and murder. As the officer responsible for the home defence of a large and vital part of the country, he could not therefore sit in his office and wait for their arrival. A proper, secure, war headquarters had to be found. Using maps and documents followed up by ground reconnaissance, a suitable disused bunker –formerly used by the now-disbanded Civil Defence Corps – was eventually located near Reading.[51]

A major preoccupation each year was the Aldershot Army Display, which was held on the great open space adjacent to Queen's Avenue. The display, which was produced by Major

Michael Parker and run by a team under the direction of Smyth-Osbourne, included a preliminary equipment exhibition and tattoo and ran for a week during June. It involved at least 5,000 soldiers and was the successor of the old pre-war Aldershot Tattoo and, as such, was a major fundraising event for the Army Benevolent Fund. There were arena displays which included massed bands, pipes and drums; The King's Troop Royal Horse Artillery and mounted displays by the Royal Military Police or the Household Cavalry; tactical demonstrations, parachute freefall drops, helicopter landings, working dogs and the like. There were also static demonstrations provided by every arm and service and showcasing the officers, soldiers and equipment of the army. As well as being a huge draw for up to 400,000 visitors, it attracted at least one Royal visit and usually most of the Army Board at some point. Although the planning and execution was in the hands of a permanently established team, TFH took a close personal interest in it – hardly surprising given its profile   and looking after the most senior visitors was his sole occupation while it was running. Among the principal guests in 1978, for example, were the Prince of Wales; Secretary of State for Defence Fred Mulley; and Generals Sir Roland Gibbs, Sir Napier Crookenden, Sir Kenneth Darling and Sir Philip Ward. Because of commitments – principally Northern Ireland – the show was reduced to a display every other year and was not therefore held in 1979.[52]

With so few Regular troops under his full command, much of TFH's energy was directed towards the TA, which was growing steadily. In 1969, the then Labour Government had reduced the TA to a small number of units, known as 'Volunteers', who would reinforce Regular formations in BAOR in wartime. The rest of the TA had clung on for a couple of years as 'Territorials' before these units were reduced to small cadres. The Conservative Government elected in 1970 had, however, resurrected the TA for home defence duties; an expansion that included 77 infantry battalions as well as other arms and service units.[53] These were still difficult times, however, as permanent staff and equipment remained short; the brigade level of command had not been re-established; and most units were still working hard to fill their ranks. TFH encountered these same issues as Colonel of the Parachute Regiment, for although 44 Parachute Brigade (TA) had been disbanded, the regiment still had three Volunteer battalions: 4 Para in the English North and Midlands, 10 Para in London and 15 (Scottish) Para in Scotand.

TFH therefore had a two-tier TAVR (which reverted to its old title, TA, in 1979) in his area of responsibility: in the top tier were the NATO-roled units like the Royal Yeomanry, 5 Queen's, 4 RGJ and 1 Wessex (the last was, in effect, a Volunteer battalion of the Royal Hampshire Regiment). These units were organised and equipped just like Regular units, with a generous allocation of permanent staff and plenty of exciting training with the Regular Army. 5 Queen's, for example, formed part of 6 Field Force. A TA unit committed to a field force formation in Britain or, like 4 RGJ in Germany, could expect to be conducting some kind of interesting and demanding training every weekend. In the second tier were units like 6/7 Queen's, with no heavy weapons, little transport and limited communications. To give these units some sense of purpose, TFH organised major training events, such as Exercise *Tiger's Teeth* in October 1977, which concentrated on internal security.

6 Field Force and several TA units took part in Exercises *Bowbell* in Norway and the NATO exercise *Avon Express* on Salisbury Plain; HQ South-East District had to find the enemy force for *Avon Express* – and as well as 5 Queen's and other units, TFH gave the job of preparing the enemy force to his Deputy Assistant Military Secretary, Lieutenant-Colonel Roy Giles of the

TA soldiers from 6/7 Queen's on exercise in 1977. (Queen's Regimental Archive)

Glosters, who had spent a good deal of his career on the staff of the British Military Mission to the Commander-in-Chief, GSFG, or Brixmis.[54] TFH wanted to give the British Army a view of what it would be like to be attacked by overwhelming numbers, just as he had been in Korea. The enemy force therefore consisted of the TA Volunteers, and every available cadet in the district – a total of at least 2,000 young men. The force was assembled at Knook Camp the day before and briefed by Roy Giles, who was dressed in the full uniform of a Soviet General, and then rehearsed by their own officers. The following morning, after a long approach march in the dark, the defending force saw – coming out of the mist – three lines of advancing troops, with vehicles at regular intervals simulating tanks or APCs. The lines were up to 1,000 yards wide and those watching never forgot the impression of an overwhelming, unstoppable mass rolling over them and enveloping their flanks.[55]

In September 1978, 6 Field Force went to Schleswig-Holstein on Exercise *Bold Guard*.[56] TFH took a close personal involvement in the UKMF and its deployment to Denmark, taking his core military staff and establishing in effect a divisional tactical headquarters in the field. His first call, however, had been the embarkation of the troops at Harwich. What he saw horrified him: the bulk of the second and third line transport was Second World War-era 10-ton lorries; while the infantry battalions had no organic lift for the troops, who would have to walk. That the British Army should go to war in such a state was appalling and unacceptable. For the duration of the exercise, the bulk of the 10-tonners were given to the infantry to provide lift. Rob McAfee, the Brigade Major, recalled much the same conditions:

> On the first exercise, arranged by my predecessor, I was taken aback to find that communications relied on a few HF radios, man-packs and *in extremis*, despatch rider

or forked stick. 'Manoeuvre' meant A to B by parachute or truck and Shanks's Pony thereafter. An hour before last light, everything – and I mean *everything* – came to a standstill while each individual (including the BM) cooked his 24-hour ration on a *hexamine* stove. Had the ration packs failed to arrive, I daresay we would have foraged in the villages abutting Hankley Common. However, the brigade senior Gunner was so embarrassed by my obvious bewilderment, that he lent me sufficient 1-ton Land Rovers and VHF sets to form a mobile HQ thereafter.

In the aftermath of the deployment, TFH began a personal crusade first for more support helicopters – work he had begun while DCD (A); secondly to provide protected mobility for the infantry; and third to bring in modern logistic lift for the UKMF. His preferred solution for the problem of protected mobility was an off-the-shelf buy of the American M113-tracked armoured personnel carrier. By coincidence, at the same time, the Berlin Infantry Brigade had been addressing the same issue and had concluded that an off-the-shelf buy of the German *Fuchs*-wheeled APC would solve the problem. This could be bought from the Berlin budget, at no cost to the British taxpayer. This latter proposal, however, raised ill-informed protests in Parliament and the result was that a search began for a British-wheeled APC which could be issued to the non-mechanised formations: the Berlin Infantry Brigade, the UKMF and, slightly later, 19 and 24 Infantry Brigades. The only available vehicle was an armoured 4-ton truck, the AT-104, which had been developed by *GKN Sankey* for the Malaysian Police as an internal security vehicle. From this, a variant – the AT-105 – was rapidly built and it was this that was issued to the British Army. It was better than nothing and it was simple to drive and maintain – although it came with no NBC decontamination kit, no camouflage set, no proper radio fit and only limited spares; it was also top-heavy – especially when fitted with a machine gun turret – thus the British Army was stuck with the vehicle it knew as the *Saxon*.

On Exercise *Bold Guard,* however, things went from bad to worse. First, the Soviet equivalent to Brixmis – Soxmis – was invited to view the start of the exercise, which was to be a parachute drop by a full battalion group. Because of the massive reductions in capability, this drop was little short of a fiasco, much to the amusement of the Soviets and to the mortification of TFH.[57] Then the Dutch reconnaissance company had to be removed from the exercise by the orders of the Corps Commander, being so much under the influence of drugs as to be more a danger to themselves and their allies to any enemy.[58] Rob McAfee recalled that:

> On Exercise *Bold Guard,* TFH turned up unexpectedly in my CV – just as I was on the radio – trying to unravel some major cock-up. He sat quietly beside me until the call ended and when I apologised for both the drama and for keeping him waiting, he replied: "*Dear boy, that's precisely what exercises are for.*" He got my vote … I very much liked his no-nonsense, professional style and felt he was a senior officer from whom one could seek advice or be trusted not to shoot the messenger.[59]

What can be said, however, is that over the next five years – beginning with TFH's insistence on modernisation – the UKMF increased in size and capability, its equipment was brought up to date, and by the last phase of the Cold War, it was capable of holding its own against at least the Soviets' first operational echelon.

TFH's interest in cooking showed no sign of abating and formed part of his usual routine of business. He would spend the day visiting a unit or in his office and then at about 4:00 p.m. he would go home, where he would spend an hour or so with Pat on whatever literary project he was engaged with at the time. He would then cook supper or, if he was giving a more formal party, make sure the cook had matters in hand and even prepare one dish himself before changing; the ADC would arrive at this point to make sure visitors were met and entertained and the party would start. On other occasions, he and Pat would be invited out to dinner. Bryan Webster recalled one all but disastrous dinner party at his own home, when the first course was shellfish – to which it turned out that Pat was allergic; the main course was a crown of lamb, which his wife had mistimed and which was, therefore, raw (this was long before the modern fad for eating raw meat and calling it 'pink'). TFH gave a short demonstration on how to cook the joint quickly – 'in the nicest possible way' – all ended well except that poor Mrs Webster was mortified. Some time later, both the Farrar-Hockleys and the Websters went to a dinner given by one of the GSO1s. No sooner had they arrived than the Calor Gas stove blew up, slightly injuring their hostess. TFH immediately took the lady to Frimley Park Hospital in his staff car; made sure she received the right treatment; returned; and finished cooking the dinner. The Websters were, by this time, convinced that they should probably stay away from dinner parties.[60]

After the first year in Aldershot, David Keenan handed over as ADC to Mike Motum of the Glosters. Motum recalled that as usual, TFH was in demand as a speaker, usually on the subject of leadership. His audiences ranged from the Staff College to groups of Army Cadets, but interestingly he usually kept these talks general and did not often refer to his personal experiences to the depth that his audiences might have expected – perhaps from modesty. Invariably he would turn the tables on the audience and ask them to suggest characteristics or qualities of a leader. One such quality – seldom mentioned, but important in his eyes – was ambition. He had always been ambitious himself and saw it as important in others: ambition for the group, or the organisation – in this case, the army – not just for the individual mattered to him and he would have condemned absolutely an ambition that led any officer to exploit the efforts of the team for his own advancement.[61]

Surprisingly, perhaps, TFH's writing career was quiet during these years and for the first time since his return from Korea, he published nothing. He had, however, been asked by the Cabinet Office to undertake the official history of the Korean War. He and Pat – who was, as usual, acting as his assistant – began collecting material for this history and his daily programme shows frequent visits to the MOD Archives at Hayes in Middlesex, usually when he was also visiting the MOD or Kensington Palace. He realised straight away that this would be a task beyond the two of them given the demands of his career, so he demanded – and got – the services of a civil servant as full-time researcher. This task was given to Linda Wood, who had worked for TFH in Combat Development and who therefore knew him and his style. Linda was seconded to the Cabinet Office on full pay and began work under TFH's direction, collecting papers and testimony. At least some of this was anecdotal, as TFH was President of the Korean War Veterans' Association, in the form of veterans' remembrances. He was, interestingly, consulted on the role of official historians and the availability of source material at this time. A letter to Mr G.J. Aylett of the Public Records Committee said that in his view, while material in the main stream of government – such as Cabinet papers – were accessible, recorded and easily retrieved, other items such as war diaries and correspondence were not. Overly-rigid recording practices, poor referencing, crudely-weeded files, the absence of key folios, a mass of useless repetition and clerical staff in the Public Record Office, Army Historical Branch and the MOD records depository at Hayes all conspired to make the historian's task far more difficult than it need be.[62] This indicates pretty clearly that he was looking hard in official records at this time; it also rings horribly true to anyone conducting research today – although the establishment of The National Archives at Kew have overcome the clerical issues and the retrieval problems.

In 1979, the Prince of Wales was appointed Colonel-in-Chief of the Parachute Regiment, a few months before his 30th birthday. The Prince immediately asked TFH if he could take a parachute training course, feeling – as he remarked later to his biographer, Jonathan Dimbleby – that he 'could not look them in the eye', nor wear the Parachute Regiment's red beret and wings, unless he had done the course. 'I felt I should lead from the front or at least be able to do some of the things that one expects others to do for the country', he said, 'so they all put their hands up in horror – or rather the RAF did – but somehow it was organised and I did it'.[63]

TFH duly arranged the matter. Subsequently, a portrait of the Prince was commissioned, along with portraits of Gerald Lathbury, 'Windy' Gale, 'Roly' Gibbs and TFH himself, who had all served as Colonel.[64] When the Prince came to Aldershot to make his first visit, he went first to Wellesley House to change, where TFH presented him with a silver badge for his beret. Ted Olive was then given the task of fixing the badge to the beret, which he did, but then found he needed some backing to stiffen the cloth behind the badge. What was there? Rooting in his pockets, Olive found a packet of Player's No. 6 cigarettes, complete with a Royal 'By Appointment' logo. This was obviously suitable and he quickly emptied the smokes, cutting off a piece of the packet (with Royal Coat of Arms) with nail scissors. This sorted the problem, but Olive wondered quietly to himself for many years afterwards just how long a piece of fag packet survived in the Prince's beret.

As it happened, two of the three Regular battalions were away from Aldershot at the time of the Prince's first visit, either in Germany or in Northern Ireland; only 1 Para under David Charles was available. However, the Colour parties of all six battalions, Regular and TA, were brought to Aldershot along with a great contingent of the Regimental Association, 7 Para RHA, the depot staff and the recruits under training. The parade included the passing-out of the Senior Recruit Platoon, followed by a display from the freefall parachute team, the Red Devils.[65] The Prince of Wales subsequently visited 1 Para at the South Cerney mounting base, where they were preparing for an airborne drop in Norway in support of a 3 Commando Brigade RM exercise. TFH was there, of course. At one point the Prince went to see the kitchen and dining room arrangements; TFH, with his keen interest in cooking, made straight for a young chef busy with something in a large bowl.

'What's that you have there, young man?' asked TFH.

'Custard, Sir' replied the soldier.

This reply brought raised eyebrows and a sideways look from TFH, who picked up a spoon, dipped it into the bowl, tasted it, gagged – but swallowed. Once he had regained the power of speech, he said: 'If ever I become Quarter Master General, the Army Catering Corps is getting a new recipe for custard!'

The Prince of Wales, Colonel-in-Chief, with men of the Parachute Regiment. (Paradata)

The Prince of Wales visiting 2 Para, accompanied by TFH. In the foreground is David Leigh, before his injuries in Northern Ireland. (Farrar-Hockley family)

TFH's command of South-East District was remarkably brief, for he handed over command to Sir George Cooper* – after little more than 18 months – in July 1979.[66] Mike Motum recalled that TFH burst in to the office one morning even more full of enthusiasm than ever, to say that he was being promoted and sent to Oslo.

"Do you want to come with me as ADC for the first year and help me settle in?" he asked. This meant an extra year in the job, but it was a very simple decision indeed to reply *"Yes please!"*[67]

Although he had been a Lieutenant-General for less than two years, TFH had been selected for a post in the rank of General. This was not a post in the highest echelons of the army in Britain for the reasons already discussed. He had, however, been chosen for a NATO post, as Commander-in-Chief Allied Forces Northern Europe. As Frank Kitson remarked, TFH deserved to be a full General; this was recognised – and in a big army within a bigger organisation like NATO, this was how that recognition could be made a reality.[68]

---

*   Later General Sir George Leslie Conroy Cooper GCB MC DL (b 1925). He had, like TFH, served in the Korean War. He was later Adjutant-General of the Army.

21

'There were no more parties' C-in-C Allied Forces Northern Europe, 1979-1981

TFH took over his new command on 30 July 1979 from General Sir Peter Whiteley, of the Royal Marines,[*] on promotion to the rank of General.[1] In the following year, he was appointed as one of the Aides de Camp General to Her Majesty The Queen – an appointment that he would hold for the next five years.[2] TFH and Pat moved into the C-in-C's residence at Holmenkollverein 88, known as 'H88' in the suburb of Besserud, above Oslo and close to the famous ski-jump. Originally, the C-in-C had been allocated a house which had belonged to the wartime Nazi collaborator, Vikund Quisling; however, the connotations being what they were – allied to which the place was chronically damp – a new house had been requested and found. H88 had been a bordello for senior German officers during the wartime occupation – something which gave TFH a good deal of wry amusement when entertaining some of his guests – and still showed some signs of its former glory: many of the bedrooms, for example, had small stages built into them and most were inter-connected. There were also a fair number of colourful telephone calls, as the phone number had not been altered after its change of use.[3] Having this splendid house meant that the family, who were not far away, could easily come and stay, for Dair – now a Major – and his family, which included TFH's grandson Henry, born on 1 June 1979, were in Berlin and Hilary – now a Flying Officer – was at RAF Shawbury for a time before moving to Laarbruch in Germany. Close by, too, was Hilary's godmother, Pat's cousin, Mary Morning, who was married to a Dane – Henry Morning – and lived in Copenhagen. As C-in-C, TFH was also granted an official residence in Copenhagen, where he called regularly on Queen Margrethe II and her ministers, and an office in the Danish MOD, to encourage him to spend time in Denmark.

In Norway, TFH became a Theatre Commander, one of three major subordinates of the Supreme Allied Commander Europe (SACEUR) – initially US General Alexander Haig[†] and very shortly after TFH's arrival, Bernie W. Rogers[‡] – along with the Cs-in-C of Allied Forces

---

[*]   General Sir Peter John Frederick Whiteley GCB OBE DL (b. 1920).

[†]   Alexander Meigs Haig, Jnr (1924-2010) served in Korea and Vietnam – winning the Distinguished Service Cross, the Silver Star with oak leaf cluster, and the Purple Heart. He was Secretary of State under President Reagan and White House Chief of Staff under Nixon and Gerald Ford. He also served as Vice-Chief of Staff of the Army.

[‡]   Bernard William Rogers (1921-2008) was Chief of Staff of the US Army and, as well as being SACEUR, he was also C-in-C US European Command.

Central Europe, based at Brunssum in the Netherlands, and Allied Forces South, based at Naples in Italy. Although he had been a Divisional Commander in the Central Region, he had not commanded a corps nor held any senior NATO post. His qualifications were, therefore, not quite what they might have been – nor was the command in a theatre of active operations – so TFH never had the opportunity to show his practical grasp of generalship. However, he began immediately to establish his intellectual grasp of the theatre level of command by studying the current situation, the enemy, his own forces, the state of play in the host nations of Germany, Norway and Denmark, and the lessons of the successful German attack on the two countries in 1940.

Allied Forces Northern Europe (AFNORTH) was the most northern NATO command, headquartered at Kolsås, outside Oslo, in Norway – although TFH also had an office in the Norwegian MOD. In the event of war, AFNORTH would assume command of all Allied forces in Norway and Denmark, and in that part of Germany north of the River Elbe and Hamburg – in Schleswig-Holstein – along with the surrounding sea territory and airspace. For much of its existence, its C-in-C was a British Admiral or General, while the Chief of Staff was a British Major-General. During TFH's time as C-in-C, the Chief was first Major-General Roy Dixon[*] and later Andrew Watson.[†] Unsurprisingly, the Germans lobbied hard for this post, but TFH – aware of the sensitivities in Norway and Denmark after the wartime German occupation – steadfastly refused to give ground and the most senior German officer was a deputy to the Chief of Staff, Rear Admiral Ebs Noodt. The post of Chief of Staff was, however, handed over by TFH's successor.[4] The Air Force Commander Northern Europe, who would assume command of all NATO air forces in AFNORTH's area in wartime, was also the C-in-C's deputy and was a Major-General from the Danish Air Force. In 1979, this was Major-General J. Brodersen. There was also a US Major-General with national air and intelligence responsibilities, Walter H. ('Buzz') Baxter.[‡] The AFNORTH command group also included a Land Deputy, Major-General Ole Miøen; and a Sea Deputy, Rear Admiral Ole Berg. These posts were always held by either Danish or Norwegian officers, about whom there were mixed feelings. Even before he had taken up his post, he received a letter from Dixon[5] on this subject, since it was potentially troublesome and would confront him on the first day. Dixon explained that when AFNORTH was first established at Holmenkollen, it had had separate service components, but when it moved to Kolsås, the headquarters had became fully integrated. However, the contributing nations had only accepted integration on the proviso that they could keep their 2-star posts for national representation and as 'advisers' to the C-in-C. Although a US airman was needed for nuclear and other American-related matters, the naval and land deputies really had no job at all, said Dixon, and their removal would improve the efficiency of the HQ. They had been given jobs to do with unit testing to keep them occupied; the C-in-C usually held a command group meeting every two months to allow the deputies 'to blow off steam and hear what the C-in-C had to say about key issues, but the structure leads to confusion of thought and the current C-in-C advises that they will seek to play a larger role in decision making, which would be dangerous'.

---

[*]   Major-General Roy Laurence Cayley Dixon CB CVO MC, late of the Royal Tank Regiment.
[†]   Major-General Andrew Linton Watson CB was Colonel of the Black Watch (Royal Highland Regiment).
[‡]   Walter H. Baxter III (1926-2004) was an acting Lieutenant-General. He had served in Korea and in Vietnam.

General Alexander Haig, SACEUR, with TFH and Italian General Cucino shortly before he handed over the supreme command. (Farrar-Hockley family)

Dixon was right to warn TFH of the lobbying and inefficiencies in the command structure. However, if he thought that this was going to change, he must have been very naive indeed. All NATO headquarters were overstaffed; all had to have representation from every nation in every branch; and all had too many senior officers – but that was part of the politics of the alliance.

Just as annoying was an attempt, in January 1980, at Norwegian nationalisation of TFH's post – although this was met with ridicule in the Norwegian domestic media. Norwegian Defence Minister Thorvald Stoltenberg had proposed that C-in-C AFNORTH should be a Norwegian, to which an article in the newspaper *Aftenpost* poured scorn on this idea, pointing out that Norway's contribution to its own defence was minimal and its reliance on reinforcing nations huge. Moreover, to nationalise the post would encourage the Soviets to increase pressure on Norway to introduce restrictions on NATO activity:

> Norway is the largest net receiver of security in the Alliance, and therefore it does not seem reasonable that we should express this surprising wish ... without having aired it with our allies in advance ... explanation is the Defence Minister's wish for creating an image for himself and a wish from his generals for a new and important post – but they have chosen a wrong case at a wrong time.[6]

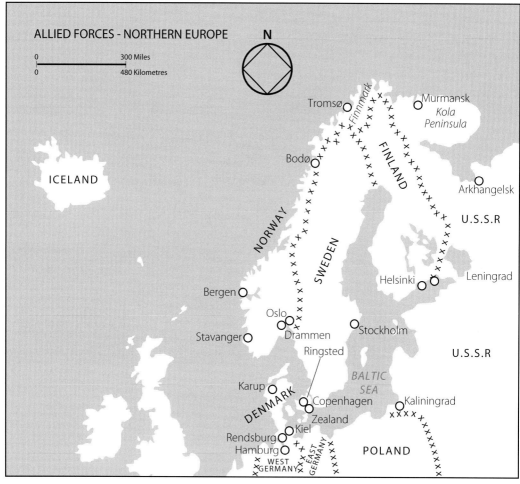

ALLIED FORCES - NORTHERN EUROPE

0 ——————— 300 Miles
0 ——————— 480 Kilometres

N

Tromsø
Murmansk
Kola Peninsula
Finnmark
Bodø
ICELAND
FINLAND
Arkhangelsk
U.S.S.R
NORWAY
SWEDEN
Bergen
Helsinki
Leningrad
Oslo
Stavanger
Drammen
Stockholm
Ringsted
U.S.S.R
BALTIC SEA
Karup
Copenhagen
Kaliningrad
Zealand
DENMARK
Kiel
Rendsburg
Hamburg
EAST GERMANY
POLAND
WEST GERMANY

Allied Forces Northern Region.

TFH was well supported by his team of personal staff. In addition to Mike Motum of the Glosters he was – unusually – joined by a second ADC, Captain David Leigh of the Paras. There were two reasons for this: first, TFH was not only a senior NATO commander, but also Colonel of two regiments and Colonel Commandant of The Prince of Wales's Division and had, therefore, a great deal of extra work; the second reason was that Leigh had been a Platoon Commander in Major (later General Sir) Rupert Smith's[*] company in Northern Ireland. While TFH, as Colonel of the regiment, was visiting the battalion, David was caught in the blast of a large car-bomb and suffered horrendous burns. Rupert Smith had pulled him clear, saving his life and losing a finger in the process, for which he was awarded the Queen's Gallantry Medal.[7] By great good fortune, the RMO was airborne in a helicopter at the time of the attack, while at Aldergrove an RAF aircraft was available for tasking. This whisked Leigh

---

[*]   General Sir Rupert Anthony Smith KCB DSO OBE QGM (b. 1943) commanded the 1st Armoured Division in the Gulf War of 1990-1991, UN forces in Bosnia 1995 and was subsequently DSACEUR.

to the BMH Woolwich, where he was looked after by one of the top specialists in burns. He was one of the worst burns patients ever to survive his injuries.

Having been close by at the time of the incident, TFH naturally took a close interest in Leigh and visited him in Woolwich on several occasions, where Leigh was, for quite a time, in a saline bath and in great pain – but there was more to it, for Leigh was the son of a Warrant Officer in the Paras who had received a Quarter Master's commission. TFH knew him well and had backed him in encouraging his son to try for a place at Sandhurst and a commission in the Paras. When the attack took place, TFH was therefore mortified. He felt responsible, in part at least, for having delivered David into the hands of the IRA; whatever he could do to help manage the effects, therefore, he would do. Leigh's life was despaired of, but Leigh was made of sterner stuff and he survived – minus his eyelids, dreadfully scarred, and with one of his fingers so badly splayed from his hand that he had it removed, so as not to interfere with his saluting. When TFH heard that a medical discharge was pending he wrote to the Adjutant-General suggesting that Leigh should accompany him to Norway, as the climate would be good for his healing skin, and he might not therefore have to leave the service – which indeed was the case.[8] Leigh later commanded a parachute company, was promoted to Lieutenant-Colonel and married Elizabeth Lamb – the stunningly beautiful daughter of the British Ambassador to Norway – whom he met at the British Officers' Ball while serving with TFH in Oslo. Leigh's mother, Jane, subsequently wrote to TFH saying that 'I have never thanked you for the very large part you played in assisting my son to make the remarkable recovery that he did … As a family, we acknowledge the debt we owe you'.[9]

TFH would never have seen this in such terms. To him, there was no debt; he had simply done his duty as one regimental officer should to another, but there is no doubt that TFH's involvement and the use of his position and authority gave both David Leigh and his family enormous moral strength and optimism. In Oslo, Leigh and Motum shared a flat in central Oslo. Leigh was an excellent cook and with plenty of local overseas allowance to supplement their pay, the two decided to enjoy life. Their flat became a regular party venue with, on one later occasion, embarrassing consequences.

TFH also had the services of a Military Assistant, Lieutenant-Colonel Graham Farrell – also a Para – who went out six months ahead to prepare for TFH's arrival. Farrell had served in the ranks, like TFH, and been the CO of the Para Depot while TFH had been GOC in Aldershot. The two got on well and when TFH invited Farrell to go to Norway as MA, Farrell accepted with alacrity.[10] There was also a secretary, Mrs Pam Øgaard. Finally there was Linda Wood, who also went out to Oslo periodically as a Cabinet Office staff member, to continue the research work on the Korean War history. Much of her time was spent travelling between Britain and Norway collecting, organising and transcribing material at TFH's direction.

Ted Olive had retired from the army at the end of TFH's time as GOC South-East District, but remained in TFH's employment as his assistant, confidant and comrade-in-arms. He based himself at Pye Barn, continuing the work of improving the house and being ready to pick TFH up on his arrival on visits to Britain and look after him. The old Dodge *Dart* had long since been superseded by a Daimler, which was in turn replaced by a three-litre Volvo Estate capable of a highly illegal 130 mph. In Oslo there were two drivers, Sgt Arthur Sullivan and LCpl Allan Tipping from the RCT and this allowed for leave – as well as being able to send one driver ahead on visits within the theatre to prepare for his arrival. On his frequent return trips to London, TFH was often collected at the airport by a Daimler Limousine from the MOD

TFH visits the Norwegian Home Guard in 1979 with his MA, Graham Farrell.
(Farrar-Hockley family)

pool of staff cars. These cars were highly suitable, as many people and much baggage could be loaded into them. Sometimes the car would remain at TFH's disposal for the duration of the visit – which was always based on Pye Barn – thus saving the hotel bill for the taxpayer. One day, however, TFH was dropped off for a meeting at the MOD and the car went off, taking Pat to a meeting of the Guild of St Helena. By great ill luck, Margaret Thatcher saw the car with Pat in the back seat and drew the wrong conclusions. A great stir followed, with accusations of flagrant misuse of public property – senior officers' wives going shopping – poodle-faking and similar harsh words. It was not until after TFH's return to Oslo that he was able to give a short explanation of the actual facts, at which point the hue and cry died.[11]

* * *

AFNORTH Headquarters was organised along standard NATO lines with the main subdivisions of Operations, Intelligence, Command and Control, Communications, Public Information, Personnel, Budget and Finance, Joint Exercises and Command support. As well as the main headquarters, there was a wartime complex built into a system of tunnels under the mountainside above Oslo, in which the headquarters could withstand a nuclear strike.[12] TFH, with his enthusiasm for energising and organising everything, tried his best to put the headquarters and the command on a war footing. His enthusiasm was not, however, always matched by that of the staff. He was also prone to forget that until war actually broke out, the

His Majesty King Olaf of Norway visits HQ AFNORTH. (Farrar-Hockley family)

Armed Forces assigned to AFNORTH remained under their own national commands and that exercises, conferences and so on needed to be cleared with national command authorities. On one exercise he did, however, invite King Olaf of Norway to visit at the very start and hand over command of his forces to NATO in recognition of this reality.[3]

TFH produced two major pieces of analytical writing that summed up his views and understanding of the situation in AFNORTH – the first of which was a paper given at the end of his time in command at RUSI in which he summarised the component parts of AFNORTH as consisting of three major, but inter-dependent, territorial divisions: North Norway, South Norway and the Baltic Approaches. The latter was included in AFNORTH on the principle that both sides of any major water gap should be under the same military command and included Hamburg, Schleswig-Holstein, Jutland and the Danish Islands as well as the Kattegat and the Skagerrak maritime passages from the Baltic into the North Atlantic.[14]

BALTAP, with its headquarters in Karup and commanded by General Christian Vegger,* comprised air and naval commands which included the whole of the Danish Navy and Air Force as well as the whole of the Navy of the Federal Republic of Germany; with the addition of US and British forces in the western approaches, this represented a formidable array of maritime

---

* Anders Christian Bugge Vegger (1915-1992) was a Danish Army officer and a Second World War resistance fighter.

and air power. On land, BALTAP consisted of two territorial commands: LANDZEALAND, in Ringsted, under Major-General D.K. Lind, responsible for the land defence of the island of Zealand and the other Danish Islands; and Allied Land Forces Schleswig-Holstein and Jutland, or LANDJUT, under *Generalleutnant* Gunter Kießling.* From 1962 LANDJUT had been responsible for the land defence of the Baltic Approaches from a headquarters at Rendsburg, West Germany. It was a corps-sized formation which comprised NATO's largest division, the 6th (German) *Panzergrenadier* Division, commanded by *Generalmajor* Egil Ingebritsen, and the Danish Jutland Division. LANDJUT was to be reinforced in time of war by the United Kingdom Mobile Force, including 6 Field Force – later 1 Infantry Brigade – along with a divisional slice of armoured reconnaissance, artillery, engineers, air defence and logistics. The UKMF operated on a four-yearly rotation of command post and field training exercises, alternating between Jutland and Zealand.

This large force structure was made necessary by the knowledge that in the event of a major Soviet attack in the Central Region, AFNORTH would have a major impact on the plans of both SACEUR and the Commander of the Group of Soviet Forces in Germany (GSFG). For the Soviets, an unsecured right flank on the south bank of the Elbe River would pose considerable risks, for NATO could well use this flank to mount a devastating counter-attack into their flank and rear. Securing the Danish Islands – and especially the Jutland Peninsula – were therefore of critical importance. It was for this purpose that the Soviets maintained a large amphibious force in the Baltic.[15] However, there were additional advantages for the Soviets in capturing this area: not only the ability to gain access to the Atlantic, but also the capture of the airfields around Hamburg and in Jutland – and with them the ability to attack NATO's tactical air forces from the rear; the use of the main ports of North-Western Germany and the denial of them to NATO for trans-Atlantic reinforcement; and the breaching of the main *Hawk* and *Patriot* high-level air defence missile belts while also deepening their own air defence zone.[16]

The maritime environment was also of critical importance to both sides here. The main effort of the Allied Atlantic fleet was to prevent the break-in of a reinforced Soviet surface and sub-surface fleet into the Atlantic, from the Baltic, once they had secured the Baltic Approaches. If this Allied fleet were unsuccessful, or was badly damaged, the Soviets would establish sea control and wreck merchant shipping. The capture of Iceland by a Soviet air-landed force would certainly form a critical part of this operation.[17] At the same time, the Soviets would try to capture the airfields of Northern Norway – giving them bases from which to establish air superiority over the Faroe – Iceland gap, the Western Approaches and much of the North Atlantic. Should Denmark be lost, the Baltic Approaches too would pass under Soviet control. TFH summed this up in the second of his two major pieces of analytical writing on the command, *Opening Rounds*: 'Maritime considerations aside, there will be no air defences between Russian aircraft operating from Danish airfields and the United Kingdom's shores'.[18]

Denmark, the major partner in BALTAP, was a staunch NATO partner – contributing proportionately well above its size to the defence of Europe and regularly spending at least

---

*   Günter Kießling (1925-2009) had served in the Second World War. In 1983 Kießling was secretly accused of homosexuality, which, in his position, was in those days regarded as a security risk and led to his premature retirement. The allegations were later found to be without foundation and he was rehabilitated – being briefly reinstated before retiring with full honours.

TFH accompanies Her Majesty Queen Margrethe II of Denmark on a visit to HQ BALTAP.
(Farrar-Hockley family)

two percent of its GDP on its military – but there were dissenting voices. One Danish politician suggested that in the first hour of a Soviet offensive, a brief recorded message should be sent to Moscow: 'We surrender'. Surrender because, after a week or so of conventional battle, SACEUR would be forced to tell the heads of all NATO governments that he could not hope to continue the fight without nuclear weapons. In the view of this Dane, nothing justified that. In December 1981, the Second Secretary of the Soviet Embassy in Copenhagen, Vladimir Merkulov, was exposed in the Scandinavian press as a KGB officer and case officer for the left-wing poet and writer Arne Herlov Pedersen, who was tried for espionage in 1981 soon after a Soviet submarine had been found spying inside neutral Swedish territorial waters.[19] However, in spite of these isolated dissenters, the Danes continued to contribute naval and air forces to BALTAP; and a corps headquarters, corps troops and one-and-a-half mechanised divisions to the ground defence of Jutland and the Danish Islands.[20]

The land mass of the second major partner in AFNORTH, Norway, extended from the Baltic Approaches to the Arctic Circle where, since the end of the Second World War, it had a common border with the Soviet Union – the only place apart from Turkey where NATO territory was actually contiguous with that of the Russians and where the second of TFH's major subordinate commands, North Norway, was located. Norway was acutely conscious of its geography, that the airfields in Troms could be used to dominate the sea-lanes through which the Soviet fleet must pass into the Atlantic. In consequence, these airfields were the objective of six Soviet motor-rifle divisions and one airborne division stationed in peacetime in the Kola Peninsula – running north from Leningrad to the Arctic Ocean – and of a naval amphibious force, strategic and tactical air forces. In the desolate tundra of the Kola, the Soviets had constructed 19 major airfields with runways capable of operating every class of aircraft then in service, with a full suite of ground-based air defences, underground fuel and ammunition storage, radar and air traffic control. Squadrons stationed further south were regularly rehearsed in deploying to the region.[21] This mighty array was opposed by the sparse defences of neutral Finland along with those of Norway, whose population was barely four million and which had only a single regular brigade on its peacetime military establishment – and that based hundreds of miles from the northern border; nor did Norway permit the basing of foreign troops, other than for exercises, on its territory.

North Norway was under the command of first Major-General Fredrik Bull-Hansen* and, from 1981, Major-General Tønne Huitfeld. Huitfeld had escaped from German-occupied Norway and joined the British Army before being attached to the Red Army as an intelligence and liaison officer in Finland. With them he had entered North Norway in 1945 in the wake of the Germans' scorched earth withdrawal – the result of which was that German atrocities seemed far closer than the Soviet threat; Germans, allies as they now were, were not especially welcome. The Soviets, by contrast, had liberated North Norway and then when asked to return home, had done so. TFH and Huitfeld became close friends and remained so long afterwards; this was especially helpful when Huitfeld joined the NATO Military Committee in Brussels.

North Norway also lay close the port of Murmansk, the main base of the Soviet Northern Fleet – the only Russian fleet with full access to open water without (like the Black Sea and Baltic fleets) having to pass through a narrow and defensible defile. The Soviet fleet included one or two aircraft carriers and 80 other ships including cruisers, frigates and destroyers. 'This', wrote TFH, was 'an ocean-going battle fleet far in excess of Russian needs to defend its interests in the Barents Sea which are, in any case, well within the striking radii of the Kola airfields'.[22]

The Soviet submarine fleet, with its 40 nuclear missile-carrying boats and 138 attack boats, was greater than the German fleet in 1940 – and did not include the 152 hunter-killer submarines in other Soviet fleets. However, the approaches to Murmansk were dominated by observation from North Norway. In order to ensure freedom of action for this fleet in wartime, therefore, the Soviets would have to secure the area immediately that hostilities commenced.[23] If they did so, Warsaw Pact submarines and surface warships had the potential to destroy much of the shipping – bringing men and materiel across the Atlantic to reinforce the NATO commands in Northern, Central and Southern Europe

NATO's problem was, therefore, how to secure the area with limited resources; Norway's problem, allied to this, was how to make a proper contribution to that effort with limited population and a small standing military force. The solution reached was that Norway would secure its own coastal waters – including the prevention of hostile amphibious landings – in order to ensure that reinforcements could be brought in. The Norwegian Navy consisted therefore of submarines, a few frigates and several squadrons of fast attack craft; and its Air Force

---

*   Later General Fredrik Vilhelm Bull-Hansen. In 1981 he set up the Multinational Force Observers in the Sinai and was later Chief of Defence Staff.

The C-in-C up with the point section on an AFNORTH exercise in North Norway, 1981. (Farrar-Hockley family)

a number of squadrons of American F-4 and F-5 aircraft. SACEUR's reinforcement plan, published in 1982, allocated a reinforced US Marine brigade, with a large air component: the 4th MAB under Brigadier-General Ernest C. Cheatham;* a Canadian Air / Ground Force of battalion group size; and the British 3 Commando Brigade Royal Marines, reinforced with a Dutch battalion, and an air component.[24] In addition, the introduction of the E3A airborne warning and control system (AWACS) aircraft allowed NATO to put in place a stand-off airspace control system that could continue to operate even if ground stations were lost.

Southern Norway had excellent port and naval support facilities at Stavanger and Oslo, and good airfields. However, South Norway – commanded by Lieutenant-General Kristian Borg-Hansen – was the poor relation to BALTAP and North Norway in resource terms,[25] defended largely by Norway's single standing brigade and its reserve formations. This highlighted TFH's major problem: that he had very few forces immediately available and was critically dependent on large-scale reinforcement. As well as the forces already mentioned, there was also the Allied Command Mobile Force (Land), under US General Alexander Weyand – including a British infantry battalion, armoured reconnaissance squadron, artillery battery and supporting units – which could be committed to AFNORTH and which exercised there regularly. If there was sufficient political will to mobilise and reinforce in the event of crisis, then he could probably hold his ground; if the Warsaw Pact was able to mount a surprise attack, or seize the initiative, the game would be over before it started.

---

* Later Lieutenant-General Ernest C. Cheatham, Jnr (b. 1929). Cheatham had seen active service in Korea and Vietnam.

The Soviet leadership at this period remained in the hands of Leonid Brezhnev, who had ousted Nikita Khrushchev in October 1964.[26] This was a period when Soviet Communism appeared to be relatively successful: educational and living standards rose, but so too did bureaucracy and centralised control. Brezhnev became not only Party leader, but also President. Repression too increased, with the denial of even basic human rights, as Alexander Solzhenitsyn's *Gulag Archipelago* exposed when it was published in the West in 1973. The Soviets clearly despised the Presidency of Jimmy Carter, seeing in him weakness and decline of US power in the wake of the humiliation of Vietnam, without, at first, taking heed of the transformation of American military power that began almost at once. There seemed no chance of a thaw in the Cold War.

TFH's command coincided with the second round of bilateral US – Soviet Strategic Arms Limitation Talks (SALT), which was an early attempt to bring about such a thaw. Negotiations had begun in Helsinki, in neighbouring Finland, in November 1969. SALT I led to an Anti-Ballistic Missile Treaty and an interim agreement between the two countries. The SALT II Treaty banned new missile programs (a new missile defined as one with any key parameter five percent better than in-service equipments), so that both sides were forced to limit their new strategic missile development. However, the US preserved their most essential programmes such as the *Trident* ICBM and *Cruise* missile developments. In return, the Soviets retained over 300 SS-18 medium-range launchers. An agreement to limit strategic launchers was reached in Vienna in June 1979, just a month before TFH took over his new command, and was signed by Leonid Brezhnev and Jimmy Carter. Six months after the signing of SALT II, the Soviets invaded Afghanistan; and in September of the same year, the US discovered that a Soviet combat brigade had been covertly stationed in Cuba since the missile crisis of 1962. In light of these developments, which greatly increased tension, the treaty was never ratified by the US Senate.

If the Soviet invasion of Afghanistan was intended to raise the stakes, the main players who were emerging on the NATO side of the table were ready to accept the play. Margaret Thatcher had been elected as Conservative Prime Minister in Britain on 4 May 1979. She was a leader whom TFH evidently admired and who made her opposition to Soviet Communism plain from the very beginning. In the face of the customary economic ruin left by the previous Labour Government – in keeping with all its predecessors and successors – she was committed to raising defence spending by three percent in real terms every year, which for the next six years, she did. The Soviet Armed Forces weekly *Red Star* dubbed her 'the Iron Lady' – a title she accepted and took as a compliment. In January 1981, Ronald Reagan was elected as Republican President of the USA; Reagan was committed not just to limiting Soviet power, but to confronting it and, if at all possible, bringing it down. The two leaders forged a strong personal relationship which was to be pivotal in the final years of the Cold War.

The emergence of a more hard-line political stance in the West in the early 1980s coincided with rapid advances in weapon technology which had the potential to reduce somewhat the Soviets' numerical superiority. These developments also had the effect of placing the Soviet economy under great pressure, as it strove to match NATO capabilities in, for example, *Cruise* and *Pershing* missile technology. In 1982 and 1983, the Soviets made great play against the deployment of these systems, aided by their willing dupes in CND and similar organisations in the West, while denying the fact that ever greater numbers of Soviet tactical nuclear missiles were being deployed in Europe. The Soviet smokescreen of a proposed Nordic nuclear-free zone, which would include the Kola Peninsula, fooled no-one. In the early 1980s, the Soviets were engaged in upgrading the firepower of their forces in Europe by around 30 percent, including the introduction of 2,300 new T-72 and T-80 main battle tanks among its overall total of more than 52,000 tanks, as well as the construction of new 65,000-ton aircraft carriers. The cost of this was remarked on in 1982 by Major-General Professor Aleksander Gurov:

> ... the inter-relationship between military matters and the economy has been unusually close, and demands on material provision for troops and naval forces have increased sharply ... an unprecedented increase in the volume and a substantial alteration in the structure of the military consumption of material facilities and resources ... more complex systems of weapons and military hardware ... virtually renewed every 10 to 12 years ... an increase in manpower costs ... substantially greater demands have been made on the ... technical and professional training both of workers ... and Armed Forces personnel.[27]

The nuclear issue always hovered near the surface in AFNORTH and was something that TFH had to work around, even though there were no nuclear weapons on his patch in peacetime. Since the Berlin Airlift, both US and Soviet policy makers had confronted symmetrical, complimentary, security problems in what was a bi-polar world. The US aimed to station a large enough force in Europe to block any limited conventional threat; to stiffen European partners; to prevent the Germans from developing an independent nuclear force to defend themselves from the Soviets; and to act as hostages, whose destruction would trigger a US nuclear response. However, it had also to ensure that if at all possible, there was no hot war in Europe: the six weeks needed to field the full American field force from continental USA made it too vulnerable to interdiction. The Soviets could not permit the US to enjoy immunity in the event of war and so intercontinental ballistic missiles were the only way to take the threat of war to the American homeland and so deter American attack in Europe, no matter how remote that possibility was. It also had to deploy a large enough Ground Force to deter uprisings in its client States – and prevent these being exploited by NATO – and to coerce Western Europe by the threat of force. However, the Soviets had to show restraint, since conventional war would inevitably unleash nuclear war, which would devastate the Russian homeland – and this was an outcome that no Soviet leader would ever countenance.[28]

To undermine the West's will to use nuclear weapons, should this become necessary, the Soviets covertly encouraged and sponsored so-called 'peace' movements in the West, which were at best naïve and at worst subversive – especially the Campaign for Nuclear Disarmament (CND). TFH was well aware that CND was active in Scandinavia, even though neither Denmark nor Norway owned nuclear weapons, nor permitted them to be deployed on their territory in peacetime.[29] CND was not content with this, however, and in spite of the close proximity of the Soviet threat, pressed Scandinavian governments – including Iceland and the neutrals, Sweden and Finland – to amend their position to deny nuclear weapons under all circumstances. This, the governments of Denmark and Norway were never likely to do, conscious as they were that the only power with nuclear weapons routinely deployed in the region was the Soviet Union.

TFH himself had no doubt, as his earlier speeches and writing had indicated, that the West should be prepared to use nuclear weapons if attacked; indeed deterrence would only work if it was credible to the enemy. There was, he wrote in the German newspaper *Kieler Nachtrichten*, no question that nuclear deterrence had kept the peace for many years and there was 'no question of not living with nuclear weapons for many years to come'.

He went on to warn of the Soviets' potential in chemical warfare as well as nuclear, suggesting that NATO should also be prepared to use nuclear weapons in retaliation for a chemical attack – since only the US possessed stocks of chemical weapons and these were not readily available in Europe.[30]

*   *   *

Inevitably, TFH was propelled into a punishing round of visits to subordinate commands following his arrival. He also had to make contact with, and establish a relationship with, the British Ambassadors and the political leaders and senior military officers in the three host nations of AFNORTH – especially Norway – and with the senior NATO commanders (notably SACEUR, SACLANT and CINCHAN). He visited SACLANT, Admiral Harry D. Train* of the US Navy, and his British deputy, Vice-Admiral Sir Cameron Rusby,† at Norfolk, Virginia in February 1980.[31] The British Ambassador, Sir Archie Lamb,‡ proved a great ally and help in establishing communications with King Olaf and Crown Prince Harald, Thorvald Stolenberg, and the Chief of Defence Staff, Sverre Hamre – who, like Huitfeld, had served in the British Army during the Second World War and had won a Military Cross, of which he was immensely proud.

During the winter of 1979-1980, King Olaf and Crown Prince Harald dined with TFH at H88. The Royals arrived very punctually – so punctually that neither TFH nor Pat was waiting for them – and they were shown into the empty drawing room by Ted Olive. Luckily, Mike Motum walked cheerily in shortly afterwards and kept the King and the Prince amused. Pat was still dressing, and as for TFH? Why, he was in the kitchen, attending to his culinary *pièce de résistance* from which not even royalty could distract him: the soufflé.[32] This was typical; he continued to enjoy cooking, and getting the meal right was always top priority no matter who was coming to dinner. Even with a very senior group it was quite usual for TFH to disappear into the kitchen to make sure everything was progressing. Quite how the chef felt about this degree of harassment can only be imagined.

David Charles recalled another Royal mishap with Queen Margrethe in Copenhagen. The Queen was being entertained to dinner in TFH's flat and all went well until the pudding – which was seen to be a delicious *crème brulée*. This was not, however, a series of individual servings, but one large dish, which was offered to the Queen along with a silver spoon. Her Majesty gave the hard sugar crust a sharp tap in order to break it – nothing; another, harder whack; still nothing. After several vain attempts to break through, the dish had to be whisked away, the crust broken in the kitchen and the dish returned. The Queen took all in good part – but TFH's face was a picture.[33]

---

*   Harry Depue Train II (b. 1927) commanded the John F. Kennedy Battle Group; and from August 1976 to September 1978, the United States Sixth Fleet in the Mediterranean.

†   Vice-Admiral Sir Cameron Rusby KCB LVO (1926-2013).

‡   Sir Albert Thomas (Archie) Lamb KBE CMG DFC (b. 1921) had been a fighter pilot in the RAF during the Second World War before joining the Foreign Office.

TFH with General Sverre Hamre, the Norwegian Chief of Defence Staff.
(Farrar-Hockley family)

General Alexander Haig visited TFH early in his command, on what was Haig's farewell round of calls, and dined at H88. This was quite soon after the attempt on Haig's life. A creature of habit, Haig took the same route to SHAPE every day – a pattern of behaviour that was soon picked up by terrorist groups. On 25 June 1979, a land mine blew up under the bridge on which Haig's car was travelling – narrowly missing the car but wounding three of his bodyguards in a following vehicle. The attack was later attributed to the Red Army Faction, and in 1993 a German Court sentenced Rolf Clemens Wagner – a former RAF member – to life imprisonment for the assassination attempt. TFH kept this dinner very low-key, with very few other guests. Usually the MA or ADC attended dinners of this sort, but not this time. This may have been so that once any business relating to the northern flank of NATO had been dealt with, they could talk about Korea. As well as helping to forge a personal connection, talking about the war would have been useful to TFH's official history project, for this was never very far from his mind, whatever else was going on. TFH particularly admired Douglas McArthur and was especially interested in hearing about the Inchon landings from anyone who could add points of detail.

Once the introductory round had been completed, the tempo never really left off. Every week there would be two or three days away for a visit, or an exercise, or a study period; or there would be a high-profile visit to the headquarters; or a speaking engagement somewhere. To allow him to cover the ground, TFH was allocated the use of an RAF *Andover* aircraft based at Oslo. Managing the aircraft was never simple, as Mike Motum recalled. The crew was captained by Squadron Leader John Daniels from an office close to the C-in-C's. They were capable and professional people, but their responsibilities began on take-off and ended on landing. Getting people and baggage to the right place at the right time was therefore the lot of TFH's personal team. Not too difficult? Maybe so in Britain, but frequently landings were in different countries, so that arranging baggage movement on the apron while avoiding too much delay from customs and immigration could be tricky. On one celebrated journey from Oslo to Copenhagen, the two ADCs had rather unwisely thrown a tremendous party the night before and were consequently somewhat shabby. Things began to unravel when the crew's baggage appeared at the C-in-C's apartment while his kit went to the crew hotel. The ADCs narrowly avoided disaster by sorting out this muddle in time for TFH to change into evening clothes and greet his guests for the evening – but they were now marked men. Next day, all seemed to go well until the aircraft, now bound for Britain, was over the North Sea – at which point TFH demanded toast and marmalade. After a flurry it became clear that the aircraft was totally uncontaminated by marmalade and the RAF steward – regardless of the stipulation that after take-off, the crew was responsible – could not care less. An offer of Marmite instead was dismissed with contempt. Mike Motum then recalled that TFH 'proceeded to give me the biggest bollocking of my entire life … the thought of a quick leap across the aircraft and a dive into the North Sea seemed most appealing …' This was not, of course, really about marmalade at all, but TFH's rule that small mistakes were fine, big mistakes were not – and only one big mistake would ever be forgiven. The big mistake here was not the lack of marmalade, but a want of professionalism; party all you like, was TFH's unspoken message, but not to the extent that it interferes with duty: 'so there were no more parties before going on trips!'[34]

Because AFNORTH relied so heavily on reinforcement from outside, the exercise regime was unrelenting – especially in winter – when the ACE Mobile Force, the US Marines and the British 3 Commando Brigade would all come for winter warfare training. At the strategic level, AFNORTH held an annual, or at most biannual, conference and study period: Exercise *Viking Shield*. TFH ran one of these in January 1980, on 'Northern Command in the Eighties', attended by the King and Crown Prince and a stellar cast from all major NATO commands. Major elements of this study looked at the probable political-military balance of the world during the forthcoming decade, with a keynote speech from Marshall D. Schulman, Special Adviser on Soviet affairs to the US Secretary of State. Ake Landqvist, the Director of the Norden Association of Sweden, spoke on the Nordic dimension; German, Danish and Norwegian speakers all laid out the defence philosophies of their nations. The second day considered technical developments in defence, the military state of NATO, a review of AFNORTH by TFH himself and a final speech on crisis management by Sir Clive Rose,* the British Permanent Representative to NATO.[35] King Olaf also hosted a spectacular dinner for the participants at the Akershus Castle on Oslo's waterfront. Soon afterwards, in March, there was *Anorak Express* in North Norway – a large international exercise designed to practise the deployment and employment of the ACE Mobile Force (Land and Air), 3 Commando Brigade Royal Marines, the 15th (US) Regimental Combat Team and a large number of American, British, Danish and Norwegian Army, Navy and Air Force units. TFH wrote in the exercise newspaper that: 'I find a definite value in bringing Allied forces together in this way … it is particularly important for foreign units to come to Norway to experience problems we would be faced with in a possible war'.[36] The exercise included four phases: warning and alerting

---

* Sir Clive Martin Rose GCMG (b. 1921).

from 28 February to 4 March 1980; deployment and deterrent operations from 5 to 13 March; employment of the AMF and other reinforcing formations alongside host nation forces from 14 to 19 March; and redeployment from 14 to 19 March – a phase which included post-exercise review, and artillery and air range practices.[37]

TFH, of course, continued to be in great demand as a speaker on a variety of subjects. In February 1980, for example, he lectured at the University of Newcastle; and in May he gave the Kermit Roosevelt Lectures in the USA on the subject 'Will Democracy Continue to Defend Itself Effectively?' This gave him the chance to travel to the USA, taking Pat with him, and going first to New York; then on 12 May to the Army War College at Carlisle, Pennsylvania to give an evening lecture. On 13 May he was able to take part in a tour of the nearby Gettysburg battlefield, before going on to the Army Staff College at Fort Leavenworth, Kansas. From there he flew to the Joint Forces Staff College in Norfolk, Virginia. From Norfolk it was on to Washington DC for a visit to the Pentagon and a lecture at the National Defense University. The final lecture of this bruising schedule was at West Point on 20 May before leaving for home. As usual, TFH wrote no script and so posterity has no record of his remarks. However, Lieutenant-General Robert Gard,* Director of the Joint Staff College, wrote to him on 27 May saying that:

> Our students were fascinated with a number of your ideas, including the necessity for a slower pace and increased time for 'meditation' by senior military leaders! … Many thanks for striking just the right balance among erudition, professionalism and good humor throughout your visit here.[38]

The matter of public speaking was clearly contentious in some circumstances, for as early as February 1980, TFH was writing for clarification on certain issues to the MOD in London – probably concerning his status, for TFH was always clear that in terms of the chain of command he was, first and foremost, a NATO officer;[39] not a British officer – and it is possible he had been taken to task over some reported remarks. Relations had not, it seems, improved between TFH and John Stanier – who was by then VCGS – and this may have been the cause. Although the original letter does not survive, the then CDS, Admiral of the Fleet Sir Terence Lewin† answered:

> Let me assure you that there is no intention nor any national regulation which would restrict you in what you wish to say on purely NATO matters … on the other hand you will be aware that the terms of Queen's Regulations … do require you to consult the MOD whenever material of political concern is involved … I should imagine that Germany, Norway, Denmark and all the reinforcing nations for AFNORTH would also expect you to clear material…

---

*   Lieutenant-General Robert G. Gard, Jnr (b. 1928) later became Chairman of the Board at the Center for Arms Control and Non-Proliferation.

†   Admiral of the Fleet Sir Terence Thornton Lewin, Baron Lewin KG GCB LVO DSC (1920-1999) had served in the Second World War and commanded the Royal Yacht and an aircraft carrier before becoming First Sea Lord and later CDS.

There is, though, another side to this. We are now fortunate in having a Secretary of State and indeed a government which favours creating an informed public opinion about defence. This has not always been the case and you will recall the last government imposed rigid controls on all military speakers. In this new situation, there is a clear obligation for us all to conform to both the spirit and the letter of the law ... if we are to avoid a similar attitude developing.

It follows that there is a requirement for officers in international posts to let the MOD know, in good time, when they are going to speak ... [40]

This exchange resulted in a standard letter on the subject being sent to all senior British officers in international posts.

The demands of his regiments continued to absorb much of TFH's time. He was at the annual Airborne Forces' Day in Aldershot in 1980 with the Prince of Wales; in June he found time to be with the North Wales branch of the Parachute Regimental Association on 6 June 1980; and in July he was at the annual Comrades' Reunion of the Glosters in Münster, West Germany on the anniversary of the Battle of Salamanca. The comrades were the guests of the 1st Battalion of the regiment under the command of Lieutenant-Colonel Robin Grist[*] – son of Digby, who had been Second-in-Command to Carne in Korea and who had had to re-form the battalion after the Imjin.[41] The Glosters returned to Britain in April 1980 and TFH was among the guests at a welcoming luncheon in the Mansion House, given by the Lord Mayor of Bristol.[42] The pace slackened somewhat, however, when he completed his tenure as Colonel Commandant of The Prince of Wales's Division on 1 June 1980 – handing over to Brigadier Lennox Napier.[43] In advance of this handover, he wrote to all the COs of the division, saying that: 'The reputation of each of our regiments is dependent on the officers and soldiers serving in them. Occasionally one or another unit stumbles or falls through omission, but looking back at the record of service in the 1970s, errors have been few, triumphs many'.[44] Responding, Brigadier Mike Dauncey,[†] Colonel of the Cheshires, wrote that as Colonel Commandant he had 'brought the regiments together as good friends ... you have been so generous in giving your personal advice and help'.[45]

There was some encouraging news on the subject of Airborne Forces. The evident gap in capability and the effect on morale brought about by the disbandment of 16 Parachute Brigade had resulted in very poor recruiting and retention in the Parachute Regiment in the late 1970s – further exacerbated by the issue of low pay highlighted during the firemen's strike. In April 1981, with the return of the Brigade level of command, 8 Field Force was re-designated as 5 Infantry Brigade, and included two in-role parachute battalions with supporting arms and services. Brigadier Tony Wilson, the Commander, wanted to include the word 'Airborne' in the title of the brigade – slightly odd, as 'Airborne' was the correct designation for a division – but his intention was a good one. The request was refused, but the basis of a new parachute or air assault brigade was at least in place.

---

[*]   Later Major-General Robin Digby Grist CB OBE DL (b. 1940), Colonel of the Glosters.
[†]   Brigadier Michael Donald Keen Dauncey DSO DL (b.1920) had taken part in Operation *Market Garden* in 1944.

After the first year, David Leigh was well enough to assume all the ADC duties, and Mike Motum returned to the Glosters. He later recalled TFH's relationship with his personal staff:

> As ADC, one was always welcome at dinner parties and everything else. If the F-H family was together, it was not unusual to be invited to the party; indeed one almost became one of the family. One evening, while staying in Copenhagen, TFH paid for his whole party, including two ADCs, the MA and his wife – Graham and Gloria Farrell – to see a performance of *Hamlet* in Helsingor Castle. When I left and returned to 1 Glosters, I received a sterling silver tankard from Garrards, inscribed 'to MJM from AF-H'. He was also generous to the house staff, who could help themselves to tea, coffee and so on; and for whom there was always food set aside – the same as for the most senior guests – at dinner parties.[46]

David Charles also recalled TFH's generosity to the staff. He would, for example, always pay for dinner during trips; and he would always give lifts home to staff or wives in the *Andover* aircraft if there were free seats.[47]

At the very height of his profession, however, TFH and his family were the victims of unexpected personal tragedy. At Christmas 1980, TFH and Pat had gone to Berlin to visit Dair and his young family. For some time, Pat had not been on top form – she was always a little fragile in her constitution – and this had been remarked on by many people.[48] During the visit, she became very poorly – feeling bloated and complaining of severe pain. She was at once taken to the BMH in Berlin, where she was quickly diagnosed with advanced, malignant and aggressive ovarian cancer. From there she was evacuated to the BMH in Woolwich and began treatment both in Britain and later in an excellent clinic in Norway. At first, she seemed to respond well to the medication. In May 1981, TFH wrote to Pat Beaumont that 'Mercifully, I believe that she has survived this dreadful scourge and shows every sign of recovery. She has been in London for the past five months but I have high hopes that she will be back in Oslo this month'.[49]

It is clear that while Pat was having treatment in London, TFH was juggling the demands of his job in AFNORTH, speaking engagements and appointments abroad, and seeing Pat whenever he could make a trip to London. This was no easy time for any of the family, but everyone was determined to carry on as close to normal as possible, since looking ahead to the future was an important part of the mental conditioning required in treating cancer patients. TFH travelled to Korea in April with a contingent of veterans on the 30th anniversary of the war. His notes on the visit record his impressions: 'For those – the greater number – who had not been back to Seoul since the end of the war, the most remarkable sight was the city itself. In 1953, it was small and partly ruined by fire and high explosive. The outcome of rebuilding 30 years later is … a mass of large modern buildings which have been designed and laid out without distracting overwhelmingly from the old city'.

He also went to Imjin for the second time, noting that: 'The spurs up which numbers of Chinese soldiers had swarmed on to A and across the road, D Company, were empty in the sunlight … There were faint wheel marks in the gravel on the river bank; surely not those of the old CV?'[50]

Pat was just well enough for the wedding of Hilary and Kim that summer. However, the appearance of recovery was nothing more than a cruel deception. In mid-August it was clear that she had very little time left. TFH telephoned Hilary, who was stationed in RAF Shawbury; Hilary was in Oslo four hours later. Dair was telephoned in Berlin and left straight away and arrived the same evening. Mary Morning too was seldom far from Pat's side. Two weeks later, on 24 August, Pat died. Her funeral took place in the Anglican Church of St Edmund in Oslo on 28 August – where she and TFH had worshipped – attended by the King and the Crown Prince, and the South Korean Ambassador, among many others. Her body was then cremated and interred in the churchyard at Moulsford, close to Pye Barn, where a memorial service was also held – led by Mr Leighton Thomas, Vicar of Moulsford and family friend.

It is difficult to convey just what a tremendous shock Pat's death was to TFH, even though he – and the family – had prepared themselves mentally for this eventuality. He feared nothing and thought he could do anything, but he could not conquer Pat's cancer and this realisation hit him hard; very hard. They had married at a young age, had been together for 40 years, and had endured much together while TFH was serving during the Second World War, in Korea – especially in Korea – and elsewhere. Much of the shock came from the inversion of every expectation that he had always held, for living the life he did, he had always assumed that he would die or be killed before Pat – even though she was several years his senior. Messages of condolence flooded in from the great and good, as well as from the lowly; TFH replied to them all. The support of Dair and Hilary was, not surprisingly, a crucial factor in getting him through; so too was the love of his grandchildren. Having been a somewhat distant father, TFH was a loved – and loving – grandfather; he adored his grandchildren and they adored him. The second factor that brought him through the loss and sorrow of this time was his work. For TFH, there was no point in sitting around moping; he had work to do. He threw himself back into his command and his other duties with frenetic energy – not taking a single day off work once Pat's funeral and memorial service had been completed.[51] The work did not make him forget, but at least it distracted him. The third factor that brought him through was his faith, for he had not one iota of doubt that there was a continuing life of the spirit after death, and that he would one day see Pat again.

22

'A mass of appeals for help' Warrenpoint, the Falklands War and their aftermath, 1979-1982

In the shadow of Pat's death, TFH did everything he could to fill his time in late 1981. This was not hard, as can be seen in his surviving correspondence, for there was a mass of appeals for help from old soldiers and families asking for assistance with pensions and welfare; then there was a growing number of funerals and memorial services for veterans of the two World Wars and the accompanying letters of condolence; and of course letters of congratulation from him on honours and awards, which TFH never missed. He also continued to fulfil representation duties, attending the Queen as ADC at the State Opening of Parliament, for example, on 4 November 1981. As was usual in those days, he was advanced in the orders of knighthood – being made a Grand Commander of the Order of the British Empire (GBE) in the New Year's Honours of 1982.[1]

The demands of both his regiments also continued to absorb TFH's time – something which, with his writing, caused a deal of muttering among the NATO deputies in the headquarters, who sometimes made comments to the effect that TFH was a part-time C-in-C. No-one else believed this, for his phenomenal commitment and energy were well known. Not that any of the deputies would dared to have said anything to TFH in person, for they were in awe of his abilities and his fighting record.[2] TFH was, at this time, especially concerned with the continuing after-shocks which followed from the IRA attack at Warrenpoint on the banks of the narrows of Carlingford Lough, just inside Northern Ireland, which had taken place not long after he had arrived in Norway on 27 August 1979. He had returned almost at once to read one of the lessons at the memorial service in Aldershot for those killed at Warrenpoint, where the IRA had ambushed a convoy from 2 Para using a large roadside bomb which killed six men and badly injured two others. The only trace to be found of one man – a driver – was his pelvis, which was welded to the driver's seat by the heat and strength of the blast. A second bomb targeted the follow-up force sent to deal with the incident, for the IRA had analysed British tactics and placed the second device where they believed the incident control point would be established. They did their work well: the second blast killed the Commanding Officer of The Queen's Own Highlanders, Lieutenant-Colonel David Blair, and his radio operator, along with another 10 officers and men from 2 Para. In all, 18 British soldiers were killed – little or no trace was left of several of the victims, so huge were the explosions, which were described as being like a napalm attack. Six more were seriously injured, making it the deadliest attack on the British Army during the Troubles.[3] A civilian was also killed and another injured when troops fired across the border into the Republic of Ireland after the first

TFH in the robes of a Grand
Commander of the Order
of the British Empire, 1982.
(Farrar-Hockley family)

blast. This attack had taken place on the same day as the murder of Lord Louis Mountbatten. Thereafter, TFH spent many weeks following up matters of compensation for the victims of the attack and their families.[4] This was especially important in the light of many delays and inconsistencies in dealing with cases of criminal injury compensation to servicemen by the Northern Ireland Office, as well as the shockingly low levels of awards.[5]

Then, without warning, on Friday 2 April 1982, Argentina invaded and occupied the Falkland Islands, South Georgia and the South Sandwich Islands in an attempt to establish the sovereignty it had long claimed over them. On 5 April, the British Government dispatched a Naval Task Force to engage the Argentine Navy and Air Force before making an amphibious assault to recapture the islands. The land component of this force was under the command of Major-General Sir Jeremy Moore* of the Royal Marines, with Brigadier John Waters of the Glosters as his deputy. The initial force package was based on 3 Commando Brigade Royal Marines, with three RM Commandos and 3 Para. On 15 April, after a reassessment of likely tasks, the PM announced that 2 Para would also join them. It was later followed by 5 Infantry Brigade, with three more battalions.[6] This was a matter of huge moment for TFH, not only as

---

*   Major-General Sir John Jeremy Moore KCB OBE MC (1928-2007) had served in Malaya, Cyprus and
     Northern Ireland and but for the bomb attack that injured Lieutenant-General Sir Steuart Pringle, would
     have retired by the time the Falklands War began. See his obituary in *The Daily Telegraph*, 18 September 2007,
     for more details.

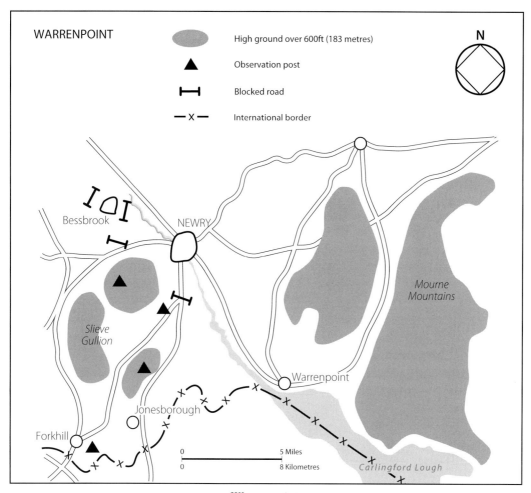

WARRENPOINT

High ground over 600ft (183 metres)

▲ Observation post

⊢⊣ Blocked road

—x— International border

N

Bessbrook

NEWRY

Mourne
Mountains

Slieve
Gullion

Warrenpoint

Jonesborough

Forkhill

Carlingford Lough

0   5 Miles
0   8 Kilometres

Warrenpoint.

Colonel of the Parachute Regiment, but also because Dair was now commanding a company in 2 Para under Lieutenant-Colonel H. Jones. Having lost his wife, TFH had to confront the possibility that he might also lose a son – not that there was any doubt about where duty lay.

1 Para did not sail with the Task Force, for the battalion was already committed to operations in Northern Ireland and could not be withdrawn, retrained and replaced without significant operational impact in what was a difficult time in the campaign against the IRA. Morale in 1 Para was, of course, shaken and the officers and men felt horribly left out while their comrades went off to war; it seemed a re-run of the Suez operation when the battalion had again been left on IS duties in Cyprus. TFH at once sent a message to the battalion, saying that:

> I dare say that there may be some among you who feel that the1st Battalion is going to a task of lesser importance or, at least, one that is less demanding. Neither of these latter views would be correct … all three battalions will be committed to operational tasks, none more important than another, all of a demanding nature.[7]

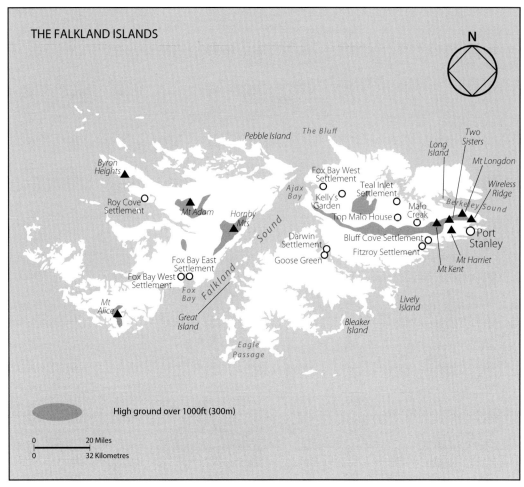

The Falkland Islands.

The two parachute battalions were embarked on the car-ferry MV *Norland* and the assault ship HMS *Intrepid* for the voyage down to the South Atlantic – and before they left, TFH went down to see them off. Although he probably did not realise it, this backfired. Lieutenant, later Lieutenant-General, 'Jacko' Page[*] recalled that TFH called the junior officers together on the car-deck of the *Norland*, having sent the field officers away:

> He told us that this would be a real war and a hard fight, not like anything else we had known before, and that we had better be ready. He then said that he did not expect to see us all again. This did not have the intended effect, as we all went away feeling that somehow he thought that we as individuals would fail the test of combat.[8]

---

[*] Lieutenant-General Jonathan David 'Jacko' Page CB OBE MA (b. 1959). He was later a Commander 16 Air Assault Brigade, Divisional Commander in Afghanistan and Director Special Forces.

The Task Force sailed southwards after an initial pause and then conducted preliminary operations. 3 Commando Brigade, under Brigadier Julian Thompson, landed on beaches around San Carlos Water on 21 May, on the north-west coast of East Falkland, in the Falkland Sound. 2 Para was put ashore from the *Norland* at Blue Beach, San Carlos while 3 Para was landed from the *Intrepid* at Green Beach, Port San Carlos. The brigade then began to advance across the rugged terrain of East Falkland, aware that the sub-Antarctic winter was approaching. With very little helicopter support, there was nothing for it but to slog it out on foot, or 'yomp', as the Marines called it.

Graham Farrell maintained close contact with the MOD throughout the whole period, briefing TFH every day on the progress of the battalions and on Dair's whereabouts. 2 Para had been sent on what was effectively a deception operation, while the main body of 3 Commando Brigade advanced towards Port Stanley. From early on 27 May until 28 May, 2 Para – with the support of 8 (Alma) Commando Battery, Royal Artillery – approached and attacked the small settlements of Darwin and Goose Green, which were held by the Argentine 12th Infantry Regiment. The BBC announced the capture of Goose Green on the World Service before it had actually happened. It was during this attack that H. Jones, the Commanding Officer, was leading his battalion into the attack against the well-prepared Argentine positions – a feat for which he was posthumously awarded the Victoria Cross. After Jones's death – and that of the Adjutant – the Second-in-Command, Major Chris Keeble, took command and a fierce struggle continued all night and into the next day. The British won the battle, losing 17 dead and killing 47 Argentine soldiers. Keeble forced the Argentine garrison to surrender and took 961 Argentine troops prisoner, a feat for which he was later awarded the DSO.

Casualties or not, the advance continued. 5 Infantry Brigade had by now arrived at the beachhead and because of a shortage of helicopters, was moved forward by landing ships and landing craft. It was this that resulted in the heavy casualties in 1 Welsh Guards near Fitzroy. On the night of 11 June, after several days of reconnaissance and preparation, Moore launched a brigade-sized night attack against the heavily defended ring of high ground surrounding Port Stanley. Two battalions and a Commando – supported by naval gunfire – simultaneously attacked Mount Harriet, Two Sisters and Mount Longdon. All were successful, but with heavy loss on both sides. In the last of these attacks, Sgt Ian McKay of 3 Para died in a grenade attack on an Argentine bunker, winning a posthumous VC. Then on the night of 13 June, the second phase of attacks was mounted. This time, 2 Para – now under the command of Lieutenant-Colonel David Chaundler –[*] captured Wireless Ridge with the loss of three men, killing 25 Argentine soldiers. After the dearth of fire support at Goose Green, Chaundler argued persuasively for additional firepower. Light armoured vehicles of the Blues and Royals, and artillery and naval gunfire support proved their worth. Simultaneously, the 2nd Scots Guards captured Mount Tumbledown with the loss of 10 men killed, inflicting 30 deaths on the Argentine garrison.

With the last natural defence line captured, the Argentine defenders in Port Stanley lost heart. A ceasefire was declared on 14 June and the Commander of the Argentine garrison in Stanley, Brigadier-General Mario Menéndez, surrendered to Moore the same day. The war had

---

[*]   Later Brigadier David Robert Chaundler OBE.

lasted 74 days and ended with the return of the islands to British rule. In all, 649 Argentines, 255 British and three Falkland Islanders died during the fighting.

From then on, TFH was heavily involved in the aftermath of the war. A Service of Thanksgiving for the Liberation of the Islands and of Remembrance of the Fallen, which TFH attended, took place on 26 July. There was then the question of burial for the dead. Until this time, it had always been the rule that British officers and men were buried where they fell. However, a promise had been made that in the event of death, families could choose to have the bodies of their soldiers brought home. Many families opted for this and in some cases, the bodies went back to the men's home towns – always accompanied by a burial party from the regiment. A significant number of families opted for burials in the Aldershot Military Cemetery and TFH arranged for them all to be buried together in November, before which the bodies lay in state in an improvised Chapel of Rest – a gymnasium in Montgomery Lines which had been suitably and reverentially decorated for the purpose. Every coffin was covered with a Union flag and the man's beret and medals. One of the dead was just 17 years old; another had been killed the day after his 18th birthday; there was a Jew and a Muslim, Christians of all denominations and some of no religion at all; it did not matter. All the families were brought to Aldershot by the regiment – sometimes bringing a whole extended family, or even most of a street of neighbours; that did not matter either. TFH was determined that everyone would be properly looked after. On the day of the ceremony, the media had to be kept from harassing the widows and families by a posse of tough-looking Paras, but one thing even TFH could not control was the weather. There had been heavy rain and the freshly dug graves had begun to subside. Before the mourners arrived, the Engineers did some rapid shoring-up and covering the wet earth around the site with timber, which was then turfed over. No-one was ever any the wiser. Later, a memorial service was held at Aldershot football ground in the presence of the Prince of Wales. In an absolute hush, the names of all the dead were read aloud. The two battalions then marched through Aldershot to a greeting that was, by contrast, truly deafening.[9]

The costs of the burial ceremonies were covered by the South Atlantic Fund, another matter which concerned TFH greatly. He was one of a number asked to give advice on how compensation should be calculated. His opinion – along with others, which was accepted – was that in every case of death, or disability which resulted in medical discharge, the potential career prospects of each man should be projected; his likely earnings and pension entitlements calculated; and awards made on the basis of the resulting amount. Much of this work fell on Graham Farrell and the Regimental Colonel, Jim Burke, but because of the workload, TFH was extended for a year as Colonel of the Parachute Regiment until October 1983. The Prince of Wales remained very much engaged in TFH's support over both the aftermath of Warrenpoint and the South Atlantic Fund. He had clearly been intensely frustrated at not being able to get close to the conflict and afterwards, the Chief of Defence Staff wrote to him, thanking him for his 'support and concern for our people during and after the Falklands Campaign. That you should devote so much of your time to meeting returning units, and the manner in which you did it, has been an inspiration to us all, and enormously appreciated'.

The Prince later wrote that 'I have had several letters, as Colonel-in-Chief of the Paras, from distressed relatives of dead soldiers who received their son's or husband's Falklands medals through the post in a jiffy bag and with a printed slip attached to it. You can imagine how dreadfully bitter they feel'.

This was just one example of the way that the Prince badgered ministers and civil servants on behalf of the interests of his regiments.[10]

TFH also spent much time in pursuit of the interests of the living, as well as the dead. In July, TFH had occasion to write to the Military Secretary on behalf of Keeble, who had not been selected for promotion to Lieutenant-Colonel – always a problem in those days for an officer who had not passed the Staff College, as Keeble had not. TFH reminded the MS, however, that:

> I am concerned about this officer's future, most particularly since he confirmed some sterling qualities in his professional and personal character in the Falklands Campaign … and has not been selected for Lieutenant-Colonel in 1983. I guess this is due not least to his having failed to get into the Staff College (his fault), and having had his reports at BALTAP written by someone who scarcely knew him (not his fault). He has since acquired better reports while instructing at Netheravon.
>
> In the Falklands, he took command of 2 PARA when H Jones was killed, pulled things together most effectively and finally brought about the surrender of the formidable numbers in the Goose Green defences.
>
> I shall be most grateful if you will let me know how Chris Keeble looks for promotion, assuming he gets (as I expect he will) a first rate report for 1982.[11]

All turned out well when in 1984 Keeble was promoted and took command of 15 (Scottish) Para. He also later had to take a hand in the case of David Chaundler, who, alone of all the commanding officers, received no recognition at all for his service – this in spite of having commanded 2 Para through a difficult and dangerous night-and-day battle which successfully opened up the back door into Port Stanley. At the end of his time in command, Chaundler was made OBE – for many, an inadequate and overdue award for his achievements. Before then, however, there was much speculation about what honours and awards might be granted. In August, TFH sent a fizzer to the editor of *The Times*, writing that:

> I am dismayed to see false information manifested under your headline concerning "Paratroop VC Proposals". For example Lt-Col Jones did *not* die in a helicopter shot down; he was *not* put into a helicopter. He had *not* been leading "a small group of volunteers" immediately prior to being hit or at any other time. Captain Wood, the Adjutant, did *not* then carry forward "volunteers"; he was killed before Lt-Col Jones. Stories of this kind are not only false but are likely to be painful to bereaved families. Speculation concerning honours and awards is likely to be misleading and similarly hurtful.[12]

In the end the list of awards won by the Parachute Regiment were the greatest haul of honours won by any regiment since the Imjin River. As well as the two posthumous VCs, there were two DSOs – the first to one of TFH's former platoon commanders in the Radfan, Hew Pike (now CO of 3 Para), and the second to Keeble; five Military Crosses; five Distinguished Conduct Medals; 10 Military Medals; one MBE; and 30 Mentions-in-Despatches. To TFH's enormous pride, one of the Military Crosses had been won by his son, Dair.[13]

There were other regimental issues too. In December 1979, the Director Army Staff Duties in the MOD was tasked to carry out a study into the future of the Parachute Regiment.[14] In the course of this study, RHQ Para under Jim Burke pressed hard, with the support of Headquarters UK Land Forces, for the restoration of a two-battalion Priority 1 role for parachute troops – and this was incorporated into the proposals. However, there was a strong view elsewhere that the main role of the regiment as a general reserve in war should be home defence. The third battalion was considered for a long-term commitment to the ACE Mobile Force, but this was not pursued. TFH wrote to the VCGS, Lieutenant-General Sir Timothy Morony, in January 1981[15] setting out his views, which broadly supported the paper being put to the Executive Committee of the Army Board, with two reservations: One was that there was inadequate supervision of parachute training and that this should be taken on by RHQ Para until some proper contingency force headquarters was in being – the proposal that a small cell in the headquarters of 8 Field Force was, he thought, inadequate; the second was that the parachute force should be given a general war role as the C-in-C UK Land Forces' reserve, for deployment anywhere.

At the same time, 5 Infantry Brigade – re-formed from 8 Field Force – was moved from Tidworth to Aldershot. Brigadier Tony Wilson had previously asked that the formation should be re-titled 5 Airborne Brigade and should take both in-role parachute battalions under command.[16] It had assumed command of the two battalions, but not received the title until after the Falklands War, when the third parachute battalion – along with 7 RHA, the parachute engineer squadron and a parachute logistic battalion – were all brought together and the brigade renamed.

*　*　*

All of this aside, TFH was still a senior NATO commander with responsibilities to fulfil and a large number of subordinates who liked to see him on a regular basis. Exercise *Viking Shield* had again been held on 18 January 1982 and focused on NATO and Nuclear Deterrence in the light of the deployment of *Cruise* and *Pershing* missile systems in Europe. SACEUR visited again in September and shortly afterwards, TFH addressed a visit by the NATO Military Committee. In October, the UKMF deployed to BALTAP for the major field training exercise, *Bold Guard*. There was, too, the continuing work on the official history of the Korean War, which absorbed much of his time. Graham Farrell's tour of duty was over and TFH took on a new MA, David Charles of the Parachute Regiment, who had been warned at short notice when the expected relief, Colin Thompson, developed a malignant and aggressive cancer. TFH and the Farrells, however, remained close, lifelong friends – bound as they were by the experiences of Warrenpoint, the Falklands War and Pat's death. After some correspondence with the Director of Infantry, TFH succeeded in having Farrell selected as Jim Burke's replacement as Regimental Colonel, where he could provide much-needed continuity. David Leigh too moved on and was replaced by Captain Simon Clark of the Glosters.

He was also still writing – the Korean War history, of course – but a letter from General Shan Hackett on the subject of his book, *The Third World War*, reveals that TFH had been giving advice on the drafting of the chapter on Scandinavia: 'I have followed the line you worked out for me pretty closely … thank you for your notable contribution to its production'.[17]

TFH being awarded
the Gwanghwa Medal
1st Class in Korea.
(Farrar-Hockley family)

TFH also reviewed the book in the *Daily Mail*[18] and described it as 'sensational', pointing out that it answered very well the case made by unilateral disarmers, showing them to be deluded and setting out very starkly the dangers to life and liberty posed by the Warsaw Pact.

Although the end of his military service was approaching, TFH refused to slow down and insisted on doing taxing and dangerous things – including several more scrapes in helicopters. On a visit to Northern Ireland to see a Para company attached to the Welsh Guards in Crossmaglen, the pilots of his *Wessex* were forced so low by fog that the helicopter began to take chunks off the tops of trees – at which point TFH calmly told the pilots to abort the flight. He took a long flight in a German *Luftwaffe* helicopter, from south to north up the Jutland Peninsula, to get a proper feel for the ground over which a Soviet attack might come; again there was bad weather – this time snow – and the pilots began to be visibly alarmed. TFH calmly told them to gain height and get above the snow, then press on and clear the storm – which they duly did. A third episode involved a Norwegian helicopter from which TFH jumped into the snow close to H88, rather than divert to the airport. The snow turned out to be five metres deep and when Leigh and the driver arrived, all that could be seen was TFH's beret. Almost frantic, it took them 30 minutes to dig TFH out – wet through, but otherwise quite unconcerned.[19]

In the autumn of 1982, TFH began making his round of farewells prior to handing over. Some of these were in Northern Europe and they included, of course, the King of Norway and the Queen of Denmark. Some were in Canada and the USA and while there, he was asked by the Canadian Joint Forces Staff College to give a talk as part of their combat stress

TFH visiting Newcastle, Jamaica in 1982. (Colonel Pat Beaumont)

General Bernie Rogers, SACEUR, passes the Colours of AFNORTH to General Dickie Lawson during the handover ceremony marking TFH's departure from AFNORTH.
(Farrar-Hockley family)

studies. TFH was delighted to do so, but gave a historically-based talk about the Korean War – and although the students tried to get him to describe his personal experiences, TFH was, as usual, very loath to do so. These were memories which were still raw even after 30 years.[20] Towards the end of the trip, he telephoned his old subordinate and friend from 3 Para, Pat Beaumont – who was, by now, Defence Adviser in the Caribbean – asking if Pat could arrange for him to visit his old home in Newcastle, Jamaica, where he had been the Training Officer in 2 Glosters. Beaumont was able to secure two helicopters from the Jamaica Defence Force and the visit was duly made. TFH was able to go back to the very bungalow where he, Pat and little Dair had lived so happily.[21]

On 14 November 1982, TFH handed over his command to General Sir Richard Lawson – the same Richard Lawson who had been Commander 20 Armoured Brigade under TFH in the 4th Division. He went home to Pye Barn and, after another round of farewells in Britain and his terminal leave, he left the active list on 14 February 1983.[22] Because years before he had given a false date of birth and the army had never corrected it, he was only 58 when he retired – on the young side for a full General. A flood of letters marked his departure, for he was regarded universally as one of the foremost soldiers of the age – and he was, moreover, one of the last senior officers who had served in the Second World War.

Twenty-one of his 42 years of service had been abroad and of those, no less than 16 years had been spent in war or active military operations. He had lived rough, and had been shot, tortured, starved and beaten; he had suffered from typhoid, malaria and blackwater fever; he had received two knighthoods and won two DSOs, one MBE and a Military Cross – as well as being mentioned in despatches three times[*] and earning 10 campaign medals: two of which carried three bars for different campaigns.[†] Somehow he had also managed to earn the degree of BLitt and had written 10 books. No wonder that the Prince of Wales, summing up everyone's feelings, had written: 'best wishes for the future, after such a magnificent past'.

---

[*]   Once in Italy and twice in Greece during the Second World War.

[†]   North Africa Star, Italy Star, France and Germany Star; 1939-1945 Star for service in Greece; Defence Medal and War Medal 1939-1945; Korean War, British and UN Medals; GSM 1918 with clasps 'Palestine', 'Cyprus' and 'Suez'; and GSM 1962 with clasps 'Borneo', Radfan' and 'Northern Ireland'. In addition, he had received the 1953 Coronation Medal and the 1977 Silver Jubilee Medal.

23

'The vital importance of home defence'
TFH's second career and life to the end of the Cold War, 1983-1990

For many senior officers, leaving the army after perhaps 40 years of service is a severe shock. When all one's adult life had been spent in uniform, sometimes in war; when one was used to the certainties of command and authority, to being obeyed, deferred to and to being able to get things done; when one had become used to having a personal staff and a certain standard of living, reality could be harsh. No orderly, no driver, no house staff. Unless he went to a service event, the average person out shopping or walking the streets would have no idea who this retired General was, nor what he had done – and in many cases, even if they knew, they simply did not care; then there would be the question of 'what next?' This might be a financial necessity, but more usually it was the continuing need to be useful; to have a point to one's life, or to contribute. For someone like TFH who dominated every event, be it an exercise or an operation, or just a dinner party, and who had so many plans for the future and so many irons in the fire, this simply was not the case; time, or lack of it, was most likely to be his enemy than being without his status as an active General. The army had never recognised his real date of birth and listed him as being a year older than he actually was, so that he was almost two years away from the latest age at which general officers retired, 60, and after an active life, TFH was far from ready to sit back and look at the sunset.

On leaving the active list, TFH had something of a soft landing, for he was still Colonel of the Glosters and of the Parachute Regiment – appointments he retained until 1984 and 1983 respectively; he handed over the Glosters to Lieutenant-General Sir John Waters and the Paras to General Sir Geoffrey Howlett.* He continued to attend reunions and regimental events of the two regiments, as well as those of 6th (RW) Para in Welshpool, until the end of his life. He was also a frequent attendee at regimental parties further afield. He returned to Athens and the South of France with the veterans of 6th (RW) Para and to Korea with the Glosters. He was still also an ADC General to the Queen, in which appointment he continued until July 1984. He also remained active in the affairs of the Korean Veterans' Association and the Army Benevolent Fund. As for the business of 'what next', this was simply not an issue. Pye Barn

---

* General Sir Geoffrey Hugh Whitby Howlett KBE MC (b. 1930) was commissioned into The Queen's Own before transferring to the Parachute Regiment. Like TFH, he was C-in-C AFNORTH.

became his permanent base of operations, as well as home, and from here, helped by Linda – who was still employed by the Cabinet Office – and with the support and encouragement of his family, he enlarged and expanded the career he had run in parallel while still serving, as a writer, historian, speaker and broadcaster. He was also helped by Ted Olive, who having left the army, stayed with him and was employed by TFH personally. Together they continued to work on Pye Barn. TFH had built a workshop and bought a vast array of tools so that contractors were needed only for plumbing and electrical work. The two had put in a new first floor, replaced every door and window, made fixtures and fittings, painted and decorated. While he was still in Norway, a winter cold snap had frozen an unprotected water pipe in part of the house that had not yet been brought up to scratch. The water ran for almost a day before a neighbour noticed something amiss and turned off the flow. The flood caused a very great deal of damage – especially to the wooden parquet floors – which TFH and Olive had to put right.[1]

His first publication from this period was the updated history of the Glosters, *Cap of Honour*, in 1984.[2] This included a substantial chapter on the Korean War, which TFH largely wrote. This was followed by *Nuclear First Use* in 1985, which he co-wrote with Neville Brown.[3] This controversial work opposed the adoption of a policy of no first use of nuclear weapons by NATO, even though the clinical and ecological effects would be devastating, for the number of casualties in a short nuclear war might be considerably fewer than had been incurred during the two World Wars of the 20th century and the other conflicts that had surrounded them. In 1988, he published *Opening Rounds*, which he had begun some years before as a result of his experiences as a Commander in NATO both in the Central Region and in AFNORTH.[4] He also contributed a chapter on the Somme in *Great Battles of the British Army as Commemorated*

Pye Barn, Moulsford. (Farrar-Hockley family)

in the Sandhurst Companies, edited by David Chandler and published by Cassell Ltd under the Arms and Armour Press imprimatur in 1989.

His major preoccupation, however, continued to be the official history of the Korean War. The first volume of this monumental work was published in 1990 under the title of *A Distant Obligation*.[5] Running to more than 500 pages, this – with its companion volume later on – became his magnum opus and was, with *Goughie*, his broadest and most analytical work. In it, he set out to 'comprehend the political as well as the military aspects of participation'.[6] He brought to it both his own long experience as a soldier and his accumulated expertise as an historian. As Brian Holden Reid put it, 'His long career as a historian is crucial to understanding him as a soldier, and vice-versa; the two cardinal features of his life interlocked'.[7]

There is no doubt that his own vivid memories, his almost unbelievable powers of recall, his soldierly insights into human nature, his understanding of the tactical and operational levels of war and of decision making all combined to produce the great powers of description and explanation that are evident in this work.

In the official history, TFH described the conflict as '… a full-scale conventional war, behind which, to the end, lay the option of the atomic bomb'.[8] The first volume is concerned with the decision of Attlee's government to commit land, as well as sea, and limited air forces to the Korean War; and the British part, in association with members of the Commonwealth, in operations and in political initiatives to bring the war rapidly to an end. It concludes at the point of failure in both endeavours. He was concerned as much with the politics of the war as its military conduct, pointing out that there is a circular relationship between politics and military strategy in which 'Sometimes politics calls the tune, sometimes it is decided by the outcome of battle'.[9] He was at pains to set the record straight on some major myths of the war:

> It now appears that Kim Il-Sung, the political leader of North Korea, was never the puppet of his great neighbours. On the other hand, the false notion has taken root that the British Government went to war in 1950 because it was politically and financially dependent on the United States, though the evidence … shows there were worthier reasons for this decision, at least a determination on the part of Mr Attlee, the Prime Minister, never to use appeasement to buy off aggression.[10]

Max Hastings, reviewing Volume I, wrote that:

> He marshals far more clearly and comprehensively than any previous writer the arguments that took place between the Chiefs of Staff and between Ministers, about British participation … the author's narrative of the British military contingent's doings is as comprehensive as one would expect … My only serious reservation is that it resolutely declines to make judgements upon the performance of units and individuals.[11]

Anyone who really knew TFH would understand why he declined to make such judgements. He understood better than most that people in war make decisions in the light of what they know then, facing the circumstances they do. Their knowledge is imperfect and the pressures great. One may analyse the reasons why a decision was made and describe its results – good or bad – with the benefit of hindsight, but one may not sit in judgement.

A modern poster from Seoul, South Korea picturing TFH. (Farrar-Hockley family)

Having launched on this new career and being taken up full-time with the writing of the Korean War history – which had previously been a part-time enterprise – TFH and Linda were thrown much more together. Many people who knew him were not therefore surprised when in December 1983, a year after he had left command and more than two years after Pat's death, he and Linda were married. The wedding took place at St Mary's Church, Streatley, near Moulsford with his brother Ted – a Master Mariner – as best man. TFH had been a married man all his adult life; he was used to companionship – even when that companion was at the end of a telephone line, or a correspondence. Life as a bachelor just did not fit him and, what was most important, he and Linda were already friends in spite of the gap in their ages (he was 59, she was 33).

Being based at home, there were plenty of opportunities for TFH to keep up with his family and especially his grandchildren. In 1985, Dair followed in his footsteps by becoming CO of 3 Para in Aldershot, where it formed part of 5 Airborne Brigade. The battalion deployed to Cyprus on operations with the UN for six months in 1986 before Dair relinquished command in 1987 to join SACEUR's staff in Mons, taking Victoria and the children with him. Two years later they returned when Dair took up the command of 19 Infantry Brigade in Colchester, on promotion to Brigadier. Hilary and Kim returned home from Laarbruch in 1983 and moved to RAF Chivenor in North Devon where their first son, Damien, was born in 1984. In 1985 they moved closer to Pye Barn – to Innsworth in Gloucestershire – and here their second son, TFH's youngest grandson, Callum, was born that year. In 1987 they moved to Manston in Kent.

Kim, Hilary, Sally Wood, TFH and Linda, 1985. (Farrar-Hockley family)

*   *   *

Korea and the Korean War continued to feature largely in TFH's life during these years. While still serving, he had been awarded the Order of Diplomatic Service Merit, an award presented to foreign officials for significant contributions in strengthening friendly relations with the Republic of Korea. It is a relatively rare honour – being usually awarded to only a handful of people every year – and is one of the highest civilian awards of the Republic of Korea. The Order is divided into six grades of five classes. The highest of the five classes has two grades. The top grade within the first class is reserved for Korean Diplomats. Alongside this in the top class for the Order is the Gwanghwa Medal 1st Class. This is the highest honour (within this Order) that can be awarded to a foreign national; and it was this that was given to TFH.[12]

He made three visits to Korea to walk the ground during his authorship of the official history, and he wrote and spoke on the war regularly. Shortly after his retirement he contributed an article in *The China Quarterly* on the Chinese Peoples' Liberation Army in the Korean War;[13] and in the margins of the official history he worked to compile a definitive roll of honour of those British servicemen killed in Korea. He also gave a paper that year on 'The China Factor in the Korean War' to a conference held by the East Asia Centre in the University of Newcastle, which was published in the Proceedings. In 1987 he was retained as a consultant on an ambitious venture by Thames Television, in collaboration with WGBH

Boston, USA and the Australian Broadcasting Commission. This was *The Korean War Project*, a series of broadcast seminars that went out in 1987. The first seminar, 'Many Roads to War', considered the post-Second World War world in the Far East and how it shaped the conditions that led to the Korean War. The second and third seminars, 'An Arrogant Display of Strength', and 'There is No Substitute for Victory', considered the early strategy of the war and its initial conduct; and then the Inchon landings and the Chinese intervention. TFH took part in both of these on-screen along with other distinguished participants, who included Lord Gladwyn, former British Ambassador to the UN; Dr Robert Oliver, biographer of Syngman Rhee; Professor Chnig-whi Kim, Director of the Korean National Institute of Security Affairs; Professor Lawrence Freedman; Professor Bruce Cummings; and Dr Peter Lowe. Later seminars covered the UN retreat and the sacking of MacArthur; the stalemate and American bombing of the North; the beginning of peace talks and the exploitation of prisoners of war; the death of Stalin, Eisenhower becoming US President, the ceasefire and prisoner exchanges and the establishment of the Demilitarized Zone. The series was widely praised on both sides of the Atlantic and in Australia for its depth of insight and scholarship.

In 1986, the British Korean Veterans Association asked TFH to carry forward a project to raise money for, and install, a Korean War memorial in St Paul's Cathedral. This involved a huge number of letters, calls, speeches and events for fundraising before it was brought to a successful conclusion in March 1987 – raising £50,000 in donations from regiments, corps, RN and merchant ships' associations, RAF squadrons, and individuals. A site was agreed with the Cathedral authorities and the memorial – black Korean granite engraved with the badges of army regiments, and the other services, and the inscription: 'Not one of them is forgotten before God', from St Luke's gospel, engraved on it – was designed by David Kindersley. The numbers of casualties were too great for every name to be inscribed – which was partly what lay behind TFH's work on the roll of honour – so the dead were recognised by their service or regimental badge. The memorial was installed and unveiled by the Queen on 11 March 1987 – coinciding (by chance) with the Thames Television series.

Given his fervent championship of support helicopters for the British Army, it was no real surprise that on leaving the active list, TFH was almost immediately retained as a consultant by Boeing, and remained with the company until 2000. TFH's work for Boeing was focused particularly on the development and utilisation of the CH-47 *Chinook* helicopter, developed for airmobile operations in the Central Region, for this was the period in which the British Army was forming 24 Airmobile Brigade which, with German and Belgian equivalent units, were later formed into NATO's first multinational formation. The driving force was the recognition that Soviet operational manoeuvre groups might break through the main defensive area on the Central Front and drive deep into the Allied rear area. The agility provided by air mobility could be used by HQ Northern Army Group, within its operational plan as developed under Nigel Bagnall, rapidly to move and position formations equipped with very large numbers of wire-guided anti-tank missiles in a counter-penetration role. With the end of the Cold War and the demise of this role, support helicopters were in heavy demand for expeditionary operations, first in the Gulf and then in the Balkans. The role of a consultant like TFH can be summarised as giving advice, but also lobbying the procurement staff; effecting introductions between military customers and industrial suppliers; hosting events; and speaking at conferences and seminars such as that at RUSI in November 1988, in which TFH addressed the subject of airmobile operations.

TFH remained much in demand by the world of military education. In March 1989 he was asked to contribute to a series of War Studies seminars, run by the Army Staff College in conjunction with Southampton University, to look in depth at the way ahead for the teaching of War Studies in the British Army from Sandhurst through to the Higher Command and Staff Course. War Studies were interpreted as being the application of the lessons of Military History to the study of the theory and practice of modern warfare. The concept being evolved was that officers would study a core campaign from the Second World War as they progressed through the various stages of their education, supplemented by other campaign studies. Those attending the session with TFH included such luminaries as Field Marshal Nigel Bagnall, Professor David Chandler, John Keegan, General Sir Hugh Beach and a raft of senior military staff.[14] The seminar did not, however, address the philosophy, but concentrated on the presentation of a series of papers on different eras – TFH's being 'Confusion to Complacency. Commitments and Campaigns of the British Army since 1945'; Korea formed a major part of this paper. Although the concept of the core campaign never took hold, the army's approach to War Studies certainly became far more serious in these years after a period in which the subject had been largely neglected. TFH's paper later found its way into *The Oxford Illustrated History of the British Army*, edited by Ian Beckett and David Chandler and published in 1993.

He was still more widely in demand as a speaker and writer. Barely a week went by in which he was not speaking at a dinner, a discussion group or a seminar. He was often pulled in to TV programmes like BBC *Newsnight* as a commentator on defence and security issues, where his pugnacious face and forthright views could be guaranteed to start a lively debate. He travelled to the USA, South Africa and Germany as a speaker on leadership at business seminars and conferences. He took part in battlefield tours and staff rides. In February 1985, he gave a lecture at the Army Staff College, Camberley which was filmed by the BBC and was interviewed afterwards. These pieces were used in two BBC broadcasts, 'Fighting Spirit' and 'Casualty' in their run of 13 programmes in the series *Soldiers: A History of Men in Battle*, which was written by John Keegan and Richard Holmes and presented by Frederick Forsyth. In September 1985, he spoke at the IISS annual conference on 'The Problems of Over-Extension: reconciling NATO defence and Out-of-Area contingencies', later published as an Adelphi Paper. He reviewed books for various publications – for example, titles by Lawrence Freedman, David E. Morris and Howard Tumber, and John Lawrence and Robert Lawrence in *The Times* Literary Supplement;[15] and Michael Carver's *Twentieth Century Warriors* for RUSI.[16]

* * *

TFH's work-rate and output were nothing short of astonishing in these years. However, he still found time for work on Pye Barn. The latter loomed much larger in his life than TFH might have wished. The damage to the flood had not long been fully repaired, and he and Linda married, when a serious fire broke out in the house. This happened on Christmas Eve 1984 when Dair and Vicki, with their children, and Frank and Joy King, were all in residence for the holiday. The fire had started due to a rodent eating through some wiring and it was some time before anything was noticed. Just after tea, the lights went out, and smoke appeared. The fire brigade was called but by now, the fire had begun to take hold. What began as a challenge for the local fire station ended with additional tenders coming

Two views of Pye
Barn after the fire.
(Farrar-Hockley
family)

from Oxford. In the end, the fire brigade was able to contain the fire to one end of the house, aided by the thickness of the main beams, which dated from the time of Queen Anne. However, smoke and water, as well as flames, had got in everywhere. Later that night, the Kings went off to open up their house so that everyone could spend Christmas there. On Christmas morning, TFH and some of the family went back to the house and forced open freezers and fridges to salvage enough food for Christmas dinner. Christmas was a gloomy time, but on Boxing Day, Linda decided that they must go home and face the mess. By great good luck, a local electrician was found who could rig up a supply to the undamaged end of the house and the whole family, with the Kings and Linda's family also rallying round, got to work scrubbing, washing and cleaning until the undamaged part of the house was habitable. Once the Christmas hiatus was over, the insurers took charge and sent in contractors to rebuild everything. Even so, it was the following October before TFH and Linda had their house to themselves once more.

In his busy second career, and in the midst of dealing with the fire's consequences, TFH embraced local issues – especially the church and Moulsford School, of which he had been a Governor since soon after moving to the village. In 1986, he became Chairman of the Governors. He continued to enjoy cricket, going to test matches at Lords at one end of the spectrum – for having put his name down years before for the MCC, he had finally been elected – and playing from time to time, in the local side (also the MCC – Moulsford Cricket Club, of which he became Honorary President) at the other. Each year, he would field his own President's XI from family and friends to take on Moulsford.

The Vicar of Streatley, the Reverend Leighton Thomas, also now looked after the Parish of Moulsford. He recalled that there had been much talk about 'the General' for years – but TFH was like an actor who never appeared on stage. However, once he retired from the army, he was very much more visible. Thomas would come to Moulsford every Thursday to hold a Communion service in the old vicarage and developed the routine of calling at Pye Barn for a chat. As a result, their friendship developed. The Parish, as it happened, had some distinguished residents as well as TFH: a parliamentary private secretary, a professor of theology, a senior consultant anaesthetist and a former headmaster of Harrow School. Thomas conceived the idea of asking these people to speak in place of a sermon from time to time, which proved highly successful; in TFH's case, he also, with the Bishop's consent, stood in for Thomas from time to time at non-sacramental services such as morning or evening prayer.[17] Being a committed churchman, TFH became a member of the Church Council and always attended meetings – even when, as sometimes happened, he had to leave after half an hour only to pop up later on the television screen. He also became a committed member of the Prayer Book Society, having a deep devotion to the forms of worship prescribed in the Book of Common Prayer, and to the Authorised Version of the Bible.

He also returned to his boyhood love of sailing. At the time of his retirement he had considered buying a yacht, but his calendar was so crowded that he would never have been able to make enough use of the boat to justify the expense, and so whenever he could, he chartered. In 1986, he sailed from Lymington to Norway in an ocean-going yacht with Ted Olive and David Leigh; Leigh went home by air from Denmark and on the return journey, Linda and her sister, Sally Wood, joined TFH and Ted Olive for the cruise through the Danish Islands and the Kiel Canal. In the North Sea, however, very bad weather struck. They made it as far as Den Helder in the Netherlands in a Force-9 gale, where the ladies disembarked – shaken but glad to be back on dry land – and flew home. TFH and Olive waited out the storm for a few days and then completed the trip, arriving back in the middle of Cowes Week.

* * *

TFH never shied away from controversy or from a fight, and for the first five years of his career after the army he was involved in an organisation that courted both: 'Defence Begins at Home', or DBH. The DBH Committee had been started by the highly-respected Admiral of the Fleet Lord Hill-Norton,* who was joined by the philanthropist and benefactor Sir David Wills† and by Air Marshal Sir Frederick Sowrey.‡ TFH had been canvassed while still serving to take on the post of Director. This he declined, due to the likely heavy load of other commitments as a writer, speaker and historian. However, he agreed to take on a role as a travelling spokesman, appearing frequently as a radio and television broadcaster and relying on his prestige and knowledge of defence and security issues. He had strong views anyway on this subject from both his days in the South-East District and his knowledge of the home defence forces of Norway and Denmark.[18] In essence, the DBH Committee felt that in the event of a general war in Europe, the home base was in grave danger of attack – not only by bombing, but also from Soviet Special Forces, or *Spetznaz*. To counter this threat, a supplementary Reserve force was needed to bolster the relatively small numbers of Regular and Territorial troops available. Like the Danish Home Guard, which TFH had known in AFNORTH, this force would act as the eyes and ears of the field army – observing and reporting incidents, and providing point protection on fixed sites; it would not be a combat field force, nor would it be used for law and order tasks. It would be equipped with small arms, CB radios, simple uniforms and NBC gear. It would have a small training liability provided by the Regular and Territorial Armies. The target was a force of 700,000, at a cost of £120 million over five years.

Unfortunately, this organisation has become wrongly targeted by various far-left conspiracy theorists, which has resulted in a great deal of complete nonsense being put about – and believed by quite sensible people – trying to tie DBH to, among other things, theories about Airey Neave seeking to set up a small group to involve itself in the internal struggles of the Labour Party; or the efforts of Walter Walker and others a decade earlier to set up an 'army of resistance' to the then Labour Government of the Wilson era to 'forestall a Communist take-over'.[19]

The extreme left-wing magazine *Searchlight* alleged that plans for secret armed cells to resist a more left-wing Labour Government were drawn up by a group that included George Kennedy Young, the former Deputy Director of MI6, and Airey Neave. *Searchlight* has even alleged

---

* Admiral of the Fleet Peter John Hill-Norton, Baron Hill-Norton GCB (1915-2004) fought in the Second World War on the Western Approaches and in the Norwegian Campaign; then the Arctic convoys and finally in the Eastern Fleet. After the war he served as First Sea Lord and Chief of the Naval Staff and then Chief of the Defence Staff in the early 1970s. He went on to be Chairman of the NATO Military Committee.

† Sir David Wills KBE TD (1917-1999) was a generous philanthropist whose principal legacy is the Ditchley Foundation.

‡ Air Marshal Sir Frederick Beresford 'Freddie' Sowrey KCB CBE AFC (b. 1922) served as Director of Defence Policy at the Ministry of Defence from 1968 to 1970 and Commandant of the National Defence College from 1972 to 1975.

that, in spite of MOD denials and a lack of any evidence, TFH actually joined with Walker in confirming that 'a secret armed network of selected civilians was set up in Britain after the war and was secretly modernised in the Thatcher years and maintained into the 1980s'.[20]

By the time that TFH became involved with DBH, Walker's proposed movement had long been abandoned. Walker himself had become a Patron of The Western Goals Institute, a body with which TFH never became associated at any time; and Walker was, in any case, suffering badly from the results of injuries during his service which greatly restricted his ability to move, let alone anything else. There is no indication in TFH's personal papers that he ever met Walker, spoke to Walker, corresponded with Walker, or shared Walker's views. Even so, the far left has continued to try to tie DBH and its supporters to Walker's objectives: this, for example, from the internet:

> More recently Admiral Lord Hill-Norton, former Chief of the Defence Staff and Chairman of the Military Committee of NATO (19747), General Sir Anthony Farrar-Hockley, former C-in-C NATO for Northern Europe, Air Marshal Sir Frederick Sowrey, the UK Representative on the Permanent Military Deputies Group CENTO, 1977-9, together with assorted groups of right-wing financiers and semi-psychopaths such as Sir David Wills, have launched a campaign to create a similar auxiliary defence force. Called Defence Begins at Home, the campaign hopes to build up a force of 700,000 reservists capable of crushing subversion from within.[21]

The truth, as always, is far less interesting than conspiracy theories and less readily believed by the gullible, even when, as with DBH, all activities were conducted openly – including in the Houses of Parliament, as well as at public meetings and in the press; and are, therefore, a matter of record – in full consultation with the government of the day and its officials who were, in many cases, very open to what was being proposed.

The facts of the campaign may be summarised quite easily. The first meeting of the committee was held on 29 September 1981. In October 1981 Michael Hickey, who had taken early retirement from the army at the early age of 51, was appointed as full-time Director of DBH and set up the office at Victoria House, Southampton Row in London with the aim of bringing pressure on the government of the day – whatever its political colour – to take home defence more seriously and to make proper provision for it. Hickey was the author of 'The Spetsnaz Threat: Can Britain be Defended' – published as an Occasional Paper by the Institute for European Defence and Strategic Studies – and he, therefore, had plenty of understanding of the issues.

In 1982 Defence Secretary John Nott acknowledged the problem highlighted by DBH, remarking that 'Where we are weakest, in some cases seriously so, is in our capacity to defend the United Kingdom base'.[22]

Consultations and lobbying by Hickey with a wide range of organisations and individuals, therefore, began at once. Among others, the Red Cross, St John's Ambulance, WRVS and the Cadet Forces were all briefed on the committee's objectives. Margaret Thatcher was written to in September 1982 and preliminary discussions were held with Defence Secretary John Nott and officials in the MOD and the Home Office. Thatcher replied to the letter, from Sir David Wills, saying that 'I should be very happy to see you myself and hear about your ideas directly' and asking for some detail on the committee's proposals, which were duly sent.

Hill-Norton, Sowrey and Wills briefed Thatcher at 10 Downing Street, with John Nott and William Whitelaw, for over an hour. The only point of difficulty was that the MOD put the cost of the proposed force considerably higher than the committee, at £357.5 million, which Wills successfully contested.

Early in 1983, Major-General Dick Gerrard-Wright, Director-General TA & Cadets, and Major-General Bill Bate, Secretary of TAVRA, were briefed. Both had seen DBH's proposals in advance and although well disposed, made it clear that they would resist any scheme that was likely to divert recruits away from the TA, or compete for resources. In reply, Hickey stressed that any Home Defence Force would be an extension to the TA, recruiting those who could not or would not join the TA. As a result, the DBH feasibility study was sent to all TAVRA associations, less Northern Ireland.

TFH joined the committee in January 1983. At the same time, Nott was succeeded as Secretary of State for Defence by Michael Heseltine. His views were unknown, so the committee met him on 4 March and gave him a full briefing. Heseltine seemed not inclined to be in favour, but did agree to see the committee again. A pamphlet was therefore prepared which outlined the committee's concerns and proposals, and this was launched at an event on in March 1983 at RUSI. It was followed by a wave of media interest – some in favour and some, like the *Daily Mail's* article 'Dad's Army plan to fight off the Russians',[23] dismissive. However, this did not prevent a determined effort by the committee to enlist grass-roots support, which went on all summer. In December, a second meeting with Heseltine was held, at which it became clear that no progress would be made while he remained Secretary of State. However, in 1983, the first steps were taken to establish Home Service Force (HSF) companies in TA battalions and to increase further the size of the TA and the Royal Auxiliary Air Force. The following year, the target for the HSF was raised from 4,500 to 7,000 and in that year's Defence White Paper, recognition was given for the first time to the threat from Soviet *Spetznaz*.[24]

Support for DBH came from some surprising quarters: Ken Livingstone, for example, interviewed by Janet Street-Porter; and Peter Tatchell in his paperback *Democratic Defence*. However, some far-right groups began to offer pirated copies of DBH material, dressing it up as their own, and this led to confusion with Walter Walker's *Column 88* of a decade before. It was some time before this problem was at least partly solved, but in the meantime, media interest continued – including a reasonably satisfactory episode of the BBC's '*60 Minutes*' in late 1983. In 1984, TFH drafted a paper which gave some alternatives to the full DBH programme, such as the formation of peacetime cadres and a national register of volunteers, or a skeleton organisation with only key personnel in place. In March, he made a tour of North-East Scotland, speaking in Aberdeen, Elgin and Inverness. This resulted in a very positive response, with more than 1,000 people expressing interest. In June, a Westminster lobby event again generated a great deal of publicity. On 17 September, TFH wrote an article for *The Times* entitled 'Call up the Home Guard', timed to appear at the same time as the start of the major NATO exercise *Lionheart*. However, it was increasingly clear that many senior TA officers were unenthusiastic, in spite of growing interest among back-bench MPs resulting from lobbying by their constituents.

In January 1985, the committee gave a briefing to the House of Lords – and there was some discussion of the concept in the debates on the Defence Estimates that June. Moreover, that year, the first major home defence exercise for many years – *Brave Defender* – was staged, involving 65,000 Regular and Reserve troops. DBH still believed, however, that the numbers were insufficient for the task and that an auxiliary third force was needed, since the mobile force currently available for contingencies amounted to only 90 men per county and more needed to be done to release fully-trained men from static duties. The *Daily Mail* subsequently reported that the RAF was considering putting out a call for 2,000 civilian volunteers to secure four air bases (High Wycombe, Brampton, St Athan and Lyneham), since during Exercise *Brave Defender*, too many trained technicians had had to be taken off their primary duty to undertake security work, which had considerably downgraded the effectiveness of the air stations in question.[25] Hill-Norton again spoke about the project publicly and at length in the House of Lords debate on the 1985 Defence Estimates.[26] In the aftermath of *Brave Defender*, a new brief was sent to Margaret Thatcher, who wrote back to Hill-Norton saying that she and her Cabinet colleagues 'are very much at one with you … on the vital importance of home defence', but pointed out that 'the main problem is inevitably one of resources'; she remained, therefore, non-committal – offering only a vague promise to look further at the enhancement of home defence after current plans for the TA had been completed.

The arrival of George Younger as Defence Secretary following the resignation of Heseltine soon after Christmas 1985 gave some cause for optimism. However, it soon became clear that in terms of resources, Younger had been left with little room for manoeuvre. A new pamphlet on *Defence Begins at Home*, heavily amended by TFH, was therefore prepared to set out the functions of the third force. In March 1986, Michael Hickey ceased full-time employment with DBH and Kenneth Jamieson agreed to take on the role of Parliamentary Liaison; however, the office was closed in September 1986. A letter from Hill-Norton to George Younger, dated 22 June 1987, suggests however that there was still cause for hope:

> David Wills passed your letter … of 16th February [1987] to us all. This encouraged me to write to you again about some of the outstanding issues that we discussed last year, but I have waited until after the election so that the future is settled …
>
> It seems to me and my colleagues that several strands are coming together to encourage the establishment of a low-cost Home Defence Force on the lines we have developed over the past five years. The welcome moves towards an arms control agreement … are bound to put greater emphasis on our conventional ability to deter war. Certainly our figures show that in defending the United Kingdom base, a Home Defence Force is by far the cheapest and easiest way of improving this capability. That one of the Armed Forces recognises this fact is clear from the Royal Air Force's pilot scheme … to stiffen the sinews of key bases by appealing to those citizens who want to participate in their own defence, but who cannot find the time to join the Territorial Army or its equivalent in the other Services … Lastly, the Home Office is taking a more robust line at local government level towards planning for a range of catastrophes.
>
> When you met us in October we suggested a meeting of minds at the RUSI, and my colleagues and I hope that you would now agree to let this go ahead. We would field a team to cover the perceived threat from *Spetsnaz*, based on information generally available, and re-iterate a solution based on Defence Begins at Home. It would make it so much more worthwhile if you could be represented by a Minister of State supported, say, by VCDS and DUS.[27]

Younger's letter had also said that Jim Spicer MP had been in touch with the department to make proposals similar to those of DBH, which were being considered. While not committing to anything, Younger was certainly not opposed to the committee's idea, although he made the point that his main consideration was still the most effective allocation of limited resources.

The hope turned out to be a false hope, however, and the DBH campaign was wound up by the end of the year. It had mobilised public awareness in home defence; it had contributed to the restoration of at least some of the lost capabilities within the Regular and Reserve forces, but it had not succeeded in mobilising political or media support for a large third force. Two years later, Communism collapsed, the Berlin Wall fell, and the Armed Forces from then on were subject constantly to attack on financial grounds – even though the world became more and more unsafe and the demands placed on them multiplied.

* * *

In the meanwhile, another long-running campaign – Northern Ireland – was drawing towards it climax, but there still remained dangers. TFH had never concealed his address and telephone number; he was listed in *Who's Who* and in the local directory. As a Parachute Regiment officer and as a former CLF Northern Ireland, he was an obvious target for the IRA during their campaign on the British mainland. Pye Barn was only three miles from the site of a massive IRA arms cache which had been recovered in 1982, and later linked to a series of attacks around that time, including the 1983 Hyde Park bombing and the Harrods bomb.[28] In 1986, TFH was said to have been on an INLA hit list found in a house search, but did not appear on a similar IRA list discovered in a bomb factory in Clapham in 1989.[29] In July and August 1990, a series of attacks by the IRA killed the Conservative MP Ian Gow, Chairman of his party's back-bench committee on Northern Ireland and a leading opponent of compromise with Republicans, and targeted former Cabinet Secretary Lord Armstrong, who only escaped death when an explosive device fell off the underside of his car.

Around noon on 13 August, TFH himself was out, but Hilary was at Pye Barn with Kim and the children. Callum, now aged five, was playing in the garden when Ted Olive, who was keeping half an eye on him, noticed him picking up the reel of a garden hosepipe which had been lying on its side. Olive could see that there was something attached to the reel which did not seem quite right. He took a closer look and became seriously alarmed, shouted 'Get away fast,' ran up, grabbed Callum and took him inside – calling out to Hilary to keep clear of the area. By the time that TFH came home soon afterwards, the police had been called.[30] The whole area had to be evacuated and an army bomb-disposal team called in. Although the Chief Constable of Thames Valley Police, Colin Smith, would only say that the device was 'consistent with previous devices',[31] it soon became clear that this was the work of the IRA. The device contained 3 lbs of *Semtex* commercial explosive which should have been activated by a mercury tilt switch. Mercifully, the switch had failed to operate. At a later press conference, TFH pointed out that his grandson had been 'fantastically lucky' and 'would have been blown to smithereens' if the switch had worked. By an odd chance, a hosepipe ban had been imposed in the area the previous week because of the unusually dry summer weather that year, so that the hosepipe had not been used. TFH added that 'We try to keep our eyes open and take the common-sense advice about such matters'.

Ted Olive, TFH and Hilary after the failed IRA bomb attack at Pye Barn.
(Farrar-Hockley family)

He went on to say that 'I have been shot at and had people attempt to end my life on various occasions in one way or another', but 'I don't care for people who leave explosive devices in my garden'.[32]

Much care was taken to recover the device intact, rather than destroy it by a controlled explosion, so that it could be subjected to forensic investigation. It was the first time a domestic object had been booby-trapped on the mainland – and even in Northern Ireland, this sort of device was rare.

24

'An Honourable Discharge' TFH's last years, 1991-2006

In the changed world after the Cold War, TFH showed no signs of slowing up or changing direction. New circumstances meant new opportunities as far as he was concerned. However, his main preoccupation remained the Korean War history – the second volume of which, *An Honourable Discharge,* was at last published in 1995. This volume opened with an evaluation of the unsuccessful strategy of the first part of the war, which provided a bridge between the two parts. The rest of the volume examined the extent to which the British contribution, within the United Nations' extended effort between 1951 and 1953, was successful.[1] Warren I. Cohen, reviewing it in the journal *History*, remarked that 'no-one who reads this book will ever again refer to the British military contribution as 'token'.'

Other reviews acknowledged the depth of research, the meticulous reconstruction of events and the pride in the performance of the troops; but although they were all respectful, they were not universally glowing – some note that the book would be difficult for the layman; others seem to have expected a somewhat racy narrative. In spite of that, there is no doubt that the work remains probably the best, but least reviewed, account of any British military campaign since official histories began to be written.

One aspect on which TFH looked for confirmation was the involvement of Soviet pilots flying Chinese combat aircraft during the war. It so happened that the chance came to talk to someone who might provide the information. This was KGB General Dmitri Antonovic Volkogonov, who had written the official history of the KGB, but then seen his work suppressed by Brezhnev. The knowledge of what had been done in his name and the millions of deaths brought about by Communism had changed Volkogonov's outlook. He had later, after the collapse of Communism, been Co-Chairman of the joint US-Russian body investigating the fate of those US airmen who had fallen into Russian hands when their aircraft had made forced landings in Soviet-controlled territory during the Second World War bombing of Japan. He had, therefore, a reputation in the West as a decent fellow. In the early 1990s he was given the task by President Boris Yeltsin of reporting to NATO on the fate of decommissioned Soviet nuclear weapons and facilities. As part of this, he visited Britain to give a series of briefings. Roy Giles, who knew him from Brixmis days, invited him to Oxford and suggested to TFH that they should meet. TFH saw his chance and put on a good dinner at Pye Barn for Volkogonov, with Roy Giles and several other Russian speakers. The two got along very well and, as a result, Volkogonov provided chapter and verse on TFH's questions – the first proper confirmation that this had actually occurred. Volkogonov had spoken Russian throughout the evening, giving no sign that he understood English, and making Roy Giles work hard as interpreter. It was not until bed time that he brazenly said good-night and passed a few pleasantries in perfect, idiomatic English. Clearly he had understood everything – as one might expect of a KGB officer – and much as those present had enjoyed the encounter, Volkogonov's want of manners remained a talking point for years afterwards.[2]

At the same time as continuing the work on the official history, TFH was still much in demand as an authority on the Korean War. In October 1992, he contributed an article on the British part in the Korean War for Garland's *Encyclopedia of the Wars of the United States*, Korean War Volume; and in March 1995 he was asked by RUSI to write an essay on the Korean War for inclusion in their volume to mark the 50th anniversary of VJ Day, linking the origins of the conflict back to the close of the Second World War. He also continued to visit Korea or to meet Koreans visiting Britain. In April 1991, he led a visit to Korea on the 40th anniversary of the Imjin battle with Korean War veterans; in March 1995, he was a guest during the visit to Britain by the President of Korea, Kim Dae-jung; he spoke on a panel giving an assessment of the strategy of the war at an international conference on *The Korean War: an assessment of the historical record* in Washington DC in July 1995, held by the Korea Society. On 20 April 1997, he was present at the dedication of a Korean War memorial window in Gloucester Cathedral, designed by Alan Younger; and in September 1997, he attended the *Korea-UK Forum for the Future* meeting and conference in Seoul where he gave the opening address. This was a body which usually met at Chatham House. TFH had joined it in 1996, becoming a member of the Forum's Steering Committee. In April 1999, the Queen and the Duke of Edinburgh made a State Visit to South Korea – during which TFH was invited to a number of the main events of the visit, including the UK-Korea Celebration of Music and Dance and a reception thereafter; a dinner given by President Kim Dae-jung for the Queen and the Duke; and the garden reception at the British Embassy in Seoul.[3]

Korea was not his only destination on visits and tours, however. In July 1992 he was the special guest on Holt's Battlefield Tour's 75th anniversary tour of Passchendaele. In August 1994, he organised the party from the Parachute Regimental Association to attend the 50th anniversary visit to the South of France and be present at the Liberation celebrations; the enthusiasm for liberation was a good deal more evident in 1994 than it had been in 1944. The following May, he was present at a ceremony in the Hellenic Cultural Centre in conjunction with the Greek Embassy in London, to mark the 50th anniversary of the end of the Second World War and the liberation of Greece. TFH and nine others were honoured with the award of the Medal of the City by the Mayor of Athens.

His written output on other issues and his contribution to conferences and seminars also continued unabated. When not travelling, or engaged in work on the house with Ted Olive, he would begin work after breakfast – summoned for short coffee, lunch and tea breaks by Linda – and continue until he had to be dragged away from his study in the evening for dinner and a little relaxation. Throughout these years he was working on a major history of the Army Air Corps from its formation, which was published in 1994 as *The Army in the Air*.[4] In August 1991, he joined the Editorial Board of *The D-Day Encyclopaedia*, led by David Chandler at Sandhurst and James Lawton Collins in the USA, published by Simon Schuster Academic References Division, New York. In 1992, he contributed an overview of events in 1991-1992 for the *Defence Ministries Specifiers Guide*; and an article on infantry warfare and comments on airborne warfare for the *Oxford Companion to the Second World War*, under the editorship of I.C.B. Dear and M.R.D. Foot. In June 1995, he spoke at a conference on 'Obeying Commands in a Democratic Setting' in Tel Aviv – during which he addressed the British position on this issue of morality versus obedience to orders – following keynote speeches by

General Klaus Naumann, Chief of Staff of the *Bundeswehr*, and Ehud Baraq, Chief of Staff of the Israeli Defence Force.

In 1998, TFH wrote contributions to *The Companion to Military History*, published by the Oxford University Press and edited by Richard Holmes on the Korean War and the Inchon landings; and in October of that year he joined Generals James McCarthy and John Shand of the USAF, and General Andrew Goodpaster of the US Army, on a panel addressing the subject of 'The Future of NATO' at the Eighteenth Military History Symposium, held at the US Air Force Academy, Colorado Springs. He also wrote a series of entries on people he had known for the *Dictionary of National Biography*: Sir George Lea in 1999; Sir Nigel Poett and Sir Charles Keightley in 2000; Sir Ken Darling in 2001; and Sir Hugh Stockwell and Field Marshal Lord Carver in 2004. In 2000, he contributed material on Palestine to Volume VI, and wrote the foreword for Volume VII, of the Royal Welch Fusiliers' regimental records.[5]

TFH's media and broadcasting career also continued to flourish. He wrote on the Gulf Crisis in January 1991 for the *Evening Standard*, setting out a robust view that the Iraqi Army could be beaten, and also contributing articles on the export of weapons to Iraq before the invasion of Kuwait. As the Balkan War grew in intensity, he contributed a piece to the *Daily Mail* on 22 April 1993, pointing up the dangers for Kosovo long before that province was on anyone else's radar. He suggested in the article that if NATO rather than the UN was serious about stopping the fighting in the former Yugoslavia, it must field a force sufficient in numbers and capabilities to intervene effectively.

The surviving Commanding Officers of 3 Para at the Presentation of New Colours to the regiment in 1998. Back row, from left: Lt-Col A.C.P. Kennet, Col F.H. Scobie, Maj-Gen C.D. Farrar-Hockley, Lt-Col R.H. Gash, Col H.M. Fletcher, Col T.W. Burls.
Front row, from left: Col E. Coates, Maj-Gen J.A. Ward-Booth, FM Sir Roland Gibbs, Maj-Gen M. Forrester, Brig P.E. Crook, Gen Sir Rupert Smith, TFH, Maj-Gen P.I. Chiswell, Maj-Gen K. Spacie. (Farrar-Hockley family)

Northern Ireland continued to feature in TFH's dealings with the media. In February 1992 he appeared on BBC Radio 4 in a discussion on the Northern Ireland peace process; and on 28 October 1993, he wrote an article in the *Evening Standard* entitled 'The true face of treachery', marking the burial of IRA terrorist Thomas Begley, who had blown himself up while planting a bomb. His coffin was carried by, among others, *Sinn Féin* leader Gerry Adams. This act, while negotiating a settlement to the violence in Northern Ireland, was the treachery – as TFH saw it – in the title of the piece. His principal concern was in defending the role of the Parachute Regiment in Northern Ireland, while always underscoring the need for the police and army to act within the law. In the build-up to the Saville Tribunal's enquiry into allegations that the regiment had shot dead 13 unarmed Catholic protestors during a civil rights march in Londonderry in 1972, after he had left the Province, TFH robustly defended the regiment and voiced the view that some forensic findings had been released early as a deliberate ploy to portray the soldiers as murderers – suggesting as it did that the view of independent technical experts appointed to advise the committee, to the effect that several of the dead had been in contact with firearms residue – was worthless. The findings also suggested that some of those people killed had handled firearms and that it was very likely one of those killed was shot while lying on the ground. TFH said on the record that this was:

> … all part of a long-running public relations exercise to work public opinion up in favour of saying that the soldiers were all murderers and nothing was done wrong by the people on the other side… It is piecemeal evidence and should await full examination in relation to all the other evidence. I am sure the army and Ministry of Defence will not attempt to fudge any evidence and will not attempt to hold anything back.[6]

He also voiced strong concerns following the ruling by the judges sitting on the tribunal that the former soldiers could not rely on being granted anonymity, even though the High Court had granted this right.[7]

He also intervened robustly on the issue of women being employed in the British infantry, to which he was completely opposed on spiritual as well as physical grounds, being certain that it would diminish both morale and standards. He was also an outspoken opponent of the European Court of Human Rights ruling that the British Armed Forces were obliged to permit avowed homosexuals to enlist – a sign perhaps that he no longer understood the contemporary world. In taking this stance, he maintained that the military was an unique institution which should be allowed to run its own affairs, and that the concession would damage morale and discipline – telling the BBC that 'Two surveys have disclosed that the overwhelming majority of those in military service today find homosexuality abhorrent'. What he had not noticed was that seven out of 10 people responding to a National Opinion Poll were in favour of giving equal rights regardless of sexual orientation, and there were few resignations when the measure was adopted by all three services.[8]

As well as contributions on current defence and security issues in the newspapers, on radio and on television, TFH took part in several serious historical studies. The first of these was the Flashback Television production of 'The Curragh Incident – A Question of Loyalty' for the BBC's *Timewatch* in 1992. The second was the 1997 Channel Four series *Game of War* presented by Angela Rippon. This was a series considering three battles (Balaklava, Waterloo and Naseby), during which each battle was recreated and re-contested on a mock-up of the original ground and with the original forces, from the same start point – but thereafter, the commanders were free to make any decisions they wished. The rival armies were commanded by contemporary senior military figures representing the historic figures, conducting the action from their own war room, where they were advised by two guest experts. TFH took part in Waterloo, playing Napoleon, with Major-General John Kiszely, then GOC 1st Armoured Division, playing Wellington. He was advised by journalist Peter Almond and Julian Humphreys from the National Army Museum. He won, of course – something which gave him enormous pleasure. In April 2001, he took part in a programme by Atlantic Productions for the BBC and the Discovery Channel on Thermopylae – giving an interview on both his perspective as an historian and his personal experience of battle to help bring the story to life in a compelling, but realistic way.

As well as entering the lists on behalf of the Paras, TFH continued to keep abreast of matters related to his other two regiments, attending reunions and events whenever he could. There was bad news, however. In the 1991 *Options for Change* Defence Review, the post-Cold War down-sizing of the army was felt largely by the infantry, which was reduced from 55 regular battalions to 36.[9] In the Prince of Wales's Division, where General Sir John Waters of the Glosters was now Colonel Commandant (as well as being C-in-C UK Land Forces), a reduction of two battalions had to be found. The Royal Welch Fusiliers escaped un-amalgamated once more. However, the Royal Hampshires left the division and were amalgamated with The Queen's. The Glosters, saved from amalgamation once before and always finding recruiting difficult, could no longer avoid change. In 1994, the regiment was amalgamated with the Duke of Edinburgh's Royal Regiment (Berkshire and Wiltshire) to form the Royal Gloucestershire, Berkshire and Wiltshire Regiment.[10] In putting his own regiment on the line in this way, General Waters acted with great integrity.

Like all who had served in the Glosters, TFH was deeply saddened by the loss of his regiment but, although he was consulted on the way ahead, he did not intervene. The new regiment, at least, retained the Back-Badge and the Presidential Citation for Korea on its uniform and was recognisable as the successor of the Glosters, as well as of the DERR. There was much worse to come, however, for in 2004, further reductions led to the regiment being re-designated as a regiment of light infantry and moved from the Prince of Wales's Division to the Light Division. The Devonshire and Dorset Regiment followed suit. In 2007 these two regiments were again amalgamated and merged with the Light Infantry and the Royal Green Jackets into a new regiment called The Rifles. TFH never lived to see this, although he knew it was in preparation, and it almost broke his heart. He had begun his service as a very young Private in the Glosters, had served with them in war and endured almost unimaginable hardship with them. Now they were gone.

There was better news for the Parachute Regiment, even though its three Volunteer battalions were reduced to one. On 1 September 1999, 16 Air Assault Brigade was formed by the amalgamation of 5 Airborne Brigade and 24 Airmobile Brigade.[11] Based in Colchester, Essex the Brigade Headquarters was formed from both army and RAF personnel – enabling it to integrate air and land operations. Its order of battle included three Army Air Corps regiments, equipped with both *Lynx* troop-carrying helicopters and *Apache* attack helicopters. It became the British Army's largest brigade with some 6,200 soldiers, combining the speed and agility of airborne and air assault troops with the potency of the attack helicopters. Its units included two parachute battalions and an infantry battalion; 7 Regiment RHA; 23 Engineer Regiment;

logistic support, medical and REME battalions; provost company and signal squadron; and a pathfinder platoon. The third regular parachute battalion took on a new role as the Special Forces Support Group – moving under the command of the Director, Special Forces – and taking Royal Marines and RAF Regiment soldiers into its ranks. In essence, its role was to provide protection, reaction forces and support to SAS or Special Reconnaissance Regiment operations worldwide.[2]

Aside from all this work, TFH loved time with his family – especially his grandchildren, who were growing up all too quickly, in the way of these things. Hilary and Kim had moved from Manston in Kent in 1990 to High Wycombe, where they stayed until 1993 – at which point Hilary decided to leave the RAF and go into business. Dair and Victoria left Colchester in 1993 when Dair became Commander Infantry Training at Warminster; in 1995 they moved to Prague and in 1996, Dair was promoted to Major-General and appointed to command the 2nd Division in York, where he stayed until 1999 when he too left the service for a second career in business.

*   *   *

Remarkably, as TFH approached his 80th birthday, he had changed little in looks for more than 30 years: not tall, but deep-chested and strongly built; bald from a very early age with twinkling eyes, a ready smile and a booming voice. He was still physically active – working

TFH inspecting a parade in York
with Dair as GOC 2nd Division.
(Farrar-Hockley family)

on Pye Barn and its garden, sailing, walking and occasionally playing cricket. Mentally his powers were unimpaired, although he had been so long away from the military – and the world had changed so much – that he was less in demand as a commentator than in former times. His output in terms of writing, broadcasting and speaking had been remarkable. He was, at this time, considering writing his own autobiography. Having tremendous recall, but never having really collected material in an organised way, this would have been a major task. However, he was lured away from this by the opportunity to write a biography of Douglas MacArthur for Wiedenfeld and Nicholson's *Great Commanders* series.[13] This was something he had long wanted to do, having as he did a great regard for MacArthur's generalship.

He began the task of writing this book and in March 2003 he made a guest appearance as a senior mentor on the Higher Command and Staff Course. However, not long afterwards, Linda and others noticed that all was not well. He suddenly lost confidence in himself and began to worry about things. For the first time in his life, he needed the help of his friends and family – other than Ted Olive – to do routine work around the house. In September he spoke at the annual service for the Korean War veterans in St Paul's Cathedral, but it was very obviously exhausting. From here on, he cut back radically on work and entertaining.

Initial medical advice put his symptoms down to a heart condition and he was referred to the John Radcliffe Infirmary in Oxford for further investigation. Here, something triggered the clinician to ask if his handwriting had changed. It had. It had never been easy to read, but it had become tiny, cramped and very hard to decipher. He was then given a series of reflex and

TFH at his last major public appearance, delivering the address at the annual service for the Korean Veterans Association in St Paul's Cathedral, 2004. (Farrar-Hockley family)

co-ordination tests, from which he was diagnosed as being in the early stages of Parkinson's disease – a progressive neurological condition which kills nerve cells in the brain and limits the production of the chemical dopamine. There was, and is, no cure – nor is it known why some people develop this condition. TFH began to exhibit the classic symptoms of Parkinson's disease: his movements became slower and it took him far longer to do things. He began to have tremors and his face went rigid – although that was successfully treated by medication. He became tired, his joints hurt and he became depressed and very anxious over small things.[14]

By 2005, he had begun to have hallucinations – seeing first quite minor illusions like a dog or an old woman (perhaps the ghost of Pye Barn), but by the New Year of 2006, he was seeing tanks coming up the drive. He had, by now, stopped cooking, for not only could he not physically do the work, but he had also lost his sense of taste. He had stopped writing the biography of MacArthur; although he would sit down to his task, he would do little but stare into space, and the task remained unfinished. That Christmas, the family had, as usual, gathered at Pye Barn but TFH hardly recognised anyone and he began speaking a mixture of languages. Parkinson's itself does not kill, but it opens the gateway to other things that do. In TFH's case, he had developed dementia with Lewy bodies. As his grip on reality loosened, he was, in his own mind, back once more in the hands of the Chinese. Being once more a prisoner of war, he began to escape from the house and take refuge with neighbours in the village.

At this point he was taken back to the Radcliffe for observation and tests. Very confused – and now very thin – he was admitted to a ward and, of course, tried to escape. After a while Linda took him home again, where a nurse came in every night to help care for him. He could not recognise anyone, however, and all he wanted to do was escape. There was no option but to take him back into the Radcliffe, where the doctors, nursing staff and the other patients cared for him as well as anyone on this earth could have done. He stayed in the Radcliffe for seven weeks. For the last two weeks, he was heavily sedated and in no pain. Even so, it seemed to those who saw him that he was still struggling. TFH had no fear of death – he had seen it too often – and anyway, he *knew* that there was a life to come; he often spoke of death as his last great adventure. However, in his own estimation, he was not an old man; he had work unfinished and he was not ready to leave the world, but this was one battle he could not win. He died on Saturday, 11 March 2006. His had been a full, hard life. It was unwillingly surrendered.

25

'I did like being in the army'
The aftermath and TFH's legacy

TFH's body was taken from the Radcliffe to Pye Barn, for the family were determined that he was to go home one last time. His funeral was a small and simple affair in the tiny church in Moulsford, attended only by the family and very close friends. His friend, Leighton Thomas, who had retired to Locarno in Switzerland, came home to conduct the service – at the conclusion of which, he was buried in the same grave as Pat, in Moulsford Churchyard. It was followed by a much larger service of Thanksgiving for his life in the Royal Memorial Chapel at Sandhurst, on 28 June 2006, for there were many, many people who wished to remember him and do him honour.

Here, in the chapel in which he had first worshipped 60 years before as a Cadet at the Sandhurst OCTU, the service was conducted by the Chaplain, Grant Ashton, assisted by the Chaplain of St Peter ad Vincula in the Tower, Paul Abram. The band of the Parachute Regiment played before and after the service and the Colours of the Royal Gloucestershire, Berkshire and Wiltshire Regiment, and the 1st Battalion of the Parachute Regiment, were marched to the altar. Following them, TFH's orders, medals and decorations were carried up the nave to the sacrarium by his old comrade-in-arms, Sgt Ted Olive. There were hymns and prayers: 'be Thou my vision', 'Who would true valour see', 'Dear Lord and Father of mankind', and 'Praise, my soul, the King of Heaven'; the Glosters' collect, read by General Sir John Waters, and the Airborne Forces' collect, read by General Sir Geoffrey Howlett; there were readings: from *Pilgrim's Progress*, by his grandson, Piers; from *The Wisdom of Solomon*, by the Chairman of the Governors of Moulsford School, Brian Lee; and from St Paul's *Letter to the Hebrews* by Sir John Morgan, a former Ambassador to the Republic of Korea; there were solos and choral pieces from Fauré's 'Requiem' and Mozart's 'Ave Verum Corpus Natum'. The centrepiece of the service was, however, the eulogy, delivered by Lieutenant-General Sir Hew Pike, who had served as a Platoon Commander under TFH in the Radfan in 1964. In this eulogy, Sir Hew pulled off the all-but impossible task of summing up TFH's life and character, with all its facets and contradictions, and of pleasing everybody.

Those who packed the chapel at Sandhurst, and mingled afterwards in the Old College dining room, all remembered TFH in different ways. They, and all those who knew him but were not there, remembered him first for his body of published work and, in particular, the official history of the British involvement in the Korean War. There are other books among his bibliography that will also endure, and of these, *Goughie* is probably the one that best stands the test of time – followed by the Hamilton papers and his biography of Kurt Student. *The Edge of the Sword* is, of course, timeless, for it is a personal memoir that stands alone and cannot be capped. It remains his most powerful and most moving book – hard to read in some passages, even now. Some of his other works have, however, been superseded by modern scholarship: *The Somme, Airborne Carpet* and *Death of an Army*; superseded in terms of research material they may have been, but they remain valid because they are written from the point of view of a practitioner, not an academic. TFH knew about war, at first hand; he knew about the pressures on commanders, be they political, or moral, or the result of limited resources; and he knew about the courage required in decision making. He loved being a soldier and he loved writing about soldiers – and it was this that gave his books their authentic, fluent and luminous style. As he himself once remarked, 'I enjoyed it every day. I had found something I loved, having been a lazy boy at school … I did like being in the army.'

Because of this body of work, he joins that number of distinguished soldier-scholars of the 20th century army whose works will endure for posterity: men like Shan Hackett, Peter Young, David Fraser, Michael Carver, Nigel Bagnall, Richard Holmes, and Rupert Smith.

He will also be remembered as a speaker, as well as a writer. Generations of officers and men were enlightened and inspired by his speeches and lectures on various topics: operations, leadership, courage, or the history of war. That these talks were never written down or recorded remains a lasting gap in the collective memory of the British Army. Even had they been written down, we would have learned little about his inner feelings on these matters in the light of his personal experience, for he was ever loath to express his own feelings in public, or recount his personal experiences of combat, imprisonment and torture. Part of this, no doubt, was that he had buried these memories very deeply and did not wish to bring them to mind again. Part of it was a very real desire not to be thought of as being boastful.

As well as being remembered as an inspiration, many will also remember his personal kindness, as well as his truly devilish sense of humour. There are many anecdotes about this throughout this biography and there is no need to rehearse them again – not that he was either tolerant of failure, or unwilling to dish out some tough love when it was required. Those who shared his religious faith will also remember him for his deep conviction and profound sense of belief in the Christian gospel. This, as much as anything, underpinned his personal approach to others even if they themselves could not, at the time, see it. However, he firmly believed that an officer's primary duty was the care and nurture of his subordinates and he placed deep trust in those that he trusted, in return for the trust placed in him.

He will be remembered for his contribution to the development of the British Army's doctrine and equipment, both as a field commander in Northern Ireland and in Germany, in the South-East District, and as Director Combat Development. He was one of the driving forces in making the army recognise modern counter-insurgency and then transform to meet it. He pushed the concept of air mobility through his championship of support helicopters. He made the army recognise the threats and opportunities posed by electronic warfare. He made sure whenever he could that training was as hard and as realistic as it could possibly be, in order to prepare those who went through it for the sort of life he had lived; for he had early in his life been taught by that greatest of all teachers: War.

He will, of course, be remembered as a field commander – for he was, and remains, a great soldier and a great commander. One cannot say, however, that he was a great General. Generalship is about the command of fighting formations, of combined arms, engaged in operations. Above and beyond this, generalship encompasses the planning and execution of campaigns, or the command of an extended theatre of operations. This includes the conduct of the war, the management of the line of communications, the sustainment of the troops and the balancing of national, alliance and host-nation interests. At the highest level, a General will be responsible for managing the military aspects of his country's policy and strategy in the context of war, and the spending of its blood and treasure. TFH prepared himself meticulously for this through study and reflection during his peacetime commands as a General, and no-one who knew him will ever doubt that had he been called upon to do so by war, he would have shown great abilities as a General – but as such, he was never put to the test by war. One might argue that Northern Ireland was an operational command; however, TFH was not in overall charge of the theatre, nor did he ever have to manoeuvre the command as a formation. His Directives and Orders were put into effect at low level, over time, and according to local circumstances. Northern Ireland was a campaign fought at the very highest level of strategy on one hand, and at the very lowest level on the other. TFH sat somewhere in the middle, charged with turning policy and strategy into tasks for others and directing resources so that these could be achieved – but in the absence of any coherent campaign plan.

Where he had been put to the test by war was as a Commander at battalion level and below. He commanded on operations as an NCO, as a Subaltern in command of a platoon, as a Company Commander and as a CO. Every time he did so, the results were eye-watering. His personal courage – moral and physical – whether on the battlefield or in captivity; his willingness to assume responsibility and make decisions; his acceptance of risk; his compassion and care for the welfare of the troops; his enthusiasm and sense of humour ('if you can't take a joke, you should not have joined') – all these were second to none; and there is no doubt that soldiers followed him in the certainty that he would *win*. He could be difficult, argumentative, overbearing, stubborn, pig-headed even; but he was physically and morally imposing, strong in mind and body, tough, brave and decisive. TFH could always find the key to any problem; he always demanded the initiative; he insisted on being kept informed and in keeping those below him in the picture – no doubt a lasting legacy from his time in the ranks – and he could always be relied on to do the unexpected; to exploit the unorthodox. He got results – and his people trusted him. The army was in his blood, as Ted Olive remarked, but his reactions to matters like the possibility of women serving in the infantry, homosexuality, the disappearance of his regiments, and the cult of what is called 'political correctness' – which he viewed as the denial of free speech to everyone except the extreme left – showed that he was out of sympathy with the direction that the world was taking in the 21st century. It is as well that his star blazed in another, more robust, age: a past that was another country, and they did things differently there.

Notes

Chapter 1

1   General Registry Office certified copy of an entry of birth, document no. 38/1891.
2   GRO Census Returns for 1901 and 1911.
3   His record of service in the RFC, later the RAF, is in T.N.A. AIR 79/201/18256. He may also be the same Hockley serving before 1918 in the RFA, T.N.A. WO 372/9/220516.
4   Much of the material in this chapter is derived from a long interview with members of the Farrar-Hockley family on 8 October 2013: TFH's widow, Linda; his sons, Dair and Hilary; his daughter-in-law, Victoria; his niece, Briony Smith; and his first cousin, Rosemary Howell.
5   Civil Registration Index, Brentford Register Vol 3a, p 238, 1921.
6   They moved some time between early 1922 and mid-1924, according to the birth-places of Pamela, who was registered in Brentford, and TFH, who was registered in Coventry (Civil Registration Index, Brentford Register Vol 3a, p 238 and Coventry Register Vol 6d, p 1,154.)
7   The *Army List* says 1923. This is because TFH enlisted under age and gave a false date of birth, as will be explained in Chapter 2.
8   Anthony Farrar-Hockley, *Opening Rounds. Lessons of Military History, 1918 – 1988* (London, 1988), p 1.
9   Brevet Colonel Charles John Wilmer (Jack) Tatham OBE RAMC, b. 5 November 1860 (*Army List*).
10 *The Exonian*, March 1941, p. 4.
11 www.exeterschool.org.uk retrieved 19 January 2014; R.J.E. Bush, *Exeter Free Grammar School, 1633 – 1809* (Devonian Association, 1962), p 94; Lloyd H. Parry, *The Founding of Exeter School: A History of the Struggle for freedom of Education within the City of Exeter* (Exeter and London, 1913).
12 *Exeter School, 1880 –1983* (Exeter, 1984), pp 57-58, 141-142.
13 Interview with the Farrar-Hockley family, 8 October 2013.
14 *The Exonian*, March 1941, p 4.
15 *The Exonian*, March 1939, p 71.
16 Cyril Tuckfield, *Spirit of Adventure. 1st Lympstone Sea Scouts River Dart Cruise* (1939).
17 Cyril Tuckfield, *Spirit of Adventure*.
18 *The Exonian*, January 1961, p 16-17.
19 *The Exonian*, March 1939, p 106.
20 Brian Le Mesurier in *Exeter School*, p 188-189.
21 Interview with the Farrar-Hockley family, 8 October 2013.
22 Interview with TFH by Peter Liddle for the WW2 Experience Centre, July 2001.
23 *The Exonian*, January 1961, p 15-16.
24 *Opening Rounds*, p 1.
25 Interview with TFH by Peter Liddle for the WW2 Experience Centre, July 2001.
26 *The Exonian*, March 1940, p 106.
27 P. Head in *Exeter School*, p 190.
28 The school certificate was established in 1918 by the Secondary Schools Examinations Council (SSEC). The School Certificate Examination was usually taken at age 16 and it was necessary to pass Mathematics, English and at least three other subjects in order to gain the certificate. The examination results were graded Fail, Pass, Credit and Distinction and to gain a certificate, the pupil had to achieve a minimum of six Passes or five Credits; anything less meant an overall Fail.

Chapter 2

1   Interview by Peter Liddle, July 2001.

2   Interview by Peter Liddle, July 2001.

3   *The Exonian,* March 1941, p 4; interview with Peter Liddle, July 2001.

4   *The Exonian,* March 1941, p 4.

5   *The Exonian,* March 1940, p 48.

6   *The Exonian,* March 1940, p 83-84.

7   AF B 271a, TFH's Attestation Notice in his record of service.

8   AF E 531, TFH's Enlistment Form in his record of service.

9   H.C. Wylly, *History of The Queen's Royal Regiment, Volume VII, 1905 – 1924* (Aldershot, 1928), p 280-281.

10 P.K. Kemp and John Graves, *The Red Dragon. The Story of the Royal Welch Fusiliers 1919 – 1945* (Aldershot, 1960), p 370-371.

11 R.C.G. Foster, *History of The Queen's Royal Regiment, Volume VIII, 1924 – 1948* (Aldershot, 1953), p 550.

12 *A Company 70th (Young Soldiers) Battalion the Gloucestershire Regiment,* in the Gloucestershire Regiment Archives; David Scott Daniell, *Cap of Honour. The story of The Gloucestershire Regiment (28th/61st Foot) 1694 – 1975* (London, 1975), p 395.

13 Foster, p 550; Kemp and Graves, p 371.

14 Interview by Peter Liddle, July 2001.

15 *A Company 70th (Young Soldiers) Battalion the Gloucestershire Regiment,* in the Gloucestershire Regiment Archives.

16 Interview by Peter Liddle, July 2001.

17 *The Exonian,* July 1941, p 53; December 1941, p 8; AF B166a and AF B 271a in TFH's record of service.

18 Interview by Peter Liddle, July 2001.

19 Interview by Peter Liddle, July 2001.

20 Interview with Colonel Mike Motum, 20 November 2014.

21 Interview by Peter Liddle, July 2001.

22 T.N.A. WO 32/4461 dated 6 September 1937.

23 T.N.A. WO 32/4461, Second Report.

24 T.N.A. WO 32/4544, August 1938.

25 For a detailed examination of officer selection in the army from 1936 to 1945, see Jeremy A. Crang, *The British Army and the People's War 1939 – 1945* (MUP, 2000). See also Jonathan Gaythorne-Hardy, *The Public School Phenomenon* (London, 1977).

26 Crang, p 25-27.

27 Crang, p 28.

28 Crang, p 31-33.

29 *Sandhurst Cadet Register* (RMAS Archives).

30 Interview with Colonel J.W. Sewell, 16 December 2013.

31 Interview with Colonel J.W. Sewell, 16 December 2013.

32 Standing Orders of the 161 Infantry (Royal Military College) OCTU.

33 Interview with Colonel J.W. Sewell, 16 December 2013.

34 Interview by Peter Liddle, July 2001.

35 'Never a Dull Moment'; interview with TFH in *Soldier* Magazine, 7 November 1983, p 18-19.

36 *London Gazette (Supplement)* No. 35836, p 5,630, 14 November 1942.

37 RMC Cadet Record Sheet in TFH's record of service.

38 Interview with Colonel J.W. Sewell, 16 December 2013.

39 RMC Cadet Record Sheet in TFH's record of service.

40 *Army List.*

41 *London Gazette (Supplement)* No. 35997, p 1,949, 30 April 1943; Royal Military College Sandhurst Cadet Register (Sandhurst Collection).

Chapter 3

1   Much of the information in this chapter, and subsequent chapters on the Second World War, is drawn from P.K. Kemp and John Graves, *The Red Dragon. The Story of the Royal Welch Fusiliers 1919 – 1945* (Aldershot, 1960), p 305-334, which TFH helped to write.

2   T.N.A. WO 166/8557, 169/10348, 175/530: 6th (RW) Para War Diary 1942 – 1943, August – September 1942.

3   For more details see David Erskine, *The Scots Guards 1919 – 1955* (London, 1956) and J.P. Riley, *From Pole to Pole, The Life of Quintin Riley, 1905 – 1980* (Chippenham, 1980), p 115-23.

4   *Pole to Pole,* p 123-133; Jonathon Riley, *The Life and Campaigns of General Hughie Stockwell* (Barnsley, 2006), p 44-62 and Christopher Buckley, *Norway, The Commandos, Dieppe* (London, 1951).

5   T.N.A. WO 170/1343: 6th (RW) Para War Diary 1 January – 31 December 1944; entry for 9 July 1944 contains an instruction on the wearing of the Flash on SD, BD and KD jackets, or bush shirts when worn outside the shorts or slacks.

6   Interview with Fusilier Jack Ellis, 13 November 2014.

7   R.J.M. Sinnett, 6th (RW) Para Summary (RWF Archive).

8   Interview with Major Cliff Meredith, 29 December 2013.

9   Peter Harclerode, *Go To It: The Illustrated History of the 6th Airborne Division* (London, 1990), p 27.

10   Anthony Crosland to Philip Williams, July 1942 in Kevin Jefferys, *Anthony Crosland* (London, 2000), p 17.

11   T.N.A. WO 166/8557, 169/10348, 175/530: 6th (RW) Para War Diary 1942 – 1943, August – September 1942.

12   T.N.A. WO 166/8557, 169/10348, 175/530: 6th (RW) Para War Diary 1942 – 1943, April 1943.

13   Interview with TFH by Peter Liddle, WW2 Experience Centre Leeds, July 2001.

14   Interview with Fusilier Jack Ellis, 13 November 2014.

15   Interview with Peter Liddle, July 2001.

16   For more on parachute training see *The Red Dragon*, p 306-307 and Harclerode, p 27-29.

17   Harclerode, p 37.

18   Interview with Fusilier Jack Ellis, 13 November 2014.

19   Interview with Peter Liddle, July 2001.

20   Reminiscence by Grafton Maggs online.

21   Interview with Major Cliff Meredith, 29 December 2013.

22   Interview with the Farrar-Hockley family, 8 October 2013.

23   Interview with Fusilier Jack Ellis, 13 November 2014.

24   T.N.A. WO 166/8557, 169/10348, 175/530: 6th (RW) Para War Diary 1942 – 1943, January 1943.

25   Interview with the Farrar-Hockley family, 8 October 2013.

26   T.N.A. WO 166/8557, 169/10348, 175/530: 6th (RW) Para War Diary 1942 – 1943, April 1943.

27   Training Instruction No. 20, Appendix E to T.N.A. WO 166/8557, 169/10348, 175/530: 6th (RW) Para War Diary 1942 – 1943, 26 April 1943; interview with Fusilier Jack Ellis, 13 November 2014.

28   Training Instruction No. 21, Appendix F to T.N.A. WO 166/8557, 169/10348, 175/530: 6th (RW) Para War Diary 1942 – 1943, April 1943; Training Instruction No. 22, Appendix F to T.N.A. WO 166/8557, 169/10348, 175/530: 6th (RW) Para War Diary 1942 – 1943, May 1943.

29   T.N.A. WO 166/8557, 169/10348, 175/530: 6th (RW) Para War Diary 1942 – 1943, May 1943.

30   Return of Officers and Field Return of Other Ranks in T.N.A. WO 166/8557, 169/10348, 175/530: 6th (RW) Para War Diary 1942 – 1943, June 1943.

31   Interview with Peter Liddle, July 2001.

32   Tristan Lovering, 'Sicily. Operation HUSKY, July – August 1943' in *Amphibious Assault. Manouevre from the Sea* (Woodbridge, 2007), p 193-199.

33   6th Battalion (Royal Welch) Parachute Regiment OO No.1 dated 5 July 1943 (Operation *Glutton*).

34   Interview with Major Cliff Meredith, 29 December 2013.

35   Interview with Peter Liddle, July 2001.

36   Return of Officers and Field Return of Other Ranks in T.N.A. WO 166/8557, 169/10348, 175/530: 6th (RW) Para War Diary 1942 – 1943, September 1943.

37   See especially Corelli Barnet, *Engage the Enemy More Closely: The Royal Navy in the Second World War* (London, 2001), p 685 and FM Lord Alanbrooke, Alex Danchev (ed.) and Daniel Todman, *War Diaries*

1939 – 1945 (London, 2001), p 438-451; Brigadier C.J.C. Molony with Captain F.C. Flynn RN, Major-General H.L. Davies and Group Captain T.P. Gleave, *The Mediterranean and Middle East, Volume V: The Campaign in Sicily 1943 and The Campaign in Italy 3rd September 1943 to 31st March 1944*. History of the Second World War, United Kingdom Military Series (HMSO, 1973).

38 See especially Carlo d'Este, *Fatal Decision: Anzio and the Battle for Rome* (London, 1991), p 32-33.

39 Lovering, p 216 *et seq.*

40 T.N.A. WO 166/8557, 169/10348, 175/530: 6th (RW) Para War Diary 1942 – 1943, September 1943.

41 *The Red Dragon*, p 310-311.

42 Interview with Peter Liddle, July 2001.

43 6 (RW) Para Roll of Honour, 18 May 1995 in RWF Mus/Archive.

44 Diary, 9 October 1943 cited in Jefferys, p 19.

45 T.N.A. WO 166/8557, 169/10348, 175/530: 6th (RW) Para War Diary 1942 – 1943, September and October 1943.

Chapter 4

1 This chapter is based on material from *The Red Dragon*; recordings made by TFH and other veterans, interviews with survivors and a ground reconnaissance by the author in December 2013.

2 Cliff Meredith, 'The Sinking of HMS Abdiel', *Y Ddraig Goch*, 1994, p 88.

3 Pearson, 'The Tragedy of HMS Abdiel 1943', p 92.

4 T.N.A. WO 166/8557, 169/10348, 175/530: 6th (RW) Para War Diary 1942 – 1943, August – September – October 1943.

5 Interview with Peter Liddle, July 2001.

6 T.N.A. WO 166/8557, 169/10348, 175/530: 6th (RW) Para War Diary 1942 – 1943, October 1943; Return of Officers dated 30 October.

7 George Macdonald Fraser, *Quartered Safe Out Here. A Recollection of the War in Burma, with a new Epilogue, 50 Years On* (London, 1993), p 293.

8 Fraser, p 294.

9 'A Parachute Battalion', X/127/2 in Army Council Instructions 3 June 1942 (Establishment table for 1942 – 1943).

10 Interview with Peter Liddle, July 2001.

11 T.N.A. WO 166/8557, 169/10348, 175/530: 6th (RW) Para War Diary 1942 – 1943, November 1943; *The Red Dragon*, p 313.

12 T.N.A. WO 166/8557, 169/10348, 175/530: 6th (RW) Para War Diary 1942 – 1943, December 1943.

13 *Fifth Army at the Winter Line 15 November 1943 – 15 January 1944* (United States Army Center of Military History Publication 100-9, Washington DC, 1945); Field Marshal Lord Carver, *The Imperial War Museum Book of the War in Italy 1943 – 1945* (London, 1945).

14 T.N.A. WO 166/8557, 169/10348, 175/530: 6th (RW) Para War Diary 1942 – 1943, December 1943.

15 Interview with Peter Liddle, July 2001.

16 Interview with Peter Liddle, July 2001.

17 Reminiscence by Grafton Maggs online, retrieved 20 January 2014.

18 T.N.A. WO 166/8557, 169/10348, 175/530: 6th (RW) Para War Diary 1942 – 1943, December 1943.

19 Interview by Francesco di Cinito with Major Paddy Deacon and Major Richard Hargreaves of 4 Para, August 2013.

20 'Account of a Patrol to Guardiagrele Area, 17th – 19th December 1943'. Appendix 3 to T.N.A. WO 166/8557, 169/10348, 175/530: 6th (RW) Para War Diary 1942 – 1943, December 1943.

21 T.N.A. WO 166/8557, 169/10348, 175/530: 6th (RW) Para War Diary 1942 – 1943, December 1943.

22 2 Independent Para Brigade Group Operation Order No.19, dated 24 December 1943. Appendix 4 to T.N.A. WO 166/8557, 169/10348, 175/530: 6th (RW) Para War Diary 1942 – 1943, December 1943.

23 Interview by Francesco di Cinito with Major Paddy Deacon of 4 Para, August 2013.

24 Jefferys, p 20 citing Crosland's Diary 8 – 20 December 1943.

25 Interview with Peter Liddle, July 2001.

26 Interview with Peter Liddle, July 2001.

27   T.N.A. WO 170/1343: 6th (RW) Para War Diary 1 January – 31 December 1944.

28   T.N.A. WO 166/8557, 169/10348, 175/530: 6th (RW) Para War Diary 1942 – 1943, December 1943.

29   2 Independent Para Brigade Operation Order No.22 dated 3 January 1944. Appendix 3 to T.N.A. WO 170/1343: 6th (RW) Para War Diary 1 January – 31 December 1944.

30   T.N.A. WO 170/1343: 6th (RW) Para War Diary 1 January – 31 December 1944.

31   Interview with Peter Liddle, July 2001.

32   Interview with Peter Liddle, July 2001.

33   *The Red Dragon,* p 319-320; T.N.A. WO 170/1343: 6th (RW) Para War Diary 1 January – 31 December 1944.

34   T.N.A. WO 170/1343: 6th (RW) Para War Diary 1 January – 31 December 1944.

35   1944 Diary of Major D. Fleming Jones, transcribed by his family in January 2002.

36   1944 Diary of Major D. Fleming Jones.

37   T.N.A. WO 170/1343: 6th (RW) Para War Diary 1 January – 31 December 1944.

38   1944 Diary of Major D. Fleming Jones.

39   1944 Diary of Major D. Fleming Jones.

40   T.N.A. WO 170/1343: 6th (RW) Para War Diary 1 January – 31 December 1944.

41   *The Red Dragon,* p 322.

42   Interview with Fusilier Jack Ellis, 13 November 2014.

43   Appendix 1 to T.N.A. WO 170/1343: 6th (RW) Para War Diary 1 January – 31 December 1944, Warning Order dated 2 Aril 1944; 1944 Diary of Major D. Fleming Jones.

44   Christopher Tuck, 'Salerno, Operation AVALANCHE, 9 September 1943' in Lovering (ed.) *Amphibious Assault,* p 227.

45   1944 Diary of Major D. Fleming Jones.

46   1944 Diary of Major D. Fleming Jones.

47   *The Red Dragon,* p 323.

48   T.N.A. WO 170/1343: 6th (RW) Para War Diary 1 January – 31 December 1944.

49   1944 Diary of Major D. Fleming Jones.

50   Interview with Peter Liddle, July 2001.

51   T.N.A. WO 170/1343: 6th (RW) Para War Diary 1 January – 31 December 1944.

52   T.N.A. WO 170/1343: 6th (RW) Para War Diary 1 January – 31 December 1944.

53   Jefferys, p 22 citing Crosland's Diary 11 August 1944.

54   1944 Diary of Major D. Fleming Jones.

55   Jefferys, p 23 citing Crosland's Diary 9 January 1945.

56   T.N.A. WO 170/1343: 6th (RW) Para War Diary 1 January – 31 December 1944.

57   T.N.A. WO 170/1343: 6th (RW) Para War Diary 1 January – 31 December 1944, entry for 18 June 1944.

58   Interview with Major Cliff Meredith, 29 December 2013.

59   Interview with Peter Liddle, July 2001.

60   T.N.A. WO 170/1343: 6th (RW) Para War Diary 1 January – 31 December 1944.

61   Attachment to T.N.A. WO 170/1343: 6th (RW) Para War Diary 1 January – 31 December 1944, dated 18 June 1944.

62   Steve Weiss, 'The Invasion of Southern France: Operation ANVIL-DRAGOON, August 1944' in Lovering (ed.) *Amphibious Assault,* p 333-347.

63   6th (RW) Para Op Order No.6 (Operation *Dragoon*) dated 12 August 1944 in T.N.A. WO 170/1343: 6th (RW) Para War Diary 1 January – 31 December 1944.

64   T.N.A. WO 170/1343: 6th (RW) Para War Diary 1 January – 31 December 1944, entry for 15 August 1944.

65   Letter Chatham to R.J.M. Sinnett dated 27 June 2007 in RWF Mus/Archives.

66   Interview with TFH by Max Arthur in *Men of the Red Beret: Airborne Forces 1940 – 1990* (London, 1990).

67   Letter Cliff Meredith to Arthur Watkins (undated) in RWF Mus/Archives.

68   T.N.A. WO 170/1343: 6th (RW) Para War Diary 1 January – 31 December 1944, entry for 15 August 1944.

69   1944 Diary of Major D. Fleming Jones.

70   Interview with TFH by Max Arthur in *Men of the Red Beret: Airborne Forces 1940 – 1990* (London, 1990).

71   Letter Chatham to R.J.M. Sinnett dated 27 June 2007 in RWF Mus/Archives.

72   1944 Diary of Major D. Fleming Jones.

73 *The Red Dragon,* p 326.
74 T.N.A. WO 170/1343: 6th (RW) Para War Diary 1 January – 31 December 1944, entry for 15 August 1944.
75 Jefferys, p 23 citing a letter from Neill Boys dated 17 March 1977; see also 1944 Diary of Major D. Fleming Jones.
76 Interview with Peter Liddle, July 2001.

Chapter 5

1   Winston S. Churchill, *The Second World War; Volume III, The Grand Alliance* (London, 1950), pp 14 – 17, 27.
2   Churchill, Vol III, pp 198-206, 263.
3   Winston S. Churchill, *The Second World War; Volume VI, Triumph and Tragedy* (London, 1954), p 63-71.
4   Churchill, Vol VI, p 97.
5   Churchill, Vol VI, p 248.
6   T.N.A. WO 170/1343, 6th (RW) Para War Diary 1 Jan – 31 Dec 1944, entry for 1 September 1944.
7   T.N.A. WO 170/1343, 6th (RW) Para War Diary 1 Jan – 31 Dec 1944, Op Instruction No 3 dated 10 Sep 1944.
8   T.N.A. WO 170/1343, 6th (RW) Para War Diary 1 Jan – 31 Dec 1944, entry for 1 September 1944.
9   T.N.A. WO 170/1343, 6th (RW) Para War Diary 1 Jan – 31 Dec 1944, entry for 13 September 1944.
10 T.N.A. WO 170/1343, 6th (RW) Para War Diary 1 Jan – 31 Dec 1944, entry for 25 September 1944.
11 T.N.A. WO 170/1343, 6th (RW) Para War Diary 1 Jan – 31 Dec 1944, entry for 1 October 1944.
12 T.N.A. WO 170/1343, 6th (RW) Para War Diary 1 Jan – 31 Dec 1944, entry for 10 October 1944.
13 *The Red Dragon,* p 328.
14 T.N.A. WO 170/1343, 6th (RW) Para War Diary 1 Jan – 31 Dec 1944, entry for 14 October 1944.
15 T.N.A. WO 170/1343, 6th (RW) Para War Diary 1 Jan – 31 Dec 1944, entry for 15 October 1944.
16 1944 Diary of Major D. Fleming Jones.
17 Interview by TFH with Max Arthur in *Men of the Red Beret* (London, 1990).
18 T.N.A. WO 170/1343, 6th (RW) Para War Diary 1 Jan – 31 Dec 1944, entries for 20 – 23 October 1944; 1944 Diary of Major D. Fleming Jones.
19 Letter Ian Chatham to R.J.M. Sinnett dated 27 June 2007 (RWF Archive).
20 Interview with Peter Liddle, July 2001.
21 T.N.A. WO 170/1343, 6th (RW) Para War Diary 1 Jan – 31 Dec 1944, Report on General Situation in Thebes, 28-29 October 1944.
22 *The Red Dragon,* p 329.
23 1944 Diary of Major D. Fleming Jones.
24 T.N.A. WO 170/1343, 6th (RW) Para War Diary 1 Jan – 31 Dec 1944, entry for 10 November 1944.
25 Interview with Max Arthur in *Men of the Red Beret* (London, 1990); interview with Peter Liddle, July 2001.
26 'Never a Dull Moment', interview with *Soldier* Magazine, 7 November 1983.
27 Interview with the author, 6 October 1998. He said the same in his interview with *Soldier* Magazine, 7 November 1983.
28 T.N.A. WO 170/1343, 6th (RW) Para War Diary 1 Jan – 31 Dec 1944, entries for 14 November 1944.
29 T.N.A. WO 170/1343, 6th (RW) Para War Diary 1 Jan – 31 Dec 1944, entries for 24 November 1944; Movement Order No 14 dated 22 November 1944.
30 T.N.A. WO 170/1343, 6th (RW) Para War Diary 1 Jan – 31 Dec 1944, Orders for the move from Thebes dated 23 November 1944.
31 1944 Diary of Major D. Fleming Jones.
32 1944 Diary of Major D. Fleming Jones.
33 T.N.A. WO 170/1343, 6th (RW) Para War Diary 1 Jan – 31 Dec 1944, entry for 3 December 1944.
34 *The Red Dragon,* p 330; 1944 Diary of Major D. Fleming Jones.
35 T.N.A. WO 170/1343, 6th (RW) Para War Diary 1 Jan – 31 Dec 1944, entries for 3 and 4 December 1944; 1944 Diary of Major D. Fleming Jones.
36 Interview by TFH with Max Arthur in *Men of the Red Beret* (London, 1990).
37 1944 Diary of Major D. Fleming Jones.

38   1944 Diary of Major D. Fleming Jones.

39   Letter Ian Chatham to R.J.M. Sinnett dated 27 June 2007 (RWF Mus/Archives).

40   1944 Diary of Major D. Fleming Jones.

41   Letter Cliff Meredith to R.J.M. Sinnett (undated) (RWF Mus/Archives).

42   Interview with Peter Liddle, July 2001.

43   Churchill, Vol VI, p 260.

44   T.N.A. WO 170/1343, 6th (RW) Para War Diary 1 Jan – 31 Dec 1944, entry for 17 December 1944.

45   Interview with Max Arthur in *Men of the Red Beret* (London, 1990).

46   T.N.A. WO 170/1343, 6th (RW) Para War Diary 1 Jan – 31 Dec 1944, entry for 20 December 1944.

47   1944 Diary of Major D. Fleming Jones.

48   1944 Diary of Major D. Fleming Jones.

49   T.N.A. WO 170/1343, 6th (RW) Para War Diary 1 Jan – 31 Dec 1944, entry for 29 December 1944.

50   Interview with Max Arthur in *Men of the Red Beret* (London, 1990).

51   T.N.A. WO 170/4973, 6th (RW) Para War Diary 1 Jan – 29 June 1945, entry for 1 January 1945.

52   T.N.A. WO 170/4973, 6th (RW) Para War Diary 1 Jan – 29 June 1945, entry for 3 January 1945.

53   Notes on the CO's Conference held 3 January 1945, Clearing of Omonoia Square – North in conjunction with 4th & 5th Para Bns. T.N.A. WO 170/4973, 6th (RW) Para War Diary 1 Jan – 29 June 1945.

54   T.N.A. WO 170/4973, 6th (RW) Para War Diary 1 Jan – 29 June 1945, entry for 4 January 1945.

55   T.N.A. WO 170/4973, 6th (RW) Para War Diary 1 Jan – 29 June 1945, entry for 5 January 1945.

56   T.N.A. WO 170/4973, 6th (RW) Para War Diary 1 Jan – 29 June 1945, entry for 10 January 1945.

57   Interview with Max Arthur in *Men of the Red Beret* (London, 1990).

58   Interview with Max Arthur in *Men of the Red Beret* (London, 1990); interview with Peter Liddle, July 2001.

59   T.N.A. WO 170/4973, 6th (RW) Para War Diary 1 Jan – 29 June 1945, entry for 30 January 1945.

60   Special Order of the Day by Lt-Gen R.M. Scobie, January 1945 (Parachute Regiment Archive).

61   Interview by TFH with Max Arthur in *Men of the Red Beret* (London, 1990).

62   Richard Sinnett, '6th (RW) Para Honours and Awards' (RWF Mus/Archives); David Buxton, *Honour to the Airborne, Part I, 1939 – 1948* (Bury, 1993). No citations are held for TFH's awards. However, immediate awards frequently had very brief, if any, citation.

63   *London Gazette,* 10 May 1945 and 21 June 1945. Also reported in the Battalion War Diary entry for 5 March 1945.

64   T.N.A. WO (MS3) BM/2674/3/(MS3) (V) dated 26 April 1946, letter from the Military Secretary to Pat Farrar-Hockley, covering the citation for TFH's Military Cross.

Chapter 6

1   T.N.A. WO 170/4973, 6th (RW) Para War Diary, 1 January – 29 June 1945, entry for 1 February 1945.

2   *The Red Dragon,* p 334.

3   T.N.A. WO 170/4973, 6th (RW) Para War Diary, 1 January – 29 June 1945, entry for 4 February 1945.

4   T.N.A. WO 170/4973, 6th (RW) Para War Diary, 1 January – 29 June 1945, entry for 1 March 1945.

5   The Op *Earlsdon* series. Operation Order No. 1 in T.N.A. WO 170/4973, 6th (RW) Para War Diary, 1 January – 29 June 1945, annexed to the entries for April 1945.

6   Op *Earlsdon* series in Airborne Forces Archives.

7   T.N.A. WO 170/4973, 6th (RW) Para War Diary, 1 January – 29 June 1945, entry for 22 April 1945.

8   T.N.A. WO 203/1209; WO 203/2821; CAB 192/8-14. See also *Hansard*, 16 March 1945. See also J.P. Riley, *Regimental Records of the Royal Welch Fusiliers, Volume VI*, p 2-3.

9   Carl-Maria von Clausewitz, *On War* (Princeton University Press, ed. Michael Howard and Peter Paret, 1976), p 105.

10   J.F.C. Fuller, *Generalship: The Disease and Its Cure* (Harrisburg, Pennsylvania, 1936), p 22.

11   See – for example – Dave Grossman, 'Human Factors in War: the Psychology and Physiology of Close Combat' in Michael Evans and Alan Ryan (ed.), *The Human Face of Warfare: Fear, Killing and Chaos in Battle* (St Leonard's, Australia, 2000) p 5-11.

12   See, among others, RMAS Study on Morale, Leadership and Discipline, 1950, p 20; General Sir John Hackett, 'Looking for Leadership', BBC Home Service Broadcast, February 1968; Fuller, *Generalship*, p

20-22; Lord Moran (C MacM Wilson), *The Anatomy of Courage* (London, 1945), Chapter 1.

13   Sir John Fortescue, *History of the British Army, Vol I* (London, 1909), p 68.

14   Interview with Peter Liddle, July 2001.

15   Norman Dixon, *On the Psychology of Military Incompetence* (London, 1976), p 168.

16   Richard L Gregory (ed.), *The Oxford Companion to the Mind* (OUP, 1991), p 389; Arthur S. Reber, *The Penguin Dictionary of Psychology* (London, 1995), p 388.

17   Interview with Peter Liddle, July 2001.

18   T.N.A. WO 170/4973, 6th (RW) Para War Diary, 1 January – 29 June 1945, entry for 21 June 1945.

19   *The Medals Year Book* (London, 1999), p 90-94.

20   Interview with the author, 6 October 1998.

21   Interview with the author, 6 October 1998; Harclerode, p 178. The War Diary concludes at the end of June 1945 and re-starts in October.

22   *Army List;* AF B 199a in TFH's record of service.

23   *London Gazette (Supplement)* No. 37052, p 2,222, 21 April 1945.

24   Interview with the author, 6 October 1998.

25   *Regimental Records of the Royal Welch Fusiliers, Vol VI,* p 435; *Who Was Who, Vol 4.*

Chapter 7

1   For a summary of the British position, see Lawrence James, *The Rise and Fall of the British Empire.* (London, 1994), p 562-564. See also Thomas Mokaitis, *British Counterinsurgency in the Post- Imperial Era* Vol I (MUP, 1995) p 654 *et seq.*

2   Peter Hennesey, *Never Again. Britain 1945 – 1951* (London, 1993), p 238.

3   Margaret Macmillan, *Peacemakers. The Paris Conference of 1919 and its Attempt to End War* (London, 2001), p 434-435.

4   Martin Gilbert, *A History of the Twentieth Century* (London, 1998), p 217.

5   Churchill, *The Second World War,* Vol VI, p 654.

6   Interview with Major-General R.D. Wilson, 24 June 2003.

7   For a summary of Bevin's views, see Tom Segev, *One Palestine, Complete* (London, 2000) p 492; and Hennesey, p 239. See also Martin Gilbert, p 224.

8   Mokaitis, i, p 122.

9   Information on the 6th AB Division and 2 Para Bde was supplied by the Airborne Forces Museum.

10   Gregory Blaxland, *The Regiments Depart. A History of the British Army 1945 – 1970* (London, 1971,) p 129.

11   For a full account of Abdullah's dealings, see Avi Shlaim, *Collusion Across The Jordan; King Abdullah, the Zionist Movement, and the Partition of Palestine* (Oxford, 1988).

12   For a full summary of deployments, see David A. Charters, *The British Army and Jewish Insurgency in Palestine, 1945 – 1947,* (Basingstoke, 1980), p 88-89; see also Harclerode, 6*th Airborne Division* pp 178-179, 186.

13   Trevor Royle, *Glubb Pasha. The Life and Times of Sir John Bagot Glubb, Commander of the Arab Legion* (London, 1992), p 172-175.

14   I am grateful to Brigadier Ahmed Aideed Al Masareh, Director of Moral Guidance, JHQ Jordanian Army; Mr Amjad Adaileh, Director of the Arabic Press Department, Communications and Information Division at the Royal Hashemite Court, Amman, Jordan; and Ms Alia Al-Kadi, Press Officer at the same department, for their assistance in research in the Jordanian Archives.

15   6th (RW) Para Movement Instruction No. 5 dated 9 Oct 45, in T.N.A. WO 169/20083, 6th (RW) Para War Diary 1 October 1945 – 31 December 1945.

16   6th (RW) Para CO's Training Directive No. 1 dated 13 Oct 45, in T.N.A. WO 169/20083, 6th (RW) Para War Diary 1 October 1945 – 31 December 1945.

17   T.N.A. WO 169/20083, 6th (RW) Para War Diary 1 October 1945 – 31 December 1945.

18   Peter Haclerode, *Para! Fifty Years of the Parachute Regiment* (London, 1992), p 194.

19   WO 169/20083, 6th (RW) Para War Diary 1 October 1945 – 31 December 1945.

20   Interview with Major-General Peter Cavendish, 26 June 2003.

21   Letter J.W. Sewell to the author dated 1 January 2014.

22   Blaxland, p 51.

23   Blaxland, p 51.

24   T.N.A. WO 169/20083, 6th (RW) Para War Diary 1 October 1945 – 31 December 1945.

25   T.N.A. WO 169/23227, 6th (RW) Para War Diary 1 January 1946 – 30 June 1946.

26   T.N.A. WO 169/23227, 6th (RW) Para War Diary 1 January 1946 – 30 June 1946.

27   T.N.A. WO 169/23227, 6th (RW) Para War Diary 1 January 1946 – 30 June 1946.

28   T.N.A. WO 169/23227, 6th (RW) Para War Diary 1 January 1946 – 30 June 1946. See also the Reminiscence by Grafton Maggs online.

29   Training Directive No. 4 in WO 169/23227, 6th (RW) Para War Diary 1 January 1946 – 30 June 1946.

30   AF B 199a in TFH's record of service.

31   T.N.A. WO 169/23227, 6th (RW) Para War Diary 1 January 1946 – 30 June 1946.

32   Field Marshal Montgomery of Alamein, *Memoirs* (London, 1958), p 428-429.

33   Montgomery *Memoirs*, p 388.

34   *Army List.*

35   Interview with Peter Liddle, July 2001.

36   *Field Service Pocket Book,* WO/GS Publications/8 January 1940. See also David T. Zabecki (ed.), *Chief of Staff, vol 2* (Annapolis, MA, USA, 2008), p 15-16.

37   *Operations – Military Training Pamphlet 23 Part I.* WO 26/GS Publications/602 (1942), p 9.

38   Harclerode, *6th Airborne Division,* p 181.

39   Peter Haclerode, *Para!* p 201-202.

40   Harclerode, *6th Airborne Division,* p 181; see also Tom Segev, *One Palestine, Complete; Jews and Arabs Under the British Mandate* (London, 1999); Part III, for more details of this period.

41   *Army Gradation List.*

42   Messenger, p 151.

43   AF B 2078 dated November 1946 in TFH's record of service.

44   Maurice Tugwell, interviewed in David A. Charteris, *The British Army and Jewish Insurgency,* p 176.

45   T.N.A. WO 0154/7678 (SD2) dated 12 March 1948; Riley, *Life of General Stockwell,* p 169.

46   Interview with TFH by the author, 16 May 2003.

Chapter 8

1   AF B199a in TFH's record of service.

2   AF B199a in TFH's record of service.

3   Information provided by the Parachute Regiment Museum.

4   *Army Gradation List.*

5   AF B.2078 dated 21 January 1948 in AFH's record of service.

6   2 Glosters Unit Historical Report (Glosters Museum/Archives).

7   *Cap of Honour,* p 328.

8   'The 61st in Jamaica' in *The Back Badge, Journal of the Gloucestershire Regiment,* December 1948.

9   J.P. Riley, *Regimental Records of the Royal Welch Fusiliers, Volume VI, 1945 – 1969* (Gomer, 2000), p 131.

10   *The Back Badge,* December 1948.

11   TFH's substantive rank w.e.f. 8 November 1945 was still only Lieutenant. He became a Substantive Captain on 8 April 1950 (*Army Lists*).

12   'The 61st in Jamaica' in *The Back Badge, Journal of the Gloucestershire Regiment,* December 1948.

13   AF B2077 dated 26 February 1949 in TFH's record of service.

14   Montgomery of Alamein, *Memoirs* p 441.

15   Gregory Blaxland, *The Regiments Depart. A History of the British Army, 1945 – 1970* (London, 1971), p 113.

16   *Army List.*

17   *The Back Badge,* December 1948.

18   2 Glosters Unit Historical Report (Glosters Museum/Archives).

19   *Services of the 28th/61st Foot* (Glosters Museum/Archive).

20   AF B2077 dated 27 November 1949 in TFH's record of service.

21   *A Brief History of 29 Infantry Brigade Group from September 1949 to October 1951* (Glosters Museum/Archive).

22   Interview with the Farrar-Hockley family.

23   Interview with Colonel Roy Giles, 16 February 2015.

Chapter 9

1   For a detailed examination of the Korean War, see Anthony Farrar-Hockley, *The British Part in the Korean War: Vol.1, A Distant Obligation* (HMSO, London 1990) and Max Hastings, *The Korean War* (London, 1987) and *Vol II: An Honourable Discharge* (London, 1995).

2   David Scott Daniell, *Cap of Honour. The Story of The Gloucestershire Regiment (28th/61st Foot) 1694 – 1975* (London, 1975), p 331.

3   Digby Grist, *Remembered With Advantage. A personal account of the Korean campaign August 1950 – December 1951* (Gloucester, 1976), p 7.

4   United Nations Security Council Resolutions 82, 83, 84, 85 and 88 of 1952.

5   Cmnd 9075, *Statement on Defence,* 31 August 1950.

6   Donald W. Boose, 'Portentous Sideshow: The Korean Occupation Decision'. *Parameters: US Army War College Quarterly* (US Army War College) Vol 5 No. 4 (Winter, 1995 – 1996), p 112-129.

7   See, for example, David Dallin, *Soviet Foreign Policy After Stalin* (New York, 1961), p 60 and Douglas J. Macdonald, 'Communist Bloc Expansion in the Early Cold War,' in *International Security*, Winter 1995 – 1996, p 180.

8   Kathryn Weathersby, 'Should We Fear This?' Stalin and the Danger of War with America', *Cold War International History Project: Working Paper No. 39,* (2002) p 10.

9   Barbara Barnouin and Changgeng Yu, *Zhou Enlai: A Political Life.* (Hong Kong, 2002), p 139-140.

10   Weathersbury, p 29-30.

11   Weathersbury, p 14.

12   Weathersbury, p 15.

13   For a detailed breakdown of the North Korean forces, see *The Armed Forces of North and South Korea,* US Army Centre for Military History.

14   William J. Webb, 'The Korean War: The Outbreak' (United States Army Center for Military History, 2011).

15   David Rees, *Korea: The Limited War* (New York, 1964), p 22.

16   Carter Malkasian, *The Korean War, 1950 – 1953* (London, 2001), p 16.

17   Rees, p 24.

18   Rees, p 26.

19   Anthony Farrar-Hockley 'The Significance of the British Commonwealth in the Korean War', speech given at the War Memorial service in Seoul, June 25-27 1990.

20   *Cap of Honour,* p 332.

21   Lofty Large, *One Man's War in Korea* (Wellingborough, 1988), p 140.

22   *A Brief History of 29 Infantry Brigade Group from September 1949 to October 1951* (Glosters Museum/Archive).

23   Grist, p 7.

24   *A Brief History of 29 Infantry Brigade Group from September 1949 to October 1951* (Glosters Museum/Archive).

25   *Cap of Honour,* p 332-333.

26   Grist, p 8.

27   *Cap of Honour,* p 333; *Services of the 28th/61st Foot* (Glosters Museum/Archive).

28   Robert O. Holles, *Now thrive the Armourers. A Story of Action with the Gloucesters in Korea (November 1950 – April 1951)* (London, 1952), p 11.

29   Interview with the Farrar-Hockley family.

30   Holles, p 12.

31   James L. Stokesbury, *A Short History of the Korean War* (New York, 1990), p 61.

32   Stokesbury, p 68.

33   Wientraub, p 58.

34   Stokesbury, p 81.

35   Stokesbury, p 90; Anthony Farrar-Hockley, 'A Reminiscence of the Chinese People's Volunteers in the Korean War' in *China Quarterly,* June 1984, p 294.

36   Holles, p 15.

37   *Services of the 28th/61st Foot* (Glosters Museum/Archive).

38   *Cap of Honour,* p 335; Holles, p 21; *Services of the 28th/61st Foot* (Glosters Museum/Archive).

39   Stokesbury, p 83.

40   Arnold A. Offner, *Another Such Victory: President Truman and the Cold War, 1945 – 1953.* (Stanford University Press, 2002) p 390.

41   Chinese Military Science Academy, *History of War to Resist America and Aid Korea* (Beijing, September 2000), p 160.

42   'A Reminiscence of the Chinese People's Volunteers in the Korean War', p 293.

43   'A Reminiscence of the Chinese People's Volunteers in the Korean War', p 294.

44   'A Reminiscence of the Chinese People's Volunteers in the Korean War', p 294.

45   Holles, p 25; *Services of the 28th/61st Foot* (Glosters Museum/Archive).

46   *Cap of Honour,* p 336.

47   *Cap of Honour,* p 336; Holles, p 29-31.

48   Holles, p 42.

49   Stokesbury, p 104-111.

50   Holles, p 45; see also Grist, p 25-26.

51   Grist, p 33.

52   *Cap of Honour,* p 338.

53   'A Reminiscence of the Chinese People's Volunteers in the Korean War', p 300.

54   Stokesbury, p 117.

55   Holles, p 82.

56   Holles, p 99.

57   *Cap of Honour,* p 342; Holles, pp 105, 112.

58   Stokesbury, p 122.

59   'A Reminiscence of the Chinese People's Volunteers in the Korean War', p 301.

60   *Cap of Honour,* p 343.

61   *Edge of the Sword,* p 16.

62   Grist, p 40.

63   Grist, p 41.

64   *Edge of the Sword,* p 15.

65   *Edge of the Sword,* p 17.

66   *Edge of the Sword,* p 20.

67   *Cap of Honour,* p 346; Holles, p 150.

68   *Cap of Honour,* p 347; *Edge of the Sword,* p 22.

69   *Edge of the Sword,* p 23.

70   *Cap of Honour,* p 347; *Edge of the Sword,* p 29.

71   *Cap of Honour,* p 347; *Edge of the Sword,* p 30.

72   'PoW tells of capture at Imjin battle' in *The Daily Telegraph,* 31 August 1953.

73   *Edge of the Sword,* p 32.

74   *Cap of Honour,* p 349; *Edge of the Sword,* p 32-34.

75   Grist, p 42; *Edge of the Sword,* p 35.

76   *Cap of Honour,* p 351.

77   *Cap of Honour,* p 352; *Edge of the Sword,* p 39.

78   *Cap of Honour,* p 352; *Edge of the Sword,* p 40.

79   *Cap of Honour,* p 353; *Edge of the Sword,* p 43.

80   *Edge of the Sword,* p 47; Large, p 51.

81   Holles, p 152; *Edge of the Sword,* p 48-49.

82   *Cap of Honour,* p 354; *Edge of the Sword,* p 51.

83   *Edge of the Sword,* pp 51, 53. In a letter to the Glosters' Regimental Secretary dated 13 June 1973, TFH points up serious errors in the 29 Infantry Brigade operations log – including an entry at this time that says that the battalion was told to fight its way out if necessary, the decision to be left to the CO – an entry probably relating to 1 RNF (Glosters Regimental Museum/Archives).

84 Holles, p 154.

85 Grist, p 33.

86 *Cap of Honour*, p 355-356; *Edge of the Sword*, p 57.

87 Holles, p 156.

88 'PoW tells of capture at Imjin battle' in *The Daily Telegraph*, 31 August 1953.

89 *Edge of the Sword*, p 58.

90 Interview with Colonel Mike Motum, 14 November 2014.

91 *Edge of the Sword*, p 62.

92 *Edge of the Sword*, p 64; E.J. Kahn, 'No one but the Glosters. A Reporter in Korea' in *The New Yorker*, 26 May 1951; TFH's citation for the DSO in his record of service.

93 Interview with Colonel Mike Motum, 20 November 2014.

94 *Edge of the Sword,* p 66.

95 *Cap of Honour,* p 356.

96 *Cap of Honour,* p 357; Grist, p 46.

97 John Ridley 'Col. Carne 'In Solitary' for 19 Months' in *The Daily Telegraph*, 2 September 1953.

98 *Edge of the Sword,* p 69.

99 *Edge of the Sword,* p 70.

100 Lieutenant-Colonel Roy E. Appleman to Mr Jeffrey Grey, University of New South Wales, dated 8 October 1985 in Farrar-Hockley Papers.

101 *An Honourable Discharge,* p 136.

Chapter 10

1   Anthony Farrar-Hockley, *The Edge of the Sword* (London, 1955), p 79. The account of TFH's time as a Prisoner of War is based on a précis of this book, supplemented by other sources as noted – especially A19/PW/Korea/1005, Interrogation Report No. A19/K/BRIT 38, August 1953 – which is the transcript of TFH's debriefing. This must have been carried out immediately after his release and it is the narrative on which *The Edge of the Sword* is based.

2   *Edge of the Sword*, p 79.

3   Colonel E.D. Harding DSO, *The Imjin Roll* (Gloucester, 1976), p 39.

4   *The Imjin Roll*, p 35.

5   *Edge of the Sword,* p 88.

6   *Edge of the Sword,* p 89.

7   *Edge of the Sword*, p 95.

8   *Edge of the Sword*, p 96.

9   See *The Imjin Roll,* p 30-33 for their stories.

10 *Edge of the Sword*, p 103.

11 *Edge of the Sword*, p 108.

12 *Edge of the Sword*, p 111; *The Imjin Roll*, p 32-33.

13 *The Imjin Roll*, p 32-33.

14 Derek Kinne, *The Wooden Boxes* (London, 1955), p 43.

15 Kinne, p 42.

16 Davies, p 104.

17 *Edge of the Sword*, p 116.

18 Kinne, p 44.

19 Kinne, p 44.

20 Lofty Large, *One Man's War in Korea* (Wellingborough, 1988), p 126.

21 *Edge of the Sword*, p 118; Kinne, pp 44, 46.

22 Kinne, p 47.

23 Kinne, p 48.

24 *The Daily Telegraph*, 1 June 1951; *The Echo* (Gloucester), 1 June 1951.

25 Kinne, p 49.

26 Large, p 81.

27 *The Imjin Roll*, p 41.

28 Kinne, pp 47, 51; see also the account by Padre Sam Davies, *In Spite of Dungeons* (London, 1954), p 40 and the account by Sgt F.S. Mathews (ed.), Francis S. Jones, *No Rice for Rebels* ((London, 1956).

29 Anthony Farrar-Hockley, 'A Reminiscence of the Chinese People's Volunteers in the Korean War', in *China Quarterly,* June 1984.

30 Large, p 85.

31 Kinne, p 52-53.

32 Kinne, p 54.

33 Kinne, p 55.

34 Kinne, p 56.

35 *Edge of the Sword*, p 125.

36 *Edge of the Sword*, p 129.

37 E. Katongole-Mbidde, C. Banura, and A. Kizito (1988-03-19). 'Blackwater fever caused by *Plasmodium vivax* infection in the acquired immune deficiency syndrome', *British Medical Journal (Clinical Res Edition)* No. 296 (1988), p 827 *et seq.*

38 Large, p 80.

39 Large, p 82.

40 *The Imjin Roll,* p 42.

41 *Edge of the Sword*, p 136.

42 Farrar-Hockley, 'A Reminiscence of the Chinese People's Volunteers'.

43 *Edge of the Sword*, p 150.

44 *Edge of the Sword*, p 155.

45 *Edge of the Sword*, p 160.

46 *Edge of the Sword*, p 166.

47 *Edge of the Sword*, p 179.

48 *Edge of the Sword*, p 181.

49 *Edge of the Sword*, p 188.

50 *Edge of the Sword*, p 190.

51 *Edge of the Sword*, p 190.

52 *Edge of the Sword*, p 194.

53 *Edge of the Sword*, p 196.

54 *Edge of the Sword*, p 198.

55 A19/PW/Korea/1005, Interrogation Report No. A19/K/BRIT 38, August 1953.

56 *Edge of the Sword*, p 199.

57 Interview with Colonel Mike Motum, 20 November 2014.

58 *Edge of the Sword*, p 204.

59 'Never a Dull Moment', interview in *Soldier* Magazine, 7 November 1983.

60 *Edge of the Sword*, p 220; see also the description by Cpl Alfred Holdham in 'I escaped from a Korean prison camp' in *John Bull,* November 1953; also Davies, p 49.

61 *Edge of the Sword*, p 221; see also Ministry of Defence, *The Treatment of British Prisoners of War in Korea* (HMSO, London, 1955).

62 *Edge of the Sword*, p 226.

63 Raymond B. Lech, *Broken Soldiers* (Chicago, 2000) pp 2, 73.

64 *Edge of the Sword,* p 231.

65 'Never a Dull Moment', in *Soldier* Magazine.

66 *Edge of the Sword*, p 238.

67 Large, p 127.

68 Davies, pp 116, 120.

69 Notes held by the Gloucestershire Regiment Archives.

70 Davies, p 126.

71 *Edge of the Sword*, p 250.

72 Davies, p 134.

73 *Edge of the Sword*, p 252.

74 *Edge of the Sword*, p 253.
75 *Edge of the Sword*, p 255.
76 *Edge of the Sword*, p 257.
77 'Set at Hazard' (MS) in Farrar-Hockley Papers.
78 A19/PW/Korea/1005, Interrogation Report No. A19/K/BRIT 38, August 1953, p 32.
79 Donald W. Boose, Jnr, 'Fighting While Talking: The Korean War Truce Talks'. *Organization of American Historians Magazine of History*, (Spring, 2000).
80 Large, p 126.
81 *Edge of the Sword*, p 271; Kinne, pp 137-139, 152-153; Large, p 126.
82 *Edge of the Sword*, p 275.
83 *Edge of the Sword*, p 277.
84 *Edge of the Sword*, p 278.
85 *Edge of the Sword*, p 279.
86 *Edge of the Sword*, p 281; see also *The Daily Telegraph*, 'Col. Carne "in solitary" for 19 months' in *The Daily Telegraph*, 2 September 1953.
87 *Edge of the Sword*, p 284.
88 *Edge of the Sword*, p 286.

Chapter 11

1 *Cap of Honour*, p 359; Holles, p 174.
2 Grist, p 47.
3 *Cap of Honour*, p 358.
4 Grist, p 56.
5 *Cap of Honour*, p 364-365.
6 Letter Carne to Colonel R.M. Grazebrook dated 10 September 1953 in Glosters Museum/Archive.
7 Telegram to Mrs M.B. Farrar-Hockley from War Office ODO (Troopers) dated 30 August 1953 in TFH's record of service.
8 A19/PW/Korea/1005, Interrogation Report No. A19/K/BRIT 38, August 1953, p 43.
9 Statement made by Lieutenant-Colonel J.P. Carne DSO to the British Ambassador in Tokyo, 7 September 1953 in Farrar-Hockley Papers.
10 Letter DPA – Pat Farrar-Hockley dated 15 September 1953 in TFH's record of service.
11 Farrar-Hockley Papers.
12 Letter Grist – Pat Farrar-Hockley dated 29 April 1951 in TFH's record of service.
13 Letter Grist – Pat Farrar-Hockley dated 17 May 1951 in TFH's record of service.
14 P/251309/ODO/Cas, Letter DPA – Pat Farrar-Hockley dated 5 June 1951 in TFH's record of service.
15 No. 1 Independent Field Records Office D III/E/36687/8 dated 8 August 1951 in TFH's record of service.
16 DPA P/251309/ODO/Cas – Pat Farrar-Hockley dated 21 December 1951 in TFH's record of service.
17 Signal BRITCON Japan to War Office Stanmore, IU/1002 150930Z June 1952; Letters DPA – Pat Farrar-Hockley dated 6 December and 23 December 1952 in TFH's record of service.
18 Letter from Hickey in TFH's record of service.
19 Letter DPA – Pat Farrar-Hockley dated 30 August 1953 in TFH's record of service.
20 AF B 199a in TFH's record of service.
21 Davies, p 151.
22 *Cap of Honour*, p 366-367.
23 *London Gazette (Supplement)* No. 40036, p 6,654, 8 December 1953.
24 *London Gazette (Supplement)* No. 40146, p 2,207, 31 August 1951.
25 *London Gazette*, 13 April 1954.
26 Dr William R. Shadish, 'Presentation to the Korean ex-P.O.W. Group, Camp 2, Saturday September 27, 1986' in Farrar-Hockley Papers.
27 Shadish, p 5.
28 Interview with the Farrar-Hockley family.

29   Michael Carver, *Out of Step. The Memoirs of Field Marshal Lord Carver* (London, 1989), p 350.

30   AF B 2077, interim confidential report for 1954 in TFH's record of service.

31   *Army Gradation List*; AF B 199a in TFH's record of service.

32   RMCS Form BS No. 16, final report on TFH dated 20 December 1954 in TFH's record of service.

33   Brevet-Major AR Godwin-Austen, *The Staff and the Staff College* (London, 1927), p 279 citing Army Order 189 of 1920.

34   The figures are calculated from information in Jeremy Crang, *The British Army and the People's War 1939 – 1945* (MUP, 2000), pp 46, 144; Godwin-Austen, *The Staff and the Staff College*, p 280; and Blaxland, *The Regiments Depart*.

35   Godwin-Austen, *The Staff and the Staff College* gives the curriculum on p 280 *et seq*. The author and indeed any officer of the post-war army who attended Camberley will remember the regime.

36   John Masters, *The Road Past Mandalay*, pp 78, 85, 104.

37   David French, 'An Extensive Use of Weedkiller', in David French and Brian Holden Reid (ed.), *The British General Staff. Reform and Innovation 1890 – 1939 (London, 2001)*, p 168.

38   David French 'An Extensive Use of Weedkiller', p 168.

39   J.P. Riley, *Unpublished PhD Thesis* (Cranfield University, 2006).

40   Interview with Major-General Peter Chiswell, 26 April 2014.

41   D. Kinne, *The Wooden Boxes* (London, 1955).

42   General Sir Ian S.M. Hamilton (ed. Anthony Farrar-Hockley), *The Commander (A Study of his Art)* (London 1957).

Chapter 12

1   AF B 199a in TFH's record of service.

2.   No staff lists for the headquarters are extant; the curator and volunteers at the Parachute Regiment Museum have been able to identify only the commanders, BMs, DQs and GSO2s Air.

3.   For more discussion, see the discussion in Stockwell's biography – who was the Divisional Commander at the time these decisions were made by the author.

4.   Parachute Regiment and Airborne Forces Museum/Archives.

5.   Frank Kitson, *Bunch of Five* (London, 1977), p 207-209.

6.   Thomas R. Mockaitis, *British Counterinsurgency Vol I, 1919 – 1960*, (New York, 1990), p 113.

7.   T.N.A. CO 926/454, an appreciation of the situation in Cyprus by Grivas dated 5 July 1956 (captured document). See also Nancy Crawshay, *The Cyprus Revolt: An Account of the Struggle for Union with Greece* (London, 1978), p 322.

8.   General Sir Kenneth Darling, Director of Operations, Cyprus, *Cyprus – The Final Round. October 1958 – March 1959.*

9.   J.P. Riley, *Regimental Records of the Royal Welch Fusiliers, Vol VI* citing material from the CO of 1 RWF, Lieutenant-Colonel R.O.F. Pritchard.

10. For a fuller discussion, see Trevor Royle, *Glubb Pasha. The Life and Times of Sir John Bagot Glubb, Commander of the Arab Legion* (London, 1992), Chapter 13.

11. See, for example, David Tal (ed.), *The 1956 War: Collusion and Rivalry in the Middle East* (London, 2001), p 6-10; Rami Ginat 'Origins of the Czech-Egyptian Arms Deal' in David Tal, p 145-168; Rami Ginat, *The Soviet Union and Egypt, 1945 – 1955* (London, 1993), pp 111-112, 171, 176, 188, 189, 209.

12. Robert Jackson, *Suez, the Forgotten Invasion* (Shrewsbury, 1996), p 11.

13. T.N.A. FO 371/118997 Minutes of the Egypt Committee, 30 July 1956.

14. HCS's MS account in KCL/Stockwell/8/6/12-13. See also 'The Suez Crisis, Operation MUSKETEER, November 1956' in Lowering, *Amphibious Assault*, p 421 *et seq*.

15. Alastair Horne, *Harold Macmillan, Vol I, 1895 – 1956* (London, 1988) (citing Macmillan's diaries), p 398.

16. PRO ADM 205/154, Psychological Warfare PSW (56), August 1956; PRO FO 371/118997 JE 11924/76, Draft note by the Egypt (Official) Committee; PRO CAB 134/1217 *Terrapin* EC(56) 47, dated 10 September 1956; PRO WO 288/77, HQ II (British) Corps Report on Operation *Musketeer*, Part III. See also Jonathon Riley, *The Life & Campaigns of General Hughie Stockwell* (Barnsley, 2006), Chapter 18.

17. AF B 199a in TFH's Record of Service.

18. Peter Haclerode, *Para!* p 218.
19. Peter Haclerode, *Para!* p 218.
20. Peter Haclerode, *Para!* p 219.
21. Peter Haclerode, *Para!* p 220.
22. Interview with General Sir Anthony Farrar-Hockley, 12 February 2004.
23. General Sir Frank King, interviewed by Max Arthur in *Men of the Red Beret.*
24. The terms of the treaty are in Maan Abu Nowar, *The Struggle for Independence 1939 – 1947: A History of the Hashemite Kingdom of Jordan* (Reading, 2001), p 307-313.
25. Interview with Sir Thomas Prickett, 19 July 2004.
26. Kennett Love, *Suez – The Twice-Fought War* (London, 1970), p 565.
27. John Cloake, *Templer: The Tiger of Malaya* (London, 1985), p 352-353.
28. General Sir Frank King, interviewed by Max Arthur in *Men of the Red Beret.*
29. *Supplement to the London Gazette*, 12 September 1957.
30. T.N.A. WO 288/77, HQ II (British) Corps Report on Operation *Musketeer*, Part III.
31. *London Gazette* (Supplement), 12 September 1957.
32. Paul Crook, *Came the Dawn: Fifty Years an Army Officer* (London, 1989).
33. HCS's MS account in KCL/Stockwell/8/6/12-13.
34. T.N.A. WO 288/77, HQ II (British) Corps Report on Operation *Musketeer*, Part III.
35. HCS's MS account in KCL/Stockwell/8/6/12-13.
36. PRO WO 288/77, HQ II (British) Corps Report on Operation *Musketeer*, Part I.
37. AF B2077 dated 20 January 1957, annual confidential report for 1956, in TFH's record of service.
38. *London Gazette* 12 June 1958. The citation AF W 3121 is in TFH's record of service.
39. AF B199a in TFH's record of service.
40. AF B199a in TFH's record of service.
41. *Field Service Regulations, Volume I (Organisation and Administration) 1930.* WO 26/Regs/1849, p 20.
42. *Field Service Pocket Book 1926.* WO 26/863, p 3.
43. AF B2077 dated 14 December 1957, annual confidential report for 1956, in TFH's record of service.
44. *Dictionary of National Biography.*
45. 3 Para War Unit Historical Report (Airborne Forces Museum/Archives).
46. Peter Haclerode, *Para!* p 234.
47. *Pegasus, Journal of the Parachute Regiment*, Vol XIII No. 3, 1958.
48. Parachute Regiment and Airborne Forces Museum/Archives.
49. Parachute Regiment and Airborne Forces Museum/Archives.
50. *Pegasus*, Vol XIII No 3.
51. *Pegasus*, Vol XIII No 3.
52. 16 Para Brigade OpO, 20 August 1958.
53. *Pegasus*, Vol XIII No 3.
54. Cyril Churchill, 'First Paratroops Fly Home From Jordan', *News Chronicle*, 27 October 1958.
55. AF B 2077 dated 7 December 1958, annual confidential report for 1956, in TFH's record of service.
56. AF B 199a in TFH's record of service
57. Interview with Colonel Roy Giles, 16 February 2015.

Chapter 13

1   K.C.L. LH 1/278/1, 12 May 1958.
2   K.C.L. LH 1/278/5, 6 July 1958.
3   Course Report for the 21st Course, JSSC, in TFH's record of service.
4   AF B199a in TFH's record of service.
5   For a fuller discussion of Stockwell's re-shaping of Sandhurst, see Jonathon Riley, *The Life and Campaigns of General Hughie Stockwell.*
6   Brigadier Sir John Smythe, *Sandhurst* (London, 1961), p 210.
7   *The Wish Stream*, summer 1947. Foreword by FM Montgomery.
8   Hugh Thomas, *The Story of Sandhurst*, p 226.

9   Smythe, p 214-216.

10   Interview with Major-General Peter Cavendish, 26 June 2003.

11   *The Wish Stream, Journal of the R.M.A. Sandhurst,* autumn 1959, p 66.

12   Interview with Major-General Peter Chiswell, 26 April 2014.

13   David Chandler (ed.), *Great Battles of the British Army as Commemorated in the Sandhurst Companies* (London, 1991), Annex A.

14   Interview with Lieutenant-Colonel P.A. Crocker, 12 March 2014.

15   Major Peter Cronk to the author, 13 March 2014.

16   Charles Messenger to the author, 16 July 2014.

17   *The Wish Stream,* autumn 1960, p 75-78.

18   *The Wish Stream,* spring 1961, p 12-15.

19   Charles Messenger to the author, 16 July 2014.

20   *The Wish Stream,* spring 1960, p 5-6.

21   *The Wish Stream,* autumn 1960, p 68-69.

22   *The Wish Stream,* autumn 1960, p 70-71.

23   AF B2078, annual confidential report for 1960 in TFH's record of service. The actual remarks from Lloyd Owen are missing.

24   Blacker to The Under-Secretary of State (MS4) dated 23 December 1960 in TFH's record of service.

25   DO/BR/797/DMS (B) dated 11 January 1961 in TFH's record of service.

Chapter 14

1   SCO 24/61 in TFH's record of service.

2   *London Gazette,* 12 September 1961.

3   *The Daily Telegraph,* 2 November 2004.

4   Lt-Gen Sir Hew Pike's eulogy to TFH at his memorial service in the RMA Sandhurst Chapel; interview with Colonel David Charles, 28 January 2015.

5   Richard A. Mobley, 'Gauging the Iraqi Threat to Kuwait in the 1960s – UK Indications and Warning'. (US Central Intelligence Agency, 2007).

6   Yitzhak Aron (ed.), *Middle East Record, Vol 1,* 1960, p 98.

7   AF B199a in TFH's record of service.

8   AF B2078, annual confidential report (interim) for 1961 dated 3 August 1961 in TFH's record of service.

9   AF B199a in TFH's record of service; *London Gazette,* 25 December 1962.

10   Army Doctrine Publication *Command,* p 1-5.

11   FM Montgomery of Alamein, cited in *Serve To Lead* (RMA Sandhurst), p 21.

12   Lt-Gen Sir Hew Pike's eulogy to TFH.

13   Susan Hickman to the author, 19 December 2014.

14   *Soldier* Magazine, 7 November 1983.

15   Hils Farrar-Hockley, 21 April 2014.

16   Jonathan Sale, 'Passed/Failed: An education in the life of Brigid Keenan, journalist' in *The Independent,* 30 March 2006.

17   Interview with Major-General Michael Walsh, 26 May 2014.

18   AF B2078, annual confidential report for 1962 dated 18 January 1963 in TFH's record of service.

19   Lt-Gen Sir Hew Pike's eulogy to TFH.

20   AF B2078, annual confidential report for 1963 dated 1 October 1963 in TFH's record of service.

21   *Dictionary of National Biography.*

22   Lt-Gen Sir Hew Pike's eulogy to TFH.

23   Interview with Lieutenant-Colonel Peter Walter, 3 October 2014.

24   AF B199a in TFH's record of service.

25   Brian Holden Reid in TFH's *DNB* entry.

26   Brian Holden Reid in TFH's *DNB* entry.

27   Interview with Major-General Michael Walsh, 26 May 2014.

28   Interview with Lieutenant-Colonel Peter Walter, 3 October 2014.

29   3 Para Annual Historical Record for 1964-1965; interview with Lieutenant-Colonel Peter Walter, 3 October 2014.

30   Harclerode, p 237.

31   Aaron Edwards, *Mad Mitch's Tribal Law. Aden and the End of an Empire* (London, 2014), p 79.

32   Interview with Lieutenant-Colonel Peter Walter, 3 October 2014.

33   Francis Graham-Bell, *Helicopter on the Heights*, MS in TFH's papers of the story of 653 Squadron AAC, no page numbering.

34   Harclerode, p 238.

35   The following section of this chapter – except where otherwise footnoted – is drawn from TFH's account of the action, first published in *The Elite*, Volume 5, Issue 53, 1986 supplemented by the text of a presentation given to 2nd Para after the battle (author unknown), in the Parachute Regiment Archives, Duxford; the Annual Historical Record of 3 Para for the year ending 31 March 1965; Brigadier R.S. Mountford, *The Actions of 'J' (Sidi Rezegh) Battery Royal Horse Artillery in the Aden Protectorate 1963 – 64* (Ipswich, 2013); '3 Battalion Group The Parachute Regiment in Action in The Radfan', *Pegasus*, 1965 (with photographs by courtesy of *Life International*); Peter Harclerode, *Para! 50 Years of the Parachute Regiment* (London, 1996).

36   TFH in *Men of the Red Beret*, p 337; Edwards, p 72-75.

37   Letter from TFH (undated) in Parachute Regiment Archives, Duxford.

38   Letter from TFH (undated) in Parachute Regiment Archives, Duxford.

39   Letter from TFH (undated) in Parachute Regiment Archives, Duxford; Edwards, p 78-79.

40   Letter from TFH (undated) in Parachute Regiment Archives, Duxford.

41   Letter from TFH (undated) in Parachute Regiment Archives, Duxford.

42   Letter from TFH (undated) in Parachute Regiment Archives, Duxford.

43   Harclerode, p 241.

44   Edwards, p 80.

45   TFH in *Men of the Red Beret*, p 337.

46   Interview with Major-General Michael Walsh, 26 May 2014.

47   Parachute Regiment Archives, Duxford.

48   *Operations of 3 PARA Gp in the Radfan 17 – 20 May 64*, OP 110/1 dated 23 May 64, in Parachute Regiment Archives, Duxford.

49   Letter from TFH (undated) in Parachute Regiment Archives, Duxford.

50   *Helicopter on the Heights*, no page numbering.

51   Edwards, p 80; interview with Major-General Michael Walsh, 26 May 2014.

52   Interview with Major-General Michael Walsh, 26 May 2014. TFH's manuscript notes for his orders are preserved in his personal papers.

53   *Operations of 3 PARA Gp in the Radfan 17 – 20 May 64*.

54   *Operations of 3 PARA Gp in the Radfan 17 – 20 May 64*.

55   *Pegasus*, summer 1965, p 40.

56   Edwards, p 81.

57   *Report on Operations in the Radfan by 3 PARA Gp, 19th – 27th May 1964* in Parachute Regiment Archives, Duxford.

58   TFH in *Men of the Red Beret*, p 337-338.

59   *Report on Operations in the Radfan by 3 PARA Gp, 19th – 27th May 1964* in Parachute Regiment Archives, Duxford.

60   *Helicopter on the Heights*, no page numbering.

61   *Helicopter on the Heights*, no page numbering.

62   *Report on Operations in the Radfan by 3 PARA Gp, 19th – 27th May 1964* in Parachute Regiment Archives, Duxford.

63   *Report on Operations in the Radfan by 3 PARA Gp, 19th – 27th May 1964* in Parachute Regiment Archives, Duxford.

64   TFH in *Men of the Red Beret*, p 339.

65   Lt-Gen Sir Hew Pike's eulogy to TFH.

66   Dair Farrar-Hockley, 21 April 2014.

67   *Helicopter on the Heights*, no page numbering.

68   Interview with Major-General Michael Walsh, 26 May 2014.

69   Interview with Major-General Mike Tillotson, 2 October 2014.

70   Cubbon to Lt-Gen Sir Kenneth Darling, GOC/DO/1 dated 12 March 1965.

71   Pat Beaumont to the author, 28 October 2014.

72   Lt-Gen Sir Hew Pike's eulogy to TFH.

73   AF W3121, Citation for the DSO dated 1 June 1964 in TFH's record of service; *LG*, 30 April 1965.

74   Interview with Major-General Peter Chiswell, 26 April 2014; interview with Major-General Michael Walsh, 26 May 2014.

75   Interview with Major-General Michael Walsh, 26 May 2014.

76   Pat Beaumont to the author, 28 October 2014.

77   AF B2078 annual confidential report for 1964 dated 15 December 1964 in TFH's record of service.

78   Lt-Gen Sir Hew Pike's eulogy to TFH.

Chapter 15

1   No British Official History of the Confrontation has been written, although there is an excellent Australian history. I am indebted to Dr Brian Farrell for his very considerable help and access to his published material in helping to frame this chapter. TFH himself left no record of his time in Borneo.

2   AF B199a in TFH's record of service.

3   Interview with Ted Olive, 17 February 2015.

4   Interviews with Major-General Mike Walsh and the Farrar-Hockley family.

5   For a full account of this forgotten campaign, see Christopher Bayley and Tim Harper, *Forgotten Wars. The End of Britain's Asian Empire* (London, 2007, Chapter 4.

6   T.N.A. PREM 11/4907, INTEL Report No. 39, 20 March 1964.

7   Brian P. Farrell, 'What do we do now? British Commonwealth and American Reactions to the Separation of Malaysia and Singapore' in Malcolm H. Murfett (ed.), *Imponderable but Not Inevitable: Warfare in the 20th Century* (Westport, 2010), p 78 (2005).

8   Brian P. Farrell, 'What do they want and how can we respond? Commonwealth Intelligence and Confrontation with Indonesia 1963'; Tan Tai Yong, *Creating Greater Malaysia: Decolonization and the Politics of Merger* (Singapore, 2008), Chapter 1.

9   Australian War Memorial, 125, Item 2, CBB4/12/1, Report by Maj-Gen. W.C. Walker, Director of Operations Borneo, 'The Operations in Borneo 22 December 1962 to 15 March 1963'; H.A. Majid, *Rebellion in Brunei: The 1962 Revolt, Imperialism, Confrontation, and Oil* (London, 2007); Nicholas van der Bijl, *The Brunei Revolt 1962-1963* (Barnsley, 2012).

10   Brian P. Farrell, 'Quadruple failure? The British-American split over Collective Security in Southeast Asia, 1963-1966'.

11   National Archives of Australia (N.A.A.) A1209/1962/1010, CRO to the British High Commission Canberra, 35, 12 December 1962; T.N.A. CO 1035/164, JICFE Weekly Review of Current Intelligence, 24 January 1963; CAB 158/48, JIC(63)8, 17 January, JIC(63)14, 31 January 1963; CAB 158/46, JIC(62)58(Final), 28 January 1963.

12   T.N.A. CAB148/1, Defence and Overseas Policy Committee minutes, 8 April, 23 April, 29 April, 8 May, 14 May 1964; CAB 148/2, DO(64)29, 7 April 1964.

13   See, for example, Tom Pocock, *Fighting General – The Public & Private Campaigns of General Sir Walter Walker* (London, 1973), p 11.

14   Neil Smith, *Nothing Short of War: With the Australian Army in Borneo 1962–66* (Brighton, 1999) p 41; Peter Dennis, Jeffrey Grey, Ewan Morris, Robin Prior and Jean Bou, *The Oxford Companion to Australian Military History* (OUP, Melbourne, 2008), p 232-233.

15   Christopher Pugsley, *From Emergency to Confrontation: The New Zealand Armed Forces in Malaya and Borneo 1949–66* (OUP, South Melbourne, 2003), p 255.

16   Pocock, p 196.

17   Interview with Colonel J.W. Sewell, 16 December 2013.

18   As late as spring 1966, Far East Command remained nearly as strong as BAOR in manpower: T.N.A. DEFE 5/166, ANZAM Defence Committee minute 1/1966, Review of British Defence Policy, 22 March 1966.

19   T.N.A. DEFE 5/155, COS 295/64, Appendix 1, Disposition of UK Fighting Units on 29 Oct 64; see also Denis Healey, *The Time of My Life* (New York, 1989).

20   Interview with Brigadier Anthony Vivian, 20 November 2013.

21   T.N.A. CAB134/555, CPC (57)6, 28 January 1957; CAB 134/1644, DSE(60)9, 1 July 1960; CAB134/1645, DSE(60)30(Final), 3 November 1960; CAB163/22, COS(62)131, 27 March 1962.

22   Brian P. Farrell, 'Quadruple failure? The British-American split over Collective Security in Southeast Asia, 1963-1966'.

23   David Easter, 'British Intelligence & Propaganda during 'Confrontation', 1963 – 1966' in *International Security,* Vol 16 No. 2 (summer 2001), p 83-102.

24   Interview with Brigadier Anthony Vivian, 20 November 2013.

25   Interview with Brigadier Anthony Vivian, 20 November 2013.

26   Lieutenant-Colonel E.N.W. Bramall 'Borneo in Perspective', in KRRC Annals, Vol 6, p 5.

27   AF B2078, annual confidential report for 1965/66, dated 17 March 1996 in TFH's record of service.

28   Interview with Brigadier Anthony Vivian, 20 November 2013.

29   Peter Haclerode, *Para!* p 247.

30   Bramall, p 3.

31   Bramall, p 4-5.

32   Bramall, p 6.

33   Peter Haclerode, *Para!* p 262.

34   'Paradata', by permission of Max Arthur, from *Men of the Red Beret.*

35   'Paradata', by permission of Max Arthur, from *Men of the Red Beret.*

36   Peter Haclerode, *Para!* p 264.

37   Interview with Brigadier Anthony Vivian, 20 November 2013; interview with Colonel J.W. Sewell, 16 December 2013.

38   It remains unclear who orchestrated the coup and why such an obvious target as Suharto was not attacked. See, for example, two recent studies: Helen-Louise Hunter, *Sukarno and the Indonesian Coup* (Westport CT, 2007); and Jusuf Wanandi, *Shades of Grey: A Political Memoir of Modern Indonesia 1965-1998* (Singapore, 2012).

39   As late as spring 1966, Far East Command remained nearly as strong as British NATO forces in manpower: T.N.A. DEFE 5/166, ANZAM Defence Committee minute 1/1966, 22 March 1966.

40   Letter Bramall to Lieutenant-General Sir Brian Horrocks, 19 June 1967.

41   AF B199a in TFH's record of service.

42   Interview with Colonel J.W. Sewell, 16 December 2013.

43   T.N.A. CAB 158/63, note re JIC(66)45 and JIC(66)46, 13 June 1966; CAB148/28, OPD(66)68, 14 June 1966; PREM13/1454, Healey and Razak meeting, minutes, 7 July, Healey to Wilson, 19 July 1966; CAB164/19, Wilson and Lee Kuan Yew meeting, minutes, 25 April 1966; DEFE 5/171, COS 140/66, 2 January 1967; NAA A1838, TS682/22/1 Part 7, CINCFE meetings with High Commissioners, February through July 1966.

44   www.measuringworth.com – retrieved 17 April 2014.

45   See, for example, J. Baylis, *Ambiguity and Deterrence: British Nuclear Strategy 1945-1964* (Oxford, 1995); M. Jones, 'Up the Garden Path? Britain's Nuclear History in the Far East, 1954-1962', in *The International History Review,* Vol 25, No. 2 (2003).

46   T.N.A. DEFE 4/202, COS minutes, 12 July 1966; DEFE 4/205, COS 1893/31/8/66, 31 August, COS minutes, 8 September 1966; DEFE 4/206, COS 1969/23/9/66, 23 September, COS minutes, 27 September 1966.

47   Interview with Major-General Mike Tillotson, 2 October 2014.

48   AF B2078, annual confidential report for 1965/66 dated 17 March 1966 in TFH's record of service.

49   Lt-Gen Sir Alan Jolly, C-in-C FEC writing Part II of AF B2078, annual confidential report for 1965/66 dated 17 March 1966 in TFH's record of service.

50   Bramall, p 10.

Chapter 16

1   AF B199a in TFH's record of service.
2   Paradata, Airborne Forces Museum. There is no annual historical report for HQ 16 Parachute Brigade at this period lodged with the National Archives.
3   Letter TFH to FM Montgomery dated 21 February 1967 in TFH's personal papers.
4   Interview with Major-General Peter Chiswell, 26 April 2014.
5   Peter Harclerode, *Para!* p 269-279.
6   Interview with Major-General Mike Walsh, 26 May 2014.
7   Annual confidential report for 1966 dated 7 January 1967 in TFH's record of service.
8   Interview with Major-General Peter Chiswell, 26 April 2014.
9   Interview with Major-General Peter Chiswell, 26 April 2014.
10 Interview with Major-General Peter Chiswell, 26 April 2014.
11 Annual confidential report for 1966 dated 7 January 1967 in TFH's record of service.
12 Interview with Major-General Peter Chiswell, 26 April 2014.
13 Interview with Major-General Peter Chiswell, 26 April 2014.
14 Annual confidential report for 1966 dated 7 January 1967 in TFH's record of service. The matter of his care for the men was made plain in every interview that I conducted for this biography.
15 Brian Holden Reid in TFH's *DNB* entry.
16 Various correspondence in TFH's personal files.
17 Death Certificate.
18 Farrar-Hockley family to the author, 14 August 2014.
19 See the coverage available from *British Pathé.*
20 Chateris to TFH, 25 April 1967, in TFH's personal files.
21 Annual confidential report for 1966 dated 7 January 1967 in TFH's record of service.
22 Annual confidential report for 1967 dated 16 October 1967 in TFH's record of service.
23 P/251309/MS(SB) dated 3 September 1968 in TFH's record of service.
24 Annual confidential report for 1968 dated 10 July 1968 in TFH's record of service.
25 2052/1 MS dated 15 November 1967 in TFH's record of service.
26 Letter dated 8 November 1967 in TFH's personal files.
27 P/251309/MS (SB) dated 25 February 1968 in TFH's record of service.
28 AF B199a in TFH's record of service; *Army List;* Paradata, Airborne Forces Museum.
29 Letter from Moulsford Parish Council in TFH's personal files.
30 www.exeter.ox.ac.uk – retrieved 27 July 2014.
31 Introduction to 'National service and British society, A Study by Major-General A.H. Farrar-Hockley DSO MBE MC BLitt', (unpublished BLitt thesis, Exeter College Oxford, 1968-1970).
32 'National service and British society', p 127.
33 Interview with Ted Olive, 17 February 2015.
34 Various correspondence in TFH's personal files.
35 MS D/WW/318/69 dated 1 April 1969; AF B199a, both in TFH's record of service.
36 D/DS15/512/5/6 dated 6 December 1974 in TFH's record of service.
37 *R.U.S.I. Journal* Vol 114, Issue No. 656, November 1969.
38 Letter TFH – Liddell Hart in KCL LH 1/278/17 – 20.
39 AF B199a in TFH's record of service.
40 Major-General W.G.F. Jackson, ACDS (OR), to TFH, 12 November 1969 in TFH's personal files.

Chapter 17

1   *Army Lists*
2   Stephen Badsey, 'In the Public's Eye: The British Army and Military-Media Relations', *R.U.S.I. Analysis*, 21 September 2009.
3   'Derry clears the debris', *Belfast Telegraph*, 7 October 1968; 'Steel-helmeted police in New Derry clashes', *News Letter*, 7 October 1968; 'Derry rocked by further riots and baton charges', *Irish News*, 7 October 1968.

4   Mary Holland, 'Police Wagons ablaze in Ulster Battle', *The Observer*, 12 January 1969; 'Ulster's Misery', *The Economist*, Vol 230, No. 6542, 11 January 1969, p.14-15; 'Ulster: Who's in charge?' *New Statesman*, 10 January 1969, p.33.

5   'Conclusions of a Meeting of the Cabinet Security Committee, Stormont Castle, 17 July 1969'. http://cain. ulst.ac.uk/proni/1969 retrieved 17 July 2014; Devenny died three months after he and his family were attacked in their home by police officers; an Independent Enquiry was conducted by Chief Superintendent Kenneth Drury of the Metropolitan Police.

6   See, for example, Russell Stetler, *The Battle of the Bogside* (London, 1970).

7   PRONI Public Records HA/32/2/55: 'Formal message to Mr Cairncross of the Home Office given to him on the telephone at 3:15 p.m. on 14th August, 1969'; 'Formal government decisions … use of … (a) RUC, (b) USC and (c) Army, … information and evidence placed before Ministers, 14 August 1969; Letter from A. Peacocke, then Inspector-General of the RUC to General Officer Commanding, 14 August 1969.

8   3 LI's account in *The Silver Bugle*, the journal of the Light Infantry, cited in Gregory Blaxland, *The Regiments Depart*, p 479.

9   *Report of the Advisory Committee on Policing in Northern Ireland,* Cmd 535, October 1969; *Disturbances in Northern Ireland,* Cmd 532, October 1969.

10   Tony Geraghty, *The Irish War* (London, 1998), p 23.

11   See, for example, Tim Pat Coogan, *The IRA* (London, 1993).

12   There is a series of papers on this subject in T.N.A. DEFE 13/1398 – however, the subject is outside the scope of this biography.

13   C/1514/AUS (GS) to D.P.R. (A), T.N.A. DEFE 13/1398.

14   *The Times*, 3 April 1970.

15   T.N.A. DEFE 13/1398, 2 April 1970.

16   Minute to DPR 6 April 1970, T.N.A. DEFE 13/1398, 2 April 1970.

17   Freeland to Callaghan, 6 April 1970, T.N.A. DEFE 13/1398.

18   DPR (A)/70/6 9 April 70, T.N.A. DEFE 13/1398.

19   PS/US Army to D.P.R. (A) 29 April 1970, T.N.A. DEFE 13/1398.

20   DPR (A) 207/1/9 28 April, T.N.A. DEFE 13/1398.

21   CGS/401 20 April 1970, T.N.A. DEFE 13/1398.

22   T.N.A. DEFE 13/1398.

23   T.N.A. DEFE 13/1398, 7 May 1970.

24   20/Misc/5409 (ASD 2a) 22 April 1970, T.N.A. DEFE 13/1395.

25   www.politics97@bbc.co.uk retrieved 21 July 2014.

26   A/BR/20201/MO3 9 Jun 1970, T.N.A. DEFE 24/1908.

27   A/BR/20201/MO3 15 June 1970, T.N.A. DEFE 24/1908.

28   C/1937/AUS (GB) dated 22 June 1970, T.N.A. DEFE 24/1908.

29   Jonathon Riley, *Soldiers of the Queen* (Chippenham, 1992), p 432-433.

30   DPR (A) dated 30 June 1970, T.N.A. DEFE 24/1611.

31   For various accounts of this series of events see, for example, Martin Dillon, *The Dirty War: Covert strategies and tactics used in political conflicts* (London, 1999), p 212-213; Sean Ó Fearghail, *Law (?) and Orders: The Belfast 'Curfew' of 3–5 July 1970* (Dundalgan, 1970), p 10 *et seq*; Brian Hanley and Scott Millar, *The Lost Revolution: The Story of the Official IRA and the Workers' Party* (London, 2009), p157-159.

32   Eamonn Mallie and Patrick Bishop, *The Provisional IRA* (London, 1988), p 159.

33   Cited in Steve Chibnall, *Law and Order News: An analysis of crime reporting in the British press* (London, 2002) p 176-177.

34   Peter Taylor, *Provos: The IRA and Sinn Féin* (London, 1979), p 79.

35   *An Phoblacht* (*Republican News*), 4 July 1970.

36   Mallie and Bishop, p 159.

37   970/35 *Conclusions of a meeting of the Cabinet held at Stormont Castle on 7 July 1970 at 11.00 a.m.,* T.N.A. CAB/4/1532/15.

38   *Irish News*, 10 July 1970.

39   Brian Hanley and Scott Millar, *The Lost Revolution: The Story of the Official IRA and the Workers' Party* (Dublin, 2009), p 157-159.

40   *Irish News*, 10 July 1970; *An Phoblacht* (*Republican News*), 4 July 1970.
41   Maille and Bishop, p 160; Geraghty, p 33.
42   Andrew Saunders, Ian S. Wood, *Times of Troubles: Britain's war in Northern Ireland* (Edinburgh University Press, 2012).
43   DPR (A)/181/5, T.N.A. DEFE 24/1611.
44   T.N.A. DEFE 24/1611.
45   TFH to the CGS, August 1970, in CLF NI – DO1 file, TFH's personal papers.
46   AF B199a in TFH's record of service.

Chapter 18

1   A copy of the Directive is in T.N.A. DEFE 13/921, attached to a visit programme for the Secretary of State for Defence.
2   Freeland to TFH, 20 July 1970, in TFH's personal papers.
3   Interview with General Sir Frank Kitson, 30 September 2014.
4   CLF NI – DO 1 file in TFH's personal papers.
5   T.N.A. DEFE 25/261.
6   CGS/828 15 Oct 1970, T.N.A. DEFE 25/261, agreed by Ministry of State 26 October 1970.
7   A/BR/224/15/10/4/1 (ASD 1/5c) 5 October 1970, T.N.A. 25/261.
8   Interview with the Farrar-Hockley family, 8 October 2013.
9   C/2360/AUS (GS) 29 September 1970, T.N.A. DEFE 25/261.
10 *Army Lists*.
11 Interview with General Sir Frank Kitson, 30 September 2014.
12 Frank Kitson, *Bunch of Five* (London, 1977), p 281.
13 *Bunch of Five,* p 283.
14 *Bunch of Five,* p 283-290.
15 Minute to the S of S for Defence, 12 August 1971, T.N.A. DEFE 13/915.
16 MO3/25001/F186 10 September 1970 and DOP 712/70 (Final) 19 January 1971, T.N.A. WO 32/21795.
17 Carver, p 405.
18 S/2457 (AUS(GS)), December 1970, T.N.A. DEFE 13/676.
19 MO 19/3/1, 2 October 1970, T.N.A. DEFE 25/261.
20 CGS/828, a detailed paper on force levels, 12 October 1970, T.N.A. DEFE 25/261.
21 CGS/828, T.N.A. DEFE 25/261.
22 MO 19/3/1, briefing note to the Prime Minister, 26 October 1970; the acceptance was given by S of S at a meeting on 19 October minuted in MO 19/3/1, all in T.N.A. DEFE 25/261.
23 MO 19/3 1 December 1970, T.N.A. DEFE 13/676.
24 NISEC 11, 3 November 1970. TFH to Brig J.A.C. Cowan Comd 8 Bde, Brig F.E. Kitson Comd 39 Bde, Lt-Col K. Dodson CO 3 Queens, T.N.A. DEFE 24/1611. TFH's personal files (CLF NI – DO 1) contain a series of handwritten notes that seem to form the preparation for this Directive.
25 Interview with Major-General Bryan Webster, 18 September 2014.
26 Colonel P.E. Butler to the author, 27 August 2014.
27 Interview with Colonel Clive Brennan, 2 October 2014.
28 Interview with Colonel Malcolm Ross-Thomas, 19 November 2014.
29 TFH – Lloyd Owen, 2 October 1970, in CLF NI – DO 1 file in TFH's personal papers.
30 Robert English, *Armed Struggle. The History of the IRA* (London, 2008), p 137.
31 Geraghty, p 40.
32 Geraghty, p 40.
33 www.philipjohnston.com retrieved 13 August 2014.
34 TFH's *DNB* entry; TFH's obituary in *The Times*, 14 March 2006; TFH's obituary in *The Daily Telegraph*, 14 March 2006.
35 Saunders and Wood, p 49.
36 Geraghty, p 40.

37 Interview with Major-General Peter Chiswell, 18 August 2014; interview with Major-General Bryan Webster, 18 September 2014.

38 Sir Frank Kitson to the author, 21 December 2014.

39 John Ware, 'Britain's Secret Terror Force', *Irish Republican News*, 23 November 2013.

40 Frank Kitson, *Gangs and Counter Gangs* (London, 1960).

41 Interview with Colonel Malcolm Ross-Thomas, 19 November 2014; see also Ed Moloney, *A Secret History of the IRA* (London, 2003), p 119.

42 CLF NI – DO 1 file in TFH's personal papers.

43 Interview with Colonel Malcolm Ross-Thomas, 19 November 2014.

44 Interview with Major-General Peter Chiswell, 18 August 2014.

45 Interview with General Sir Frank Kitson, 30 September 2014.

46 Interview with Colonel Malcolm Ross-Thomas, 19 November 2014.

47 S/2428/AUS (GS), 9 November 1970, T.N.A. DEFE 13/676.

48 2431/AUS (GS), T.N.A. DEFE 13/676.

49 Signal CLF to DMO 17 December 1970, T.N.A. DEFE 25/261.

50 T.N.A. DEFE 13/676.

51 Cabinet meeting minutes, 29 January 1971, T.N.A. DEFE 13/676.

52 Minute by P.J. Woodfield to S of S for Defence dated 3 February 1971 in Summary of Ops 3 – 7 Feb 71 VCGS/28 covering NISEC 6 7 Feb 71, T.N.A. DEFE 13/676.

53 Seán Mac Stiofáin, *Memoirs of a Revolutionary* (Daly City, 1979), p 146.

54 Brendan O'Brien, *The Long War – The IRA and Sinn Féin* (Dublin, 1995), p 166.

55 Interview with Colonel Clive Brennan, 2 October 2014.

56 Summary of operations 3 – 7 February 1971 VCGS/28 covering NISEC 6, 7 February 1971, T.N.A. DEFE 13/676.

57 Geraghty, p 40.

58 *Hansard*, vol 813, p 597-605, 11 March 1971.

59 Geraghty, p 41.

60 CGS/S28 11 January 1971, T.N.A. DEFE 13/676.

61 Summary of Operations 3 – 7 February 1971, T.N.A. DEFE 13/676.

62 Letter Carington to TFH dated 2 February 1971, in DEFE 13/676.

63 Interview with General Sir Frank Kitson, 30 September 2014; interview with Malcolm Ross-Thomas, 19 November 2014.

64 CLF NI – DO 1 file in TFH's personal papers.

65 Interview with the Farrar-Hockley family, 8 October 2013.

66 Letter Carington to Freeland, 2 February 1971, DEFE 13/676.

67 CLF NI – DO 1 file in TFH's personal papers; interview with General Sir Frank Kitson, 30 September 2014.

68 *The Independent*, 9 August 1998.

69 Michael Carver, *Out of Step. The Memoirs of Field Marshal Lord Carver* (London, 1989), p 402-403.

70 Carver, p 403.

71 Minutes of a telephone conversation between Heath and Chichester-Clark, 19 March 1971, T.N.A. DEFE 13/915.

72 Carver, p 403.

73 Carver, p 403.

74 Minutes of the Cabinet meeting, 1 April 1971, T.N.A. DEFE 13/915.

75 T.N.A. WO 32/21795.

76 39/G/BOR 1 May 1971, T.N.A. WO 32/21795.

77 CLF NI – DO1 file in TFH's personal papers.

78 TFH – Ian Dobbie dated 20 August 1971 in TFH's personal files.

79 Geraghty, p 41.

80 CLF NI – DO1 file in TFH's personal papers.

81 Signal 10 July 1971 GOC to VCGS, T.N.A. DEFE 13/915.

82 Carver, p 404.

83   CLF NI – DO1 file in TFH's personal papers.

84   Carver, p 405.

85   Interview with General Sir Frank Kitson, 30 September 2014.

86   Interview with General Sir Frank Kitson, 30 September 2014.

87   CGS/828 22 July 1971, T.N.A. DEFE 13/915.

88   A/BR/2021/14/MO3, T.N.A. DEFE 13/915.

89   Carver, p 405-406.

90   The Ambassador's cable summarising the meeting is in T.N.A. DEFE 13/915.

91   Carver, p 408.

92   Interview with Colonel Clive Brennan, 2 October 2014.

93   Interview with Colonel Malcolm Ross-Thomas, 19 November 2014.

94   T.N.A. DEFE 13/915.

95   Jonathon Riley, *Soldiers of the Queen* (Chippenham, 1992), p 341.

96   Interview with Colonel Clive Brennan, 2 October 2014.

97   Riley, *Soldiers of the Queen*, p 30.

98   Sir Frank Kitson to the author, 24 December 2014.

99   Jonathan Tonge, *Northern Ireland* (London, 2013), p 66.

100 Interview with Major-General Bryan Webster, 18 September 2014.

101 *Report of the enquiry into allegations against the Security Forces of physical brutality in Northern Ireland arising out of events on the 9th August, 1971* by Sir Edmund Compton GCB KBE, *November, 1971,* Cmnd 4823; *Report of the Committee of Privy Counsellors appointed to consider authorised procedures for the interrogation of persons suspected of terrorism by Lord Parker of Waddington*, March 1972, Cmnd 4901.

102 Carver, p 412.

103 Geraghty, p 41.

104 Rupert Smith, *The Utility of Force. The Art of War in the Modern World* (London, 2005), p 18.

105 Kitson, *Bunch of Five,* p 299-303.

106 Simon Winchester, 'Promoting General Confusion', in *The Guardian*, 2 August 1971.

Chapter 19

1   General Sir Richard Gale, *A Call to Arms: An Autobiography* (London, 1968), p 192-200; Riley, *Life of General Hughie Stockwell,* p 221-228; Kenneth Macksey, *A History of the Royal Armoured Corps, 1914 – 1975* (Beaminster, 1983), p 203; Desmond Bastick, *Spearhead: The Story of the First British Corps* (Bielefeld, 1977), p 120-121.

2   Graham E. Watson and Richard A. Rinaldi, *The British Army in Germany (BAOR and After): An Organizational History 1947 – 2004* (Orbat.com 2005).

3   *Statement on the Defence Estimates 1975* (Cmnd 5976).

4   *Notes on the Soviet Ground Forces,* Army Code No. 70735 (Ministry of Defence, January 1972 edition), p 1-2 to 1-3.

5   *Opening Rounds,* p 146.

6   Interview with Major-General Peter Chiswell, 26 April 2014.

7   AF B199a in TFH's record of service.

8   Interview with Desmond Bowen, 5 February 2015. TFH left no record of his period in command of the 4th Division, nor did the Divisional Headquarters carry out its requirement to submit an annual historical report to the MOD Historical Branch (Army), as none can be found in the National Archives.

9   Interview with Desmond Bowen, 5 February 2015.

10   Interview with Desmond Bowen, 5 February 2015 and with Ted Olive, 17 February 2015.

11   Interview with Field Marshal Lord Bramall, 19 November 2014.

12   *Rates of Pay for the Regular Army, 1970,* MOD Army Personal Services Code 6551, published annually.

13   Interview with Desmond Bowen, 5 February 2015.

14   Hilary Farrar-Hockley to the author, 28 October 2014.

15   Interview with Field Marshal Lord Bramall, 19 November 2014.

16   T.N.A. WO 305/3325, I (BR) Corps Historical Report January – December 1971.

17   T.N.A. WO 305/3325, I (BR) Corps Historical Report January – December 1971.

18   Sixth Sense, 17 March 1972, p 8.

19   Sixth Sense, 17 March 1972, p 8.

20   T.N.A. WO 305/3325, I (BR) Corps Historical Report January – December 1972.

21   Various Correspondence, 1971 – 1977 in TFH's personal files.

22   Interview with Field Marshal Lord Bramall, 19 November 2014; interview with Desmond Bowen, 5 February 2015.

23   T.N.A. WO 305/3325, I (BR) Corps Historical Report January – December 1972.

24   T.N.A. WO 305/4195, I (BR) Corps Historical Report January – December 1973.

25   *Journal of The Queen's Regiment,* Vol 7, No. 2, September 1973, p 19.

26   T.N.A. WO 305/3325, I (BR) Corps Historical Report January – December 1972.

27   Interview with Desmond Bowen, 5 February 2015.

28   T.N.A. WO 305/4195, I (BR) Corps Historical Report January – December 1973.

29   T.N.A. WO 305/4195, I (BR) Corps Historical Report January – December 1973.

30   Interview with Desmond Bowen, 5 February 2015.

31   *Student,* Ballantine's Illustrated History of the Violent Century 1973, Barrie Pitt (ed.): 'War Leader' book No. 15 (Ballantine Books Inc., USA, 1973).

32   Interview with Desmond Bowen, 5 February 2015.

33   Brian Holden Reid in TFH's *DNB* entry.

34   T.N.A. DEFE 48/222, 'Survivability of Army Field Formation Headquarters in 1st British Corps post 1980'. Defence O.A. Establishment Report 7204.

35   *Opening Rounds,* p 151-153.

36   Brian Holden Reid in TFH's *DNB* entry; *Student,* Ballantine's Illustrated History of the Violent Century, 1973, Barrie Pitt (ed.): 'War Leader' book No. 15 (Ballantine Books Inc., USA, 1973); *Goughie. The Life of General Sir Hubert Gough* (Hart-Davis MacGibbon, London 1975).

37   AF B199a in TFH's record of service; *Army List.*

Chapter 20

1   AF B199a in TFH's record of service.

2   ACDC (WP)/P (67) 3 in T.N.A. WO 32/21264.

3   Interview with Colonel John Stevens, 20 November 2012.

4   T.N.A. WO 32/21799.

5   *Army Lists.*

6   T.N.A. WO 32/19332, Combat Development Establishment in the War Office.

7   Interview with Colonel John Stevens, 20 November 2012.

8   *The Times*, 14 March 2006.

9   Interview with Major-General Rob McAfee, 3 April 2015.

10   Brian Holden Reid in TFH's *DNB* entry.

11   ACDC (WP)/P (67) 3.

12   Interview with Colonel John Stevens, 20 November 2012.

13   T.N.A. WO 279/667.

14   Interview with Colonel John Stevens, 20 November 2012.

15   Interview with Colonel John Stevens, 20 November 2012.

16   DCD (A)/27/4/2 in TFH's personal papers.

17   AF B 199a (ADP) in TFH's record of service.

18   Various letters in TFH's personal files.

19   Elizabeth Monroe and A.H. Farrar-Hockley, *The Arab-Israel War, October 1973, Background and Events* (Adelphi Papers, No. 111, RUSI, Winter 1974-75).

20   *Infantry tactics, 1939 – 1945* (Almark Publishing, London, 1976).

21   *Infantry Tactics,* p 70.

22   D/DPR/233/1/26, 13 August 1973 in DCD (A)/27/4/2, TFH's personal files.

23   Interview with Colonel John Stevens, 20 November 2012.

24   'Never a Dull Moment'; interview with TFH in *Soldier* Magazine, 7 November 1983.

25   AF B 199a (ADP) in TFH's record of service; *LG Supp*, 16 August 1977. He was appointed on 12 May 1977, with seniority 12 May 1976 – there was some confusion over this date, which was clarified in a letter from the Military Secretary (P/251309/MS1 (a) dated 31 July 1977.

26   Various correspondence in TFH's personal papers.

27   Charity Commission information.

28   Interview with Colonel Mike Motum, 14 November 2014.

29   Interview with Hilary Farrar-Hockley, 28 October 2014.

30   Michael Carver, *Out of Step*, p 394-395.

31   The author from David Keenan, 21 October 2014.

32   *The Guardian*, 23 February 1972.

33   Statement on the Defence Estimates, Cmnd 5976 (1975).

34   *Paradata*, Airborne Forces Museum.

35   D/DMS (B)/44/40/MS 3 dated 24 October 1977 in TFH's personal papers. The appointment was wef 18 December 1977, for five years.

36   Interview with Colonel Graham Farrell, 20 November 2014.

37   Interview with Colonel Mike Motum, 14 November 2014.

38   Interview with Major-General Bryan Webster, 18 September 2014.

39   See, for example, *The Daily Mail*, 14 November 1977.

40   *The Daily Mail*, 23 November 1977, p 3.

41   Interview with Brigadier David Keenan, 21 November 2014.

42   *The Sun*, 23 November 1977.

43   *The Daily Mail*, 23 November 1977, p 3.

44   *Rates of Pay for the Regular Army.* MOD Army Personal Services Code 6551 published annually.

45   *Manchester Evening News*, 24 November 1977; *The Daily Telegraph*, 10 December 1977; *Daily Express*, 25 November 1977; *Liverpool Daily Post*, 29 November 1977.

46   *The Times*, 25 November 1977.

47   Interview with Major-General Rob McAfee, 3 April 2015.

48   Interview with Colonel Roy Giles, 16 February 2015.

49   Interview with Major-General Bryan Webster, 18 September 2014.

50   Interview with Brigadier David Keenan, 21 November 2014.

51   Interview with Colonel Roy Giles, 16 February 2015.

52   Event programme supplied by Colonel Mike Motum.

53   *Soldier* Magazine, July 1971, p 21; MOD A/79/Gen/4067 (ASD 1/5c), Expansion of the Territorial Army Volunteer Reserve, dated 29 January 1971 in RWF Museum/Archives.

54   Interview with Major-General Bryan Webster, 18 September 2014; interview with Brigadier David Keenan, 21 November 2014.

55   Interview with Colonel Roy Giles, 16 February 2015.

56   Riley, *Soldiers of the Queen,* p 535-537.

57   Interview with Brigadier David Keenan, 21 November 2014.

58   Interview with Colonel Roy Giles, 16 February 2015.

59   Interview with Major-General Rob McAfee, 3 April 2015.

60   Interview with Major-General Bryan Webster, 18 September 2014.

61   Interview with Colonel Mike Motum, 14 November 2014.

62   T.N.A. CO 27/89, Evidence of Official Historians to G.J. Aylett Esq., Public Records Committee, dated 24 May 1979.

63   Jonathan Dimbleby, *Prince of Wales: A Biography* (London, 1996), p 161.

64   RHQ Para 16A dated 30 April 1981 in TFH's personal papers.

65   Interview with Colonel David Charles, 28 January 2015.

66   AF B199a in TFH's record of service.

67   Interview with Colonel Mike Motum, 14 November 2014.

68   Interview with General Sir Frank Kitson, 30 September 2014.

Chapter 21

1   P/251309/MS1(a) dated 10 October 1978 in TFH's record of service.

2   D/DMS (B) 43/1/1/MS3 dated 10 March 1981 in TFH's record of service.

3   Interviews with Colonel Mike Motum, 14 November 2014 and with Colonel Graham Farrell, 20 November 2014.

4   Interviews with Colonel David Charles, 28 January 2015 and with Major-General Andrew Watson, 3 February 2015.

5   COS AFNORTH – TFH dated 3 July 1979 in TFH's personal papers.

6   'A wrong thought at a wrong time', *Aftenpost*, 18 January 1980.

7   *The London Gazette* (supplement) No. 48837, 30 December 1981, p 6.

8   Brigadier David Keenan to the author, 21 October 2014.

9   Jane Leigh to TFH dated 7 August 1980 in TFH's personal papers.

10 Interview with Colonel Graham Farrell, 20 November 2014.

11 Interview with Colonel Mike Motum, 14 November 2014.

12 Interview with Major-General Andrew Watson, 3 February 2015.

13 Interview with Major-General Andrew Watson, 3 February 2015.

14 Anthony Farrar-Hockley, 'Dynamic Defence: The Northern Flank', a lecture given at the RUSI on 4 March 1983 in *RUSI Journal*, August 1983.

15 'Dynamic Defence', p 7.

16 'Dynamic Defence', p 7.

17 Farrar-Hockley, *Opening Rounds,* p 153.

18 Farrar-Hockley, *Opening Rounds,* p 153.

19 Michael Arthur Ledeen, *Superpower Dilemmas: The U.S. and the U.S.S.R. at Century's End* (New Brunswick, 1992), p 224-225.

20 'Dynamic Defence', p 9.

21 'Dynamic Defence', p 9.

22 Farrar-Hockley, *Opening Rounds,* p 144.

23 'Dynamic Defence', p 7.

24 'Dynamic Defence', p 8.

25 'Dynamic Defence', p 9.

26 William Taubman, *Krushchev: The Man and His Era* (New York, 2003), p 5-13.

27 Aleksander Gurov, 'the Effectiveness of Logistics', *Krasnya Zvezda* [*Red Star*], 9 December 1982.

28 Philip Bobbit, *The Shield of Achilles. War, Peace and the Course of History* (London, 2002), p 49.

29 'Dynamic Defence', p 10.

30 *Kieler Nachtrichten*, 12 November 1981.

31 The visit programme is in TFH's personal files.

32 Interview with Colonel Mike Motum, 14 November 2014.

33 Interview with Colonel David Charles, 28 January 2015.

34 Interview with Colonel Mike Motum, 14 November 2014.

35 Ex *Viking Shield* programme in TFH's personal papers.

36 *Anorak Express* No. 7, 7-19 March 1980 in TFH's personal papers.

37 *Anorak Express* exercise programme supplied by Colonel Mike Motum.

38 Gard – TFH dated 27 May 1980 in H's personal papers.

39 Interview with Colonel Graham Farrell, 20 November 2014.

40 Letter CDS – TFH 1164/1 25 Feb 1980 in TFH's personal papers.

41 *Gloucester Evening Echo*, 29 July 1980; interview with Brigadier Martin Vine, 14 November 2014.

42 *Daily Mail*, 23 April 1981, p 30.

43 D/DMS (B) 44/22/MS3 dated 14 April 1980 in TFH's personal file.

44 TFH to all COs dated 7 March 1980 in TFH's personal papers.

45 Dauncey – TFH dated 7 May 1982 in TFH's personal papers.

46 Interview with Colonel Mike Motum, 14 November 2014.

47 Interviews with Colonel David Charles, 28 January 2015 and with Major-General Andrew Watson, 3 February 2015.

48   Interviews with Colonel Mike Motum, 14 November 2014 and with Colonel Graham Farrell, 20 November 2014.

49   TFH – Lt-Col P.M. Beaumont dated 12 May 1980 in TFH's personal papers.

50   Visit notes in TFH's personal files.

51   Interview with Major-General Andrew Watson, 3 February 2015.

Chpater 22

1   *London Gazette* No. 48837, p 5, 30 December 1981; *Who's Who*, 2006.

2   Interview with Major-General Andrew Watson, 3 February 2015.

3   John Bowyer Bell, *The IRA, 1968-2000: Analysis of a Secret Army* (London, 2000), p 305; Roger Falligot, *Britain's Military Strategy in Ireland: The Kitson Experiment* (London, 1983), p 142; David Barzilay, *The British Army in Ulster*, Vol 4 (London, 1981), p 94.

4   Interview with Colonel Graham Farrell, 20 November 2014.

5   See, for example, RHQ Para A/14/4; Burke (Colonel Parachute Regiment) to the NI office dated 28 May 1981.

6   The story of the campaign is fully described in Lawrence Freedman's *Official History of the Falklands Campaign* (London, 2005).

7   Signal to 1 Para in TFH's personal papers.

8   Conversation with Lieutenant-General 'Jacko' Page at the Afghanistan Memorial Service, 13 March 2013.

9   Interviews with Colonel Graham Farrell, 20 November 2014 and with Colonel David Charles, 28 January 2015.

10   Dimbleby, *The Prince of Wales,* p 517-518.

11   TFH to the Military Secretary dated 12 July 1982 in TFH's personal papers.

12   *The Times*, 10 August 1982.

13   *London Gazette* 12846, 8 October 1982.

14   D/DASD/115/13/8 (ASD 2a) dated 12 December 1979.

15   CINC 260/12 dated 5 January 1981 in TFH's personal files.

16   Appreciation by Wilson dated 9 March 1981 in TFH's personal files.

17   Letter Hackett to TFH dated 8 December 1982 in TFH's personal files.

18   *Daily Mail*, 24 June 1982.

19   Interviews with Colonel Mike Motum, 14 November 2014 and with Colonel Graham Farrell, 20 November 2014.

20   Interview with Colonel David Charles, 28 January 2015.

21   Colonel Pat Beaumont to the author, 28 October 2014.

22   *London Gazette*, No. 41257, p 7,531, 8 October 1982; AF B199a in TFH's record of service.

Chapter 23

1   Interview with Ted Olive, 17 February 2015.

2   David S. Daniel, *Cap of Honour: the 300 years of the Gloucestershire Regiment* (Sutton, Stroud, 1989).

3   Neville Brown and Anthony Farrar-Hockley, *Nuclear First Use* (Buchan and Enright, London, 1985).

4   *Opening rounds: lessons of military history 1918–1988* (Deutsch Press, London, 1988).

5   *The British Part in the Korean War: Vol.1, A Distant Obligation* (HMSO, London 1990).

6   *A Distant Obligation*, p viii.

7   *Dictionary of National Biography.*

8   *A Distant Obligation,* p vi.

9   *A Distant Obligation,* p viii.

10   *A Distant Obligation,* p viii.

11   *The Daily Telegraph*, undated cutting in TFH's personal files.

12   Information supplied by the Soldiers of Gloucestershire Museum.

13   *The China Quarterly,* issue No. 98, 1983.

14   Staff College DS/SC/26 dated 24 October 1988 in TFH's personal files.

15   *TLS* 16 – 22 September 1988.

16   *RUSI Journal*, June 1988.

17   Interview with the Rev Mr Leighton Thomas, 17 February 2015.

18   The narrative that follows is largely taken from a typewritten history of the campaign in TFH's personal files, supplemented by other letters and documents as noted.

19   'The Airey Neave File', *Independent*, 22 February 2002.

20   Institute for the study of globalisation and covert politics.

21   www.Libcom.org retrieved 10 February 2015.

22   Hedgehog '86 (DBH news) in TFH's personal files.

23   *Daily Mail*, 8 March 1983, p 11.

24   Cmnd 9227-1, Statement on the Defence Estimates 1984.

25   *Daily Mail*, 10 September 1986.

26   House of Lords Debate, 3 July 1985 in *Hansard*, Volume 465, cc 1199 – 1270.

27   Personal letter from Lord Hill-Norton to George Younger, 22 June 1987.

28   Wendy Holmes, 'IRA attack on former Ulster general foiled', *Daily Telegraph*, 14 August 1990.

29   Terry Kirby 'Garden hose bomb at general's home', *Independent*, 14 August 1990.

30   Interview with Ted Olive, 17 February 2015.

31   *Daily Telegraph*, 14 August 1990.

32   *Independent*, 14 August 1990.

Chapter 24

1   Anthony Farrar-Hockley, *The British Part in the Korean War: Vol 2, An Honourable Discharge*, (HMSO, London, 1995).

2   Interview with Colonel Roy Giles, 16 February 2015.

3   Korea papers in TFH's personal files.

4   *The Army in the Air: the History of the Army Air Corps* (Far Thrupp, Stroud, A. Sutton Publishing, 1994) ISBN 0-7509-0617-0.

5   J.P. Riley, *Regimental Records of the Royal Welch Fusiliers, Volumes VI and VII* (Llandysul, 2001).

6   BBC News, 17 September 1999, retrieved online 25 February 2015; see also TFH's obituary in the *Daily Telegraph*, 14 March 2006.

7   BBC News, 14 June and 21 June 1999, retrieved online 25 February 2015.

8   BBC News, 27 September 1999; see also TFH's obituary in the *Daily Telegraph*.

9   Chief of the General Staff MOD (A) D/CGS/44/1, 4 June 1991.

10   HQ Prince of Wales's Division G3161, 19 June 1991.

11   Cmnd 4446, December 1999.

12   The Parachute Regiment – British Army website: www.army.mod.uk retrieved 25 February 2015.

13   Anthony Farrar-Hockley, (Unfinished, *MacArthur (Great Commanders Series)* (Weidenfeld & Nicolson, London) ISBN 0-297-84684-1.

14   http://www.parkinsons.org.uk retrieved 18 February 2015.

Bibliography and Sources

ORIGINAL SOURCES

The National Archives

SECOND WORLD WAR
T.N.A. WO 32/4461 dated 6 September 1937.
T.N.A. WO 32/4461, Second Report.
T.N.A. WO 32/4544 dated August 1938.
WO 166/8557, WO169/10348, WO175/530: 6th (RW) Para War Diary 1942–1943.
T.N.A. WO 169/20083: 6th (RW) Para War Diary 1 October 1945–31 December 1945.
T.N.A. WO 169/20083, 23227 and 261/404: 6th (RW) Para War Diary 1 October 1945–31 December 1946.
T.N.A. WO 170/1343: 6th (RW) Para War Diary 1 January–31 December 1944.
T.N.A. WO 170/4973: 6th (RW) Para War Diary 1 January–29 June 1945.
T.N.A. W.O. Memo 20/Inf/3725 AG2 (b) dated 29 November 1946.
T.N.A. WO 0154/7678 (SD2) dated 12 March 1948, reduction of 6th Airborne Division.

KOREAN WAR
T.N.A. W.O. A19/PW/Korea/1005, Interrogation Report No. A19/K/BRIT 38, August 1953, which is the transcript of TFH's debriefing immediately after his release from captivity.

MIDDLE EAST
T.N.A. ADM 205/154, Psychological Warfare PSW (56), August 1956.
T.N.A. CAB 134/1217 *Terrapin* EC(56) 47, dated 10 September 1956.
T.N.A. CO 926/454, an appreciation of the situation in Cyprus by George Grivas dated 5 July 1956 (captured document).
T.N.A. FO 371/118997 Minutes of the Egypt Committee, 30 July 1956.
T.N.A. FO 371/118997 JE 11924/76, Draft note by the Egypt (Official) Committee.
T.N.A. WO 288/77, HQ II (British) Corps Report on Operation *Musketeer*.
Annual Historical Record of 3rd Para for the year ending 31 March 1965.

FAR EAST
CO 1035/164.
PREM 11/4907, 13/1454.
CAB 134/555, 134/1644, 134/1645, 148/1, 148/2, 148/10, 148/17, 148/26, 158/46, 158/48, 158/63, 163/22, 164/19.
DEFE 4/174, 4/202, 4/205, 4/206, 5/148, 5/154, 5/155, 5/156, 5/161, 5/166, 5/171.

NORTHERN IRELAND
CAB/4/1532/15.
DEFE 13/676, 13/915, 13/921, 13/1395, 13/1398, 24/1611, 24/1908, 25/261.
WO 32/21795.

BRITISH ARMY OF THE RHINE
DEFE 48/222, Survivability of Army Field Formation Headquarters in I (British) Corps post-1980. Defence Operational Analysis Establishment Report No. 7204.
WO 305/3325, HQ I (BR) Corps Historical Report, January–December 1971.
WO 305/4195, HQ I (BR) Corps Historical Report, January–December 1972.
WO 305/4195, HQ I (BR) Corps Historical Report, January–December 1973.

DIRECTORATE OF COMBAT DEVELOPMENT (ARMY)
WO 32/21799, DCD (A) Working Party on Army Department Organisation.
WO 279/667, Tactical Doctrine Working Party Study into Counter-Revolutionary Operations post-1975.
WO 32/21264, British Army Concept of Operations, 1971–1980.
WO 32/19332, Combat Development Establishment in the War Office.
ACDC (WP)/P (67) 3, Army Combat Development Guide
CO 27/89, Public Records Committee.

Liddell Hart Centre, King's College London
Correspondence between TFH and LH, LH 1/278/1; 278/3; 278/5; 278 17–20.

General Registry Office
GRO certified copy of an entry of birth, document no. 38/1891.
Census Returns for 1901 and 1911.

Australian Archives
AUSTRALIAN WAR MEMORIAL
CBB/12/1, 121/25/J/1.

NATIONAL ARCHIVES OF AUSTRALIA
A1209/1962/1010,   A1209/1963/6668,   A1209/1964/6647,   A1838,   TS682/22/1,   A1838,
   TS682//22/1.

Public Records Northern Ireland
HA/32/2/55.
Conclusions of a Meeting of the Cabinet Security Committee, Stormont Castle, 17 July 1969.

Private Papers of General Sir Anthony Farrar-Hockley

GENERAL
Record of Service of 251309 A.H. Farrar-Hockley, supplied by the Adjutant-General of the Army.
General Correspondence, 1964–1967.
Personal Correspondence, 1966–1968.
Correspondence on Lectures and Talks.

KOREAN WAR

'The Significance of the British Commonwealth in the Korean War', speech given at the War Memorial service in Seoul, June 25–27 1990.

Dr William R. Shadish, 'Presentation to the Korean ex-P.O.W. Group, Camp 2, Saturday September 27, 1986.'

Letters of Lieutenant-Colonel Roy E. Appleman to Mr Jeffrey Grey, University of New South Wales, dated 19 July and 8 October 1985

Statement made by Lieutenant-Colonel J.P. Carne DSO to the British Ambassador in Tokyo, 7 September 1953.

16 PARACHUTE BRIGADE

16 Para Brigade personal file, 1967.

Correspondence on lectures, talks, reviews and articles.

NORTHERN IRELAND

CLF NI-1 DO file 1969–1971.

DO file Northern Ireland, 28 August 1970.

Monthly Reports from HQNI 1971.

Monthly Reports and Statistics from HQNI 1972–1973.

Bound Report on Operations in Northern Ireland.

4TH ARMOURED DIVISION

Correspondence on lectures, talks, reviews and articles.

4th Armoured Division personal file.

DIRECTORATE OF COMBAT DEVELOPMENT

DCD(A)/27/4/2 Correspondence on lectures, talks, reviews and articles.

AFNORTH

Correspondence on lectures, talks, reviews and articles.

C-in-C AFNORTH personal files.

C-in-C AFNORTH exercises and study periods.

CORRESPONDENCE RELATED TO BOOKS AND PUBLICATIONS

Papers relating to the publication of *The Edge of the Sword*.

Various files on the Korean War official history.

Papers relating to the publication of *Goughie*.

Papers relating to the publication of the Hamilton Memoirs.

Papers relating to the publication of *The Somme*.

Correspondence related to the publication of *Opening Rounds*.

GENERAL PAPERS

Papers relating to Boeing Inc.

Papers relating to *Defence Begins at Home*.

Papers relating to BBC and commercial TV stations, various broadcasting contracts and programmes.

Liddell Hart Archives, King's College London
General Sir Hugh Stockwell's Suez papers in KCL/Stockwell/8/6/12-13.

Royal Welch Fusiliers Archives
R.J.M Sinnett, 6th (RW) Para Summary.
Letter Ian Chatham to R.J.M. Sinnett dated 27 June 2007 (6 (RW) Para).
Letter Cliff Meredith to R.J.M. Sinnett (undated) (6 (RW) Para).
MOD A/79/Gen/4067 (ASD 1/5c), Expansion of the Territorial Army Volunteer Reserve, dated 29 January 1971.

Gloucestershire Regiment Archives

SECOND WORLD WAR
Correspondence related to Horfield Barracks, Bristol–especially 112/Southern/4367 (QMG1) dated 9 July 1938.
A Company 70th (Young Soldiers) Battalion the Gloucestershire Regiment.

KOREAN WAR
2 Glosters Unit Historical Report, 1948–1949.
A Brief History of 29 Infantry Brigade Group from September 1949 to October 1951.
The Back Badge. Journal of the Gloucestershire Regiment (28th/61st Foot), June 1948, December 1948, December 1949, December 1950, December 1951, December 1953.
Letter TFH to Colonel E.D. Harding, Regimental Secretary, dated 13 June 1973.
Letter Carne to Colonel R.M. Grazebrook dated 10 September 1953.
Letter John Watkins-Williams to Colonel R.M. Grazebrook dated 10 September 1953.

Parachute Regiment Archives

SECOND WORLD WAR
Special Order of the Day by Lt-Gen R.M. Scobie, January 1945 (6th (RW) Para, Greece).

MIDDLE EAST
Annual Historical Record of 3 Para for the year ending 31 March 1965.
'Notes for a Lecture to 2 Para: The Radfan Operations Jan–Jun 64' (anon).
'Operations in Radfan 14 Apr–30 Jun 64' (official account).
Lieutenant Pearson, 'Commanding Officer's Military History Research Project: the Radfan–1964.'

RMC and RMA Sandhurst Archives
RMC Magazine and Record, 1921 and 1922.
RMA Sandhurst Collection, Sandhurst Cadet Registers.
RMA Sandhurst Study on Morale, Leadership and Discipline, 1950 (ed. Maunsell).

Diaries and Letters
FM Lord Alanbrooke (ed.), Alex Danchev and Daniel Todman, *War Diaries 1939–1945* (London, 2001).
1944 Diary of Major D. Fleming Jones, 6th (Royal Welch) Para, transcribed by and with the permission of his family.

OFFICIAL PUBLICATIONS

GENERAL PUBLICATIONS
Field Service Regulations, Volume I (Organisation and Administration, WO 26/Regs/1849 (1930).
Service Pocket Book, WO 26/863, 1926.
Field Service Pocket Book, WO/GS Publications/8, January 1940.
Operations–Military Training Pamphlet 23 Part I. WO 26/GS Publications/602 (1942).
'A Parachute Battalion', X/127/2 in Army Council Instructions 3 June 1942 (Establishment table
    for 1942–1943).
Brevet-Major AR Godwin-Austen, *The Staff and the Staff College* (London, 1927).
Rates of Pay for the Regular Army. MOD Army Personal Services Code 6551, published annually,
    various years as cited in endnotes.

SECOND WORLD WAR
Molony, Brigadier C.J.C. with Flynn RN, Captain F.C., Davies, Major-General H.L. and Gleave,
    Group Captain T.P., *The Mediterranean and Middle East, Volume V: The Campaign in Sicily
    1943 and The Campaign in Italy 3rd September 1943 to 31st March 1944.* History of the Second
    World War, United Kingdom Military Series, (HMSO, 1973).
United States Army in World War Two: The Mediterranean Theater of
Operations, *Cassino to the Alps* by Fisher, Jr, Ernest F. (Center of Military History, United States
    Army, Washington D.C., 1977).
Fifth Army at the Winter Line 15 November 1943–15 January 1944, (United States Army Center of
    Military History Publication 100-9, Washington DC, 1945).

KOREAN WAR
The Armed Forces of North and South Korea, US Army Centre for Military History.
Chinese Military Science Academy, *History of War to Resist America and Aid Korea* (Beijing,
    September 2000).
Ministry of Defence, *The Treatment of British Prisoners of War in Korea* (HMSO, London, 1955).
Webb, William J., 'The Korean War: The Outbreak'. (United States Army Center for Military
    History, 2011).

MIDDLE EAST
General Sir Kenneth Darling, Director of Operations, Cyprus, *Cyprus–The Final Round. October
    1958–March 1959.*

UNITED NATIONS SECURITY COUNCIL RESOLUTIONS
82, 83, 84, 85 and 88 of 1952.

PARLIAMENT COMMAND PAPERS
9075, Statement on Defence, 31 August 1950.
532, Disturbances in Northern Ireland, October 1969.
535, Report of the Advisory Committee on Policing in Northern Ireland, October 1969.
4823, Report of the enquiry into allegations against the Security Forces of physical brutality in
    Northern Ireland arising out of events on the 9th August, 1971 by Sir Edmund Compton
    GCB KBE, November 1971.
4901, Report of the Committee of Privy Counsellors appointed to consider authorised procedures for
    the interrogation of persons suspected of terrorism by Lord Parker of Waddington, March 1972.

5976, Statement on the Defence Estimates, 1975.
9227-1, Statement on the Defence Estimates, 1984.
4446, Statement on the Defence Estimates, 1999.

HANSARD
House of Lords Debates, Volume 465 (1985).

BOOKS

COMMAND AND LEADERSHIP
Carver, Michael, *Out of Step. The Memoirs of Field Marshal Lord Carver* (London, 1989).
von Clausewitz, Carl-Maria, *On War* (Princeton University Press, ed. Michael Howard and Peter Paret, 1976).
Dimbleby, Jonathan, *Prince of Wales: A Biography* (London, 1996).
Dixon, Norman, *On the Psychology of Military Incompetence* (London, 1976).
French, David, and Holden Reid, Brian (ed.), *The British General Staff. Reform and Innovation1890–1939* (London, 2001).
Fuller, J.F.C., *Generalship: The Disease and Its Cure* (Harrisburg, Pennsylvania, 1936).
Kitson, Frank, *Gangs and Counter-Gangs* (London, 1960).
Kitson, Frank, *Bunch of Five* (London, 1977).
Moran, Lord, (C MacM Wilson), *The Anatomy of Courage* (London, 1945).
Smith, Rupert, *The Utility of Force. The Art of War in the Modern World* (London, 2005).
Smythe, Brigadier Sir John, *Sandhurst* (London, 1961).
Zabecki, David T. (ed.), *Chief of Staff, vol 2* (Annapolis, MA, USA, 2008).

REGIMENTAL AND FORMATION HISTORIES
Arthur, Max, *Men of the Red Beret: Airborne Forces 1940–1990* (London, 1990).
Buckley, Christopher, *Norway, The Commandos, Dieppe* (London, 1951).
Buxton, Dave, *Honour to the Airborne, Part I* (Liverpool, 1994).
Chandler, David (ed.), *Great Battles of the British Army as Commemorated in the Sandhurst Companies* (London, 1991).
Daniell, David Scott, *Cap of Honour. The Story of the Gloucestershire Regiment (28th/61st Foot) 1694–1975* (London, 1975).
Erskine, David, *The Scots Guards 1919–1955* (London, 1956).
Fortescue, Sir John, *History of the British Army, Vol I* (London, 1909).
Foster, R.C.G., *History of The Queen's Royal Regiment, Volume VIII, 1924–1948* (Aldershot, 1953).
Harclerode, Peter, *Go To It: The Illustrated History of the 6th Airborne Division* (London, 1990).
Harclerode, Peter, *Para! 50 Years of the Parachute Regiment* (London, 1996).
Kemp, P.K. and Graves, John, *The Red Dragon. The Story of the Royal Welch Fusiliers 1919–1945* (Aldershot, 1960).
Mountford, Brigadier R.S., *The Actions of 'J' (Sidi Rezegh) Battery Royal Horse Artillery in the Aden Protectorate 1963–64* (Ipswich, 2013).
Riley, Jonathon, *Soldiers of the Queen* (Chippenham, 1992).
Smythe, Brigadier Sir John, *Sandhurst* (London, 1961).
Thomas, Hugh, *The Story of Sandhurst* (London, 1961).
Wylley, H.C., *History of The Queen's Royal Regiment, Volume VII, 1905–1924* (Aldershot, 1928).

SECOND WORLD WAR

Barnet, Corelli, *Engage the Enemy More Closely: The Royal Navy in the Second World War* (London, 2001).

Carver, Field Marshal Lord, *The Imperial War Museum Book of the War in Italy 1943–1945* (London, 1945).

Crang, Jeremy, *The British Army and the People's War 1939–1945* (MUP, 2000).

Churchill, Winston S., *The Second World War* (6 vols, London, 1950–1954).

Crang, Jeremy A., *The British Army and the People's War 1939–1945* (MUP, 2000).

d'Este, Carlo, *Fatal Decision: Anzio and the Battle for Rome* (London, 1991).

Fraser, George Macdonald, *Quartered Safe Out Here. A Recollection of the War in Burma, with a new Epilogue, 50 Years On* (London, 1993).

Jefferys, Kevin, *Anthony Crosland* (London, 2000).

Lovering, Tristan, (ed.) *Amphibious Assault. Manouevre from the Sea* (Woodbridge, 2007).

Masters, John, *The Road Past Mandalay* (London, 1961).

Riley, Jonathon, *From Pole to Pole, The Life of Quintin Riley, 1905–1980* (Chippenham, 1980),

PALESTINE

Charteris, David A., *The British Army and Jewish Insurgency in Palestine, 1945–1947,* (Basingstoke, 1980).

James, Lawrence, *The Rise and Fall of the British Empire* (London, 1994).

Gilbert, Martin, *A History of the Twentieth Century* (London, 1998).

Hennesey, Peter, *Never Again. Britain 1945–1951* (London, 1993).

Macmillan, Margaret, *Peacemakers; The Paris Conference of 1919 and its Attempt to End War* (London, 2001).

Mokaitis, Thomas, *British Counterinsurgency in the Post- Imperial Era,* Vol I (MUP, 1995).

Montgomery of Alamein, Field Marshal, *Memoirs* (London, 1958).

Riley, Jonathon, *The Life and Campaigns of General Hughie Stockwell* (Barnsley, 2006).

Royle, Trevor, *Glubb Pasha. The Life and Times of Sir John Bagot Glubb, Commander of the Arab Legion* (London, 1992).

Segev, Tom, *One Palestine, Complete* (London, 2000).

Shlaim, Avi, *Collusion Across The Jordan. King Abdullah, the Zionist Movement, and the Partition of Palestine* (Oxford, 1988).

KOREAN WAR

Barnouin, Barbara and Yu, Changgeng, *Zhou Enlai: A Political Life* (Hong Kong, 2002).

Dallin, David, *Soviet Foreign Policy After Stalin* (New York, 1961).

Davies, S.J., *In Spite of Dungeons* (London, 1954).

Grist, Digby, *Remembered With Advantage. A personal account of service with the Glosters in the Korean War* (RHQ the Gloucestershire Regiment, 1976).

Harding, Colonel E.D., DSO, *The Imjin Roll* (Gloucester, 1976).

Hastings, Max, *The Korean War* (London, 1987).

Holles, Robert O., *Now thrive the Armourers. A Story of Action with the Gloucesters in Korea (November 1950–April 1951)* (London, 1952).

Hopkins, William B., *One Bugle No Drums: The Marines at Chosin Reservoir.* (Chapel Hill, N.C, 1986).

Jones, Francis S., *No Rice for Rebels, a story of the Korean War as told to the author by Lance-Corporal (now Sgt.) R.F. Mathews, B.E.M.* (London, 1956) [with an introduction by Tony Farrar-Hockley].

Kinne, Derek, *The Wooden Boxes* (London, 1956) [Edited and in part ghost-written by Tony Farrar-Hockley].

Large, Lofty *One Man's War in Korea* (Wellingborough, 1988).

Malkasian, Carter, *The Korean War, 1950–1953* (London, 2001).

Offner, Arnold A., *Another Such Victory: President Truman and the Cold War, 1945–1953*. (Stanford University Press, 2002).

Rees, David, *Korea: The Limited War* (New York, 1964).

Stokesbury, James L., *A Short History of the Korean War* (New York, 1990).

Weintraub, Stanley, *MacArthur's War: Korea and the Undoing of an American Hero* (New York, 2000).

MIDDLE EAST

Cloake, John, *Templer: The Tiger of Malaya* (London, 1985).

Crawshay, Nancy, *The Cyprus Revolt: An Account of the Struggle for Union with Greece* (London, 1978).

Edwards, Aaron, *Mad Mitch's Tribal Law. Aden and the End of an Empire* (London, 2014).

Ginat, Rami, *The Soviet Union and Egypt, 1945–1955* (London, 1993).

Horne, Alastair, *Harold Macmillan, Vol I, 1895–1956* (London, 1988).

Jackson, Robert, *Suez, the Forgotten Invasion* (Shrewsbury, 1996).

Love, Kennett, *Suez–The Twice-Fought War* (London, 1970).

Mockaitis, Thomas R., *British Counterinsurgency Vol I, 1919–1960*, (New York, 1990).

Nowar, Maan Abu, *The Struggle for Independence 1939–1947: A History of the Hashemite Kingdom of Jordan* (Reading, 2001).

Riley, Jonathon, *The Life & Campaigns of General Hughie Stockwell* (Barnsley, 2006).

Royle, Trevor, *Glubb Pasha. The Life and Times of Sir John Bagot Glubb, Commander of the Arab Legion* (London, 1992).

Tal, David, (ed.) *The 1956 War: Collusion and Rivalry in the Middle East* (London, 2001).

Ziegler, Philip, *Mountbatten* (London, 1985).

FAR EAST

Bayley, Christopher, and Harper, Tim, *Forgotten Wars. The End of Britain's Asian Empire* (London, 2007).

Baylis, J., *Ambiguity and Deterrence: British Nuclear Strategy 1945-1964* (Oxford, 1995).

Healey, Denis, *The Time of My Life* (New York, 1989).

Hunter, Helen-Louise, *Sukarno and the Indonesian Coup* (Westport CT, 2007).

Majid, H.A., *Rebellion in Brunei: The 1962 Revolt, Imperialism, Confrontation, and Oil* (London, 2007).

Van der Bijl, Nicholas, *The Brunei Revolt 1962-1963* (Barnsley, 2012).

Wanandi, Jusuf, *Shades of Grey: A Political Memoir of Modern Indonesia 1965-1998* (Singapore, 2012).

NORTHERN IRELAND

Barzilay, David, *The British Army in Ulster*, Vols 1–4 (London, 1974–1981).

Bell, John Bowyer, *The IRA, 1968-2000: Analysis of a Secret Army* (London, 2000).

Chibnall, Steve, *Law and Order News: An analysis of crime reporting in the British press* (London, 2002).

Coogan, Tim Pat, *The IRA* (London, 1993).

Dillon, Martin, *The Dirty War: Covert strategies and tactics used in political conflicts* (London, 1999).

English, Robert, *Armed Struggle. The History of the IRA* (London, 2008).

Falligot, Roger, *Britain's Military Strategy in Ireland: The Kitson Experiment* (London, 1983).

Geraghty, Tony, *The Irish War* (London, 1998).

Hanley, Brian and Millar, Scott, *The Lost Revolution: The Story of the Official IRA and the Workers' Party* (Dublin, 2009).

Ó Fearghail, Sean, *Law (?) and Orders: The Belfast 'Curfew' of 3–5 July 1970* (Dundalgan, 1970).

Hanley, Brian, and Millar, Scott, *The Lost Revolution: The Story of the Official IRA and the Workers' Party.* (London, 2009),

Mac Stiofáin, Seán, *Memoirs of a Revolutionary* (Daly City, 1979).

Maille, Eamonn and Bishop, Patrick, *The Provisional IRA* (London, 1988).

Moloney, Ed, *A Secret History of the IRA* (London, 2003).

O'Brien, Brendan, *The Long War – The IRA and Sinn Féin* (Dublin, 1995).

Saunders, Andrew, and Wood, Ian S., *Times of Troubles: Britain's war in Northern Ireland* (Edinburgh University Press, 2012).

Stetler, Russell, *The Battle of the Bogside* (London, 1970).

Taylor, Peter, *Provos: The IRA and Sinn Féin* (London, 1979).

Taylor, Peter, *Brits: The War Against the IRA* (London, 2001).

Tonge, Jonathan, *Northern Ireland* (London, 2013).

COLD WAR AND NUCLEAR DETERENCE

Bobbit, Philip, *The Shield of Achilles. War, Peace and the Course of History* (London, 2002).

Hackett, General Sir John, *The Third World War: The Untold Story* (London, 1982).

Freedman, Lawrence, *Official History of the Falklands Campaign* (London, 2005).

Leeden, Michael Arthur, *Superpower Dilemmas: The U.S. and the U.S.S.R. at Century's End* (New Brunswick, 1992).

Taubman, William, *Krushchev: The Man and His Era* (New York, 2003).

Reference Books

Dictionary of National Biography.

Reber, Arthur S., *The Penguin Dictionary of Psychology* (London, 1995).

Gregory, Richard L. (ed.), *The Oxford Companion to the Mind* (OUP, 1991).

The Medals Year Book (London, 1999).

Hansard Parliamentary Debates, Vol 813, 11 March 1971.

Articles and Journals

OBITUARIES

Y Ddraig Goch, Journal of the Royal Welch Fusiliers: March 1962, February 2007.

GENERAL SUBJECTS

Badsey, Stephen, 'In the Public's Eye: The British Army and Military-Media Relations', *RUSI Analysis*, 21 September 2009.

Tuckfield, Cyril, *Spirit of Adventure. 1st Lympstone Sea Scouts River Dart Cruise,* (1939).

COMMAND AND LEADERSHIP

Grossman, Dave, 'Human Factors in War: the Psychology and Physiology of Close Combat' in Evans, Michael, and Ryan, Alan, (ed.) *The Human Face of Warfare: Fear, Killing and Chaos in Battle* (St Leonard's, Australia, 2000).

'Never a Dull Moment'; interview with TFH in *Soldier* Magazine, 7 November 1983.

SECOND WORLD WAR

Meredith, Cliff, 'The Sinking of HMS Abdiel–9th/10th September 1943' in *Y Ddraig Goch, Journal of the Royal Welch Fusiliers*, March 1994, p 88.

Pearson OBE, Lt Col John, 'The Tragedy of HMS Abdiel 1943' in *Y Ddraig Goch, Journal of the Royal Welch Fusiliers*, March 1995, p 91-92.

Review of Camilla Whitby Films, 'A Summer in Provence: The Story of Operation Dragoon (1944)'. *British Army Review* No. 110, p 105.

KOREAN WAR

'Captivity in Korea: How Officer and Sergeant Prisoners of War Lived, A Record in Drawings', *Illustrated London News*, 5 January 1954.

Boose, Donald W., 'Portentous Sideshow: The Korean Occupation Decision'. *Parameters: US Army War College Quarterly* (US Army War College) Vol 5 No. 4 (Winter, 1995–1996).

Holdham MM, Corporal Alfred, 'I escaped from a Korean prison camp' in *John Bull*, November 1953.

Kahn, E.J., 'No one but the Glosters. A Reporter in Korea' in *The New Yorker,* 26 May 1951.

Macdonald, Douglas J., 'Communist Bloc Expansion in the Early Cold War', in *International Security*, Winter 1995–1996.

Weathersby, Kathryn, '"Should We Fear This?" Stalin and the Danger of War with America', *Cold War International History Project: Working Paper No. 39,* (2002).

FAR EAST

Easter, David, 'British Intelligence & Propaganda during "Confrontation", 1963–1966' in *International Security* Vol 16 No. 2 (Summer 2001) p 83-102.

Farrell, Brian P., 'What do we do now? British Commonwealth and American Reactions to the Separation of Malaysia and Singapore' in Murfett, Malcolm H. (ed.), *Imponderable but Not Inevitable: Warfare in the 20th Century* (Westport, 2010), p 78.

Farrell, Brian P., 'Quadruple failure? The British-American split over Collective Security in Southeast Asia, 1963-1966.'

Farrell, Brian P., 'Escalate to Terminate: Far East Command and the need to end Confrontation', in Dennis, P. and Grey, J. (ed.), *Entangling Alliances: Coalition Warfare in the Twentieth Century* (Canberra, 2005).

Jones, M., 'Up the Garden Path? Britain's Nuclear History in the Far East, 1954-1962', in *The International History Review,* Vol 25, No. 2 (2003).

NORTHERN IRELAND

'Ulster's Misery', *The Economist*, Vol. 230, No. 6542, 11 January 1969.

'Ulster: Who's in charge?' *New Statesman*, 10 January 1969.

Ware, John, 'Britain's Secret Terror Force', *Irish Republican News*, 23 November 2013.

Winchester, Simon, 'Promoting General Confusion', *The Guardian*, 2 August 1971.

COLD WAR AND NUCLEAR DETERRENCE

Gurov, Aleksander, 'The Effectiveness of Logistics', *Krasnya Zvezda* [*Red Star*], 9 December 1982.

BOOKS, ARTICLES AND PAPERS BY ANTHONY FARRAR-HOCKLEY

Books

The Edge of the Sword (Frederick Muller, London 1954) (later edition ISBN 0-352-30977-6).

True Book about the Second World War (Frederick Muller, London 1959).

The Somme (Pan Books, London 1966) (later edition ISBN 0-330-28035-X).

Death of an Army (Barker, London 1968) (later edition ISBN 1-85326-698-1).

The War in the Desert (Faber & Faber, London 1969). ISBN 0-571-08949-6.

Airborne Carpet: Operation Market Garden (London, Macdonald & Co. 1970). ISBN 0-356-03037-7.

Arnhem: parachutisten vallen uit de hemel. (Standaard, Antwerpen 1972).

Student, Ballantine's Illustrated History of the Violent Century1973, Pitt, Barrie (ed.): 'War Leader' Book No. 15. (Ballantine Books Inc, USA, 1973).

Goughie. The Life of General Sir Hubert Gough (Hart-Davis MacGibbon, London 1975). ISBN 0-246-64059-6.

Infantry tactics, 1939–1945 (Almark Publishing, London, 1976). ISBN 0-85524-255-8.

Opening rounds: lessons of military history 1918–1988 (Deutsch Press, London 1988). ISBN 0-233-98009-1.

The British Part in the Korean War: Vol.1, A Distant Obligation (HMSO, London 1990). ISBN 0-11-630953-9.

The Army in the Air: the History of the Army Air Corps. (Far Thrupp, Stroud, A. Sutton Publishing 1994). ISBN 0-7509-0617-0.

The British Part in the Korean War: Vol 2, An Honourable Discharge (HMSO, London, 1995). ISBN 0-11-630958-X.

Unfinshed: *MacArthur (Great Commanders Series)* (Weidenfeld & Nicolson, London). ISBN 0-297-84684-1.

With others

Brown, Neville, and Farrar-Hockley, Anthony, *Nuclear First Use.* (Buchan & Enright, 1985). ISBN 0-907675-26-3.

Farrar-Hockley, Anthony, chapter in: Daniell, David S. (2005) *Cap of Honour: the 300 years of the Gloucestershire Regiment.* (Sutton, Stroud, 1989). ISBN 0-7509-4172-3.

Hamilton, Ian S. M. (ed. Farrar-Hockley, Anthony), *The Commander* (Hollis & Carter, London 1957).

Contributions

The D-Day Encyclopaedia, Chandler, David (ed.), 1991.

'The British Part in the Korean War' in Garland's *Encyclopaedia of the Wars of the United States, Korean War Volume* (New York, 1992).

'Infantry Warfare' in *The Oxford Companion to the Second World War,* (ed.) Dear, I.C.B., and Foot, M.R.D. (OUP, 1992).

'Confusion to Complacency. Commitments and Campaigns of the British Army since 1945' in *The Oxford Illustrated History of the British Army,* (ed.) Beckett, Ian and Chandler, David, 1993.

The Companion to Military History, (ed.) Holmes, Richard, (OUP, 1998).

Mathew, H.C.G., and Harrison, Brian, *Oxford Dictionary of National Biography* (OUP, 2004) entries on Sir George Lea, Sir Nigel Poett, Sir Charles Keightley, Sir Ken Darling, Sir Hugh Stockwell and Lord Carver.

Articles

Farrar-Hockley, Anthony, 'The Chinese Peoples' Liberation Army in the Korean War', *China Quarterly,* issue No. 98, 1983.

Farrar-Hockley, Anthony, 'A Reminiscence of the Chinese People's Volunteers in the Korean War', *China Quarterly,* June 1984.

Farrar-Hockley, Anthony, 'News from the 1st Battalion', *The Back Badge, Journal of the Gloucestershire Regiment,* Summer 1951, p 136 *et seq.*

Farrar-Hockley, Anthony, 'Dynamic Defence: The Northern Flank', a lecture given at the RUSI on 4 March 1983, in *RUSI Journal,* August 1983.

Papers

Farrar-Hockley, A.H., 'National service and British society', (unpublished BLitt thesis, Exeter College Oxford, 1968–1970).

Farrar-Hockley, A.H., and Monroe, Elizabeth, 'The Arab-Israeli War October 1973' (Adelphi Paper 207).

Farrar-Hockley, A.H., 'The Problems of Over-Extension: reconciling NATO defence and Out-of-Area contingencies' (Adelphi Paper, 1986).

Reviews

Michael Carver's *Twentieth Century Warriors* in *RUSI Journal,* June 1988.

Various titles by Lawrence Freedman, David E. Morris and Howard Tumber, and John Lawrence and Robert Lawrence in *The Times Literary Supplement* 16–22 September 1988.

Newspapers and Magazines

London Gazette
14 November 1942 (Supplement); 30 April 1943 (Supplement); 8 April 1945 (Supplement); 10 May 1945; 20 June 1945; 21 June 1945; 31 August 1951; 8 December 1953; 13 April 1954; 12 September 1957 (Supplement); 12 June 1958; 30 April 1965; 30 December 1981 (Supplement); 8 October 1982.

The Daily Telegraph
1 June 1951; 2 September 1953; 10 September 1977; 14 August 1990; 14 March 2006; 18 September 2007.

The Times
3 April 1970; 31 March 1976; 1 April 1976; 25 November 1977; 10 August 1982; 14 March 2006.

The Daily Mail
23 November 1977; 23 April 1981; 24 June 1982; 8 March 1983; 10 September 1986; 22 April 1993; 28 October 1993.

Daily Express
25 November 1977.

The Sunday Times
12 April 1970.

The Sunday Telegraph
12 April 1970.

The Observer
12 January 1969.

The Independent
14 August 1990; 9 August 1998; 22 February 2002.

London Evening Standard
29 June 1970; 16 January 1999.

The Sun
23 November 1977.

The Guardian
2 August 1971; 23 February 1972.

New York Herald Tribune
29 June 1970.

Manchester Evening News
24 November 1977.

Liverpool Daily Post
29 November 1977.

Bristol Evening World
Thursday 24 September 1957.

The Echo (Gloucester) and *Gloucester Evening Echo*
1 June 1951; 29 July 1980.

Belfast Telegraph
7 October 1968.

News Letter
7 October 1968.

Irish News
7 October 1968; 10 July 1970.

An Phoblacht (Republican News)
4 July 1970.

Aftenpost, (Norway)
18 January 1980.

Kieler Nachtrichten, (Germany)
12 November 1981.

The Exonian
March 1939; July 1939; March 1940; July 1940; December 1940; March 1941; July 1941; December 1941; January 1961; May 1961.

Sixth Sense [originally the newsletter of 6 Armoured Brigade, but later the weekly newspaper for British forces in Germany]
No. 19, 17 March 1972.

The Back Badge, Journal of the Gloucestershire Regiment
December 1948; summer 1951.

Pegasus, Journal of the Parachute Regiment
Vol XIII No. 3, 1958; summer 1965.

The Wish Stream, (RMA Sandhurst)
Summer 1947; autumn 1959; spring 1960; autumn 1960; spring 1961; autumn 1961.

Theses and Unpublished Papers

Graham-Bell, Francis, *Helicopter on the Heights*, MS in TFH's papers of the story of 653 Squadron AAC. No page numbering.
Riley, J.P., 'Instinctive leadership, Intuitive decision-making: a command study of General Sir Hugh Stockwell' (unpublished PhD thesis, Cranfield University, 2006).

Film and TV

COMMAND AND LEADERSHIP

General Sir John Hackett, 'Looking for Leadership', BBC Home Service Broadcast, February 1968.
BBC broadcasts, 'Fighting Spirit' and 'Casualty' in their series of 13 programmes in the series *Soldiers: A History of Men in Battle* written by John Keegan and Richard Holmes and presented by Frederick Forsyth, 1985.
Flashback Television, 'The Curragh Incident–A Question of Loyalty' for BBC *Timewatch*, 1992.
Channel Four, 'Game of War', *Waterloo,* presented by Angela Rippon, 1999.
Atlantic Productions for the BBC and the Discovery Channel, 'Thermopylae', 2001.

SECOND WORLD WAR

Camilla Whitby Films, *A Summer in Provence: The Story of Operation Dragoon (1944).* Tony Farrar-Hockley is among those thanked for their assistance with the making of this film.

KOREA
Thames Television, in collaboration with WGBH Boston, USA and the Australian Broadcasting Commission, *The Korean War Project*, 1987.

NORTHERN IRELAND
BBC *Panorama*, 6 April 1970; 7 November 1970; 5 February 1971.
Columbia Broadcasting (USA), April 1970.
BBC News, February 1992; 14 June, 21 June, 17 September and 27 September 1999.

GENERAL NEWS
Central Television News, 14 March 2006, reporting TFH's death.

Websites and Online Resources
www.exeter.ox.ac.uk – website of Exeter College Oxford.
www.exeterschool.org.uk – website of Exeter School.
www.measuringworth.com – for comparative values and worth of money over time.
www.paradata.org – the Airborne Forces Museum Archive Service.
www.philipjohnston.com
www.politics97@bbc.co.uk
http://cain.ulst.ac.uk/proni – Public Records Northern Ireland.
http://www.parkinsons.org.uk
http://www.army.mod.uk – the British Army website.

Interviews and Letters

INTERVIEWS WITH TFH and HIS FAMILY
Max Arthur with TFH in *Men of the Red Beret: Airborne Forces 1940–1990* (London, 1990) (Italy, the South of France and Greece).
Peter Liddle of the WW2 Experience Centre, Leeds with TFH in July 2001.
By the author:
  With TFH for Regimental Records of the Royal Welch Fusiliers, 6 October 1998.
  With TFH for the biography of General Sir Hugh Stockwell, 16 May 2003.
  With TFH for Operations in Suez, 12 February 2004.
  With the Farrar-Hockley family on 8 October 2013: TFH's widow, Linda; his sons, Dair and Hilary; his daughter-in-law, Victoria; his niece, Bryony Smith; and his first cousin, Rosemary Howell.

SECOND WORLD WAR
Francesco di Cinito with Major Paddy Deacon and Major Richard Hargreaves of 4 Para, August 2013.
The author with Colonel J.W. Sewell, 16 December 2013.
The author with Fusilier Jack Ellis, 13 November 2014.
Major Glyn Hughes on behalf of the author with Sergeant, later Major, Cliff Meredith, 29 December 2014.

PALESTINE
The author with Brigadier Ahmed Aideed Al Masareh, Director of Moral Guidance, JHQ Jordanian Army; Mr Amjad Adaileh, Director Arabic Press Department, Communications

and Information Division at the Royal Hashemite Court, Amman, Jordan; and Ms Alia Al-Kadi, Press Officer at the same department by the author in 2003.
The author with Major-General Peter Cavendish, 26 June 2003.
The author with Colonel J.W. Sewell, 16 December 2013.
The author with Fusilier Jack Ellis, 13 November 2014.

MIDDLE EAST
The author with RAdm Teddy Gueritz, 28 January 2004
The author with with Sir Thomas Prickett, 19 July 2004.
The author with Major-General Peter Cavendish, 26 June 2003.
The author with Major-General Peter Chiswell, 26 April 2014.
The author with Major-General Mike Walsh, 26 May 2014.
The author with Lieutenant-Colonel Peter Walter, 3 October 2014.
The author with Colonel Pat Beaumont, 28 October 2014.
The author with Major and Mrs Jeremy Hickman, 19 December 2014.

RMA SANDHURST
The author with Lieutenant-Colonel P.A. Crocker, 12 March 2014.
The author with Major Peter Cronk, 13 March 2014.
The author with Charles Messenger, 16 July 2014.

NORTHERN IRELAND
The author with Major-General Peter Chiswell, 18 August 2014.
The author with Colonel P.E. Butler, 27 August 2014.
The author with Major-General Bryan Webster, 18 September 2014.
The author with General Sir Frank Kitson, 30 September 2014.
The author with Colonel Clive Brennan, 2 October 2014.
The author with Major-General Mike Tillotson, 2 October 2014.
The author with Colonel Malcolm Ross-Thomas, 20 November 2014.

GERMANY
The author with Field Marshal The Lord Bramall, 19 November 2014.

MOD
The author with Linda Farrar-Hockley, 28 October 2014.
The author with Colonel John Stevens, 20 November 2014.

SOUTH-EAST DISTRICT
The author with Linda Farrar-Hockley, 28 October 2014.
The author with Hilary Farrar-Hockley, 29 October 2014.
The author with Colonel Graham Farrell, 20 November 2014.
The author with Brigadier David Keenan, 21 November 2014.
The author with Colonel Roy Giles, 16 February 2015.
The author with Major-General Robert McAfee, 3 April 2015.

NORWAY
The author with Linda Farrar-Hockley, 28 October 2014.
The author with Hilary Farrar-Hockley, 29 October 2014.
The author with Colonel Mike Motum, 14 November 2014.

COLONELCIES
The author with Brigadier Martin Vine, 14 November 2014.
The author with Colonel Graham Farrell, 20 November 2014.

SECOND CAREER
The author with Sgt Ted Olive, 17 February 2015.
The author with the Rev Mr Leighton Thomas, 17 February 2015.
The author with the Farrar-Hockley family, 18 February 2015.

Index

INDEX OF PERSONAL NAMES

INDEX OF PLACES

INDEX OF MILITARY UNIT AND FORMATIONS

INDEX OF GENERAL SUBJECTS